YNGRESS®

HOW TO CHEAT AT
IT Project
Management

Susan Snedaker

Nels Hoenig Technical Editor

KEY	SERIAL NUMBER
001	HJIRTCV764
002	PO9873D5FG
003	829KM8NJH2
004	J98444FRRT
005	CVPLQ6WQ23
006	VBP965T5T5
007	HJJJ863WD3E
008	2987GVTWMK
009	629MP5SDJT
010	IMWQ295T6T

PUBLISHED BY
Syngress Publishing, Inc.
800 Hingham Street
Rockland, MA 02370

How to Cheat at IT Project Management

Printed in Canada
1 2 3 4 5 6 7 8 9 0
ISBN: 1-59749-037-7

Publisher: Andrew Williams   Page Layout and Art: Patricia Lupien
Acquisitions Editor: Jaime Quigley Copy Editor: Amy Thomson
Technical Editor: Nels Hoenig   Indexer: J. Edmund Rush
Cover Designer: Michael Kavish

Distributed by O'Reilly Media, Inc. in the United States and Canada.
For information on rights, translations, and bulk sales, contact Matt Pedersen, Director of Sales and Rights, at Syngress Publishing; email matt@syngress.com or fax to 781-681-3585.

Acknowledgments

Syngress would like to acknowledge the following people for their kindness and support in making this book possible.

Syngress books are now distributed in the United States and Canada by O'Reilly Media, Inc. The enthusiasm and work ethic at O'Reilly are incredible, and we would like to thank everyone there for their time and efforts to bring Syngress books to market: Tim O'Reilly, Laura Baldwin, Mark Brokering, Mike Leonard, Donna Selenko, Bonnie Sheehan, Cindy Davis, Grant Kikkert, Opol Matsutaro, Steve Hazelwood, Mark Wilson, Rick Brown, Leslie Becker, Jill Lothrop, Tim Hinton, Kyle Hart, Sara Winge, C. J. Rayhill, Peter Pardo, Leslie Crandell, Regina Aggio, Pascal Honscher, Preston Paull, Susan Thompson, Bruce Stewart, Laura Schmier, Sue Willing, Mark Jacobsen, Betsy Waliszewski, Dawn Mann, Kathryn Barrett, John Chodacki, Rob Bullington, and Aileen Berg.

The incredibly hardworking team at Elsevier Science, including Jonathan Bunkell, Ian Seager, Duncan Enright, David Burton, Rosanna Ramacciotti, Robert Fairbrother, Miguel Sanchez, Klaus Beran, Emma Wyatt, Chris Hossack, Krista Leppiko, Marcel Koppes, Judy Chappell, Radek Janousek, and Chris Reinders for making certain that our vision remains worldwide in scope.

David Buckland, Marie Chieng, Lucy Chong, Leslie Lim, Audrey Gan, Pang Ai Hua, Joseph Chan, and Siti Zuraidah Ahmad of STP Distributors for the enthusiasm with which they receive our books.

David Scott, Tricia Wilden, Marilla Burgess, Annette Scott, Andrew Swaffer, Stephen O'Donoghue, Bec Lowe, Mark Langley, and Anyo Geddes of Woodslane for distributing our books throughout Australia, New Zealand, Papua New Guinea, Fiji, Tonga, Solomon Islands, and the Cook Islands.

Author

Susan Snedaker (MBA, BA, MCSE, MCT, CPM) is Principal Consultant and founder of VirtualTeam Consulting, LLC (www.virtualteam.com), a consulting firm specializing in business and technology consulting. The company works with companies of all sizes to develop and implement strategic plans, operational improvements and technology platforms that drive profitability and growth. Prior to founding VirtualTeam in 2000, Susan held various executive and technical positions with companies including Microsoft, Honeywell, Keane, and Apta Software. As Director of Service Delivery for Keane, she managed 1200+ technical support staff delivering phone and email support for various Microsoft products including Windows Server operating systems. She is author of *The Best Damn Windows Server 2003 Book Period* (Syngress Publishing, ISBN: 1-931836-12-4) and *How to Cheat at Managing Windows Small Business Server 2003* (Syngress, ISBN: 1-932266-80-1). She has also written numerous technical chapters for a variety of Syngress Publishing books on Microsoft Windows and security technologies and has written and edited technical content for various other publications. Susan has developed and delivered technical content from security to telephony, TCP/IP to WiFi, CIW to IT project management and just about everything in between (she admits a particular fondness for anything related to TCP/IP).

Susan holds a master's degree in business administration and a bachelor's degree in management from the University of Phoenix. She also holds a certificate in advanced project management from Stanford University. She holds Microsoft Certified Systems Engineer (MSCE) and Microsoft Certified Trainer (MCT) certifications. Susan is a member of the Information Technology Association of Southern Arizona (ITASA) and the Project Management Institute (PMI).

Technical Editor

 **Nels Hoenig** (CSQE, MCP, CPIM, Project+, Network+, MS-Project Expert) is a QA Project Leader and Senior Application Analyst with TDCI, Inc. where he provides expertise in the verification of correct functionality of their software products and supports external users across the US and international locations. TDCI develops e-commerce solutions to support the "engineer to order" business model. He is an expert in web product usability issues. His background includes implementations in the US and abroad of ERP solutions, developing and managing e-commerce sites, and implementing QA processes to improve user experience and reduce costs and development time. His past positions include Senior Application Specialist with Avalon Software and E-Commerce Project Leader with The Stanley Works.

He holds bachelor's degrees in operations management and management information systems from the University of Arizona and is a member of the American Society for Quality and the Project Management Institute. He lives in Ohio with his wife, Patty, and their three great children, Phoebe, Noelle and Maisie.

Author Acknowledgments

Writing a book is a rewarding experience, but it's certainly not a solo venture. Thanks first to my immediate friends and family—Lisa, Amy, Dee Ann, Rosie, Jackie Brown, and Bailee. Thanks for putting up with me, book writing and all. Thanks to my mother, Anne, for early instruction in English grammar (it started at birth and continues to this day…) and for ongoing support of my writing efforts. Thanks to my father, Richard, for instilling in me a love for all things technical. Special thanks to my dear friend Shirley for a lifetime of encouragement.

I'd also like to thank my MBA friend Patty Hoenig for introducing me to Nels, the talented technical editor for this tome. Sincere gratitude and thanks to Nels—you did a great job on the technical editing. I enjoyed our virtual conversations and the book benefited from those shared insights. You contributed to the depth and breadth of this book and the content is that much stronger for it. It was an insightful collaborative experience and I'd do it again in a heartbeat.

Thanks also to the friends and colleagues who agreed to supply real world examples for the book including Amy Buttery, Chris Compton, Gary Frost, David Getman, Lorraine Gutsche, Nels Hoenig, Chris Landi, Lisa Mainz, Kim Nagle, Sonal Rana and Ralph Spitzen.

I'd also like to thank Nick Mammana for demanding excellence earlier in my life and Sensei Ken Carson for teaching me the real meaning of *kaizen* (continuous improvement). Both were instrumental in helping me develop the professional and personal skills I have today.

Finally, I'd like to thank the brilliant folks at Syngress who do what they do to bring these books to fruition. Andrew, thanks for making this book possible and Jaime, thanks for making this process as enjoyable as you do and for your diligent efforts on all fronts. I think I'll take a couple days off now; I encourage you to do the same.

—*Susan Snedaker*

Contents

Foreword

By Susan Snedaker

Unlike any other book you'll find, this IT project management book synthesizes project management fundamentals, IT processes and procedures, and the bare bones of business. Many IT professionals are incredibly bright people who have a passion for technology. If they're really good, they also get along well with others. If they're exceptional, they also understand the business implications of their department, their technology initiatives and their projects. In this book, you'll learn how to become an exceptional IT professional. Whether you're an IT manager who oversees the department *and* manages IT projects, or a member of the team who is sometimes an IT project manager, you'll learn how to align your projects to the company's strategic objectives, how to develop a strategic plan for your IT department, how to pick the right projects to solve the right problems and how to add value to your company. And if you've ever wondered how to get on the fast-track to CIO…you might just be holding the answer in your hands.

As a business and technology consultant, I examine and explore businesses everyday. Based on my observations, you should know that the way your company runs projects is probably like 98% of all the other companies out there—often a bit disorganized, very stressful, and less-than-successful. I'm always surprised by how many people tell me that they've already had project management training. When I ask how much of it they still use, most tell me they use none of it. This begs the question: Why has past PM training failed to be integrated into the project process? Most will tell me in a round about way that the system was too complex, took too much effort, or required too big of a change. Human nature is such that we tend make small changes more effectively than large, wholesale changes. If you've ever tried to lose weight, start eating better or get more exercise, you know this is true. If you're completely sedentary, you might be able to consistently add a 10 minute walk during your lunch hour, but you're not likely to stick to a stringent daily hour of power aerobics at the gym.

The same holds true for IT project management fundamentals. Most people will not implement the system end-to-end unless there is tremendous pressure and support from within the company at the executive level. Failing this, PM systems (and any other improvement processes) become nothing more than the flavor of the month and this syndrome quickly engenders a cynical view of process improvement in general. So, I take a different approach. Don't try to implement the system end-to-end if that doesn't work for you. Pick one thing and do it consistently; then add another—continuous improvement. As I've taught this in various training seminars, I've encouraged students to pick one thing and do it consistently, then add to their repertoire until they are practicing textbook project management…one step at a time. Sure, it would be great if they could simply do everything right today, but that's not likely to happen. My goal is to gradually get you to improve your IT PM skills, even if it takes 6 or 12 or 18 months. Eventually is better than never.

This book is not intended to provide the most exhaustive look at IT PM ever written. It *is* intended to get you up and running in IT PM with the least amount of effort and the most amount of improvement possible. For those of you looking for the encyclopedia of formal IT project management, you won't find it here (I refer you to the PMBOK). This book and the IT PM process it describes is not process-heavy. Anyone aquainted with me knows I'm a real results-oriented person, and I loathe process for process' sake. The only process I am comfortable with is that which drives the outcomes I want, so this book takes a minimalist approach to process (less *is* more). Where processes are defined, they are the shortest, least complex ways to get from Point A to Point B.

I've trained in Shotokan karate for many years and my sensei, Mr. Ken Carson, always says "Power comes from good fundamentals, speed comes from practice." As 6th dan black belt (karate *and* judo) who has trained and taught for over 60 years, if Sensei Carson says it's so, *it's so*. Companies (and IT professionals) that implement consistent project management practices will build a solid foundation. As the organization becomes familiar with the processes and internalizes them, they will also gain speed and knowledge. Companies that are stronger, faster and smarter win in the end. It's not just a one-shot effort, either. It is a process of continuous improvement (*kaizen*). As you consistently implement project management practices, you, your IT projects, your department and company will continuously improve as well. This book gives you a shortcut to those skills so you can get the basics quickly and start using them today.

Yoki Shuppatsu Wa Hanbun Michi O Sugitaru Go Gotoshi
(Well begun is half done.)

Chapter 1

What's Project Management Got To Do With IT?

Solutions in this chapter:

- Business Process Improvement Systems
- Overview of Project Management
- Project Success Factors
- Four Project Constraints
- Projects, Programs, Portfolios

☑ Summary

☑ Solutions Fast Track

☑ Frequently Asked Questions

Introduction

If you read the introduction to this book, you already know what project management has to do with IT, but now we're going to break it down a bit further and look at how Information Technology (IT) projects benefit from project management and by extension, how your career will benefit from project management. In this chapter, we'll begin by looking briefly at business process improvement and how project management fits into that world. We'll also look at some of the brutal facts about project success (or rather, failure) rates as well as the factors that can have the most impact on project success. We'll close out the chapter by looking at project constraints and elements to give you a solid foundation for the subsequent chapters. Let's start by looking at business process improvement systems and where project management fits.

Business Process Improvement Systems

Business process improvement (BPI) has been around in different "flavors" for decades. Companies continually look for ways to become more efficient, and with efficiency often comes competitive advantage. If a company can create a computer program or a part for a car at a lower cost than another company, it has a distinct advantage. It can sell the part for less than its competitors, which often leads to greater market share. That company also has the option of selling the product for the same as its competitors, but making a larger profit on each unit. With more profit comes the ability to pick and choose markets, pricing, profit margins, etc. So, it makes sense that companies are constantly looking for ways to improve their business processes to gain that advantage. In a moment, we'll take a look at some of the more popular business process improvement methods being used by companies today. To tie it all in, we'll begin with project management since project management is, essentially, one aspect of improving business processes. Project management is a structured methodology for evaluating, defining, and managing projects, so it clearly fits into the business process improvement arena.

The Project Management Institute

As with other BPI systems, *project management* (PM) also has many different flavors, but essentially, project management is project management. Numerous companies develop and sell proprietary systems and approaches to PM, but ultimately those systems all use the same fundamentals. That's not to say that some companies haven't developed extremely effective systems. It's just that the fundamentals are the same, regardless of which system you use. Projects are projects: small, large, simple, complex, short, long, economical, expensive, and everything in between. All projects, regardless of size, complexity, or cost can benefit from using PM principles, but there are other quality programs that companies use as well—sometimes in conjunction with PM and sometimes in place of PM. Regardless of the approach you take, implementing a consistent, quality-focused process will improve your results.

The *Project Management Institute* (PMI) is widely recognized in the United States as a leader in the project management field and an organization that sets forth project management standards. PMI states they have over 150,000 members in 150 countries. PMI provides two certifications in project management, both of which are currently considered the gold standards in project management. PMI also publishes the *Project Management Body of Knowledge*. PMI sponsors seminars, events, and training related to project management. There are other international organizations such as the International Project Management Association, which is based in the Netherlands. There are many other reputable PM training and certification programs on the market today including those from leading universities and colleges around the country. Some programs and certifications are more accepted than others. PMI certifications are the accepted standard, but remember that in many cases PM *certification* is not required for the job. If you want to get a job as a project manager, a PMI certification can help, but experience and knowledge in PM will often suffice. After reading this book, you'll have a better understanding of what's involved in PM, and if you're interested in pursuing a career as a project manager you can look into formal training and certification. You can find out more about PMI on their website at www.pmi.org.

CMM and CMMI

The *Capability Maturity Model* (CMM) and the *Capability Maturity Model Integration* (CMMI) are not project management systems but process improvement methodologies. Carnegie Mellon University's *Software Engineering Institute* (SEI) developed these models as approaches to process improvement in software development. Currently, CMM is being phased out in favor of CMMI. The CMMI system focuses on various disciplines such as software engineering, system engineering, integrated product and process development, and supplier sourcing. For example, according to the SEI website, the CMMI process in software engineering focuses on "applying systematic, disciplined, and quantifiable approaches to the development, operation, and maintenance of software." Applying a systematic, disciplined, and quantifiable approach sounds a lot like project management. There is clearly overlap and both PM and CMMI processes can co-exist synergistically in an organization. For more information on CMMI, visit the Software Engineering Institute website at www.sei.cmu.edu.

Six Sigma

Six Sigma is another process improvement system that seems to have taken corporate America by storm. Six Sigma is defined as a highly disciplined process that helps companies focus on developing and delivering near-perfect products and services. The term *six sigma* is a statistical term that measures how far a given process deviates from perfection. From a mathematical standpoint, six sigma specifies fewer than 3.4 defects per million. Stated the other way, it means that 99.99966% of all output meets quality standards. The idea behind Six Sigma is that if you can measure how many defects you have in a process, you can systematically figure out how to eliminate them and get as close to zero defects as possible. This quality improvement process can be traced back to Motorola in the 1970's when it was facing serious quality problems. The project was developed by Mikel Harry, a senior staff engineer at Motorola's Government Electronic Group and he named the process Six Sigma. Motorola states it saved $250 million the first year it implemented Six Sigma practices. Later, Jack Welch, CEO of General Electric, evangelized Six Sigma within his organization and Six Sigma gained momentum quickly after that. GE claims it saved $750 million in 1995 alone and Allied Signal claims $165 million in savings through implementing Six Sigma practices.

There are those who think that Six Sigma is just another management or business improvement "flavor of the month." Indeed, Six Sigma builds upon a lot of previous quality work including that of Edwards Deming, the architect of post-World War II industrial revival in Japan. Another consideration is the cost to organizations. Individuals in the organization must be trained in the system and these individuals, depending on their skill levels are dubbed "white belts," "green belts," "black belts," "master black belts," and "champions." GE reportedly spent over $465 million to have over 10,000 employees trained and certified in this system.

To complicate matters, there is no one single governing body as there is with CMMI. Instead, Six Sigma was driven by industry and is therefore defined by various companies. While there are defined best practices, Six Sigma certifications and business processes vary from company to company. For instance, if you achieve "black belt" certification at one company and then go to another company, you may have to undergo recertification or retraining. Another implementation, *Lean Six Sigma*, is also gaining popularity in the market. For more information, you can query "Six Sigma" on your favorite Internet search engine and come up with many companies offering Six Sigma information and certification.

While formal Six Sigma may not be for every company or every person, significant process improvement gains can and have been made by implementing Six Sigma processes. Business or management improvement programs typically only become "flavor of the month" when corporate executives fail to fully support, fund, and implement the chosen process.

ISO 9000

The *International Standards Organization* (ISO) is a non-profit organization dedicated to developing and maintaining standards in a wide variety of areas. One well-known standard is ISO 9000, which has become an international reference for quality requirements in business-to-business dealings. Another emerging "generic standard" (meaning it is not industry or business-specific) is ISO 14000, which is trying to achieve at least as much recognition and acceptance as ISO 9000 (if not more) in helping organizations to meet environmental challenges. Recent changes to the ISO 9000 standard have resulted in the merging of the ISO 9001, ISO 9002, and ISO 9003 standards into the new ISO 9001:2000, which is the sole certification standard in the ISO 9000 family. ISO 9001:2000 is now the only standard in the ISO 9000 family against whose requirements a company's quality system can be certified by an external agency. The standard recognizes that the word "product" applies to services, processed material, hardware, and software intended for, or required by, your customer.

Like CMM, CMMI, or Six Sigma, the ISO standards are focused on developing consistent, defined, and repeatable processes to improve quality. For more information on ISO, you can visit their website at www.iso.org.

Overview of Project Management

Now that you've learned a bit about business process improvement systems, you can see that project management can be viewed either as an integral part of these other systems or as a business process improvement system itself. Regardless of where you want to place it in the scheme of things, there is hard data to support the premise that all companies can benefit from implementing project management processes. Unlike some of the BPI systems, project management fundamentals can be learned quickly and implemented almost immediately. As with these other systems, there are many levels of expertise and once you begin learning the basics, you may find you want additional information or formal training to continue to improve your skills and project results. Now, let's take a more in-depth look at project management. We're going to start with some of the research that's been done on projects, project success and failure rates, and how project management can help. If you need to sell your manager or top executives on why the company should implement project management or pay for project management training, memorize this next section.

Project Success and Failure Rates

In 1986, Alfred Spector, president of the Transarc Corporation, co-authored a paper comparing bridge building to software development. The paper stated that bridges are normally built on time, on budget, and do not fall down. Conversely, software rarely, if ever, comes in on time or on budget and software almost always breaks. Spector proposed that bridges come in on time, on budget, and do not fall down because design detail and specifications are locked down and the building contractor has little flexibility in modifying the specifications. Of course, that and 3,000 years of collective bridge building experience have something to do with it. Software development is a relatively new endeavor in the scheme of things. We don't have 3,000 years' experience, more like 60 or 70 years. Like all fledglings, software development has changed by fits and starts and in many ways is still an awkward toddler—sometimes running at lightning speed and others times stumbling and falling for no apparent reason.

The world of software development is certainly a bit different than, say, upgrading the corporate network infrastructure. However, the problems found in software development projects are pretty common to all kinds of IT projects, so we'll examine some data collected by the Standish Group International, Inc. on software development.

The Standish Group International (Standish Group) began researching the success and failure of software projects back in the 1990's. Since then, they have published a report called the *CHAOS Report* every two years. Each time it's released, it contains updated statistics on many different aspects of software projects. What's interesting is that the first report, reflecting 1994 data, indicated that only 16% of all software development projects *succeeded*, 31% failed outright and 53% were deemed "challenged." The term *challenged* is used to indicate a project that is running behind schedule, over cost, or does not contain the original set of required features (reduced scope or reduced quality). *Successful* is defined as being on time, on budget, and containing substantially all the required features and functions originally specified. *Only 16% of projects were successful in 1994.*

There are a few other noteworthy statistics that drive home the cost of failure. In 1995, U.S. companies spent about $250 billion on software development. The average cost of a development project in a large company was about $2.3 million. The average cost in a mid-sized company was about $1.3 million and in small companies, the cost was about $430,000. Those are large numbers, especially for small companies. Now, let's do the math. In 1995 dollars, cancelled development projects cost $81 billion (U.S. companies and government combined). If each software project for small companies cost $434,000 and only 16% were successful, think about the millions of dollars lost by small businesses. Certainly the numbers for large and mid-sized companies are also significant, but small businesses in particular can ill-afford to waste millions of dollars on failed and challenged projects.

Six years later, in 2000, the Internet boom was in full swing and software startup companies were a dime a dozen (in retrospect, even at a dime a dozen, many would now be considered overvalued). You'd think software development would have significantly matured with all that time, money, and effort being expended in development. According to the Standish Group, in 2000 a whopping 28% of all software projects were successful. Not a bad improvement for six years, but here's the bad news. 23% of all projects still failed and 49% were still challenged. It would be a hard sell to go into your senior management and say, "Let's spend $500,000 on this IT project, it has a 28% chance of success," but that's exactly what people do when they implement projects without a defined project management process.

Now some more bad news: most projects in the successful category (28%) had inflated cost estimates. According to the Standish Group, "IT executives told us that they get their best estimate, multiply by two and then add a half!" So, projects can have a 28% success rate if the estimates are roughly tripled. That 28% success rate sounds like it's still closer to the 1994 number of 16%, but that IT professionals have simply gotten better at "guestimating" the true cost of development. The good news is that through the use of project management processes, all IT projects, including those pesky software development projects, have a better chance of coming in on time, on budget, and with the required features and functions. Since you're reading this book, it's assumed that that's exactly what you want to do and as you read through the remainder of the book, you'll gain the knowledge you need to improve your projects from start to finish.

The problem is definitely *not* just within the software development arena, so don't sit comfortably by pointing the finger at the development folks. As you'll see in a moment, there are many organizational factors that contribute to the project failures (and successes) and it's everyone's responsibility to contribute to the success of the project. Now that we've examined the bad news, let's look at some of the things companies and IT managers *can* do to improve the chance for the success of all IT projects, including software development projects. After all, if there wasn't some good news in all of this, we'd be in big trouble.

Enterprise 128...

Too Much, Too Late, Too Bad

Throughout this book, you'll see these small segments that discuss topics related to the material in that section. The segments that describe what went wrong with projects and why are titled "Enterprise 128". Here's the story of Enterprise 128 and why it is an apt name for these segments.

In the early 1980's, a British company was set up to create a home computer just when it appeared home computers might become a viable market. The computer was based on the Zilog Z80 processor and boasted 128K of memory, an astounding amount of RAM for that time. It also had ports galore—RS232/RS432 serial ports, RGB output port, Centronics printer port, two external joystick ports, a cassette interface, a ROM cartridge slot, and an expansion slot. It also featured 4-channel stereo sound. Years ahead of its time, it also had a graphics coprocessor (named "Nick" after one of the designers) and a sound coprocessor ("Dave", the other designer) to take some of the load off the Z80 processor. Pretty advanced features for a 1983 product.

The company announced its flagship product, the Enterprise 128, in September 1983. The units didn't actually go on sale until the spring of 1984. At that time, the company was taking pre-orders because the units weren't actually ready to ship. The company did manage to pull in 80,000 pre-orders, which at that time was a pretty good trick given the fledgling home computer market.

Unfortunately, that's where the good news ends. The computers, announced in late 1983, didn't actually ship until 1985, by which time there were many more competitors in the market. The competitions' computers had fewer features, but were less expensive. Within a couple of years after the release of the Enterprise 128, the company folded and was lost in space forever. The units that were eventually built and sold found a market in Hungary and there was a strong Enterprise 128 contingent there for years.

Lesson Learned: Projects that come in late, over budget, and with features no one really cares about (or understands) are very likely to fail. The folks of the Enterprise learned that lesson just a bit too late. For more information on the Enterprise, visit http://en.wikipedia.org/wiki/Enterprise_128.

Project Success Factors

There are numerous things companies and IT managers can do to increase the chance of success for any IT project. We'll look at these success factors in the order in which they currently impact project success. Over time, these factors tend to shift positions, but the list itself has remained fairly constant. If you're trying to make the case for implementing project management in your company, you may want to pay special attention to this section. It will provide you with critical data that you can use to present the case to your senior management team or to convince other stakeholders in the company of the importance of PM practices. In each of the segments below, you'll learn about a different success factor and how you can use or implement it in your organization. We'll return to each of these items in later chapters in the book and provide detailed steps you can take to improve your project outcomes.

Success Factor 1: Executive Support

Executive support is the number one factor impacting project success. Of course, that probably doesn't come as much of a surprise. If executives are not supportive, they're unlikely to assign needed resources (labor hours, dollars, equipment, etc.) to the project. Additionally, they're less likely to defend the project if it runs into trouble or gets bogged down in corporate politics. Executive support can also help ensure that cross-functional teams deliver on their assignments, especially when projects cross departmental and divisional corporate lines. Finally, executive support can give a project company-wide visibility, which can be good or bad, depending on how the project turns out.

APPLYING YOUR KNOWLEDGE

As you'll learn in later chapters, having a project sponsor is important to project success. Often the project sponsor is an executive in the company. Your job is to provide that sponsor with accurate, useful, and appropriate information about what the project will look like, what the project will cost, how long the project will take, and perhaps most important, why the project should be undertaken. You can and should use your team members as resources when compiling project details and you'll learn exactly how to do this when we discuss project planning later in the book. Even if the person that assigned you the project is the project sponsor, it's still important for you to provide the information he or she will need to support and defend your project in the future. You'll learn more about this later in this book.

Success Factor 2: User Involvement

The lack of user involvement is number two on the list only because if the project never gets out of the gates, it won't succeed, so executive support is the first success factor. However, coming in a close second is lack of user involvement. Here's what typically happens: Someone comes up with an idea for a project. A team is put together to evaluate and implement the project. The project starts up and about three-quarters of the way through, someone might mention getting the users trained. In the worst-case (and fairly common) scenario, once the project is complete, it is implemented and dropped on the users. Often user input and training comes after the fact or not at all. In a better scenario, users are involved in designing the project and trained sometime before the project goes live. If you're like most IT folks, right about now you're saying "Yes, but...." Read on.

Many IT managers find it difficult to involve users early on for two key reasons. First, users are typically uneducated about IT processes, whether it's software development or infrastructure upgrades. Without understanding how things work in IT, most users come up with fairly unrealistic expectations about how and when things should be done. Think of it as a culture clash—each culture (IT and user) is right within its own sphere, but a lot gets lost in translation. Users' requirements can seemingly change from day to day and their understanding of what it takes to get the job done is limited. If users don't understand the process, they may inundate IT with a barrage of questions the IT staff is unprepared (or unable) to answer at that point in time. To avoid this onslaught of user questions, IT staff often delay communicating with users.

A second big complaint from the IT department is *scope creep*—the requirements for the project keep growing even as the project is underway. The source of this scope creep is often the user community. On the other side, users complain that they are left out of the loop until it's too late to make any meaningful changes to the project. As a result, both IT staff and users become frustrated.

From a user perspective, the IT department often comes in, asks a few questions and months later unveils the new system, application, or solution. Users are not asked about requirements ahead of time, are often not involved in usability and functionality testing, and sometimes are not trained until after the fact. This leads to user confusion and dissatisfaction. There is a better way. We'll discuss how to turn users into allies rather than opponents later in this book.

APPLYING YOUR KNOWLEDGE

Involve users early but through a very well-defined and managed process. Look for subject matter experts (SMEs) within various user segments and work with these user representatives. Set clear expectations about their participation, and when the requirements are agreed upon, they should be "etched in stone" to prevent scope creep. Developing requirements documents is not a simple task and it will take practice to get your skills where they need to be, but it is well worth the effort. We're going to devote a fair amount of discussion to this topic later in the book because getting users on board with the project early on will absolutely impact your project's chance of success. You'll learn how to effectively manage user involvement so you don't get yanked in every direction, and we'll discuss specific methods you can use to gather user input while managing the project requirements. We'll discuss scope creep in more detail when we discuss project planning and change management later in this book.

Enterprise 128...

Users, Users Everywhere...

The following is a true story. No names are used to protect, well, everyone involved. A software company was developing an advanced application to manage financial data for non-profit organizations. The target market had been making do with a handful of homegrown applications built on legacy platforms (DOS, for example). This new application was going to transform the marketplace and would be in huge demand, or so went the story. As the first couple of beta customers tested the product, the response was overwhelming. "Where is the reporting capability?" Didn't customers notice the new, easy-to-use interface? No. Didn't they notice the ease with which they could manage funds from different accounts? No. What they noticed was the *one* (missing) feature every customer had mentioned during customer meetings, focus groups, and surveys: reporting.

What went wrong? The development team prioritized the bells and whistles higher than reporting features. In every development meeting, user requirements (reports) were de-prioritized to make way for either critical fixes or features that

Continued

some believed would be a deciding factor in future sales. Though the client side was represented by two or three lonely voices, there was little support at the top of the organization for these user requirements. As a result, the engineering department took their cue from the top and repeatedly de-prioritized the reporting features.

There is a happy ending. Once engineering focused on getting the users 90% of the reports they needed and wanted, the client's resistance to the product melted away and the new application was enthusiastically received in the marketplace.

Lesson Learned: Find out what the users need and want. Spend time listening, not talking. Understand how users currently use the technology and discuss what needs to change. Then, prioritize the items on the user lists. Confirm the required and optional features with subject matter experts. Make sure you understand what the "must have" features are and deliver on those. Get agreement from the users on the final list. You may have to negotiate because often you can't deliver on everything. It's better to have 100% of 10 features than 10% of 100 features. Next, lock down that list. If you need to, shorten the list for the first iteration and work on subsequent priorities in later releases. Although this software company spent time gathering user input, it never incorporated that into a firm list of "must have" user-side requirements, sometimes referred to as *acceptance criteria*. If they had, the product probably would have gained traction in the marketplace about 18 months earlier than it did. Not all stories end as happily.

Success Factor 3: Experienced Project Manager

In recent years, it's become clear that having an experienced project manager at the helm has a significant impact on the success rates of IT projects. In the 1990's, there was little call for formally trained (or experienced) project managers only because project management as a business practice was not as in demand as it is today. While project management has long been utilized in many large, industrial companies and governmental agencies, it has now become almost a *de facto* requirement even in small and mid-sized companies. The evidence is clear and overwhelming—having a trained, experienced project manager has an enormous impact on a project's chance of success. Experience becomes a more important factor as the project size, cost, and timeline increase. In fact, according to the Standish Group's research, 97% of all successful projects have an experienced project manager. We'll discuss the role of project manager and what skills and traits are important for success as a project manager later in this book.

APPLYING YOUR KNOWLEDGE

This data gives you a great selling point if you need to get top management to pay for formal project management training for you, your team, or your company. Even if formal training isn't on your agenda, you can get buy-in for assigning strategic projects to the most experienced project managers. While that sometimes means shifting in-progress projects to other project managers, your goal should be to assign your most complex, strategic, and/or critical projects to your most experienced project managers. If you want less experienced project managers to gain expertise, assign them as team members on important projects and let them learn from the best. If you're an experienced project manager, applying the processes defined in this book will add consistency to your projects.

Success Factor 4: Clearly Defined Project Objectives

For most people familiar with project management, success factor 4 is painfully obvious. If that's the case, however, it's hard to explain why a vast majority of projects don't have clearly defined objectives. It's one of those things like daily exercise—everyone agrees it's good for you, but it's just such a nuisance to actually do it. There are a number of reasons why projects lack defined objectives. Laziness is one explanation, of course, but not the best one. Most of the time there are numerous organizational factors including politics, shifting priorities, cash flow/financial problems, extremely tight timelines, and organization restructuring that sometimes make defining project objectives difficult or impossible. Project objectives essentially define the scope of the project. The *scope* is the total amount of work to be accomplished. If these are continually changing, it's like trying to hit a moving target. Later in this book, we'll take a close look at objectives and give you specific tools you can use to create well-defined project objectives. We'll also discuss how to get buy-in from appropriate stakeholders so those objectives don't shift on you (too much).

APPLYING YOUR KNOWLEDGE

Clearly defined project objectives comes in at number four on the list of key success factors. The first three success factors have to do with people—the executives, the users, and the project manager. This is the first factor internal to the project itself that appears on the list and is the most important project-specific aspect. Knowing this will help you get all the stakeholders (anyone impacted by the project or the project's out-come) aligned with the project's objectives. As with other elements, it may take some negotiating on your part to lock down these details, but if everyone understands the impact of clearly defined objectives on the project's success, you're more likely to gain agreement on the top-level items.

Success Factor 5: Clearly Defined (and Smaller) Scope

Studies have shown that the longer a project runs (scheduled duration), the less likely it is to be successful, so there is an inverse relationship between project success and time. *Scope*, defined as the total amount of work to be accomplished, is inextricably linked to time—the more work that needs to be done, the longer it usually will take. The scope of the project is reflected in the project's objectives. Some IT project managers prefer to start with objectives to see how those define the scope; others prefer to start with the scope and develop the objectives from there. We'll discuss the process of defining scope and objectives later.

Clearly, there is only so much that can be accomplished in a given amount of time. Despite our impulse to throw more bodies at some problems, studies have shown that in many cases there is an inverse relationship between the number of people working on the problem and the time it takes to resolve the problem. To put that in plain English, in some cases the more bodies you throw at a problem, the longer it will take to fix it. This might explain why you always see six highway con-struction workers standing around while one guy does all the work…OK, that might not apply, but how many people *can* write one section of code or install one server? You may be familiar with the expression, "a camel is a horse designed by committee," which sums up the challenge of having too many people working on one problem.

Typically, the only way to reduce the amount of time spent on a project is to limit the scope of the project. Scheduling efficiencies may reduce the timeline, but rarely reduce the amount of effort required to complete the project tasks. In many cases, it is worthwhile to break large projects down into smaller, shorter projects. Smaller projects are more manageable and often give the project manager and project team more flexibility with limited resources.

APPLYING YOUR KNOWLEDGE

Resist defining or managing big, complex projects. Some people see these as a chance to make a name for themselves. That's true, but it won't be a name you like when the project fails. If you're assigned a large, complex long-running project, try to break it down into smaller projects (sub-projects or phases) in a manner acceptable to senior management. Work diligently to define scope and prevent scope creep. One method that works is to define both what the project *does* and *does not* include. When you define what the project does not include, there's less room for confusion about the actual scope of the project. We'll discuss this in greater detail later in the book.

Success Factor 6: Shorter Schedules, Multiple Milestones

You just read that time is the mortal enemy of project success, so it should come as no surprise that the next success factor is shorter schedules with more frequent checkpoints. Scope defines the total amount of work to be accomplished and the schedule defines the shortest possible path to accomplishing that work. If the schedule starts getting longer, there's a good chance your scope is creeping on you and that will directly reduce your chances for success. The schedule is developed based upon the availability of resources and the skills of those resources. We'll discuss scheduling and resources when we look at the planning phase of project management.

Studies have also shown that projects with more milestones placed closer together are more successful. This also makes sense when you think about it (of course, most of us just don't stop and think about it). *Milestones*, by definition, are tasks in your project plan that have no duration. They are simply markers to help you navigate through your project plan and indicate important checkpoints or events. They can be project phase transition points; points at which external data, resources, or decisions must be gathered, or simple checkpoints. It makes sense, then, that the more often you have a checkpoint, the more successful your project is likely to be. The sooner you notice the project is heading off-course, the easier it is to make small adjustments. Of course, all things (including milestones) in moderation—too many checkpoints and you'll drive yourself and your team members crazy.

Applying Your Knowledge

Take a look at the average or typical project length at your company or within your IT department. Then look at the success rates of those projects. Since there is no specific definition of "short" or "long" duration, look for the intersection of project duration and project success in your department. While there are numerous other factors at play, you might be able to find the optimal project duration for your purposes. If not, break big projects into smaller projects then set shorter schedules with multiple milestones. We'll discuss schedules and milestones later in this book.

Success Factor 7: Clearly Defined Project Management Process

Has it struck you yet that "more time, more money, more people" are *not* on the success factor list? What is on the list includes getting the right people involved and clearly defining some key project elements. Sound basic? It is, though it is certainly easier said than done. Having a clearly defined project management process comes in at number seven on our countdown, but odds are good that if you have an experienced project manager (success factor three), he or she is using a clearly defined PM process already. If that describes you, hang on. We'll discuss that process and ways you can improve your own PM methods throughout this book.

A clearly defined project management process is important for project success for several reasons. First, when processes are clearly defined, you avoid reinventing the wheel each time and you can re-use processes that worked and tweak those that didn't. Over time, this leads to improved processes that can easily be implemented by members of the project team. Also, clearly defined processes reduce or eliminate some of the project re-work. Think about the last time you went to the hardware or grocery store. If you had a list, you had close to a 100% chance you'd leave the store with all the items you needed. On the other hand, if you didn't have a list, you had close to a 100% chance that you'd leave the store without something you did need and with several things you really didn't need. The same holds true in project management. Having well-defined project management processes helps you do the right things in the right order without having to give too much thought to the process.

There's also an efficiency that comes with having well-defined, easy-to-use processes. If the process by which you got paid by your employer changed each pay period, imagine the confusion it would cause. The time wasted tracking down missing paychecks and responding to frantic or irate employees would take far more time than the payroll department could handle. Instead, there is a consistent process and everyone knows not only when and how paychecks are distributed, but they also know what to do in the event a paycheck is missing.

Before we leave this topic, let's make one thing perfectly clear. Process for process' sake is a waste of time. We're going to focus on simple, easy-to-use processes that actually make your job easier. The processes in this book are excellent tools for managing your project, not excellent ways to waste more of your valuable time.

APPLYING YOUR KNOWLEDGE

First, you can use this information to generate buy-in for using a project management process. Some companies are more reluctant than others to implement new processes or systems. However, using the information in this chapter, you should be able to create a compelling case for using project management. Also, once you've read through this book, you'll be able to develop clearly defined project management processes for your department or team. You'll then be able to implement and modify the project management processes your IT team uses to reflect the unique needs of your situation. You should learn the process from start to finish before you decide to modify anything, but once you have a good feel for the processes, feel free to tweak them to suit your company's needs and business methods.

Cheat Sheet...

What Projects Really Cost

It's been estimated that 50% to 75% of the *total* cost of any project is directly attributable to errors, omissions, and re-work. Think about that for a moment. A project that's estimated to cost $500,000 will cost almost $1,000,000 or more and all of the difference is probably directly related to errors, omissions, and re-work. While having well-defined project management processes won't prevent all project problems, if you could reduce errors and re-work by half, you'd save 25% to 38% of the total cost of the project.

Here's another estimate related specifically to software development. It costs approximately 100 times more to fix a software problem after the product has been released to customers than it does to fix the problem during the development phase. Clearly, cost savings (and numerous other benefits) come from testing and quality processes built into the project management process so problems and errors are detected and resolved early.

The best part of the deal is this: if you implement these processes and reduce errors, omissions, and re-work, you not only reduce the total cost of your project, you also probably reduce the time it takes to complete the project and deliver higher quality as well. There aren't too many free rides in life, but this is one of them. We'll discuss these processes in detail throughout the remainder of this book.

Success Factor 8: Standard Infrastructure

The last major success factor we'll discuss is using standard software infrastructure. Clearly, this applies directly to software development initiatives, but it can also be applied to other IT projects. According to the Standish Group research, 70% of all application code is considered infrastructure, which means that the other 30% is the custom code. Standardizing the infrastructure of the code's foundation leads to both efficiency and stability in the code. Some of the infrastructure code is unique to the application, but often there are components that can be purchased from an infrastructure vendor to alleviate the need to develop unique infrastructure solutions. Relying on off-the-shelf infrastructure components increases the chance the development project will come in on time, on budget, and with required features. Developers can focus on the competitive or strategic elements of the code (what separates your product from your competitors) instead of developing the infrastructure.

If you're not developing software, this success factor still applies to you. Projects that use standard infrastructure components are more likely to be successful. Most IT pros who work on the hardware end of things will tell you that things almost always work better when the infrastructure components are standardized on particular platforms and even with particular vendors. Mixing and matching often creates compatibility issues that hardware folks hate to chase down. Standardizing the infrastructure used in your project, regardless of where in the IT world your project falls, will generate greater success.

APPLYING YOUR KNOWLEDGE

When developing your project plan, look for opportunities to use standardized components—from software infrastructure elements to hardware infrastructure elements to templates and off-the-shelf solutions. Carefully analyze the cost of purchasing infrastructure versus creating your own. Small and medium-sized companies often fall victim to the "it costs too much" mentality when looking at off-the-shelf solutions to incorporate into their products or projects. However, if you add in the cost of errors, omission, re-work, and cost and schedule overruns, you'll more than likely find that purchasing these components or elements is a better business decision—even if it costs you more initially than you expected. When we look at developing a project budget, we'll discuss how to evaluate some of these items.

The IT Factor...

Using Standard Components

Remember the software company that ran into trouble because it lacked the reports customers required? A missed opportunity was to purchase a report engine and incorporate it into the product. At the time, the company was tight on funds, as are many startups, and top executives made the decision that developing the code for reports would be more cost effective than purchasing a report engine. On the surface, that appeared to be true when you look at the cost of that kind of component. However, there are a number of things they did not

Continued

consider. For instance, how many programmer hours did it take to develop these reports? How much expertise did the programmers have in developing reports versus a company whose business it is to develop and sell a report engine? How likely or possible would it be to continue to upgrade and improve the reporting functions as technology changed? What was the opportunity cost of developing those reports in-house (meaning, what did those programmers NOT work on because they were busy developing reports)? Finally, what sales/marketing benefit (if any) would there be to using a well-known, widely used report engine? Had these factors been considered, it's possible the company may have chosen to use a standard report engine, despite the high initial price tag. There are times using standardized components makes sense and there are times when it does not. The key is to clearly define objectives, identify alternatives, evaluate the feasibility (including cost, risk, etc.) of each alternative and implement the best solution. We'll discuss identifying departmental strengths and weaknesses in Chapter 2 and evaluating alternatives in later chapters.

Four Project Constraints

Before we move on, let's look at the four project constraints. Don't confuse this with task constraints, which is a separate matter altogether. The project constraints are *scope*, *time*, *cost*, and *quality* (quality is sometimes referred to a *functionality*, *performance*, or *features*). They're often written as a formula to denote the *relationship* between the elements. You typically can't take these four elements and perform a mathematical calculation on them based on the formula, but it does describe the relationship between these elements:

Scope = Time x Cost x Quality

Let's define each term here.

- **Scope**   Previously, we defined *scope* as the total amount of work to be accomplished in the project. Scope is often defined both by what will and will not be done in the project. Defining what will not be accomplished can be a great reality check for all involved.

- **Time**   *Time* clearly is the total amount of time the project will take. As mentioned earlier, there is a direct relationship between scope and time—the more you want to get done, the longer it will usually take.

- **Cost**   *Cost* is the cost of the project including all direct and indirect costs.

- **Quality or Performance** *Quality* is sometimes a confusing term. It typically refers to the features of the project or the performance requirements. Quality is often sacrificed when projects get behind schedule or sideways with their funding. Quality is also reduced when there are errors, omissions, and re-work due to poor project planning. Both *scope* (how much gets done) and *quality* (how well the project meets expectations or requirements) are reduced when one or more required or desired features are not included in the final project deliverables.

The relationship describes how these elements are related because if you increase the scope, either intentionally or via the insidious scope creep, you will have to modify at least one of the three elements on the other side of the equal sign. For instance, if you want to increase scope, you will either have to spend more time or more money (or both) to accomplish the additional work. Alternately, if you increase scope and you cannot increase the time or cost, you will most likely have to reduce the quality. If a project is set to go and you're suddenly told you must do the project for 30% less money or in 20% less time, something has to change. The relationship among these elements is important to understand and we'll spend time working on this concept and give you specific tools to use.

Here's a corollary to that concept—you cannot initially define all four variables. If you were to randomly select four numbers—10, 2, 4, 9—and plug them into this equation, it won't work. You need to have one or more variables to make the equation work with the other randomly selected numbers. In this case, we'll use 10, 2, 4 and y. Now, if you try to make the equation work, you solve for y and you can always solve the equation, regardless of what those three numbers are. The same holds true for the relationship between scope, time, cost, and quality. You can't define all four at the front end of the project and expect that the project will succeed (achieve all four metrics). There is a very high likelihood that it won't.

Often when you're handed a project, you're told what to accomplish (*scope*), how quickly you must complete it (*time*), what the budget will be (*cost*) and what features the project must include (*quality*). That's the best recipe for project disaster ever devised and yet it's done every day in companies all over the world. It's important to note that we're talking about projects that are just dropped in your lap with these four parameters defined for you without any research or planning behind the numbers. If the project has been thought through and experienced subject matter experts have worked to develop these four parameters, it is possible you might hit these numbers. As the project manager, your job is to do the planning that will allow you to more accurately define all four elements. Once those are defined and the project begins, those are the metrics you're going to try to meet. Once you've planned your project, it is not only possible to define all four elements, it's expected. Later in this book, we'll look at these elements and how to negotiate so that at least one becomes your "variable" so you actually can solve your project equation and how to develop these four variables when you're in the planning phase of your project.

Projects, Programs, and Portfolios

Projects are discrete efforts that define and deliver a single result such as a software release or a hardware upgrade. Many companies have multiple projects underway at any given point in time. Collectively, these projects are referred to as *programs*. *Program management* is the management of multiple projects that share resources, tools, time, and talent. *Portfolios* are collections of projects and/or programs, and in large companies, portfolio management is a major undertaking. There's been increasing talk about portfolio management in the IT arena, so you may want to research this topic further if you work in a large company that's likely to have a Program or Portfolio Management Office. Companies are also starting to create Program (or Portfolio) Management Offices and appoint Program (Portfolio) Management Officers. As you can see, you can drown in the alphabet soup of acronyms. Don't worry about the letters, just be sure to watch developments both in your company and in the larger market so you stay up-to-date with the latest trends and initiatives in your industry.

The IT Factor…

Portfolio Management—What's All The Buzz About?

A January 2005 article by Dean Meyer in CIO Magazine explains portfolio management in the IT arena in this manner: "In IT circles, *portfolio management* is being used to describe a wide range of initiatives, from project-approval processes to project management methods and tools." While your IT department may not be that large or you may not be CIO (yet), you might benefit from reading up on this emerging trend in the IT field. You can find the CIO Magazine article at www.cio.com/leadership/buzz/column.html?ID=1926. Please keep in mind that URLs change from time to time, so you may have to dig around in your favorite search engine if the article has moved.

The Gartner Group, a research organization, estimated that the portfolio management market (selling products and services related to portfolio management) would grow from $186 million in 2001 to over $1.7 billion in 2005. Project

Continued

portfolio management is big business aimed primarily at IT projects. As IT departments have to evaluate, plan, and implement a wider and wider range of projects, portfolio project management will likely gain in importance. Today, unlike even five or ten years ago, IT has to contend with supply chain management (SCM) including procurement and distribution applications; enterprise resource planning (ERP) including operations and finance applications; and customer relationship management (CRM) including sales, marketing and customer service applications. It has to deal with infrastructure, security, and e-commerce issues as well. With IT now reaching into every corner of the organization and touching almost every business process, new methods are needed to effectively manage the entire range of projects. Project portfolio management may be the next best thing since sliced bread, but only time will tell if it reaches its promised potential.

Summary

Businesses are looking for any competitive advantage they can find and IT departments are looking to squeeze more productivity out of the same (or fewer) budget dollars. As a result, there have been renewed efforts to improve business processes. Business process improvement (BPI) is a broad category that includes methodologies such as CMM, CMMI, Six Sigma, ISO9000, and more. Project management fits well into the category of business process improvement because standard project management methodologies can be applied to any type of project in any business or industry. While the particular processes may be further refined or specified by broader business process improvement systems, project management is a great starting point.

As you learned in this chapter, there are eight fundamental success factors for any project. It's important to understand these success factors because if they're missing, your project has an increased chance of failure. Successful projects may not have all eight success factors present, but the more you have, the better your chance of success. As you review the projects you already have in progress, you can see which are on track and which are at risk, then review the success factors. Chances are good you'll find those projects that are at risk are missing one or more of the eight key success factors.

We also introduced the relationship of the four project constraints—scope, time, cost, and quality. You may have already looked at your current IT projects and discovered the relationship between these elements. You may have seen that when you were asked to include six more features, you had to extend the timeline to accommodate for that change. You may have realized that when your budget was cut by 20%, you had to go back and re-negotiate the amount of work you were going to include in the project. As you become more familiar with these concepts, you'll have some excellent tools to more effectively negotiate project details with stakeholders. We'll discuss this in greater detail later, but you can ponder these relationships in past, current, and upcoming projects in the meantime.

Project, program, and portfolio management are buzzwords you may have heard about recently. They're gaining popularity and it's good to be familiar with trends and terminology that impact your job and industry.

Solutions Fast Track

Overview of Business Process Improvement Systems

☑ Companies are implementing business process improvement systems in order to gain efficiencies and competitive advantage.

☑ Project management fits into business process improvement by improving the manner in which projects of all kinds are managed.

☑ The Project Management Institute has developed the Project Management Body of Knowledge (PMBOK), which is widely accepted as the standard for project management practices.

☑ CMM and CMMI are software process improvement methodologies specified by Carnegie Mellon University's Software Engineering Institute.

☑ Six Sigma is a business process improvement program that has its roots in Motorola quality problems in the 1970's and was evangelized by Jack Welch, former CEO of General Electric.

☑ Six Sigma lacks a centrally managed set of specifications and certification authority.

☑ ISO specifications pertain to different industries and different business arenas. The current ISO9001:2000 is primarily concerned with business to business dealings and the ISO 14000 specification has to do with environmental impact.

Overview of Project Management

☑ Software development projects are successful about 28% of the time.

☑ 50%–75% of the total cost of any project is due to errors, omissions, and re-work.

☑ Errors found early are less expensive and easier to fix than those found by the customer.

☑ Eight success factors have been identified. Projects that have these factors tend to be more successful than those lacking these success factors.

☑ Executive support, user involvement, and experienced project managers are the first three success factors and all involve people.

☑ The remaining five success factors involve processes: clear objectives, smaller scope, shorter schedules with more milestones, clearly defined project management processes, and standard infrastructure.

Four Project Constraints

☑ There is a relationship between project scope, time, cost, and quality. If any one element changes, it changes the equation.

☑ Projects are often assigned with all four elements specified without any supporting research. When this occurs, the project team must work to validate the assumptions or negotiate changes.

☑ Be prepared to respond to changes in any of the constraints by practicing good PM skills and ensuring the project sponsor is aware of the change and how it will impact the other constraints and the project as a whole.

Projects, Programs, Portfolios

☑ Multiple projects are often referred to as programs. Portfolios are corporate-level collections of project or programs.

☑ Large companies often use program and portfolio management to balance competing demands for resources including time, talent, and funding.

☑ Portfolio management is currently a popular buzzword in IT and should be on your professional radar screen.

Frequently Asked Questions

The following Frequently Asked Questions, answered by the author of this book, are designed to both measure your understanding of the concepts presented in this chapter and to assist you with real-life implementation of these concepts. To have your questions about this chapter answered by the author, browse to **www.syngress.com/solutions** and click on the **"Ask the Author"** form.

Q: If I have a green belt in Six Sigma, do I need project management training?

A: Six Sigma is a business process improvement system that is implemented slightly differently at each company you go to. Project management is similar in that while there is a standard body of knowledge, PM is implemented slightly differently every place you go. Having a strong understanding of project management fundamentals will help you no matter what job or industry you end up working in and you'll find that, like Six Sigma, project management fundamentals will improve everything you do—even projects at home or in your community. It's a portable and transferable skill set that's definitely worth getting.

Q: My company has just achieved ISO9001:2000 certification. Do I need project management training?

A: ISO9000 is another rigorous business process improvement methodology. Unlike Six Sigma, ISO standards are centrally managed and archived. ISO9000 standards are the same wherever you go. However, just as with Six Sigma, you can always benefit from understanding project management fundamentals. Standards in companies are sometimes applied only to development or manufacturing processes. Being able to implement a consistent project management methodology is certainly part of business process improvement even if it's outside the scope of the BPI methodology your company is using.

Q: If I learn the project management fundamentals in this book, will I have to learn someone else's system later on?

A: No. The project management fundamentals in this book are just that—the fundamentals found in any project management system. Though the terminology or specific implementation will change from company to company (and from project management system to project management system), once you know and understand the basics, you can build on that knowledge and adapt to any system that your company uses.

Q: We have no executive support for many of our IT projects. What can we do about that?

A: As you learned in this chapter, executive support both for a project management methodology and for the IT projects you undertake is critical for project success. In the next chapter, you'll learn how to make the business case for your projects by tying them into strategic corporate initiatives and by providing various business analyses that will have your top executives ready to sign on the dotted line and ready to support your initiatives.

Q: I've run a lot of projects in the past, some have failed, some have been cancelled, and some have been successful. Does that make me an "experienced" project manager even if I have no formal training?

A: Experience takes many forms, so yes, you probably are an experienced project manager (project success factor #3). After reading through this book, you might want to review some of your successful and failed projects and see what went right and what went wrong in light of your new knowledge. This will help you improve your skills and provide you excellent material for your next job interview, should you apply for a new position using your experience as a project manager. Using the information presented in the remainder of this book will supplement your skills and fill in gaps. It will also provide you with a thorough, systematic process to use if you don't already have one.

Q: The projects at our company are large and complex. Will the project management fundamentals in this book be of any use?

A: Absolutely. For instance, in this chapter alone you've learned that smaller projects, shorter time frames (schedules), and smaller scope (amount of work to be done) all contribute to project success. You might take this knowledge and see if you can divide up any of your current projects—perhaps looking for projects that are off-track and seemingly headed for disaster, failure, or cancellation. Splitting them into smaller projects might save those precarious projects and make you look good in the process. Even if you can't split up your projects, understanding these fundamentals will allow you to understand any other, more complex projects. Larger, more complex projects typically have more "moving parts" and are more difficult to coordinate and manage. You may need more advanced project tools to keep everything on track, but the basics don't change.

Q: You mentioned the four constraints of any project—scope, time, cost, and quality. In our company, quality is always of utmost importance, how does that impact this "equation"?

A: Any company in business today should be concerned with delivering the highest quality possible. However, quality can be relative. If you are building a house and your budget gets tight, you might choose polished brass fixtures over 18K gold plated fixtures. They both do exactly the same thing and may work exactly alike (same *functional* quality) but one isn't quite as luxurious as the other and by downgrading from gold to brass, you have reduced quality without impacting the overall quality of the finished product. Note that *quality* is sometimes referred to as *performance, functionality*, or *features*. When we discuss quality and grade later in this book, we'll talk more about this.

Q: Our company is small and we have a very tight IT budget. You haven't really talked about project management software tools. Are we going to have to purchase something like that in order to use the concepts in this book?

A: No, you will not *have* to purchase project management tools to learn and use the concepts in this book. Many companies (and IT managers) find these tools helpful, but they are not required. That said, the bigger and more complex the project is, the more likely you are to see significant savings and efficiency gains by using various PM tools. There are numerous Web-based tools you can use, many with reasonably monthly subscription rates. Several enable collaboration for geographically disbursed teams, while others provide additional communication tools. However, if you're running smaller projects, you can do so with a pen and paper, Microsoft Excel, Microsoft Outlook, Lotus Notes, etc. While those may not be optimal, they're certainly adequate for many smaller projects. One final note: Having project management software doesn't make you a project manager any more than having Microsoft Excel makes you an accountant. Learning project management fundamentals is the first step to using any project management tool more productively and effectively.

Chapter 2

What's Corporate Strategy Got To Do With IT?

Solutions in this chapter:

- Overview of Corporate Strategy in Today's Environment

- Aligning IT with Corporate Strategy: Taking It One Step Further

- Understanding Your Company's Strategies

- Developing Your IT Strategy

- Assessing Your Current IT Environment

- Developing Your IT Operational Roadmap

☑ Summary

☑ Solutions Fast Track

☑ Frequently Asked Questions

Introduction

Many IT professionals look back on the 1990's as "the good old days." Money was flowing like water from an endless fountain and IT increasingly was viewed as the Holy Grail of business. Within a year or two of the dawning of the new millennium, things took a distinct turn for the worse, especially if you were in the IT field. All of those promising startup companies wilted as that endless fountain of venture capital and IPO profits ran dry. Reality set in and irrational exuberance gave way to rational moderation, which left many IT departments caught in a bind. During the late 1990's, they couldn't deliver on some of these pie in the sky dreams and they couldn't find enough qualified people to help them meet demand. Once the boom went bust, just the opposite was true. IT was asked to deliver more with less—less staff, less funding, and fewer resources. The tables had turned completely in just a few short years.

Many IT departments are facing cutbacks and outsourcing. In order to remain competitive, IT departments must add value to companies. If the IT department is seen as a cost center or a utility function, it's likely not going to get the funding, the resources, or the support needed to be truly effective. If all you want to do is maintain the corporate network and provide 99% uptime, then you may not need to worry about strategy. If you're interested in taking your department, your company, and your career to the next level, you'll need to begin to understand and contribute to the larger corporate vision. Strategy is the road that will take you there. If you're anxious to get right into the heart of IT project management, you can head right into Chapter 5, but do so with caution. These first four chapters lay the foundation for IT project management by helping you understand the environment that surrounds all IT projects. By understanding the environment, you'll be better prepared to define, plan, implement, and manage any project that comes your way.

Overview of Corporate Strategy in Today's Environment

If you're an avid reader of online IT news, blogs, etc., you may have read a lot in the past year or so about "aligning IT with corporate strategies." That concept is well-intended, but stops just short of the target. Certainly, any IT department out-of-step with its company's strategies is in jeopardy, but the issue is deeper and wider than that. The issue is not simply whether or not IT aligns with corporate strategies or not, but how IT initiatives *can* drive (or at least contribute to) corporate strategies and perhaps provide competitive advantage. That's a slightly different take on the current alignment discussion, but in order for IT to be seen as a valued-added component of the business, it has to do more than jump in line with the corporate strategies (though, admittedly, that alone would be a big improvement for some). From a corporate viewpoint, it's fair to say that if your IT initiatives are not aligned with your business initiatives, your company will be in serious trouble within a few years. Technology is increasingly an integral part of the business environment. How well and how fast your firm can implement technology to drive efficiency is what will separate companies. Technology touches every part of the business today. Not only are internal functions dependent upon technology, but increasingly, customers want to reach directly into your company to get the data they want or need. It used to be that the customer might call you and ask for information on financial transactions for the previous quarter. Now the customer wants to be able to log into a secure server and grab the information in real time. Couple that with the fact that the lone employee in a remote part of the world needs to be just as connected as those at corporate headquarters and you begin to understand not only how pervasive technology has become, but also how integral it is to the company's success.

In this chapter, we're going to explore these issues so you can navigate through the sometimes confusing world of corporate strategies and ultimately, corporate IT funding. If you're not a business or finance type person or you think this topic is really boring, then this chapter is a must-read for you. The information presented will make you smarter about how companies work without boring the daylights out of you.

The IT Factor...

Fast-Track to CIO

The April 2005 issue of CIO *Insight Magazine* presented the findings of a research study on the role of the CIO. Although a large percentage of CIOs still come from a strictly IT background, there's been an increase in recent years in CIOs with what the study calls a "hybrid" background - people who have experience in both IT and business. Not surprisingly, these hybrid CIOs are more likely to be in charge of or involved in corporate strategy. They are more confident that they have enough business experience to do their jobs well and they earn, on average, 9% more than their counterparts. Women with a combination IT and business background are 15% more likely than their female IT counterparts to move into the CIO position, though women still account for only 9% of all CIOs out there. Hybrid CIOs are found in small, medium, and large companies in equal measure. So, if you were wondering what corporate strategy has to do with IT....these

Continued

statistics show a very clear trend toward hiring and rewarding those with both IT and business experience.

If you're looking to get on the fast track to CIO, you should absolutely improve your business skills. The material in this chapter will give you a running start; the rest is up to you.

Source: The CIO Insight Research Study, The Role of the CIO, *Meet the Hybrid CIO: Well-Paid and Powerful*, April 2005, Number 52, pp. 65-76. Copyright 2005, Ziff Davis Media, Inc.

Aligning IT with Corporate Strategy: Taking It One Step Further

Much has been written about aligning IT activities with corporate strategy. That is a good first step, but not the whole answer. Aligning IT with corporate strategy can imply a passive role—the company charts its course and the IT department, the ready second mate, steps up and says, "I'm behind you 100%." Always nice to have that support, but what about the scenario where the IT department actually contributes to developing the corporate strategy? That's taking it one step further. In this chapter, we'll discuss ways you can work on contributing to corporate strategy, but we first need to understand what the current environment is like.

Many IT departments today are realizing they must run as other departments do in the organization. More and more, IT departments are being held accountable for metrics and budgets; some are charging IT costs to internal corporate departments to account for IT expenditures; some are comparing internal costs to outsourcing costs to determine where savings can be gleaned. Though IT departments are beginning to use standard business tools and metrics, there's still work to do in this area. Here are some interesting statistics from 2002 (according to *The Business of I.T. Portfolio Management: Balancing Risk, Innovation and ROI*, Meta Group White Paper, January 2002):

- 89% of companies are flying blind, with virtually no IT metrics in place except for finance.

- 84% of companies either do not do business cases for any of their IT projects or do them only on select, key projects.

- 84% of companies are unable to adjust and align their IT budgets with business needs more than once or twice a year.

Given the lackluster success rates for projects (discussed in Chapter 1), you can see that making sure IT efforts are, at minimum, aligned with corporate strategies is important—the statistics clearly show there is ample room for improvement. By working actively to create this alignment (and we're going to take it one step further later in the chapter), you can:

- Maximize the value of your company's IT investments while minimizing the risk (hint: corporate executives usually prefer to avoid risk whenever possible).

- Reduce or eliminate redundancy in IT projects.

- Schedule corporate and IT resources more efficiently.

- Better integrate the IT function into the company so the mentality shifts from "us versus them" to "all of us."

- Improve the business skills of the IT team and improve the understanding of IT in the business teams.

In this economic climate, IT departments are being required to deliver more with less. CIOs and IT departments are being asked (or required) to demonstrate a return on technology investments. Yet, looking at the statistics cited earlier, that's a difficult task. So how do we bridge the gap? Part of the answer is looking at how corporate strategy and operations interact so you can begin to line things up. Once you've started to align with corporate strategy, you may find opportunities to take it a step further and actually help drive corporate strategy. Once strategies are defined, you create your operational plan, which includes all of your IT projects and other operations. Yes, these are ambitious objectives, but if you don't stretch, you'll never grow.

Strategy Versus Tactical

Let's take a moment to discuss the difference between strategy and operations. A strategy is a high-level vision of where the company is headed. Typically it describes *where* it's headed, not *how* it will get there. The *where* (and sometimes *why*) is the strategic component. The *how* is the operational, or tactical, component. In this chapter, we'll use the terms *operational* and *tactical* interchangeably. Even though they're not exactly synonymous, they describe the ongoing operations and methods used to achieve strategic goals. For example, if you say that you want to go to Santa Fe, NM, clearly that's the *where*. It does not describe *how* you're going to get there. You could drive a car, take a bus, take a train, walk, ride a bicycle, take a plane, or even some combination. These are all various ways that describe *how* you'll meet your objective. It's important to make this distinction because as soon as you start describing *how* you'll get something done, you've moved into the operational or tactical realm. When trying to define strategy, continually check to make sure you're describing *what* must be done or *where* you're headed. Figure 2.1 depicts the ideal relationship between strategies and operations in an organization.

Figure 2.1 Corporate and IT Strategies

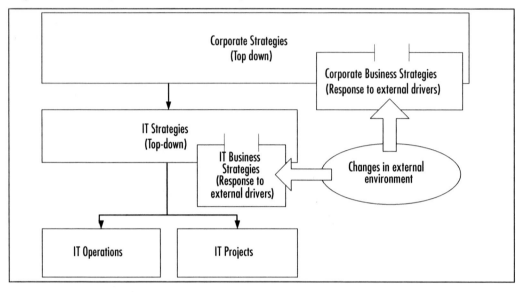

Competitive Advantage

During the heady *dot-com* days of the late 1990's, there were opportunities to use technology to develop competitive advantages because not all companies were able to implement technology-based solutions with equal finesse or speed. Largely because of the dot-com boom, technology as a business tool became a *de facto* or required element in all businesses. Today, just about every company—small, medium and large—uses technology in some form or another. Some small companies may just have one or two computers running e-mail, an Internet browser, and office applications (word processing, spreadsheets, etc.). Medium and large companies must have a computer network, and employees must have e-mail and Internet access at minimum. In most cases, a wide variety of business applications must also be deployed and maintained. It's reasonable, then, to state that technology by itself no longer provides any meaningful competitive advantage because all companies are using IT to some extent.

That said, there are opportunities to develop competitive advantages within the IT arena. Let's look at three key opportunities for creating competitive advantage using technology.

Execution and Efficiency

How well a company is able to execute its strategic and operational plans can be a distinct competitive advantage. Any company that can gain significant efficiency in operational execution will likely beat out its competitors—until their competitors learn how to replicate those results. Technology can often be a key element in creating those operational efficiencies. Here's a great example. There was a time when the only way to get a letter across the country was by putting a first class stamp on it and popping it in the mail (U.S. Postal Service). Then one day, a company named Federal Express (FedEx) proposed something more radical—if you were willing to pay approximately 30 times the cost of a first class stamp, they would get your letter to the recipient overnight, guaranteed. They could do this because they'd implemented technology that allowed them to track every single package at every single stop. At a moment's notice, they could tell you exactly where that package was and when it would be delivered or the time of delivery and recipient's name. That's a great example of operational efficiency through technology. It was a distinct competitive advantage for a while—that is, until the increased use of e-mail and the implementation of similar technologies at companies like UPS and the U.S. Postal Service (among others). At that point, the competitive advantage shifted away from the technology itself to the ability of the company to expertly *utilize* that technology more effectively than its competitors—that's where execution and improved business processes play a role. It's possible that one company may still have a better technology implementation than the others, but if they all are using a similar technology, it comes down to who can utilize that technology more effectively. And as we all know, technology doesn't stand still, so the continued opportunity is to expand and reach into new areas with the same or new technology.

Efficiency gains through the effective use of technology may create a competitive advantage, but that type of competitive advantage is often short-lived. Today, there are a number of express delivery services all using some sort of tracking and routing technology solutions. How well they fare is now more a result of how well they *utilize*, *manage*, and *leverage* that technology rather than the technology itself.

Leveraging Technology to Lower Costs

As we've seen repeatedly in the past five or ten years, technology can clearly be used to lower costs and create a competitive advantage. Again, sometimes this advantage is short-lived, other times it has a longer shelf life. To continue the previous example, FedEx had an interesting proposition—pay us a lot more for the security of knowing your letter will arrive tomorrow. Companies were willing to pay a lot more for the ability to know exactly where an important package or document was at any given time. As e-mail became more ubiquitous, companies discovered that e-mailing a document was faster, cheaper, and just as reliable as FedEx. Those companies leveraged technology to lower certain shipping costs. Did companies stop shipping things? No, there were still documents (and everything else imaginable) crisscrossing the globe in the belly of express delivery airplanes, but the number of letters it carried certainly may have dropped with the advent of e-mail. Of course, people have now become so accustomed to "instant" everything that express delivery companies are often used when a plain old stamp would do just fine, but that's another story altogether.

Major cost-cutting initiatives in recent years have also driven the expectation that technology should be leveraged to lower costs. Initiatives such as Total Cost of Ownership (TCO) have forced IT departments to look at how the very technology they're using can cost even less, so it's a double spiral: using technology to lower costs, lowering the cost of using technology. It is a prevalent trend and one that's not likely to change anytime soon.

Innovation

Innovation using technology can lead to a competitive advantage. Depending on the nature of the innovation, that competitive advantage can be short- or long-term. An example of a short-term advantage is the Web-based retailers who in the late 1990's were able to deliver easy, secure online shopping for consumers. Amazon clearly got a running start and defined some of the standards for e-commerce used today. However, some of the technological innovations were replicated and some of the competitive advantage of technological innovation was reduced or eliminated. Amazon continues to look for ways to leverage technology to gain efficiency in execution and leverage technology to reduce costs knowing that its competitors will copy (or attempt to copy) its technology innovations.

Another excellent example is Netflix, the online movie rental company. They went head-to-head with bricks-and-mortar outfits like Blockbuster. Their innovative strategy used the Internet for movie renters to look for and reserve movies. They used the old-fashioned U.S. mail service to deliver movies right to the movie renter's door, which oddly enough, was an innovative idea. They used technology to manage their regional distribution centers to make sure that it took no more than 2 days to get a movie from any distribution center to the customer. Innovation using a mixture of approaches and technologies gave Netflix a significant competitive advantage. It took about 18 months before Wal-Mart and Blockbuster, among others, tried to compete with Netflix. While the jury is still out on how Netflix will fare, Wal-Mart recently announced they were handing over their movie rental business to Netflix to manage for them. Wal-Mart with all its technological savvy perhaps realized Netflix had the technology and the operational know-how that Wal-Mart wanted. Rather than fight them, Wal-Mart clearly decided to join them. The innovative use of technology provided a distinct competitive advantage to Netflix for a few years. As the innovative technology and technology-driven processes are copied, Netflix will need to focus on execution, efficiencies and costs to maintain a competitive advantage.

There may be other examples you can think of where technology provides a competitive advantage to a company, but chances are good that those examples ultimately fit into one of the three categories just mentioned. The expectation that technology itself will create the competitive advantage has been mostly relegated to the category of "short-term advantage", but the current expectation is that technology can and should help drive corporate efficiencies and lower costs.

With that as the backdrop, then, it's clear that your IT projects will have to meet one (or a combination) of these expectations. As you select IT projects for your department to undertake, these elements should be kept firmly in the forefront. However, as you'll see in a moment, you can take it one step further.

APPLYING YOUR KNOWLEDGE

Understanding the expectations for technology and the IT department in your company, in the industry, and in the market is critical in today's environment. The more you understand these requirements, the better chance you have of keeping your IT department (and your career) on the right track. Most of us don't want to just sit back and go along for the ride, especially when there are new and exciting technologies right around the corner that can make a huge difference in the ways companies do business. Many IT pros are in this field for just that reason—to be on the cutting edge of technology and to be part of the evolutionary (sometimes revolutionary) process.

Take time to understand how technology is viewed and implemented in your company and in your competitors as well. It will give you some idea of where the competitive advantage is and where it might be headed. It's all about competitive advantage and you and your IT department *can* make a meaningful contribution.

At the conclusion of Chapter 1, we briefly touched on the concept of portfolio management. Portfolio management is the management of all IT projects in the company and the alignment and allocation of resources for those projects. It's the latest in a long line of attempts to quantify, measure, and evaluate the contribution

IT makes to an organization. Other departments, like sales, marketing, and production more clearly contribute to the company's bottom line. On the other hand, IT is often viewed as a financial "black hole", a necessary evil, or the source of the latest electronic gadgets. In some cases, IT is seen as a solid business partner providing "utility" services such as e-mail, Internet connectivity, and business application support. In rare cases, IT is seen as a strategic component of the business, but our goal in this chapter is to catalyze change in that area so your IT efforts can become more strategic in nature. Many IT projects are all about "keeping the lights on" and have no clear value proposition. Think of it this way: When you hire an employee, you usually don't look for someone who will come in, do an average job and go home. You want someone who will contribute to making your department and the company better than it is today. This attitude should hold for your IT projects. Yes, you have to get the job done, but you don't want to settle for *just* that. Later in this chapter and throughout this book, you'll learn more about how to identify strategic projects from operational ("keeping the lights on") projects so you stand a better chance of making a meaningful contribution to your company (and let's face it, to your own career as well). While there is a growing trend toward charging for internal IT functions as a way of exposing or accounting for the true cost of IT, it's not clear which way this trend will go. You might find it useful to calculate the internal cost and apportion it to the various corporate departments, but unless IT is adding value and seen as strategic, all you're really doing is buying yourself a bit of time or shifting costs around on the balance sheet. There's nothing wrong with accurately accounting for costs, but don't look to this to save your IT department.

IT managers need to manage differently in today's world. It's not enough to come up with a budget and do a great job with service levels. Successful IT managers understand that they must find ways to add value to the company and to effectively communicate that value to key corporate executives and managers. Otherwise, the long-held perception that IT is nothing but a cost center will continue to thwart genuinely innovative and strategic IT initiatives.

Understanding Your Company's Strategies

In this next section, we're going to discuss ways to look at and uncover your company's current strategies. We're doing this for two reasons. First, corporate strategy is not always well defined and second, it's sometimes not formally stated. In order to align your IT strategies with corporate strategies, you have to know what those corporate strategies are. The expectation isn't that you're going to go on a mission to develop your company's strategies, just that you're going to do a bit of research and a bit of thinking about these issues so you can begin to align your IT efforts in that direction. Don't get overwhelmed thinking you have to go *do* all these things—these are tools you can use if and when you need them. Your job is not to single-handedly develop your company's strategies, but if you don't understand where your company is headed, you have a very slim chance of aligning your IT strategies to your company's strategic objectives. Read through this section, but don't turn it into a big action item for yourself. The action part comes later.

Cheat Sheet...

Corporate Strategy

Volumes have been written about corporate and business strategy and our goal is not to rehash everything ever written. However, there are a few key things you can learn about corporate and business strategy that will help you better understand your company's direction and how IT can play an important role. Here's the short version.

Corporate strategy is typically created at the top of the organization and it should be relatively stable. Companies that continually change corporate strategies are often floundering looking for the right answer. A strategy may involve using (or even trying out) different *tactics*, but the overall direction should remain relatively stable over time. Let's look at an example. Microsoft developed a corporate strategy that was summarized by, "A computer on every desk and Windows on every computer." Their strategy was to dominate the desktop market. How did they plan on dominating the market? They used a number of different tactics to do so. In some cases, they bought their competitors; in other cases, they added features or slashed the price of Windows. Microsoft's detractors would say that Microsoft sometimes used heavy-handed tactics, but the point is that Microsoft created a long-term strategy to dominate the desktop computer and they are succeeding. Their methods or tactics along the way changed based on changes in the market, but their overall strategy did not waiver. With new technologies on the horizon, Microsoft may have to modify its strategy, but that would come after years of successfully holding fast to a single strategic vision.

Corporate Strategies and IT

If you want to create a more strategic vision of your IT department, the first step is to learn about your company's corporate strategies. In some companies, there is a clearly defined plan shared with top executives and sometimes middle management. If you're not privy to the company's strategic plan, sit down with your boss or a top executive and learn about it. If you aren't sure how to begin this quest, think of it as a corporate job interview. Do some research—much of the information is just a few search engine clicks away. If you are going to sit down with corporate executives, make sure you've done your homework. Answer as many of these questions on your own as possible. If you're well prepared, you'll create a positive impression and you'll likely get better answers from the top execs. Research the answers to these questions:

- What industry or niche is this company in?

- Where is the company headed? Where does it want to be in 3–5 years?

- What are the company's mission, vision and core values?

- Who are the key competitors and what are they up to?

- What's happening in the broader market or market niche that will potentially impact the firm?

- What impact do economic cycles have on the company? Does it do well in growing or shrinking economies or is it not particularly vulnerable to economic fluctuations?

- Does your company lead or follow its market? (Some companies are always out front innovating, others are always back in the pack, less innovative but often more stable. There is no "good" or "bad" answer here.)

- If the company is publicly held, what do the quarterly and annual reports say about the company, its goals and direction?

- If the company is publicly held, how has the stock price fared compared to its competitors and compared to the overall market? How has it done year-to-date (YTD), in one, three, and five years? Are securities analysts recommending buying, holding, or selling your company's stock?

- How are the company's financials? Strong, weak, improving, deteriorating?

- What do your company's press releases say the company is up to?

Even if you're not particularly strong in business and finance, if you understand your company and the business it's in, you should be able to understand the fundamental concepts related to your firm. For instance, some companies track very closely with the economy. Others don't at all. How does your company fare when the economy is running full-speed ahead? How has it done in the past three or four years when the economy was in recession? Here's an example. The adult education market is a multi-billion dollar market in the U.S. with a wide variety of companies providing degree programs for working adults during evening or weekend classes. During lean economic times, people often choose to get further education to help them keep their jobs or find new jobs in a tight market. During expansive economic times, people seek further education in order to qualify for new jobs and new opportunities that arise as businesses expand. Therefore, when you look at demand for education in that partic-ular niche market, you see it's almost impervious to economic fluctuations. Other busi-nesses do track with up or down economic cycles. You don't need to have a Ph.D. in economics to understand how the economy could impact your business and by taking time to consider these higher level issues, you'll learn a lot and be able to develop a better IT plan. We'll discuss devising your IT strategy later in this chapter.

Obviously, the company is not going to come right out and announce to the world (and consequently, to its competitors) what all of its short and long-term strategies are, but the overall direction can certainly be discerned by asking questions and doing some research. Answering the questions posed above will give you a better than average overview of your company. Once you've answered all the questions you can, request a meeting with someone above you in the organization who is likely to answer your questions. If you prepare the answers to the above information in a brief document and bring it with you to this meeting, you'll impress the boss with your preparation and won't waste his or her time asking questions to which you could have (and should have) gotten the answers on your own. You can use this document and the data you collect as the basis of a conversation about where the company is headed. The point is to gather enough information so you can create an IT strategy that does better than just align with the corporate strategy—it contributes to it in a new, substantive, or innovative way.

Sound like a tall order? It is, but it might be the most important thing you do as head of your IT department. Yes, the day-to-day projects, initiatives, and crises will continue and you'll still have to deal with those, but if you can find a way to take the information you glean from this process, synthesize it, and create a strategic IT plan that contributes to and improves upon the corporate strategy, you're going to find that there is far more executive support for IT projects than ever before. And, if you recall, executive support is number one on the list of success factors for a project. If you are an IT project manager and not the IT manager, these same principles apply even though you are not responsible for the overall direction of the IT department.

Business Strategies and IT

Business strategies are those strategies that are a response to changing market conditions. Businesses don't exist in a vacuum and though they may spend a lot of time and effort developing their *corporate* strategies (which should remain fairly stable through time), *business* strategies will have to be modified by changing market conditions. In some circles, these strategies are called *business strategies* to differentiate them from long-term *corporate strategies*. If a company's main competitor suddenly reduces its prices by 30%, the *business* strategy might have to shift overnight to respond to this change. The overarching corporate strategy remains unchanged. For instance, GE had as its goal to be number one or number two in every market it was in. This meant that the business strategies could change to respond to market conditions as long as the result was to keep GE in the number one or number two slot. Business strategies will change and flex as the market shifts, but overarching corporate strategies should remain fairly constant.

So, what does all this have to do with IT? The strategies you implement via your IT strategic plan should contribute to (or be aligned with) the overall corporate strategy, but the business strategies you implement will change to respond to changes in the external marketplace. This is important to understand, especially when looking at IT projects. While your project may contribute to the long-term corporate strategy, it's also likely it will have to align with business strategy to ensure the projects help the company respond quickly and effectively to changes in the market. This is a tall order to fill, but understanding these elements helps you discern where your IT projects fall in the scheme of things and it might help you manage them more effectively down the line.

Cheat Sheet...

The Skinny on Corporate and Business Strategies

Corporate strategies come from within the company and do not change based on what's happening in the outside world. *Business* strategies derive from changing forces in the external marketplace and may influence the corporate strategies and corporate (and IT) operations.

Now that we've defined corporate strategies and business strategies, we're ready to jump into the specifics of developing IT strategies. If you're not the head of the IT department or not your company's CIO, you can still use this information to improve your business skills as they relate to IT. Even if you are not responsible for developing these plans, thinking about these issues will make you a more valuable contributor.

There are numerous methods you can use to develop strategies and a thorough discussion of them is outside the scope of this book. However, there are some common elements to these methods and we'll discuss these to give you specific tools to use to devise your IT strategies. Also keep in mind that you may already have a solid understanding of your company's strategies and some excellent ideas about what your IT strategies are or should be. If so, feel free to use this information rather than going through the exercises described in the next section. The methods described next are simply tools to help you look at the current environment so you can develop strategies based on the information you uncover. Remember, any method simply provides a framework in which to think—it will not do the thinking for you nor will it provide you a list of strategies when you're finished.

Methods To Assist In Developing IT Strategies

The first step in developing your IT strategies is to take some time to think about where your company is headed and what its strategies are or have been. If you've ever thought, "If I ran this company, I would…" then this is a great opportunity to put those ideas to the test. Although there are probably numerous factors to which you are not privy, your evaluation of the company's direction is the best place to start. One way you can do this is to look at what your company has accomplished in the past three to five years. You can also look at any public corporate documents such as news articles, press releases, and stockholder information if the company is publicly held, as mentioned earlier in this chapter. All of this information gives you an idea of not only what the company intended to do, but also what it was able to accomplish. Take time to review what role (if any) IT played in the intended and actual results of the company in the past three to five years. Did IT contribute significantly? Did IT play a "utility" role? Did IT projects get cancelled, delayed, funded, extended? Answering these questions will help you begin to see the role of IT in the company in the recent past.

Core Competencies

Companies often try to define core competencies as a way to continually focus on what they do best and leave the rest to someone else. Sometimes they outsource these non-core competencies; sometimes they simply stop doing them altogether. The same holds true for IT core competencies. Whether your IT department primarily manages the network and its users or develops custom software solutions, you should look at your core competencies. Here's a good example. A company in the hotel business has a great IT department that manages the reservations system, hotel inventory system, and restaurant services system. Is developing an integrated software program that includes these three key functions part of the IT department's core competencies or not? There is no simple yes or no answer here. If the IT department has a group of talented, experienced software developers, the answer might be yes. If the IT department is primarily focused on deploying, maintaining, upgrading, and repairing these three core applications and its related infrastructure, the answer might be no. If it's not a core competency and the company wants/needs an integrated solution, the IT department can either develop the requirements and have an external company develop the application, or it can develop the skills internally through targeted hiring. As you can see from these examples, there are often several approaches that might be feasible, but usually only one or two solutions that leverage core competencies.

Identifying the core competencies of your IT staff and department will help you develop an appropriate strategy for moving forward. If you can't define your core competencies, you may have an IT department in transition from one role to another or you need to step back and really focus on what core competencies it *should* have and work to develop/acquire those. Understanding your IT department's core competencies will also help you make smarter decisions when planning new IT projects. We'll discuss that in more detail later in the book.

SWOT Analysis

Another useful planning tool is the SWOT analysis, which stands for *strengths, weaknesses, opportunities*, and *threats*. This is a commonly used technique in all types of business planning. Some like to view strengths and weaknesses as internal to the company and opportunities and threats as external to the company. In truth, you can do a SWOT analysis on just about anything and this includes your company, your competitors, and the marketplace. For instance, after looking at your company's strengths and weaknesses (internal), you might also see some opportunities and threats that are internal to your company. Internal opportunities might be those related to leveraging your core competencies. Internal threats might be politics, significant changes in top management, or a change in corporate ownership, for example. You don't have to spend days or weeks on this exercise, but you should give these factors some thought. What does your company do well (strength)? What does you company not do as well as its competitors, or not do well at all (weakness)? Based on your company's strengths and weaknesses, what are the opportunities in the marketplace that will leverage your company's strengths? Based on your company's weaknesses, what are the external threats that exist? Are there any opportunities or threats that are internal to your company (pending take over, change in direction, etc.)?

Next, do a SWOT analysis on your IT department. Be brutally honest and be willing to look at the good, the bad, and the ugly. What is your IT department very good at? What is it not so good (or terrible) at? What are the current or possible opportunities for your IT department, and what are the known or possible threats to your IT department? By looking at these elements, you'll begin to see the picture come into focus. If you're really brave (or secure), you may want to ask department outsiders for their view of the IT department's strengths and weaknesses. You might be quite surprised by what you learn and you can incorporate that feedback into your planning process.

For each strength you identify, you should look for corresponding opportunities. You want to play to your strengths and minimize your weaknesses. You also want to correlate each of your identified weaknesses to potential opportunities and threats. For instance, if there is a great opportunity, but it really hits you in your weak spot, you might choose to forgo the opportunity or take steps to strengthen that weakness. Similarly, if you spot a threat that plays right into a weakness, you'll need to take decisive action to mitigate the threat or improve strength in that area. Knowing these four elements will help you align your priorities, activities and projects so you take full advantage of your strengths while managing the downside (weaknesses and threats).

Trend Analysis

Another method of developing a strategic IT plan is to look at trends in the market. These can be broken down into four main quadrants and it's possible that there may be a slightly different set of four for your company's specific industry or market. The four quadrants are:

- Customer
- Competition
- Technology
- Regulation

Customer

What's happening with your customers? What are customers looking for in general? How does IT play into this? Trends these days include customers increasingly looking for more value at a lower cost, judging a company by the service it provides, and demanding higher quality (lower tolerance for poor quality). In some cases, brand is also an issue. Understanding the trends in your customer market is vital to a good plan because without customers, you are out of business. Remember, in the IT world, you often have two (or more) customers: the internal corporate customers for whom you provide IT services and the external corporate customers who purchase your company's products and services. If your IT department develops software that your company sells as well as manages the network infrastructure, you probably have two distinct customer sets—internal users and external paying customers. You'll need to look at all IT customers in developing your IT plans.

Competition

What are the trends with your competitors? Are they gaining or losing market share? Are they equally impacted by economic trends? How are they responding to changing customer demands? How are they responding to globalization? What is the impact of technology on their business? How are your competitors managing their business knowledge? Are they outsourcing? How are they using technology in their business? How are they innovating with technology? Have they created any key alliances? Finally, are there any new competitors now or on the horizon? What are the "new guys" doing? When looking at your company's competitors, you also want to try to find out what technology they're using, how their IT department is structured and/or functioning and anything else you can glean from your competitors about their IT efforts.

Technology

How do the changes in technology impact your company (and your competitors)? How has the Internet changed your business and how will it drive change in the future? How has technology impacted your relationship with your customers (internal and external)—for better or worse? (*Press 1 if you've ever been trapped in a voice mail system, Press 2….*). How have increased mobility demands impacted your company? How have changes in the security environment impacted your company? How has the competition implemented technology? What technologies are "industry standards" in your field? What types of emerging technologies might give your company a competitive advantage if implemented early and well?

Regulation

How has the regulatory environment impacted your company? Has the opening of new trade markets (NAFTA, etc.) helped or hindered your company? Have the regulations regarding health care privacy (HIPAA—Health Insurance Portability & Accountability Act) or financial reporting (Sarbanes-Oxley) impacted your company? How have these or other regulations impacted your IT department?

APPLYING YOUR KNOWLEDGE

The methods mentioned here are only a sampling of ways you can go about analyzing where you are and where you need to be, but they are among the most user-friendly ones. While it won't hurt you to use all of these methods (and some of you very detail-oriented people out there *will*), you can keep it simple by selecting one method that aligns best with the way you prefer to think and work. Set aside a time to meet with key team members and gather input and ideas. Spend time processing the results of the meeting and reconvene again in a week or so and gather team responses, comments, and insights. Just dedicating time to this activity and making it a priority is a great start and will likely generate ideas and information you can use. If possible, include as many members of your team (or better yet, a cross-departmental team) as possible to help you avoid blind spots in your planning process. The old adage "two heads are better than one" is doubly true in the planning process.

Developing Your IT Strategy

Let's recap for a moment. We looked at the importance of aligning IT strategy to corporate strategy and even suggested you might be able to do one better by developing IT strategies that further the corporate strategy, taking it to the next level. Then, we looked at corporate strategy and tools you can use to unearth the strategies in your company. Sometimes they're written down and easy to find; other times you have to reverse engineer some information to figure out what the corporate strategy is. You're doing this because you want to make sure IT efforts are lined up in the same direction that the company's headed. Next, we looked at business strategies that come from changes in the external market and how these integrate into corporate strategies. At a high level, the corporation has strategies and business strategies, so too does the IT department. Finally, we looked at ways you can begin to figure out what your IT strategies might be.

At this point, you should have some ideas regarding what your IT strategies should be. However, you may still be pondering these questions. Take all the information you have and see if you're missing anything. Any big, crazy ideas you'd like to throw in the pot? Thinking big at the strategic level is good. You can always dial it back into reality later, but we tend to miss opportunities for innovation when we think too small. If Microsoft had said, "We'd like to be the operating system running on business desktop computers throughout the U.S." they would have missed the enormous opportunity to be on desktops in homes *and* in businesses all over the *world*.

After you've generated your ideas on what your IT strategy could look like, decide which ideas are truly innovative, play to your strengths and minimize (or mitigate) your weaknesses. Decide which ideas will help drive the company forward toward its strategic goals. Begin to look at these ideas in a more concrete way and discard any ideas that seem truly unreasonable or outside the realm of possibility, but do this *very* carefully. Sometimes innovative ideas are scrapped because initially they may not be well formulated or well articulated. While we can't always see the future clearly, pondering big, "impossible", innovative ideas can lead us to unexpected strategies that are feasible either near- or long-term. Sometimes it's just a matter of perspective.

Next, we're going to discuss several methods you can use to sort through your ideas on IT strategy. You can use all of them or just some of them. If you have a method you prefer, feel free to use it. Again, the idea is not to overwhelm you with process—just the opposite. By giving you several different methods you might use, you can pick and choose those that fit best with your business or your way of seeing things. It's not an exhaustive review of methods, just a few that are relatively user-friendly that can generate a sense of order and clarity when trying to put together your IT strategies.

APPLYING YOUR KNOWLEDGE

When you look at innovative strategic ideas (which can include ideas for innovative projects as well), you can use these four keywords as your guides: *logical, feasible, desirable,* and *affordable.* As a baseline, business activities (including all IT efforts) should be logical—do they make sense at this time in this situation? Next, are they feasible? Some great ideas are just not feasible—either now or in the future. Next, is it desirable? Again, some ideas will knock your socks off, but they're actually not desirable for any one of a number of reasons (serious downside risk is one). Something can be feasible (do-able) but not desirable. Finally, is it affordable? Sometimes we have to make the final decision between two or more competing ideas (or activities) based on which is most affordable.

If you use these four concepts in evaluating ideas and proposals, you'll be able to decide from among competing demands in a more rational manner.

One method of looking at strategy ideas (potential strategies) is to use a grid with four quadrants, each with a different risk and reward (payoff) level. This commonly used planning method provides a more tangible method of placing ideas with regard to risk and reward and you can begin sorting out which ideas are worth pursuing and which are probably not. The grid is shown in Figure 2.2.

Figure 2.2 Risk-Reward Grid

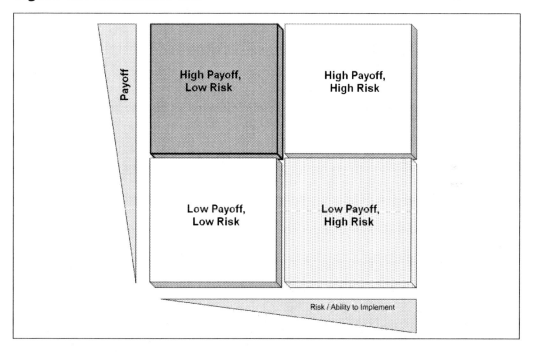

Clearly, when you're assessing both the potential payoff and the potential risks, you want to aim for the "sweet spot" where you get the greatest payoff for the lowest risk. However, there are times when you might select projects with a lower payoff and less risk or a higher payoff and more risk. Things are relative and though it would be nice if all projects fell neatly into these categories, there are always judgment calls you'll have to make. If you begin by sorting your ideas into these four quadrants or sections, you should get a clearer picture of how your ideas fit together. If you're looking toward big, innovative ideas, you're usually going to have to look in the high payoff/ high risk category. Remember that innovative use of technology can create a competitive advantage, but these days it's typically not a long-term advantage. Keeping that in mind will help when evaluating risk and reward so you can choose your projects wisely. If you don't have the final authority to pick and choose strategies or project ideas, categorizing projects according to risk/reward will help decision-makers sort through ideas and will underscore your business savvy with folks who are likely to notice.

Once you've developed your short list of ideas, approaches, and directions, look at the broader market again. How will these ideas fit into what is happening now and likely to happen in the future? If you're not looking ahead, you're going to be blind-sided by something, so make sure you look into the short and long term to see what is likely to occur. If you fail to take into account what's happening in the market (which, as you recall, drives *business* strategies or how you run the business), you're missing a large portion of the picture. If you fail to address market issues when you present your project ideas to decision makers, you'll undermine your credibility.

When you've moved all these puzzle pieces around, you should have an excellent start on your IT department's strategic direction. How you record it is up to you, but you should write it down, save it and print it out so you can look at it every day. You may want to boil it down to a few key words or phrases so that when you glance at it on your wall, cubicle, or computer monitor you instantly remember to align everything you do to these strategies. Next, you need to build a bridge between your strategies and your day-to-day activities through developing business strategies and an operational plan.

The IT Factor...

Urgent? Important?

Steven Covey, the popular business guru, talks about categorizing our day-to-day tasks into four main categories:

- Urgent and important
- Urgent and not important

Continued

- Not urgent and important
- Not urgent and not important

Many of us spend a lot of time responding to *urgent and not important* things. Many interruptions, phone calls, and e-mails fall into this category. They grab our attention and demand our time. We'll always have to deal with these kinds of tasks, but keeping an eye out for these time killers is important so we can keep them to a bare minimum. To be most effective on the job (or anywhere, really), you should make sure you leave time in your day and week to work on things that are *not urgent but important* because these are things like *planning*, *relationship building*, and *learning*. These add value and help you look at a slightly longer time horizon. And, if you're spending a lot of time on *not urgent and not important* tasks, you're wasting valuable time. People often work on *not urgent and not important* tasks when they're overwhelmed or burned out. If you (or a member of your team) spends a lot of time on *not urgent and not important* tasks, take a long hard look at what's going on because it's certainly not productive and it's absolutely not driving the company (or your career) forward.

Moving From Strategy To Operations

For many, it's easier to just jump in and start doing things than it is to step back and strategize first. The dot-com bubble of the late 1990's proves that point. Many companies were built on great ideas or technological possibilities, with the belief that operations would follow. Not so. Numerous online startup companies at the time approached the market with a cool website and maybe even innovative technology, but no operational plan that might have addressed supply chain management, distribution channels, or delivery methods. What investors and dot-com companies alike learned was that operations do not just naturally follow strategy (the word *strategy* is used loosely here because it's clear in retrospect that some of the dotcom companies lacked a coherent strategy).

In order to maximize a business's chances for success, strategy should drive operations. In order for that to happen, though, you must first do the following:

- Develop a corporate strategy

- Translate strategy into tangible terms

- Implement work efforts that support strategy

- Align resources with prioritized work efforts

- Define operational performance indicators that support strategies

- Manage change

It's relatively easy to list these items and a bit more difficult to do them. Let's talk about these six key elements briefly.

Develop a Corporate IT Strategy

We've already discussed corporate strategy and corporate IT strategy at great length, so we won't reiterate that information here. In order to translate strategy into operations, you obviously have to start with a strategy. We'll assume you have one based on the material presented earlier in this chapter.

Translate Corporate and IT Strategy into Tangible Terms

Your job as IT manager is to take that corporate strategy and begin to define the details of how the strategy will be accomplished. Again, this is the translation from strategy into operations—the *where we're headed* into the *how we'll get there*. Some companies like to define two separate stages: implementation and operations. Using this model, *implementation* is how you achieve strategic objectives and *operations* are the ongoing maintenance activities of these implementations. However, we're going to talk in relatively simple terms: strategy and operations. Someone has to develop plans as to how strategic objectives will be met. Your opportunity as the IT manager (or part of the IT team) is to look at how IT and technology can play a part in achieving strategic objectives. A good starting point is to look at each strategic objective and ask (and answer), "How can IT (or technology) support this objective?" You can also ask, "What IT current or new activities would support this strategy best?"

Cheat Sheet...

One Goal, Many Roads

Often there are many different operational activities that can support or further strategic objectives. The trick is figuring out which ones are the most desirable. Earlier we discussed the four keywords you can use when looking at projects: *logical*, *feasible*, *desirable*, and *affordable*. Even after you've looked at your options in this light, you may still need additional input on the direction to head since there may be several options that meet your criteria. At this point, executive input or feedback can be helpful. In some companies, this is a real challenge because

Continued

the top executives may mistakenly believe that you have all the information you need to translate the strategies into operational plans. If you don't, you'll need to discuss your options with them and get their input. While they may not understand operations as well as you do, they can be instrumental in helping you discern the best options. Along the way, they may learn operations a bit better and you'll certainly come away with a stronger understanding of the corporate strategies and how you can ensure your IT operations support and further those goals. You may also get a few bonus points for recognizing the need to choose wisely and ask for executive input. Don't go in with an open-ended question "What should we do?" Instead, lay out your options (using risk/reward discussed earlier or any other useful method of categorizing opportunities) and ask which of the options presented best suits the business.

Executive support is key to project success and the same holds true here. If you go off and plan your operations without executive support, you may find that you've selected the wrong options or that you used the wrong criteria when selecting from among your options. Getting executive buy-in early helps prevent misunderstandings later.

Implement Operations that Support IT Strategy

This might seem incredibly obvious, but it's worth stating. Once you figure out what the strategy is and you've defined ways you can accomplish those strategies, you need to ensure that work efforts actually support the strategy. It's not uncommon to find companies that have defined strategic plans and who have even taken the time to translate strategy into operational plans—and then proceed to ignore them. They take on projects or perform work that doesn't align with the strategy. It's a good idea to step back from time to time to ensure your efforts are aligned with where the company is headed. Otherwise you could find yourself, your department, or your job headed out into left field all alone.

You'll also need to figure out your priorities. In an ideal world, we could manage "triorities" (translation: "Do these three things first.") but in truth, we must prioritize. Part of the trick is in knowing which criteria to use for prioritizing. Do you do so based on how closely something fits with the strategy or which will have the most impact on strategy? Do you choose based on that which is least expensive or involves the least risk or that which can be accomplished most quickly? These are decisions you'll need to make and your company may have guidelines to help you through this process. If not, sit down with your boss and say (in essence), "Here are all the things we need to do, here are the things that align best with corporate strategies. Here is what I think our priorities should be, what do you think?" Also be aware that despite your best efforts, your plans (short or long-term) could end up being tossed aside for a completely new direction or new set of priorities.

Unfortunately, change sometimes happens quickly and quietly at the top of the organization and can take a while to filter down to you. Changes that impact your planning may require you to re-think your strategies, which can be discouraging. However, if you have strategies, priorities, and plans, you're certainly better off than if you didn't. And, you're more likely to get noticed (in a good way) from top executives when you are well prepared and understand that planning, prioritizing, and flexibility are all important skills for business.

Cheat Sheet...

Communication is the Key

One key concept you'll see throughout this book is communication. It's critical at every juncture and good communicators are often more effective in organizations than poor communicators. In the May 23, 2005 issue of Baseline magazine, CIO Trude Van Horn says that, "I've been in organizations where the best presenters got the funding as opposed to those who needed it but couldn't articulate that need appropriately." (Baseline Magazine, May 23, 2005, Issue 044, p. 62). It's clear that communicating effectively not only gets the job done, it gets the job funded. It's a good idea to sit down with your manager, the CIO, or even the senior management of the company (whichever is most appropriate to your particular situation) and talk about priorities. Every company is different and if you create a prioritized list based on cost and your company is more concerned with time-to-market, you're going to have problems. Instead, ask for explicit agreement on priorities. In fact, if you can get agreement in writing (e-mail is a good tool for this), all the better. If things change down the road, you'll have support (or at least evidence of prior support) for the decisions you made and the priorities you set. If you're working in a highly political organization, be sure to read Chapter 3 on navigating the murky waters of corporate politics.

Align Resources with Prioritized Operations Efforts

Once you have your priorities figured out and agreed to, you have to align available *resources* with those priorities. Resources include people as well as tools, technologies, and funding. Companies are dealing with finite resources, so making sure the right resources are applied to the right projects and other efforts is important to ensure success. As we'll discuss later in this book, applying the right resources to the right tasks is an important element of IT project management, so proper resource allocation will be a theme you'll hear more about.

Define Performance Indicators that Support IT Strategies

The adage "You get what you measure" holds true here. Once you've defined what you're going to do to support corporate strategies, you need to define performance metrics that support those strategies. It's often good to get those involved with the delivery (operations) involved with defining those performance indicators because they know what is reasonable and what is not. They can also alert you to inherent problems with chosen performance indicators that you might not spot immediately.

Enterprise 128...

Be Careful What You Ask For...

You do get what you measure, so you need to choose your measurements carefully. Here's a great example of how measuring the wrong thing will get you the wrong result.

A software company hired an outsourcer to handle the bulk of its technical support call volume for a particular product line. Most of the calls were considered Level One or Level Two calls, meaning that they were easy to moderately difficult to resolve. The Level Three calls, those that required significant expertise or even engineering changes, were always routed to the software company's senior technical staff. The software company had decided to outsource these Level One and Level Two calls as a way of saving money. They believed that the outsourcer's economies of scale would result in significant cost savings. That, and the outsourcer's staff were paid about 60% of the average of the software company's technical staff.

The software company set up metrics for call times, average time to answer a call, and number of available technicians per half hour. Guess what happened? Call times met the call time length, but that meant that calls that needed more time to be resolved were being "dumped." Maybe you've had this happen to you—the support person says, "I need to check on some things, is it O.K. if I put you on hold for a moment?" You grudgingly agree and next thing you know, you're disconnected. If the support person is being held to a specific call time metric, he or she might dump calls that threaten to raise the call time over the acceptable threshold (most companies have metrics in place to prevent this and most support folks—outsourcers and internal folks alike—do a great job and respond to the caller's needs. To all you support folks out there who do a great job, this does not refer to you!).

Continued

There is a happy ending here. The software company agreed to a more rea-sonable average call time and began measuring and *paying* for higher quality results. Thus, the staff at the outsourcer was also measured and rewarded for higher quality results, which lead both to fewer dropped calls and to record-set-ting quality results.

<u>Lesson Learned:</u> Be sure that what you're measuring is what you really need to be measuring and) doesn't have a hidden downside. Think through scenarios to determine if your measurements will actually drive the outcomes you want. Talk to the folks who will be held to these metrics to find out if there are prob-lems you hadn't anticipated. Be willing to modify metrics if they do not drive the outcome(s) you want.

Manage Change

The final element is managing change. Though a thorough discussion of change management is outside the scope of this book, it is important to discuss it briefly here. Change is a constant factor in any plan. Although you should avoid constantly changing or re-evaluating the strategic plan, the operational plan (also known as the tactical or business strategy) should change to address changes in the marketplace. Companies that cannot respond effectively to change are at a significant disadvan-tage, especially if their competitors manage change well. Revising operational plans and business strategies as market and competitive forces dictate is important. As the saying goes, "Manage change or it will manage you." There are additional elements of change management and we'll discuss some of those elements later in the book when we discuss how projects create change and how to communicate and manage that change.

Assessing Your Current IT Environment

After all is said and done, you still need to know exactly where you are today. Once you have a corporate IT strategy defined and you've gone down into the next layer and defined your priorities, you should take a step back and audit your current IT department and IT projects. Gather all the information you can on all IT projects and (ideally) pop it into a database. Be sure to include details such as the project name, project objectives (or business objective it's addressing), project length, esti-mated cost, project risk, and even the business benefits. If you can't define or identify one of those elements just mentioned, it should raise a red flag for you. This com-prehensive inventory of IT projects gives you the big picture view and if this is the first time you've ever taken inventory of your IT projects, you might be shocked by what you see. On one hand, you might see a beautiful array of perfectly aligned IT projects…on the other hand, you might see a random assortment of projects that don't seem get you anywhere at all.

The process might seem tedious, but the results are often worth the effort. It's through this process that you often find redundancies that you might have missed before. You can see overlaps, resource conflicts, and a wealth of other information when you step up to the "40,000 foot view."

Evaluating Your IT Projects

There are numerous ways one can evaluate IT projects and for our purposes in this chapter, we're talking about evaluating IT projects as it relates to corporate strategy. As you're taking inventory of your IT projects, you can put each proposed or current IT project in one of three strategic buckets: supports corporate strategies, supports IT strategies, or does not support strategies. Clearly, projects that support both corporate and IT strategies (which, for your IT department, are now closely aligned or the same) are those that should continue to get the most focus and resources. Those that meet corporate but not IT strategies will be second on your list. However, if these types of projects exist, it's a good idea to step back and find out why it aligns with corporate, but not IT strategies. It's possible it was started before you aligned these goals or it's possible that it's a unique project that fits appropriately or is a pet project of a senior manager in the company. Third on your list of projects should be those that align with IT strategies but not corporate strategies. These you should take a hard look at. If it aligns with IT but not corporate, there's a strong chance the project is the wrong project. There's also an excellent chance the project will run into some sort of political problem (see Chapter 3 for more on corporate politics and projects) because top executives will be unable to rationalize or support a project that doesn't further corporate goals. Finally, at the bottom of your list are the projects that don't align with either corporate or IT strategies. The question must be asked: why on Earth are you doing this project at all? Of course, sometimes there are leftover projects that should be completed; sometimes politics are at play and it's a favorite project of someone in a powerful position. If it doesn't align and it's not a political hot potato, consider dropping it, suspending it, or finishing it up quickly (reduced scope or quality, perhaps). There are no hard and fast rules here, but clearly you can see that it's much easier to support, define, and defend projects that align, support, or even further corporate and IT strategies.

Categorizing Your IT Projects

There are several high-level categories you can use to look at your projects as well. When you evaluated your projects (previous section), you looked at them in terms of strategic fit with the organization. Now, you look at them from an IT perspective. While not exhaustive, here's a starter list for you to work with:

Strategic or Operational

Projects are either strategic or operational in nature. Strategic projects are those that map with the corporate and IT strategies we've been discussing. Operational projects are those that provide maintenance or utility function. Remember, a project is a one-time solution to a defined problem, but projects can address strategic or operational issues. Although a project may not be viewed as strategic, how well it's carried out can have a significant impact on the business, so all projects that are planned and implemented must be executed flawlessly. Here's an example. Suppose you've determined that three of your key network servers are too slow and don't have enough storage capacity. You've looked at the costs and various solutions and determined that in the long run, replacing those three servers with the latest models will save the company time and money by:

- Reducing or eliminating network bottlenecks (which translates into slow user response, wasted user time, and increased user frustration).

- Reducing or eliminating failures and repairs (which translates into no user response, wasted user time, and increased user frustration).

- Providing opportunities for additional storage, additional or upgraded applications (which translates into faster user response, efficient use of user time, and reduced user frustration).

Clearly, this is routine maintenance in an IT department—making sure network resources meet or exceed corporate (user) needs. However, if this is implemented poorly, it might take the network down for too long during the upgrade or it could provide intermittent, unreliable service for weeks or months after the conversion. If these servers store data needed for a huge client proposal and users are either unable to get the data or not certain of the data integrity, this conversion could shift from a maintenance task to an escalated nightmare in a hurry. Though this may appear to be a normal operational issue, it may also be defined as a project because it is a one-time solution to a defined problem. Just because a project is deemed operational doesn't make it any less important. Later in this book, you'll learn the steps to take to make sure every project you undertake has a much better chance of success.

Long or Short-Term

IT projects may be long or short-term in nature, that's not news to you. However, it's often a good idea to categorize your projects by duration for several reasons. First, as you read in Chapter 1, projects with a more limited scope and a shorter duration are often more successful than longer, more complex projects. In addition, projects of short and long duration often share resources. In some cases, it's desirable to mix long and short duration projects so that you make the most efficient use of resources. Shorter projects can often be scheduled in between other tasks or projects when resources are available or are not being used at maximum capacity. While this may sound like a pie-in-the-sky concept (when compared to your every day reality), if you've taken some time to categorize projects by duration, you may just find opportunities to better utilize your limited resources. If you don't, at least you'll know exactly how much time your various projects are slated for (scheduled). Later in this book, you'll look at managing resources to maximize efficiency.

Hardware or Software

Another useful category for projects is hardware or software. Clearly some projects may fall in between and you may find additional categories in this area helpful. The point of separating hardware from software projects is simply to help you get a good feel for the types of projects you have. It's like cleaning off your desk. The amount of work hasn't changed but your ability to more quickly organize and complete your work goes up dramatically. Later in this book when we discuss project plans, we'll delineate areas where hardware project plans and software project plans may have slightly different steps involved.

Develop or Deploy

Experienced IT project managers usually recommend separating the discovery phase from the implementation phase. Another way of saying that is don't try to implement something you have yet to invent. If you have projects that are in trouble, it might be useful for you to determine if any of them have fallen victim to this type of planning. If so, these projects might do well broken into multiple projects that separate discovery (or invention) from deployment (or implementation). If you are going to upgrade your company's entire infrastructure and use a new program you're developing, which is based on a new security algorithm, you might do well to create three project plans:

- Test security algorithm

- Develop and test new program using security algorithm

- Lab test and deploy new infrastructure components

Finally, it's important to know which projects involve development effort and which involve deployment effort. When you're talking about a software project, it can be particularly useful to determine which is which. Here's an example. If you have an application that is new and you have clients willing to test it out, you may have development and deployment going on simultaneously. It might be useful to identify your development projects separate from your deployment projects. Although deployment projects may also require development, they are specifically related to deploying the application. This might include writing a custom interface to map or import client data from an old system to yours. It might involve writing code to improve the installation and configuration of your application on a variety of platforms. It could entail creating a Web interface for your application and developing a hosted application model. All of these are certainly development tasks, but they are also part of deployment. As you can see, there may not be any black and white answers here, but taking the time to classify projects can help you see what's going on in your IT department.

Project or Process

We'll mention one last categorization that might be useful—determining whether something requires a project or a process. It's a fundamental question that should be asked before undertaking *any* project and we'll give you the tools to evaluate this later in this book. However, here's a preview. A project is a solution to a stated problem. A process is a set of procedures used to address ongoing operations. Sometimes new processes are needed to address operational issues. Before jumping in and developing a whole new project plan, you should determine if the solution should be in the form of a project or a process. Projects can produce new business or operational processes, but sometimes projects have been created when a process is really all that's needed. Evaluating current and proposed projects in this light can help you avoid creating projects when a process is all that's needed.

Applying Your Knowledge

This mapping process can be a great opportunity for you to meet with people in your organization representing the various business units. As you work together to map or categorize projects, you can derive some great benefits. The opportunity to build relationships with your business unit counterparts will help you when the going gets tough (see Chapter 3 on corporate politics for more on the value of building relationships). You will also have the opportunity to learn about your company and its business from the experts in each business group. As you've read, the stats are favoring IT pros that have both IT and business experience and learning from this expert group can jump-start your understanding of the important business elements in your firm. And the reverse is also true—your counterparts in the business units will have the opportunity to learn a bit more about IT operations. Perhaps the most powerful outcome from this type of meeting is the opportunity for business unit managers to identify IT projects that are redundant, useless, or clearly no longer needed. By working with this group to map IT projects to strategic objectives, you'll reduce (or eliminate) resistance you might otherwise encounter when suggesting scrapping (or mothballing) a project.

Once you've gained agreement on the projects that should continue, you'll need to prioritize those projects. They can be prioritized using different methods, but a good starting point is trying to determine how much each project contributes to the strategic objectives and perhaps how many strategic objectives a project addresses. You'll also need to look at other constraining factors such as how effectively projects use assigned resources or how quickly a project needs to be completed. You're bound to end up with a list of projects beyond what the company can implement or fund today or in the near future. By mapping projects to strategic objectives and prioritizing them with your business counterparts, you can make a much stronger case for funding the projects that align with strategies and get less resistance for scrapping the ones that don't align (or never made much sense in the first place).

Developing Your IT Operational Roadmap

Once you have your IT strategies and your project inventory in hand, you can develop your operational roadmap—your ops plan. This is where you identify *how* IT will achieve both corporate and IT strategic objectives.

The first step is to map each project that is either slated to start soon or is already underway to your corporate and business IT plans. If a project can't be mapped to defined strategies, it might not be an appropriate project to work on. You'll need to take a hard look at those projects to determine if they should be continued to completion, put on hold, or scrapped altogether. While most of us are reluctant to just take a project and dump it in the virtual trashcan, it's sometimes the only rational choice once you've taken an objective look at your strategic objectives and your current efforts. With limited time and resources, it's critical to ensure that each project helps move you forward toward your strategic objectives—or better yet, pushes your strategic objectives into a new realm altogether. Dead or drifting projects create organizational drag that slow the company (and your department) down, losing precious competitive advantage.

Depending on the organization, some non-conforming projects are implemented because of political pressure, because of favors promised or owed to key clients, or because of personal aspirations (and many other crazy reasons). By *non-conforming*, we mean that these projects came from or live somewhere out in left field and they do not now, nor have they ever supported the ongoing mission of the IT department or company. Certainly after reading and digesting the information in this chapter, you may be looking with fresh eyes at your IT projects. In many companies, there are projects that just don't make sense. If they can be re-aligned to support business objectives, they might be worth completing. If not, scrap the project. If it's a political minefield, you may be able to use all the data you've collected and prepared in this chapter and present it to those with the political influence. Quite often, *logic* and *finances* trump politics (often, but not always).

After gaining agreement on project priorities, you can develop your operational plan. If you also took time to categorize your current and proposed projects, you have an excellent feel for all the work currently expected of the IT department. At this point, you can put all of this into a plan that describes how you'll achieve these results. If you're not sure how to develop this plan, there are numerous books, websites and articles available to you. However, this plan should include all current and proposed projects *as well as* ongoing operational/maintenance activities. Though our focus is on IT projects, we all know that the day-to-day problems, minor and major crises, and unexpected issues have to be dealt with. An operations plan should recognize and account for these activities along with the operational and strategic elements. The plan should identify existing IT resources including staff (and staff expertise), equipment and funding (budget). It should describe the processes you'll use to manage the day-to-day activities and projects. It should be a useful document you can use on a daily basis to keep you on track when all the forces of the universe seem to be pulling you in opposing directions.

Summary

We covered a lot of ground in this chapter. For some of you, it might be old hat. For others, it might be new and a bit confusing. If this is all very new to you, take time to come back and read this chapter again later, after the dust has settled. It will begin to come into focus if you take your time and digest it in small segments. Perhaps reading this summary will tie it all together for you.

It's more important than ever before that IT departments contribute to corporate success. The use of technology itself no longer provides a competitive advantage by default. Companies are looking for IT departments to contribute to the forward progress of the company. The best way that can happen is if the efforts of the IT department are aligned with corporate strategies and objectives. A notable benefit from this type of alignment is that your projects and your department are more likely to gain much needed executive support if your efforts are contributing to the greater good of the company. If in that process you can also find a way to extend or expand corporate strategies through IT efforts, you're even better off. That's a tall order but if you don't look for it, you'll certainly never find it.

It may take some work to figure out what your company's strategy is—it's not always written down, it's not always openly discussed. In this chapter, we provided you with some tools you can use to research and reverse engineer corporate strategy if you have to. Corporate strategies (and IT strategies as well) are impacted by what's going on in the external market place. Strategies that originate from these external drivers are often called business strategies. The IT department may or may not have business strategies, but it's worth looking at because IT is often impacted by what's happening in the broader technology market and by what's happening with vendors, customers and competitors.

Once you've got some idea what the corporate strategy is, you can begin to develop your IT strategies. We talked about various methods people use to begin to formulate ideas for strategies including evaluating core competencies, doing a SWOT analysis and looking at trends. This is not an exhaustive review, but a good starting point. And, if you already have a good idea of what your IT strategies should be and how they align with corporate strategies, you can use those tools to test, evaluate, or strengthen your thoughts.

After you've come up with your thoughts and ideas, you'll need to organize those ideas. In this chapter we provided tools for you to begin doing that including the risk/reward grid. We also discussed the importance of talking about priorities with your boss or senior management to make sure everyone is making the same assumptions about priorities. We also discussed four keywords you can use in evaluating ideas:

logical, feasible, desirable, and affordable. You can add to or subtract from this list to suit your needs, but this is a good start.

Once you've developed your prioritized list of strategies or objectives, you have to find a way to translate that into reality. Strategies tell you where you're headed; next you have to determine how you'll get there. We talked about ways of assessing your current IT environment and mapping that to your prioritized objectives. That helps you sort out where current activities belong in your new framework. Finally, we discussed methods for taking all of that and creating an operational roadmap that can be used on a daily or weekly basis to keep you on track. It would be a shame to expend so much effort on creating a well-aligned strategy only to have the operations drive off in a different direction.

If this whole topic is new to you, it might seem like a tall order on top of everything else you have to do. But, to paraphrase Steven Covey, if you don't spend time on important, non-urgent planning activities, you'll sell yourself and your department short. Learning to plan and strategize is an important part of being effective in the business world and to be effective as an IT project manager. Hopefully now you have a few new tools to help you on your way.

Solutions Fast Track

Overview of Corporate Strategy in Today's Environment

- ☑ Due to economic changes in the past decade, IT departments and IT activities no longer provide a *de facto* competitive advantage.

- ☑ To be successful in today's business climate, you need to run your IT department more like a business. Your IT efforts must support or extend the corporate mission.

- ☑ CIOs today have a blend of business and IT experience, so it's desirable to improve your business skills.

Aligning IT with Corporate Strategy: Taking It One Step Further

- ☑ IT strategies and operations must, at minimum, support the direction the company is headed.

☑ Ideally, you should look for ways that IT can be leveraged to create new, innovative strategies that further your corporate strategies rather than simply align with them.

☑ Competitive advantage can come through the use of technology by driving efficiency in execution, by lowering costs, or by innovation.

☑ Competitive advantage through technology innovation is often short-lived in today's fast-paced IT environment.

Understanding Your Company's Strategy

☑ Most companies have a strategy, but not all have well-articulated strategies, and not all have well-communicated strategies.

☑ In order to align IT activities with corporate strategies, you have to have some understanding of your company's strategic direction.

☑ There are numerous tools you can use to reverse engineer your company's strategies, though your best bet is to sit down with your boss or senior management and simply ask.

Developing Your IT Strategy

☑ Before you can develop your IT strategy, you have to understand what's what. You can use various tools to analyze the current state of your IT department (and your company, if you so choose) to give you a solid starting point.

☑ Analyzing core competencies, performing a SWOT analysis or trend analysis will help you determine what your department is good at and what your strategic direction should be.

☑ Once you've analyzed where you are and where everything else is (customers, competitors, technology, threats, opportunities, etc.), you can finalize your strategic objectives.

☑ You can use the risk-reward grid as one way of categorizing your strategic objectives.

☑ Your objectives or strategies should be prioritized based on agreed upon priorities. If you're not sure what should be first, second, and third priorities, sit down with your manager and discuss this. Mismatched expectations about priorities cause lots of problems down the road.

Assessing Your Current IT Environment

☑ Once you have an idea of your strategic IT direction, you need to look at your current IT environment and match things up.

☑ There are many ways you can categorize your IT efforts including strategic versus operational efforts, long-term versus short-term, development versus deployment, and more. Categories simply help you see what's what.

Developing Your Operational Roadmap

☑ Your operational roadmap is the document or plan that tells you what activities you must undertake in order to reach your strategic objectives. It helps you choose the right activities based on limited time and resources.

☑ An operational roadmap (or ops plan) provides a day-to-day guide for managing IT functions in a manner that will keep them aligned with IT and corporate strategies.

Frequently Asked Questions

The following Frequently Asked Questions, answered by the author of this book, are designed to both measure your understanding of the concepts presented in this chapter and to assist you with real-life implementation of these concepts. To have your questions about this chapter answered by the author, browse to **www.syngress.com/solutions** and click on the **"Ask the Author"** form.

Q: I've got an IT background and all this business information is making my head swim. Isn't there an easier way?

A: I'm assuming that you have a really strong IT background and I'm also assuming you didn't learn everything you know in one sitting. It takes time to learn new skills and these skills might be using a few new brain cells. Take your time, parse out the data into small chunks, and don't move on until you feel like you've got a handle on it all. You can't learn about TCP/IP until you understand binary math, right? You can't develop an application until you understand how to write an if/then loop. Take it one step at a time.

Q: Our company holds long planning retreats to come up with corporate strategy. The information in this chapter makes it seem like it shouldn't take that long.

A: Developing a corporate strategy can be a long, complex, and difficult task. When markets and technologies and customers are changing rapidly, it can be difficult to see the road ahead. So, yes, it can be a long, difficult task for corporate leaders. That said, it's not always that tough. It depends on many different factors including the market you're in, the strengths of your company, the company's position in the marketplace, and more. However, if your company has a strategic plan to which you have access, your job is half done. Creating the IT strategy is just that much easier because you already know the direction the company is headed. Thus, you can develop your IT strategies by using your corporate strategies as your starting point.

Q: I'm still not clear on the difference between a corporate strategy and a business strategy. Can you clarify that for me?

A: Corporate strategy is developed from the top of the organization. It is a vision of where the company is headed, what the company should be (or become). However, companies don't exist in a vacuum. They have to interact with the outside world every day. That outside world is comprised of customers, competitors, changing technology, regulations, and more. When companies have to respond to these outside influences, they must develop business strategies. Business strategies come from the business units or the operations areas and influence corporate strategies. In a sense, they are a unique subset of corporate strategies.

Q: What's the difference between corporate strategies and IT strategies?

A: Corporate strategies set the course for the entire company. They describe where the company as a whole is headed. IT strategies are a subset of corporate strategies. They are, essentially, corporate-level strategies that deal only with the IT area of the business.

Q: What's the difference between business strategies and business IT strategies?

A: Business strategies are developed in response to the external environment. Companies must develop business strategies in order to remain responsive and relevant in the marketplace. Business strategies might involve competing on cost or increasing the level of service based on demands from the market. Business IT strategies also arise as a response to the external market, but are specifically related to IT. This might involve a decision to implement a particular application or use a particular technology platform because of demand in the marketplace. Once these are determined you can create operational plans to guide you through the day-to-day tasks required to accomplish these strategies.

Q: Where can I find out more about creating a strategic IT plan?

A: There are many resources available on strategic planning and almost any one you choose can be applied to IT planning as well. There are books, courses and Web resources available. A good place to start is with well-known, reputable websites such as CIO.com, eWeek.com, ComputerWorld.com, and TechRepublic.com, just to name a few. You can also work with an experienced consultant to assist you in the development of your strategic plan. Sometimes having a person external to the organization can be helpful because they'll approach things with a fresh perspective.

Chapter 3

Navigating Corporate Politics

Solutions in this chapter:

- **Corporate Politics: A Primer**
- **Understanding Sources of Power**
- **Understanding Methods of Influence**
- **The Power Paradox**
- **Working Effectively in a Political Environment**
- **Breaking Up Political Logjams**
- **Effective Countermeasures**

☑ **Summary**

☑ **Solutions Fast Track**

☑ **Frequently Asked Questions**

Introduction

In Chapter 2, we discussed what corporate strategy has to do with IT. Now we're going to look at how corporate politics impact IT projects and project management. As an IT project manager, you often lack formal, organizational authority to accomplish your project's objectives. This means that you have to know how your organization works, both formally (organizational chart) and informally (politics) in order to get the best possible results. Politics affect which projects get priority or get funded; politics impact which people and resources are assigned to projects, and politics certainly affect whether or not projects are successful. In this chapter, you'll learn why and how politics operate in organizations and you'll gain insight and knowledge that will help you navigate corporate politics more effectively. If you're anxious to jump right into IT project management, you can skip ahead to Chapter 5, but be sure to come back and read these first four chapters. They introduce you to critical concepts about the environment that surrounds all IT projects and will help your IT projects be more successful.

Some people thrive on corporate politics; others (including many in IT) would rather chew nails than get involved in company politics. The truth is, if you work for any company—small, medium or large—politics are a fact of life. Rather than hiding your head in the sand, you can actually learn how to handle politics with confidence and grace (well, most of the time). If you hate everything about corporate politics, this chapter is a must-read for you. You'll learn how to navigate the sometimes murky political waters and avoid most of the dangers along the way. After reading this chapter, you'll have the tools you need to succeed in a political environment, even if you really dislike company politics.

Corporate Politics: A Primer

We all know corporate politics have a huge impact on which projects do and do not get funded and even on the success of those projects, but few people ever want to talk about it. Corporate politics are a fact of life and every company has a different personality and different political dynamics. Most IT pros would be happiest if there were no politics—after all, it's all about the technology, isn't it? Still, we all have to work together toward a common goal and understanding the impact of politics on the IT department can help you achieve your objectives. Though *power* and *politics* are often seen as "dirty words" in the corporate world, they are a natural aspect of life—in and out of the corporate world—and the more you know about how things work, the better off you'll fare. Most of us form a negative impression of politics and power when they are used simply for self-promotion or ego enhancement. When they're used for the good of the company and everyone involved, they actually are positive traits. A thorough discussion of corporate politics could fill volumes, so we're only going to look at a few elements that might impact your IT department and make a few suggestions for navigating the muddy waters of corporate politics.

First, let's define three words: *power, influence* and *politics. Power* is, quite simply, the ability to produce change or to get results. *Influence* is the exercise of that ability to produce change. *Politics* has been defined as the study of who gets what, when and how. Politics is power and influence in action. Now, before you turn away in disgust, let's look at the positive uses of power, influence, and politics.

- When someone uses his/her power and influence to persuade top executives to support an IT infrastructure upgrade because it will improve everyone's ability to get their jobs done.

- When someone uses his/her power and influence to persuade department heads to support doing a project for a local charity at no/low cost.

- When someone uses his/her power and influence to convince employees of the Marketing department to cooperate with employees in the IT Development department to create an award-winning application for the company.

You'd be hard-pressed to think that anyone misused power and influence to accomplish these results. In fact, it's typically only the negative experiences we have that call attention to the darker side of power and influence. When things go well, we tend to attribute that to other factors and ignore the fact that power and influence can work toward positive, desirable outcomes. Throughout this chapter, words and phrases such as "politics" or "highly political atmosphere" are used to indicate the negative aspects of these types of activities. Unfortunately, we don't have words that describe the great things that happen when power and influence come together for the common good. Though we talk about success, teamwork, or innovation, we rarely (if ever) attribute these to a positive political environment. As you read through this chapter, keep this in mind because power, influence, and politics don't have to be negative. In fact, if you talk to 100 people, 98 of them would probably say they prefer to work for a powerful, influential boss. Why? Because powerful, influential people get things done and people like to be around success.

The problems most people run into, though, are often the results of the misuse of power and influence. The best defense is a good offense in this case, so we're going to look at the elements of power and influence and later in the chapter we'll look at specific methods you can use to analyze the political environment and tools you can use to achieve your objectives.

Understanding Sources of Power

One of the most useful things you can do in a political environment is take time to understand the sources of power. In this section, we'll look at the basics and you can use this knowledge to assess your own organization. You'll find that once you understand the sources of power, you're well on your way toward having the knowledge and tools you need to work effectively in a political environment. Let's look at these sources of power:

- Position
- Information
- Resource
- Expertise
- Performance
- Personal traits

Positional Power

The most commonly recognized source of power is *positional* or *organizational* power. Your boss has power over you because he or she is your boss. The organization bestows upon each position a certain amount of organizational authority. A person's position provides a set of responsibilities, access to information, and access to resources. The position also provides a certain amount of authority to make change, to act, and to direct the actions of others. If you recall our earlier definition of power, it is the ability to enact change or to get things done. Thus, one's position in the organization comes with a certain amount of built-in power.

However, there are additional elements to positional power that are important to recognize. These are:

- How critical you are to a particular outcome
- How relevant your position is to the organization's priorities
- How visible you are in the organization
- How much discretion you have in your position

As you can imagine, someone who is very *critical to an outcome* is more powerful that one who is not. If a particular engineer or software architect is key to a project's success, that person has more power than a peer who is not key to a project's success.

One whose position is *closely connected to the company's priorities* will have more power than someone in a position that is not aligned with priorities. For instance, if the company's major focus is to improve efficiency and your IT group comes up with a series of initiatives aimed at improving not only IT efficiency, but corporate productivity as well, you'll have more power and influence. Conversely, if you're working on a project that is highly innovative, but no one is sure yet if it will work or if it will improve efficiency, the project could easily run into political interference if the current focus is on efficiency.

Another element of positional power is the position's *visibility* within the organization. The more visible a position is in a company, the more power it typically holds. Visibility is often part of how people get promoted in companies. Visibility can come from the position itself or from performance within the position (see the section entitled, "Performance Power"). Visible positions may always be visible, as many executive positions are, or they may be visible for a certain period of time. Accountants are highly visible during the budget development cycle. An IT project manager may be highly visible during the design, implementation, and management of a key IT initiative. Working on cross-functional teams is often a way to gain some visibility in the organization and can be a good way to improve your career progress.

Finally, the amount of *flexibility* or *discretion* in your position also generally correlates directly to the amount of power the position holds. Most managers have a certain amount of flexibility or discretion designed into their jobs. Back in the 1980's there was a movement toward empowering employees—to give them more flexibility or discretion. If you've ever called your credit card company to dispute something on your statement, you've probably experienced folks who have almost no flexibility or discretion in their positions. On the contrary, companies known for the great service they provide, including Nordstrom, Federal Express, LLBean, and ShopNatural, among others, all empower their service staff to make decisions. They give them the flexibility and discretion needed to resolve all but the most difficult customer service problems. These folks do have power and the teams are more productive as a result (you'll read more about the benefits of sharing power later in this chapter).

These additional components of positional power are important because it helps us understand why some positions are (or appear to be) more powerful than others. Positional power also comes from the fact that people in those positions often have access to information and resources that others do not. This leads us to the next two major sources of power in an organization.

Information Power

Information is power in most companies. It is often, but not always, tied directly to position. The more we know, the more we are able to work effectively in an organization. There are all kinds of information in organizations and almost all of it can be useful. Knowing who's preparing a key client presentation, knowing the current quarter's financial results, knowing who the boss is looking at for the next big project, knowing when the next round of budget cuts is coming, and so on, are all types of information that can provide power in an organization. Here are two examples. Purchasers for a company have information about suppliers, order status, or availability that others within the organization may need. An administrative assistant for an executive has informational power because he or she knows the executive's schedule and can grant or deny access or information. In these cases, these positions have access to needed information and this bestows upon the person in that position a certain amount of power.

Information power, of course, is not absolute. Information tends to get stale pretty quickly these days, so information power is often time-sensitive. If you know that the boss is about to approve a budget for a new project, that might provide some measure of power until your boss announces it. Other types of information power are less transitory. If you're part of a cross-functional team that meets monthly to discuss a particular corporate initiative, you have information that is not generally available to others in the company, even if a meeting summary is distributed.

It's important to understand the nature of information power because information flow is often used in political maneuvers. Sometimes information is withheld in order to make others less informed and therefore more vulnerable to misinformation or manipulation. Sometimes misinformation is disseminated in order to make others look bad or to throw others off the track. Unfortunately, these negative aspects of information power are used in organizations, which is why it's important to understand this source of power so you can use it in a positive, beneficial manner and counteract those who might try to use it for lesser purposes.

Resource Power

Most managerial positions have resource power because these positions have access to and control over organizational resources. These positions have the ability to grant or deny raises (money is one of the most important resources), promotions, key assignments, excused absences, and work assignments. Non-managers may also have resource power—the clerk responsible for purchasing office supplies, the administrative assistant responsible for submitting reimbursement requests, the purchaser who can get special deals from a vendor—all of these people have resource power to some degree or another. As with other forms of power, misuse of this source of power can lead to problems. If your key vendor's invoices are being held up or if your ability to purchase spare computer parts is limited by a purchasing clerk, your ability to get your job done effectively can be diminished. If this is the case, you may try to determine what you can do to convince the person with resource power to use their power to your benefit. Later in this chapter, we'll discuss methods of influence and ways you can negotiate with this person to get better access to needed resources (hint: this typically involves giving something the other party needs in exchange for getting what you need).

Expertise Power

Expertise is the specialized knowledge someone has, whether it was gained through experience, training, or formal education. Clearly, someone with needed expertise has a certain amount of power. The IT technician who knows how to fix your e-mail problem has power when your e-mail goes down. The copier technician is in a powerful position when the copier jams on copy 125 of 800. Financial analysts have a lot of power around budget time. Notice that few sources of power are fixed—they are relative to many other factors. The copier technician may have power when the copier jams but has very little power if there are five other suitable copiers nearby or a copy shop on the corner next to your office.

One important thing to note about the power that comes from expertise is that it is often the only power a new hire has. He or she does not have a network of relationships upon which to rely, so he or she probably doesn't have information or resource power. This is good to understand because a new hire must leverage his or her expertise in order to gain other forms of power within the organization, so you may see someone new to the company overusing his or her expertise power. Overuse of this power can cause someone to come off as an overbearing "know-it-all." As with other forms of power, the overuse or over-reliance on this form of power can have an opposite effect. Instead of respecting the expert, people in the organization may come to ignore or shun that person because he or she is aggressively asserting his or her expertise and perhaps not allowing adequate room for discussion, dissent, and team input.

Performance Power

Performance power is just as you might expect—you can derive a certain amount of power from turning in exceptional results. A track record of outstanding performance can give you the ability to influence not only your own future, but that of the project, department, or company. For instance, you might be asked to participate in an innovative new project or you might be asked your opinion on a variety of topics. Strong performance also enhances your reputation with peers and perhaps others outside your direct sphere of influence as well. Just as people typically enjoy working for a powerful boss, people also enjoy associating with top performers. This inclination to view strong performers in a positive light is the source of performance power and influence.

The downside of performance power is similar to expertise power. If you perform above and beyond normal expectations on a consistent basis, you may be threatening to some people, especially poorer performers. It's possible you don't need to be concerned with poor performers, but what if that person is your manager? Then your outstanding results might only serve, by contrast, to highlight the poor or mediocre job your manager is turning in and this could be a problem. Most of the time, however, when you deliver outstanding results, it's not only good results for the company, but for you as well.

Personal Traits Power

You might call this personality power or personal attraction power, but whatever term you use, it has to do with personal traits that provide power within an organization. The first that might come to mind is physical appearance. An interesting note about looks is that it is true that "good looking" people tend to get more breaks and opportunities, but people who are "too good looking" are often seen as less intelligent. Fair or not, these are biases that impact personal power. How one dresses is also part of personal traits and is related to personal power. Again, there are some interesting dichotomies here. If you dress "above" your position, you're more likely to be considered for a promotion, but less likely to be accepted by your peers. If you dress impeccably, whether your company requires casual or formal business attire, you may be seen as less capable. The thought is that people who are "*too* well groomed" are less intelligent or less capable. If you consistently dress in a manner that is outside the norms for your company, you may be seen as less of a team player. For instance, if you work at a company where jeans and t-shirts are the norm and you consistently wear a suit, you may be seen as snobbish, not a team player, or someone only interested in moving up the ladder. This can work against you. However, if the dress code is jeans and a t-shirt and you wear khakis and a polo shirt, you're more likely to be viewed as a part of the team, even if you stand out in a positive way. The obvious statements also hold true. If you dress "below" your position, your work may be viewed in a more negative light. If you consistently dress below company standards, you may have trouble getting your work to be taken seriously or to be judged fairly. It's quite relative to the norms of your company or department.

Beyond the physical characteristics, there are several key attributes that bestow personal power to individuals. Research indicates that there are behaviors and traits that we associate with "likeability" and the more likeable someone is, the more personal power he or she has. Some of the traits that may cause us to like someone are honesty, acceptance, supportiveness, similarity of values, and willingness to endure costs for the relationship. People who are seen as likeable are judged to be more effective speakers and they are more likely to get the benefit of the doubt in a performance appraisal. So, it may literally pay to be nice.

There is a downside to being too likable or too nice and that is the danger of being perceived as gullible or naïve. While being likeable is a positive trait and can be the source of a certain amount of power, it must be balanced with getting the job done. As a manager, being likeable is tricky. On the one hand, if your boss or others in the organization consider you to be likeable, you can derive a certain amount of power and influence from that. On the other hand, as a manager, it's not your job to be liked. New managers often are torn because they want their team to like them, but they often find that things like reprimanding and managing run contrary to being liked. It is a fine balance, but as a manager, you can do your job effectively and still have you staff like you. Just don't get trapped into being a manager who is well-liked first and effective second. This holds true for IT project managers as well.

APPLYING YOUR KNOWLEDGE

Now that you understand the various sources of power in an organization, you can start taking inventory. How much power do you have? What about your manager? As you probably can see by now, if your manager lacks several of these sources of power, you may be at a disadvantage because power is relative. If your boss's position is seen as powerful, then your position bestows upon you more power than a peer who works for a less powerful manager. You may also discover other sources of power such as expertise, information, resources or personal power that you weren't aware you had. Most powerful people in organizations have developed multiple sources of power since few sources of power are absolute and unchanging. Understanding who has what types of power (including you and your manager) will give you a much better feel for how things run in your company. It gives you insight into why things are the way they are and how you might influence them (see next section) for better results.

Understanding Methods of Influence

Power is the ability to get things done, and *influence* is using power to get things done. We've all felt *influence* at work in our jobs, whether it was a department manager trying to persuade us to move her project to the top of the priority list or one of your staffers trying to get a key assignment. Influence is used all the time and is really how things get done. In this section, we're going to look at three key methods of influencing people and we'll discuss which ones work best and which are best to avoid. As with power, these methods can be used appropriately to generate results or they can be overused or abused. Understanding methods of influence helps you spot them when they're being used on you and also helps you use them effectively to get better results.

Threats

The least desirable method of influencing is to threaten someone. You can threaten someone directly or indirectly. You can say, "Your raise depends upon how well you do at the client site," or you can say, "I'm expecting a lot from you tomorrow." While threats as a method of influence may sound very negative and manipulative, the fact is there is a certain amount of threat built into every corporate structure. We all know on a very basic level that if we don't perform, if we don't do as expected that we aren't likely to get a raise, bonus, or promotion, or worse, that we can lose our jobs. That's an implicit threat and we all pretty much accept that. However, when used to manipulate us into doing something we don't want to do, threats are perceived as negative. In fact, that's true about any use of power. When we are forced to do something against our will or against our own self-interest, we typically view power negatively. Conversely, when we do something aligned with our desires or that furthers our own self-interests, we view power in a positive light.

Here's the downside of using threats: they will force *compliance* but not *commitment*. Think about it. If you have the power to force someone to do something, they will likely comply. However, they are not likely to be committed to the action or decision because they were forced into it. Compliance may be all you need in a particular situation. If the report needs to be completed by noon, you don't need a commitment, you need the report completed by noon (compliance). If you need all e-mail users to log off by midnight on Friday so you can upgrade the server, you don't need commitment, you need compliance. The threat in that case is that if you don't log off, we're taking the server down and anything you were working on might be lost. The threat, in this case, is rather benign. Notice that you can present this information in one of two ways. You can send out an e-mail that says, "The e-mail server is going down at midnight on Friday. Log off before then or lose anything you're working on. E-mail will be back up by Saturday 10:00 A.M." That e-mail will force compliance, but is perhaps not the best presentation. To make the threat more palatable, you could instead send this e-mail: "In order to provide faster e-mail response and more storage space for your e-mail, we're upgrading the server this weekend. Please log off e-mail prior to Friday at midnight so you don't lose any important work. We anticipate bringing the new server back up and restoring e-mail service to you no later than Saturday 10:00 A.M. If you have any questions, please contact IT at extension 1234. Thanks for your cooperation. Signed, your friendly IT group." Both e-mails *threaten* to cut off service at midnight, but one will be seen as curt and the other seen as a positive, friendly message. Threats need not be heavy handed and as you can see, they're sometimes quite appropriate.

You typically need *commitment* when you need to get something done over a longer period of time or you need to gain agreement before proceeding. We'll discuss gaining commitment in a moment. Making threats will almost never result in commitment, so generally speaking, threats are not your best option most of the time. They generate short-term compliance. They can be delivered in a positive manner that generates willing rather than resentful compliance. As you can see from the previous example, a threat is sometimes exactly what's needed. It wouldn't be helpful to try to get commitment from people to log off their e-mail, all you need is compliance and the threat (presented in a polite and positive manner) gets the best result. That should be your goal whenever using threats as your method of influence—to generate compliance without generating resentment.

Exchange or Barter

There are many commonly used expressions for the normal (and desirable) exchange or barter that operates in all companies. Some of these expressions are, "Help me out today, will you?" "You owe me big time!" "What's it going to cost me?" "How long am I going to have to pay for this one?" or "I'll put in a good word for you." These kinds of expressions demonstrate the normal exchange between individuals in a company. This type of exchange is a form of influence. We use whatever power we have—information, resources, position—and attempt to exchange it for what we need. Again, there's nothing sinister in this unless it's used for purely selfish power-building reasons. Otherwise, it's how business gets done; it's the art of the deal. We negotiate every day for what we need and this exchange system works pretty well. The informal balance of trade in organizations helps people extend and call in favors. If you owe someone a favor, you can be influenced to take action on that person's behalf. That wipes out the debt and the person to whom you owed a favor was able to influence your behavior for that interaction. Similarly, we can use exchange or barter for future benefit—I'll do this today in exchange for you doing something for me later on. It's a good system and is actually the primary influence system at work in most companies today.

Here's the downside to using exchange as a method of influence: you have to have something the other person needs. Just like any exchange or barter system, what you have to offer and what the other person needs must match up in order to make an exchange. In an organization, you have to figure out how your "inventory" matches up with others' needs in order to make an effective exchange to get what you need. In addition, it's helpful to know what you have that others need so you can make an exchange. The exchange can be immediate or it can be banked for future use. If you can't discern what the other person needs or what you have that might be of value in an exchange, you'll have difficulty using exchange effectively in your organization. Since this is a very common (and typically fair and aboveboard) method of wielding power and influence, it's worth understanding it consciously. Most of us have worked, with varying degrees of success, using the exchange and barter methods, but we perhaps have never taken time to examine the inner workings. In order to use this method successfully, you'll need to figure out who you need to influence and the balance of trade in that relationship.

It's also worth noting that sometimes the exchange can be simple human interaction. When you are consistently nice to the receptionist as you come in each day and you later need a favor, he or she may be more inclined to help you out than if you walked by and nodded every day. Do you know the receptionist's name? Do you talk with him or her on occasion? It's not always *what* we can give someone on a tangible level that creates the exchange, but what we give through human interaction. And let's face it, techies are sometimes so engrossed in their current technological challenge that they fail to notice the people around them. Paying attention to your personal interactions can generate this exchange "currency" as well.

APPLYING YOUR KNOWLEDGE

Since exchange or barter is the primary currency of influence in an organization, you can begin to look at your exchange balance with a critical eye. Are you usually on the giving or receiving end of the exchange? Do you know how to call in favors? Do you know how to extend a favor "with strings attached"? Some people are good at the outgoing exchange part, but not so good at the incoming exchange part. Learning to effectively call in and extend favors will increase your effectiveness. And no, this is not manipulative; this is simply how business gets done. If you're the one who's constantly doing things for others but never collecting on the balance due, you're losing out on an important source of influence. This type of influence works up, down, and across the organization, so it's one of the most versatile tools you have available to you. There are many resources available to you—in books and on the Web—to learn to improve your ability to negotiate and influence people. It might be valuable to you to learn how to manage this process more effectively than perhaps you have in the past. Managing this process simply helps you be more effective and successful and if you're working for the good of your team, department, and company, it's likely to yield the desired, positive results.

Appeals to Values, Emotions, or Reason

If the U.S. Presidential election of 2004 is any indication, appealing to values and emotions works. People across the political spectrum were bombarded with appeals to their values and emotions. While in politics these appeals often are or appear to be disingenuous, in corporate politics they can be another viable way of wielding influence. Think about this. If your boss comes to you and says, "You agreed to complete this code in time for the upcoming release and I know you always keep your word," your manager is appealing to your values—that of keeping your word, of being honest. Your boss might also be appealing to your emotions—your desire to avoid feeling bad for not keeping your word, your desire to feel good about yourself (ego). Let's look at another example. Your company is in a competitive bid process and you feel you're the best person to develop the proposal. You remind your boss that the last time he or she let someone else complete the proposal it was poorly done, late, and lost the contract for the company. This is an appeal to emotions and perhaps to reason. The emotional part is your boss wanting to avoid another embarrassing situation (which he or she will almost certainly have to explain to someone up the ladder) and the reasoning part is that it is reasonable to assign someone more capable to a key project if the previous person failed or underperformed. Again, these can be used in very manipulative ways, but they can be used for positive reasons as well. When charities raise money, they have no direct power over you or your checkbook. They wield the only power they have—an appeal to shared values, an appeal to emotion or an appeal to reason. These are very effective, legitimate tools and they're used with good results all the time. When done in an open, honest manner, you have a choice to respond to these appeals or not. Therefore, this method of influence is less likely to be perceived as manipulative, though there's still ample opportunity for this method to be used in an underhanded manner. When someone appeals to your values, emotions or reason when they themselves do not believe what they're saying, it is often manipulative (or will be perceived as such). Appealing to values and emotions can certainly inspire commitment and get you to go "above and beyond" to generate results beyond mere compliance.

Appealing to reason is another way to inspire commitment. As mentioned earlier, using threats gets compliance but not commitment. Using reason gets commitment (and usually also compliance) and when commitment is critical (as it is in most IT projects), appealing to reason is a good tool to have at your disposal. The other attractive quality to appealing to reason is that it typically is all aboveboard. It's harder to manipulate (or be manipulated) if you're appealing to reason because the other party can think through the logic and agree or not. This is exactly why appealing to reason fosters commitment—the other party has thought about it and agreed with your perspective. Now your cause is their cause, in a sense, and this can generate a longer-term commitment than other types of influence might.

The downside examples of appealing to values, emotions, or reason are the ones that people tend to remember and fixate on. Most charismatic leaders appeal to values and emotions and can manipulate people quite effectively, especially if the leader does not actually share those values but simply uses them to get you do as they wish. I'm sure we can all think of people who have used this type of influence for personal gain, but that doesn't make the method inherently bad. Another downside of this type of influence is that you have to know what someone's values are before you can appeal to them. You also have to know what emotions are likely to get that person fired up. If you've ever been in a team meeting where you left feeling fired up and ready to take on the next challenge, you've been influenced via an appeal to values, emotions or reason. Were you manipulated? Not unless the reason for someone getting your team all fired up was malicious, self-serving, unethical, or illegal. Is it unethical or manipulative for an NFL coach to give an inspiring speech in the locker room before a big game? No, but he's certainly appealing to values and emotion to get the job done. Appropriate appeals to values, emotions and/or reason can help foster a strong, cohesive team.

Applying Your Knowledge

You probably have appealed to people's values, emotions, or reason in the past and achieved the results you wanted. The question is: did you do so for the common good or for your own good? It's not always easy to tell and sometimes we fool ourselves into thinking it's for the common good when it's not. However, now that you understand this source of influence and power, you can monitor your own behavior and make sure you always stay "inside the lines." On the other side of things, you'll be much better armed to deflect disingenuous appeals to your values, emotion, or reason now that you understand a bit more about this type of influence. Later in this chapter, you'll read an example of how this is commonly used in the project management arena—appealing to emotions (and ego is part of that) to get you to take that project that no one wants.

The Power Paradox

Power is an interesting and complex subject to study, especially in organizations, because it is full of contradictions. Here are two good examples: Have you ever known someone with positional power who was completely powerless? Have you ever known an administrative assistant (or equivalent) that was the "go to" person and had tremendous informal power? Most of us have experienced these two extremes. There are several interesting dynamics related to power that are worth discussing so you understand the power dynamics in your company as well as how to (or not to) wield your own influence.

- **Organizations work better when people have more power.** When people are powerless, they are less motivated, have less commitment, and tend to dislike their jobs. They tend to rely heavily on rules and regulations and the environment becomes petty or dictatorial. Most people prefer working for a powerful boss because he or she does not rely solely on rules and regulations, but fosters an environment of interest, commitment, and appropriate professional challenges (opportunities to learn).

- **Overuse of organizational power reduces that power.** These are the people who often inspire contempt because they don't know how to use any type of power except that bestowed upon them by their position. They often lord that power over people and as a result, their effectiveness diminishes. Again, they may be able to demand short-term compliance, but that's all they'll get and even that will diminish over time.

- **Frequent use of power leads to a distorted sense of power.** People that often use power inappropriately to get results tend to develop an oversized sense of power and self. They tend to see themselves as more important and more key to the organization than they really are. The ancient expression "Pride goeth before the fall" is appropriate here. The overuse of any form of power eventually backfires, especially when that overuse stems from self-serving motives.

- **The more you share your power, the more powerful you become.** This is a very interesting notion, especially for those power misers who believe just the opposite. Managers who share power with subordinates generate increased commitment and improved group performance. Shared power helps people learn to make better decisions, which not only helps them as individual performers, but helps the group perform at a higher level as well. As an IT manager, a team that is empowered will help you make better decisions by "pushing back" when you propose something flawed (or flat out wrong). As individuals and the team perform better, the manager is perceived as a better manager and is bestowed more organizational power (typically in the form of information and resources).

Working Effectively in a Political Environment

Now that we've taken a good look at power and influence, we can begin to see what politics is all about. People are complex beings and they often blend good and not-so-good intentions all in the same mix. In order to effectively navigate the politics in your company, you first have to understand sources of power and influence, which we just covered. Next, you need to develop strategies for maintaining (or increasing) your power in genuine ways that benefit the organization. Here's a good analogy: If you donate money to charity, do you take a tax deduction? If the answer is yes, does taking the tax deduction make the donation any less noble or good? Of course not. When the actions we take serve the company *and* our own self-interests, there is (generally speaking) no inherent problem just as there is no problem doing something noble (charitable donation) and taking the tax deduction (self-serving). At the risk of repetition, none of these concepts or actions is inherently good or bad; it's how they're used that determines their ultimate "goodness" or "badness." In this section, we're going to look at several strategies you might choose to use to navigate through the political waters. These are not the only methods, just a few to get you started.

Accept That Politics Exist

The first tool you'll need in working effectively is to accept that politics exist wherever there are two or more people working together. As mentioned, most of people's discomfort around power and influence stems from the abuse or misuse of power. At its worst, power is an end in itself. At its highest form, power can be used to create positive change in an organization. When we refer negatively to power and politics, we're typically discussing an environment in which political activity is devoted to the acquisition of personal power, which is a waste of time and resources that could be better applied toward accomplishing organizational goals.

However, when power and politics *are* applied toward accomplishing organizational goals, they produce much better results. When they are aligned with organizational goals, people tend to feel motivated, connected and energized. So, if you understand that power and politics themselves are not necessarily bad, you can learn how to use them to accomplish organizational goals. Forewarned is forearmed, so learning about how power and politics work in your organization will contribute to your ability to get things done. If you blithely refuse to admit that politics exist or that they impact your chances for success, you'll be far less effective than you might otherwise be.

Develop Positive Relationships

One of the easiest ways to survive corporate politics is to develop genuine, positive relationships with people inside and outside of your department. Have coffee or lunch with people outside your immediate circle. Greet the receptionist or the shipping/receiving clerk by name. Get to know others in your organization besides the ones you work with on a daily basis. Take time before or after meetings to engage in appropriate conversation with people you don't always come in contact with. Not only will you meet a few folks you might genuinely like, you'll build important relationships with people across your organization. Now, those of you who are naturally suspicious might be thinking, "That's not very sincere—to get to know people so you can get something from them." That's true; it's not sincere if you do it for that reason. That's not what's being suggested. Get to know people and develop positive relationships because it's interesting, because it makes your job easier, because you'll enjoy going to work, and because it may also benefit you at some point in the future.

Another way IT folks can develop positive relationships is to take time to really understand what others in the company do. People love to talk about themselves and their jobs, so take time to listen. You might also gain genuine insight into that job or department that you can use when you implement a related IT project in the future. The more you understand what everyone in the company does, the better you can do your job, so taking time to develop relationships is a great starting point.

In any business relationship, there's always some give and take. Doing favors and helping out others in need can not only foster positive relationships, but can help you out in times of political turmoil. Of course, setting appropriate boundaries for favors is important, too. Some are small favors of convenience and have little residual impact other than the person "owes you one." Other favors are bigger and may have a negative impact on other departments or on the organization as a whole. If you favor one person or group over another and it has a negative impact on those that did not receive the special treatment, resentment will usually result. That's when you begin to tread dangerously close to our definition of negative politics. You need to be careful about how favors and special treatment may impact others. Finally, some favors cross all boundaries and are unethical or illegal. Don't even go there. That said, we do favors for each other everyday and this is part of the exchange/barter system that naturally helps things get done at work.

Develop Your Exchange

Understanding how you exchange information, resources, and influence in the organization can help you understand what you have to offer and what you have to gain through these kinds of mutually beneficial transactions. Most of us do this naturally, but doing so more consciously may lead to better results. For example, though not in your job description, you're really good at Microsoft Access and you assist a colleague in the purchasing department with creating a small database. Your expertise in Microsoft Access is part of the exchange. The next time you need purchasing to expedite a purchase order for an IT purchase, you will likely find that the purchaser is happy to do so because you helped him/her out previously.

It's also good to know what you will and will not exchange. For instance, though you might be really good with Microsoft Access, as director of IT for your company, it is probably not appropriate for you to develop a database for a purchaser. In this case, you might offer to have one of your staff develop the database so the purchaser still "owes" you, but it's not a direct trade. Again, we don't usually do things so that someone will owe us—we do it because we have the skills, time, or talent to help out and helping out others greases the wheels of the company. The residual effect is that the purchaser is more inclined to help out in the future and there's nothing wrong with that. Avoid using your balance of trade to strong-arm people into returning a favor that puts them in a bind. The exchange or barter can be powerful ways to get things done, but be aware that you can take this too far and put people in difficult situations by demanding they return a favor in a specific manner.

Listen Carefully

Listening is a skill that takes a bit of practice. You might hear the words, but are you really listening to the meaning? Along with words come tone of voice, speed, choice of words, choice of content (what to say and what not to say), positioning (also known as "spin"), and body language, to name just a few variables. Make a habit of listening to the speaker for words, content, and tone. You might be surprised by how much more information you glean about the political environment by listening in this manner. Sometimes it's not what someone says, but what she doesn't say that becomes important, especially in highly political organizations. This kind of listening takes practice because it requires that you look for what's not there—and sometimes there's no way to know that. However, if you simply spend more time really listening, you'll improve your listening skills and you'll know more than you might otherwise. Someone once said, "Listen twice as often as you speak," and in a political environment, you might want to bump it up to a three to one ratio.

Communicate More, Not Less

When things aren't going so well, we tend to want to either close ourselves in a room to think or take decisive action to resolve the problem. Regardless of what the situation calls for, make sure you communicate clearly, honestly, and effectively. Communicating too little allows rumors, half-truths, and flat-out lies to travel at the speed of light through the company. Communicating frequently, especially when there's a problem, will cut those rumors off at the knees and give you the opportunity to bring the truth into the light of day. While you might not be comfortable with the truth when things are going wrong (especially if it's your fault), it's always better than the alternative. Learning how to communicate bad news can also help. For instance, there are two ways you can notify people of a system problem. You can say, essentially, "The server is down and we don't yet know when it will be back up," or you can say, "We're working on the server that went down this morning at 10:00 A.M. and we'll keep you informed of our progress in diagnosing and repairing the problem." Which one sounds better to you? They're both true, but one has a positive "spin" on it, which leaves people with a sense of confidence that the problem is being handled. The first example leaves a lot to be desired in terms of effective communication, but it's the most common type of communication people get when there are problems. IT people often prefer to go work on some code or rebuild a server to talking with people, so working on developing and improving this one skill can go a long way in helping you survive corporate politics.

Know What Not To Say

Sometimes enthusiastically endorsing something or someone turns out to be a terrible decision. Other times making disparaging remarks turns out to be a bad decision. If your corporate climate is such that the winds shift from time to time, make sure you know what's going on before you jump in with your opinion. Often knowing when to speak up and when to remain silent is one key to success in organizational politics. We've all been in a situation where we speak up because we believe we have good information only to later discover our information was incorrect or incomplete. These kinds of situations are sometimes caused by people intentionally misinforming us, but other times it's just a matter of bad data. In either case, make sure you have the information you need and are confident it's correct before speaking too strongly either for or against a proposal. That doesn't mean you can't voice a strong opinion, just stop and think about the potential political consequences before speaking. This goes back to the first suggestion—admitting that politics exists.

Knowing what to say and what not to say also relates to choice of words. We've all had the experience of saying something that was correct or accurate, but was said in an unfortunate way. Afterward, we sit wondering how we could possibly have said it in that manner (the old "open mouth, insert foot" routine). We're especially prone to misspeaking when under pressure—during job interviews, difficult meetings, or uncomfortable confrontations. Take a moment to stop and think about what you want to say and then think about how you want to say it. An awkward silence is always better than an unfortunate comment. If the network goes down because someone really made a huge mistake, you might choose to say it was due to "an oversight" rather than "an error." Both are probably accurate, but the word *oversight* leaves the listener with more confidence than the word *mistake* does. The intent is not to deceive, but to avoid throwing gasoline on an already smoldering fire. Your choice of words can certainly be used to misdirect or deceive, but they can also be used to set the appropriate tone so sensitive situations remain under control.

If you accept that you work in a political environment, you're more likely to think about political consequences before jumping headlong into the fire. That said, don't let awareness of the political environment paralyze you. You'll take your lumps when you're wrong, but if you've developed genuine relationships and an awareness of the political environment, you're likely to survive with only a few bumps and scratches.

Share The Power

Those who share power end up with more power, in most situations. While you may need to exercise care when sharing power, it's a good idea to look at where you can and should share power and when it's best to hold on to it. Look around the organization for examples of people who've shared power. Were they managers or non-managers? Did it benefit them or did it hurt them? In some highly negative, political environments, sharing power can be tricky. However, if you can find appropriate ways to share power, you're more likely to end up on the winning end of the deal. The saying "trust, but verify" is a good one to keep in mind here. Start off with small increments of shared power and verify that the trust and shared power is used appropriately. Once you see a track record of your team (or individuals) being trustworthy, you can give them more power. As you do so, you empower them to do a better job and most of the time your results will improve as well.

Know Your Personal Values

It's a good idea to sit down and think about what you would or would not do in hypothetical work situations. Playing "what if" can give you insights into your personal values and limits. When you know firmly what your own limits are, you can make sure that when you run into a political situation, you make decisions based on your own values. While you might not make the most politically correct decision, it will be one you can live with later on. Sometimes the only right answer is the one you can live with.

Plan On Politics Impacting Your Job

In most companies, you'll be judged by two criteria: quality and politics. If you plan on politics playing a role in how your work is perceived, you won't take the naïve stance that your work should or will be judged solely on quality. In a perfect world, our work would be judged only on its merits, but that rarely is the case. Pretending politics doesn't exist or won't affect you is the best way to be blindsided by political events within your company. Making some effort to understand the political environment and accepting that your job performance will be perceived through the political filter will help you come out ahead.

Be Aware of Political Change

Political change can happen slowly over time or it can happen quickly overnight. This change can help or hinder you. If you're associated with someone with a lot of political power and he or she leaves the company suddenly, you could be left out in the cold. Unfortunately, people who are aligned with someone who falls out of favor also tend to fall out of favor. On the other hand, if someone leaves and that creates a gap in the organization, you could be standing in just the right spot. Being aware of what's going on around you and which way the political winds are blowing is important. While you may not always be able to gauge what's going to happen next or who's going to fall out of favor, you often can see signs of change and be prepared. If a project is suddenly cancelled (for political reasons or otherwise), you may see an opportunity to use those now idle resources for another project. There's a saying that luck is when preparation and opportunity meet, so if you're keeping your eyes open and you're prepared, you may find that changing political environments actually create opportunities for you.

Enterprise 128...

Beware of Ego-Boosters

In every company, at one time or another, there comes a big, complex project that no one else seems to have taken on or a project that is on the brink of failure. Your boss (or top corporate executive) comes to you, appealing to your company loyalty, your supreme project management expertise, and the promise of glory if you'll just take on this project. *Beware*. First, make sure you notice when someone is appealing to your ego. We all love it, but it's sometimes just a way of getting us to feel so good about ourselves we *are* ready to take on the world (and that very ugly project). These folks may be appealing to your values, emotions, or reason in an attempt (legitimate or not) to get you to do something they want you to do.

Projects that have not found a suitable home, that have not gotten a "good" project manager to sign on, or that have failed and are now being revamped and offered around can be signs of serious political issues. Though it's not always the case, it's good to keep your eyes open and your ego in check when this comes up. If others have failed on a project, why? Was it really because that project manager was not able to successfully complete the project (as you might be told) or were there corporate politics at play that caused the failure? While you may not be able to find out the whole story, start asking appropriate questions before you sign on. Otherwise, you might find yourself holding a political bombshell with nowhere to run and nowhere to hide. If possible, it's better to respectfully decline. If that's not an option, do your homework to find out the

Continued

politics behind the scenes so you don't run into the same problems your prede-
cessor(s) did. If you are able to discern the reasons for failure and believe you can
address these issues effectively, you may still choose to take on these "challenged" projects. Just don't be fooled by flattery and ego-boosting chats - look
at the *facts* and make informed decisions.

Breaking Up Political Logjams

Corporate politics and power determine which projects get funded, which get priority, which get support, which get the best people, etcetera. IT projects are often "politically challenged" for two primary reasons. The first is that IT is seen as a cost center. From a political standpoint, few people are going to stand up and staunchly defend something that is seen as doing little more than costing a bundle of money. We discussed this to some extent in Chapter 2 when we looked at aligning IT strategy with corporate strategy. IT projects also run into political problems when IT is not seen as important (or strategic) to the business. Again, if you take the steps delineated in Chapter 2, IT will be viewed as a more integral and necessary (not necessary evil) part of the company. If the IT projects are seen as strategic, those with political capital are more likely to defend or support them. In this section, we're going to discuss strategies you can use to break up some of the political logjams that might be hindering your IT projects. These methods might not solve every political problem you encounter, but they'll give you a great set of tools to use as a starting point.

High-Level Sponsorship

In Chapter 1, you learned about the top eight reasons projects tend to succeed or fail. Executive sponsorship was listed as the most important factor for project success. So it should be no surprise that having high-level support in the organization, both for yourself and for your projects, is an important element in overcoming political obstacles. Executives have organizational, information, and resource power. They can work on your behalf to ensure projects get the resources they need when they need them. Executive support can also help you overcome politics lower in the organization. It's unlikely that your boss (or your boss's peer) is going to try to block something that a senior executive supports.

One very important note about executive support is this—always attempt to go *through* your manager or direct supervisor. Going around or above your boss's head is seen as a power play (and in truth, it almost always *is* a power play) and it almost always results in negative consequences. There may be times when it's appropriate to go directly to senior management. For example, your boss might tell you that it would be a good idea for you to pitch the project to his or her boss directly since you understand the details of the project. These types of situations depend a lot on how your company is run and what the political climate is. If there is a lot of trust and cooperation, it's possible you can go directly to a senior executive without your boss's explicit permission. In other organizations, that's what's termed a CLM—a *career-limiting move.* You'll need to figure out how to get high-level support for your project one way or another. Using the information you gleaned from Chapter 2, you should have a more versatile set of tools to use now.

Making The Business Case

Another very practical and effective method of blowing through political logjams that are impacting your IT projects is to do an excellent job making the business case for your project. While politics may still impact your project, it's much more difficult to argue when the facts and figures are clearly laid out. Going back to Chapter 2 material, you learned that one effective way to influence people is with reason. In this case, the business case you make for your IT project will appeal to reason. If you can also find a way to appeal to values and emotion, you'll make a stronger case. Create a strong business case, be prepared to present it in a way that generates interest and maybe even excitement.

The IT Factor...

Generating Support for IT Projects

Making the business case is a good way to generate support for an IT project, but often the presentation of the material falls flat. You don't need to go out and hire someone to create a dazzling Flash-based presentation to make the material interesting. Spend time thinking about the IT project and what you hope to accomplish. Think about its impact on the company, the internal users, the customers—whoever the project will impact most. Think about the positive potential for this project. Now you're ready to present your case. Don't bore people with infinite details about the project. Be prepared with details in case someone asks, but like a good first date, keep it short and sweet. Be honest and forthcoming, but present information in a positive, energetic manner. How you perceive the project and how you present the information has a lot to do with how others receive the proposal. Earlier, you read CIO Trude Van Horn's comments that in some organizations, those who were the best presenters often got their

Continued

projects funded. Presentation has a lot to do with perception, so learn to state your case in a manner that is both compelling and convincing (if you can't do it, find someone on your team who can).

Avoid presentations that are either all flash and no substance or so boring even *you* want to fall asleep. Beware of Microsoft PowerPoint presentations (which often fall to either extreme). PowerPoint is fine as a tool, but don't jam your slides full of detailed data and then read every slide to your audience. Use bullet points to remind yourself of your key points and then speak to the audience. That's the short course on presentations, you know the rest. Generate interest and excitement. If you can't, you might want to have someone else do the presentation or go get some coaching to learn how to give better presentations. Many innovative projects have failed to get off the ground because the presentation failed to make the case in a way that got anyone interested.

Calculated and Demonstrated ROI (Reduced TCO)

Calculating and demonstrating a *return on investment* (ROI) or a reduced *total cost of ownership* (TCO) can also help a project move through political waters. This is closely related to making the business case, but this focuses specifically on the financial aspect. If finances are not your strong suit, try to get one of your company's Finance people to assist you in these calculations. This will be critical for several reasons. First, if you can show that your IT project not only has a strong business case (makes sense, supports or extends the company's strategies, etcetera), but also has good financials (ROI, TCO), you're much more likely to reduce political opposition. If the IT project has a weak ROI (or no ROI), you might need to re-evaluate it. If it supports or extends the company's mission, it might have a different type of ROI. For instance, it might not save the company money or pay for itself in *x* number of years unless you look at it from a more corporate perspective. Does this project improve efficiency that could save the company money over time? Does this project help generate additional revenue? Does this project help keep your company at the forefront of the market? Even if these benefits are difficult to calculate or are intangible, you can still delineate them. Helping executives understand the business case and the financial elements is one of the best ways to prevent negative political activity. It's not a cure-all—certainly there are some companies that don't let facts get in the way of decision-making, but most companies are fairly rational when it comes to spending money. Use that to your benefit. Of course, you'll still need to use all your political savvy (developed, of course, from reading this chapter) to make sure your projects stay on the fast track to success.

Effective Countermeasures

The methods discussed in the previous section are good at breaking up a political logjam once it has occurred. However, there are numerous countermeasures you can take that help reduce the political charge of an environment. More accurately, they turn the political activity from negative, self-serving power grabbing to positive, group-serving, power sharing. These suggestions don't work in all companies all the time and these are not the only techniques you can use. Most of these will work when applied in the right situation and as you read, you'll certainly be able to think of situations now or in the past that could have used a dose of one or more of these countermeasures.

The Politics of Service

Providing excellent service is often a great way to overcome political standoffs or political fights. While it's not a cure-all, it can be very effective in many situations. Many IT departments are good at keeping their company up-to-date with or even ahead of the technology curve, but just as many IT departments are viewed as out-of-touch with their customers. As any doctor knows, fixing the physical problem is only part of the cure—dealing with the non-physical factors can often effect a more powerful and lasting cure. Taking medication for high blood pressure without modifying your diet or exercise will result in mediocre results. The same holds true in IT. Fixing the physical problem is often only half the cure. Dealing with the customers, whether internal or external, is what results in both the reality and the perception of excellent service. We've all dealt with a variety of service people in our lives that were probably competent, but didn't say more than two words to us. Lack of information leads to concern, distrust, and even suspicion. This can lead to a situation where the problem was resolved, but the customer's perception of the situation is still negative. Improving service (assuming your IT department provides some sort of service to the organization) can help calm turbulent political waters.

Partnering with Business Unit Counterparts

This is one of the most powerful countermeasures to interdepartmental politics. When you actively seek out and partner with business unit counterparts, you are sharing organizational, information, and resource power with them. As you learned earlier in this chapter, when you share power, you tend to get more of it (power shared is power gained), but that's not the reason you'd use this method. Partnering with business unit counterparts (those in other departments at roughly the same organizational level you are) yields the opportunity for you to gain knowledge about what the company and other departments are up to, which helps you do a better job aligning your activities with the direction the company is headed. When you do this, you make your department, your staff and your IT projects more relevant to the company and this increases your power. As they say, the best defense is a good offense, and when you genuinely forge relationships with others in the company, you create a positive political environment.

Nowhere in our discussions do we imply, suggest, or outright state that these activities should be undertaken for purely political purposes—just the opposite. The goal is to reduce the negative political implications and the only way that can be done is by undertaking these activities in a positive, genuine manner. To partner with business unit counterparts for the sole purpose of gaining information to make yourself or your department more powerful would be to further the negative political environment and those types of maneuvers typically backfire anyway. These countermeasures are intended to help reduce political maneuvering through activities and behaviors that create win-win situations.

Partnering with your counterparts also creates another interesting dynamic. Once you actually know one another, you can find and forge alliances outside your normal sphere of influence. If you need a favor or support for a key project, you may find allies in these counterparts who can use their power and influence to help get things done. And, when push comes to shove, you may find support where you least expected to find it.

The Project Team

Selecting your project team can also help counter negative political activity in a company. However, in some companies, this can be tricky, since adding the wrong members to your team could cause even bigger problems. Certainly, you'll need to weigh the pros and cons of adding outside members to your project team, but often, adding key stakeholders and business unit counterparts to the team helps tremendously. For example, adding a person from another business unit that has often opposed your project could help or hurt. If the person is genuinely interested in finding an optimal solution, it could be a real bonus for your team to have that person's involvement. On the other hand, that person could simply undermine everything you do. Keeping an eye toward building relationships and adding key people to your project team might be a good move. It's especially wise if you, your department, or team is frequently criticized for not including the right people or getting enough input prior to implementing a project. In this case, adding the right people to the team can reduce that tension and provide a venue for meaningful and timely input and advice. Later in this book, we'll discuss how to determine the best outside people to add and why, and we'll discuss subject matter experts and how their input and support can catapult a project toward success.

Customer/User Involvement

Another related method for creating a more positive political environment is to involve key users or customers in the projects that will impact them. In this case, the word *customers* refers primarily to internal customers, though there may be instances when involving external paying customers makes sense. Internal customers and users can be the source of political unrest if their needs are not being met. Information is power and if users (we'll refer to internal customers as *users* here) feel they do not have access to needed information, they can often become political liabilities. By involving users in a meaningful way, you accomplish two key objectives. First, you share information, which in itself might resolve or reverse negative political trends. Second, you gain valuable information about your users that you can use to address concerns, build trust, and over time build stronger alliances. Again, because these methods can be used in negative, manipulative, power-grabbing ways, you might find resistance at first, even if your intentions are good. When you involve users and you have a genuine desire to improve business relationships, your department and projects will benefit. We'll specifically discuss when and how to involve users in the project planning, testing and implementation phases of the project.

Communications Plan

Another potentially useful tool for skirting the usual political skirmishes is to create a communications plan that addresses issues that are likely to arise. Many negative political maneuvers become less effective when information is shared openly because power plays often rely upon limited information. If you determine who might be impacted by the project and in what manner, you can begin to plan your communication strategy. We'll discuss this in more detail later in the book when we look at planning your IT project. For now, however, keep in mind that the more information you can share, the better off you're likely to be. Remember that information is power and that when you share power, you increase you own power. Clearly, there are times when you want to limit which information you share, such as when a project is confidential or when you're trying to fly "under the radar." There are also times when you want to limit the scope of the information you share so you don't give political players additional fuel. However, if you can communicate proactively and as openly as possible, you'll thwart many political maneuvers. And let's face it, unfortunately, not all IT departments are known for their outstanding communication skills, so this is one are where there's usually room for improvement.

Cheat Sheet...

Half Full, Half Empty

Some people naturally look at things with a positive attitude, while others seem to always see the downside. Often, there is no absolute truth, simply a matter of perspective. The same holds true of our behaviors at work (and elsewhere). While there certainly are some absolutes we can point to, much of what we do is open to interpretation based on one's perspective. A CEO who cuts jobs is seen as the bad guy to those who are losing their jobs, but the good guy to those who are keeping their jobs because the company isn't simply closing its doors. This problem with perspective can impact you as you try to navigate the political waters of your company. Each of the methods discussed in this chapter can be used in negative, political, power-grabbing ways. Each of them can also be used to build alliances, reduce political friction, and accomplish mutually acceptable goals. That's the ideal situation, but if your organization is already highly political (we use that phrase with negative connotations throughout the chapter), your actions may be seen as suspect or as self-serving. Sometimes it seems you can't win for losing, but if you work to build alliances and your outcomes consistently generate positive results for you, your team, your department, and the company, your actions will gradually be seen as genuine and positive. Who knows, you might single-handedly change your organization from one that uses negative political maneuvers to one that uses power and influence to everyone's benefit. Don't laugh. It could happen.

Summary

Power, influence and politics are incredibly useful tools in every organization, especially when used to generate positive results for yourself, your team, and your company. When used in an open, genuine manner, these methods can help you utilize the various sources of power and the various methods of influence to generate exceptional results. Don't let the stigma of the words *power*, *influence*, and *politics* rub off. Use the information in this chapter to become more effective in your organization and generate results that benefit everyone.

Solutions Fast Track

Corporate Politics: A Primer

☑ Politics are a fact of life and are present in all companies.

☑ *Power* is the ability to create change or to get things done.

☑ *Influence* is the exercise of that ability to produce change.

☑ *Politics* has been defined as, "the study of who gets what, when and how." Politics is power and influence in action.

☑ Politics is viewed negatively when it is self-serving and does nothing more than provide opportunities for increasing one's own power. Power, influence, and politics, when positively applied, provide the ability to get things done that benefit all involved.

Understanding Sources of Power

☑ Power can be derived from numerous sources. The primary sources are: organizational, information, resources, performance, expertise, and personal traits.

☑ Each source of power can be used in positive or negative ways.

☑ Organizational power often includes information and resource power.

☑ Performance and expertise are often power sources over which you have some control. In other words, you can improve performance and expertise through effort. Both are sources of power that can be useful in gaining access to other sources of power.

☑ Personal traits are often things over which we have some control such as how we dress, how we speak, or how genuine we are (or are perceived to be).

Understanding Methods of Influence

☑ Influence is the use of various forms of power to achieve goals or objectives.

☑ Threats, exchange/barter, and appeals to values, emotions, and reason are the three primary methods of influence.

☑ Threats work for short-term, "emergency" situations. They generate *compliance*, but not *commitment*.

☑ Exchange and barter are effective methods because they cut across the entire organization. There need not be a one-for-one exchange or an in-kind exchange for this method to work.

☑ Appeals to values, emotions, and reason can be used in a variety of settings. These can generate the type of commitment that threats cannot.

☑ Appeals to values and emotions, when misused, are seen as manipulative or underhanded in most situations.

☑ Appeals to reason work well, but may not generate the level of commitment needed for certain undertakings.

The Power Paradox

☑ Power has some very interesting contradictions that are important to understand.

☑ Organizations work more effectively when more people have more power. When power is limited or restricted, the environment can become negative, self-serving, and limiting.

☑ Overuse of organizational power diminishes that power. If you constantly use "because I'm the boss" as the method of getting results, you'll erode your power and authority.

☑ Overuse of power leads to a distorted sense of power. These people tend to overestimate their importance of in the organization.

☑ Sharing power increases your power. Managers who share power with subordinates generate increased commitment and improved group performance. It helps people learn to make better decisions and helps the group perform at a higher level.

Working Effectively in a Political Environment

☑ Accept that politics exist. Ignoring it will not make it go away.

☑ Plan on politics being a part of your job. Just about everything you do will be judged based on both quality and politics.

☑ Develop positive, genuine relationships. Getting to know your counterparts in the business, your customers, your users, and your co-workers creates a positive environment and can counteract a lot of political maneuvers.

☑ Learn to listen. This prevents you from talking too much and provides you valuable opportunities to gain insights and information. It's also important to communicate effectively and let people know what's going on. This also circumvents political maneuvers that rely in misinformation.

☑ Know your own values. You'll need to know what you think and believe so you can follow your own internal values when it comes to working in a political environment. When you encounter negative political behaviors, it's important to know in advance what you will and won't put up with.

☑ Be aware of the changing political landscape. Not only will you fare better if you keep an eye on what's happening, you may also find unexpected opportunities. Be aware and be prepared to leverage those opportunities.

Breaking Up Political Logjams

☑ Within the business environment, there are specific things you can do to break up a political logjam.

☑ Executive support is important to project success and it can be particularly helpful if the project is being held up by political maneuvering.

☑ Making the business case for a project is another useful tool for getting an important project underway. If it's been bogged down in the organization's politics, developing a clear and concise business case document may just get things moving again.

☑ Calculate the return on investment. If a project gets logjammed in the decision-making process, showing the ROI (or in some cases, the reduced total cost of ownership) can jump-start a stalled project.

Effective Countermeasures

☑ In a political environment, finding ways to create win-win situations often is your best countermeasure.

☑ Delivering excellent service can be an effective countermeasure to a political situation. It addresses a number of organizational power bases including organizational, information, and resource.

☑ Developing strong relationships with business unit counterparts will help on a number of levels. Sharing information helps increase your power and reduce the political maneuvers that rely on lack of information. It also can give you genuine allies that can support your IT projects or lend their influence to your projects. It can also just make work more interesting and enjoyable.

☑ Involving the right people in IT projects—whether it's subject matter experts from within the company or internal users/customers—you can increase your ability to get the job done by forging these kinds of alliances as well.

☑ Information is power and sharing power increases your power. Therefore, sharing information will increase your power and reduce political activities that rely on misinformation or information hording.

Frequently Asked Questions

The following Frequently Asked Questions, answered by the author of this book, are designed to both measure your understanding of the concepts presented in this chapter and to assist you with real-life implementation of these concepts. To have your questions about this chapter answered by the author, browse to **www.syngress.com/solutions** and click on the **"Ask the Author"** form.

Q: I often find out important data after the fact. Any suggestions for getting more information sooner?

A: Withholding information can stem from one of two basic causes: someone forgot or someone purposely didn't tell you. We all can forget to share critical information from time to time, but most of us know when we see a pattern or when it seems intentional. In these cases, you might choose to talk to the person directly to let them know you're aware of the problem. We're assuming, for this problem, you do not have organizational power over the person (that is, you are not his or her boss or in their chain of command). By letting the person know you're aware of the withholding of information and politely confronting him or her, you provide the opportunity for him to explain, but you've also put him on notice. If the person continues this behavior, you may need to have the conversation in a more public setting, such as in a meeting with other key people present. Often people trying to gain power through withholding information will do so on the sly. If you call them on it in a meeting, especially if you've gotten hammered for not having the information, you can sometimes resolve these issues. The best approach is to be polite and direct, stick to the facts as you know them and be careful how you word things. Leaving the other person with some dignity is always your best bet and sometimes phrasing these inquiries as polite questions rather than accusations can yield better results.

Q: My manager is an executive with the company. She frequently has us pitch project ideas directly to her boss, the CEO. I always feel like I'm "talking out of school" when this happens. Any comment?

A: It seems your boss is comfortable with sharing power and is happy to let you loose with her boss—that's a real vote of confidence. Of course, because you do have the ear of her boss, you need to be cognizant of the political implications here. If her boss, the CEO, says to you after a presentation, "So, tell me, how do you like working for Lisa? Any problems?" you need to *think* before you speak. If there are problems, this is probably not the right time or place to air them. For instance, have you talked with your boss to try to resolve the problems? If not, mentioning them to her boss first will undermine her and will cause a serious trust problem between you two. If there are problems and you have talked with your boss about them, this is still probably not the best time or place to address these issues. Again, while the CEO may genuinely want information, he or she should understand that the question puts you in an untenable position. In this case, your best bet is to say as little as possible. If you are facing a serious, difficult problem with your boss and this is your one shot at taking it up with the CEO, you may choose to do so, but be aware that this path is fraught with peril.

Q: All this talk of politics makes me want to hide in the computer lab someplace. Can't we ever work in a non-political environment?

A: Yes and no. First, it's interesting to note that when a company's political environment is negative, it is considered political. When a company's political environment contributes to the greater good of the company, the employees, shareholders, and customers, it's not seen as political at all. Thus, when we say a company is highly political, we often mean that the more negative aspects are at the forefront. Companies vary widely in how political they are. Some companies frown upon the negative aspects of politics while others seem to thrive on power plays and intrigue. Often this behavior is encouraged, modeled, or at least blindly accepted at the top of the organization. If your organization is highly political, you really only have three choices: play along; ignore politics and just try to get your job done; or leave the company. Many people find the first choice unacceptable. However, ignoring the political environment puts you at a disadvantage. Your work will rarely, if ever, be judged solely upon its quality and content. The perception of the quality of your work will always be influenced by the political environment. You might get lucky, but if not, your overall work performance will likely be judged as adequate or mediocre if you're not participating in managing the political aspects of your job. You can always quit and look for a company that is not as political, but you're likely to find that every company has its own unique blend of politics and problems and you have to take the good with the bad. The good news is that you now know how to counter and defuse political moves to make them less effective in your world.

Q: I'm currently interviewing with several different companies for a new job. How can I tell if the organization is highly political or not?

A: When interviewing, you have the responsibility to do your own due diligence to make sure the job and the company are right for you. One way to view the political environment of the organization is to talk with people. Talk with the receptionist, talk with the person that interviews you, talk with people in the parking lot. Asking them if the organization is political is probably not going to yield meaningful information. Instead, using the knowledge you gained in this chapter, ask questions related to how people get things done in the company. Ask questions that will help you determine if people share or hoard information or resources. Ask questions that help you determine if organizational power is the primary method of getting things done. While you may not know for sure until you're well into your 90-day probationary period, you can often get a feel for things by seeing how open, honest, and forthcoming people appear to be, how negative or biting they might be about their peers or the company in general, and by how often they use words like team, we, share, flexible, cooperate, etc. and actually mean it. Every company has a unique personality and politics is part of the mix. Finding one that seems to suit your approach to work and life is your best bet. And remember, they're taking a risk on you as well—it's in everyone's best interest to make sure it's a good fit.

Chapter 4

Managing the IT Project Team

Solutions in this chapter:

- **Today's Management Environment**
- **What People Really Want**
- **Work Styles and the Project Team**
- **Culture Matters**
- **Men, Women, and Technology**
- **Developing High Performance Teams**

☑ **Summary**

☑ **Solutions Fast Track**

☑ **Frequently Asked Questions**

Introduction

Projects don't fail, people do. That basic statement sums up the challenge every project manager faces. Any research done in this area returns time and again to the underlying cause of project failure: people. Most technology projects are complex and lack of funding, lack of staff, and lack of time or focus are all blamed in equal measure for project failure. Projects don't arise from the dust and run themselves—someone has to define them, fund them, staff them, and run them. The people involved are responsible for the success (or failure) of the project. As the project manager, you're ultimately responsible for the success of the project. For that reason, we're devoting a chapter to managing the project team. We're taking a slightly different approach than you may have seen in the past. We're going to explore not only how people tend to work (work styles) but also how you, as the project manager, can be more effective in managing teams that may be geographically, culturally, or technically diverse. In today's wired world (and increasingly, wireless world), we work with people around the globe in different time zones, different countries, and different cultures. While one chapter won't give you all the tools you need to perfect your multicultural management skills, it will help you better understand some of the challenges and give you some tools you can use immediately to improve your team management skills.

Project management, by definition, is the process of working with a team of people to solve a problem. In a vast majority of projects, the project manager (PM) must manage people over whom he or she has no direct (organizational) authority. Much of the PM's job, then, is using influence to generate the desired results. As you learned in Chapter 3, there are many sources of power and many methods of influencing people. Understanding these basics will help you as you manage your project team.

If you've ever wondered what makes people tick or what makes some managers so good at getting people on board with their projects, this chapter will give you some insight into those skills. If you manage a team that is across the continent or across the world, you'll learn highly useful information that will make your job a bit easier. And, if you've ever felt like your team was simply running you ragged, this chapter is a must-read for you.

Today's Management Environment

It has been estimated that the amount of information contained in one issue of the Wall Street Journal or the New York Times is more information than people processed in a year a century ago. We're all hit with the onslaught of information—from television, radio, newspapers, magazines, books, e-mail, to the Internet news and blogs. We get information instantly and we scan, absorb, reject, and move on. A century ago, a manager was in the position to have all the needed information and could make informed decisions for the people who worked for that manager. Today, managers are more like traffic cops, trying to direct the efforts of those in the organization toward a common goal while avoiding head-on collisions. The manager is no longer in the best position to know everything and make all the decisions. Instead, a manager must rely upon the people on his or her team to have expertise and to take initiative. However, at the same time this is needed, people are more mobile and less committed to employers than they were one hundred years ago. Today's manager needs to find a way to foster commitment and initiative with employees who are likely to change careers five times and hold ten or more jobs over their lifetimes. In order to manage this workforce, an effective manager must use new tools to achieve desired results.

Commitment and initiative are more important when managers have to process so much information that they are no longer the "experts" but the "generalists." Increasingly, companies must depend on highly skilled employees to think and act intelligently on behalf of the company since they have the technical knowledge, the imagination, and the connection with customers, vendors, and the marketplace. Technology has had a significant impact on the way we work and process information. A successful manager today must be able to mobilize employees to figure out how to get more done with less; a successful manager must find ways to inspire commitment and initiative to get the best possible results; and a successful manager must understand what challenges employees face to clear roadblocks and provide the best possible environment for success. That's a tall order, but in this chapter, we're going to look at some of the ways you can do just that.

What People Really Want

Let's start with the basics. Most people work because they have to earn a living. Hopefully, they also enjoy what they're doing and their job or career brings them a sense of accomplishment and satisfaction. Some people like the power or importance they derive from their jobs and others enjoy the daily interaction with co-workers, vendors, and clients. Some people like the problem solving and the challenges they get at work and others work for a personal sense of fulfillment or personal mission. Regardless of the reason people work, there are common elements about what people want when they're at work. Naturally, people want to be well compensated for the work they do, but every Management 101 class will tell you that money is not a motivator, but a demotivator. What does that mean? It means that you can't pay someone enough to like their job, but you can pay them too little to enjoy their job. Think about the last time you got a big raise or promotion. You were probably thrilled with the increase in pay—for a while. After a time, you adjusted to your new income and that raise lost its luster. On the contrary, think about a job you may have had where you were asked to assume a larger role or greater responsibility and were not given additional compensation. At some point, you were probably a bit irritated (or downright dissatisfied) that you were not being paid more money. So, let's cross money off the list of what people want. Everyone wants more money, but if one is adequately compensated, money rarely solves the underlying problems. We'll assume that the folks that work with and for you are adequately compensated and that, like everyone else, they'd love a hefty raise or bonus this year.

Causes of Job Dissatisfaction

There are issues that can cause dissatisfaction, but once they're taken care of they don't buy you much *satisfaction*. These are often termed *hygiene* issues or *housekeeping* issues. Like housekeeping, if the room is a mess you might be dissatisfied, but once it's cleaned up, it begins to blend into the background and is viewed in a relatively neutral manner. You rarely come into your office and think, "Wow, this office is *so* clean, I am so productive!" though you may occasionally think to yourself, "If I don't clean off the top of my desk soon, I won't get anything done, I'll spend all day looking for paper!" So, let's run through some of these housekeeping issues. As an IT department manager, you may have control over some or all of these. If you're an IT project manager without direct control or authority over any of these things, it is still good to be aware of these issues. When these things are lacking, people become disorganized and frustrated. Anything you can do to reduce disorganization and frustration is a good thing. Let's take a look:

- Company and administrative policies
- Salary
- Supervision
- Working conditions
- Interpersonal relationships

Company and Administrative Policies

Policies and procedures that don't make sense drive everyone nuts. Some companies have lots of crazy policies that seem to have been written back in 1965 and haven't changed for forty years. Other companies are flying by the seats of their pants and have few, if any, written policies and procedures. Neither extreme is good or desirable.

Policies and procedures can be an excellent part of making your company (or in your case, IT department or IT project) run smoothly and efficiently. Policies and procedures can clearly delineate common areas of confusion, responsibility, or legal requirements and help everyone stay on the same page. The flip side is you can create so many policies and procedures that it takes a Ph.D. to understand and apply them.

We'll discuss setting up policies and procedures for your IT project later in the book. Again, it's not so that we can create a tangle of red tape, but to provide a framework in which team members can work more efficiently. If a policy or procedure doesn't drive efficiency, it should be re-evaluated. There are policies and procedures that are required by law, but one could argue that they drive efficiency by keeping the company out of court. If you're an IT manager, you certainly have to abide by and enforce company policies and procedures. However, you also have to create and enforce policies related to IT—both internal and external to your department. Creating policies and procedures that help your staff get their jobs done more efficiently should be your goal. Gather input from your staff and get rid of any that just don't make sense or that make things unnecessarily more difficult. If you start bumping up against company policies or procedures that don't make sense, take them up with your boss or the appropriate person in the company and try to get them changed. In order to be competitive in today's fast-paced environment, working through useless or nonsensical policies and procedures slows things down and causes unnecessary confusion, frustration, and often, expense. Lack of coherent policies also creates confusion and slows things down as well.

Salary

We've already briefly touched on the salary issue. As a project manager, this is out of your hands, but if you're also the head of your IT department, you may have some control over this. Of course, we'd all love to make huge salaries, but that's just not going to happen in IT anytime soon. That said, if your company pays below market salaries, you'd better have some pretty cool perks to add on to the salary if you hope to attract and retain top-level talent. If you pay B or C-level rates, you're going to retain C or D-level staff. While you may not have much control over salary ranges in your company, you can make a business case for paying market (or better) rates. Someone with more skills and experience will ultimately cost your company less than someone with fewer skills and experience (assuming those skills and experience are relevant and necessary).

Another related issue is one that's been facing IT departments in the past four or five years and that is one of shrinking staff and expanding responsibilities. You and your staff may be tasked with more work and with higher levels of responsibility than ever before, but salaries don't necessarily get boosted to accommodate that. In some companies, the unfortunate attitude is akin to "You're lucky to have a job." In other companies, it's a bit more benign—closer to "We'd love to pay you more if we could afford it, but things are tight right now." Just take one look at what the stock market has done in the past few years and you can see that many businesses are simply going sideways—earnings were flat, revenues were flat (or down) and were in no position to grant large increases. Still, you may be able to make a business case for increasing salaries for key members of your staff to retain that talent. The mantra is *retain or re-train*, and training new hires (even those with equivalent skills, experience, or talents) generally costs far more than a raise for key employees.

Finally, another trap companies get locked into—and this is more common for smaller companies—raises don't keep pace with the market. You end up with these incredibly talented company veterans with 5 or 10 years' of excellent experience and they're making less than if they quit and got hired elsewhere (or re-hired at the same company). This is one way that companies lose talented employees, and it goes back to the policies and procedures issue we discussed earlier. If your policies prevent you from keeping key employees' salaries at (or above) market, you'll lose them to your competitor.

As IT manager, you should lobby hard to ensure your team's wages are up to par. If you're an IT project manager, this may impact you because you may have staff being asked to take on more and more "special projects" and they may feel tapped out, over-loaded, or just resentful at having to take on one more project for no additional pay. As companies continue to try to get as much productivity as possible out of each indi-vidual contributor (and that's a good thing, to a point), it's important that you also lobby to hire additional positions as the work expands. CEOs, VPs, and other senior managers often have the mistaken impression that as technology marches forward, the costs should go down (as efficiency goes up). Not so. For the most part, costs shift from one place to another and sometimes costs increase. It's important that you help your senior management understand this by preparing and presenting an effective busi-ness case. In this case, delineating the cost of errors, omissions, and rework due to short staffing might justify hiring (temporary or permanent) additional help.

Supervision

Supervision is another housekeeping issue that can be the source of dissatisfaction. Often people selected to move into supervisory roles are those deemed "good workers." The problem is that a good worker is not always a good supervisor. A good supervisor is one that interacts well with others and is able to be fair, impartial, and rel-atively unemotional about employee behavior. A good supervisor also needs leadership skills, especially the ability to get commitment (and compliance) from employees being supervised. If you're an IT project manager, you are essentially supervising project team members during the project, so this applies to you as well. If you don't have supervisory experience, you should consider taking a supervisor's course or reading up on what constitutes good supervision. Since this is a primary work relationship, your supervisory skills will have a significant impact on the people you work with. If you're an IT department manager, you should carefully evaluate who you make a supervisor and be clear about the skills you're looking for. Poor supervision is often a source of employee dissatisfaction. Inexperienced supervisors tend to be micro-managing control freaks or hands-off no-boundaries types that let staff walk all over them. Neither is helpful or desirable, and good, consistent, fair supervision is key to job satisfaction.

Working Conditions

Working conditions are another area that you may or may not have much control over, but that have an impact on employee productivity and satisfaction. If every time someone goes to make a copy, the copier breaks, jams, or catches on fire, you're losing valuable time and money. Not every company can afford first-class accommodations, but that doesn't mean it should skimp on important parts of the work environment. Adequate heating and cooling (you'd be surprised…), comfortable chairs (especially for programmers and folks that spend their 10-12 hours a day sitting), and reasonable personal space are all key elements. As an IT department manager, you can do your best to create a comfortable work environment within your sphere of influence. If necessary, lobby to get some of the corporate budget allocated for these things applied to your department. Even if you're such a geek (and that term is used with the highest respect) you only notice whether or not the network is up, decent working conditions are important to the vast majority of people.

Let's add another dimension to working conditions—information overload. In today's world, the amount of new information we need to process is accelerating and we have to deal with more data than ever before. It's not your imagination—the technological revolution over the past fifty years has caused more information to be generated than ever before in human history. Sorting the "need to know" from the "nice to know" from the "don't need to know" can itself be time consuming. There may be very little you can do to reduce information overload (some call it "data smog") but you can try to help your department staff or project team by not contributing unnecessarily to the overload. Be aware of the information demands and work to reduce non-critical information for your team. If you're interested in reading up on this, a thorough academic discussion of this problem can be found online at http://icl-server.ucsd.edu/~kirsh/Articles/Overload/published.html, but don't feel compelled to read it—it may only contribute to your information overload.

Interpersonal Relationships

Just the words "interpersonal relationships" brings fear to many IT types—after all, it's about the technology isn't it? Sure it is, but in this context, we're talking about the importance of people being able to interact with one another. Ensuring that the work environment affords adequate time for social contact is an important aspect of work for almost everyone. Socializing during a break, at lunch, or between meetings should be allowed and encouraged—to a point. Clearly, work has to get done, but there are some managers (though it's more often inexperienced supervisors) that expect people to work with their nose to the grindstone for 10 continuous hours a day. Breaks for socializing recharge people's batteries and bring enjoyment to the job.

The flip side of this is also important to note. You should not allow rude or offensive comments, inappropriate behavior, or threats of any kind. You should take immediate and appropriate action to curtail this type of activity. Some of this behavior crosses the line from simply rude to illegal when it creates a hostile environment, so making it clear that this type of behavior will not be tolerated is very important. As an IT department manager, you'll be bound to the company's policies and procedures regarding this type of behavior, but you can also model and foster a positive environment that encourages positive interactions and provides a framework for dealing with problems in an acceptable manner. As an IT project manager, you'll also encounter situations where people may behave in inappropriate (or illegal) ways within the project environment and you'll need to take appropriate action as well. When this negative type of behavior is not challenged and stopped, it becomes a major source of job dissatisfaction for those who are the frequent targets of this bad behavior. Again, these activities, if unchecked, could constitute harassment or worse and could land you and your company in legal trouble if you're aware of it and do nothing to stop it. If you're an IT project manager without direct authority to take action, notify your supervisor or manager or notify your Human Resources manager for assistance.

When these "housekeeping" items are in order, employees won't be distracted by basic elements of the job. If you don't deal with these issues effectively, the most likely result is that excellent employees will leave and you'll end up with mediocre employees (all the B and C-level folks, none of the A-level folks). Now, let's turn our attention to what helps people feel satisfied with their jobs.

Cheat Sheet...

Keep Your Eyes and Ears Open

As an IT project manager, the things that cause job or work dissatisfaction are often outside your direct control. While you can't control them, you *can* be aware of them and understand how they impact your team. If any of the items listed in the previous section are causing your team to be less productive or effective, you can and should try to take steps to work with someone in the organization that does have direct control over these elements. Though you might not be able to effect change in these areas every time, it's important that you understand and recognize these problems if they arise because they will likely impact your team's overall success. However, make sure you remember the lessons you learned in Chapter 3 about managing in a political environment to make sure you approach the problem in a positive and effective manner.

Foundations for Job Satisfaction

If money is not what people want, then what do they want? A motivation theorist by the name of Frederick Herzberg proposed that people are motivated and their needs are satisfied by just a handful of things:

- The work itself
- Achievement
- Recognition
- Responsibility
- Advancement

Keep in mind that people will only be motivated or satisfied by these things if the basic elements of a good work environment are present. As we discussed, those include money (compensation and benefits), working conditions (hours, physical surroundings, workload), relationships with supervisor and peers, and company policies and procedures. Any of these can create dissatisfaction when not present or when not positive, but once these items are present and accounted for, they become part of the background. Understanding the basics of why people work and what they want is important because it will help you as a project manager learn to manage people more effectively and will certainly help when you have to manage project team members over whom you have no direct or organizational authority. It's especially important to understand it's not really about the money because as a PM, you usually have no control over the project team's paychecks. Now that you understand you have several other highly effective tools at your disposal, let's look at how these various motivators come into play on an IT project team.

The Work Itself

Many people seek out jobs that utilize their natural skills and talents. Whether they're landscapers or psychologists, plumbers or dancers, everyone will make a best effort to find a job aligned with his or her skills and interests. That said, not everyone has the opportunity to find a job aligned with his or her skills and talents. Hopefully, in your organization, people are in jobs at which they can perform at or above expectations. Most people, then, find satisfaction from the actual work they perform. That doesn't mean they enjoy all aspects of it. An IT manager may love designing the network infrastructure and hate giving performance reviews to staff or dislike having to develop a departmental budget every year. Every job has elements we don't enjoy, but the overall job responsibilities and tasks are a source of great satisfaction for many people, especially those in professional vocations.

APPLYING YOUR KNOWLEDGE

As an IT manager or project manager, you should try to assign people to projects or tasks that align with what they enjoy doing. Although it's not always possible, if you can find someone who enjoys finance to be part of developing the project budget, you're going to get a much better result than if you get someone who *can* do it, but hates that aspect of their job. Aligning skills, interests, and talents with project needs will yield better results with less effort. A task that one person dislikes might be a task that someone else really enjoys, so make sure you understand your team and which tasks are likely to appeal to each team member. While you can't always make a good match, you can achieve higher quality at a lower cost just by consciously aligning people and project tasks.

Achievement

Another area that brings job satisfaction is a sense of achievement. There are two key aspects to a sense of achievement—the actual work (accomplishing a difficult goal) and the recognition of that accomplishment. We'll discuss recognition separately in a moment, but remember that a sense of achievement contains those two elements. As people become more self-confident and mature, they often derive enough satisfaction from the achievement itself, but having someone be aware of or witness your achievement is often important. Olympic athletes certainly revel in their achievements, but when they do something spectacular in front of a crowd or on television rather than during their Tuesday morning workout, it becomes more meaningful. Thus, providing opportunities for achievement and recognizing that achievement often go hand-in-hand.

Applying Your Knowledge

As an IT manager or project manager, you should look for opportunities for people to stretch, grow, and learn. These opportunities provide people with a sense of achievement and can contribute to a strong sense of job satisfaction. While you don't want to put your project or department in jeopardy, you can help people take measured, calculated risks that help them learn new skills. This not only helps that person feel a sense of achievement, but it also helps you learn what the members of your team can or cannot do. If necessary, assign tasks to a junior person with a more senior person overseeing the task. This allows the more junior person to grow and provides the more senior person the opportunity to learn and grow in supervision and management, so everyone wins.

Recognition

How is a "job well done" recognized in your organization? Every company has a different culture and unfortunately, many are not good at giving recognition. Some people seem to think that if you praise someone's work, it will cause them to slack off, but just the opposite is true. Recognition of good or excellent work can be a real motivator. People want praise and recognition for work they do that meets or exceeds expectations. Recognition is one of the easiest methods of keeping employees motivated and the good news is that, unlike a bonus or raise, it doesn't cost a nickel. Think of the last time your manager praised you for work you did. You felt good and that recognition probably made your day, week, or month.

Sadly, some managers are terrible at recognizing great work. As a result, staff feel their efforts aren't valued or noticed and they tend to perform at lower and lower levels until their work simply *meets* standards (at best). To produce high-performance teams, the manager must be able to give appropriate recognition to team members' work. What's appropriate recognition? That depends a lot upon your company's work environment, your team members, and the nature of the task receiving recognition. However, some general ideas include verbal or written recognition, either privately or in a more public setting (team or department meeting, for instance). You can send an e-mail to the person or to the entire team touting someone's accomplishments. You can also recognize outstanding accomplishments with small rewards such as an afternoon off from work or tickets to the movies. If appropriate and you have the authority to do so, you can also give someone a bonus or raise due to truly outstanding effort. Remember, though, the rewards and bonuses are NOT a substitute for verbal and/or written praise. Verbal or written recognition is less expensive than rewards or bonuses and it's also far more effective.

Enterprise 128...

Keepin' It Real

A manager of an IT department had been promoted into the position during a time when the company was having financial problems. As a result, he wasn't really the best suited to the job, but was there because he'd been in the right place at the right time. We'll call him Hamilton. Hamilton was very personable and many people who interacted with him found him to be funny, interesting, and charming—except the people that worked for him. He was known to have an explosive temper with his staff and they alternately feared and resented him. Unfortunately, when they did a good job, Hamilton turned on the charm and was effusive in his praise. It was rarely proportionate to the work done. Even more unfortunate was that Hamilton, lacking even basic management skills, would shower an underperforming employee with lavish praise to the same degree he would for a super star. This got him into trouble with the HR department on more than one occasion because he'd bestow high praise on someone and then turn around and fire them for poor performance a week or two later. This was confusing to existing staff and lead to reduced productivity and increased tension.

Avoid bestowing praise on underperforming staff unless it's really warranted. Make sure the praise is commensurate with the task and effort. Make sure the praise is real and meaningful. Don't tell someone you're thrilled they're part of the team when they are barely making the grade. When you give disproportionate or over-the-top praise, especially when it's not warranted, you'll lose credibility and the trust of your team.

Applying Your Knowledge

Genuine, meaningful recognition makes people feel valued and enhances their sense of accomplishment. Make sure you're specific and honest when recognizing accomplishments and make every effort to do so in a timely manner. It's far more effective to give public recognition at a team meeting a week after the accomplishment than to add it as a note in someone's performance review 8 months later. Also, avoid giving glowing recognition to underperformers—it creates a mixed message and can cause legal problems if the employee is later let go ("My boss told me I was a great asset to the team and a week later I was fired!"). If you're the type that's not comfortable giving recognition, focus on the facts and practice saying it a few times before you have to deliver it. The more you do it, the easier it gets, but keep it real.

Responsibility

Some people thrive on taking on additional responsibilities. This is another source of job satisfaction for some. Remember that not everyone wants to move up in the organization and not everyone will enjoy additional responsibility, so unlike recognition, this does not always have universal appeal. However, most people enjoy having more power, authority, and responsibility, so finding ways to provide that for staff who are performing above expectations is a real motivator. Keep in mind that you should almost never give more responsibility to someone who is underperforming. You might think the person is bored or underutilized (and he or she might tell you that), but you shouldn't reward bad behavior. So, additional responsibility should only be given to those who have proved themselves. In the real world, that may not always be possible, but it should be your goal.

Applying Your Knowledge

Sometimes real "go-getters" are chomping at the bit for more responsibility, but they ignore the responsibilities that they currently have. This is often the case with younger, less experienced staff. While helping staff to focus on current responsibilities, you can increase job satisfaction by providing small opportunities for additional responsibilities and see how things go. For instance, you might assign someone the task of gathering and analyzing weekly call volumes or weekly satisfaction ratings for help desk calls and see how they accomplish the task. If they start ignoring other work, you can scale their responsibilities back without having a huge, disruptive impact on the organization. Look for small additional tasks to assign for those you're not sure about. Look for permanent transfer of large responsibilities for staff who've not only proven they're up to it but who deserve the opportunity. Giving huge opportunities to unproven staff can backfire. Experienced staff will be resentful at missed opportunities and inexperienced staff may falter in their new duties—both scenarios cause disruption in the team or department.

Advancement

Advancement is another source of job satisfaction for many people. They want to know that their efforts will be rewarded with additional responsibility, which often comes with career advancement. A big thank you and an occasional raise work wonders in the near to mid-term, but over the long haul, many people want to see that they have the opportunity to advance.

As a project manager, you may have limited control over this part of someone's job, but you may be able to provide staff with the opportunity to advance within the framework of the IT team or project team. As people demonstrate their abilities to define, organize, and manage tasks and projects, you can begin to reward them with additional responsibilities or roles on the project team. You may define project team leaders or project team supervisors and this may be an area that provides some sense of advancement, even if it's not a job promotion. Giving people the opportunity to advance within the bounds of your authority (team, project, department, etc.) will help motivate some people because they'll see the possibility and path to advancement. The opportunities you provide for your team to learn new skills and grow professionally might also lead to career advancement for them due to their efforts on your project team. Strong performance on a project team may lead to opportunities for promotion outside the project team.

Cheat Sheet...

IT Projects and Job Satisfaction

We all know that some IT projects are highly coveted and others are run-of-the-mill (or worse). As an IT department manager or IT project manager, keep in mind that everyone should have a shot at the coveted projects, but everyone should also have to participate equally in the dreaded projects (splicing 600 cables that were cut when the landscaper accidentally dug up the buried cabling...). Remember the sources of job satisfaction we just discussed and try to assign people to projects in a manner that will drive job satisfaction. While it's important to assign the right resources to the right projects, when you have a bit of leeway, look for opportunities to drive job satisfaction among your team members. You'll find the work is done faster and with higher quality when you can do so. It only takes an extra couple of minutes to consider these factors when making project or job assignments and it can make a world of difference for you, the team and the team member.

Work Styles and the Project Team

It's clear that people have different work styles—from how they like to receive information to how they like to manage their work; from how they interact with others to how they like their manager to communicate with them. In this section, we'll look at four common work styles that you can use to begin to understand how each of the members of your team approaches work. These four styles are used as you might use the four primary colors. Each can be used alone, but is often mixed with one or two others to create new, unique colors. Work styles are similar in that they rarely show up purely as one of the four styles. More often, they are blends of two or three styles. As with color, though, you can almost always discern the primary work style preference. This is useful because when you understand how someone (primarily) approaches work, you can work with him or her to leverage his or her strengths and minimize weaknesses.

Some of you may be familiar with work styles assessments such as Myers–Briggs or DiSC profiles. Myers–Briggs is a useful tool, but can be somewhat more complex or comprehensive than needed in some instances. Myers–Briggs looks at four areas. These are:

- Where do you primarily direct your energy? The two polarities used to describe these traits are *extrovert* and *introvert*. The extrovert is externally focused and the introvert is internally focused.

- How do you prefer to process information? The two polarities used here are *sensing* and *intuition*. Those who prefer sensing prefer facts, figures, and things that can be measured and known. Those that prefer intuition prefer ideas, possibilities, and the unknown.

- How do you prefer to make decisions? The two polarities in this case are *thinking* and *feeling*. Typically a person is more comfortable thinking through decisions or more comfortable following the "gut" response.

- How do you prefer to organize your life (and work)? The two extremes used in this instance are *judgmental* and *perception*. Those that are judgmental (without the negative connotation) are those that prefer things to be planned, stable, and organized. Those preferring to organize their lives based on perception like to be flexible, responsive, and to "go with the flow."

As with any assessment or system, it's rare that someone is totally to one extreme or the other in their behaviors and preferences. More often, people fall somewhere along the continuum. We all know people who prefer rules and regulations and order and stability. Some of them on the extreme may seem incredibly rigid or uptight to us, but that's where they're most comfortable. We all also know people who couldn't seem to care less about the rules and would love nothing more than to sit down and reveal their innermost thoughts to you. Almost everyone else falls somewhere in between and you'd have to get to know them well or work closely with them to come to any conclusions about their natural preferences. The key to any of these systems that categorize human behavior is that almost no one fits neatly into any *one* area and in order to be effective at work (and in life), we need to expand our repertoire to include as least a few of the traits from outside our normal preferences. If you are an extroverted, intuitive, feeling, perception type, you're going to either find a job that requires those skills and traits or you're going to have to learn a few new tricks. Most of the time, our jobs and lives require us to flex between traits in order to be successful and most of us do pretty well.

Another very popular and useful system is the DiSC profile system, which is a bit more oriented to the work environment. Some people find it less threatening than Myers-Briggs because it is more focused on work styles and behaviors. DiSC uses four main traits to describe primary work styles, though don't get thrown off by the terminology. These are:

- **Dominance** The person who primarily exhibits *dominance* is someone who wants to get things done—they are outcome-oriented and they want to get results. In shorthand, these folks are called "D's."

- **Influence** The person who primarily exhibits *influence* is someone who wants to influence or persuade others. They tend to like to interact with others. In shorthand, these folks are called "I's."

- **Conscientiousness** The person who primarily exhibits *conscientiousness* is someone who likes to work within existing circumstances to ensure quality and accuracy. They tend to be highly organized and rule-oriented. These folks are often referred to as "C's."

- **Steadiness** The person who primarily exhibits *steadiness* prefers to get results through teamwork and cooperation. They tend to be very good with people and are good at keeping the team together and functioning well. These folks are called "S's."

Many CEOs, business leaders and entrepreneurs are primarily D's—they want to get the job done and they're all about the results. The expression "Ready, fire, aim" can describe a D who's in a frenzy since D's often want to act first and think later. In the extreme, they can disregard or break rules to get results, which is not a desirable expression of the D work style. Some leaders who are also quite charismatic might be termed "DI's" meaning they tend to use both dominance and influence in equal measure.

The influence pattern without any other letters (no D, S, or C) is someone who is highly interactive and needs to have a job in which they interact regularly with others. They typically avoid going into technical fields because they want to work with people, not machines. They make great counselors, but if they lack any other "letters," they'll probably have a tough time in the IT world.

The world of programmers, engineers, and accountants is filled with people whose primary trait is C (conscientiousness). They are organized, like to think through problems before tackling them (just the opposite of the D personality) and like structure, quality, and accuracy first and foremost.

Finally, the last trait is the person who exhibits steadiness, the S. He or she is the person that always makes sure everyone in the room knows each other's names, will make sure everyone has a chair to sit in or will make sure everyone feels included in the meeting. They're natural hosts and hostesses and they typically work well alone or in a group.

As you can see, the Myers-Briggs and the DiSC terminology are different, but they have a lot in common. They describe how people prefer to work, what their natural tendencies are. You might be sitting here thinking this is all a bunch of psychological mumbo jumbo, but read on. Understanding these tendencies does two important things for you. First, you will be able to leverage people's natural styles and get them working in ways that are most comfortable for them. When you can do this, you increase their job satisfaction and their productivity while reducing their stress (and yours). Sound interesting now? The second benefit is that your job of managing the department or project team will be much easier if you understand how each team member naturally operates. You can assign them appropriate tasks and leverage their natural styles while minimizing or mitigating their shortcomings. This is really much easier than you might at first think. In the next section, we're going to talk about these work styles, using the four primary work traits. You'll learn how to discern someone's primary style and then you'll learn what the pros and cons are of each style. You'll also see how these traits can be used in positive ways and how they sometimes show up as negative traits.

Before we jump into that, let's look at an example that will drive this concept home. If you have a huge IT project and you're working on putting together the project plan, you obviously need to take some time to plan. (OK, most of us know we should, not all of us do, but more on that later in the book). If you have a bunch of people who are *doers*, they want to jump in and get the job done and you're going to have to restrain them until it's time to actually go *do* something. On the other hand, if you have folks that we'll call the *analysts*, they're the ones who enjoy, in fact, need to plan and get all the details locked down. You want to leverage their natural abilities to enhance your project plan, but you'll also have to make sure they don't get "analysis paralysis" and fail to get to the "doing" stage. When you have a mixture of folks on a team, you can see now that these various traits can really help you plan, define, organize, implement, and manage your project. Your job as the project manager becomes slightly easier when you can rely upon people's natural traits rather than asking someone to do something so far outside their natural abilities that it's difficult (or impossible) for them to do. Don't misinterpret this—we all have to do things in our jobs that we'd rather not do or that we're not as skilled at. The point is that anytime you can assign a task or job to someone that aligns with their natural abilities, they'll be more likely to deliver a high-quality result in a timely manner. It's just another tool in your IT project manager tool bag that you can use to make everyone's life just a bit more productive without added stress.

While the systems described earlier are helpful, they're not required in order to understand basic work styles or work behaviors. These types of assessments can be helpful in understanding your own work style as well as that of your team. However, rather than refer specifically to one "system", we'll paint the picture with broad strokes so you can learn how understanding work styles can greatly benefit you and your team. Remember that none of the work personalities described is absolute—

most people have a predominant trait or style and one or more subordinate traits. The predominant trait is the one that almost always shows up under pressure because it's what's most natural and least stressful. The subordinate traits often are used when the situation is more relaxed and the person can take time to determine the best course of action. The terminology used is not specific to any one system and is used to describe the predominant work style.

Many people fall under the broad category of *doers*. They want to get things done, they jump into action at the first opportunity. These folks are often the ones that get initiatives going, that take steps to put plans into action. The downside of this type of work personality is that they often don't take time to think and plan. They simply jump into the action that seems most appropriate at the time. Sometimes that's fine because the action didn't require much planning. Other times, they have to either re-think or re-work what they've already done because they failed to take time to plan before acting.

A second major category of work personalities is that of the *interactive* personality. This person almost always wants to talk things through and the conversation often centers around that person and their relationship to the work. This is the kind of person that can help bring the *doer* back to earth and get a conversation going about how to approach the project or problem. This type of person will often call or stop by your office to respond to an e-mail you sent because they prefer personal interaction to e-mails or phone calls. Typically, these people are found in jobs that involve interacting with others people frequently and are less represented in the IT field. The downside of this personality type is that they can focus the conversation on them and distract the group from discussing the more relevant issues. They can also be time wasters because what could have been a quick three-word response in e-mail from them becomes a 20 minute conversation in your office.

The third work personality type is that of the *team player*. This person often works to assess the team environment and works to ensure that everyone on the team is participating. The team player will be interactive, as will the interactive person just discussed, but the point of the interaction is to ensure the overall functionality of the team. It's not about the team player, it's not about any one individual on the team; it's about everyone working together in as an efficient team. This person will often subordinate his or her own needs to ensure the team's needs are met. The downside of this type of personality is that they can overlook their own needs or become too involved with the team and its dynamics to be effective. They sometimes can be too nice in trying to get the team together.

The fourth major work personality type is that of the *analyst*. This person is the type (often found in IT and very often in programming, engineering, and accounting positions) that enjoys understanding every last detail so he or she can organize things.

He or she is often excellent with detail and will spend time keeping things orderly. This type of work personality is useful for analyzing data, for dealing with details on a daily basis, and for organizing large amounts of detail. This type of person may often be seen as the person that says "that's not going to work" because they have already given thought to a topic and have drawn their conclusions. The downside of this personality type is that they can be seen as the naysayers in the group, throwing a wet rag on every proposed idea as they point out the shortcomings. They may also have difficulty finishing tasks on time (or at all) because they may feel they do not have sufficient data to make a decision or come to a conclusion.

Managing Different Work Styles

One of the first things to understand about work styles is that there is no good or bad, right or wrong work style. Certainly some work styles are more appropriate or helpful in certain positions. For instance, if you have someone who's primarily *interactive* and needs to discuss things at length, he or she may not fare well as a programmer whose primary job is to sit in a room and write code six hours a day. If someone is a *doer* and is prone to just jumping in and getting things started, he or she might not be the best person to manage the corporate finances unless that person also has the ability to deal with detail. Someone who is a team player may not do well as a sole contributor at a remote corporate location because they are most comfortable (and most effective) as part of a highly functioning team. Your job, as IT manager or project manager, is to leverage the skills, talents, and personalities of your team in order to get the best possible result. That means learning to maximize the strengths of each work style and minimize the weaknesses of that style. In this section, we'll briefly look at how you can best manage people with these predominate work styles.

Managing A Doer

The doer prefers action to talk, planning, or waiting. Managing these folks means learning to temper their desire to jump right in without completely removing their ability to take action. When these folks want to just get started, your job will be to ask them to do some planning first. Since planning *is* an action, it is compatible with this work style; it's just that planning is not their natural first course of action. Helping them to understand that planning will allow them to move forward faster and more effectively is often all it takes. These folks are usually outcome-oriented, meaning they are most interested in the outcome or end point. As a result, they're often willing to flex their personal style in order to get the job done. Helping the *doers* to take time to think and plan before acting will make them far more effective in the long run. Asking the *doer* for a plan of action prior to implementation will help slow them down just enough to help them get their thoughts in order. Since errors, omissions, and re-work are a major source of expense in any project, it's critical that these *doers* are engaged in the planning process early on to avoid potential problems later. A summary of traits is shown in Table 4.1. The traits are divided into personal tendencies, environmental factors, and team composition. Each trait has positive characteristics, shown on the left side of the table, and each trait has negative potential, shown on the right side of the table. The types of people on a team that balance out this work style are listed at the bottom of the table. Remember that no one is absolutely all one style, so these are broad descriptions that should be helpful in identifying the primary work style.

Table 4.1 The *Doer* Work Style

Positive Traits	Potential Negative Traits
Personal Tendencies:	
Action-oriented	"Bull in a china shop"
Immediate results	Acts without a plan, has to go back and redo some portion of work
Accepts challenges, comfortable with ambiguity or the unknown	Arrogant, selfish, self-centered
Quick decisions, (sometimes acts before thinking), solving problems	Disorganized, scattered
Taking authority, natural leaders	Lacks facts and figures to support efforts
The Environment:	
Power, authority, prestige, challenge	Challenges authority, breaks rules
Opportunity for individual accomplishment	Finds opportunities to take power and authority away from others
Hands-off manager	Can be disorganized or too hands-off as a manager
New and varied activities	Can have a short attention span, gets bored too easily to complete required tasks

Table 4.1 The *Doer* Work Style

Positive Traits	Potential Negative Traits
Works well on a team that includes others who:	
Are more detail-oriented	Attends to the needs of the team
Will research facts, figures, risks	

Managing An Interactive

An interactive person prefers talk to action, planning, or waiting. Managing these folks means you'll need to provide an outlet for discussion and provide ample opportunity for this person to engage with others. Again, these kinds of people are typically under-represented in IT, so you may know of people like this, but do not directly manage them. These kinds of folks often gravitate toward sales and marketing, which are highly interactive positions (for the most part). To effectively manage these folks, you need to provide them the opportunity to interact with others. You'll also need to keep an eye on the discussion to ensure it drives the meeting objectives and doesn't get bogged down in chit chat. Interactive types can be great on a team because they often bring a natural ease with people and can have a valuable role on the team in terms of getting people talking and interacting. Just don't let it get out of hand. Provide the interactive person with opportunities to work with others in a structured (or outcome-oriented) environment and provide specific deliverables to keep interactions on track.

Table 4.2 delineates the interactive work style. As with the previous table, the three main categories are the personal tendencies, the environment, and the team. Any of the personal or environmental traits can be positive, but they both have their negative potential. The bottom section of the table shows you what kinds of people they should be around and work with to balance their natural tendencies.

Table 4.2 The *Interactive* Work Style

Positive Traits	Potential Negative Traits
Personal Tendencies:	
Talks with and to people	"All talk, no action"
Creates a motivating environment	False motivation based on flash, not substance
Articulate, entertaining, enthusiastic	Unaware of time, can waste time (their own and others'), can be disorganized and scattered
Views people and situations optimistically	Unrealistic view of obstacles and challenges
Participates well in groups	Self-centered, conversation always steered back to them
The Environment:	
Public recognition for accomplishments	Can become unmotivated or mean-spirited if recognition is withheld or wrongfully assigned
Freedom from control and detail	Can miss deadlines, make errors in detail work
Popularity, acceptance, social interaction	Can become ineffective, unproductive or scattered
Opportunities to socialize outside of work	Can spend too much work time socializing and talking
Works well on a team that includes others who:	
Are more detail-oriented	Are more action-oriented
Will research facts, figures, risks	

Managing A Team Player

A team player prefers working as part of a team to working individually. He or she will strive to make sure the needs of the team are met. In or out of work, they're often the person described as "nice" (in a good way). They're the person that is often sought out for advice or consolation, the person that makes everyone in the room feel comfortable. As a member of a team, they'll strive to work with others to achieve the group's goals. That doesn't mean that he or she is not a solid sole contributor—just the opposite in most cases. The team player will hold up his or her end of the bargain by getting their work done on time and to specification. They often believe that their job is to be the best team member they can while helping to iron out differences between other team members. If you have someone on your team that is a team player, leverage their ability to bring team members together, but watch that they do not overextend themselves helping others. Sometimes they'll take on others' duties in an effort to be helpful, but this can lead to burn out, resentment, and lack of accountability. You'll need to keep team players focused on their own jobs, their own responsibilities and duties, and you may need to help them draw boundaries to avoid them taking on too much or taking on tasks for someone who is underperforming. Encourage team players to report team problems to you so you can resolve them rather than having the team member take them on.

Table 4.3 shows the traits of the team player work style. Again, the table shows the personal tendencies, the work environment, and the type of team members that complement this style. The positive and negative potentials are shown to help you recognize these traits.

Table 4.3 The *Team Player* Work Style

Positive Traits	Potential Negative Traits
Personal Tendencies	
Work with and help others, good listener	"Doormat", may have trouble saying no or setting firm boundaries
Perform in consistent, predictable manner	Uncomfortable with change or uncertainty
Create harmonious, stable work environment	May take on others' responsibilities to help maintain stability
Develop specialized skills	Narrow, specialized skill set
The Environment:	
Little change or change that is managed	Unable to cope with rapidly changing environments
Predictable routines	Unable to deal with non-routine events
Minimal conflict	May avoid or suffer through (hide from) conflict
Sincere appreciation	May lose motivation or effectiveness if work effort is not noticed and appreciated

Table 4.3 The *Team Player* Work Style

Positive Traits	Potential Negative Traits
Works well on a team that includes others who:	
Take risks, enjoy change	Can become involved in multiple tasks and priorities
Are flexible in work procedures	

Managing An Analyst

The *analyst* is someone who prefers to think rather than act. This work style is sometimes unfairly labeled as negative because he or she can often see what's wrong with a particular course of action—sometimes long before anyone else sees it. Human nature being what it is, most of us are reluctant to be told we're wrong and we often resist information proving us so. The *analyst* is sometimes seen as gruff or rude though that is usually not their intent. As a result, their information can sometimes be discarded because of how it's delivered. If you manage this work style (and chances are good you do, because this work personality is often found in the IT arena), you may need to help this person work on his or her delivery so the message is more accepted. Others with this work style are very diplomatic and precise in their delivery—it all depends on how they display these analytical traits. They'll often need to learn to present their ideas and opinions in ways less offensive or abrasive to the group, but once mastered, they can be highly diplomatic.

You may also have to work with these *analysts* to provide specific details on deliverables as well as deadlines. Those with a strong analyst work style can feel there is insufficient information to draw conclusions or complete a project and as a result, they can fail to deliver on time. Create multiple checkpoints and ask questions that elicit information from them so you can help them move toward conclusion. Asking yes/no questions or making blanket demands ("I need that report by Friday morning, ok?") will probably not work. Instead, say "I need the XYZ report by Friday at noon. What will it take for you to complete this?" They may need to go back to their desk, think about it, analyze it, and then return with an answer. Allowing them to do so will result in far better outcomes.

Table 4.4 delineates the analyst's traits. The personal tendencies and the work environment show that there are both positive and negative traits that can surface. Clearly, aiming for the positive traits is the goal for each work style. The bottom section of the table shows the types of team members that will complement the *analyst* style so your team can be highly productive.

Table 4.4 The *Analyst* Work Style

Positive Traits	Potential Negative Traits
Personal Tendencies:	
Think analytically and logically	Can become paralyzed and fail to act
Work accurately with detail	Can be seen as nitpicking, gruff, or rude
Analyze performance critically	Can be seen as negative or not a team player
Can be diplomatic	Avoids conflict, agrees just to get away from conflict
The Environment:	
Clearly defined expectations about performance	Spends too much time defining framework, not enough on content
Reserved, unemotional business environment	Avoids personal interaction, especially conflict or difficult situations, may not be viewed as a team player
Opportunity to ask "why"	May not do well with time-sensitive tasks that require immediate, decisive action
Control over aspects that impact performance	May try to be "perfect" and fail on key deliverables
Works well on a team that includes others who:	
Action-oriented risk takers	Encourage team work
Deal with uncomfortable situations	Are flexible in their approach to work

Enterprise 128 …

Managing For Success

This is a true story, though all the names have been changed to avoid embarrassing anyone.

A director of client services (we'll call him David) for a large, international company was having trouble with an employee we'll call Chris. Chris was very bright and had come up through the ranks quickly. He was well qualified for his job as a department manager overseeing service delivery for three clients and managing a staff of about 200. The problem David was having was that Chris was missing deadlines for deliverables left and right. Here's one conversation:

David: Chris, we discussed getting these quarterly reports ready before the last week of the quarter, but yours is late again. What's going on?

Chris: Well, I was working on it but I wasn't able to get it done on time.

David: We've discussed the importance of timeliness a number of times, haven't we?

Chris: Yes.

David: Alright. I need this report by Friday at noon at the latest. OK?

Chris: OK. Sorry.

David: Let me know if you need any assistance with this. OK?

Chris: OK.

If you're a quick study, you can imagine what happened on Friday. No quarterly report. David was irate, as you can imagine, because he thought he had Chris's buy-in on the timeline. Where did David go wrong? What could he do differently in the future?

David himself is predominately a *doer*, as you might be able to tell from the rather quick, no-nonsense discussion he had with Chris. He wants results and he wants them now. This, in itself, can be a bit intimidating to some of his staff, especially those *analyst* types like Chris who want to think long and hard about things and get organized and get every possible detail before proceeding. These two styles can be diametrically opposed to one another and can spell trouble unless David figures out how to manage a style so different from his own.

David was frustrated and called a consultant, Patty, whom he had worked with in the past and asked if she could help. Patty came to the rescue. She knew that David was on the verge of firing Chris and she made David promise her that no such action would be taken until she'd had a chance to talk with both of them privately. David promised, but was highly skeptical. He was reluctant to have to completely change his own management style to accommodate one of his staff. Patty assured David he would not have to completely change, but he *would* have to make a few minor changes to his approach. David agreed to give it a shot.

Continued

After talking with Chris, Patty set up a meeting with David. Though she did not share any specifics from the private conversation she'd had with Chris, she did share her impressions. She told David she thought Chris was competent and highly motivated to do a good job. David almost screamed, "Then why can't he do anything I ask of him?" Patty explained that Chris was, underneath, a bit afraid of David's fast-paced, get-it-done style and was reluctant to say no to anything David asked. Patty also explained that Chris was often not sure exactly what was being asked of him and that David rarely gave him much detail to work with or time to think things through. David's perspective was that either Chris knew or would ask, but that was apparently not the case.

Patty's suggestion to David: Don't ask Chris yes/no questions such as "OK?" or "Got it?" Instead, give Chris an assignment then ask Chris to go think about it and come up with a plan, suggestion, or proposed course of action. Have Chris come back in a day or two, having had time (but not too much time) to think about it and to have a *discussion* about the deliverable including what else Chris might need, additional details Chris might ask about (that David may not have even considered), or potential pitfalls (that David may not have been aware of). David agreed to try this. Chris's assignment from Patty was to ask questions to clarify assignments, to raise issues as he saw them (which he now understood David actually valued) and to say "Yes" only when he meant it.

The next time David met with Chris, he gave Chris the assignment and then asked how soon Chris would be ready to come back and discuss how to proceed, knowing the report was due in three weeks. Chris came back a few days later fully prepared, asked some excellent questions, got needed clarification and boundaries (what the assignment included and did not include) and went off to do his project. David checked in with Chris a week later and Chris reported making good progress. A week later, on the due date, Chris presented David with the report he needed. It was an excellent, thorough, and comprehensive report that not only provided David with the required information, but some additional analysis that was quite helpful. Needless to say, David was thrilled with the turnaround and Chris was relieved to finally have been able to complete his job according to David's specifications.

This is a true story. With just a minor adjustment to how David approached Chris's assignments, both were able to get what they needed. David simply had to slow down a bit (which, ultimately, was a good thing for him anyway) and allow Chris (and his other *analyst* types) to think, plan, analyze, and ask questions. The end of the story is that Chris went on to be a stellar performer on David's team and was promoted two years later into a key role.

Lesson Learned: If you're not getting the results you need or expect from a team or staff members, they may need to be managed slightly differently. Think about how the person tends to work and interact and try to find ways to give them more of what they need. In this case, Chris needed more guidance and time to think about a project than David had given him. In other cases, someone might need more time to talk a project through or to work with the team to figure out the best options. While you can't (and shouldn't) completely change

Continued

your natural management style to accommodate each member of the team, you should find ways to flex your management style to get the best possible result from each individual team member. Sometimes an outside consultant can help you and your team make those minor adjustments that improve productivity and job satisfaction significantly if you're unable to determine the best course of action. However, very often with a bit of thought and observation, you *can* figure these primary traits out and work more effectively—either as the project manager or even as a team member. Just keep in mind that almost no one is all one trait, we are usually some blend of two or three primary traits. By learning to work with your team's work styles, your stress and the stress of your team will go down while the quality goes up. How's that for a win-win situation?

Culture Matters

We've talked about traits on a personal level—what creates job satisfaction (and dissatisfaction) and how people tend to approach work. Another important element in understanding and managing your team is to recognize that we often operate in a multicultural environment. Today's teams are likely to be diverse. That diversity includes people of different races, religions, national origins, ethnicities, gender, ages, and languages. If you're managing a team across geographic boundaries, you know how time differences and cultural and language differences can all make managing a highly productive team that much more difficult. In this section, we'll discuss some of the challenges and discuss ways to address those challenges. If you manage a diverse team, this section will give you several important skills as a starting point to improving your cross-cultural management skills.

Managing People From Different Cultures

Managing people from different cultures is becoming more and more common as technology brings together people from across the globe in real time. It's not unusual in some companies to have a project team comprised of people from several countries. This leads to challenges that involve time, language, and culture. While we can't address every possible nuance of communicating across cultural boundaries, this section will highlight some of the common challenges and give you tools to begin to explore and address these challenges.

Culture and Language Differences

Language and culture play a huge part in how people communicate. Though English is becoming more universally accepted as a primary language in business, that doesn't mean that everyone who speaks English as a second language is comfortable with

English. If you took a few Spanish or French classes in high school, think about how comfortable you would have been sitting in a restaurant in Spain (or Mexico) or a high-powered business meeting in France having a conversation with native speakers. It's important to remember that even though others may speak English, they may not be entirely comfortable with the language. This is critical to recognize because it means that business conversations that take place over communication links (phone, video conferencing, etc.) must be paced so that native and non-native speakers are comfortable. One of the common observations made about Americans in international business settings is that we talk a lot and we talk fast. We like to talk ideas out, think out loud, discuss, debate, and conclude. To those whose culture does not emphasize that, it can be daunting. Couple that with English as a second language and these non-native speakers can quickly get lost in a rapid-fire business conversation. It also means that phrases, idioms, and slang that we might use without thought will be confusing and perhaps even offensive to these non-native speakers. To avoid these potential problems:

1. Learn to pronounce and spell names. OK, this is incredibly basic, but you'd be surprised how many people say, "Hey, will you get that UNIX guy from Bangalore on the phone—what's his name, I can't pronounce it, it starts with a P." Learn to pronounce your team member's names. Even if you have to ask twenty times how to properly pronounce someone's name, it's better than saying, "Hey, is the Indian guy on the line right now?" Ask them if they use that name or another name. For instance, in the Philippines, it's not uncommon to have two first names and several surnames. As a result, names are often combined into unique nicknames. Maria Luisa Hernandez Fuentes Marquez might be known as "Malu" (a combination of Maria and Luisa). You may also run into difficult situations where the person's name is not a desirable name in the U.S. such as names that are slang words in the U.S. or names such as "Baby" or "Boy" that seem odd or inappropriate to use to address a team member or employee.

2. Create meeting agendas that are short and concise. This helps keep everyone focused on the important topics and helps prevent rambling and straying off course.

3. Keep conversation focused on the meeting agenda. If it rambles and includes unrelated topics, non-native speakers may become confused about the conversation.

4. If discussion is needed, make sure to specifically ask your team members from around the globe for their input. Some cultures are reluctant to speak

up unless directly spoken to. Make sure you consciously request their input. This will also help ensure they comprehend the discussion and are participating fully.

5. Clarify terminology. Don't assume that others understand what you mean by words such as "meeting," "report," "presentation," or "deliverable"—these things may mean entirely different things in other cultures and making everyone comfortable with the common business language you use is critical for success.

6. Avoid yes/no questions. Ask questions that require an answer. This helps ensure the questions are understood and that the responses are based on understanding rather than confusion. Some cultures are naturally more inclined to say "yes" to a yes/no question, even if they're confused or don't understand.

7. Avoid jokes and sarcasm. Jokes and sarcasm usually don't translate well and non-native English speakers may become confused, or worse, insulted if they do not understand the tone or the nature of the humor.

8. Listen more than you speak. Americans like to talk and talk some more. If you're the project manager and your team is comprised of people from around the world, spend time actively listening to what is being said and to what is not being said.

9. Ask for negative information. In some cultures, it's rude to mention problems; it's considered a sign of failure. Americans are fairly open about discussing problems and brainstorming solutions, so make sure you take time with people from other cultures to encourage their honest assessments. This is critical because with a global team, you may not find out about a problem until much later than you might if you were working with a local team.

10. Communicate frequently. Managing a successful project involves making small, incremental changes throughout the course of the project so it stays on course (more on that later in this book). These small changes are even more necessary when you're working with a global team. If part of the project team is 6,000 miles away, it will be harder to notice when the project is slipping off course. Frequent communication is part of the key to keeping a global project on track.

11. Learn about the culture. You'd probably be surprised by how many global project team managers don't bother to learn about the cultures of their team members. Things that Americans consider normal business matters may not be so normal in other countries. Asking someone to work on one

of their national holidays without regard for that holiday would cause the same problem as if you were asked to work on Memorial Day or July Fourth. You might still need to have that person work on that national holiday, but you would recognize it the same way you would with an American team members—"I'm sorry you have to work on that day, I know you were looking forward to a day off." Learn about "hot button" issues and behaviors that are considered polite (or rude) so you can interact with team members in a manner conducive to getting results.

12. Invest in cross-culture awareness training for your team. If you're going to be working with people from other countries for extended periods of time, you would do well to get some formal training to develop openness and awareness of cultural perspectives. You and your team will not only learn a lot about how other cultures work, live, and think, but you'll also learn a tremendous amount about the assumptions you make about how people work, live, and think. It can be a deeply enriching experience and it will certainly improve your team's efficiency and success.

13. Learn to use meeting time and non-meeting time wisely. Many productive global teams use face-to-face (or virtual face-to-face) meetings to handle hot issues or to develop group understanding and personal commitment. They use non-meeting time to work on tasks and to perform tasked-based communication. By understanding the best use of meeting and non-meeting time, you can use precious meeting time for developing the group and allow the task-based communication to happen through e-mail, document collaboration, instant messaging, etc. Don't rush through the process and team building parts to get right to the tasks. Spend time building a cohesive team; it will be an investment that pays back major dividends for you.

14. Invest in communication technology. It almost goes without saying that you need your cross-cultural teams to be able to communicate effectively—in real time when possible (though with time differences, this is clearly a challenge). Using collaboration software, communication technologies such as net meetings, video conferencing, instant messaging, e-mail, blogs, wikis, and collaboration management tools will greatly enhance the team's efforts. While nothing can replace the occasional need for face-to-face meetings, intelligent use of these communication and collaboration technologies will help bridge the gap. And remember that the lone guy/gal in the outskirts of Belfast or Mexico City needs to be just as connected as the team in Atlanta, Georgia.

The IT Factor...

R-E-S-P-E-C-T

If you learn to value and respect cultural differences, you'll manage cross-cultural teams more effectively. People around the world want to be respected—for who they are and what they bring to the table. Showing respect by learning to pronounce difficult names, understanding what's important to various team members, and including everyone on your team equally is not all that difficult—it just takes time and willingness to make a conscious effort. Once you do, you'll be rewarded by a broader global view and a cohesive team that is ready to take on the challenges of the project.

Values Differences

Americans work hard and play hard. Other cultures take a different view of work, play, and life. Even within the U.S., different regions and subcultures view work, play, and life slightly differently. We cannot simply assume that what is important to us, our company, or our clients is the same in other cultures, whether those cultures are across town or across the world.

Successful cross-cultural teams work well together by recognizing and respecting the various cultures. The IT project manager must ensure the team is productive in a culturally appropriate manner. He or she must also know which issues are performance-related and which are cultural. It's also important that the project manager avoid alienating employees or accidentally offending them. Part of this involves understanding the values and mores of other cultures and working with those in an effective manner. Again, there are numerous challenges here, but we'll highlight a few to get you started.

1. When *yes* means *no*. In many cultures, it's rude to say no. When posed a yes/no question, some people will answer yes when they actually mean no. As mentioned earlier, one of the ways to avoid this and to get better information is to ask questions that require an explanation rather than yes/no.

2. Work ethic. Many Americans work long hours and put their lives and families second. In many countries, family is far more important than work or career advancement. Understanding the relative importance of work and family (or work/non-work time) is important in terms of motivating and

rewarding a cross-cultural project team. Asking someone to work overtime or not allowing time off for an important family event can be absolutely unimaginable in some cultures.

3. Managing conflict. Americans, for the most part, are fairly comfortable with debating a topic or disagreeing with someone in a business setting (assuming the right environment). In other cultures, disagreement, conflict, or heated discussions are avoided. Understanding how to manage conflict on a cross-cultural team is important because some of the conflict may not surface in ways you're accustomed to. Many Americans will voice their dissatisfaction, in private or in public, in order to hammer out a resolution. In some cultures, there may be no outward sign that there is a problem. Well, let's revise that. To you, the American project manager communicating from 6,000 miles away, there may be no recognizable sign there is a problem. It's entirely possible that folks from that other culture in the same room may instantly recognize the problem, even if it's not verbalized. Understanding how to recognize dissent and conflict on a cross-cultural team and how to manage it is critical to success.

4. Personal information. The amount of personal information people are willing to share about themselves varies widely—not only from culture to culture, but even within cultures. Many Americans are seen as being fairly open about themselves and this can lead to embarrassment or discomfort by other team members. Conversely, Americans may tend to view other cultures as standoffish, distant, remote, closed, or secretive if they are not naturally inclined to talk about themselves (or talk as much as we do about anything). Some Americans may view other cultures as being too emotional, too "touchy-feely," or too open. Ensure that all team members respect appropriate boundaries.

5. Criticism. How and when constructive criticism is given varies widely from culture to culture. In some cultures, any negative feedback is devastating and is a sign of abject failure. In other cultures, that same feedback is just part of the job. Learning the language of criticism and constructive feedback is vital since not everyone on your project team will be perfect all the time. Your criticism should be delivered in a way that corrects the problem without demotivating (or devastating) the recipient. This can be tricky, but taking time to learn how this can be handled smoothly will make your team more effective. We'll look at that in more detail later because you'll need to manage your team's performance and do so without destroying people's egos along the way.

6. Individuality. As much as we might want to lump everyone from a particular culture into one category, that's not any more appropriate than lumping all Americans into one category. Are all Americans the same? Of course not. Every individual is different and may not follow all the cultural norms you expect. Remember that when dealing with cross-cultural teams—understand and respect their culture and work with each person as an individual.

Feedback In A Diverse Environment

Successfully managing your cross-cultural team means investing time and resources into understanding other cultures and informing your team about the various cultures represented. It also means learning to effectively guide your team through the project cycle. This frequently requires giving feedback to team participants—both positive and negative—to get the needed results. In this section, we'll look at some of the common problems encountered with feedback and then provide specific solutions you can evaluate using with your cross-cultural team.

If you've managed a cross-cultural team, one of these scenarios has probably already happened to you. If you haven't yet managed such a team, this is an example what you might encounter:

- A newly hired team member continues to skip an important step in a critical procedure. Each time you try to correct the problem, you meet with subtle resistance.

- One of your team members gave the wrong information to a client. When you corrected him/her, he/she left the room quickly and quietly.

- A deliverable turned in by a team member is way off the mark even though you believe you clearly and repeatedly explained what was expected.

These are all examples of situations that required feedback, but that didn't turn out as expected. If you've encountered one of these types of situations, you may have walked away shaking your head in confusion. What happened? What went wrong? Let's look at some of the common cultural elements related to receiving feedback:

- **Saving Face** Team members from some cultures may view negative feedback as shameful. You may notice inappropriate laughing, smiling, or blushing. They may try to avoid feedback by not making eye contact, by missing meetings where criticism might occur, or by simply clamming up.

- **Maintaining Harmony** In some cultures, maintaining a harmonious environment is paramount. This can contribute to people saying yes when they mean no. If a team member continues to say yes, but repeats the mistake or undesirable behavior, chances are good there's a communication problem going on.

- **Respecting Authority** Some cultures have an absolute respect for authority, which means they are likely to follow your feedback, instructions, or criticisms to the letter. In the U.S., it's not uncommon for someone to discuss or even disagree with feedback from an authority figure if they believe the feedback is incorrect. Some cultures will not question the instruction or feedback, even if it is blatantly wrong, out of respect.

- **Blaming Fate** Some cultures believe strongly in outside or external control of events. They may truly believe that fate (or something similar) was at work. Americans typically believe they control events and often view the blaming of external factors as avoiding responsibility.

- **Relating vs. Working** Some cultures value the relationship between people at work as much or more than the tasks they are assigned. Americans are typically fairly task-oriented; we want to get the job done as quickly as possible. Other cultures may find this off-putting, rude, or cold. In other cultures, creating and maintaining the relationship is as important as what gets done. Employees from these cultures may feel that their relationship with the boss, their seniority, or their status in the group is more critical to success than following the task-oriented procedures given in the feedback.

- **Separating Self From Results** Some cultures view results and self as inseparable, so to criticize one's work is to criticize that person. In the U.S., managers are taught to correct the behavior and not to make it personal. In some cultures, correcting the behavior is inherently personal and you cannot criticize work without also criticizing the person.

- **Emphasizing Group versus Individual** Americans are known to be focused on the individual. While we may work well in groups, we fundamentally define ourselves by our individual uniqueness. In other cultures, the group is far more important than the individual and individual tastes, desires, and preferences are sublimated to the group. In this setting, having one's performance singled out, for positive or negative feedback, is embarrassing and to them, perhaps even inappropriate. If they are singled out for praise, they may be viewed as disloyal to the group.

Now, as you've read through this list, you might be thinking, "How am I ever going to successfully manage a cross-cultural team?" Well, the good news is that with a bit of effort on your part, you can understand, appreciate, and leverage cultural differences to create a highly effective team. Let's discuss a few ideas you can consider using when you have to provide feedback in a cross-cultural team setting.

1. **Build a relationship first.** If you have developed a relationship with your team members before giving feedback, you're more likely to understand their cultural biases and conditioning so you can find the most effective way to provide feedback.

2. **Assure the individual of your respect.** This is closely related to building the relationship, but it's important that the individual receiving feedback understand that you provide the feedback out of respect. This can help mitigate some of the negative cultural values associated with criticism.

3. **Try to emphasize how the feedback will benefit the recipient.** If the person understands what value or benefit is in it for them, he or she is more likely to be receptive to the feedback. This applies to anyone in any culture, but is doubly important in cross-cultural communication.

4. **Use the passive rather than active voice.** In the U.S., we're taught to write and speak in the active voice, which can be intimidating to people in cultures that are used to the passive voice. The active voice starts with the word "I" or "You". The passive voice omits these. Here are some examples (active then passive):

   - "You didn't finish the report on time" versus "The report was not finished on time."

   - "I asked you to report back to me by 3:00 P.M." versus "The report was needed at 3:00 P.M."

   - "You gave the wrong information to the client" versus "The wrong information was given to the client."

   - "You were asked to help Noelle with that task last week" versus "Noelle needed help with that task last week."

5. **Use an intermediary**. In some cultures, authority and criticism are a difficult combination. In some instances, you may be able to use an intermediary to deliver the feedback. While we in the U.S. might view that as ducking a responsibility, in some instances, it can allow the recipient to save face. You might ask an appropriate intermediary, "I'd like to help Jawara, but

I'm don't want to offend him. What would you suggest?" or "Yi Min, would you work with Jawara to find a way to address the vendor issue?"

6. **Keep it private**. In an American meeting, it might be fine to say, "Hey, Bill, what were you thinking when you told the vendor they could deliver the computers two weeks late?" Bill might take it as a friendly jab, but get the message that he'd made an error. In cross-cultural teams, you should avoid these kinds of exchanges. Instead, talk with the person privately and in a low-key manner. Keep your voice soft, slow your rate of speech, and reduce the potential for embarrassment or defensiveness.

7. **State what you *do* want**. Rather than stating the negative—"Don't do this again"—frame the feedback in a more positive manner. "In the future, please use this new procedure." Again, this is subtle, but can avoid someone losing face. And it never hurts to state exactly what you do expect so there are no assumptions made about expectations.

8. **Give feedback to the group**. If you are dealing with a culture that is very group-oriented, you would do well to give the feedback to the entire group rather than the individual. Though to our American minds this may not make sense, to some it is the only acceptable method of providing feedback.

The IT Factor...

Slow Down

The American culture is known for being fast-faced and results-oriented. There's nothing wrong with that except when it clashes with the culture of key project team members. Then it becomes counter-productive. Rather than changing your style, work to tone it down a bit. If you slow down, listen a little more and communicate in a more deliberate manner, you'll probably do just fine.

Amy Buttery is a global training director for a large, international outsourcing firm that supports numerous global technology companies. In her job, she manages people (staff and project teams) from several countries, including India and the Philippines. Her team is multinational, multigenerational, and multicultural. As a natural leader and communicator, Amy had the skills she needed to be successful in this type of global setting, but she still had her work cut out for her. Her advice to global IT project managers: "Whatever you know about

Continued

> communications and managing a team goes triple for global teams. Communicate more often using more methods. Be very aware of the language you use, make sure everyone has the same understanding of terminology, commonly used phrases and jargon, and listen more than you talk."

Though this is not an exhaustive list of potential pitfalls and solutions, it will give you food for thought. Taking time to understand the culture(s) you're dealing with shows respect and will help generate far better results than if you ignore cultural differences and assume everyone is operating under the same set of assumptions you are.

Managing Across the Generations

We've looked at working with teams that include people from different cultures, but what about when those different cultures are generational? In the U.S., we have Boomers, GenX, GenNext, Echos, and many other terms for the various generations currently in the country (and consequently, in the work force). Dealing with teams that include people in their 20's, 40's, and 60's can make for a very interesting team dynamic. In this section, we'll explore some of the differences between the generations and discuss strategies for working effectively regardless of age. The good news is that some of what you learned earlier in this chapter about dealing with cross-cultural teams can be applied toward working with generational differences.

We all know that there are certain stereotypes about different generations. Younger people may see older people as too cautious or too slow; older people may see younger people as too reckless or too fast-paced. Certainly, generational stereotypes have some basis in truth, but not everyone in a generation behaves in the same manner. When we discuss generational differences in this section, we will be relying on stereotypes based in truth. Still, many people in the generations we'll discuss might not fall into this neat definition. If you can find ways to recognize and leverage generational differences, you'll have a more functional team when it's all said and done.

- **The Silent Generation** The group was born in the U.S. before 1946. In business today, they are the oldest workers. Their generation generally believed in honesty, loyalty, and an honest day's work for an honest day's wage. They are generally reliable workers who arrive on time to work and to meetings and enjoy taking the *whole* weekend off from work.

- **The Boomer Generation** The Baby Boomers were born roughly between 1946 and 1960 (there are various opinions about the exact years on all of these, all years are approximate). These folks were children of the

1960's and 1970's with the counterculture, hippies, Woodstock, and the Vietnam War in the forefront of their formative years. Many have maintained some of the values from those times—openness, tolerance, and acceptance. They are often noted for their desire for material success and their pursuit of spiritual experience or knowledge. They have been portrayed in the media as the "Me" generation due to their focus of personal success and pleasure.

- **Generation X** These folks were born between 1965 and 1977 (those between 1960 and 1965 are sometimes termed "cuspers" because they fall into either group). They are typified by a strong connection to tradition and traditional values, which in some ways is a response to their parents' rejection of traditional values. Their parents were often busy with themselves (they were, after all, the "Me" generation) and their care was often left to others—daycare, after school programs, babysitters, nannies, extracurricular activities, and self-care (the term "latch key kids" was coined for these kids). This resulted in a generation that was highly self-reliant. In addition, they grew up with technology and are more comfortable than any preceding generation with computers, the Internet, cell phones, and other emerging technologies.

- **Generation Y** These folks were born roughly between 1978 and 1988. They came of age during an expansive economic cycle and as a result, they tend to be a bit more optimistic than their older GenX siblings. Like GenX'ers, they are also very comfortable with technology, having been raised with PCs, the Internet, tiny cell phones, and television remotes. They tend to be more oriented toward the "common good" and work to make positive change in the world.

There are other variations, different terms, and additional segments of the population that researchers may define and describe, but we'll stick with these large segments that are commonly discussed. Now that we've identified broad trends, you may begin to imagine some of the inherent problems you might find on a team that has a mix of generations. Some of the common "complaints" are described:

- Older people are too rigid, too slow and don't understand technology.

- Middle-aged people are in it for themselves and don't "get" technology.

- Younger people act before thinking, they don't care about the rules, have no respect for authority, and have short attention spans.

You may have heard these types of comments; you may have thought them yourself. You probably know people that fit these stereotypes completely and others who don't in any way fit their generational description. As a project manager, you'll have to learn how to manage these different types of people in order to get your team up and running. Here are a few suggestions:

1. Have the team members talk about themselves, what they value, how they approach work. Understanding differences makes them more manageable.

2. Ask team members to identify their strengths and weaknesses and pair up team members so they can learn from one another in two-way mentoring.

3. Define your team's mission clearly and concisely. Generational issues are less likely to rear their heads when everyone understands what must be done and why.

4. Define each person's role clearly so that everyone understands who's doing what and why.

5. Leverage uniqueness. Find ways make the best use of each team member's background, skills, experience, temperament, work style (as discussed earlier in this chapter), and interests. By making it about the work and not the personal style, you can develop a much more effective team.

6. Ditch job descriptions and titles. Sometimes on a team, it's more effective to divide up roles, responsibilities, work, and tasks based on skills, interest, ability, and availability rather than by job title or job description. This can provide a bit more latitude for everyone to gravitate toward what they can do best rather than what their job title says they should do on the team.

7. Help the team create conflict-resolution guidelines. The possibility for conflict arises anytime two or more people work together. On a cross-generational team, the natural methods for addressing conflict may vary widely. Having the team discuss and develop methods for resolving conflict before it arises can help bridge generational gaps, especially those related to communicating and dealing with interpersonal conflict.

8. Create a team environment that fosters respect, courtesy, and kindness. With or without generational issues, working in a courteous environment brings out the best in everyone.

Learning to recognize and respect generational differences will make you a better project manager. Learning to leverage generational differences will make your team a more effective project team. While everyone from one generation may not be exactly alike, the culture and environment in which they were raised does have a significant and lasting impact on people of a particular generation. That said, it's also important to understand these same generational boundaries do not apply generically to people of other cultures. For instance, 20-year-olds in India or Japan may be equally adept at technology, but their view of the world and their approach to authority, team members, and job responsibilities may be dramatically different than their U.S. counterparts. If you're working with a multigenerational, multicultural project team, you certainly have your work cut out for you. If you can find ways to encourage and enhance the best traits of each, the team will have a rich, rewarding experience and you'll have a highly effective team.

Cheat Sheet...

The Pace of Work

Younger workers, for the most part, are always connected. They regularly check e-mail, talk on cell phones, and surf the Internet to find information, entertainment, and answers. It's not unusual for them to mix a bit of business with pleasure—on the weekends they may be likely to log in from home and respond to a few e-mails then go out for pizza with friends. Older workers typically like more defined boundaries between work and home. Neither style is good or bad, but as an IT project manager, you'll need to learn to balance this. If your own style is to be always connected, you must be careful not to negatively judge team members who choose to "disconnect" over the weekend (unless, of course, there's a specific need for them to check in). Conversely, if you're the type that likes those defined lines between work and home life, don't expect your younger team members to do the same. Recognizing those preferences and allowing them to co-exist within a project team can be a bit of a challenge at first, but over time it will add to the team's productivity. Watch for signs that one group is negatively influencing or judging another group. For instance, if younger team members are always connected, watch that they don't begin excluding team members who don't check in even on days off. A sub-group culture can begin to form that excludes others and that can be detrimental to the team. Keep your eyes open to different work styles and make sure the team remains cohesive.

Men, Women, and Technology

Dr. Lawrence Summers, president of Harvard University, found himself in hot water not long ago for making negative statements about women in science and technology.

One thing he *was* right about is that women are underrepresented in science and technology fields. According to the U.S. Department of Labor, women make up about 45 percent of the workforce, but represent only 13.6 percent of boards of directors running Fortune 500 companies in the U.S. They represent only 9.3 percent of boards of directors of technology companies. In 2003, women accounted for 10.4 percent of all computer hardware engineers and 7.1 percent of electrical and electronics engineers in the United States. Women hold just 9% of all CIO jobs in the U.S. They fared better as computer and information systems managers, making up 30 percent of the work force in this category, according to an article in the June 6, 2005 issue of Red Herring magazine (www.redherring.com/Article.aspx?a=12217). The point is that women are underrepresented in science and technology and those that are there have learned to work effectively in a predominantly male environment.

The reason we're discussing this is because you may or may not have a technology team that includes women. If you work with a cross-cultural team, you may or may not have women from other countries on your team. How you deal with men and women on your team has a lot to do with cultural norms. Understanding what is and is not appropriate in various cultures is another important aspect of your job as a manager or IT project manager. Certainly, treating everyone with respect is a great starting point, but you'll need to understand cultural differences between men and women in other countries if you have a cross-cultural team. Some of the common biases women may face on any IT team are difficulty having ideas taken seriously, lack of credit for work done and lack of choice assignments. If you're managing a team that includes women, make sure you create an environment that takes advantage of the best each person has to offer and pay special attention to cultural norms that may come into play with cross-cultural teams that include both women and men.

Developing High Performance Teams

In this chapter, we've discussed work styles as well as cultural, generational, and gender differences. There are many other kinds of differences we experience including race, religion, political orientation, and more. The reality is that everyone is unique and brings a unique world and self-view to the team. Since work is about accomplishing results (and hopefully enjoying it along the way), your goal as the IT project manager is to find ways to get the very best out of each team member with the least effort on everyone's part. The old adage "Work smarter, not harder" certainly applies. If you can find ways to fully utilize individual team member's skills, talents, interests, work styles, and experience, you'll be getting optimal team results that should translate into optimal project results. In this section, we'll look at some generally recognized methods for creating highly functional teams. We won't reiterate the information presented earlier on work styles, culture, language, and generation differences, but keep them in mind as you go because they form the foundation for outstanding team performance. Many of these topics will be revisited later in this book when we discuss forming your project team and defining procedures and guidelines for team performance.

Ensure the Team Composition Matches the Task

High performance teams have team members whose background, skills, experiences, and work styles are varied. Having a homogeneous group leads to lopsided thinking and often results in errors and omissions because everyone has the same perspective. Whenever possible, include people on the team that are different—from different stakeholder groups (customers, users, managers, hardware, software, testing, quality, etc.), with different work styles, experiences, and talents. While you don't want to create diversity for diversity's sake (except in some instances), diversity almost always yields a better result, so strive to find a good mix of people with the right skills for the team.

Clearly Define the Project and Team Purpose

We'll discuss defining the project and the team's purpose in more detail later in the book, but an integral part of any high performance team is a clear understanding of purpose. When the project and its purpose are clearly understood and when the team clearly understands what is expected of it and what its deliverables are, the project will be far more successful. In cross-cultural teams, this is even more important to ensure that teammates working around the world can collaborate successfully toward a common goal.

Clearly Define Team Member Roles, Leveraging Unique Skills and Talents

Each member of the team should also understand his or her unique role on the team. Ideally, these roles should, ideally, leverage the individual's skills and talents. As we discussed earlier in this chapter, when a person can work inside his or her comfort zone, he or she is often far more effective. That said, a project is a great opportunity for people to stretch and learn new skills, so team roles should offer the opportunity to learn new skills and to work with new people, if at all possible.

Clearly Define Team Member Responsibilities to the Team

We'll also discuss this more later in the book, but it's important that each team member understand exactly what his or her responsibility is to the team. Often teamwork is just a group of individuals coordinating or parsing out a chunk of work rather than truly collaborating on a solution. Team members should be encouraged to work as a team. They should also be very clear about their responsibilities to the team, including speaking up if problems arise within the team.

Create Clear Guidelines for Deliverables

Highly effective teams understand clearly what is expected of them. Clearly defined deliverables help everyone know what is expected and when it's expected. Quality comes from clearly defined work that is delivered according to clear guidelines, so defining what a quality deliverable looks like is an important building block for your project. We'll spend a fair amount of time later in the book discussing how to build quality into your project through clearly defined deliverables.

Work as a Team to Define a Team Culture and Identity

Many project managers approach a project team as a temporary collection of people that have to get a job done. While that is, in fact, the mission of many teams, they can be far more effective when people begin to identify as part of the team, to form team bonds, and to create a team culture. Shared experiences help create bonds, so developing opportunities for the team to get to know one another (in work and/or non-work settings) can help forge relationships important to the success of the project. You can be creative in creating a team identity—have the team come up with a name, make team t-shirts, have lunch or coffee together as a team, etc., to develop a high functioning team.

Work as a Team to Develop Problem Solving and Conflict Resolution Guidelines

Any team will have problems and conflicts arise at some point in time. Rather than sitting down and laying out these guidelines, work with the team to develop them. This not only gets needed buy-in, but it will take into account cultural, generational, and work style differences. What might have seemed like a good conflict resolution

solution to you might be completely unacceptable to your multigenerational, cross-cultural team.

Create an Environment that Fosters Respect and Courtesy

Respect and courtesy can be in short supply when we're under immense pressure to start, run, or complete a project. Added to all the other job responsibilities we might have, we can forget our manners pretty quickly. As the project manager, your job is to set the tone for the team. When you create an environment that fosters courtesy and respect and quickly addresses any lapses, members of the team will be more likely to want to contribute fully. Knowing that team activities will be respectful and courteous also encourages team members to speak up and raise contrary information and opinions that might be critical to the success of the project.

Recognize Individual and Group Achievement

As you read earlier in this chapter, recognition is one of the things that drives job satisfaction. This is a fairly universal human need, so cultural and generational differences melt away for just a moment. However, how that recognition should be delivered will be highly influenced by cultural and generational factors. As you learned, some cultures are very group-oriented and for you to single any one individual out for positive (or negative) feedback could be bad both for the group and the individual. Provide genuine recognition of achievements in whatever culturally acceptable method(s) you determine. The important thing is to provide that recognition.

Manage Team Time Efficiently

How many team or project meetings have you attended that were a complete waste of time? Too many to count, probably. Unfortunately, too many project managers (and other managers) don't manage team time effectively, causing team members to duck out of meetings early or not show up at all. Set an agenda for the meeting and make sure everyone knows the agenda. Make sure everyone is clear about their roles in the meeting (are they expected to make a presentation, deliver an analysis, bring ideas to solve a problem, etc.?). Make sure the meeting starts and ends on time and stays on topic. Allow time for socializing before or after the meeting, not during. If team or project meetings are clear, concise, and useful, people will actually attend and participate. It might be a foreign concept in your company, but give it a shot—you'll be surprised how effective a meeting can actually be when it's well facilitated. We'll talk later in the book about how to run effective project meetings in more detail.

Establish Communication Guidelines

Setting guidelines and expectations about communications is another important facet of high performance teams. As project manager, you may have some guidelines you'd like to establish (and that's fine). You should also work with the team to determine what's feasible and reasonable. Some companies expect e-mail to be responded to within a few hours, other companies seem to expect responses sometime in the next week or two. Time zones, cultural, and generational differences also come into play. For instance, some team members may be reluctant to log into e-mail on the weekends to check on and reply to e-mail (unless they have a specific need to do so). Other teammates may log in nights, weekends, and holidays just to keep their fingers "on the pulse." An e-mail sent at 8:00 A.M. in the U.S. might arrive just after normal working hours in another country and may not be replied to until the next day. In addition to issues of timeliness, your team should set guidelines about how they'll communicate. How often will they meet, do they need to talk by phone, net meeting, video conferencing, face-to-face meetings, etc.?

Implement Technology to Enhance Real-Time Communication and Collaboration

High performance teams have team leaders who work to reduce barriers to productivity and success. Looking for ways to implement and leverage technology to enhance real-time communication and collaboration among team members can have a huge impact on the success of the team. Utilizing existing tools more effectively can be part of your strategy and the implementation of new tools might be needed as well. Also, make sure everyone has access to the tools the team will use. If one part of the team has access to video conferencing and another part of the team doesn't, it can cause problems with communications and keeping the team in sync. In today's wired world, we all expect to have e-mail, phones, and access to the Internet, but these amenities are not universally available. If you have lone team members in remote locations, don't assume they're as connected as other team members. Assess which technologies the team can all utilize to communicate effectively.

Cheat Sheet...

IT Team Performance

With the rapid pace of IT change, it's hard just to stay on top of technology, much less stay on top of managing a diverse team. However, remember the saying, "Projects don't fail, people do." The key to any successful project is the project team. Certainly there are times when more money or more time makes a big difference, but regardless of your budget or schedule, if you don't have the right people on the team performing at their optimal levels and fully utilizing their skills and talents, your project will fall short of the mark. Learning to manage others effectively, especially through influence (rather than direct authority) is the most important thing you can do as an IT project manager. There are numerous resources—books, websites, newsletters, training courses—available to help hone your skills as a manager. Investing in these skills will enhance your career regardless of where you're headed.

Summary

Managing a project team has become increasingly more complex as we work with people of different work styles, different languages, different cultures, and different generations. We are expected to work in real time with people from around the world and generate cost-effective results to help our companies remain competitive in the global market. IT project management is a complex task that requires a solid depth and breadth of skills that include business, management, and technical skills. As a project manager, you'll garner far more success if you work to understand people a bit better. No doubt you've got a handle on the latest technology; you're in IT after all. But understanding what makes people tick and how to get the best out of people is often a skill that's neglected in the IT world. As an IT project manager, you need to find ways to get people engaged in the team and committed to a successful project—often without direct or formal authority over your team members. Understanding work styles, cultural and language differences, generational and gender differences, and what actually makes a team perform well will set you apart from your peers and give you a huge head start on project success.

Solutions Fast Track

Today's Management Environment

- ☑ With the vast amount of information we have to process every day, managers are no longer accepted as "the experts."

- ☑ Corporate culture has changed and people no longer have jobs for life; individuals no longer assume they'll always have only one job or career in their lifetimes.

- ☑ Technology has changed the way we work. The lone employee in a rural area must be as connected as employees at the corporate headquarters.

- ☑ A successful manager must help remove roadblocks to high performance and help foster commitment and initiative.

What People Really Want

☑ There are numerous factors that impact job satisfaction or dissatisfaction.

☑ Factors that create job dissatisfaction if not attended to are often referred to as "hygiene" or "housekeeping" issues. These include salary, company policies, and the work environment. If these are lacking, employees may become dissatisfied. If these are adequate, they will not create job satisfaction.

☑ Factors that create an environment that fosters job satisfaction include meaningful work, the opportunity for achievement and advancement, and recognition for a job well done.

☑ As a project manager, you often lack the ability to address the "housekeeping" issues, especially salary, but you can have an enormous impact on the job satisfaction factors.

Work Styles and the Project Team

☑ There are numerous systems that define work and personality traits. Myers-Briggs and DiSC are two of the more widely known systems.

☑ Everyone has a work style that comes naturally to them. When they can work primarily within that style, they are more productive, generate higher quality, and typically experience less stress.

☑ As a project manager, learning to recognize and leverage various work styles will make your job easier. Relying on individuals' strengths and minimizing their weaknesses creates the strongest possible team.

☑ When putting together your project team, try to include various work styles on the team and then utilize those strengths for the good of the team.

☑ Create an environment that accepts and respects various work styles. Each style has its strengths and potential pitfalls, so no one style is "good" or "bad".

Culture Matters

- ☑ If you're managing people from other cultures or other countries, you'll need to learn about those other cultures in order to effectively manage those people.

- ☑ Following some basic guidelines such as learning to pronounce difficult, foreign names and understanding the values and norms of another culture will show respect, the most important factor in managing cross-cultural teams.

- ☑ Make sure all members of the team understand terminology, jargon, and expectations. English may be a second language for other team members and culture, countries, and distance all can add to confusion.

- ☑ Communicate clearly and frequently. Make sure all members of the team are involved and are participating.

- ☑ Feedback is a normal and required part of any team management process, but providing negative feedback in a multicultural environment can be tricky. Make sure you understand the culture and the most appropriate way to provide feedback before proceeding so you don't accidentally cause embarrassment or worse.

- ☑ Multigenerational teams also can be challenging because older and younger workers typically have different work styles.

- ☑ Learn to respect different work styles and leverage their best traits. Pair or team up workers of differing styles so they can learn to respect and understand each other's strengths and can offset each other's weaknesses.

- ☑ Don't confuse cultural issues for performance issues, but don't let cultural issues prevent you from addressing performance issues. Learn to address the work and the expectations in culturally appropriate ways, but do address performance issues.

Men, Women and Technology

- ☑ Women are underrepresented in science and technology fields.

- ☑ If you manage a team that includes women, create an environment that takes advantage of everyone's skills and talents equally.

- ☑ Be aware of cross-cultural issues related to gender when managing an international team.

Developing High Performance Teams

☑ High performance teams start with the right mix of people. Make sure you have the right people for the project and rearrange jobs, titles, and tasks to leverage everyone's best talents.

☑ Clearly defining the project, the project's objectives, the team's mission, and the roles and responsibilities of each team member is critical to a high performance team. People work more effectively when they clearly understand the project's objectives and their role within the team.

☑ Make sure your team meetings are well run. Use meeting agendas, keep conversations on topic, and avoid wasting people's time discussing or rehashing prior deliverables or events (unless needed). Provide opportunities for informal talk or socializing outside of the formal confines of the team meeting.

☑ Utilize any and all appropriate technology to enhance team communication and collaboration. This is especially critical when your project team is geographically dispersed.

Frequently Asked Questions

The following Frequently Asked Questions, answered by the author of this book, are designed to both measure your understanding of the concepts presented in this chapter and to assist you with real-life implementation of these concepts. To have your questions about this chapter answered by the author, browse to **www.syngress.com/solutions** and click on the **"Ask the Author"** form.

Q: There's a guy on our project team who always says, "That won't work." We're getting a bit tired of his negative attitude. Any suggestions?

A: Some people always see the downside to everything. While this can be a drag on the team's momentum, it can also be useful to the team by helping the team (and project) avoid pitfalls no one else has discovered. If you're the project manager, you need to manage this behavior so it's productive and not just a constant negative voice. One of the best ways to do this is to give this guy time to think about whatever's being proposed then set a team meeting to discuss the pros and cons of the proposal. This gives him a legitimate outlet for raising his concerns. Another technique that can be very helpful is to allow him to say, in essence, "That won't work," then press him for ideas on what *would* work. When someone poses problems without solutions, it's not helpful, so asking anyone who raises potential problems to also suggest ideas for solutions will yield a more positive outcome. In fact, you can make that part of your team process—whenever you raise a problem you must also offer potential solutions. While there are times when people might raise a legitimate problem and not be able to offer a potential solution, it will separate out the perpetually negative people from those who are raising legitimate concerns.

Q: My project team's meetings are a complete waste of time. We just sit around and rehash what we talked about before. Any suggestions?

A: It's possible that your team's project manager is just not good at running meetings. He or she may have a work style that is less organized than others. If you're more organized, you may offer to be in charge of creating team meeting agendas. By proposing both the problem and solution, you'll give the PM a break and you will use your strengths for the good of the team. For instance, you could say, "I know others are comfortable with less structure, but I think there are some on the team, myself included, that could use a bit more structure in our team meetings. Would it be ok if I developed an agenda for each meeting and submitted to you for approval before the meeting? That would help me stay focused and organized during the meetings." If the PM isn't good at organizing and running meetings, he or she will probably be quite thankful for the assistance and because it's positioned as a team aid (rather than addressing the PM's shortcomings), it is more likely to be accepted. It's also important to recognize that you, as a team member, play an important role in the team, not only as a subject matter expert, but as a member of a team that needs to get results. By taking steps to improve the effectiveness of your team meetings, you're demonstrating an important team trait. If every member of the team takes responsibility for ensuring a highly functional team, chances are good it will be one.

Q: I have someone on my team who's from another country and I can't pronounce her name. I gave her a nickname to make it easier. Was that ok to do?

A: That depends. Some people understand that their names are difficult for others outside their country or culture to pronounce and are fine with nicknames. Others may be offended. You might ask this person if the nickname or some other name is her preference. Remember, avoid a yes/no type of question since she may be reluctant to say no, even if she does not like you using a nickname for her.

Q: I have a guy on my team who's in his late 50's and he's a real rules-and-regulations guy. He seems to annoy a number of the younger team members. Any advice?

A: Your approach to this situation is important because you indicated that you only have one older worker on the team. If this is the case, he may feel like the "odd man out." This may actually cause him to become even more focused on what he's comfortable with, which in his case are the rules and regulations. Recognizing his expertise and talents, making sure he's included in non-work team activities, or finding situations to specifically include him or rely upon his talents may help diffuse the situation. Talking as a team about what the rules and procedures are can also help clarify for everyone what's expected. You may also need to talk privately with him about his behavior if he is imposing his views and work style on others. Again, respect his contribution and focus on what you'd like him to do and how he can best contribute.

Q: My IT project team is comprised of several people who are much younger than I am. They're late to meetings, they miss meetings, and they can't seem to deliver results on time. It's driving me nuts. What should I do?

A: Well, there are some interesting dynamics you just described. First, you lumped all of these younger team members into one. Are all of them always late to meetings and miss meetings and deadlines, or are you seeing them as one unit even though they are three or four distinctly different individuals? It's possible your discomfort with their work style is causing you to miss some of their individual differences, so that's one place to begin looking. However, if this is a generational kind of work style issue you're noticing, there are several things you can do. First, make sure your meetings are not a waste of time. Younger team members, in particular, move quickly and have the ability to multitask, which means they can get bored more quickly. If the meetings they're skipping aren't particularly relevant, you may want to make some changes to your meetings. Make them focused by having specific agendas and sticking to them. Make them effective by using everyone's time in the most efficient manner possible. Finally, you may have a performance issue with one or more of these folks. Don't confuse poor performance with other issues. Setting clear performance guidelines and making sure everyone understands what's expected and when is important in all business settings. If team members do not perform to these expectations, you may have to address individual performance.

Q: I've been managing a project team that I "inherited" from a previous project manager. The team is in disarray and is far from being a high functioning team. There are sub-groups and in-fighting, and territorial and political issues running rampant. I don't even know where to start. What do you suggest?

A: Well, you've certainly got your work cut out for you. One way to move through this type of situation is to stop whatever you're doing and completely disassemble the team's structure—not the project, just the team. Privately, you may want to evaluate all the team members to see if you have the right mix of people. It's possible you don't and that's causing some of the problems. Make sure everyone on the team is contributing something needed and if not, remove him or her from the team (yes, politics do come into play and you may not be able to remove some members of the team without major problems. You'll have to use your best judgment in these cases). Essentially, try to wipe the slate clean. Get rid of job descriptions and titles, and get rid of current groupings. Get the team together and tell them you want to start from scratch. Have everyone look at the project and the project team and start by redefining your project and the team's mission or objectives (that's specifically addressed later in this book). It's also possible that the project definition was poor or misguided in the first place or that it has changed over time. When the team has a clear understanding of the project, its objectives, and the team's responsibility, you can begin to create a shared vision of the project. Next, work with the team to clearly define roles and responsibilities based on work styles, subject matter expertise, and skills (and other relevant factors). Realigning the team based on roles and responsibilities can also help break up these sub-group issues. Finally, you may need to get the leaders of these sub-groups aligned with the project's new definition and mission or remove them from the team. It's possible to turn around your rag-tag team, but it will take some work.

Chapter 5

Defining IT Projects

Solutions in this chapter:

- **Project Management Process Overview**

- **Project Origins**

- **Validating the Project Proposal**

- **Defining the Project**

- **Developing the Project Proposal**

- **Identifying the Project Sponsor**

- **Gaining Validated Project Proposal Approval**

- ☑ **Summary**

- ☑ **Solutions Fast Track**

- ☑ **Frequently Asked Questions**

Introduction

In the first four chapters of this book, we defined and discussed the environment that surrounds and influences IT projects. If you skipped over those chapters, make sure you go back and read them at some point. They help put things in perspective and give you some great tools for more effectively navigating in your corporate culture. In this chapter, we're going to start digging into IT project management itself. We're going to look at each phase of project management beginning with the definition phase. This is an element of IT project management that is often skipped or short-changed, but it is in the definition phase that you begin to build success into your project. Some project management methodologies begin with *project initiation.* We'll keep it simple and include initiation and definition together in this chapter. We'll begin by discussing project origins and we'll briefly discuss types of projects. We'll discuss the important elements in defining a project so that you build the foundation for success. Think of it this way—if you don't define the problem, you are likely to solve the wrong problem. A great solution to the wrong problem is like a bicycle with an airbag—it might be interesting, but it's not very useful.

Project Management Process Overview

Throughout the remaining chapters, we'll use a diagram (Figure 5.1) showing the project management process to help you visualize where you are. You'll be reminded of where you've been and what your next steps are by referring to this diagram, which you'll also find at the beginning of subsequent chapters. You can refer to this as you plan your project and you can download the template showing all the steps and the details of each step from www.syngress.com/solutions. It's important to understand that IT project management is an iterative process meaning you'll have to do some of the steps more than once, refining your project as you go. You usually can't just do each step once and leave it at that. While it might be nice if you could engrave your project plan in granite, it's far more likely that you'll have to re-work and revisit various project elements throughout the project planning and project management process. Expect that you'll have to do that. Don't become defensive or irritated when something needs to change. Accept that change is part of what you're managing and the better you manage change, the better you'll be able to manage your project. This is especially important in the early stages of project planning, including the stage we're going to discuss in this chapter, defining the project. If you bring your thoughts and ideas back to the project sponsor and he or she does not validate your findings, that's a good thing. It means that you have successfully rooted out assumptions or misunderstandings that later might have completely blown the project out of the water. Knowing that now rather than 10 months and $10 million later is a good thing, don't you think?

Figure 5.1 IT Project Management Process Overview

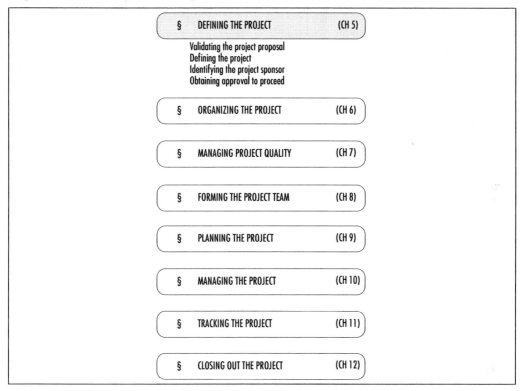

We're starting with *Defining the Project*. Within this section of the overall IT project management methodology, there are defined *inputs*, *actions*, and *outputs*. In plain English, that means that there is a specific starting point (input), specific steps we'll take (actions), and specific results of our actions. For each of the steps show in Figure 5.1, there are inputs, actions, and outputs that we'll discuss. If this language is new to you, don't be put off. It will quickly become familiar and using these concepts (*input*, *action*, and *output*) will help you keep track of each step in the project more easily. Figure 5.2 shows the inputs, actions, and outputs for the project definition step of IT project management. Let's quickly define a few terms before we continue.

- **Duration** The length of time allotted for a particular task to be completed.

- **Effort** The actual amount of time expended completing a task.

- **First use penalty** The additional length of time (or cost) that stems from the first time something is done (cost of the learning curve).

- **Parametric estimating** Using parameters from previous projects to develop estimates for the current project.

- **Project** A unique solution to a problem.

- **Project lifecycle** Each project has seven phases: define, organize, form the team, plan, manage, track, and close the project. Together, these form the project lifecycle.

- **Project proposal** A project overview document given to you to begin project implementation. Ideally, a project proposal contains certain elements, discussed later in this chapter. A project proposal is not always required, though if one exists, it should be validated.

- **Proposed solution** A solution to a problem that is suggested as a project or approach to the project.

- **Problem to be solved** A problem to be solved by creating a project plan.

- **Project sponsor** Typically the person who assigned the project to you and appointed you project manager. The project sponsor is the person to whom you must go to get formal and informal approval for project parameters such as the project proposal, the cost, time, and other details of the project.

- **Validated project proposal** An initial project plan that defines several basic elements of a project plan.

Figure 5.2 Inputs, Actions, and Outputs for Project Definition Step

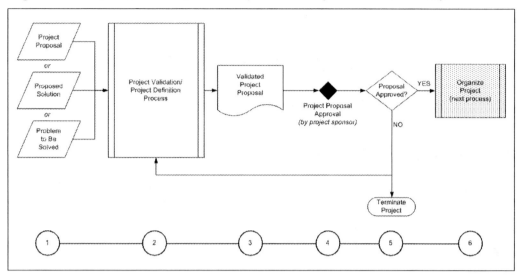

Within the project definition step or phase, there are 6 steps. Let's discuss each one briefly so the diagram will become clear if it's not already.

1. **INPUT** The input in this case is one of three things. Either you have been given a project proposal, you have been handed a proposed solution (a less defined project proposal), or you have identified a problem to be solved. We'll discuss where projects come from more in a subsequent section of this chapter.

2. **ACTION** Using one of these three inputs, you'll then go into the project validation or project definition process. This process is a defined set of steps you'll use that will result in a validated project proposal. If you were handed a project proposal, following the steps in this process will result in a proposal that has been validated by research and investigation. If you were handed a proposed solution or an identified problem, following the steps in the project validation/project definition process will result in the creation of a formal (or not-so-formal) project proposal.

3. **OUTPUT** The output from this phase or step is a validated project proposal. Notice that regardless of which of the three inputs we have, we use the same steps to validate or create the project proposal and the result is a validated project proposal. Whether this is generated from reviewing an existing proposal or from creating a new proposal from scratch, the result is the same.

4. **CHECKPOINT**   In many of the steps in IT project management, there are one or more checkpoints. These are points at which you need to stop and make sure everything is on track. Within a project schedule, these are typically referred to as *milestones*. Outside of the project schedule, you can call them milestones, checkpoints, or input points, just as long as you have them and use them. For this step, the validated project proposal is brought to the project sponsor for approval. We'll discuss how to do this later in this chapter.

5. **DECISION POINT**   Based on the response of your project sponsor, you'll either need to go back and rework parts of your project proposal or continue on to the next step, organizing your project. If the sponsor gives the proposal the go ahead, you continue. If not, you will have to address the project sponsor's specific concerns and revise the validated project proposal and submit it for approval again. This may be an iterative process where you'll need to make several revisions before the project sponsor agrees to the proposal. It's also possible that based on the information gathered thus far, the project sponsor (or project manager) recommends terminating the project. This occurs when it becomes clear that factors have changed such as the project would be too late or too costly, etc. We'll discuss this in more detail later in this chapter.

6. **NEXT STEP**   Once you have approval from the project sponsor for the validated project proposal, you can continue in the project planning process and begin organizing your project. These steps are discussed in Chapter 6.

Project Origins

In organizations, there are essentially two different types of projects arising from different needs. The bottom-up project is typically *needs-driven*. Someone in the organization sees a problem or need and a project is born to solve the problem. The second type is the top-down project and that is typically *solution-oriented*. Someone at the top of the organization wants something to exist and creates a project to make it happen. Sometimes a project has already been proposed and defined (it may have already been planned) and is then placed on hold or modified in some way before it's handed to you. We call these *project proposals* to differentiate them from a solution that's been handed to you or a problem that's been identified. While this may seem like splitting hairs, it's important to differentiate because these are your project inputs (see Figure 5.2, Step 1) and each requires a slightly different approach.

Some projects are driven by internal needs, while some result from external needs (client, customer, or perhaps vendor). These external projects are often projects for which clients are paying, so while the overall process is the same, there may be different checkpoints, approval points, and signatures required. We'll point out the places where these differences exist as we go.

Notice in Figure 5.2 that regardless of your inputs (where the project comes from), the steps are the same. If you're starting with a project proposal, which assumes much of the project information has been developed, you'll be validating instead of creating data. If your input is a solution or a problem, you'll be creating the project data related to the definition step to validate the problem, solution, and approach.

As we discussed in Chapter 3, corporate politics have a lot to do with project success and how you manage the political environment is key. When a project is needs-driven, it's often (though not always) easier to get the project approved, especially when everyone feels the pain. An example of that would be the need to upgrade the desktop operating system to a newer version because everyone (including the CEO or company owner) experiences the "blue screen of death" or other symptoms of system instability. The downside is that if the project is needs-driven and it's not a need that is clearly defined or directly felt by top executives, it may be hard to gain project approval. An example of this type of project is rewriting part of an internal application to provide more seamless integration with a financial package so less manual work occurs (and therefore fewer errors). This type of project is invisible to almost everyone in the organization and can be difficult to sell unless you make a strong business case (see Chapter 2 on aligning IT with business strategies).

The second type of project is the assigned project, or proposed solution. These typically come about because an executive wants to see some sort of result. This might be in response to a unique opportunity in the market that an executive wants to capitalize on or it could be a pet project of someone at the top. While this type of project may still be responding to a need, it is often assigned based on a desired outcome or proposed solution. The good news for these types of projects is that they typically have strong executive support (though there may be politics at a higher level in the organization that could cause problems later on) and that executive will use political and organizational influence to ensure the project is a success. The downside to these projects is that they are rarely researched or validated and some (or all) of the objectives may be unrealistic. We'll talk more about this in just a moment.

The third project type is the project proposal. This type of project has already been formalized to some degree. It might be a project that was planned six or twelve months ago and put on hold or it could be a project that was defined and planned and handed to you. Regardless of how much work has been done on the project, you should spend time validating the project proposal. Probably the only exception would be if you were handed a full-blown project plan that had been developed by a competent project team and you are assigned as the project manager. Even in that case, it wouldn't hurt to go back over the project plan and validate each step. After all, you're the project manager and you're the one who will be held accountable for results. It would be good to know, going in, that the project was feasible and positioned for success rather than an impossible project for which you'll be the fall guy (or gal).

Whether your project comes from the bottom up or the top down, your steps are going to be almost the same. There are a few key differences and when we run into them, we'll discuss them so you know exactly how to proceed. We're going to look at all of these elements in detail in this chapter.

Validating the Project Proposal

When a project is assigned to you, it often comes with additional project information. A project proposal may be complete or not, but a thorough project proposal will contain all or most of these elements:

- Business case
- Financial analysis
- Market factors or requirements
- High level scope and requirements
- Assumptions and exclusions
- High level resources
- High level schedule
- Success criteria
- Risks
- Alternatives
- Recommendations

Whether you're given a project proposal that has some or all of these elements, you'll need to spend a bit of time validating the project proposal. The intent is not to second-guess anyone but to validate the information in the project proposal for which you'll be held accountable. Sometimes project proposals are developed and the project is placed on hold for month or sometimes years. Sometimes project proposals are developed and the cost of the project components changes dramatically or the required resources or expertise are no longer available or the technology itself has changed. Validating a project proposal is critical because things change constantly. If the project proposal is up to date and was developed by those with enough expertise to develop a valid proposal, you're probably in good shape, but we all know the danger of making assumptions. Rather than assume things are fine, spend time validating the project proposal. How? In two ways: first, by following the project definition steps discussed in this chapter you'll be able to validate the project at a high level—are we solving the right problem, have we selected the optimal solution, etc. Second, you may need to do research or market analysis to validate or develop a complete project proposal.

The primary difference between validating a project proposal and developing one from scratch is that with the former, you're not reinventing the wheel, just making sure the wheel has all its spokes. Using the project definition process we'll discuss in this chapter will allow you to validate each part of the project proposal and to come up with alternatives if things have changed. If the project proposal itself is no longer feasible or desirable, going through the project definition steps should result in solid data supporting the decision to scrap or redefine the project proposal you were given. Without validating the project proposal, you're essentially signing a blank check because you have no way of knowing in advance what you're actually signing up for or whether or not it has any chance of success.

One more note about project proposals before we continue: sometimes it is both necessary and desirable to create a very abbreviated project proposal. In some cases, no project proposal is needed or wanted at all. These may be cases where there is a short window of opportunity or compelling evidence that a project should absolutely move forward. An executive might say, "I don't care about these (project proposal elements), just get it done now!" In those cases, don't spin your wheels developing data that won't be used or needed. However, rather than spending time developing a project proposal, you should spend time defining your project. The lack of need for a formal project proposal does not mean you can or should skip the project management steps listed in this chapter and subsequent chapters; just the opposite. You'll need the data you develop from these steps even more if there is no project proposal prepared to support the rationale for the project.

Form a Small Preliminary Project Team

Regardless of the type of project you're undertaking, it would be helpful at this point to put together a small team of experts to help you define the project, including reviewing the existing project proposal (if one exists). When working through the early stages of project definition, it can be very helpful to have several people working with you. This avoids the pitfalls you might run into such as not seeing your own (perhaps faulty) assumptions and not having access to more than your own point of view. A small team can plow through these initial steps quickly and efficiently and can help build a better foundation for the project. Keep in mind that the folks you gather now may not end up working on the project when you're ready to begin. However, they should be a reliable team that you trust to help you develop these initial concepts. After you've read through this chapter, you'll have a better idea of the kinds of people you might want to ask to assist you in these preliminary tasks.

Review the Existing Project Proposal

The existing project proposal, if one exists, may be short or quite lengthy. The first step is to review any and all project documentation that exists. Make sure you have all the information called out in the existing project proposal including attachments, exhibits, contracts, memos of understanding, and anything else mentioned in or needed by the project proposal document. If the proposal is missing any elements, especially those discussed throughout the remainder of this book, make sure you create them. Any missing element is a potential error waiting to happen, so make sure you have all the data you need to deliver a successful project. If you recall, it's been estimated that 50% to 75% of the total cost of any project is due to errors, rework, and omissions, so validating the project proposal at this point will save time and money down the road.

Validate the Project Information

Now that you've got all the information you need, you can validate the project proposal. There may be some instances where the project sponsor wants to get a project going very quickly to take advantage of favorable market conditions or to address a critical need. While you may have to do an abbreviated "power planning" process (purposely choosing to shorten, condense, or skip steps in the interest of time), you should be aware of the risks of doing so. The risks include errors, omissions and incorrect data and/or assumptions that cause rework, delays, or quality problems later on. You'll have to decide how much planning is appropriate to the situation and keep in mind there are often political factors that must be taken into consideration as well. Not all projects are large and complex, nor do they all require a lot of planning and documentation. Later in this book, we'll discuss the concept of *precision*, which includes how much planning and effort should go into a project plan. If you are working on a short, two week project that involves three people and $8,000, far less planning is needed than for a massive project involving hundreds of hours and thousands (or millions) of dollars.

One important note here is that some companies run in "emergency" mode all the time. This would cause the average IT project manager to skip the project *planning* steps and jump right into the project *managing* steps. Again, there may be isolated instances when this is ok (or required), but don't get caught in the trap of feeling there is no time to plan. Planning now will result in consistently better, more predictable project results. If you're assigned as the project manager to a project already underway, it would be well worth your time to go back through the project, using the steps we'll detail in this and subsequent chapters, to validate your project. You may discover new data that helps the project succeed or that simply keeps you from being the captain of a sinking ship.

Enterprise 128 …

No Time For Planning?

Have you ever noticed that few people (or companies) think they have enough time to plan, but they *always* find time to correct mistakes, errors and omissions once the project is underway?

Take time to plan the project using the steps described in this book. Otherwise, you'll be wasting time and money when you do go back and fix the problems that occurred due to lack of planning. It is a proven fact that the amount of time you spend planning will pay for itself by reducing errors and rework later in the project, when you'll somehow have to find time to make needed corrections.

Defining the Project

Whether your IT project is needs-driven, assigned, or handed to you as a project plan, you should begin with defining the project. Remember, if the project is assigned as a project proposal or project plan, you'll need to review the proposal to validate the various project parameters included in the assignment. If there are any critical changes, they'll have to be submitted to the project sponsor for approval. If the project is solution-oriented or needs-driven, you'll need to create the project proposal to develop the project parameters and submit them for approval. In any case, you'll need to do your homework to make sure the project starts off on solid footing.

Let's begin with defining the initial steps for defining a project, regardless of its origins.

- Problem Statement

- Project Mission Statement

- Potential Solutions

- Selected Solution/Approach

- Project Proposal

This doesn't have to be a long, drawn-out process. In many cases, you and a small team can go through the steps to define these five project elements in an hour or two. While the amount of time this takes varies with project size and complexity, it should not be a painful and arduous process. If you can't define the problem, mission, potential solutions, and selected solution within a reasonable amount of time, it should raise a flag for you that something is wrong.

- **Problem Statement** All projects should begin with a problem statement. Whether the project is needs-driven or solution-oriented (assigned), the project should begin with identifying the unique problem to be solved. This helps validate the project assumptions and makes sure you're solving the right problem in the right way. If you work in an organization that assigns projects and doesn't expect (or accept) someone questioning the project, you should still do this step so you know where you stand and because it's good to get into the habit of managing each project using the same defined steps. In some cases, this step can take 5, 10, or 15 minutes—it need not be a long, involved process to define the problem.

- **Project Mission Statement** If you've ever worked in a company that sent people away for week-long retreats to develop the corporate mission statement, you might be cringing right about now. Some people love those types of activities, but others (including many in IT) find them tedious and unproductive. Let's erase those images from your mind now. When we talk about the project mission statement, we're basically saying, "Let's define what we're trying to accomplish." When you define the problem *and* the mission (which can also be called the *desired outcome*), you will have basically defined a gap between what exists and what is desired. From there, you can develop potential solutions. The mission statement should be a simple statement that includes the desired outcome. If you can attach metrics to your mission, that's even better. For instance, you might say that you want to reduce user downtime (or increase user uptime) by x % or by x number of hours per month. You may not be able to come up with that level of detail at this time, which is fine, but if you have that detail, add it to your mission statement.

- **Potential Solutions** If you've been assigned a project, you already have the identified solution in your hands. However, that does not mean you should skip these steps. In fact, it's important you do these steps because you'll either validate the proposed project or you'll find that it's a disaster waiting to happen (or something in between).

  In this project definition step, which we'll discuss in more detail later, you begin by brainstorming all potential solutions that address the defined problem and the desired outcome. You can be creative in this phase, even if your project is assigned. It's in this phase that brilliant ideas sometimes pop out, so skipping this is a lost opportunity. Once you've listed all potential solutions, you'll go through them and identify the best solution that fits both the problem and desired outcome(s).

- **Selected Solution** We'll discuss this in much greater detail later because there are several methods you can use to identify the best solution to both the defined problem and the desired outcomes (project mission statement). However, once you've developed your list of potential solutions, you have a whole host of options open to you. This is one way you optimize organizational performance—by testing and validating projects before they move forward. Since many projects are scrapped by companies for a variety of reasons, we can assume that some (or many) of these scrapped projects should not have been undertaken in the first place. While it's often difficult to be the bearer of bad news ("This project is not solving the problem" or "This project is not feasible based on current data", etc.., if you can offer up an alternative solution, you'll be seen as someone adding value to the organization by trying to solve the right problem in the best way possible.

- **Project Proposal** If you were handed a project proposal, you can use the list earlier in the chapter to see if all the requisite elements are there. If not, you may want to fill in the gaps. Some companies want all the elements included in a project proposal, while other companies may want to skip over certain elements. You'll have to adapt to your organization's basic formula, but also keep in mind that each element is included for a specific reason and to skip over any element is to have a less-than-complete project proposal document, which leaves things open for interpretation, discussion and, unfortunately, finger-pointing. The project proposal is not a required element, especially because some companies don't yet understand the value of things like making the business case for an IT project. However, in most cases, you'd do well to at least create a small project proposal. This is discussed in more detail later in the chapter.

Defining the Problem

We briefly mentioned the importance of defining the project problem. In this section, we'll look at the needs-driven project and the solution-oriented (assigned) project and why you should take time to define the problem. If your project came to you in the form of a project proposal or a full-blown project plan, you can review the solution-oriented or assigned project section. Then, we'll look at how to actually define the problem so you get your project off on the right foot.

Defining the Needs-Driven Project

Needs-driven projects are sometimes the easiest to work with only because they typically start with someone identifying a problem to be solved. The reason this is a bit easier to work with is because a good project definition begins with defining the problem to be solved. A *project*, by definition, is a unique solution to a problem. So, the ideal starting point is the problem statement. In a needs-driven project, this is often the process of clarifying the problem that's been identified. Using the example cited earlier, a needs-driven project might be upgrading all desktop systems to a newer, more stable operating system version. The original problem might have been raised this way, "Do you know the help desk staff has spent over 70 hours this month fixing system problems?" or an executive may have said "I'm really tired of my desktop hanging when I'm in the middle of working on a big project. I'd like you to find a better solution than constantly rebooting my system." In either case, a problem was identified—the desktop systems are unstable. Notice, however, that these problems are not necessarily stated in clear, defined ways. Someone on the IT team may come to you and mention that an executive was upset with system performance and wants a more permanent solution, or you may discover through routine report analysis that an excessive number of help desk hours are spent on a particular type of problem (in this case, system instability issues). You might decide that the problem is large enough to warrant upgrading the systems, so you decide to look into a project to accomplish this.

Defining the Solution-Oriented Project

Solution-oriented projects (including those that are handed to you as project proposals or project plans) are often assigned projects. Someone notices a problem and decides the best course of action and assigns a project to someone. These come about in two distinctly different ways. If you're the IT manager and you assign a project to someone on your team, you may very well assign the scope, time, cost, and quality metrics for the project. Based on your skills, experience and understanding of the assignment, there's a very good chance you can assign these four variables with a fair amount of accuracy. Still, the project manager for the assigned project should work through every step, including defining the project, to validate the project.

A second and very common scenario is when someone outside the IT department, typically an executive, assigns a project to the IT department or assigns a project to someone that includes a major IT component. In this case, it's entirely possible (or even likely) that the four assigned metrics are not based on experience or history, but are instead based on a business need. If this is the case, there is a strong chance that the four variables assigned will not be realistic or achievable. Now you're faced with a dilemma. You can move forward with the project knowing that at least one of the four metrics (scope, time, cost, quality) will *not* be achieved (unless you are incredibly lucky) or you can step back and define the project from the ground up. After defining the project problem as well as other steps, you may have to go back to the person who assigned the project and let him or her know what is realistic or achievable. While this might sound like bucking the chain of command, most reasonable executives want to know if there's a problem *before* it costs time and money. If you work in the type of organization where this type of dialog with those higher up in the organization is unacceptable, then you may have to simply have to continue along with all the project definition and planning steps, even if you are unable to change any of the project parameters. By going through every step, you'll at least know what you're up against and how close or far the assigned project is from reality. These steps should be followed regardless of whether or not you can change the parameters, and these steps may give you leverage to get the project modified or at least to record data for future use. However, in most organizations, you have the opportunity to clarify and provide additional information that may change the project parameters so that you and the project can be successful.

It is at this point in the project planning stage that you have your best shot at beginning to educate your higher-ups in the chain of command. While they may not want to hear the details of the project, you should make every reasonable attempt to help these executives understand the project planning process and why it's important that they listen to your feedback. Again, not all companies are going to allow this, but it doesn't mean you shouldn't give it a shot. Help the executive understand the process and most importantly, show what's in it for the company and the executive. Make the business case: "We can reduce the errors and rework in this project by following this defined process. The first step is validating the project proposal and these are the variances we've found." While you may not always be successful in these attempts, it is true that you "pay now or pay later." If a project must be completed in four months, it may well be completed in four months. It is also highly likely that the project will lack key functionality (scope) or may have errors (quality). It might also cost four times as much because it had to be done so quickly (cost). We'll talk more about the relationship of these elements in more detail later, but keep in mind that every chance you have to get your project sponsor and/or the executive team on board with the project management process should be fully utilized.

Defining the Problem Statement

Whether the project is needs-driven or assigned, you should begin with defining the problem to be solved by the project. When the project is needs-driven, it's often easier to see the problem to be solved and to develop a problem statement. With assigned projects, it might be more difficult to discern the problem and if possible, you might want be able to talk with the person who assigned the project and ask what problem he or she is trying to solve. The reason for doing this is simple. A project is a unique solution to a defined problem. If you define the wrong problem, you'll develop a solution that solves the wrong problem and might ultimately cause more problems than it solves. Starting at the very beginning is an important step for all projects so you can be clear about where you're headed.

Let's look at the example of system instability we used earlier. The problem was stated in two different ways. Someone saw that 70 hours of help desk time was spent during one month on dealing with system instability issues such as blue screen of death and other related issues. A second problem statement is the executive asking for a better solution to the computer problems since rebooting is inefficient and frustrating. Both describe the problem and can be used as the basis for defining the problem, though neither is an adequate problem statement.

The problem statement should be a clear, concise statement of the problem to be solved. Using this example, we can say the problem is "system instability is causing excessive help desk effort and user downtime. User downtime causes organizational inefficiency and user frustration." You might word it differently, but this is the essence of the problem. Another way to look at defining the problem is to ask the question, "Why should we care about this problem?" You might answer that question by stating that user downtime is inefficient and costs your company both in terms of inefficient use of help desk hours (that could be better spent doing something more productive) and loss of time and increased frustration for users. *Defining the problem doesn't describe the solution.* Notice that nowhere in our problem statements have we said that the solution should be to upgrade the desktop systems. So far, all we've done is say, "here's the problem" or "here's the reason we care about this problem." The result of this step is a project problem statement, shown in Figure 5.3. As you can probably tell, this step doesn't need to take hours. It might be a ten-minute exercise in some cases. Throughout the remainder of this book, you'll see these images. The shape on the left indicates a document. Within the shape is the name or title of the document. To the right of the shape are words describing the contents or nature of the document. So, the document that results from the preceding process is a problem statement. We'll continue to identify the type of document and the document contents at each step. Look for these icons throughout this and subsequent chapters to help identify tangible deliverables or outcomes from discrete steps. While each of these discrete deliverables should be captured in a document, they can all be captured in the same document, the project plan.

Figure 5.3 Project Problem Statement

APPLYING YOUR KNOWLEDGE

Begin all projects by defining the problem to be solved. Describe either the problem itself or why the company (or you or your department) should care about the problem. This will help you not only make sure you're solving the right problem with your project, but will give you a solid foundation for validating the project and project parameters later. Remember, whether your project is needs-driven or solution-oriented, you should begin with the problem definition.

It's possible you are thinking that since most of your projects are assigned and you're not expected to question the project assignment that you can skip this step. Don't. Even if you are powerless to modify the project parameters, you need to know how close (or far) this project is to reality. If you don't start with the project problem statement or definition, you'll never know if you're solving the right problem or not. Remember to take every opportunity to manage up the chain of command by educating higher-ups about the process and why it makes good business sense to do it in the manner described. You might not always win, but you'll never have someone say, "Why didn't you say something earlier?"

The IT Factor...

A Well-Defined Problem

Starting with a well-defined problem can make all the difference in the world. For many people just learning project management, it can be so effective that convincing others to use project management processes becomes an easy sell. For Lisa Mainz, Operations Manager for ShopNatural.com, a well-defined problem statement made all the difference when she first introduced these processes to her team. She asked her team to work with her to define the problem they were trying to solve. She reported, "Not only was defining the problem statement easier than anyone thought it would be, it gave us all such a clear understanding of the problem that finding the optimal solution was actually easy." For anyone just learning IT project management or for anyone who's a bit overwhelmed by having to implement many new steps or processes, Mainz recommends beginning with a well-defined problem statement. "Even if you don't ever implement another PM step, you'll find your projects are more successful just by implementing this one fundamental step," Mainz suggested. "Though implementing all the steps in this defined IT project management process will ultimately yield the best results, you can always start small and add one step at a time. Incremental improvement is better than none at all."

Defining the Project Mission Statement

After you've clearly defined the problem to be solved, you can then create the project mission statement. The project mission statement is really the desired outcome of the project. Remember, you're still not defining *how* you'll accomplish this project—that comes in just a bit. For now, we're essentially performing a gap analysis. "Essentially, here's the problem and here's the desired outcome."

The project mission statement should be a short, concise statement about the outcomes to be achieved, not *how* those outcomes will be achieved. While this may sound a bit like verbal nitpicking, it's not. It's important that you define each element independently so that you don't make any very basic errors in your assumptions. A mistake in this definition process will be amplified so that later in the project, an error here will be very costly to reverse or repair. This is also used to state the exit criteria or how you will know when the project is successfully completed. Later, you'll define success criteria for the project, but a very concise statement here will also help avoid scope creep later on.

Using the example mentioned earlier, we'll use the problem statement regarding system instability and we'll develop a mission statement for it. The problem was stated in this way: "System instability is causing excessive help desk effort and user downtime. User downtime causes organizational inefficiency and user frustration." What would be the desired outcome then? We might state our project mission (or desired outcome) as, "To reduce user downtime and help desk staff hours related to desktop operating system faults and failures." Notice that we have not defined how we'll do this; we have not defined the solution. We have only defined the problem and the desired outcome. At this stage, you may not be able to define specific, measurable outcomes and that's ok. However, if you can, you'll be ahead of the curve later in your project planning. For instance, if you can state that you want to reduce down time by 85% from current levels, you have a much more specific statement about what you're trying to accomplish. If you can't yet define it this specifically, that's fine—later activities will help you more clearly define specific measurable goals for your project.

A clearly defined mission statement is another very critical step in the project definition phase of project planning. It is possible that once you define the problem and the mission that you find your assigned project (whether it comes in the form of a suggested solution or a project proposal) is just flat out wrong. If you find that through defining the problem and mission that you come up with a different view of the project altogether, there's a disconnect somewhere that should be addressed. It's always easier to fix these gaps earlier than later, even if it means braving the potential irritation of higher-ups who may just want the project to get under way.

Notice that this process doesn't have to take forever. In many cases, once you've defined the problem clearly, the project mission statement almost writes itself because it's just the other side of the coin, so to speak. In some cases, you and your small, expert team can identify the problem and mission statement in just a few productive minutes together. Figure 5.4 shows the project mission statement as a defined result of this step.

Some people like to think of the project mission statement as the statement of work or the project charter. They're not exactly equivalent because the project mission statement simply defines the desired outcome(s). A statement of work or project charter certainly should contain (or summarize) the problem statement and the mission statement, but they are not interchangeable. We'll discuss statement of work and project charters in the next chapter.

Figure 5.4 Project Problem Statement

APPLYING **Y**OUR **K**NOWLEDGE

Begin all projects by defining the mission statement or desired outcome(s). After you've defined the problem you're trying to solve, you should develop your mission statement, which identifies the desired outcome(s) for the project. This essentially is a gap analysis—where are we and where do we want to be? By defining the beginning and end points, you can then discuss all the potential ways to solve the problem and hopefully come up with the best solution for the situation. If you don't describe the end result, you won't ever know if your project hit the mark or not.

Identify Potential Solutions

If you haven't yet put together a small team to work with you on defining the project, you might want to do so now. They can validate the problem and mission statements (if you created them on your own or with your project sponsor) and they can help you identify all potential solutions. Schedule this meeting for an hour, bring food (always a good way to invite lively participation) and encourage folks to get creative. If you have fun with this and allow all potential solutions to be listed, you may find that someone has a brilliant idea that at first glance seemed outlandish or just plain crazy. It happens.

You'll want to begin by reviewing the project problem statement and mission statement. Then, ask the team to take ten minutes to write ideas down on a piece of paper. This allows everyone to think freely without outside influence or judgment. Once everyone has brainstormed on paper, have people share their ideas with the team. Write them all down and don't eliminate any just yet—even if they seem completely off-the-wall or unrealistic. If people think of other ideas while you're writing, encourage them to make a note of them and add them to the list since sometimes one person's idea sparks another new, unique idea for someone else.

Once you have a list of all potential solutions, make sure the list is complete. If you have a list of very sane, doable solutions, you haven't thought hard enough or big enough. You should have some crazy, over-the-top solutions on your list if everyone is being creative and participating fully. It doesn't matter that at first glance you might dismiss a handful of ideas for one reason or another. Sometimes it takes a crazy idea to spark a related thought. If you've heard the theory that there are only six people between any two people on this planet, such as you and the Dalai Lama (the *six degrees of separation* theory), it might also be true that there are only six crazy ideas between a bland one and a blockbuster. It's worth a shot, isn't it?

The Do Nothing Option

Add "do nothing" to your list of potential solutions. One trap many companies get caught in is knee-jerk responses to problems or crises either internally or in the marketplace. Sometimes you may find that doing nothing is actually the best solution. Rather than racing around creating a project, sometimes simply allowing a situation to resolve itself is the best option. This option should be considered, but it should be a conscious choice, not the result of vacillation or over-thinking a problem (that is, don't confuse "analysis paralysis" with an active "do nothing" choice).

Project Versus Process

Another trap that IT project managers and companies can fall into is that they define a whole new project when a *process* is what's needed. A project, by definition, is a unique solution to a problem. A process, on the other hand, is a defined set of repeatable steps taken to address an ongoing circumstance or problem. For instance, payroll is a process in most companies. You wouldn't create a new project every two weeks so people could get paid. Instead, you create a process to address how and when people get paid, how checks are delivered, and how problems with payroll are addressed. These are all processes because even though they may address problems, they are ongoing and are not unique (even if a unique problem pops up within the payroll process, it usually requires an adjustment to the process, not a project). You should make sure that the problem you're trying to solve requires a project and not a process.

Not to confuse matters, but sometimes a project is needed to develop a new process, and sometimes new processes are derived from projects. The key to keep in mind is that a process is used for ongoing activities and a project is a solution to a unique or one-time problem. While the lines can get blurry at times, make sure you stop and ask, "Would a process solve this problem better than a project?" If so, talk to the project sponsor and make your case for developing a new process rather than defining and implementing a new project.

Figure 5.5 Potential Project Solutions

APPLYING YOUR KNOWLEDGE

Identify all potential solutions. After you've clearly defined where you are (problem) and where you want to be (mission), you can brainstorm all potential solutions (see Figure 5.5) that fit both the problem and mission statements. Being creative and even over-the-top in this step can some-times yield surprising, innovative solutions that might otherwise be over-looked. Don't cross anything off the list at this point, but do make sure that all listed solutions address both the problem and mission state-ments. If not, they're off the mark and should be added to the list only if the team thinks the potential solution is a blockbuster. Ideas that are off the mark can also be recorded for future use or to develop other projects. Don't let a great idea slip away, but don't be distracted by great ideas that are not appropriate for your project's problem and mission.

Selecting the Optimal Solution

You and your small, expert team have developed the problem statement, the project mission statement and a list of potential solutions, even if you were handed the solution initially. Now, you will go through a process of looking at all potential solutions and rank them based on certain criteria (which we'll discuss in a moment). Even if you have been handed the solution you should still go through this exercise. If the solution bubbles up to the top, you've validated the solution. If the solution falls low in the list, you have invalidated the solution and perhaps found an even better solu-tion to the stated problem. Of course, this can be tricky politically, but we'll deal with that later. For now, let's focus on finding the optimal solution.

Developing Ranking Criteria

You've got a long or short list of potential solutions that you and the team have developed. The next step is to develop the criteria against which you'll rate or rank these potential solutions. For instance, the project sponsor may have told you the project must be completed in less than six months or for less than $50,000. The pro-ject sponsor or the project proposal may have stated that certain requirements must be met such as the use of a particular technology, programming language or security algorithm. In some cases, these requirements are just that—requirements that must be included in or addressed by the solution. In other cases, however, requirements are mentioned but they're really closer to suggested solutions. If you can discern the difference (or you know the difference based on how your organization works), so much the better. Don't work to meet requirements that are really suggested solutions if you and your team believe a better solution exists.

There is no standard set of criteria that we can give you to say, "Use this list to rank your potential solutions," because every situation is different. However, you can begin by looking once again at corporate and IT strategies and determining which of the potential solutions aligns best. You can also look at which potential solution(s) have the best business case or which approach seems most appropriate. You can also look at the market and determine if there are particular market requirements that must be met or potential market opportunities that can be exploited via your proposed solutions. These all help align the IT project to the business and market, which will make them easier to support and defend down the road if the going gets tough. These are all elements that can and should go into a project proposal if you're developing one, so this data will be put to good use.

Next, you should develop your target scope, time, cost, and quality metrics or definitions. Often these are assigned with a project. If they're not, you may need to discuss these elements with your project sponsor before you try to rank your potential solutions. For instance, if the project sponsor says that time is the most critical element and the project must be completed in less than four weeks, then any potential solution that you can intelligently estimate taking more than four weeks would be placed at the bottom of the priority list. Notice we placed them at the bottom of the list rather than tossing them aside. Things change and your sponsor might come back and say, "Well, maybe eight weeks at the most if you have a better idea." You'll be ready with a few alternatives.

Target scope, time, cost, and quality can be difficult to estimate, but often your project sponsor has a good idea on these targets. It's rare that a project is handed to you with absolutely no preconceived notion of duration and cost, though it does happen. If there are no set targets, then you can prioritize your potential solutions based on the approach that seems most *logical, feasible, desirable,* and *affordable* (see Chapter 2 for more on this). Logical, feasible, and desirable are all inexact labels based on judgment calls made by your and your team. However, in the absence of other, more exact criteria for your project, these may be good substitutes. Affordable is also a judgment call but it's usually a bit easier to determine for each potential solution. It's relatively easy to discern the difference in affordability between advertising in a few trade publications versus advertising during the Super Bowl.

Ranking Your List

Once you have developed your ranking criteria, you should rank each potential solution. You may find that a weighted ranking system works better than a simple ranking system. For instance, one or more criteria may be far more important than several other criteria. You may choose to assign a value of 5 for each important criteria and a value of 1 for other criteria. Each potential solution can then be ranked according to several criteria and the solution(s) that have the highest overall score should be those that meet the most critical criteria. Whatever ranking system you use, make sure it's clear, concise, and that everyone doing the ranking has the same understanding of the system.

Selecting Your Solution

If you have been able to create a ranked list of all potential solutions, the best solution(s) should be at or near the top of the list. Of course, there's nothing like a little human intelligence to optimize results, so if your ranked list doesn't seem to match the reality of the situation, you and your team should take steps to figure out why the ranking system didn't identify the optimal solution. If you and the team believe there is an optimal solution that is not at the top of the list, you can and should examine both your assumptions and your ranking criteria to make sure you're not just trying to promote the politically correct solution. It's possible that in some cases, you will still have to go with the politically correct solution, but you should at least know whether or not that solution is the best one.

Once you have identified Figure 5.6's optimal solution (and, unfortunately, we'll include the politically correct or *required* solution in here as well), you should identify the target scope, time, cost, and quality for that solution. Your next step is going to be to bring the problem, mission, and selected solution to your project sponsor for approval, so make sure you've got all the supporting data you'll need to back up your decision, especially if it differs from what was assigned. If that's the case, go back and review Chapters 2 and 3 to make sure you're ready to deal with the business and political realities in your company.

Figure 5.6 Optional Solution Identified

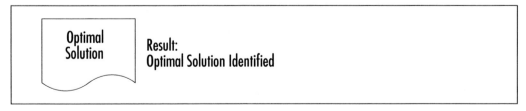

Applying Your Knowledge

Select the optimal solution. Once you've listed all potential solutions that address both the problem *and* mission statement, you can narrow down your choices to the most optimal solutions. Ranking them in order based on defined criteria can help, especially if more than one solution appears to be feasible. If you don't know enough about the project constraints at this point (budget, timeline, etc.), you can bring this ranked list to your project sponsor for discussion and/or approval. Keep in mind that too much information can slow the process to a halt, so you may want to limit your ranked list to the top three solutions and capture the other potential solutions in an appendix or separate document. This way your project sponsor can choose from among the best three solutions based on the research you and your team have done rather than rehash the entire list of potential solutions.

Developing the Project Proposal

Earlier in the chapter, we listed the ideal elements for a project proposal. If you were handed a proposal to validate or if you were developing one from scratch, you now should have enough preliminary information to develop your project proposal. Let's review the list one more time:

- Business case
- Financial analysis
- Market factors or requirements
- High-level scope and requirements
- Assumptions and exclusions
- High-level resources
- High-level schedule
- Success criteria
- Risks
- Alternatives
- Recommendations

In Chapter 2, we discussed the importance of aligning IT projects with corporate strategy and for making the business case for your projects. Here's where it comes into play. If after looking at the problem and desired outcome(s), if after listing all potential solutions and developing either a ranked list or a selected solution, if after all of that you can't make a business case for the project, you need to rethink your direction. Granted, you may not be in a position to change or cancel the project, but you will be in a position to discuss the potential problems with your project sponsor. Throughout this book, we'll continue to discuss ideal scenarios and best practices, not because we're unaware of the real world, but because we want to create an opportunity for you to grow and learn and hopefully create these best practices out there in the real world.

In some cases, you need to get the project up, running, and completed in a very short amount of time. This can occur for numerous reasons, but typically it's because there is some opportunity that someone wants to capture before it goes away. While it's not an ideal situation, it's certainly common in the corporate world. If you're pressed to get a project underway very quickly or you know that certain data will be seen as extraneous, bothersome, or presenting it would be considered an act of insubordination, you can create an abbreviated project proposal. In those instances, you can instead create a project proposal that includes:

- Purpose of the project

- High-level scope (what *is* and *is not* included)

- Target schedule

- Target resources

- Target budget

Clearly, if you create an abbreviated proposal, you're missing the opportunity to ensure the project aligns with corporate strategy (the business case). You're also missing the opportunity to identify market requirements that might impact or influence the project. You're missing a lot of opportunities to clearly identify the project, but sometimes you just have to get the job done and do as you're told. If you aren't going to develop a full-fledged project proposal, make sure you at least cover the basics because this will be the foundation of the project as well as the basis for determining project success. As you read subsequent chapters of this book, you'll gain the skills to develop the remaining data for the project proposal. We'll discuss target schedule, resources, and budget in more detail.

If you do not have all the information you need to develop a solid project proposal, especially the more thorough version listed earlier that includes business case and financial analysis among others, don't worry. In the next chapter, we're going to continue to develop our project plan and define some of these additional elements.

In some companies, you're expected to justify the business case or show the cost/benefit of the project long before you've had a chance to develop project details. It's difficult to develop the project budget (which describes the cost of the project in the cost/benefit analysis) before you've defined all the work that has to go into the project. At the same time, you can't just expect to be handed a blank check for this yet-to-be defined project. So you have a bit of a dilemma. Let's take a minute to discuss estimating at this point in the project lifecycle.

Creating Estimates

At this point in the project planning process, you really only have a wild guess about what the project will cost and how long it will take unless it's similar to projects you've done in the past. Therefore, any estimate you toss out at this point would really be a guess, so informal or ballpark estimates are usually a waste of time at best and potentially dangerous at worst. You can really tank your reputation by consistently tossing out bad estimates, so try to avoid this whenever possible.

When you need to create a more formal estimate for your project proposal, you can do so in a number of ways. Again, your estimate will still be just that—an estimate—until you actually break down the work into recognizable tasks (we'll do that in Chapter 9). The estimate you'll create at this point should get you closer to reality and will often be used as a *go/no go* decision point.

Elements of a Formal Estimate

For an initial, high-level estimate, you should include three key elements:

1. A list of assumptions that were used to create the estimate. This might include what is included and excluded and other assumptions that would impact scope, time, cost, or quality.

2. A range of variance for the estimate. How far off could you reasonably be? Sometimes you're so uncertain that your variance might be 100%, other times you might be reasonably confident (especially if it's similar to another project you've done) and the variance might be as low as 20% or 30%.

3. A time period for which the estimate is valid. Obviously, an estimate created today will likely be completely invalid in three or six months due to changes in technology, staffing, and market costs. Make sure you attach an expiration date to your estimate so it doesn't come back to haunt you eight months later.

Developing an Estimate

If you have any historical data you can use in your estimating process, this is the best place to start. Historical data can help you not only determine costs more closely, but can also help you review variances and problems that impacted similar projects in the past. For instance, if a similar project was bogged down because it depended on one technical "guru" who is in constant demand and this current project requires the same resource, you'll need to either build in extra time to work around this expert's schedule or build in extra cost to hire an external expert.

It's also important to understand that the closer you get to actually starting the project work itself, the more reliable your estimate will be. At each point in the project plan lifecycle, your confidence in estimates should increase. For example, at *this* point in the project planning process, your confidence in any estimates is (and should be) fairly low. Once you've fully developed functional and technical requirements for the project, your confidence in your revised estimates should increase significantly. Once you create the work breakdown structure (WBS) for your project, your revised estimate should become your target. It is at that point you will have to (and should) commit to your estimates and these become your goals or targets for the project.

In some cases, it's impossible to know how long one phase of a project will take until you have more confidence in your estimates for an earlier phase. In larger projects, phased estimating is often used to continually refine the project estimates because as each phase is better defined, the confidence in those estimates increases and provides input data for later phase estimating. There are three commonly used methods of developing cost estimates that might be helpful for you: *parametric, bottom-up* and *top-down*.

- **Parametric Estimates** A parametric estimate uses the *parameters* of other, similar projects as the basis for the estimate. These often are broken down into recognizable units such as cost per unit or labor hours per unit. If you can determine, for instance, the prior cost per user and you know how many users you'll have in this project, you can determine the estimated total cost. If you also know the total time per user, you can multiply the number of users and the total time to determine the estimated schedule. This is most useful when you've done other similar projects in the recent past.

- **Bottom-up Estimates** Bottom-up estimating is the most time consuming method of estimating, but it is also the most accurate. The biggest problem with bottom-up estimating at this point in your project planning process is that you don't have enough detail to create a bottom-up estimate.

In fact, you typically create a bottom-up estimate based on information developed from your WBS and you aren't ready to create your WBS yet. When you do develop estimates from your WBS data, you really will be closer to targets (what you'll be committed to achieving) rather than estimates. To create a bottom-up estimate, you figure out the time and cost for every project task (which is determined from the WBS, covered in Chapter 9) and add up it all up. Very accurate, very time-consuming, and not usually helpful for these early-stage estimates.

■ **Top-down Estimates** Top-down estimates rely upon historical data from past projects, so if you've never done a similar project before, you cannot use top-down estimating. It starts with an estimate for the entire project then assigns a portion to each phase. For instance, you might start with a project total of $100,000 and estimate that, based on historical data, design is 10% of the total (cost), planning is 20%, and so forth. You could do this for time *and* cost estimates. This is not a particularly accurate estimating technique unless you are confident in the total cost of the project and you have historical data to help you determine the breakdown.

Enterprise 128 …

Elevator Estimates

Be very careful when asked for project estimates, whether you're riding in the elevator or passing in the hallways. "Elevator estimates" are almost always taken at face value; the word "estimate" seems to disappear and any estimate you gave becomes "fact." Suddenly, the number you casually tossed out to the executive pressing you for "just a ballpark estimate" becomes the target. To avoid this, prepare and practice a standard response such as, "We really haven't figured out an estimate yet, we're still trying to determine how much work needs to be done." If pressed, you may have to come up with a number but there's danger here too. Guesstimate too high and you could blow a perfectly good project right out of the water ("We can't afford to do that!"); guesstimate too low and you will more than likely be stuck with that estimate. In some cases, you can hedge your risk by saying, "Well, we've *guessed* that it's going to be around $80,000 and take about 14 weeks, but it could vary by 75% or more." Essentially, you've given yourself a lot of room by using the word "guess" instead of "estimate" (this often gets people's attention) and you also gave a possible variance of 75% (though

Continued

this often isn't *heard* clearly). If at all possible, simply say, "We just don't know yet. I'll get back to you with an estimate." Remember that estimating is part science and part art and your skills will get better over time and with experience.

Developing time estimates can be similar to cost estimates, though there are a few other concepts that will help you develop better time estimates.

- **Effort versus Duration** Some people get confused between effort and duration and it's vitally important to understand when creating time estimates. *Effort* is the actual amount of work required to complete a task. *Duration* is how long you'll allow for the completion of that task. Here's an example. You might know that it takes 1.5 hours to set up a new desktop computer for a user. However, you also know that your IT staff have many other tasks to complete during any given day. Rather than scheduling that task as a 1.5-hour task (we'll talk more about scheduling later in the book), you might give it a 1 day duration. That means that anytime within that day, the tech will have to find 1.5 hours to set up that desktop computer. Now, you might actually have that tech scheduled to do 14 other things that day, but setting up that computer must be completed during that 1-day time frame. That's a duration of 1 day for an effort of 1.5 hours. If you start scheduling for effort rather than duration, you'll find your schedule gets out of whack very quickly. The same goes for estimating. Use duration, based on your assumptions about effort, to build time estimates.

- **First Time/First Use Penalty** Remember the last time you tried to upgrade a software package or install a new server for the first time? It took far longer than subsequent upgrades or installations. There's always a first time/first use learning curve and this should be taken into account if you're working on a project that is unlike anything you've done in the past. While you may not be able to quantify this, you might be able to look back on other times you've had to do something for the first time and get a feel for how much extra time you should allow for a first time/first use type of project.

- **Schedule versus Resource-Driven Projects** Some projects are schedule-driven, meaning that the overriding constraint or "must have" is a final delivery date. Other projects are resource-driven, meaning the overriding constraint is the availability of resources. As you can probably tell, these two are fairly different types of projects. A schedule-driven project means it must be completed at a particular point in time and therefore you'll need to schedule resources in a way that gets the project done on time. Scheduling a resource-driven project means that you'll have to work around availability issues with various resources and this often means the project may take longer to complete. Understanding which it the overriding constraint on your IT project will help you develop better estimates.

- **Milestones** We'll discuss milestones in more detail later, but for the purposes of time estimating, they can be helpful if you know of any milestones in advance. For instance, you might estimate the time each phase of a project will take and create milestones for each phase. You might also have external constraints that will impact your project schedule and you may want to include those. If your project relies on a new version of a software application that is supposed to be released in May, you may set a milestone in May for that event. If the software application isn't released until July, that will delay your scheduled completion date. Milestones can help you look at the calendar with a mile-high view that can be helpful in determining high-level schedules and time estimates. You can also sometimes work your way backward from a particular milestone to get an idea of when something must start or be completed.

Cheat Sheet...

IT Project Proposals

There are many elements that may come into play in an IT project proposal. At this stage of the process, you want to stick to high-level elements such as the problem and mission statements, the proposed solution, the high level scope, and information related to how the IT project aligns with corporate and/or IT strategies. You probably don't have enough detail at this point to actually get into more detail, but if there are details you know you want to include in your project, you can mention them briefly in the project proposal or keep a separate document with these reminders so you can include them later in the project. Examples of items that might not belong in this initial project proposal that you'd want to include later might be critical user data or requirements, special factors related to resource cost or availability, a statement of work, or elements of a client contract. All of these things are important to the project, but unless they are critical for determining the initial project parameters (discussed throughout this chapter), you may want to keep things simple and not include them in the project proposal. If your company has a very formal project proposal process, all of these added details may be appropriate.

Figure 5.7 Project Proposal

APPLYING YOUR KNOWLEDGE

Develop the project proposal. If you were handed a project proposal, you should now have most (if not all) of the data you need to validate that proposal. While there may be elements in the proposal, such as market data, that we did not specifically cover in this chapter, you can take time to validate those elements as well. If you were not handed a project proposal to start with, you now have some excellent data at your disposal for creating a thorough project proposal. Once this document is prepared, you should bring it to your project sponsor for approval. This is one of the first and most critical project checkpoints because misunderstandings here will multiply and become more expensive and more difficult to resolve later.

Identifying the Project Sponsor

Throughout this chapter, we've mentioned the project sponsor. At the outset of the chapter, we defined the project sponsor as the person to whom you must go to get formal and informal approval for project parameters such as the project proposal, the cost, time, and other details of the project. Sometimes the project sponsor is your manager, sometimes the project sponsor it an executive higher up in the company. Sometimes, though less often, you are both the project sponsor and the project manager. However, for the purposes of our discussion, we're assuming there is another person to whom you must go to get approval for various elements of the project.

The project sponsor is also the person who will defend the project if it gets into political, financial, or other trouble; he or she is the person who (ideally) can rally corporate resources for your project. The project sponsor is typically the person to whom you must go for budget and schedule approval and to sign for or approve "big ticket" items. Finally, the project sponsor can act as your ally to help you keep the project on course and on time. While the project sponsor may or may not be in constant communication with you about the project, there should be a clear line of communication between you and the project sponsor. We'll discuss how to set up some of the communication protocols and procedures in the next chapter.

Why are we discussing this? Because sometimes it's not clear who the project sponsor is and this creates a problem both near and long-term. To whom do you go for clarification? To whom do you go to get approval to spend $10,000 on new equipment required for the project? Typically a project manager will have the authority to spend money or assign resources within certain limits, but the project sponsor is usually the person that approves the overall project proposal, scope, budget, and schedule. It's also important to identify your project sponsor not just because he or she will be signing various requests for resources, but because if the project runs into trouble, you need someone with the authority to back you up. Ensuring you know who your project sponsor is (and that your project sponsor knows he or she is the project sponsor) is critical, so this is as good a time as any to get that squared away.

The IT Factor...

Approaching the Assigned Project's Sponsor

As you know from your experience and from reading the opening pages of this chapter, some projects are assigned from higher up in the organization. Typically, the person that assigns it to you is the project sponsor. You might at first glance think that you should simply take the project and run with it, since it *was* assigned. However, in the *ideal* world of project management, you would step back and go through the exact same steps you would as if you were working on a needs-driven project. While you must be aware of corporate politics and accepted work methods, you should still go through each project step. Here's why. Executives in companies often *rely upon* the project manager to come back and validate the project and/or its parameters. They may rely upon the knowledge, expertise, and skills of the project manager in planning the project (even if they don't specifically say so). If you and the project team go through the project definition stages and determine this is the wrong project, the wrong time, or it's solving the wrong problem, it's your job to say so. The project sponsor may still want you to move forward, but if there is a problem with the project the sponsor is not aware of, it's certainly better to find out now rather than later after hundreds (or thousands) of hours and dollars are spent pursuing a flawed project plan.

Gaining Validated Project Proposal Approval

By now, you have a solid understanding of the purpose of the project. You've done some initial work with a small expert team and you've developed your project's problem and mission statements, you've looked at potential solutions and narrowed down the list to either one selected, optimal solution or a ranked list of the top potential solutions. You've looked at the corporate and IT strategies and determined which solutions make the best business case and which ones support the direction the company is headed. If these don't all add up to the project everyone had in mind, you've got a minor problem to address. It means the results of your project planning thus far don't map with the assigned project or the project proposal or the problem that was identified. That disconnect is important information that shouldn't just be swept under the carpet. Instead, take time with your team and/or your project sponsor to identify the problem. It might be that in the process of looking at that problem you uncovered a fundamental flaw in your thinking (not necessarily you, personally). This is the best time to discover these kinds of issues because you can develop alternatives and solutions now rather than trying to patch together a solution later in the process. Of course, some companies and some executives just don't want to hear it. That's ok. Your job is to validate the project proposal and bring your findings to your project sponsor for approval. If he or she says, in essence, "I don't care about your findings, just do this project in this way," you'll probably have to do that. Be prepared, however, for problems down the road if the best solution is not the one implemented. On the other hand, also keep in mind that corporate executives often have access to information that you may not have and their rationale for moving forward with a project might be very well founded even if you are not privy to the details.

Earlier in the book, we discussed aligning your IT projects with corporate goals and objectives. If you haven't done so, you should also make the business case for your IT project. That might include doing a cost/benefit analysis or a SWOT analysis (strengths, weaknesses, opportunities, and threats) to verify this project is aligned with IT and corporate goals. Since we covered that earlier, we won't repeat it here, but your project proposal ideally will include the business case for the project as well as the other data discussed.

Once you've got all this data assembled, you should compile a project proposal. If you were handed a project proposal, you can modify or revise it as needed based on your team's findings. Documenting and summarizing your process results (problem statement, mission statement, etc.) to this point in a formal project proposal document will help you keep track of what's been done and why so you don't have to revisit this section of work again and again. Write up the project proposal using whatever format your company prefers or requires (visit www.syngress.com/solutions for a project proposal template you can download and use) and set up a time to meet with your project sponsor. If you've included a target for scope (the total amount of work to be accomplished), time, cost, and quality, make it absolutely clear these are *targets* and not *commitments* at this point. Later, after we've developed additional project detail, we will make commitments on these four elements, but for now, without extensive time and research, you should avoid committing to these targets. That may not always be possible, but it should be your goal. One of the big dangers of targets at this point is that they somehow get translated into commitments through the corporate process. Tread carefully here.

Project proposal approval, ideally, should be a signature on a piece of paper or an e-mail stating approval for the proposed project (see Figure 5.8). It's important to have your project sponsor formally agree to the work and assumptions done this far. After all, you should both have some skin in the game. If you have no formal approval here, it's possible the project sponsor might not back you up if things get political or the project goes south at a later date. Formal approval makes both the project manager and the project sponsor responsible for the project. There are numerous approval points we'll discuss in the project planning and project managing phases and each is important. However, every company has different ways of dealing with these types of activities and if you suddenly show up with a pen and paper for someone to sign when that's not how your company does business, you're going to either get some very strange looks or create a bit of paranoia. Use your best judgment, but do get formal approval in writing (paper or electronically) at each approval point whenever possible.

One last comment here. Sometimes a project makes it to this point and is scrapped. That's why the diagram shown at the opening (and end) of this chapter (refer to Figure 5.1 or Figure 5.9) shows the small oval that says "Terminate project." Sometimes you can't validate the project, other times factors have changed significantly causing you (and/or your project sponsor) to decide to scrap the project or put it on hold. So, sometimes you'll move ahead with a project at this point, sometimes you'll need to go back and rework things and sometimes you'll agree it's time to leave this project behind and move on. If you believe the project still has merit, you'll need to negotiate and make a convincing argument. Otherwise, view a scrapped project as a win—you avoided wasting precious time and resources on a project that should not have proceeded and you've done your job.

Figure 5.8 Validated Project Proposal Approval

APPLYING YOUR KNOWLEDGE

Get approval for your project proposal. Though in some cases you may not develop a project proposal, in most cases you'll at least need to get approval for your project problem and mission statement and selected solution (bare minimum). Ideally, you'll also have a target in mind for the scope, time, cost, and quality of the project and you'll be able to state the business case or show how the project aligns with corporate and IT strategies. Once that's prepared, it's critical to get formal project sponsor approval. Whether in writing or via e-mail, make sure you get the formal OK to move forward with the project as it is currently defined or you could find yourself all alone later if the project runs into problems. Remember that sometimes the project will proceed, sometimes you'll have to go back and revise certain elements, and sometimes you'll just deep-six the whole thing. That's exactly why you go through these steps in the first place—to make sure you're doing the right project(s) at the right time for the right reasons.

Summary

We began the chapter by looking at the IT project management steps that you can use to get a visual idea of where we are in the process. The first step is Defining the Project and we looked at the flowchart that shows the inputs, actions, and outputs. The summary is shown here in Figure 5.9. The documents or data that are the defined results of this step in the project planning process, **Defining the Project**, are shown in Figure 5.10.

Figure 5.9 Summary of Defining the Project Step

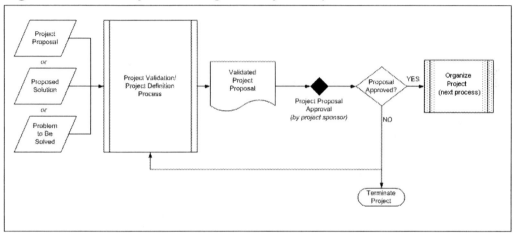

The problem statement identifies the unique problem to be solved by the project. Remember, some problems are better solved by a new or modified process rather than a project.

The mission statement describes the desired outcome. By defining both the problem and the desired outcome, you are essentially describing the gap between where you are and where you want to be. That helps define the potential solutions that will fill that gap.

Developing a list of potential solutions should be an energizing, creative undertaking if possible. Thinking outside the box can help you come up with innovative solutions that might have been missed if you'd simply listed the most logical solutions. Even if the solution has been handed to you or assigned, going through this process will either validate or invalidate that assigned solution so you'll at least know how close or far off the mark this required solution is. This may give you adequate information to go back to the project sponsor and make the case for a different, more optimal solution.

Figure 5.10 Results of Defining the Project

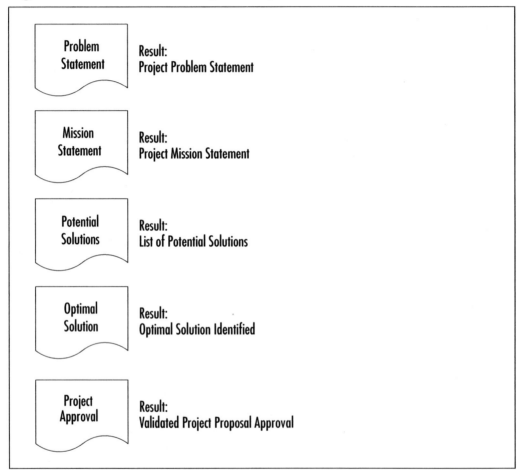

Once you have developed potential solutions, you'll need to rank them according to pre-defined criteria. These criteria vary from company to company, but some include alignment with corporate and IT strategies, alignment with market requirements or needs as well as other criteria. In the absence of formal criteria, you can also look at which solutions are the most logical, feasible, desirable, and afford-able. Once you've created your ranking criteria, you can match your solutions to these criteria and develop a ranked list of potential solutions. The most optimal solution(s) should rise to the top of the list. A bit of human intelligence might be needed to review the list and make sure the results make sense. Select your top choice(s) to submit to your project sponsor for approval or prepare data explaining why the assigned solution is not the optimal solution.

Once you've compiled all this data into a project proposal, you should bring it to your project sponsor for approval. Formal approval, whether in writing or in e-mail, is critical to ensure you and the project sponsor are in agreement about the fundamentals of the project. It's also important to have project sponsor approval in case something in the project goes wrong later. It's more difficult to start pointing fingers when things are clearly spelled out.

Solutions Fast Track

Project Management Process Overview

- ☑ The project management process has seven major steps: define, organize, form the team, plan, manage, track, and close the project.

- ☑ The project management process is iterative. You may have to repeat several steps a number of times in order to clearly define, organize, and manage your project.

- ☑ Sometimes projects are terminated after this process is complete because the data developed during the definition stage does not support moving forward with the project.

- ☑ It's better to terminate a project early before valuable time and resources are committed or expended on a project that, ultimately, is not the right project at the right time.

Project Origins

- ☑ A project, by definition, is a unique solution to a defined problem. Projects can originate from a stated problem. These are needs-driven projects.

- ☑ Sometimes projects originate from a proposed (or assigned) solution. These are solution-oriented projects. These still have to be validated and the underlying problem must still be defined.

☑ Some project managers are handed a project by way of a project proposal. This assumes that some analysis and research has already been done. If a project proposal exists, the project manager should validate the proposal to ensure that the project is still appropriate, feasible, and desirable. Things change rapidly and an old project proposal may be out of date.

Validating the Project Proposal

☑ Whether you're validating a project proposal or beginning the project definition phase, you should form a small team to help you with these initial tasks. Two (or three or four) heads are better than one.

☑ Reviewing the project proposal you've been handed is the first step toward validating the proposal. Gather all related materials so you can properly evaluate the data contained in the proposal.

☑ At minimum, a project proposal should have the problem and mission statement, the optimal or proposed solution, as well as some initial targets including scope, time, cost, and quality.

☑ A more formal project proposal could contain data that makes the business case for the project showing how it aligns with corporate and/or IT strategies, how it addresses a need in the market, or how it addresses a customer/user need.

☑ Each company may have a unique approach or attitude toward a project proposal. Follow your company's guidelines, but make sure you include the basics so you'll know what you're doing and what the project will entail.

☑ If the project cannot be validated, you've either made errors in your research or the project should not be undertaken. Sometimes projects are scrapped at this stage if they cannot be validated.

Defining the Project

☑ The definition phase includes these elements: problem statement, project mission statement, list of potential solutions, selected solution, and project proposal.

☑ A clear, concise problem statement is fundamental to a successful project. Make sure you're solving the right problem with a well-crafted problem statement.

☑ The project mission statement describes the desired outcomes or results, not *how* those results will be achieved. A well-written mission statement can help describe the gap between where you are and where you want/need to be.

☑ The list of potential solutions should begin as a brainstormed list of all potential solutions. Don't filter ideas until all have been recorded.

☑ Develop a list of criteria for the project (if possible) so you can determine optimal solutions. Criteria can include scope, time, cost, quality, market, or user requirements.

☑ Develop a ranked list of potential solutions and select the best fit for both the stated problem and desired outcome(s).

Developing the Project Proposal

☑ Develop a project proposal that outlines the problem, mission, selected solution, and the business case for the project.

☑ Include other project details in the project proposal only if they are known or relevant to making the decision to move forward at this point. Otherwise, capture that data for later use.

☑ Some companies neither require nor desire a formal project proposal. Develop the basic data for your own sake even if a formal process is not in place.

☑ There are numerous methods for creating high-level estimates that you should be familiar with. Some help you develop better cost estimates and others help you develop better time/schedule estimates.

☑ Remember that an estimate is really an educated guess, but it often becomes your project target. Avoid giving estimates until you have the data to support those estimates.

Identifying the Project Sponsor

☑ The person who assigns the project to you is typically the project sponsor.

☑ Ensure you are clear who the project sponsor is and that the project sponsor knows he or she is the project sponsor.

☑ The project sponsor is the person who can rally corporate resources on behalf of your project, approve budgets and timelines, and help you stay on course with your project.

Gaining Validated Project Proposal Approval

☑ Once you have defined the problem, mission, and optimal (or selected) solution, you should formalize this data in a project proposal.

☑ A project proposal can be short or long, formal or informal, but it should capture at least the essential elements.

☑ Sometimes the project manager and project sponsor may forgo a more lengthy or formal project proposal in favor of taking immediate action on an opportunity. The project manager and small team should still take time to define the project (problem and mission statement, potential and selected solutions) to both validate the fast action and to ensure everyone is headed in the same direction.

☑ These initial definition steps can be performed very quickly with a small, focused team.

☑ A project proposal, ideally, should be presented to the project sponsor for formal approval. This is the first of many checkpoints in the IT project management process that we'll discuss.

☑ Formal project approval is important to ensure that the assumptions under which you're operating are correct, that you and the project sponsor agree on the basic project data and direction, and to assure you that you're covered later on if the project runs into trouble.

Frequently Asked Questions

The following Frequently Asked Questions, answered by the author of this book, are designed to both measure your understanding of the concepts presented in this chapter and to assist you with real-life implementation of these concepts. To have your questions about this chapter answered by the author, browse to **www.syngress.com/solutions** and click on the **"Ask the Author"** form.

Q: We've never used a formal project management process in our company. It seems like this will be an uphill battle.

A: Remember that throughout this chapter and this book, we're describing best practices and ideal circumstances (except where noted). Clearly, many companies use little or no formal project management processes. Some would argue that things are running quite well, but if they were to take time to examine results, they'd probably see results that track with the statistics given earlier in this book (low project success rates). If you're the IT project manager, you can begin by going through these steps yourself or with a small team. If your company is resistant to these processes, you'll have to slowly educate those around you (including those higher up) as to the benefits of taking time to plan. The information presented earlier in this book should give you ample data to present your case and even if it falls on deaf ears, your improved IT project results will, over time, win over the doubters. Yes, it may be an uphill battle, but implement as many of these steps and processes as possible and your project results will absolutely be better than without.

Q: I'm an IT project manager and I'm interested in getting better project results. I just can't realistically see me or my team implementing all of these steps— like writing a project proposal—that would never fly. Any comment?

A: One of the best parts of a simple, straightforward IT project management methodology, like the one presented in this book, is that you can use it in any way that suits you. While it's true that you will get far better results from implementing the entire methodology, it's also true that you can improve any project you're working on by implementing even just one part of the IT PM process. For instance, you will find better results simply by clearly stating the problem or by brainstorming other potential solutions besides the one you were assigned. Some people find that implementing a new process one piece at a time suits their style or the company's style better—that's fine. The key is to make continuous improvement. Start by implementing one step that will have the greatest impact on your projects. Once that's completely incorporated into your process, pick another step. Don't be overly concerned with perfectly implementing an entire new process or methodology if that's not your style. And, if you have any of those *analyst* types we discussed in Chapter 4, now's the time to get them involved.

Q: I'm often handed a project with the scope, time, cost, and quality elements already pre-defined. You mentioned how to validate the project, but can you provide more advice on how to "push back" within the organization. My boss (who is usually the project sponsor) believes he has already done adequate research when he hands these projects to me.

A: Your situation is actually pretty common and if you can learn to deal with this situation effectively, you'll make real gains in improving project results. We'll discuss these four elements in more detail later in the book, but in terms of your approach to your project sponsor, it will be important to understand the environment. You might begin by reviewing past projects on your own and comparing required results (the ones your boss handed to you) to actual results. Chances are extremely high that these assigned projects' parameters (scope, time, cost, quality) have rarely, if ever, been met. Sure, you might have met a timeline if that was most important, but that probably meant you ran over on the budget or had to cut the scope. If that's the case, you can begin to look at where and how these projects varied from the required parameters. Then, you might have an opportunity to sit down with your boss and discuss these variances. Unless your boss is the type to say something like, "These projects were just never well managed," you should have the opportunity to gain agreement on the things you, your boss, and your IT team can do differently in the future to ensure the projects are more successful. If you don't try to do *something* differently, you'll just keep generating the same results. It's entirely possible that the time or cost overruns that happened on past projects is simply an acceptable and expected way of doing business in your company. If that's the case, you can learn these IT project management steps and implement them, even if you don't have formal approval of the various elements. If that ends up being the case, you can still create the information and data for the project and simply not bring them through the formal approval process if that's going to create more problems than it solves. Ideally, your boss will begin to see better results and will be more open to changes later on. Better results can be very convincing and worst case, you'll be a better IT project manager even if your boss never changes.

Q: Our company had a big push a few years back to implement IT project management and it basically failed. After spending hundreds of hours and thousands of dollars on training and methodologies and the like, everyone basically went back to doing things the way they'd always done them. I think IT PM is a great idea, in theory, but I'm having difficulty figuring out how we'd get this going in my company. Any suggestions?

A: You describe a very common scenario. Changing habits and behaviors is not an easy thing to do. Psychologists and behaviorists will all tell you that the best way to make lasting change is in small increments. Large, wholesale changes rarely take hold, though in some cases you do need to shake things up completely to break out of old patterns. Your company made an attempt to do something different, but it didn't stick for one of two reasons (well, there may be others, but these are the top two). Either the methodology was so radically different from how you currently did things that no one could implement the entire system successfully or there was lack of support for this change at the top of the organization. Lack of support can take on various appearances. For instance, if top executives never expected or required a project proposal before heading into a new project, then eventually project proposals stop being created. This lack of support for the new process eventually leads back to old behaviors and patterns. If you're trying to implement change in your organization now, you have a doubly tough task because you have the added burden of hearing "We tried that before and it didn't work." Instead of trying for wholesale change, pick one thing and do it differently. Small changes are often more manageable and once they take hold, you can move on to the next change. Take this process step by step. For instance, you might simply begin by crafting clear problem statement for every project that comes your way. Once everyone accepts that projects begin with a problem statement, you can begin trying to get everyone to come up with a mission statement by asking what the desired outcomes are for the project. Jamming an entirely new system down your team or company's throat without strong executive support is often the least effective approach, so start with small steps.

Q: We learned about defining the project in this chapter, but isn't there more to defining a project than just identifying the problem, mission, and solution?

A: Yes, there is and you'll learn about additional elements of project planning in the next chapter. At this point, you do have your project defined—meaning you know what problem it is trying to solve, what mission it is trying to accomplish, and what the potential solutions and optimal solution are. That's a pretty clear starting point and one from which we can now build. In Chapter 6, we'll develop more detail project information.

Chapter 6

Organizing IT Projects

Solutions in this chapter:

- **Identifying Project Objectives**
- **Identifying Stakeholders**
- **Identifying Project Requirements**
- **Refining Project Parameters**
- **Defining Project Infrastructure**
- **Defining Project Processes**

☑ **Summary**

☑ **Solutions Fast Track**

☑ **Frequently Asked Questions**

Introduction

In Chapter 5, you learned how to validate a project proposal that was assigned to you and to develop a high-level definition of an IT project. In this chapter, we're going to continue along that same line, adding detail and organizing the project as well. As you know, IT project management (IT PM) is an iterative process and you'll revisit various steps more than once. It's also true that in many instances, IT PM steps occur concurrently or out of order. For instance, it's possible that during the high-level definition stage, you also developed additional project definitions and data that we'll discuss in this chapter. While there is a logical flow to the IT PM steps, in the real world things don't always follow an ideal order. The key is to properly define and organize your IT project before you start actually doing the work of the project, whenever possible.

If a project is in trouble, the steps we're going to discuss in this chapter are often the ones that were skipped. If you're taking over a project, especially one that's flirting with disaster, go back and review or verify the steps listed in Chapter 5 and this chapter. You need not do all the steps with the same rigor or with the same level of detail, but you should verify these steps were performed and performed correctly if you're working on a project that is faltering. You should also review the conclusions and decisions made if the project is in trouble because it's often here that trouble begins (usually by skipping these important preliminary steps).

In this chapter, we're going to develop a bit more project detail including elements such as priorities, specifications, user requirements, and project infrastructure, to name just a few. Before we get into the details, let's review our IT project management overview diagram, shown in Figure 6.1, to keep track of where we are and where we're headed.

Figure 6.1 IT Project Management Process Overview

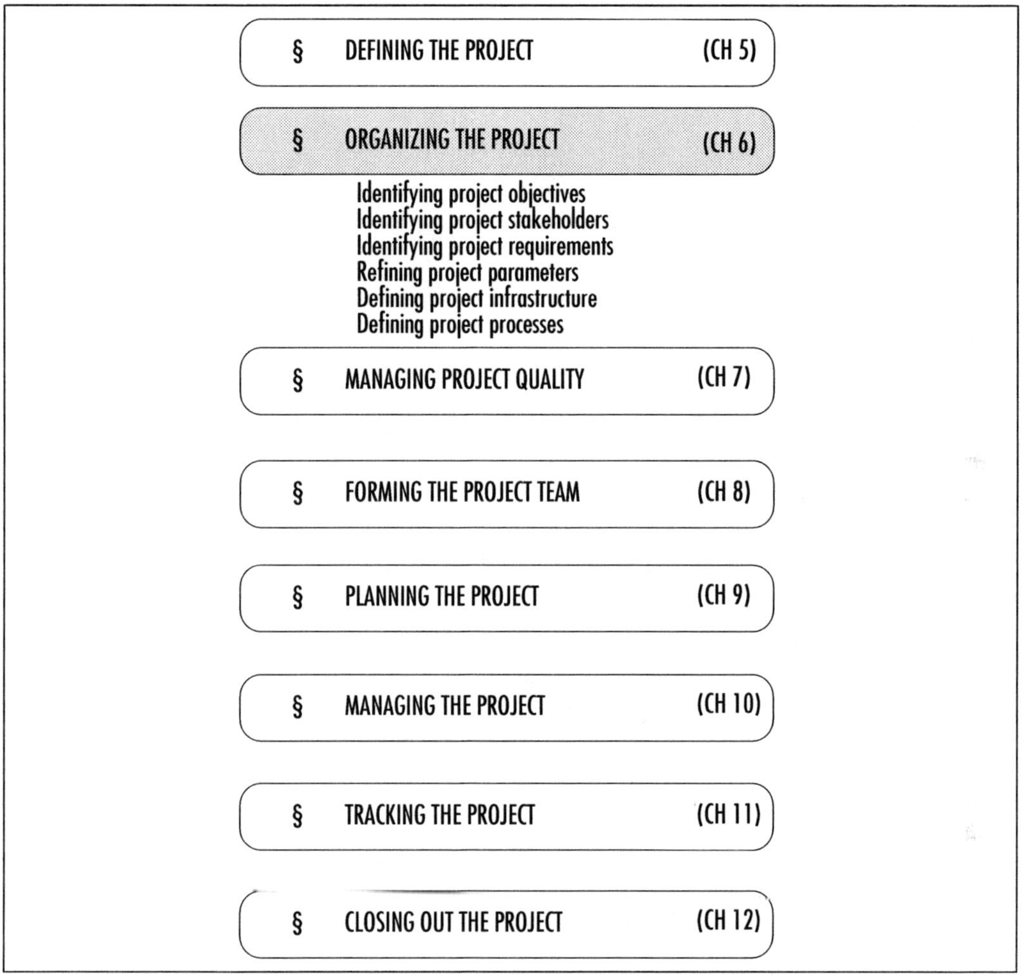

```
┌─────────────────────────────────────────────────────────────┐
│         ╭──────────────────────────────────────────╮         │
│         │  §    DEFINING THE PROJECT        (CH 5)  │         │
│         ╰──────────────────────────────────────────╯         │
│                                                              │
│         ╭──────────────────────────────────────────╮         │
│         │  §    ORGANIZING THE PROJECT      (CH 6)  │         │
│         ╰──────────────────────────────────────────╯         │
│                 Identifying project objectives               │
│                 Identifying project stakeholders             │
│                 Identifying project requirements             │
│                 Refining project parameters                  │
│                 Defining project infrastructure             │
│                 Defining project processes                   │
│                                                              │
│         ╭──────────────────────────────────────────╮         │
│         │  §    MANAGING PROJECT QUALITY    (CH 7)  │         │
│         ╰──────────────────────────────────────────╯         │
│                                                              │
│         ╭──────────────────────────────────────────╮         │
│         │  §    FORMING THE PROJECT TEAM    (CH 8)  │         │
│         ╰──────────────────────────────────────────╯         │
│                                                              │
│         ╭──────────────────────────────────────────╮         │
│         │  §    PLANNING THE PROJECT        (CH 9)  │         │
│         ╰──────────────────────────────────────────╯         │
│                                                              │
│         ╭──────────────────────────────────────────╮         │
│         │  §    MANAGING THE PROJECT        (CH 10) │         │
│         ╰──────────────────────────────────────────╯         │
│                                                              │
│         ╭──────────────────────────────────────────╮         │
│         │  §    TRACKING THE PROJECT        (CH 11) │         │
│         ╰──────────────────────────────────────────╯         │
│                                                              │
│         ╭──────────────────────────────────────────╮         │
│         │  §    CLOSING OUT THE PROJECT     (CH 12) │         │
│         ╰──────────────────────────────────────────╯         │
└─────────────────────────────────────────────────────────────┘
```

Now that you see where we are in the process, let's define a few terms we'll be using in this chapter.

- **Assumptions** The information and concepts that are assumed to be true (or false) at the outset of the planning phase of the project. Clearly identifying relevant assumptions can be helpful in avoiding mistakes later in the project.

- **Customer or user** A customer or user is defined here as anyone who will use or rely upon the output of the project. Customers/users can be internal or external, existing (current), or targeted (desired).

- **Derived requirements** The requirements that are *derived* or come from primary requirements of the project. They may be additional technical requirements that stem from stakeholder requirements.

- **Flexibility matrix** A matrix or grid indicating the relative flexibility of project scope, schedule, and resources. This is used as a decision-making tool to help the team make appropriate decisions throughout the project management process. Schedule-driven projects have the least flexibility in the schedule, for example.

- **Framework** The processes and procedures your project and project team will use to successfully implement and manage the project.

- **Major deliverables** This term is used interchangeably with *objectives* to indicate the high-level outcomes for the project.

- **Objectives** High-level statements about what the project will accomplish. These are typically *categories* of work to be accomplished in the project. This can also be called *major deliverables*.

- **Precision** The term precision will be used interchangeably with *rigor*. How precisely you execute each step of the project management process will depend greatly on the complexity, expense, and criticality of the project.

- **Project organization** The team that will be involved in the project including the project manager, project sponsor, core project team, and contributor team.

- **Project parameters** The defining of the project objectives, scope, budget, timeline, quality, success criteria, flexibility grid, and deliverables. This may also include hardware or software boundaries or requirements that set the minimum criteria for project expectations.

- **Requirements** The elements the project must deliver to meet the expectations of the stakeholder(s) and project sponsor. Also called *primary requirements*.

- **Rigor** Rigor, or *precision,* is used to define how much or how little detail and effort you apply in each step or phase. Very rigorous planning is required for complex, expensive, or critical projects. Less rigor is often acceptable for shorter, more "casual" projects.

- **Stakeholder** Anyone with a stake, or interest, in the outcome of the project. This typically includes those people outside of the project including the project sponsor, users, customers, vendors, corporate executives, and/or shareholders. Although the project management and project team have an interest in the outcome of the project, they are internal to the project and are usually excluded from the collective term *stakeholder* as it pertains to project outcomes.

- **Success criteria** The clear, concise, accurate statements that indicate how the team, project sponsor, and organization will know that the project is successful.

As we did in Chapter 5, we also have a flowchart for the inputs, actions, and outputs of this phase of the IT project planning process. Figure 6.2 depicts these elements. If you're not a flowchart kind of person, don't be put off by these diagrams. They are intended to simply help you visualize the process we'll describe in this chapter.

Figure 6.2 IT Project Organizing Phase

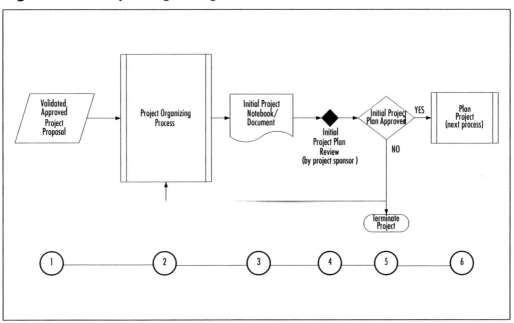

Within the *Organizing the Project* step or phase, there are six discrete steps. Let's discuss each one briefly so you know what the inputs, actions, and outputs are for this phase.

1. **INPUT** The input in this case is the validated, approved project proposal, which was the output from the previous step (see Chapter 5). If your organization does not use a formal project proposal, you should at least have the data collected during the defining stage of the process, which includes the problem statement, mission statement, potential solutions, selected solution, target scope, target timeline, target budget, and target quality.

2. **ACTION** Using your project proposal (or equivalent data) as the starting point, we'll go into the project organizing process described in this chapter. This process is a defined set of steps you'll use that will result in a more detailed project document. It is at this point that the project should begin to take form. You should have key data compiled and you should create a formal method for storing this data. You should also have defined the ways in which you and your team will work with the project sponsor.

3. **OUTPUT** The output from this phase or step is a formalized system or method of storing project data. This is referred to as the *project notebook, project workbook,* or *high-level project plan*, and it can be in the form of a physical notebook, a virtual notebook containing files stored in a folder on a shared network drive, or files stored using your company's collaboration tools (Lotus Notes, Microsoft SharePoint, corporate intranet, etc.). Regardless of the form it takes, there should be a formal document storage process in place before you go on to the next phase.

4. **CHECKPOINT** All the high-level data should be approved by the project sponsor at this point. This includes the project objectives, parameters, and stakeholders, among others. In some projects, this step may not be necessary, but typically you should gain agreement from your project sponsor on the content and frequency of project checkpoints moving forward.

5. **DECISION POINT** Based on the response of your project sponsor, you'll either need to go back and re-work parts of your project documentation or continue on to the next step, planning your project. If the sponsor gives the project the go ahead, you continue. If not, you will have to address the project sponsor's specific concerns and revise the project parameters and submit it for approval again. This may be an iterative process where you'll need to make several revisions before the project sponsor agrees to the document. It's also possible that based on the information gathered thus far, the project sponsor (or project manager) recommends terminating the project. This can occur if it becomes clear that with the additional data provided that the project just doesn't make sense. A project

can (and should) be cancelled at any point before actual work begins if the project parameters shift or if the external environment shifts in such a way that the project no longer makes sense.

6. **NEXT STEP** Once you have approval from the project sponsor for the additional project details developed in this stage, you can move on to the detailed project *planning* process. These steps are discussed in Chapter 7.

Cheat Sheet...

Defining and Organizing Your IT Project

In Chapter 5 and in this chapter, we're discussing ways to define and organize your project before you get into the detailed planning stage. The reason for this is because if you don't properly define what you're going to do, the detailed planning may either have to be redone or your project may ultimately address the wrong problem or provide a "useless" solution. Through these stages, you not only get a good idea of what the project will look like, but you have a great opportunity to get feedback from the project sponsor. Changes are very easy to make at this stage and if you can define the project clearly and concisely at this point, your detailed planning stage will be a lot easier. Lack of clearly defined project goals and objectives are a major cause of project failure, so success starts here.

Keep in mind that if you have a small project, you can abbreviate these steps and phases. You shouldn't skip any of these steps, but you can shorten them. For instance, on a small, two-week project, you may write up a one-page project proposal that identifies the problem, mission, solution, target scope, budget, and timeline. You should be able to generate this document in under 30 minutes. The project sponsor can approve this document and you can move on to the organizing and planning stages quickly. A short, easy project requires far less detail and far less structure than a large, complex project, though the steps you take each project through should always be the same. Remember, process for process' sake is a waste of time, but having a defined process or methodology that you can expand or shrink as needed will make your planning more consistent and your projects more successful.

Identifying Project Objectives

In Chapter 5, you defined the project mission statement, which was a statement of the desired outcome(s) for the project. You also selected the best solution based on various parameters. Based on both the desired outcome and the solution selected, you can now begin to define or identify several high-level project objectives. These objectives should identify *what* you want to accomplish, not necessarily *how* you're going to accomplish it. However, you will also begin to identify, at a high level, how you'll accomplish this project. The details of how to accomplish your project's objectives are discussed in detail in the next chapter.

Project Objective Statement

The first step in identifying project *objectives* or *major deliverables* is to create a project objective statement. It's similar to the project mission statement, but it should be much more specific to your project because it should incorporate the problem, the mission, and the selected solution (see Chapter 5). Here's a great rule of thumb about creating any of these statements (problem, mission, or objective): if you can't state it clearly and concisely (50 words or so) you probably don't have a good understanding of what the project is trying to accomplish. Again, this doesn't need to take days or weeks to accomplish, but if you can't describe the high-level objectives or deliverables quickly and in 50 words or less, you may need to revisit some of the steps in Chapter 5. For example, "Replace all servers used in the Marketing department with new servers to provide improved response time, reliability, and security with all new equipment in place no later than December 31, 2005." This begins to describe your *approach* to the project based on the parameters you've defined.

Project Objectives or Major Deliverables

Once you have your objective statement, you can further refine it by breaking it down into three to five high-level objectives or major deliverables that fit the project problem, mission, and solution. It's good to keep the problem and mission statements in mind when defining project objectives because it's easy to get off course otherwise. These objectives essentially define how you're going to approach the project, so spending time to develop these will help you moving forward.

We limit our objectives to three to five items for two primary reasons. First, if you cannot define your project in terms of five (or fewer) objectives or major deliverables, it's entirely possible the project is too large and should be broken in to several smaller projects. Second, if you cannot define your project's objectives in five or fewer major deliverables, you may be including too much detail in your list of high-level objectives. It's also true that three to five major deliverables may not be enough for your project. If your project demands six or eight or ten major deliverables, that's fine. Just be sure that each of the major deliverables or objectives you define is, in fact, a high-level one. It's very common for people to begin digging down into the project detail when developing objectives. All objectives at this point should define high-level categories. If all of your objectives are not at the same level of detail, you're probably going into detail in one or more areas. Later when you define the activities or tasks under each objective, you will probably delve into differing levels of detail since not all objectives will necessarily have the same level of detail. When defining high-level objectives, though, they should all be at the same level.

Define What IS and IS NOT Included

One exercise that many people find useful is to define what *is* and *is not* included in the project. When you're defining your project's major deliverables, you can begin by stating what the major deliverables are. To avoid confusion and to really help clarify the deliverables, you can also state what your deliverables are not. Other language that can be used to describe this process is to define what is *in scope* and *out of scope* or to define what the project *includes* and *excludes*. Obviously, your project is *not* a lot of things, but we're only concerned here with the things that are related to what your stated objectives are. For instance, if the project is to upgrade the network infrastructure, you might state, "Replace all network servers that were placed in service prior to July 1, 2002." That tells you what server hardware will be replaced, but it doesn't define specifically what hardware will not be replaced. In this case, you might say, "Departmental servers and application servers are not considered network servers and will not be included in this project." If the project is a software upgrade to your company's software product, you might state that, "Critical issues and hot fixes reported since the last release will be included in this project. File export and reporting capabilities upgrades and fixes will not be included."

By stating what is and is not addressed at this point in the project gives you another reality check. If you write all this up and bring it back to your sponsor (as you will do before you exit this phase), your sponsor might or might not agree with what you've stated as included or excluded. It's certainly better to know here that your project sponsor had different expectations or a different view of the project than you and your team did. If your project sponsor assumed that the software upgrade project would absolutely include fixes to the file export functionality and you state that is not part of the project, you've got a great opportunity to modify the project plan before anyone has written a single line of code. It might also be at this point that you begin to notice shifting ideas, plans, priorities, and directives from your project sponsor. Once a project starts taking shape, the project sponsor may realize that the project is not what he or she expected or that other things in the organization or external environment have shifted. That's fine as long as you are able to pin down the project details. If you can't, you will constantly be trying to hit a moving target and it's almost guaranteed that your project will fail to satisfy the sponsor or other stakeholders. If possible, don't leave this stage of project definition and organization until you have these details agreed upon and locked down. It will be harder later on to gain this level of clarity, especially if the project gets underway without these details.

You may have heard the term scope creep or you may have experienced scope creep in your projects. *Scope creep* happens when features and functionality are added without addressing the effects of these changes on the time, cost, or schedule of the project or without customer approval. These are considered uncontrolled changes that expand the scope (total work to be accomplished) of the project. Sometimes this happens through small "innocent" changes being requested and other times it happens through large changes being demanded. In either case, scope creep is one of the most important things to manage during the project and we'll discuss managing scope creep when we discuss managing change later in this book. We discuss it here because by clearly defining what is and is not part of the project, you begin to draw the lines around your project's scope. Doing so helps avoid finger pointing or confusion and helps you also avoid scope creep later on.

As with other steps we've already discussed, this should not take an inordinate amount of time. That said, the amount of time you spend on very clearly defining your project's major deliverables or objectives is time well spent. You may find that this step takes you a bit longer than previous steps took, but the payoff here is significant.

Figure 6.3 Project Objectives

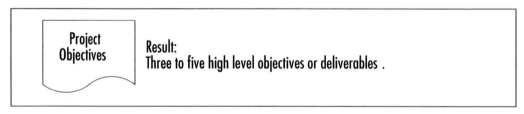

Identifying Stakeholders

Stakeholders are any individuals (sometimes companies or groups, but we'll keep it simple here) who have an interest or stake in the outcome of the project. Typical stakeholders are users, corporate executives, project team members, and the project sponsor. Different stakeholders have different needs, requirements, and expectations, so it's important to identify your various stakeholders early in the project's life. As you move through the definition and organization phases of this IT project management process, you may identify additional stakeholders. Keep in mind that stakeholders usually define (or refine) the project's requirements. Users are those who use or rely upon the project's deliverables, so clearly they have a stake in the project. The company is footing the bill for the project, so clearly corporate executives have a stake in the project's outcome. The project sponsor will be judged upon the success of the project, so clearly the project sponsor is a stakeholder. There are others who can be stakeholders in different circumstances and each company and project is different.

Identifying Your IT Project's Stakeholders

When trying to determine who the stakeholders are, you can ask a series of questions to help you identify stakeholders and to help ensure you don't inadvertently overlook an important stakeholder.

1. Who needs to know about this project?
2. Who will use this project?
3. Who is impacted by the results of this project?
4. Who is impacted by the operations of this project (the actual project itself)?
5. Who is paying for this project?
6. Who is approving this project?
7. Who is delivering this project?
8. Who needs to be trained?
9. Who else should we talk to about this project (what else do we need to know)?

We'll discuss each of these questions very briefly to help clarify exactly how these questions help you identify all potential stakeholders. Remember, though, that there are stakeholders and then there are *stakeholders*—meaning there are many different people or groups you'll identify as stakeholders, but they can then be prioritized into primary, secondary, and tertiary stakeholders. This is important to understand because later in this chapter, we'll discuss how to work with stakeholders to define, refine, and negotiate project requirements.

Who Needs to Know About this Project?

Answering this question helps you identify stakeholders in the company that will be impacted by this project. This could include groups you might not always think about such as Human Resources, Marketing, Sales, and Training to name a few. There may be groups or departments in the company that will be called upon to lend resources to the project. There may be individuals or groups whose activities will be impacted by the project. Another approach to this is to take a look at all the departments in your company (assuming your company isn't too large) and ask if that department will be impacted by your project or if anyone in any of those departments needs to know about your project.

Remember that people will have different information needs. Some individuals or groups will have to be (or should be) brought into the project planning and decision-making loop while others may just need to be notified of the existence of the project. Once you've identified your stakeholders, you can prioritize them, as we'll discuss in just a bit.

Who Will Use this Project?

The results or deliverables for your project are intended for use by someone or some group. You may already know who the users will be (current or existing) or the users may be a target market for a new product that doesn't yet exist. In either case, you will need to identify who will be using the output of this project. Getting user input and developing user acceptance criteria are crucial to the success of the project, so we'll discuss this later in this chapter. The users of the project's output are usually among the most important stakeholders, but they're not the only stakeholders you'll need to address.

Who is Impacted by the Results of this Project?

Understanding who is impacted by the results of the project is also vitally important. For instance, if you're implementing a new payroll system, the users may be the people in Finance and/or Human Resources that will actually use the system, but everyone at your company who gets a paycheck is potentially impacted by the results of this project. Understanding the answer to this question can help you understand how this project will impact your company or your client's company and to plan accordingly.

Who is Impacted by the Operations of this Project (the Actual Project Itself)?

This question may seem to overlap earlier questions in terms of identifying stakeholders and if it does, that's fine. It's better to overlap slightly than to leave large gaps, so you may start finding duplicates on your stakeholder list as you go through these questions. It's a safe bet that if someone (or some group) shows up more than once or twice on the list, the stakeholder group is very important to your project and you should treat it as such.

Understanding who is impacted by the operations of the project can include other departments that may have to lend staff, expertise, time, or other resources to your project. It can also include people whose jobs or processes may be interrupted or impacted when the project is underway. It might include who will be impacted by your project team taking over an office or conference room. Using the payroll example again, the payroll processing clerks will be impacted by this project and they are also part of the user stakeholder group. However, while you're working on the project, you may also need the assistance of accounts payable and accounts receivable clerks in entering test payroll data, verifying payroll test results, etc. While many of these activities may fall under the Quality Assurance department's line of responsibility, they may require the assistance (or resources) of others in the organization that might not normally be involved in the project.

Who is Paying for this Project?

The person paying for the project is clearly a stakeholder. The project might be funded by a client, by a potential client, by a government grant, or by the company (internally, through a departmental or project budget). Regardless of how the project is being funded, someone is going to have to approve the budget and/or project expenditures and that person or group has a vested interest in the outcome of the project. Sometimes project managers forget to take into account the person writing the check unless that person is the project sponsor or part of the user group. This is why we discussed aligning IT projects with corporate objectives earlier in the book. If the IT project is aligned, this stakeholder's needs are likely to be addressed. If the IT project is not aligned, you're probably going to have to spend time addressing this stakeholder's needs in terms of making the business case for the IT project and explaining why the project should be funded and what value it adds.

Who is Approving this Project?

Usually the person(s) paying for the project also approves the project, but not always. Make sure you know who will be approving not only the overall project plan and who will be giving the project the green light, but also know who will be approving the project's deliverables. The project plan may be approved by the project sponsor and the deliverables may be approved by the user, but there may be others such as corporate executives, steering committees, and governmental agencies that may be involved with various project approval points.

Who is Delivering or Implementing this Project?

The delivery or implementation may be part of your project or it might not be. You should be clear about who is delivering or implementing the project. An example of this might be that the software group develops the software, but the client services division actually installs and supports the software installation on the client side. If that's the case, you'd want to make sure your client service's key personnel are in the loop on this project so you can ensure that their installation and support needs are also met by this project. Delivering a software project that no one can install, implement, or use would be pointless.

Who Needs to be Trained?

IT staff rarely deliver training themselves (unless training is part of the IT function in your company) and as such, user training often is neglected. Asking who needs to be trained will help you identify training needs and make plans to address those needs. Sometimes you need to train project staff in a new technology, technique, or process. Sometimes users need to be trained. Even if it is outside the scope of the project, if someone needs to be trained, you've identified another stakeholder (the training department) and you can incorporate this information into your project plan accordingly. Often this is a simple step of adding a task to the project to contact the training department at a certain point to allow them to become familiar with the product or process and develop training materials, etc..

Who Else Should We Talk to About this Project (What Else Do *We* Need to Know)?

Asking "What else do *we* need to know?" can also lead you to additional stakeholders. If you're tasked with updating the payroll system, you may decide you want to map out or understand the current payroll process and to understand the current limitations. While some or all of this may have been discovered or discussed during your initial project discussions (Chapter 5), it's also possible you'll need additional information. Perhaps you've talked with the payroll staff, but you haven't talked with Human Resources staff who interact with payroll and with corporate employees. Perhaps you need to get input from an outside expert such as an attorney, CPA, or consultant before you have all the needed data. There may be legal, financial, or security requirements that necessitate consulting an expert (Sarbanes-Oxley financial data requirements, HIPAA (health care data) or other data security requirements. These are examples of situations that may require notification or inclusion of people you might not normally think of.

You might be thinking that if you ask and answer all these questions, you're going to have about 15,000 stakeholders on your list. Yes and no. Yes, you may generate a long list; but no, you don't have to accept input from every single stakeholder to the same degree. The point of this exercise is to find out as much as you can about who may be a stakeholder and then develop a strategy for managing stakeholders of various kinds.

Prioritizing or Categorizing Stakeholders

It would be impossible for us to specifically define the stakeholders for your projects, but we have defined three of the high-level stakeholders. Some stakeholders should help make key decisions, others may be needed from time to time or may need to be kept in the loop, and still others may just need to know about the project. We're purposely using the term stakeholder loosely here to ensure you notify and involve the right people in the project early on. How you deal with this list you've generated depends largely on the types of stakeholders you've identified and on the nature of your project. We can divide stakeholders into three categories. If you identify a fourth or fifth category specific to your company, project, or situation, that's fine. The key is to categorize your stakeholders so you can better manage expectations and requirements. The three categories we'll discuss are influential, involved, and informed.

Influential

Influential stakeholders are those that are key or critical to the project and they influence the content, deliverables, and acceptance of the project. These stakeholders typically include users of the project's deliverables as well as the project sponsor and the person or group funding the project. These are people whose input and approval is critical to the success of the project and these are the folks you're going to work closely with to ensure your project meets or exceeds expectations. In fact, these are the folks with whom you'll be setting (negotiating) expectations and who will help you develop acceptance criteria for the final project deliverables.

Involved

The stakeholders in this category need to be involved to one degree or another. This might include staff from Training, Human Resources, Sales, Marketing, or other departments that may need to be *involved* with the project from time to time or who may need to gear up to do work related to the project's deliverables once the project is complete. For instance, if a new product is going to market, the Marketing department should be brought into the loop to allow them adequate time to prepare marketing materials to get the new product to market. Of course, in some cases, the Marketing department might be part of the *influential* group if they are providing input on what users need and therefore will influence the actual project deliverables. The Training group may need to be brought into the picture 60 days before the product is released in order to give them time to develop training content and schedules. They don't influence the actual project, but they need to be involved at some point.

Informed

The last category of stakeholder includes those who need to be *informed* from time to time about the project. If your company is going to implement a new network infrastructure that will be relatively transparent to users, but that will cause downtime at certain points, you'd want to keep users informed of that. If the Sales department has a huge client presentation they're preparing and the network servers are down, that's a major problem. Typically, the informed group needs to be informed of top-level information such as key dates, milestones, or activities. If the network servers will be down from Friday 6:00 P.M. through Sunday at midnight, letting users know this a few weeks before can help avoid all those last minute, frantic help desk calls asking for assistance in preparing for the network outage, for example. Stakeholders in this group might also be corporate executives for whom you must prepare periodic progress reports. They want to know the project is succeeding, but they don't need (or want) to know the project details. Typically, people in this category are included via various communications plans, which we'll discuss in more detail later.

APPLYING YOUR KNOWLEDGE

Users or *customers* are those who utilize or employ the deliverables of the project, while *stakeholders* are those who directly or indirectly impact or are impacted by the project (*users* are also *stakeholders,* but not all *stakeholders* are *users*). You may wish to develop a different set of criteria for categorizing your stakeholders, but it's important to organize them in a clear and accurate manner. This will make planning and managing the project much easier because large segments of work such as communications plans can be targeted to specific groups of stakeholders. This will help reduce the amount of work (or redundant work) you have to do and will also help you avoid omitting or overlooking a key contingent.

Managing Stakeholder Expectations

Once you've identified and categorized your stakeholders, you will also have to create plans for managing stakeholder expectations. This may sound bigger or more cumbersome than it really is. Stakeholders in the *influential* category are those you're going to have to work closely with on many aspects of your project. It's fair to say that these are the most important stakeholders for you to manage because it is within this group that your project's definitions of specifications, requirements and success will come (hint: these stakeholders may provide all this, but it's your job as IT project manager to negotiate final specifications). Scope, time, budget, and quality are all impacted by the expectations, demands, requirements, and needs of this group.

The stakeholders in the *involved* and *informed* groups typically will be much easier to manage because they are not as key to the project's success. Those in the *involved* group will need to be managed to a lesser degree than those in the influential group, but it will still be important to develop strong lines of communication and to develop a common understanding of processes and procedures. For example, the Training department needs to be involved at some point, so you'll need to provide them with a method of gaining needed information and expertise so they can develop training materials. This might mean you have to get one of your software developers to commit to spending four hours with one of their trainers to transfer that knowledge at some point during the later stages of the project. Managing the Training department's expectations about what they can expect from your project and when they can expect it will keep everyone calm, cool, and collected as things heat up in the midst of the project.

The stakeholders in the *informed* group usually just need to be kept in the loop about events that may impact them or top-level accomplishments. It's usually easiest to create communications plans for each stakeholder group within this category. For instance, corporate staff probably don't need a monthly report on project progress (unless you're doing some major in-house PR to gain support for the change that the project will create), but they will need to know about events that will impact them, such as network outages, new logon procedures, etc.. On the other hand, corporate executives need to know about events that will impact them as well as project progress, so you'll need to create a communication strategy unique to this group. We'll talk more about all of this later in the book.

You can see that identifying stakeholders is a bit more involved than you might at first have thought, but it's not a difficult task. When you take time to identify and categorize your stakeholders, your project plan can incorporate plans (or tasks) that provide for the needs of the various stakeholders. It's much easier and faster to take a few minutes to map out your stakeholders now than to overlook at key group and find out later on.

Enterprise 128 …

Avoid the *Doh!* Factor

The Matt Groening character, Homer Simpson, is famous for exclaiming *"Doh!"* whenever he discovers an error (well, he uses it for a lot of things, that being one of them). One of the things most IT project managers absolutely hate is that moment when they discover an error or omission that could have (and should have) avoided, causing them that awful *Doh!* moment. Avoid overlooking any important individuals or groups by taking a few minutes to ask and answer the questions in the previous section. It will help you identify all potential stake-holders. Then take another few minutes to categorize stakeholders to assist you in creating plans for interacting effectively with the various stakeholders. Here's a tip: when you're talking with the stakeholders you've identified, take a moment to ask *them* who else needs to know. You might be surprised by their answers and relieved that they helped you avoid overlooking an individual or group that is important to the project's success. Asking, "Who else should I be talking to?" helps you avoid the *Doh!* factor later on.

Figure 6.4 Project Stakeholders

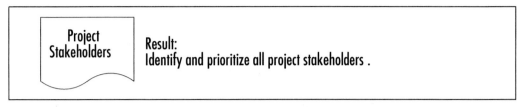

Identifying Project Requirements

Let's start with the most basic statement about your IT project's requirements. The definition of *requirements* is "something that is obligatory or demanded; something that is needed for a particular purpose." Requirements are what someone is going to hold you accountable for delivering through your IT project. That *someone* is the key here because projects have various stakeholders. As you just learned, stakeholders are those people who have a vested interest (of one type or another) in the project. For instance, users, corporate executives, and the project sponsor are common stakeholders. As you talk with stakeholders, your requirements will begin to form. As you begin to define your requirements, you may identify additional stakeholders.

If the project does not meet *user requirements*, the project is, fundamentally, a failure. Keep in mind that *users* are defined as those people who use or rely upon the results of your project; so the project must meet their needs, or it's a failure by definition. It's important to learn to listen effectively when talking with users (we're defining *users* here as those who will use the result of the project). The project should be solving the user's problem(s), which is not always the problem you think the project should solve. Keep that in mind as you develop project requirements. There's a story about a police mobile radio project where the police say there's a problem with the radio. The engineers look over the radio and the specs and find nothing wrong. They talk to a police officer who says, "The problem is that when I hit a suspect with the radio, it breaks and then I can't call for backup." Clearly, the mobile radio was not designed to withstand impact, but that was the reality of the situation. Sometimes when the police were caught off-guard and had nothing else handy, they'd use the radio handpiece to subdue a suspect and it would break, making it impossible for the officer to then call for backup. The manufacturer changed the specs for the handpiece so it could withstand greater impact. Regardless of your opinion about the use of the radio handpiece as a weapon of self-defense, the point is that the radio project had not fully taken into account the users' real-life application. The result of the project (the original mobile radio) did not meet users needs and was seen as a problem by the users. As you develop user requirements, try to suspend judgment until you fully understand the user's needs and expectations. Only then can you begin to develop requirements that meet user and business needs.

The IT Factor...

Square One: User Requirements

You might think that if you deliver a project on time and on budget that you've got a winner on your hands. Not necessarily. If the project does not meet user requirements, you've just spent a lot of time and money solving the wrong problem. When you're defining the project, the users (those who will utilize the project's deliverables) should be kept foremost in your mind. If not, your project may completely miss the mark. Then you'll have angry users/clients, a poor reputation, missed opportunities, and lots of wasted effort and dollars. A successful project is one that is perceived as successful by users, not one that simply meets the metrics and fails to deliver on user requirements.

User requirements are not the only requirements a project has. Think of a situation with which many of you are familiar—the project in which users continually request/demand new features and functionality, even while the project is in progress (also known as *scope creep*). Hypothetically, you could spend millions of dollars and thousands of hours trying to meet changing or evolving user requirements and put your company out of business in the process. You have to balance the needs of the company, the market, and the users to find the right set of project requirements. Simply meeting user requirements is not adequate, but meeting corporate requirements such as profitability or time-to-market *without* fulfilling user requirements is a waste of time. You might think that we're talking in circles here, but we're not. The key is to identify and work with stakeholders to define the optimal set of project requirements. It's often helpful to differentiate between *must-have* and *would-like-to-have* requirements because users' wish lists can get rather long. Identify the must-haves as deliverables and keep the would-like-to-haves as optional components (sometimes you can include several desirable features along with a required feature with no extra effort). The two key groups you'll need to work with are the users and the project sponsor because we're assuming the project sponsor's requirements reflect those of the corporation, which include financial, timeline, and market requirements. The key is to define requirements as quickly and as efficiently as possible and then generate a list of requirements that are manageable and measurable. Figure 6.5 shows the iterative process you can use to gather and refine project requirements.

Figure 6.5 Iterative Requirements Gathering Process

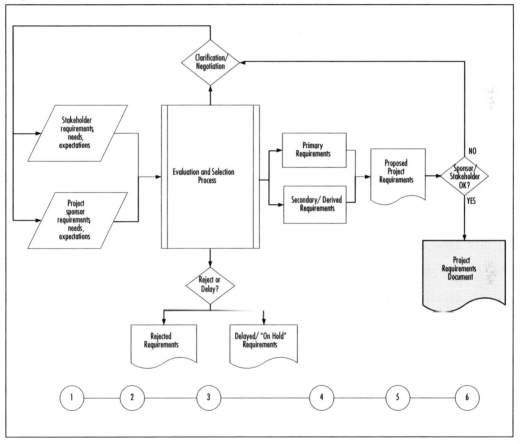

Let's take a look at each of the steps involved. Again, if you're not a fan of flowcharts, you can read through the following text and gain the same understanding of the process.

1. *Gather stakeholder and project sponsor requirements.* We're assuming that the stakeholders are those who depend upon or will use the project's deliverables. Though we've identified three categories of stakeholders earlier, you don't necessarily need to involve everyone in this process. Typically, you involve the *influential* groups and perhaps key members of the *involved* group. Don't include any more than the bare necessity or you may end up with a large, unmanageable group that may never come to agreement. We're also assuming the project sponsor represents other key stakeholder interests such as executive or corporate requirements (profitability, time to market, etc.). The first step is to bring the approved project proposal to these stakeholders and gather a list of requirements. You may have to help user groups in identifying requirements, but avoid unduly influencing this group at this time. The optimal solution is an extensive list you can hone down to help you deliver a useful project.

2. *Compile stakeholder requirements.* Compile all requirements so the project team can evaluate and discuss these requirements in an efficient, complete manner. Identify required versus optional elements (must-haves versus would-like-to-haves) so you don't get bogged down in unnecessary requirements.

3. *Review, evaluate, and select requirements.* The project team should review and evaluate all project requirements. Begin with creating evaluation criteria that will help all team members make decisions based on the same factors. Also keep in mind that user requirements are sometimes "out in left field" if they don't understand the nature or scope of the project. You don't have to (necessarily) accept all user requirements, but you will have to defend your decisions, so make sure you are using clear, sound criteria for your decisions. Obviously, these criteria should be based on the elements already present in your project proposal including problem, mission, solution, target scope, timeline and budget.

    Once you've evaluated and sorted through all stakeholder and project sponsor inputs with the team, finalize the list of requirements you believe can be delivered in this project. Remember the four criteria we used in Chapter 2? They are *logical*, *feasible*, *desirable*, and *affordable*. Those can be used here as well. Are the proposed requirements logical? Are they feasible? Are they desirable? Are they affordable? While these won't be the only criteria you use, they can be helpful when deciding from among many choices. Also keep in mind that you and your project team likely have skills and expertise your users don't, which means you often have a better (or more realistic) view of what is feasible and what is not given a target scope, cost, time, and quality requirement. This is where your negotiation skills come in handy because you may have to educate or persuade your users to accept what is realistic rather than what they'd like in a perfect world.

For requirements that don't meet the criteria you've established, you should decide whether these requirements should be put on hold (for further discussion, input, or future projects) or rejected for this project. Remember, none of this is etched in stone, but you don't want to revisit these decisions over and over again either. Place requirements either in the *rejected* or *on hold* category and be prepared to explain, negotiate, and justify your decisions to the stakeholders. Remember that the stakeholders are, by definition, the ones that will use or rely upon the outcome(s) of the project, so if you can't persuasively make your case for nixing these requirements, you may end up with a project that either fails to meet stakeholder expectations or is all over the map in terms of deliverables (too confined or too broad). Neither is a good place to land.

Also in this step, you should gather all requirements that require further discussion, negotiation, or input from stakeholders and set a time to discuss these with stakeholders. When possible, ask very specific, closed-ended questions during this process. An example of a closed-ended question is, "How exactly do you use the toolbar in this application to find customer records?" This leads to a specific answer. An open-ended question invites further input, which at this point could lead you into an endless loop of additional requirements being added at each iteration. An example of an open-ended question in this case is, "What else do you need when finding customer records?" You may want this type of input and if so, ask away. However, if you got that information from the stakeholder during the first round of requirements gathering, asking again may yield different answers based on "wish lists" or a poor understanding of the IT process rather than answers based on what the stakeholder needs. This is a judgment call, but ask your questions with the end in mind so you don't invite a free-for-all discussion.

4. *Define primary and derived requirements.* The *primary requirements* are those that were gathered from the stakeholders and agreed to by the project team, whether from the initial discussion or from subsequent clarifying discussions. The *derived requirements* are those that come from the primary requirements. For instance, a primary requirement might be data security and a derived requirement would be the storage of data in an encrypted format. You don't necessarily want to get into the detail of *how* you're going to fulfill these requirements at this point, though there are times you might do that. For instance, if you know your data has to be encrypted and you're going to use the standard file encryption used in Windows Server 2003, you can add that to the requirements. Add derived requirements (even if they describe *how*) if they are clear, concise requirements for the project and stem from the primary requirements.

5. *Proposed project requirements.* This is a document that should describe the proposed final project requirements. It's important to gain stakeholder agreement on this because this is what your project will deliver when it's all said and done. If you don't have agreement at this stage, you will likely run into scope creep, changing user requirements, and dissatisfied stakeholders during the project (you may run into those anyway, but at least you'll be doing what you can to avoid these pitfalls). If the stakeholders do not agree to these requirements, you'll have to go through another iteration of this process. While it might irk you to have to do so, keep these things in mind: first, business and markets change quickly and it's entirely possible some new data has come to light that should be included. It could be this addition makes your project far better than it otherwise would have been. Second, if you miss a key requirement (even if it's the fault of the stakeholder), it's better to know it earlier than later. You can incorporate additional or modified data at this point far more easily than you can once the project is underway. So, while you might cringe at the thought of another go-round in this process, keep the end result in mind—a successful project that you can be proud of. In Chapter 9, we'll discuss developing technical and functional requirements in detail and we'll look at the three rules of requirements: defined, discrete, and measurable.

6. *Modify or codify.* If the proposed project requirements need further modification based on stakeholder needs, you'll have to go through steps 1 through 4 again. This time it should be shorter, but make sure you look at the proposed modifications alongside your current proposed requirements list. Avoid revisiting the same issues over and over and also try to recognize

related issues. For instance, you might have a requirement for data security and a stakeholder wants to discuss user logins. These may be related and it might only take a modification or clarification to a current requirement rather than an entire review of requirements. If changes are made, check back with your original requirements to ensure you haven't inadvertently created a conflict ("add security, don't add security…")

If the stakeholders agree, you should have them officially and formally sign off on this document (in whatever manner is appropriate to your organization). You may have to revisit these agreements later on and it's good to have this in black and white. Your job as IT project manager is to ensure that your project is meeting stakeholder needs and that your project is positioned for success. That means that not only do you have to lead negotiations on requirements, but you have to educate stakeholders about the process. You don't need to go into tremendous detail on how the whole thing works, but you should make it very clear to stakeholders that once requirements are agreed upon, it should take a major event to modify the requirements. You can help them understand this by explaining (briefly) how you create and manage the project plan as well as how changing requirements will impact scope, time, budget, and quality. You can also discuss with them your change control process so that if they do request changes later, they'll understand there is a formal process for doing so. It might not completely prevent changes to requirements down the road, but you can try to nip it in the bud. Later in this book, we'll discuss change management so you don't get run over by changing demands.

We keep saying IT project management is an iterative process and here's a great example. You now have this wonderful list of user requirements. The question is, how have these requirements impacted your original estimate for scope, time, cost, or quality? Has the scope increased (or decreased) significantly? Has the amount of time required to deliver on these requirements changed? Most often, you'll find that things have expanded. If so, you'll have to adjust something. Remember, there is a relationship between scope, time, cost, and quality and if you modify one, something else has to change as well. If you increase the scope, you have to increase the time or cost or reduce the quality. Also, if something has changed, it's much easier to go back now and request more time or money (the two most common requests) because you now have a concise list of requirements rather than a more intangible "project concept."

> ## The IT Factor...
>
> ### Project Requirements Are Like A Healthy Breakfast
> A project will get off to a much better start if you make a concerted effort to gather, manage, analyze, and document your project requirements. This is an often-skipped step that really is the foundation of a solid project for several reasons. First, if you know what your project must deliver, you clearly have a better chance of delivering it. Second, if you are clear about the project requirements, you can avoid (or minimize) scope creep later on. You will certainly have to negotiate, and that sometimes means taking some of the requirements and putting them on hold for a later revision or a separate project. The third reason is that a formalized list of project requirements that the stakeholders all agree to will help manage expectations ("Hey, I thought you agreed to include...") and increase stakeholder satisfaction later (no surprises, no gaps = happier stakeholders). While gathering requirements won't guarantee project success, it will certainly get it off on the right foot. And the opposite is also true—without doing a thorough job gathering requirements, your project has a slim chance for success. You might like pie for breakfast, but you also know it's not the best way to start the day.

Managing Requirements

The reason you gather requirements before you even get into the task planning stage is that the later in the project process changes are made, the more expensive they become. If you recall our discussion from Chapter 1, you know that an estimated 50% – 70% of the total cost of *any* project is due to errors, omissions and rework. Sound familiar? By doing a thorough job on the requirements gathering and by gaining critical agreement for the project's requirements, you can reduce the cost of your project simply by avoiding some errors, omissions, or rework. You won't avoid all of them, but any reduction at this point is a good thing and will translate to the bottom line.

Timing Issues

Another important thing to keep in mind as you're developing your requirements is that you will almost never have 100% certainty as to the project's scope, requirements, etc.. You may feel confident, you may feel certain, but you may never feel like you have everything in place to move forward. That thinking style is common in the *analyst* work style we discussed in Chapter 4. These kinds of people often allow uncertainty to stop forward progress. At some point, you have to fish or cut bait, so if you (or members of your team) have a tendency to wait for additional data before proceeding, you're going to have to manage this tendency. In business, there is rarely a perfect moment when you have 100% of the information you need to make a decision or to move forward. Some people use an 80% metric—if you have about 80% of what you need, you can proceed. Waiting for perfect data can cause *analysis paralysis* and cause your project to sit in idle too long (or forever).

The flip side to that argument is that there are also times when it's best to wait. We can all think of situations where, in retrospect, we realize that if we'd waited we would have had a better outcome. This is typical for people in the *doer* category discussed in Chapter 4. These folks tend to jump in and get things going and if they plan at all, it's often after the fact (the popular "ready, fire, aim" technique). These folks probably have the most experience with the feeling of "if only I had waited a day or two." Sometimes data does evolve or come to light more slowly than we'd like. You'll need to find a balance between waiting for perfect data, which may never come, and jumping in too quickly without all the necessary information. Sometimes only hindsight will tell you if you made the right decision, but if you're cognizant of these two extremes, there's a good chance you'll find an acceptable balance.

Change Management Issues

We'll discuss this in more detail later, but this is a good place to introduce the concept of *change management*. We mentioned this briefly earlier in this section, but it bears repeating. Once you have agreement on the requirements, you should educate your stakeholders about the change management process. If you haven't yet developed your project processes (discussed later in this chapter), you can discuss the change management process in general terms. Stakeholders must understand the impact of change on a project. If you recall that scope is a function of time, cost, and quality, then you can help your stakeholders understand that if they increase the scope, something else will have to change to accommodate that increase. If they understand that the elements are interdependent, they can understand the implications of the changes they are requesting. While you may not always win, you will be better positioned to explain how requested changes will impact the project. Sometimes those changes will require that already-completed work will have to be scrapped. Other times it means those changes will delay other parts of the project. Sometimes requested changes are so significant they completely change the nature of the project. As the IT project manager, your job is to help stakeholders understand the impact their requested changes may have on a project and help the key people make decisions about how to proceed. Often these decisions are not yours to make, but you must facilitate the process of making smart, savvy decisions for the project IT department and for the business.

A long series of small changes can be as devastating to a project as one or two major changes, so don't allow small changes to be made to the requirements outside of the formal change management process. Educate both your stakeholders *and your project team* that the only changes made to project requirements are those that go through the formal change management or change control process. This helps you avoid situations where a casual conversation over coffee or after a meeting between a stakeholder and a project team member results in several changes being made on the fly. While both parties might think these changes are small and insignificant, they often can and do have a major ripple effect.

Categories of Requirements

Before we leave the topic of requirements, let's briefly talk about different kinds of requirements. It's possible that even after discussions with stakeholders and the project sponsor that there are additional requirements needed for the project. This is where your expertise and the expertise of the team come in handy. For instance, there are numerous examples of projects that may have legal, financial, regulatory, or technical requirements. Though we'll deal with project *specifications* separately, requirements might include such things as compliance with Sarbanes-Oxley (financial) or HIPAA (health care) regulations. Hopefully, one of your stakeholders has brought these to your attention, but this is a good time to step back and look for other requirements that have not yet been included. If you find any of these kinds of requirements, you should bring them back to your stakeholders for formal approval. This will ensure that you're not introducing complexity where none is needed, but also helps ensure the final project will meet all requirements. For instance, it's possible (though unlikely) that stakeholders and a project sponsor neglect to mention the requirement for HIPAA compliance in the software solution you're discussing. Perhaps they all *assumed* it was known because to them it was so obvious that they failed to mention it. If you discover requirements after the fact, go back through the process to gain formal approval for additional requirements. We won't cover all possible categories, but this list should get you started in your discovery process. Keep in mind that requirements are not specifications. To use a very tangible example, a *requirement* might be, "The car must stop within 60 feet of the application of the brake when traveling at 30 mph." A *specification* might be the thickness of the brake pads or the viscosity of brake fluid that will be used to meet the requirement(s). We'll discuss specifications later on. We'll also discuss functional and technical requirements in more detail in Chapter 9.

User Requirements

User requirements are often synonymous with stakeholder requirements since users are defined as those who will utilize the deliverables of the project. However, it never hurts to list user requirements so they're not forgotten. A good example of when user requirements are not part of stakeholder requirements is when corporate executives decide that the entire network infrastructure of the company should be upgraded and managed by a third-party company. The project that will make this happen may not take into account the front-line users who may have specific needs in terms of infrastructure. Perhaps users need wireless access or a simpler logon process. These may not initially be part of the stakeholder or project sponsor requirements, but they certainly come into play when planning the project.

Business Requirements

Clearly the project sponsor is the one who should be representing the business interests of the company, but there are times when that's not the case. Ensuring business requirements are met is an important element of your job as IT PM and whether your project sponsor covers it or not, make sure these are included in your project. Business requirements can also include legal, accounting, or other requirements that must be met by this project.

Functional Requirements

In Chapter 9, we'll discuss functional requirements in more detail, and at this point in your project planning process, you don't necessarily need to dig down into the details of functional requirements. The requirements you define are likely to be functional requirements because users (the typical majority stakeholder) often define project requirements in terms of what they need the result to do.

Technical Requirements

Technical requirements are often *derived* requirements because they are based upon the primary requirements set by the stakeholders. It's possible, though unlikely, that stakeholders will provide technical requirements. More often they'll define functional requirements ("we need it to do this") and your project team may then identify technical requirements from those. We'll discuss this in more detail in Chapter 9

The IT Factor...

It's All About the Requirements

Successful entrepreneur and business owner, Chris Landi of Tekwork.com and BestJobsInTucson.com, is a firm believer in defining requirements completely before starting on project work. "If you define what the users need and what you can deliver and get agreement on that, you usually end up with satisfied users and a successful project," says Landi. "If you don't take time to agree on requirements, your project will miss the mark and your users will be dissatisfied. It's hard to recover from those kinds of mistakes." As a successful business owner, Landi's best practices include clearly defining user and business requirements and gaining agreement on those before starting project work.

Figure 6.6 shows the result of this step is a list of all agreed upon requirements and formal acceptance of these requirements. If the requirements are lengthy, they can be referenced in the project plan and attached as a separate document, but ideally the requirements should be clear, concise, and included in the body of the project document. It's possible you'll need to develop more detailed requirements (both functional and technical), but at this stage, high-level requirements should be stated and agreed upon. Once you gain agreement on these, you can develop additional detail and gather agreement on the next iteration, if needed.

Figure 6.6 Project Requirements

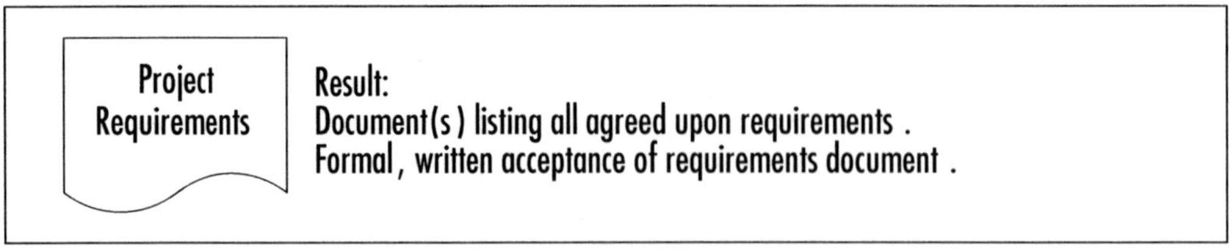

Project Requirements	Result: Document(s) listing all agreed upon requirements . Formal, written acceptance of requirements document .

Refining Project Parameters

So far, we've defined the initial project and gotten approval to proceed (Chapter 5). Then we took that initial project proposal and began to develop additional detail. At this point, you should have a list of three to five major deliverables or objectives. You should have identified and categorized your various stakeholders, and you should have an initial list of requirements. We'll continue to hone our project definition by refining the project parameters. A *parameter* is defined as "a fact or circumstance that restricts how something is done or what can be done." In this case, then, project parameters define what and how the project will be done. We'll discuss common project parameters used in IT projects in this section, but the list is not exhaustive. It's meant to cover the more commonly used elements, but you can certainly add to this list as your company and project requirements dictate. Our list is as follows:

- Success criteria

- Acceptance criteria

- Scope, cost, time, quality

- Flexibility grid or list

- Constraints and limitations

- Risks

- Milestones

- Statement of work or project charter

Success Criteria

A study undertaken in the mid-1970's on project management showed that some projects meet their scope, time, cost, and quality metrics and are still considered failures. Other projects, by comparison, missed one or more of the scope, time, cost, or quality metrics and were considered successful. The study attempted to understand why this was the case. The results were published in 1974 and later summarized in a 1988 compilation [Baker, Murphy, Fisher "Factors Affecting Project Success" in *Project Management Handbook*, Cleland and King, Eds., New York: Van Nostrand Reinhold, 1988]. The findings can be summarized by this statement:

> If the project meets technical performance specifications and/or user expectations and if there is a high level of satisfaction with the results of the project by key people in the organization, the project

is considered a success. The key people in the organization include the company, the client, the project team and the user.

At first glance, you might think this all seems a bit obvious, but let's look a bit closer at this. If the project meets technical performance specifications and stakeholders (key people) are happy, the project is *considered* a success. This means that the project may have run over budget or past its deadline. It may have not included all the functionality (scope) or it may not meet all the technical specifications (quality). Still, it's considered a success. Ultimately, if the project meets the needs and/or expectations of key people, the project is considered a success. So, while IT project managers often spend a lot of time managing the project's metrics, especially time and cost, there's another element that, when well managed, can lead to the *perception* of a more successful project. As the study results and the summary statement demonstrate, success is, at least in part, a matter of perception. We've all experienced these kinds of things. For instance, if you bring your car in for repair and the people who greet you are courteous and efficient, you're more likely to think the car repair facility is a quality shop. You're not talking with the mechanics and finding out if they're certified or what type of experience they have to come up with your perception; you're basing it on how the greeter greeted you. Smart companies understand that first impressions create customer perceptions and that's the first place to begin managing perceptions of quality and service. The same is true in IT project management. You, as the IT project manager, are responsible for managing the perception of the project with key people. Certainly you are also responsible for managing the actual project's deliverables, but it should be clear that even if you deliver on all your requirements, the project may not be perceived as a success. Now that you understand that you must manage the project and the perception of the project, we'll talk specifically about success criteria. One way to manage project perceptions is through your communications, which we'll discuss in a later chapter.

Defining Success Criteria

Success criteria are the tangible criteria you'll use to define what a successful project is (and is not) and what it includes and excludes. The criteria from any and all of the stakeholders should include elements that address scope, cost, time, and quality whenever possible so that you can identify metrics for these four elements through your success criteria. The questions you can use to define these criteria are:

1. What criteria will the *influential* stakeholders (specifically the *users*) use to determine if the project is a success?

2. What criteria will the *project sponsor* use to determine if the project is a success?

3. What criteria will the *company's executives* use to determine if the project is a success?

4. What criteria will the *project team* use to determine if the project is a success?

The influential stakeholders include other stakeholders on this list, but we're specifically talking about those who will utilize the results of this project. You gathered user requirements and can use these as a starting point for defining success criteria with the user. Work with them to develop specific criteria they'll use to determine the success of the project. To some of you, this may sound like we're defining *acceptance criteria*; they're not always the same thing and we'll discuss acceptance criteria in the next section.

APPLYING YOUR KNOWLEDGE

Here's a tip from expert Project Manager (and Tech Editor) Nels Hoenig: Use your requirements list and your success criteria together for checks and balances. If you have items listed as success criteria that are not mirrored in your requirements, something is wrong. Your requirements should determine your success criteria and your success criteria should mirror your requirements. When they match up, you know the project is starting off well aligned. You may add success criteria as you further refine your functional or technical requirements in your planning process. Once the project begins work, everything should be finalized and agreed upon so there's no guesswork about what needs to be accomplished.

You'll also need to work with your project sponsor to identify the success criteria he or she will use to determine if the project is a success. Typically the project sponsor will represent the business's objectives or priorities, but not always (which is why we'll also answer the next question in the list in a moment). As with your users, work with your project sponsor to define specific criteria he or she will use to determine whether or not your project is successful. If the project sponsor is very busy or not inclined to participate in this process, you'll have to proceed with caution. Although you may well be able to come up with a list of success criteria for your sponsor to review and approve, you run the risk of omitting some criteria that the sponsor ultimately uses but never reveals. If possible, have a discussion with the project sponsor to develop the success criteria and try to be as certain as possible that these actually are the criteria the project sponsor will use at the end of the project.

The success criteria used by corporate executives may or may not be the same as those used by the project sponsor. However, corporate executives are typically looking at the bigger picture, so the business case you made for this project will be helpful in developing the executive success criteria. Since corporate individuals are often the ones approving the budget expenditures for the project, they often have financial metrics by which they'll judge the success of the project. However, financial metrics are not the only metrics they may use. For instance, time to market or addressing a particular market niche might be part of their criteria. These may overlap with or even conflict with user success criteria, so you may have to do some negotiating.

Here's an example. If your project is to develop a software application add-on that addresses a particular need in the market, your users might say, "It will be successful if it includes the ability to generate reports quickly and easily." Based on initial research, you know that to do this will take a minimum of three months of development. Your corporate folks know that there is increasing competition in this market niche and want to get their foot in the door as soon as possible. In fact, they want the product out the door in 30 days and they don't really care if it can generate reports quickly and easily because they see that functionality as a secondary requirement. Now you, as the IT project manager, have to determine how to get everyone on the same page. You can't very well negotiate with the user group, which in this case is a new target set of users out in the world. You can't very well negotiate with the corporate folks who absolutely insist the project get out the door in 30 days. You may come up with some creative ideas, but one of the more obvious ones is to deliver the project in two parts and have your marketing folks make that clear to the market. For instance, you could deliver the initial set of functionality in the 30-day timeline and follow up with the reporting functionality within 60 days. While it might be possible to convince the corporate folks that they should wait 90 days and go in "with both feet" you might not win that battle. If you deliver in 30 days, the corporate folks might initially be happy, but will quickly realize that without the reporting functionality, the users are not happy. If you deliver in 90 days, the users may be pleased with the functionality, but your corporate folks will not only hound you for 60 days, but they may view the project as a failure. It's also possible that if you get the product out the door in 90 days, the market may have already been grabbed by your competitor, who got a competing product into the marketplace in 45 days.

The point is that you should not second-guess your target users or your corporate executives, but you may have to work to find a common area between two competing sets of demands. And ultimately, the corporate executives pay your salary, so if they say 30 days, that's what you're going to have to shoot for. Clearly, in this case we're talking about scope and timelines along with success criteria, but these things all come into play. If a project is delivered with reduced scope, it doesn't nec-essarily mean it will be perceived as a failure. If a project is delivered within scope, it doesn't necessarily mean it will be perceived as a success. Using the skills and talents you have as an IT project manager and those that you gained through understanding and applying material from earlier chapters (navigating politics, working with diverse groups of people, etc.), you should be able to define a common set of success criteria that will allow you and your project team to deliver a project that all key stake-holders define as successful. It might take some effort on your part, but defining these criteria now will help you make better decisions once the project is underway.

The last set of success criteria are those used by the IT project team itself. Talk with the project team (if you haven't yet defined your final project team, you may have to revise this list later) to define success criteria. Again, there may be many areas of overlap that correspond with user, project sponsor, or corporate success criteria, but there may be a few additional items to add to your list. You might think that the IT project team's success criteria don't really matter because they're not the users nor are they the sponsors of the project. However, their ability to perceive the project as a success is important to achieving final success because they must buy into the pro-ject and make the effort to achieve success. Remember the phrase we've used before: Projects don't fail, people do. If the IT project team can't define what success in this project means, they may not be as committed to it and therefore the overall success of the project may be in jeopardy. If the project team seems hard pressed to come up with success criteria, you may guide them toward using the requirements or the target scope, time, cost, and quality metrics as their success criteria.

Cheat Sheet...

Defining Success

How do you know your project is successful when it's all said and done? How have you judged project success in the past? If you and your IT team were happy with the results, did you assume everyone was? Defining what a successful pro-ject will look like is helpful because it not only gets everyone to agree what suc-cess looks like, but it helps make the project's success more tangible for team members. If you know what you're aiming for, you have a better chance of hit-ting it. Define your success criteria and get appropriate buy-in.

Acceptance Criteria

Acceptance criteria are similar to success criteria, but are narrower in focus. They are typically used in technical projects though they can be used in many different kinds of projects. *Acceptance criteria* define the specific circumstances under which the *user* will accept the final output of the project. In external technical projects, the acceptance criteria are often contractual obligations and are typically captured in a Statement of Work document (discussed later in this chapter). The acceptance criteria are certainly related to success criteria because the end user will be influential in creating both.

Acceptance criteria should be *specific, measurable,* and *binary.* By binary, we mean that the answer is either yes or no, there is no "maybe." Either the criteria were met or not. This helps avoid ambiguity as well as the "yes, but…" issues that arise when trying to get a client to sign off on a project's deliverables. Clients typically refuse to sign off for one of two reasons: Either the project results really do not address their needs *or* they are not clear what their needs are (there is a third and very unfortunate reason some clients don't sign off and that's to avoid paying the bill, but we're talking about legitimate reasons here). By working to clearly define what it will take for them to sign off on the project's deliverables before you write one line of code or install one router, you'll be protecting yourself, your project team, and your company. If the client is internal, you'll be avoiding political maneuvering and miscommunication.

Cheat Sheet…

Acceptance Criteria

Success criteria tell you what a successful project looks like and sometimes that's all you need. There are other times (depending on the nature of the IT project) that you will also need acceptance criteria. As mentioned, these are typically used on projects where a client is paying for deliverables or for completion of phases of the project. In these cases, acceptance criteria can make the difference between getting paid or not. Be clear that the acceptance criteria that are developed are clearly appropriate to the deliverable, are binary (either it *is* or *is not* acceptable), are measurable or tangible (whenever possible), and tied to payment (when appropriate). You'll be very thankful later on to have a clear list of acceptance criteria to which the client (or user) agreed.

Scope, Cost, Time, and Quality

As we discussed in Chapter 1, scope is a function or result of the budget (cost), schedule (time), and quality (performance or adherence to specification). Different people describe this relationship using different analogies and they're all essentially saying the same thing. Some use a triangle whose legs are cost, time, and quality and the area of the triangle is scope. Others use the image of a stool where the three legs are cost, time, and quality and the seat of the stool is the scope. Whichever image or analogy works best for you is fine as long as you understand the relationship among these various elements. As you continue to refine your project, you'll need to continue to refine your estimates for scope, time, cost, and quality. When you finalize your project plan and present it to your project sponsor for approval prior to starting project work, you will have to commit to these metrics. As the IT project manager, you'll be held accountable for these elements and you'll have to manage the project in a manner that comes as close to delivering on all four elements as possible. However, remember that perception has as much to do with project success as does hitting your metrics, so spend time managing both metrics and perceptions when the project is underway. In Chapter 9, when you create your work breakdown structure (WBS), you'll gain a much clearer understanding of what it will take to complete this project. At that point, you'll be able to really clarify your scope, time, cost, and quality commitments for the project.

Flexibility Grid or List

As you're defining and refining your project proposal, you'll need to come to an understanding with your project sponsor about the nature of the relationship between the elements of the project including scope, cost, time, and quality. In this phase, you've refined your estimates on these four elements and are beginning to gather data that will ultimately help you pin down these four elements as part of your success criteria. However, we all know that when something goes wrong in the project, something's got to give. Using the image of a triangle whose area is the project's scope, if you expand the scope, one or more legs of the triangle *will have to* grow longer in order to keep the triangle a triangle. If you reduce the length of one of the legs of the triangle, the area of the triangle grows smaller. So, if the project's time or budget is reduced, something else has to "give" in order to keep the triangle in shape. This could mean that you reduce the quality and keep the scope relatively unchanged or you drastically reduce the scope. There are many different scenarios, but the point is simply this: things change and when they change, you need to know what your priorities are to manage the change in the best possible manner.

A flexibility grid or list can be used to describe how flexible any one of the elements is in the equation. The point is not to give you wiggle room on your commitments and deliverables, but to give you an agreed-upon priority list to use to manage change to the project.

To develop the flexibility grid, you should list the four elements: scope, cost, time, and quality. Then, with your project sponsor, decide which of these elements is *least* flexible. That means that when the going gets rough, this element should remain constant. If cost is the least flexible, it means that you should manage all elements of the project to keep the project within budget first and foremost. Does that mean you're going to ignore the schedule? Of course not, but if cost is least flexible, it might mean that rather than running several overtime shifts to make up for the (inevitable) project delays, you allow the project schedule to run longer or you put another project on hold to free up extra staff to work on the project. Knowing the cost is the most important, least flexible parameter helps you make decisions that support those priorities.

Each of the four elements should be rated: Least flexible to most flexible. You may use a numbering system such as 1 = Least flexible, 2= Less flexible, 3= Somewhat flexible, 4= Most flexible. Then, when you're working on setting your schedule, developing your budget, or deciding on your quality processes, you can make decisions that map with organizational and project sponsor priorities. Figure 6.7 shows a sample grid you can use for rating and recording the agreed-upon flexibility of each element. Remember, the project sponsor ideally is the one who ok's your flexibility grid because he or she is going to have to help you manage the perception of the project throughout its lifecycle and perhaps negotiate on your behalf with executives later on.

Figure 6.7 Flexibility Grid

	FLEXIBILITY	
Scope / Work to be Done		Rate each element based on its relative flexibility. The least flexible element is the one you will have to manage most rigorously.
Time / Schedule		
Cost / Budget		SCALE 1 = LEAST flexible 2 = Less flexible 3 = Somewhat flexible 4 = MOST flexible
Quality / Performance		

Your flexibility list also comes in handy when you are deciding how much effort, or precision, each planning stage requires. Ideally, you should expend more effort (more precision or rigor) on those items that are least flexible because they are part of the project's constraints. If time is least flexible, you're going to expend more effort and be more precise in your scheduling than you might otherwise or you might expend more effort with scheduling than on budgeting if cost is most flexible. This flexibility list or grid helps both in your decision-making and your planning efforts. It helps avoid instances when your project sponsor becomes upset because you're running over budget when you assumed the schedule was more important. Clarifying these elements helps bring assumptions out into the open, and formal agreement as to the priorities of these elements will help you deliver a project that meets sponsor expectations and perceptions for success.

Precision or Rigor

The terms *precision* and *rigor* are often used in project management to indicate how precisely or how rigorously you will work on any particular step of project planning. This is directly related to flexibility, so it's included in this section. It stands to reason that if one element is least flexible, you must ensure that your project plan works around that element to make sure you deliver on that element, at the minimum. Certainly you want to deliver on all elements per your plan and agreements, but we all know that things change and when they change you need to know where to focus. If your IT project's budget is the least flexible element, then it stands to reason that you and your IT project team are going to be very precise when it comes to developing the budget. You're going to spend more time and effort ensuring the components of the budget are correct and that you can deliver on those commitments. If on that same IT project your schedule is most flexible, then you may choose to spend slightly less effort on developing a precise schedule than on developing your budget. At first you might balk and think, "Shouldn't I expend the effort to develop a highly accurate budget and schedule?" Yes, you certainly should generate accurate metrics for your project. However, if schedule is most flexible, it's highly likely that the schedule will change as the project progresses and all that time spent creating an incredibly detailed schedule will be wasted. This is one area in which rework can come into play. While you want to create a realistic schedule, if that's the element most likely to change, you may want to only develop a precise schedule for near-term work and develop a less precise schedule for work that comes later in the project.

Another element of precision or rigor is that if you're doing a project that is similar to one you've done many times, your level of precision or rigor may be less than if it's a brand-new project. You don't need to expend as much time or effort on planning a project in which many of the variables are actually known. Conversely, if you're doing a brand-new type of project, one in which none of your IT team has any previous experience, you will need to plan with far more precision (and probably also allow for more contingencies). Take, for example, the software company that installs its enterprise product at new clients. The project team that is responsible for client installations will develop a project plan for that client's installation. However, because this type of project has been undertaken many times in the past, there are not defined processes that will be used and the number of unknowns is relatively small. You might argue that client installation is a *process*, not a *project*. However, each client environment is new and unique and the definition of a *project* is that it solves a unique problem. Thus, it falls into the project category even though it relies upon many standardized processes. This is a situation in which your level of precision and planning may be relatively "low" except for the areas that are unique to the client.

There are no hard and fast rules about the level of precision or rigor in your planning processes except to note that the less flexible an element is, the more precise the planning must be and the more unknown an element is, the more rigorous the planning should be. With time and experience, you'll gain a strong sense of which parts of the plan should be precisely planned and at what point. The point is to avoid over-engineering parts of the plan and to reduce the amount of "wasted" effort and rework later on wherever possible.

Applying Your Knowledge

Flexibility is a concept some people struggle with because they think it means "wiggle room." Flexibility is important to define at this point because you *will* have to make tradeoffs during the project and it's important to have clarity and understanding with your project sponsor about how you'll handle these decisions. This saves you time because you won't have to contact the project sponsor every time you need to make a change or adjustment to the project. It also saves you from a certain amount of armchair quarterbacking that may occur during or after the project ("Why did you make that decision? You know we agreed that …"). If you have your flexibility grid approved by your project sponsor, it leaves little question as to how you should prioritize the inevitable changes and tradeoffs and it gives you backup in case your project sponsor gets a case of amnesia later on.

Constraints and Limitations

We're still in the high-level defining and organizing phase of our project, so we're not going to dig into detail on constraints and limitations at this time. However, there may be some known constraints or limitations that you want to note in the initial project plan. These constraints and limitations might be quite relevant to your project sponsor and might be critical in a go/no go decision. For instance, if a constraint is that your IT staff is in the midst of a mission-critical project and key members of the IT team will not be available for additional project work for some time to come, the project sponsor may decide that this new project should be put on hold, cancelled, or outsourced.

Another example is if you're going to have to rewire part of your building as part of the project and one of your stakeholders mentions that the company is hosting several key clients for a week at some point during the project. You'll probably want to keep this in mind as you move forward and note it as a high-level limitation. These limitations and constraints will ultimately be tied to the tasks related to rewiring the building, and they could have a huge impact on the project's timeline (and perhaps budget as well), particularly if they are not built into the project plan. Again, avoid delving into tremendous detail at this point, but do make use of the opportunity to make note of any relevant constraints or limitations you're aware of going into the project.

Risks

As with constraints and limitations, it's also important to note risks to the project that you're aware of at this stage. Project risks can include internal and external risks such as changing market demands, changing technology, changing personnel, changing corporate priorities, and more. We'll spend time later in our planning process identifying risks and coming up with strategies to deal with these risks. For now, you simply want to identify those risks about which you're already aware. Again, these may be highly relevant to the project sponsor who might decide that these early risks are too significant to even continue in the planning process. While few IT project managers want to spend time defining and organizing a project and have it cancelled, now's the time to do it if it's going to happen. And if the project is cancelled for good reason, you can feel good that you did your job, which is defining the project well enough that others (project sponsor, corporate executives) can make intelligent, informed decisions about the project before project work gets underway.

Milestones

Milestones are checkpoints set throughout the project to help monitor project progress. They are, by definition, *zero duration tasks* (a task in the project plan that is set to 0 days) in the project plan. They can be used for a number of different reasons. For instance, milestones can be used to indicate a point at which you check on the status of one phase of the project or to indicate the point at which external resources or deliverables must be received or to indicate the point at which you need to get project sponsor approval. We'll develop milestones in our project later, but there may be some high-level milestones you want to make a note of at this time so they are not overlooked later. You should be able to define the final milestone at this point, as it determines when the project is finished and has accomplished all of its objectives. Further planning may mean the project finish date moves, but you should have some idea of what that will be at this point in time.

Many people use milestones to indicate key deliverables. If that's how you and your IT project team use the term, that's fine as long as everyone has the same understanding of the definition of the word. Milestones that might be defined at this point are the deadlines for each of the major deliverables or objectives for your project. While these may not be known at this point, there are times when milestones can be set for the project during this phase. This will help you avoid missing them later when you get into the details of planning. You can also create milestones without exact dates to indicate major deliverables or events and assign specific dates to them later. For instance, you might create a milestone for development work, another milestone for testing, another milestone for quality assurance, and a final milestone for delivery to the client. These dates may not be known, but they are major markers in your project plan and if they are known at this point, they can be added.

Statement of Work or Project Charter

It seems that every project management system uses slightly different terminology, so you might find that your company or your clients or vendors use terms like *Statement of Work* or *Project Charter* to describe what we're calling the *Initial Project Proposal*. Whatever you want to call it, you should have a document that captures all of the work you've done thus far on the project. This document captures the high-level details of the project including the problem to be solved, the mission, the selected solution, the major deliverables (objectives), and the initial estimate for scope, time, cost, and quality. The document should also contain the project requirements as well as the success criteria and the acceptance criteria. Remember, all project management (including IT project management) is an iterative process, so you may have to go back through some or all of these elements as you learn more about the project. Each time you go back you should be *refining* more than *changing* the elements. If you find you're changing things rather than adding layers of additional detail, it should cause you to stop for a moment and ask why things are changing. If they are legitimate changes based on a greater understanding of the project, that's fine, but if things are changing because key elements have changed, you're aiming at a moving target and your project is at risk. If things are changing at this point, either the project environment (internal or external) has changed or you may have to spend time going back through the definition phase to really nail down the initial project statements (problem, mission, etc.).

The Statement of Work (SOW), Project Charter (PC) or Initial Project Proposal (IPP) all capture the definition and initial organization of the project. This type of document is typically used as a checkpoint to ensure the project is the right project at the right time for the right reasons. Many IT project managers set a milestone in their planning for both the *development* of the SOW, PC, or IPP and another milestone for the *approval* of the document. Once the document (SOW, PC, IPP) is approved, you have essentially entered into a contractual obligation.

You might be thinking that at this point you don't have enough information to agree to scope, time, cost, and quality metrics and you'd be right. At this point in the process, you're looking at high-level items. You should have enough information based on the requirements and success criteria to determine the project's scope. While you may develop additional detail about the elements that comprise the scope of work, it shouldn't change significantly after this point unless you've missed a major chunk of work. However, you can't reasonably know the schedule, cost, or quality until you get further into the project. You should be able to provide target estimates at this point (see Chapter 5 for estimating techniques) and most managers would expect that. For instance, you may be able to determine, based on the requirements, that the project will take about 6 months. You can estimate this based on similar projects you've done in the past. You might also know that you could be wrong by a couple of months since you don't have all the detail available yet. The data to include in the SOW, PC, or IPP should indicate that—you could state that the initial estimate is 6 months with a margin of error of 30%. Some managers may want you to lock down these numbers at this point (and if you're working with a client, they may also press for this), but until you have more information about the project, it's hard to make a more precise estimate and you'll have to use your business savvy to explain why a more precise number cannot be guaranteed at this point.

Cheat Sheet...

Formal Statement of Work

Many companies use a formal statement of work document as the project contract between the company and a client company. In these cases, it is usually a formal, written document that is signed by both parties. Companies will have different required SOW elements, so you should conform to your company's requirements and use existing templates when possible. If your company doesn't have a formal SOW template or process, you can use the following list of elements as a starting point. As you can see, we're developing the critical elements, so if you develop your initial project proposal, you'll have most of what you need for a formal SOW. In many cases, the initial project proposal can be used in place of a SOW. You can also head out to the web and find examples and downloadable templates for SOWs.

SOW Elements:

1. Background (reason for the project)
2. Scope (work to be accomplished)
3. Approach (Technical, quality, management approach, risk management, change management and issue tracking)
4. Deliverable Products
5. Roles and Responsibilities (typically used when the project is for a client)
6. Time and Cost Estimates
7. Risks and Mitigation
8. Change Process
9. Acceptance Process
10. Appendices

When you've finished listing, defining, gathering, and defining all relevant project parameters, they should be incorporated into your project plan. It's a good idea to run these by your stakeholders (if appropriate) and your project sponsor for a formal review. Doing so helps you avoid omitting important data that will help your project succeed. Figure 6.8 shows the document developed as a result of this part organizing your project.

Figure 6.8 Project Parameters

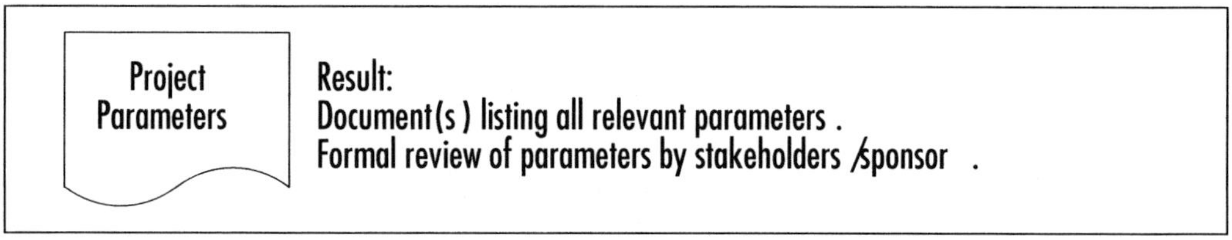

Project Parameters	Result: Document(s) listing all relevant parameters . Formal review of parameters by stakeholders /sponsor .

Defining Project Infrastructure

There are two aspects to project infrastructure—the actual infrastructure components such as an intranet, instant messaging, or e-mail and the structure of the project itself, which includes the processes and procedures your project will use. We'll discuss infrastructure in terms of the physical, tangible components and we'll discuss processes and procedures in the next section.

If you recall from earlier discussions in the book, we talked about working with a diverse project team. This diversity includes culture, geography, age, and gender, to name a few. When you're defining your project's infrastructure, you need to be cognizant of the needs of your IT project team. We'll talk about how to form that team later in the book, so you may not be able to complete this segment until you've identified your IT project team members. If they've already been identified, take a moment to think about what technology, tools, or infrastructure might be most helpful to the team. Do they need cell phones, wireless access, instant messaging, a secure, shared website? Think about how you'll run the project and which tools will help you and the team be most efficient. Clearly, you should look to leverage existing assets first such as laptops, computers, Internet access, cell phones, etc.. However, you should also step back and ask if those existing tools will be enough. If team members need to share lots of documents as part of the project, you may want to create a secure website that IT team members can access for downloading, uploading, and sharing project documents rather than e-mailing them back and forth. What kinds of hardware, software, network, Internet, and Web services will be required by the project team?

Beyond technology, you should also think about some of the more mundane but critical infrastructure elements. Do IT team members need office space, conference room space, visitor space, a testing lab, special furniture, a project office, dedicated office equipment (fax, copier, chairs, desk, storage), or communications equipment?

Again, if you have not yet formed your IT project team and are defining and organizing this project with a special team of experts that may or may not be working on the project itself, you may have to revisit these requirements once you have your IT project team. However, in many cases, you'll be able to identify many of the infrastructure needs.

Once you have this list, you'll need to talk with your project sponsor. He or she will need to approve these and provide (or provide access to) these resources. If any of your infrastructure needs are new (to the company), you'll have to take ownership of getting these resources. That might mean working with your telecommunications company to increase Internet bandwidth or provide high-speed access at several new locations. It might mean you have to select and purchase new hardware, software, or furniture. Whatever it is you need for the project and the sponsor has approved, make sure you either get it yourself or delegate this task to someone reliable and persistent. Of course, wait to purchase infrastructure components until your final project plan has been approved (or as close as possible) to avoid making large purchases for a project that ultimately gets dropped. Figure 6.9 shows the results of this step, which is a document outlining all infrastructure requirements (currently known) and approval by the project sponsor indicating the ability to use, commandeer, or purchase necessary infrastructure components. Keep in mind that each of the documents generated in each step can be compiled for approval by the sponsor in one sitting when you submit the initial project plan to the sponsor. However, some project sponsors are busy or may prefer to get these documents one by one, so work with your sponsor to determine the best approach.

Figure 6.9 Project Infrastructure Needs

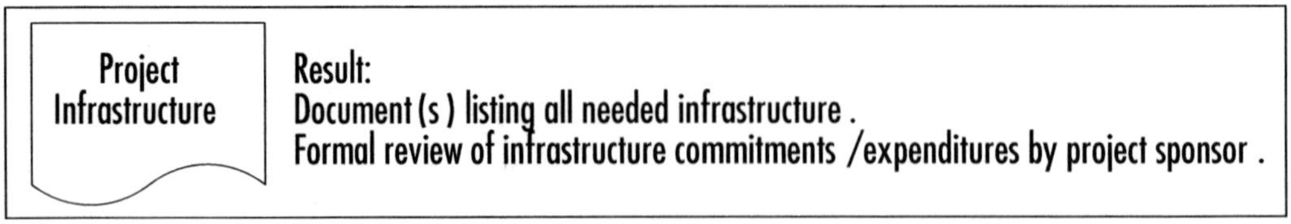

Project Infrastructure	Result: Document (s) listing all needed infrastructure . Formal review of infrastructure commitments /expenditures by project sponsor .

Defining Project Processes

We're heading down the home stretch here. Defining the project's processes and procedures is the final step in this phase of our planning. To this point, you've identified a tremendous amount of information about the project, and now it's time to define the project's processes and procedures—how the project will run and how you'll run the project.

Cheat Sheet...

Processes, Procedures, and Stress

You already know that process for process's sake is a waste of time, but when processes (and procedures) make sense, they're priceless. A renowned exercise physiologist, Michael Hewitt, has researched and written a lot about exercise (bear with us, we'll get to the point quickly). His philosophy is to find the least amount of exercise needed to remain healthy. That's an attitude you've got to love and that's our approach to process. Look for the least amount of process and procedure possible to generate a calm, consistent, and manageable project team environment. Predefined processes and procedures reduce stress because people know in advance how to handle routine situations. However, those same people can feel stressed out when there are so many processes and procedures that they literally can't get their jobs done. Find the least amount of process you can to make your project manageable and be careful not to build in so much process that everyone spends time on process and none on the project itself. Help your team be productive by defining key project processes and procedures. If possible, work with the project team to define these so that the processes will be ones the whole team can live and die by.

There are many different processes and procedures your project may need and it's impossible to define and discuss every possibility. We'll discuss many of the more common ones and discuss their components so you can develop your IT project's processes and procedures using these as a starting point. If you find yourself in the midst of your project (once it's underway) and there are areas that seem confusing or are causing errors, delays, or frustration, they may be candidates for additional processes or procedures. If you find yourself or your IT team solving the same problem over and over, it's a likely candidate for a new process or procedure. The flip side is don't define more processes or procedures than are necessary—keep your project processes lean and mean to keep your IT team moving forward on project work. The following is a partial list of processes and procedures you might want to define for your project. We'll discuss each one briefly and there are several that we'll discuss in more detail in subsequent chapters.

- Acceptance Criteria
- Risk Management Plan
- Change Management Plan
- Communication Plan
- Quality Management Plan
- Status Reporting
- Defect/Error/Issue Tracking
- Escalation Procedures
- Documentation Procedures
- Approval Procedures
- Deployment Plan
- Operations Plan
- Training Plan

You may already have some or all of these procedures and processes defined from previous projects. If so, double-check that they're applicable to your project and feel free to reuse any that make sense. Some may need to be tweaked a bit and others can be used as-is. Others may not address the current project needs and will have to be tossed aside or rewritten. Any time you can reuse work from a previous project, do so. If you (or someone you trust) took time to think through a process in the past, you may as well leverage that work, but do so only after reviewing it to ensure it's still applicable.

Acceptance Criteria

We discussed acceptance criteria earlier, so we won't cover that again. Keep in mind that acceptance criteria really define the process by which the user or client formally accepts the project's deliverables. It's critical to define these with the user or customer and to gain agreement on the acceptance criteria before the project gets underway (or as soon as acceptance criteria can be accurately developed) or you risk some confusion (or outright finger-pointing) later on.

Risk Management Plan

We'll discuss risk management in a later chapter, so for now, we'll simply mention that risk management is a process you should have in place for your project, regardless of how big or small the project is. Every project faces risks and spending time identifying those risks before you begin the actual project work will help you avoid the "running around with your hair on fire" syndrome that often hits IT project managers at some point during the project. Good risk management planning gives you intelligent, viable alternatives when identified risks occur. Great risk management can help you avoid the problem in the first place by knowing that it might happen and taking steps to avoid it altogether.

Change Management Plan

We all know that despite our best efforts to plan, things change. One of the most common changes to a project plan is that the users (those who will utilize the deliverables of the project) come back and say, "Oh, we forgot, we have to have this, that, and the other thing." This happens whether you have a hardware or software project, an internal or external project, a small or a complex project. You know changes to your project will happen, so you can choose to manage that process or not. If you choose not to manage the process, you can end up with a project that looks like spaghetti—a jumbled mess. Since there usually are many dependencies in a project, changing one thing typically changes one or more other things in your project plan, creating a ripple effect. We'll discuss creating a change management plan, or process, so you can manage how, when, and why your project changes.

Communication Plan

You'll hear a lot about communications plans throughout this book because they are some of the most overlooked processes in IT project management. Many IT departments are not very good at communicating with anyone except others within the IT department. You may bristle at that statement, but the overwhelming number of complaints registered about IT departments is that requests go in and silence comes out. If this does not describe you or your IT department, you are to be congratulated. The rest of you know who you are…and in later chapters we'll talk about creating effective (and simple) communications plans so you can break the pattern and the perception of poor communication from IT. It's possible you never thought of communicating as a process, so you've already learned something that can help you communicate more effectively by establishing processes and procedures to make your life easier.

Quality Management Plan

In Chapter 7, we're going to discuss quality. It's been given its very own chapter because quality is a critical part of all projects and managing quality touches all aspects of the project. So, while quality is built into a project from the ground up and is defined and managed at each step, we will devote a chapter to identifying this in more detail. As a process or procedure, you may also have a separate Quality Management or Quality Assurance Plan. If you're using any one of a number of quality programs (Six Sigma, ISO9000, etc.), you may have a framework for managing quality that is separate from the IT project management process. If so, it integrates well with the IT PM processes and will drive the quality of the final project results.

Status Reporting

You should identify the procedures you want the IT project team to use to report project and task status. It's important that you decide what information will help you know the project is on track. Think back to our discussion about the flexibility grid and the concept of precision or rigor. If budget is the least flexible element, your status reporting should clearly contain information about the budgetary items such as the actual versus estimated cost of each task or deliverable. If time is your most flexible element, you may not have the team track the time spent on the project down to the minute, but instead ask that time be rounded to the nearest hour or even half day.

There are several keys to effective status reporting:

1. The process for reporting status should utilize existing tools.

2. The status report should include data that already exists or is easy to compile, such as tasks completed, tasks underway, dollars spent, etc..

3. The reporting process should be well defined and should only ask for data that will help you manage the project.

4. The reporting process should not take long to complete from data gathering to reporting.

The adage "You get what you measure" certainly holds true here. The information you request in a status report is what your IT team will focus on because they'll have to report on it. Human nature being what it is, your team will strive to report positive results on the things they have to report, so they'll work hard to make sure they can report positive things. If you're measuring or monitoring the wrong things, your IT team will probably focus on those wrong things and your results won't be quite as good or on target as you'd like. Also avoid re-creating systems that are already in place. For instance, if your company has a process for people reporting their time for payroll processing, you may not need an additional time tracking tool. Look for ways to leverage existing systems before creating or adding new systems.

What To Report

Another truth about reporting is that if it is too difficult, too cumbersome, or takes too much time to complete, your team may very well "guesstimate" rather than take the time and effort to complete the status report accurately. If it takes too much effort, people will often forego accuracy (and sometimes truth) in order to just get the report done. If you've taken time to really think about what you need to know and how your team needs to report that, you can find the *least* amount of reporting that will keep you well informed. Some companies use exception-based reporting, meaning that they only want to know about work or tasks that are exceptions to the plan. If a task starts late or is running over budget, that would be reported. If a task is on time, has completed within budget, and is otherwise normal it would not be reported.

It's also important to sit down with your project sponsor and find out what kind of reporting he or she will need. Status reporting is the process of the team reporting to you, the IT project manager. However, you'll also have to report on the project status to your project sponsor and perhaps to other key executives. Reporting to your project sponsor may be a regular weekly report, for example, and reporting to key executives may well fall under the heading "Communications Plan" discussed later in this section. Many IT project managers find it helpful to develop a list of key metrics or data that fits with the flexibility and precision decisions made earlier with the sponsor and use those as the basis for discussion. If you ask the project sponsor an open-ended question such as, "What information on the project would you like to know about?" the response you receive can run the gamut from very little to everything. If your project sponsor's work style falls in the *doer* category, he or she may simply want to know that the project is on track and if there are any major problems. If your project sponsor's work style falls in the *analyst* category, he or she may ask for so much detail that you're running around preparing reports instead of actually managing the project. Rather than start with a "blank sheet of paper", start the discussion with your suggestions and ask the project sponsor to add or remove items. You'll end up with a more focused, useful list of items on which you'll need to report. It will also be another good opportunity to make sure your expectations are in line with your project sponsor's.

How To Report

You (and possibly your IT project team) should determine how the status reports will be generated and delivered. If you're using a project management software tool, you can use the tools and functionality within the tool to help your team develop and deliver reports based on data in the tool. However, not all PM tools have the same reporting capabilities. For instance, many users of Microsoft Project complain that it's very difficult to print *just* the data they want. If it's in a canned report it's fine, but if not, it can be difficult to generate meaningful reports. Other programs have limitations and you should try to avoid having the team jump through hoops to get data out of the PM tool for reporting. Some companies want hard copies of status reports, while others keep them as soft copy files on a server. Whatever method you use, make sure that everyone on your IT project team have access to the same reporting tools. If everyone but the three remote team members have access to a particular program, those three remote team members will not only be out of the loop, but they'll also have to do extra work to comply with reporting requirements. Make sure that if you use any technology for reporting that all team members have equal access or that you make specific accommodations to address any shortfalls.

When To Report

Another question you'll need to answer is how often you need status reports. Remember that more frequent milestones or checkpoints are important to a successful project, so it makes sense that frequent reporting can also contribute to a project's success—to a point. You should determine the best reporting interval based on the complexity and scale of the project as well as your company's typical reporting cycles. If you have to report to your manager or project sponsor every week, you may need to have your team update you each week. You might also decide (and get approval) to have your team update you every two weeks and you present an overview report each month. If your reporting interval is too frequent, IT project team members may "fudge" their reports because it would take too much time away from getting the project work done. You can discourage that by making the reporting interval frequent enough to ensure the project is on track, but not so frequent as to be a burden on you or the team.

Ideally, you, your IT project team, and your project sponsor should come to agreement on what has to be reported, how it has to be reported, and when it has to be reported. If you can have the team participate in this definition process, you may find that the things you were going to request are too difficult to report on regularly (due to the PM tool or other factors) or you may have overlooked something important that your team or project sponsor identifies. A collaborative approach can fine-tune the reporting process so it encourages and drives the project outcomes.

Cheat Sheet …

Reporting on Reports

Some project managers make reporting such a big deal that it becomes an end in itself. This would fall into the category of "process for process's sake", which is nothing more than the tail chasing the tiger. Create a list of things you think should be reported and take it to your team for verification, approval, or modification. Then, see if you can pare it down further. Ask yourself, "What will this information do for me?" or "What will I do with this information once I have it?" Some information may clearly be needed such as actual budget for each task or deliverable. However, there's lot of information you can ask for and have your team report on that will not help you manage the project toward success. If you can't clearly state what the information is and how you will use it, consider removing it from your list. Keep it lean and mean to encourage accurate, timely, and meaningful reporting. And don't confuse reporting with recording. You may want or require your team to record very detailed information about the project, but you may only request a small portion of that data in the form of a report. You need the detail as backup and as history, but you probably don't need all that detail in a report. Here's a staggering factoid: 80% of all documents filed (electronic or paper) are never touched again. If you think about that when looking at reporting requirements, you might well be able to pare things down.

Defect/Error/Issue Tracking

Despite your best planning efforts, you will have to have some method of tracking deviations from the plan, whether those show up in the form of defects, errors, or issues. We'll use the generic *issue tracking* to refer to all types of problem tracking in a project.

You and your IT project team should define the issue tracking process and identify procedures the team can use when these issues arise. At minimum, you should define:

1. What constitutes an issue?

2. How should the issue be reported?

3. How should the issue be tracked?

4. How should the issue be resolved?

What Constitutes An Issue?

Using a process similar to the one you developed when identifying success criteria, you can identify criteria to use to identify a problem or issue. Identify what constitutes an issue that should be reported versus normal bumps along the project road. Some issues get resolved by the person who is working on the task or deliverable. Other issues require team notification because they:

- Impact other tasks' start, finish or deliverables

- Impact the cost of the project

- Impact the project schedule

- Trigger one of the project risks

- Put the entire project at risk

There may be other categories you want to add, but you can use this list as a starting point. Once you've identified the criteria that will be used by the team to identify reportable issues (versus issues that are handled quickly and easily within the project or even the task), the team will have a clear sense of what has to be reported and what doesn't. Once the project gets underway, you may find you have to modify these criteria to adjust to the reality of your project work, but the initial definition will help you and the team with a starting point.

The IT Factor...

Starting From Scratch

In most instances, it's easier for people to respond to something than to create it from scratch. Developing the criteria for issue tracking is a good example. You may come up with a list of suggested criteria and present it to the project team so they can respond to it. This might save time and effort, and your project team will have the opportunity for input without the burden of creating the original list. Responding to something usually takes less time and effort than creating it from scratch. Giving people the option of providing input for changes is often a better use of time than trying to "design by committee."

How Should the Issue be Reported?

Once your team understands what has to be reported, you'll also have to develop a procedure for reporting issues. First, how much information should be reported about an issue? Do you want an issue report form or just a list of items to include in the report? A quick issue report might include items such as issue title, brief description, person reporting, reporting date, and the task it is associated with. A lengthier report might include a longer description, how the issue was discovered, what the potential impact is (high, medium, or low criticality) and suggested resolution, as an example. You'll also need to ask and answer questions such as: Are issues reported to the team via e-mail or via their periodic status reports? Should critical issues be reported differently than non-critical issues? Should the entire team be notified of an issue or just the project manager? Identify the methods the team will use to report issues. Again, you want to avoid flooding the entire team with constant issue reports that don't pertain to them, but you also want the team in the loop on issues that may impact them or that impact the entire project. If you're using technology for these issue notification, make sure all members of your project team have equal access to these tools and know how to use them.

How Should the Issue be Tracked?

Once issues are identified and reported, how will they be tracked? Will you, as the IT project manager, manage that process? Will that task be assigned to a member of the team? Will the task be tracked in a software tool such as a Microsoft Word document, Excel spreadsheet, or Access database? Will issues be given a unique tracking number and if so, what is that number based upon? Will issues be tied to tasks or to the resource (person) performing the task? Again, less is more, so keep the tracking methods short and simple. Also make sure you have a system in place to avoid losing track of issues. Issue tracking is a key metric directly related to the health of the project. Tracking and managing issues also helps keep the team focused on the important problems. At the end of the project, as part of the close out we'll discuss toward the end of this book, you'll need to review all issues and ensure they were either resolved or closed. Any open issues at the end of the project should be reviewed and addressed (hint: some issues become irrelevant and are simply closed or left unresolved at the end of the project, but we'll discuss that in detail later).

How Should the Issue be Resolved?

Finally, what is the process for resolving issues? As you'll learn when we start assigning tasks, a task without an owner doesn't get done, and a task with two or more owners usually doesn't get done. The rule: one task, one owner. The same holds true for issues. If you feel like you need to assign more than one person to an issue, you might want to break the issue into its components and assign each component to an individual. This way you avoid the old finger-pointing routine or the honest confusion that comes from, "Sorry, I thought Lisa was handling that." Issue resolution not only requires an owner, it requires a deadline. Issues without deadlines rarely resolved. If possible, identify the completion criteria for the issue resolution as well. Completion criteria, which we'll discuss later when we discuss our work break-down structure, are the criteria you develop so you'll know in a very clear and unambiguous way that the task was completed satisfactorily. These can also be developed for issue resolution. Sometimes the resolutions (or completion criteria) are unknown, but you can to develop these criteria as you go along. For instance, if a developer is working on a section of code and discovers that it will not integrate into the existing code in the manner that was specified or assumed, you have an issue to resolve. What would resolve this issue? The developer might have a few suggestions that can be included in the issue. For instance, she might suggest that an additional piece of code could be spec'd out to integrate these two elements or that the specifications for the code she's writing be revised to include code that will integrate these components. Often the person closest to the issue has the most realistic ideas about how the issue can be resolved, so encourage task owners or those working on the task to provide their input. Also keep in mind that it is possible for someone to be too close to a problem to see the solution, so sometimes the person closest to the issue is the most stumped for an answer (or has a vested interest in a particular solution) and you may have to turn to other subject matter experts for advice, input, or assistance.

Escalation Procedures

Escalation procedures should be put in place before problems arise, which is why you should define them at this point in your project. There are several types of escalation and each procedure should be clearly defined.

Issue Escalation

Members of your team should have a clearly defined escalation procedure to use to raise critical problems. If the procedure is clearly defined, team members don't have to think too hard to figure out how and when to escalate an issue. While your team members may be bright, motivated people, you want to minimize the amount of time and effort they expend on project tasks that don't drive the project forward. Work with your team to identify how and when issues should be escalated. If you've identified which types of things constitute issues (see the previous section) and what priority these issues are, then you're halfway to defining when to escalate an issue. Use clear, binary types of decision points. If you leave too much gray area, it will either cause confusion for the team or you risk having each team member interpret the guidelines differently.

Team Problem Escalation

You should also define how team members should resolve and escalate problems between team members. Whenever two or more people work together, the possibility for interpersonal conflict pops up and you should have clearly defined procedures for team members to escalate issues about the team itself. It's important to instill in the team members a sense of responsibility to the team so it can function at its best. Part of functioning well is addressing problems when they arise, and providing an easy-to-use escalation process for interpersonal problems will make sure that team members feel they have an outlet for resolving issues they cannot resolve on their own. As IT project manager, your job is to ensure the successful completion of the project and part of that is clearing away roadblocks to success.

Project Problem Escalation

Sometimes there is a problem with team members or with the project itself that are outside your area of influence or control. In these cases, you should define a project problem escalation procedure and run it by your project sponsor. As you know, the IT project manager often has to manage without organizational authority. That means that you have no direct control over project team members other than to try to influence them to complete their tasks or project work on time, on budget, and with the required quality. What if they fail to do that? What if they are falling behind and putting the project at risk? What if they are simply unable to deliver? What should you do? Since your job is to shepherd the project along toward successful completion, you may also need an escalation path to someone in the organization with the authority to resolve higher-level issues. That person might be your project sponsor or it might not be, but often the escalation path goes through the project sponsor for issues that you're unable to resolve through normal processes.

In additional to potential personnel issues that might impact your project, there may also be issues with the project itself that should be escalated. This might be a key vendor failing to deliver due to a payment dispute with your corporate finance folks or a key part of the project failing initial tests. Sit down with your project sponsor and identify the types of issues that should be brought to him or her for resolution. Some project sponsors are fairly hands-on and might want you to bring all issues with high or medium criticality to their attention immediately. Others might want a weekly or monthly report. Still others might tell you to only come to them when all other options fail. You'll need to develop an explicit understanding with your sponsor about escalating issues (how, what, when, where, why, who) so there are no misunderstandings. No one likes unhappy surprises and project sponsors are no exception. You know how much you hate being taken by surprise, so make sure you keep your project sponsor up to date by agreeing, in advance, on escalation procedures.

Documentation Procedures

As you've gone through the last couple of chapters, you've seen the document icon we're using to indicate when you have a tangible document as the outcome. Examples include user requirements, acceptance criteria, and the initial project proposal. All of these are examples of project documentation. Each company may have its own procedures regarding how to document a project and if yours has defined procedures, feel free to use them. Otherwise, work with your project team to define what has to be documented and why. Just like status reports, you may not need to document every last detail (then again, you may need to), and you should only document what's going to be useful in the future. Remember that there may be legal, ethical, or corporate requirements about documentation for your project and you should clearly adhere to those requirements. If nothing like that exists, think about which information will be useful to you or someone during and after the project, then decide how that information should be captured and documented.

Keep in mind that documentation can be useful during the life of the project for figuring out what was done when and by whom, but it can also be helpful later when quality testing or troubleshooting issues. Keeping thorough (but relevant) records may also end up being a very useful tool after the project is complete.

Approval Procedures

In an ideal world, the IT project manager would have full authority over the project, including the authority to approve the schedule, allocate resources, and spend money. In the real world, the amount of authority given to the IT project manager varies widely. At minimum, you should have the authority to get the project done without constantly going back to the project sponsor for approval. If that ends up being the case, the project sponsor may not clearly understand his or her role versus your role as IT project manager. If the project sponsor trusts you to run the project, he or she should also trust you, within certain guidelines, to make decisions for the project. In most situations, IT project managers have enough authority to make routine expenditures and decisions for the project and are required to go to their project sponsor for approval for unusual or large decisions.

Before heading into your project, get agreement from your project sponsor as to what does and does not require project sponsor approval. If possible, negotiate for a reasonable amount of autonomy to make scheduling, resource, and budget decisions. For budget expenditures, most companies have set rules regarding what level of expenditure requires additional approval. If those are too low for your project, make the business case for raising that limit for the project. For example, suppose your company has a limit of $500 for any single expenditure before getting higher-level approval. Suppose your IT project involves replacing all of the corporate servers, each of which you estimate to cost between $800 and $3,000. Every time you prepare to purchase a new server, your current guidelines would require you to get approval. You could be strangled by corporate red tape even before you purchase your first server. You may want to build this level of fiscal authority into the project plan itself so that within the initial project proposal you state that all expenditures for servers up to $3,000 per server will be allowed and other expenditures above $500 will go through the approval process (or whatever reasonable solution works for you). Pre-negotiate these items so your project doesn't get bogged down later on with budget review and exception requests.

Deployment Plan

Developing a deployment plan may be part of your project's deliverables, but it might be overlooked if someone outside your IT project team is responsible for deployment activities. In many software companies, especially enterprise-level software, the deployment is handled by a specialized deployment team. In other companies, the IT team is the one that does the deployment. If necessary, form a deployment team and make sure you invite key users (typically handpicked subject matter experts) to participate in developing the deployment plan since it will directly impact users. If you don't involve users in developing the deployment plan, there's a good chance you'll make incorrect assumptions, disrupt operations, and have a whole group of people really cranky with you and the IT team. It's much easier to bring the right people together to develop the plan, gain their buy-in, utilize their expertise, and develop a plan that meets the needs of both the IT project team and the users.

Operations Plan

After the project is complete and deployed, will you also need to operate or maintain the project's deliverables? For instance, if your team is responsible for developing Web content for a client, will you also be expected to maintain that content? If so, you need a post-project operations plan that delineates what has to happen next. Clearly the operations plan will be specific to each type of project and deliverable, so guidelines here won't be of too much help. However, you can use your IT project management process to create a project plan for the operations plan. Sound redundant? It's not really. If a project is, by definition, a unique solution to a unique problem, then you can use PM to solve the problem of "How do we maintain the operations of the project after it's been completed and deployed?"

Training Plan

The training plan is listed last, but it shouldn't be the last thing you think of at the end of your project. One of the most common criticisms of IT departments is that they don't think about training until it's too late or they assume it's someone else's job. Even if delivering the training *is* someone else's job, you should begin to define what will be needed by the trainers when you hand this project off to them. The easiest way to create your training plan may be to invite the key training staff to a meeting and ask them what they'll need and when. If training is up to you, you'll need to answer those questions with the *user* in mind, not with the IT project schedule in mind. User training can be accomplished in numerous ways and finding the most effective training methods, both in terms of the cost of training and the effectiveness for the user, is important. If you wait until the project is winding down to think about training, you're doing yourself, your team, and your project a disservice because the user *perception* of the project will be negatively impacted as will their actual experience. As with your operations plan, you may choose to create a separate sub-project plan that goes through all the IT PM steps to create a training plan. As you've probably already figured out, these IT PM steps are highly scalable, so you can use it for large and small projects alike. Using the same IT PM process for all your projects reinforces your skills and provides a consistent approach that everyone will appreciate, especially as they become more and more familiar with the IT PM components. A good place to start with training elements is with the project's requirements. This helps identify who might need training and what elements will be included in training.

Enterprise 128 ...

People, Technology, and Business

When you're developing your processes and procedures, keep in mind that all IT projects involve *people*, *technology*, and *business*. Make sure your processes address or accommodate these three elements. If you forget about people or business in favor of technology (the most common thing IT project managers do), your project will start to wobble. Your processes and procedures should conform to your business's requirements; they should help people get the project done quickly and efficiently (and ideally, reduce the amount of work people have to do). Once you've got those two bases covered, you can concern yourself with processes and procedures involving technology. Saving the best for last (from an IT perspective) will help you remember to address the first two.

Figure 6.10 Project Processes and Procedures

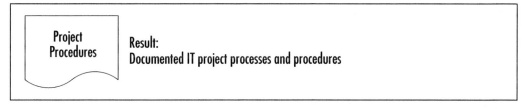

If you refer to Figure 6.11 (the same as Figure 6.2 earlier in the chapter), you can see that the output from the steps described here in Chapter 6 is an initial project plan that you should bring to your project sponsor for approval. Approval includes verifying the information and assumptions included in the project as well as giving you the green light for moving on to the next phase of your IT project planning process. You should have steps 1, 2, and 3 completed. Once you have approval from your project sponsor (steps 4 and 5) you can move on to step 6, which we'll discuss in Chapters 7 and 8.

Figure 6.11 Initial Project Plan Approval

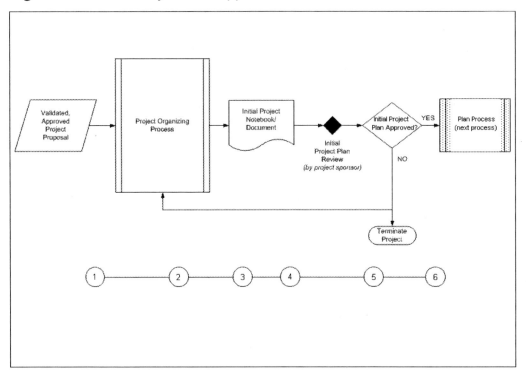

Cheat Sheet...

The Genesis of Problems

It's been said that many problems are born from solutions. If you think about that, it means that often when we think we're solving a problem, we're creating new problems. While we can't always avoid creating new problems, we can certainly reduce the number or magnitude of new problems by taking time to make sure we're solving the right problem in the right way. The steps we've reviewed in Chapter 5 and Chapter 6 will help you make sure you're solving the right problem in the best way possible. Everything we do from here on out will build upon the foundation we've built in these two chapters, so now's the best time to step back and make sure you are comfortable with what you've developed so far. If not, make a few tweaks so your project actually solves more problems than it creates.

Summary

In this chapter, we continued the process started in Chapter 5 by honing our project definition and by creating the project structure and framework. You should now have clearly defined project objectives, which are used as the project's major deliverables or are used to define the major deliverables. We spent quite a bit of time identifying and categorizing stakeholders. This often-skipped step is vital to a successful project because making sure the project meets the needs of users and the expectations of stakeholders is vitally important. Although the task of identifying all stakeholders can be a bit larger than you might at first have imagined, when you're finished, you'll know that you've likely included all the right people in the right ways.

With a complete list of project stakeholders, you can develop the project's requirements. To develop requirements before identifying all the relevant project stakeholders would simply mean you'd have to cycle through this process two or three (or more) times to refine requirements as you discovered or included new stakeholders or risk the project will not meet all *perceived* requirements. With a complete and categorized list of stakeholders, you can more easily manage the requirements gathering phase. Depending on the nature of the IT project, your project requirements will vary. You will also have to find a way to integrate or manage sometimes disparate requirements. Sometimes that means you have to negotiate with various stakeholders or work with them to agree on what might be removed or delayed so the project has a chance of success. Clearly defined, agreed-upon requirements is one of the most essential elements of a successful project and time spent on this step will pay for itself tenfold on the other end.

We reviewed a number of project parameters that you'll need to define for your project including success criteria and acceptance criteria. These help you define, in advance, what the project will look like when successfully completed and what it will take for clients to sign off on major deliverables. We also defined a number of other parameters such as the flexibility grid and the amount of precision needed for the project. These are needed when you have to make decisions regarding changes to the project later on. They help you make better, faster decisions that are aligned with the priorities of the company and the project sponsor. There are numerous other project parameters that you may want to define in order to bring clarity to your project early in the planning cycle.

Every project also requires infrastructure and this is as good a time as any to begin defining those elements. You'll need to decide what physical infrastructure needs you have such as office space, furniture, and phone lines. You'll also need to figure out your technology requirements from computers, network connections, network storage, cell phones, and PDAs to any special technology needs such as a testing lab or testing equipment. Also make sure that all the remote members of your team are as connected as those at the home office and that the remote staff have equal access to project resources.

Project processes and procedures, when well-designed, help reduce IT project team stress by providing simple, easy-to-use processes, procedures, and tools to help them manage the project workload. Consistent processes and procedures help everyone perform at a higher level, but there is a limit. Avoid creating processes and procedures that simply get in the way of getting work done. Encourage feedback from your team during the definition of processes and procedures as well as when the project is underway. Your job is to remove roadblocks for your team, not create them, so define only as many processes and procedures as will help. This varies from project to project and from company to company. If you have processes and procedures from previous projects, repurposing them can save you a lot of time—don't reinvent the wheel if you don't have to.

Solutions Fast Track

Identifying Project Objectives

- ☑ Develop the project objective statement, which helps focus you on what outcome(s) you're trying to achieve.

- ☑ Develop three to five major objectives or major deliverables based on the work you've done to this point (problem, mission and solution, target scope, time, budget, and quality).

- ☑ It's usually helpful to define what is and is not included in the project to avoid making incorrect assumptions.

Identifying Stakeholders

- ☑ *Stakeholders* are those people or groups who have a vested interest in the outcome of the project. *Users* are a particular subset of stakeholders who are most impacted by (and who impact) the project.

- ☑ Stakeholders should be identified before requirements are developed because ideally, requirements should be the result of identifying and addressing stakeholder needs.

☑ Stakeholders can be categorized to help you sort through their needs, demands, and requirements. Three categories that might be helpful to you are influential, involved, and informed.

☑ *Influential* stakeholders typically include users who both influence the project's direction and are influenced by the final result.

☑ *Involved* stakeholders are those who need to be involved at some point during the life of the project. This might include the Marketing or HR departments, for instance.

☑ *Informed* stakeholders are those who need to be informed at certain points along the way, but do not need to be directly involved in the project. This might mean keeping other departments up to date on the status of your project even if your project work or results have no direct bearing on them.

Identifying Project Requirements

☑ Identifying requirements begins with correctly and thoroughly identifying and categorizing stakeholders.

☑ Defining the project's requirements is an iterative process that may also involve negotiation. As the IT project manager, you have a good idea about what's possible and what's not given a certain scope, time, cost, and quality requirement.

☑ A project that does not meet user requirements is, by definition, a failure. Make sure you negotiate and gain agreement on user requirements before moving forward.

☑ Requirements typically fall into one of four categories: *user, business, technical*, and *functional*.

Refining Project Parameters

☑ *Success criteria* and *acceptance criteria* are two very important parameters to define for your project. Success criteria are specific (preferably measurable) measurements you, your team, and your project sponsor will use to determine that the project is/was successful. Acceptance criteria are typically used when users must accept (which often translates into *pay for*) tangible deliverables from the project. It is critical to define these criteria clearly and in a binary manner.

☑ You should refine your target or estimates for *scope, schedule, cost*, and *quality* for the project at this point. You will continue to refine these metrics moving forward, but as you more specifically define the project, you should be able to home in on these estimates.

☑ The *flexibility grid* helps you identify which elements of the project are most and least flexible according to your project sponsor. This helps you make decisions about change later in the project that are aligned with the sponsor's priorities.

☑ If you are aware of *constraints, limits*, and *risks* to the project at this point, they are worth noting. In some cases, these may be quite significant and cause you (or the project sponsor) to re-evaluate the feasibility or desirability of the project. If the project is terminated as a result, you should view this as a win for stopping a "bad" project from going forward.

☑ If you are aware of any *milestones* at this point, you can also record those. Milestones are not typically developed until later in the planning process, but if you are aware of any, they should be recorded now so they are not overlooked later.

☑ The *initial project plan*, which is the result of the steps in this chapter, may also be used as the basis for a Statement of Work or Project Charter document. Some companies use these terms interchangeably, and some have specific elements they require for such documents. All three (SOW, PC, and IPP) serve to clarify and document the high-level information about the project so the project can gain the official green light to move forward.

Defining Project Infrastructure

☑ The infrastructure needed for the project may include communication and collaboration tools for the team, communications devices (cell phones, PDAs, laptops, etc.), and other technology components needed to successfully complete the project.

☑ Infrastructure also includes the project team's needs in terms of office/desk space, office equipment (desks, cubicles, chairs, etc.), conference rooms, labs, or test equipment needed to successfully complete the project.

Defining Project Processes

☑ If you have defined project processes and procedures in the past that have worked well, reuse those.

☑ If your company has defined processes and procedures you are required to use, start with those and add only as many additional processes or procedures as needed to drive project quality and efficiency. Too many procedures can hinder productivity and quality.

☑ There are many different kinds or processes and procedures you can define. Some of the more commonly used ones include defining how status will be reported, how issues will be tracked, how changes to the project will be requested and approved, and how issues will be escalated.

☑ Additional plans related to the project may be required and these can be defined as project procedures. These may include a communications plan, a deployment plan, an operations plan, and a training plan. Not all projects require all of these plans; some projects require other plans not listed here.

Frequently Asked Questions

The following Frequently Asked Questions, answered by the author of this book, are designed to both measure your understanding of the concepts presented in this chapter and to assist you with real-life implementation of these concepts. To have your questions about this chapter answered by the author, browse to **www.syngress.com/solutions** and click on the **"Ask the Author"** form.

Q: Project planning in our company seems to go on and on and on. We seem to be able to plan something to death. What are we doing wrong?

A: IT projects are often managed by people who fall into the *analyst* category. One of the downsides to this work type is that they have a tendency to analyze things to death. They can feel as if they never have enough data to finalize the plan or make a decision. As a result, they get "analysis paralysis." Two things are important in overcoming this type of behavior. First is to acknowledge that we rarely, if ever, have "perfect knowledge" and at some point, we have enough information to move forward. The second thing is that things will change over time—they always do. Since project management is an iterative process, it means you will have to go back and tweak things later on. So, spending time to make it perfect now is a waste of time because it will more than likely change. To overcome this problem, it's often helpful to determine if you (or the team) feel you have 80% of what's needed. If so, move on. Also, set deadlines that are rigorous but achievable. Don't let the project lose momentum, find some *doers* and get them on the project team— they'll get things moving if you let them.

Q: Everyone at our company thinks P–L–A–N is a four-letter word. Any time I suggest we create a project plan, eyes roll and I get a lot of sarcastic comments about sitting around in planning meetings and never getting anything done. What can I do to counteract this attitude?

A: Many companies view planning as a waste of time and that's probably because if you plan and plan and plan and never *do* anything, planning *is* a waste of time. However, the reverse is also true. If you charge ahead without a clear idea of where you're headed and why, that's also a waste of time. There is a happy medium—planning followed by action. If you find a lot of resistance in your company to planning, try implementing one or two new practices at a time. While using the IT project management process end-to-end as delineated in this book will yield the most optimal results, implementing even one or two pieces of it will certainly help your project. For instance, maybe you start out by asking your team to help you clarify or identify the problem you're trying to solve, who you're trying to solve it for (stakeholders, users), and what the desired outcome is. You haven't used the word "planning"; instead, you've used the word "clarify" or "identify". Sometimes just changing a few words and not making a big production out of "planning" can help reduce resistance. Over time, these new habits should lead to better project results, which in turn could give you the opportunity to introduce one or two additional planning habits. Eventually, you'll have your IT project team (or company) planning without the sarcasm because you'll start with planning, but your planning will result in action.

Q: It seems that no matter how good a job we do at gathering user requirements, we always have some big change thrust upon us mid-project. What can we do that avoid this in the future?

A: Changing user requirements in mid-project is one of the most common, and most frustrating, elements of managing an IT project. The solution starts with identifying what is causing or allowing these changes in mid-project. Does your IT project team really do a good job gathering requirements? You might think so, but it's worth a second look to determine if your team can do a better job gathering requirements. One of the keys is to listen more than you talk. Listen to what users say they need and translate that into requirements. Negotiate with users only after you've gathered their requirements. Sometimes in the requirements gathering stage, someone from the project team begins to mold the requirements based on things outside the user such as the desire to use a particular technology or to implement a particular solution. Begin with listening to the user to gather the real requirements, not just the ones you and your team might like best. The other problem might be that your process for getting users to sign off on the requirements might be too weak or too ill-defined. It might be useful for you to formalize this process so users (whether internal or external) understand two key things. First, when they agree to the requirements, they are essentially "engraved in stone" and second, the cost of change goes up exponentially (while quality typically goes down) once the project is underway. Helping users to understand why it's important that the requirements be agreed to and locked in helps them understand what's in it for them. And, what's in it for them is a project result that meets their expectations in terms of scope, budget, time, and quality. In some cases, creating prototypes might help avoid mid-project changes.

Q: You defined a ton of project parameters and I get exhausted just thinking of defining all of this. Is it really necessary?

A: Each project is unique and the parameters you'll need to define for each project will also vary widely. You may not need every single parameter defined in this chapter, and you may find there are additional parameters you need to define that are not discussed here. The information listed is to give you a running start so you can define the elements that are critical to your project's success. And remember, it's about the quality of the data, not the quantity of the data. If you have a 10-page project plan or a 100-page project plan, it's only as good as the information in it, so only include the elements that will help you and your IT project team deliver a successful project. Also keep in mind that you can utilize your IT project team in the development of these parameters—parse out the work so that each team member has a deliverable and come together as a team to discuss and finalize these. It will be a better use of everyone's time, it will help reduce gaps and errors, and you won't be saddled with coming up with all of this on your own. Finally, smaller, less complex projects may need only a few of these parameters—define only what will make the project work clear and the final result successful.

Q: Our company is holding the line on technology expenditures and not all of the members of my IT project team have access to the same tools. Any suggestions?

A: That can be a tricky situation. If the technology required for the IT project's success cannot be purchased or acquired, you have to step back and ask why the company would want this project to move forward without the tools it needs for success. For instance, if you are tasked with upgrading the server infrastructure to Microsoft Windows Server 2003, but you are not authorized to create a testing lab, you have a problem. The same holds true when members of the project team do not have equal access to the tools to get the job done. Typically the most effective approach is to determine the cost of not having these tools available—the cost in terms of real dollars and in terms of lost dollars. The real dollar cost might be overtime, hiring external help, etc.. The lost dollars might be that project team members are unavailable to work on other tasks or projects or that the project itself comes in at a lower scope or quality. If you can quantify the cost and risk of not having these tools, you may be able to get your company to purchase or acquire these tools. If you can't, you may need to seriously reassess whether it's wise to move forward with this project at this time. Finally, you and your team may need to get creative about how to use existing tools to which all team members have access. Necessity is the mother of invention and you might discover a cool new way to use existing tools to help team members on the project.

Q: Our company has some very specific processes and procedures defined for projects, but they don't really seem to help me manage my IT projects any better. How should I approach this?

A: There are two parts to this question. The first is that your company has processes and procedures that don't really meet your needs. If you believe they are "process for process's sake," you can ask that your project be exempt from one or more of these processes or procedures. Remember though, choose your battles wisely. If some of the processes and procedures don't make sense but they're easy enough to comply with, you may choose to leave those for another time. Also keep in mind that some processes and procedures are there to comply with legal or regulatory requirements or to meet the needs of the business. Assess which ones might serve a higher purpose even if they're not meaningful to you. Then, try to lobby for reducing or eliminating those processes or procedures that simply get in your way and don't produce a meaningful result. The second part of this is that you must implement processes and procedures that fit your IT project. After reviewing the corporate processes, you can then determine what additional procedures you may need for your project. Avoid adding to already existing processes and procedures if the result will be redundant or just slightly different.

Chapter 7

Quality From the Ground Up

Solutions in this chapter:

- **Quality Overview**
- **Planning Quality**
- **Monitoring Quality**
- **Testing Quality**

☑ **Summary**

☑ **Solutions Fast Track**

☑ **Frequently Asked Questions**

Introduction

The title of this chapter is "Quality From the Ground Up" because it's important to build quality into your project right from the beginning. You can try to retrofit quality into your project later on, but it's just never the same. So, now that you've defined and organized your project, we're going to discuss the ways you can build quality into each phase of your project.

No one sets out to deliver poor quality results, but it happens all the time. These days, with corporate budgets being downsized and expenditures being thoroughly scrutinized and challenged, it's even more critical that projects deliver high-quality results. Lean economic times *aren't* the reason you should focus on building quality into your project, but they can certainly add pressure to do so. Whether your company is flush with cash or struggling to get by, your goal as the IT project manager should be to deliver the absolute highest quality result you can *within the constraints of the project*. It doesn't mean you necessarily deliver the absolute highest quality of all time, but the highest quality within the boundaries of your specific project. In this chapter, we'll explore this concept in more detail.

The biggest misconception about quality in any IT project is that it costs more money. That's not necessarily true and in fact, in 99.9% of the cases, it saves the company time and money far beyond the costs incurred. A study done by IBM in 1990 on the benefits of implementing Software Process Improvement (a.k.a. quality program) showed that implementing the program cost 0.005% of total corporate resources. You might immediately start doing some math, so let's make up some numbers. If the company has $1 billion in resources, the cost of the quality program would have been $5 million. As a result of implementing this quality program, the number of defects from 414 developers dropped by 50%. This saved 4 man-years (people-years, to be more exact) in software inspection time, 41 man-years in software testing time, and 410 man-years in post-release maintenance time. To simplify the math, we used a salary of $50,000 for all the people who might be involved in software inspection, testing, and maintenance. The total number of *years* saved was 455. At $50,000 each, that totals $22,750,000 saved. Spend $5M, save $22.75M. Any questions? [Source: "Using Cost Benefit Analysis to Develop Software Process Improvement Strategies", Department of Defense, 2000.]

There is a positive ROI (return on investment) for quality programs that are properly implemented and managed. How much of an ROI is dependent on several factors, but the point is that they net out in the gain column. There are also other costs associated with quality from the other side: the cost of poor quality. Think about the company's reputation, its ability to sell new software or the next version, the ability to convince people to convert to their software or product or to purchase the upgrade. All of those are dependent to a large degree (though not solely) on the quality of the product. The same holds true for hardware. If you build hardware that fails or hangs or halts intermittently (or regularly), customers will be reluctant to purchase or recommend your products. If you implement a poor quality project internally, you have to deal with downtime, repairs, maintenance, hot fixes, lost productivity, and more. There is a cost to implementing quality programs, but there is usually a higher cost associated with delivering poor quality. That factor is often difficult to quantify and it's rarely added in to the cost/benefit/risk analysis, though it should be. There are tangible examples out in the real world we can point to. One in particular makes the point painfully clear. The Denver airport stayed closed for over a year due to software glitches in the automated baggage handling system. After millions of dollars wasted, it abandoned the system. What was the total cost of failure in this case? Hundreds of millions of dollars when all the time, effort, expense, and traveler inconvenience is totaled up.

It's also important to mention that while you may want to aim for perfection, you have to work with limited time, resources, and money to achieve your project's objectives, which can make perfection an elusive and expensive goal. You have to make tough choices sometimes and you never *want* to sacrifice quality, though that is often exactly what happens. If you implement a quality management program, your goal is to improve quality to the highest reasonable degree. In this chapter, we'll look at some of the ways you can build quality into your project without implementing an additional quality management program. However, other quality management programs are compatible with IT project management, so if your company has implemented a quality program, what you learn in this chapter will fit in nicely.

Now that you've read Chapters 5 and 6 and have defined and organized your project, you're ready to look at the components of quality in your project. When you've completed this chapter, you may choose to go back and refine/redefine some of the elements you've developed so far and that's fine. IT project management is an iterative process and making a quick second pass through the existing project materials developed to this point can be helpful. On the other hand, you may find that you've already gotten your project off to a good start and can continue forward into your project planning stages.

As we did in Chapters 5 and 6, let's begin by seeing exactly where we are. Figure 7.1 shows the IT project management overview and where we are in that process.

Figure 7.1 IT Project Management Process Overview

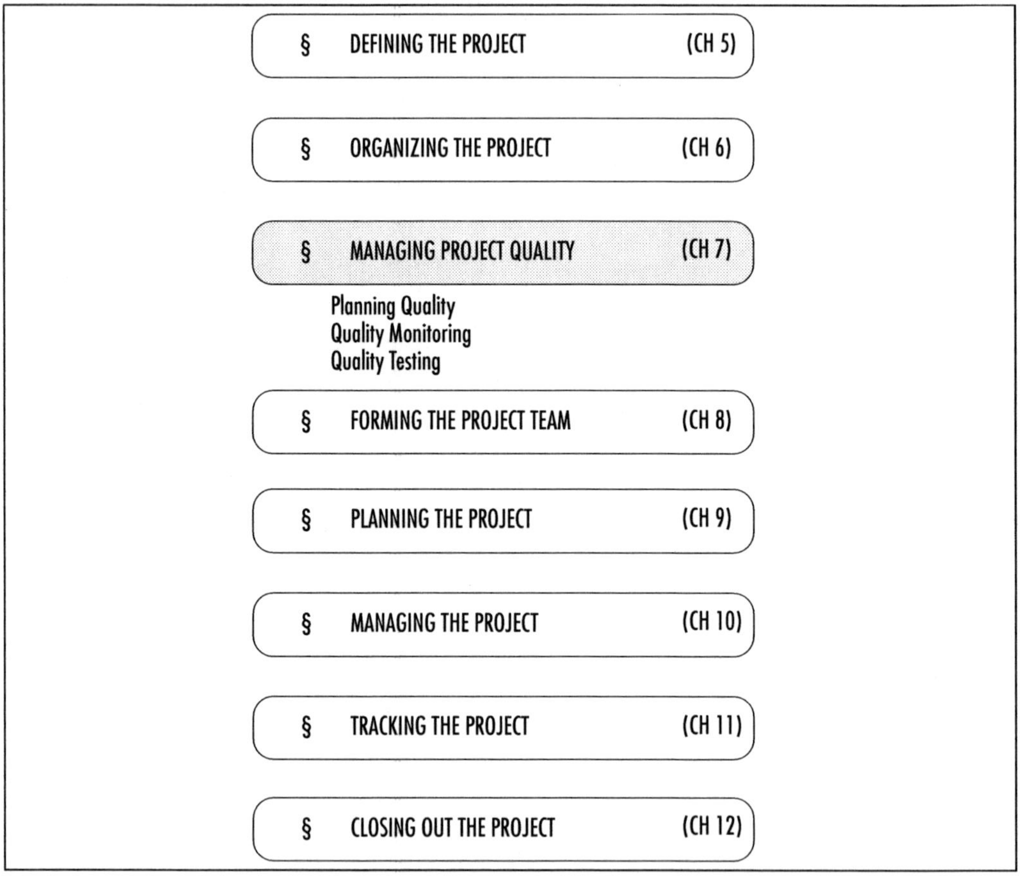

§ DEFINING THE PROJECT	(CH 5)
§ ORGANIZING THE PROJECT	(CH 6)
§ MANAGING PROJECT QUALITY	(CH 7)

Planning Quality
Quality Monitoring
Quality Testing

§ FORMING THE PROJECT TEAM	(CH 8)
§ PLANNING THE PROJECT	(CH 9)
§ MANAGING THE PROJECT	(CH 10)
§ TRACKING THE PROJECT	(CH 11)
§ CLOSING OUT THE PROJECT	(CH 12)

Quality is built into an IT project in three primary ways: *planning, monitoring,* and *testing.* We'll look at each of these areas in this chapter and then refer to them again in later chapters. The planning, monitoring, and testing elements occur in different phases of the project, so we'll revisit some of these topics again when we come to those stages of the project process. Let's also define a few terms before we head into the rest of the chapter.

- **Baseline** The data used as a reference with which to compare future observations or results.

- **Benchmarking** The process of setting a baseline or standard for analysis and comparison of future results or performance.

- **Grade** Grade refers to the category assigned to products or results to indicate similar functional, but different technical specifications. Grade A and

Grade B may work exactly alike, but one has different technical specifications than the other.

- **Quality** The degree to which a set of inherent characteristics fulfill requirements. Quality is defined through functional specifications. The user's perception of quality is influenced by both functional and technical specifications (how well the project results conform to user expectations in terms of function and errors/defects).

Quality Overview

Let's begin with a definition of the word *quality*. If you look up the word *quality* in the dictionary, you'll see a number of definitions. However, the one best suited to IT project management is "the degree to which a set of inherent characteristics fulfill requirements." Notice it doesn't say that it's the absolute pinnacle, but the *degree* to which *requirements* are fulfilled. Requirements…sounds familiar, doesn't it?

Quality Versus Grade

It's also important to distinguish between *quality* and *grade*. Low or poor quality is always a problem, but low grade is not necessarily a problem. *Grade* is the category assigned to products or results to indicate similar functional, but different technical specifications. For instance, if you're building a house and you want it to be a luxury house from top to bottom, you might specify that the fixtures will be made of 14 karat gold. However, once you develop your budget, you realize those fixtures are busting your budget and you decide to use a lower *grade* fixture made of burnished brass. *Functionally* those fixtures may be identical, but their technical specifications are different. The same is true of a software program. It might be very high quality with very few errors or bugs, but if it has very limited functionality, it might be considered a low-grade product. Conversely, we've all worked with products that might be considered high grade but low quality—they have features galore, but nothing works as well as it should or as advertised. Obviously then, *quality* and *grade* are related in the user's mind and it is the job of the IT project manager and project team to develop standards or specifications that deliver the required quality *and* grade.

Quality Management Components

There are numerous quality management systems used by companies today and everything we'll talk about in this chapter is aligned or consistent with these systems. If your company has implemented Total Quality Management (TQM), Six Sigma, or even ISO standards (to name a few), you can easily incorporate those quality systems into your IT project management process. There are four main components to quality management and these elements are consistent across all systems:

1. User satisfaction

2. Prevention versus correction

3. Continuous improvement

4. Management commitment

User Satisfaction

We've repeatedly mentioned the importance of user satisfaction. There are two components of user satisfaction. The first is one we've discussed, which is that the deliverables from the project meet user requirements. If you've done a good job defining requirements (Chapters 6 and 9), your project should deliver what you and the users agree it should deliver. The second component is that the requirements must be correct, meaning that the final result must actually satisfy the user's real (and not perceived) needs. This is the difference between "must have" and "would like to have" in the user world. If your project fails to deliver on the "must have" requirements, the project will be perceived by the user as less than successful (or a total failure altogether). Quality (errors, defects) and grade (functionality) are closely related in the user's mind as well. Grade is set through user requirements and quality is determined by how well the project conforms to those requirements.

Prevention Versus Correction

The old saying "an ounce of prevention is worth a pound of cure" is certainly true when it comes to quality. It's always easier and more beneficial to build quality into your project from the beginning. To go back once the project is underway or worse, to handle quality in the quality testing procedures as the end of your project, is the least desirable way of approaching quality. It is less costly and less time consuming to build quality into the project than to go back and try to correct things after the project is underway (or nearly completed). Quality management systems focus on preventing quality problems rather than correcting them. We'll discuss the cost of quality in more detail in a moment.

Continuous Improvement

Continuous improvement is another component of quality management. You may be familiar with the *plan-do-check-act* cycle (part of many quality systems). The point is that the process is continuous, or iterative, and you create your plans, go do your project, check the results, and take appropriate action to improve your project planning processes.

Management Commitment

If you recall from our discussion back in Chapter 1, projects that are most often successful are those with executive support. This is especially true when it comes to quality. If your company's focus is to get the project out the door as soon as possible and it does not value or emphasize planning, the quality of the finished product will likely suffer. Management or executives must be willing to make the investments in the project to ensure quality; this includes giving the project (and project team) enough time, money, and resources to get the job done right. Certainly there are limits on all of those, but a quality management approach recognizes that the project team cannot be held completely or solely responsible for quality; it is the responsibility of management to support quality efforts.

Applying Your Knowledge

If you want to deliver a quality project to your sponsor, project stakeholders, and users, you'll need to make sure management is aligned with your view of quality. Otherwise, you'll be specifying certain level of quality while your management team delays or denies requests for the resources you need to deliver on those quality commitments. If that happens, your project is going to wobble without the necessary resources to generate a quality result. There's only so much you can do with glue and rubber bands.

The process of planning for quality is depicted in Figure 7.2. As you can see, the initial project plan is one of two inputs to quality planning. The second input is your company's quality policy. If your company does not have a quality policy, you may still have some idea of the level of quality your company expects and what it will typically take to deliver that expected level of quality. If your company doesn't have a formal quality policy, you can write up your thoughts about expected level of quality and use those as the second input to this process, if desired.

Figure 7.2 IT Project Quality Planning Phase

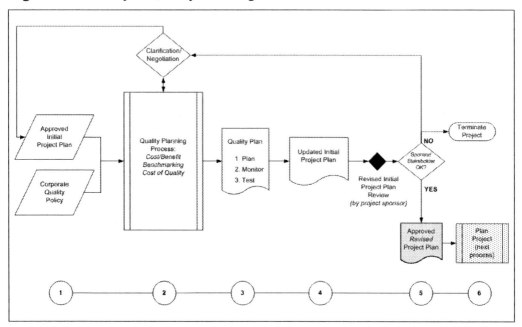

Within the quality planning phase or process, there are six distinct steps that we'll outline here and then discuss in more detail in this chapter.

1. **INPUTS** The approved initial project plan is one of two inputs for this phase. Although you could begin planning quality as you begin defining and organizing your project, you can also start at this point once you have a fairly well defined project. The second input is information or specifications from your company's corporate quality policy, if you have one. Many companies do not have a quality policy, but if one exists, you can use it as a second input to your quality planning process.

2. **ACTION** The quality planning process is an overarching process that impacts all phases of your project planning. There is always a tradeoff between the cost and benefit of quality. The benefits are typically less rework and higher user satisfaction. The cost is often captured in additional planning, monitoring, and testing. There is a balance between the two and often this balance is defined by a corporate quality policy, if one exists. Benchmarking provides a basis against which you can measure quality performance in the project. Analyzing the estimated cost of quality involves capturing the cost to build quality into the project as well as the costs of poor quality. For instance, quality costs might involve the cost of planning

to avoid errors and rework. The cost of poor quality might involve lost sales, poor company reputation, rework and after-release fixes.

At any point during the quality planning process, you may need to go back to your initial project plan to make revisions or you may need to go all the way back to your users and project sponsor for clarification and/or negotiation on certain points. If you recall from Chapter 6, when creating the requirements you may find through your quality planning process that you cannot reasonably deliver some of the requirements at the specified or desired quality levels. Remember, too, that quality is one of the four key project elements: scope, time, cost, and quality. If quality must be increased, it means that something else will have to change—usually time or cost will increase. In some cases, scope may decrease and this is where negotiating with either the users or the project sponsor becomes key to project success.

3. **OUTPUT** The result of this process is the overall quality plan. It contains the information that will allow you to plan, monitor, and test quality throughout the remainder of the project. This plan can contain a wide array of data, depending on your project and how your company operates. Three typical components of any quality plan are *quality objectives*, *quality metrics*, and *quality checklists*. We'll discuss these in more detail later in this chapter.

4. **ACTION** The overall quality plan should be integrated into the initial project plan and prepared for review by the project sponsor.

5. **CHECKPOINT** The checkpoint of this phase is the approval of the revised initial project plan (which now contains a quality component). Any revisions to the initial project plan should be approved by the project sponsor and stakeholders before proceeding. You may also need to clarify or revise additional elements of the plan based on sponsor or stakeholder feedback or requirements. Hopefully, this step will result in only minor changes to your plan and not a major revision.

6. **NEXT STEP** Once you have an approved, revised initial project plan, you can move into the planning stages where you and the project team will develop the project details. This is discussed in Chapter 9, after we discuss putting together your project team in Chapter 8. Remember, too, that there may be times when you've gone through all these steps and may have determined that the project is not viable and should be terminated. For instance, if given the scope, time, and cost you will be unable to deliver anything close to the quality expected, you may choose to delay or terminate the project. If your budget is suddenly slashed or the scope is dramati-

cally increased, you may decide to terminate this project and go back and start from scratch so you can better define and organize your project with these drastically different parameters.

The Cost of Quality

There have been numerous studies done on the costs associated with higher and lower quality. Many in the IT world have focused on software development. While there are many other kinds of IT projects that require quality, we're going to look just at software development for the moment, in part because the statistics are readily available and in part because we can all relate to using software that works well and software that drives us nuts due to errors and bugs. Many studies have been done, but the one mentioned at the opening of this chapter by IBM is significant. It's hard to argue with an ROI of over 400% for implementing a software process improvement program. There's additional data that supports the statistics cited earlier. Figure 7.3 shows the Rayleigh probability distribution (see http://en.wikipedia.org/wiki/Rayleigh_distribution for more on this subject) and a picture is worth a thousand words in this case.

Figure 7.3 The Cost of Fixing Software Defects

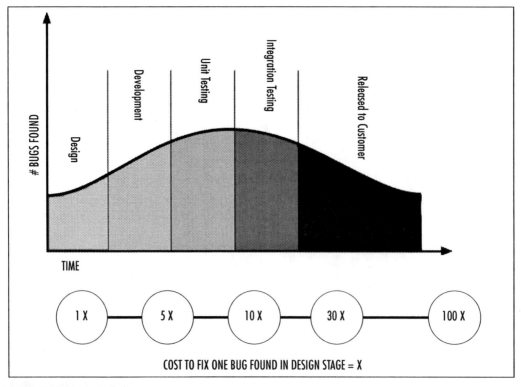

Clearly, defects in the design (which come directly from requirements) are far less expensive to fix earlier in the process. If you wait until the project result (in this case, a software program) is released to the customer, the cost is 100 times what it would have been back in the design stage for issues discovered by the user. The same type of cost structure applies to all types of IT projects. You have to begin with solid requirements and you have to use the processes, procedures, and metrics specified within the project to deliver a quality product at the other end. Whether your IT project involves improving network security through better intrusion and detection or upgrading servers or implementing supply chain management tools or integrating legacy applications with the Web, your IT project will benefit greatly from implementing an IT project management system (described in this book) and possibly other quality management systems appropriate to your company, industry, and focus.

If you recall, in Chapter 1 we mentioned that it's been estimated that 50% to 75% of the total cost of any project is due to errors, rework, and omissions. The errors, rework, and omissions happen throughout the project lifecycle, but the sooner they are discovered, the less expensive they are to repair. The corollary to that is that the fewer there are to begin with, the lower the cost and higher the quality of the final project.

Enterprise 128 …

Quality Versus Grade

Think back to our story of Enterprise 128, the early-to-market home computer that failed to find a following (see Chapter 1 for the whole story). Based on what you've learned in this chapter so far, what would you say the problem was? The problem was primarily one of *grade*. We have no idea what the quality of the product was from the perspective of whether or not it generated errors, had buggy software or hardware, halted, overheated, or crashed, and we don't know what how the requirements were written (how many errors/defects were acceptable?). We don't know any of that. What we *do* know is that the machine had all kinds of functionality the user didn't need or want. From the user perspective, then, the quality was probably not as much the issue as was the grade. It had too much functionality. The technical specifications were apparently not derived from the functional specifications generated through thorough market research or interviews with prospective users, but were apparently derived from what a few engineers thought would be fun, useful, or cool. Even if that machine had zero

Continued

errors, never crashed, and never so much as hiccoughed, it wasn't useful to users and never really took off. A lower grade product would have done the trick—if only the inventors had known, they might now be where Michael Dell is.

Planning Quality

The best way to ensure the quality of the project deliverables or results is to plan quality into each step. We've discussed this already to some degree, but let's take a few minutes here to review where this occurs in the defining, organizing, and planning stages.

User Requirements

We discussed user requirements in Chapter 6, so we won't revisit that material, but we will add some important distinctions to it. Earlier we talked about the difference between quality and grade. We said that quality has to do with the number of errors or defects in the final product and grade has to do with the functionality of the results. In the user's mind, the two may be exactly the same thing or the user(s) may have difficulty discerning the difference between the two. What matters is that you and your project team understand the difference between quality and grade and can work effectively with the users to define user requirements that are achievable by the project and project team.

Functional Requirements

Functional requirements describe what the project's deliverables must do. It includes statements and metrics about features, performance, speed, ease of use, workflow, usability (interface, look and feel), data or input requirements, access and security requirements, and output requirements (reports, exports). These are the things the user typically cares most about and these are what create the user's initial impression of quality. If the software product cannot produce reports and all the user cares about is reports, the functional requirements were incorrect or poorly developed (or the user, despite repeated rounds of interviews and questions, failed to mention reports as a "must have" requirement until the project was delivered….). How the reports are generated would fall under the technical requirements, which are derived from the functional requirements.

Technical Requirements

Technical requirements follow functional requirements. After clearly defining functional requirements for your IT project, you and your team can develop the related technical requirements. These can include all necessary requirements and specifications that allow your project team to develop the project's deliverables. These typically include things such as specific hardware, software and network requirements, error handling and logging, capacity, redundancy, reliability, interoperability, scalability, portability, security, storage, and monitoring, among many others. Clearly defining technical requirements in an IT project can only be done after the IT project is initially defined and organized and requirements (including user, functional, business, and others discussed in Chapter 6) have been gathered, compiled, and agreed upon. You may find that you can begin creating technical requirements earlier in the planning process and proceed in parallel with the other planning processes, but make sure you don't get ahead of yourself. Creating technical requirements for requirements that are not yet locked in or agreed to/approved can cause a lot of wasted time and rework.

Acceptance Criteria

We discussed developing acceptance criteria in Chapter 6. These criteria are typically used between a vendor and a client as a method of specifying what makes a deliverable acceptable to the client. This, in turn, is often used by the vendor as the trigger for billing the client for that deliverable or phase of the project. Acceptance criteria specify the essential elements and conditions for the project's deliverables to be accepted by the user. The definition of acceptance criteria clearly can increase or decrease the cost of quality. While you and your IT project team want to deliver the highest possible quality within the requirements of the project, you should use caution here when developing acceptance criteria with the user/client. Overengineering acceptance criteria can mean having to deliver more quality than is needed and at a premium. If ten errors in a million transactions are acceptable, don't sign up for five errors in a million. The incremental cost of reducing errors from ten to five could be huge *and* it's not required for the project to be successful.

Quality Metrics

Quality metrics are specific, measurable, quantifiable measurements related to the quality of the project. Metrics leave no room for guessing. For example, rather than asking whether the product shipped on time, which might yield a yes/no answer based on someone's perception, you would ask what day and time the product shipped. With an IT project, then, you might specify how much downtime is acceptable or how much uptime is required, or you might specify the failure rate threshold or the average bandwidth or speed that must be met. Metrics are used in both the quality monitoring and quality testing phases of the project, so defining them during the planning phase makes sense. As you develop additional project details, you may revise your quality metrics.

Quality Checklist

The term we use at this point in the project planning is *quality checklist*, which is a list used to verify that a required set of steps has been completed. Later in this book we'll use the term *completion criteria* when we begin talking about the specific tasks in the project. Completion criteria are usually listed (as a checklist) within the notes section of each task to ensure that each task was completed according to requirements and specifications. We can use the terms quality checklist and completion criteria interchangeably, but for our purposes, the quality checklist at this point will be much higher-level (less detailed) than the completion criteria you'll develop later in your planning process.

APPLYING YOUR KNOWLEDGE

These aren't the only tools at your disposal for managing quality in your project, but these are some of the most commonly used. The key is to determine what constitutes a quality result and figure out which processes and measurements will get you there. If you have some *analyst* types on your project team, this can be a good area to assign them to—they'll relish the opportunity to develop systems and metrics to deliver quality, but watch that they don't overdo it. Keep in mind the tradeoff between quality and time/cost to make sure your project hits the sweet spot.

Monitoring Quality

Once you've planned quality right into the project, your job as IT project manager is to manage and monitor quality while the project is underway. Some project management systems call this stage *quality assurance* (QA). In later chapters, we'll discuss managing the project once it gets started and the processes and procedures you defined in all the steps leading up to that point will come into play. We'll mention some of the tools you'll be using to monitor quality in your project, but we won't go into detail at this point to avoid redundancy. Look for these topics in later chapters.

Quality Management Plan

As the project gets underway, the quality management plan is one of the inputs to this phase as part of the overall project plan. The quality management plan describes how quality will be planned, monitored, and tested, so it should be available throughout the project life cycle.

Quality Metrics

We discussed quality metrics earlier and defined them as those specific, measurable items that define the level of required quality and the measurements used to validate those levels. These should be used during the management of the project and may also be used as part of the completion criteria for tasks that we'll discuss in Chapter 9.

Project Processes and Procedures

The processes and procedures you defined in Chapter 6 are an integral part of managing quality during the project work. Defined processes and procedures help you and the project team keep track of key data, metrics, results, and issues. Without well defined, easy-to-use processes and procedures, the quality of the project is at risk due to errors, oversights, and omissions. Quality can also suffer if there are too many useless, confusing, or contradictory processes and procedures in place because the project team may spend more time on procedure than on making sure they deliver quality results. Quality auditing may be a process or procedure in place at your company through an existing quality management program or through other means. If so, your quality auditing procedures may include process auditing to ensure that the processes used generate the required quality.

Status Reporting

Status reporting is another element that can assist in managing quality during the project. Understanding actual versus planned performance helps you and the project team make needed corrections during the project to ensure quality metrics and requirements are met. This information can also be useful during a post-project audit to locate the source of quality problems that might surface after the project's completion.

Issue Tracking

Issue tracking is critical to project quality because issues, by definition, put the project at risk. Anytime the project is at risk, the project quality is at risk as well. Tracking issues is not just a matter of defining what constitutes an issue and making a note of issues as they arise. In order to deliver a quality project result, you also need to effectively manage issues. That means that someone must be assigned as the owner so the issue is tracked, researched, analyzed, and resolved in a timely and reasonable manner. Issues that just get left behind in the logbook are quality problems in the making. An effective issue tracking system is critical to project quality.

Change Management

In Chapter 6, we discussed change management and the importance of developing a change management process that helps you manage change requests for the project. All requests for modification scope, time, cost, quality, or work methods should be analyzed for their effect on the project and in particular, their effect on project quality. All changes requests should be formally documented and submitted to the IT project manager. The project team should discuss the requested changes to determine the impact on the project and the benefits and risks of implementing the change. If the change is agreed to, it should be incorporated into the project plan. Any elements of the quality plan impacted by the change should be updated as well, including testing specifications for the changed elements. One last note about change management: poor change management almost always results in poor project quality. If you don't maintain control over the project's scope, time, budget, quality, and tasks, you have little chance of turning in a successful project.

Quality Assurance and Quality Control

Some companies use the term *quality assurance* to indicate the activities that are undertaken during the project to ensure quality results. This can be defined as *the application of planned, systematic quality activities to ensure the project meets requirements.* Some companies also use the term *quality control* (QC), which involves monitoring project results to ensure they meet requirements. These activities also occur during the project work cycle as well as at the completion of tasks, phases, or the entire project itself. If your company uses a quality management system, you may use other terminology, but the bottom line is that you have to plan quality into the project and then keep your eye on it throughout the project's life.

Testing Quality

As the saying goes, "You can't test quality into a product." During and after the project, you must test the results (interim and final) against the quality metrics and requirements specified to ensure the project is on track. No one in their right mind would create a project schedule and then look at it again on the final due date. The same holds true with quality. You can't just aim for quality then test it after all is said and done. You'll need to test for quality all along the way. In many IT projects, there is also a distinct quality testing process or phase a project goes through before the final product or deliverable is handed off to the user. It is during testing (both during and after the project work phase) that you hope to find any errors or defects that may have slipped through the process. The worst and usually most costly time to find errors or defects is once the project's deliverables have been handed over to the user, but the second worst time to find them is in the final testing phase, since it is always more expensive and more difficult to go back and fix problems at this point. As with monitoring quality, we'll discuss some of the quality testing components here to introduce you to terminology and concepts.

Prevention and Inspection

We mentioned earlier in this chapter that prevention is always more effective than inspection because you can't retrofit quality into a project; it has to be there from the beginning. Preventing errors and rework is always the goal, but there is a tradeoff between the level of desired quality and the cost. That tradeoff must be taken into account both from a user perspective and from a corporate perspective. You may be able to prevent 99.99% of all project errors, but the cost of the project results might be one hundred times what the market would pay for such a product. Inspection is how you ensure that your error/defect prevention is working and that your processes and procedures are generating the desired results. By periodically and thoroughly inspecting project results, you can ensure that the quality requirements and metrics are being met throughout the work of the project. Inspection also gives you the opportunity to make minor corrections before things veer too far off course. Inspection is sometimes referred to as project auditing, project review, and peer reviews.

Defined Quality Testing Procedures

Some IT projects require (and utilize) defined quality testing procedures. For instance, a software development project may have a dedicated quality control team responsible for designing tests that will put the software through its paces at each development stage and at the end of development. If your team or company has a defined quality testing procedure, it would be included in this phase.

Sampling

In some IT projects, sampling the project results is part of quality testing activities. Rather than inspecting every single line of code or every single network interface, you can achieve quality control at a lower cost through effective sampling techniques. Discussing sampling techniques is outside the scope of this book, but they are mentioned as a potentially useful tool you and your IT team may want to investigate.

Analysis

Analyzing project results throughout the project work cycle can also yield higher quality results. For instance, if an error or defect occurs in one area, analyzing the root cause or source may help reduce or avoid errors in another area. Analyzing the technical performance as well as the impact of errors or defects along the way can yield information you can use to finetune your project moving forward to further reduce errors.

Issue Resolution

Reviewing how issues are resolved is another component of quality testing. As you recall, issues should not only be tracked, they must also be resolved. The resolution of issues can point to areas of improvement in project processes and procedures or in other areas of the project. The action taken to resolve an issue can be helpful in improving other parts of the project and avoiding errors, omissions, and rework in subsequent phases of work. However, it's also true that the steps taken to resolve an issue may create a potential quality problem, so you should have a process in place to validate or test resolutions before they're implemented. Sometimes problems are simply solutions gone bad.

Cheat Sheet...

People, Technology, and Business

Remember that every IT project involves people, technology, and business. When you're developing your quality plans, make sure you keep these three factors in mind. Ask yourself, how can people contribute to the quality of this project? How can technology contribute to the quality of this project? How can our business contribute to the quality of this project (business processes, vendors, external relationships, and expertise are just a few ideas). When you look at these three areas for contributions to quality, you're bound to find a few that cost you nothing (or next to nothing) that you might otherwise have missed.

As the result of working through the steps in this chapter, you should have a solid quality management plan in place. This should be incorporated into you initial project plan so it can be an integral part of your project planning moving forward. Figure 7.3 depicts the outcome of this step, which is a quality management plan within the initial project plan.

Figure 7.4 Quality Management Plan

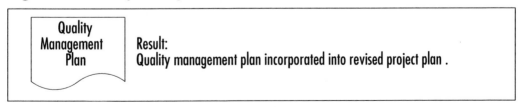

| Quality Management Plan | Result: Quality management plan incorporated into revised project plan . |

Summary

Quality and grade are two key components of the user's perception of quality, but they have distinctly different characteristics. Understanding the difference between quality and grade can help tremendously when working with users to define requirements and acceptance criteria. Quality is less expensive to plan into a project than to try to retrofit in once the project is underway, but there is always a tradeoff between the level of required quality and the cost to deliver that quality. Costs include the various efforts required to meet quality levels, including project work itself as well as quality monitoring and testing processes. The higher the level of required quality, the more rigorous the work, monitoring, and testing procedures must be, and that almost always comes at a higher cost.

The cost of poor quality must also be taken into account because this is often missed in the planning stages. What will happen if your product reaches the customer/user with too many errors, bugs, or defects? Will you have to tear things apart and redo them? Will you have lost a customer? Will your company be viewed negatively in the marketplace? Will the project team suffer negative consequences? It's important to understand the downside of poor quality as well as the cost of delivering high quality.

The three key components to quality are planning, monitoring, and testing. Based on what you've learned in this chapter, you may want to go back into your initial project plan and refine requirements, acceptance criteria, or other processes/procedures to build more quality processes into your project. As we move into the planning phase of the project in later chapters, we'll revisit some of the concepts presented in this chapter.

Don't let the relatively short length of this chapter fool you. Building quality into a project is of utmost importance, and using the defined IT project management process you're learning in this book is a major part of what drives quality. Consistent, repeatable processes that help you do a better job each step of the way is what IT project management is all about, so you're learning a methodology that will, by its very nature, help you deliver higher quality at a lower cost. The additional elements in this chapter are discussed throughout this book, so rather than bore you to tears with redundant information, we're giving you the short version here and we'll revisit these topics again in more detail.

APPLYING YOUR KNOWLEDGE

You may want to create a checklist based on the major headings in this chapter for use during your project planning and implementing phases so you are constantly reminded of the things that drive quality in your project. Many activities that drive quality in a project are fairly easy to do; they often just require an additional step or two or sometimes they simply require that you pay attention.

Solutions Fast Track

Quality Overview

☑ Quality and grade are two components of a user's experience or perception of quality.

☑ Most quality management systems include four major components: User satisfaction, prevention versus correction, continuous improvement, and management commitment.

☑ Your quality plan should be a component of your overall project plan and should be incorporated into the plan review and approval process.

Planning Quality

☑ User requirements are the basis of defining and delivering quality in a project. User requirements must be balanced against the cost of delivering the required/desired level of quality.

☑ Functional specifications define what the product or deliverable should do. Technical specifications define how the product or deliverable should achieve that functionality. Technical requirements are developed from the functional requirements.

☑ Acceptance criteria are used to gain agreement between the project team and the user/customer as to what constitutes fulfillment of requirements.

☑ Quality metrics are specific measurements to determine if the project's deliverables meet requirements.

☑ A quality checklist can be developed (detailed or high-level) to use throughout the life of the project to ensure project quality is maintained. Some people use the terms *quality checklist* and *completion criteria* interchangeably.

Monitoring Quality

☑ A quality management plan defines all the elements that will drive quality in the project including those in the planning, monitoring, and testing phases. It defines activities that will occur during the project work phase to ensure quality results.

☑ Quality metrics provide measurable ways of determining if a project deliverable has met requirements.

☑ Processes and procedures help drive quality during the work phase of the project. The processes and procedures defined throughout this book help ensure quality results by providing a framework for consistent effort and evaluation.

☑ Status reporting and issue tracking are part of the quality monitoring process during the work phase of the project.

☑ Change management helps ensure quality results by closely monitoring and managing any and all requested changes to the project's work (scope, time, budget, quality, tasks, etc.). Poor change management typically results in poor project quality.

Testing Quality

☑ Prevention is the process of planning quality into the project. Inspection is the process of verifying the planned quality is being achieved. Testing is the third component of quality in an IT project used to verify the quality of results.

☑ Defined quality testing procedures may exist for your IT project, based on the type and nature of the project. Some IT projects use a dedicated quality control (testing) team to test the results of the project at each step or phase and to test/verify the overall/final quality of the project.

☑ Sampling can be a good method of testing project results without having to spend time or money to test every single component. Testing a random sampling can generate almost the same accuracy as testing every single component, but at a fraction of the cost/effort.

☑ Analyzing project results as you go can also help increase quality and reduce the cost of the project. Determining the source or cause of a problem can help you avoid that same problem later in the project.

☑ Issue resolution can be helpful to look at during quality testing because it may point you to methods to improve quality in other areas of the project based on the resolution taken for a specific issue. On the other hand, the steps taken to resolve an issue may create a potential quality problem, so resolutions must be tested before being implemented.

Frequently Asked Questions

The following Frequently Asked Questions, answered by the author of this book, are designed to both measure your understanding of the concepts presented in this chapter and to assist you with real-life implementation of these concepts. To have your questions about this chapter answered by the author, browse to **www.syngress.com/solutions** and click on the **"Ask the Author"** form.

Q: Our company uses Six Sigma and it seems that it conflicts in some ways with IT project management. Is that true?

A: No, any quality management system can work side by side with IT project management. In some cases, you may want to modify the IT project management practices defined in this book simply to avoid redundancy. The point of Six Sigma is to reduce errors. The point of IT project management is to deliver a more successful project, part of which involves delivering the highest required quality at the lowest cost (time and money) possible. They are quite compatible, so if you find conflicting areas, examine them closely and resolve them in a way that meets your company's criteria. However, there's a good bet that upon closer examination, you won't find areas that are completely incompatible.

Q: I've had a long-running debate with a colleague about quality and the discussion in this chapter on quality versus grade clarified things greatly. Why isn't grade discussed more often? It's so important in decision making.

A: Quality and grade are closely related, as you saw in our earlier discussion, and, from a user's point of view, there may be no difference. If you purchase a financial software program for your personal use, do you differentiate between how many bugs you experience and the fact that it won't export your data to your favorite spreadsheet program? You probably don't, nor do most users. However, one is a quality issue (bugs) and one is a grade issue (lack of an export capability), but to you, as the frustrated user, they are both elements of quality. The distinction between quality and grade really becomes important in for the IT project team when helping to develop requirements and acceptance criteria. The reason why no one discusses the difference between quality and grade might be because so few IT project teams use a defined IT project management methodology (you may be the exception since you're reading this book).

Q: You mention quality metrics several times, but we've never used quality metrics. Can you explain how we can develop specific quality metrics for our IT project?

A: If you've never used specific metrics, you may have actually made things harder on yourselves than necessary. Think about connecting a new communications line to your office building. You might say that in order for it to meet quality requirements it must provide a fast Internet connection to the 1200 users in your building. That sounds good, but what happens when the line the vendor installs is so bad that the error rate is so high that the Internet connection for your users crawls to a halt? How do you quantify this with the vendor? You can't very well say, "It's just too slow!" One way to begin to develop metrics is to figure out what you'd want to use if this deliverable was being delivered to you and you were paying someone external for it. How would you measure it then? Most likely you'd use some sort of line speed test with a minimum speed threshold and a maximum erro threshold for the line. With a bit of digging, you can probably quantify some of the quality statements you've made and turn them into meaningful quality metrics.

Q: Our company always says it wants quality, but when push comes to shove, they want it cheaper and faster and quality goes out the window. Any suggestions?

A: The unfortunate reality is that many companies give lip service to quality and then do nothing to support it in the organization. Other companies truly value quality and don't realize the things they're doing don't support quality. These are two distinctly different corporate personalities so try to discern which it is first. If your company truly doesn't value quality, you have a huge uphill battle, but you may have success in explaining how low quality costs the company, directly and indirectly. If your company actually values quality, but has processes, procedures, and cultural practices in place that undermine quality, you have a better chance of catalyzing change in the organization. Take it one step at a time and begin by implementing processes and procedures in your IT projects that deliver quality. Since planning quality in is almost always less expensive (time and money) than trying to fix it later, your project results will begin to speak for themselves. You can also make the business case for quality and then work to change the processes and procedures in your company that undermine quality results. Start small and build momentum. Just implementing this IT project management methodology could improve your results so much that people come to you asking how you did it. Wouldn't that make changing habits an easier sell?

Q: I like the idea of planning first and creating code second, but what do I do with the developers on the project until I am ready for them? I don't want them to be bored or get "stolen" for another project, and I don't want my developers to appear idle to my management since I don't have anything tangible to show for the project during all this planning. Any ideas?

A: You are correct in your concerns to ensure your team is busy doing useful work while collecting requirements and developing the plan. Consider tasking the developers with designing the test plans to ensure customer requirements are met. Two big benefits: First, the developers gain an understanding of the bigger picture and may have some good ideas on ways to improve the process and second, by having your developers writing the testing plans, you can be sure the code will do what the customer requires. If your developers are still going to run out of things to do, consider doing a phased start up where the development team is not fully engaged until you are ready for them or ask the developers to help in designing a method to track issues found, but be careful here—you don't want to spawn a project within a project to design and develop a whole new bug tracking system when your company probably already has a working solution for you to use.

Chapter 8

Forming the IT Project Team

Solutions in this chapter:

- **Identifying Project Team Requirements**

- **Identifying Staffing Requirements and Constraints**

- **Defining Roles and Responsibilities**

- **Acquiring Needed Staff**

- **Forming the Team**

☑ **Summary**

☑ **Solutions Fast Track**

☑ **Frequently Asked Questions**

Introduction

Some IT projects have the same project team from start to finish, while others have changing personnel throughout the various stages of the project. At some point, whether it's at the very inception of the project or somewhere after the project definition and organization, you'll need to put together your project team. While you could theoretically put your team together after you've planned the whole project, you'd be starting it off on the wrong foot. Ideally, the project team should be involved in the defining, organizing, planning, execution, and assessment of the project. While this is not always possible in the real world, it is what you should be aiming for. Here's why: a project team provides subject matter expertise you probably lack, ideas and perspectives different from your own, information and contacts with others in the organization that are relevant to the project, and more heads and hands to help get the project work done.

While all of these are essential for success, there is one additional element that might be the single most important reason to get your project team on board early in the project life cycle: ownership. If you've ever been handed a complete plan and told to go implement it, you probably know just how your project team would feel if that happened to them. You're less than enthusiastic about the assignment because you had no part in designing, developing, and planning it. In fact, the approach to the project itself might be so different that you really have a hard time getting your arms around it, even though you understand what's outlined. People are far more likely to participate fully when they have a hand in the definition, organization, and planning of a project. They'll feel a sense of ownership and will usually work hard to ensure the project is a success. Since the IT project manager is typically managing a team over which they have little formal organizational authority, creating a sense of commitment to the team and to the project is critical to actually being able to get the project team to complete the project within the scope, time, cost, and quality required.

In Chapter 4, you learned a lot about why people work, what motivates them, and how to work within a diverse team. You also learned what it takes to create a high performance team, so if you skipped over Chapter 4, now may be a good time to go back and read (or review) it. In this chapter, you'll learn about how to put together a project team and how to assign roles and responsibilities to team members. You'll also learn about how to track and manage performance and deliverables and what to do if trouble arises. In Chapter 9 we'll begin the detailed planning tasks for the project, and having your project team in place and ready to go for these planning tasks will be essential. If you put your project team together (or if some of the team members have changed) at this point, you should review the definition and organization with them and make any needed modifications prior to moving forward. This will begin to build a sense of commitment to the project and may also provide new information that helps make the project better. If your project team has been with you from the start, you'll be ready to hit the planning stage running. But, don't skip this chapter even if your team is formed; there are a few tips and tricks you'll find helpful before moving on. Figure 8.1 shows where we are in our project planning process.

Figure 8.1 IT Project Management Process Overview

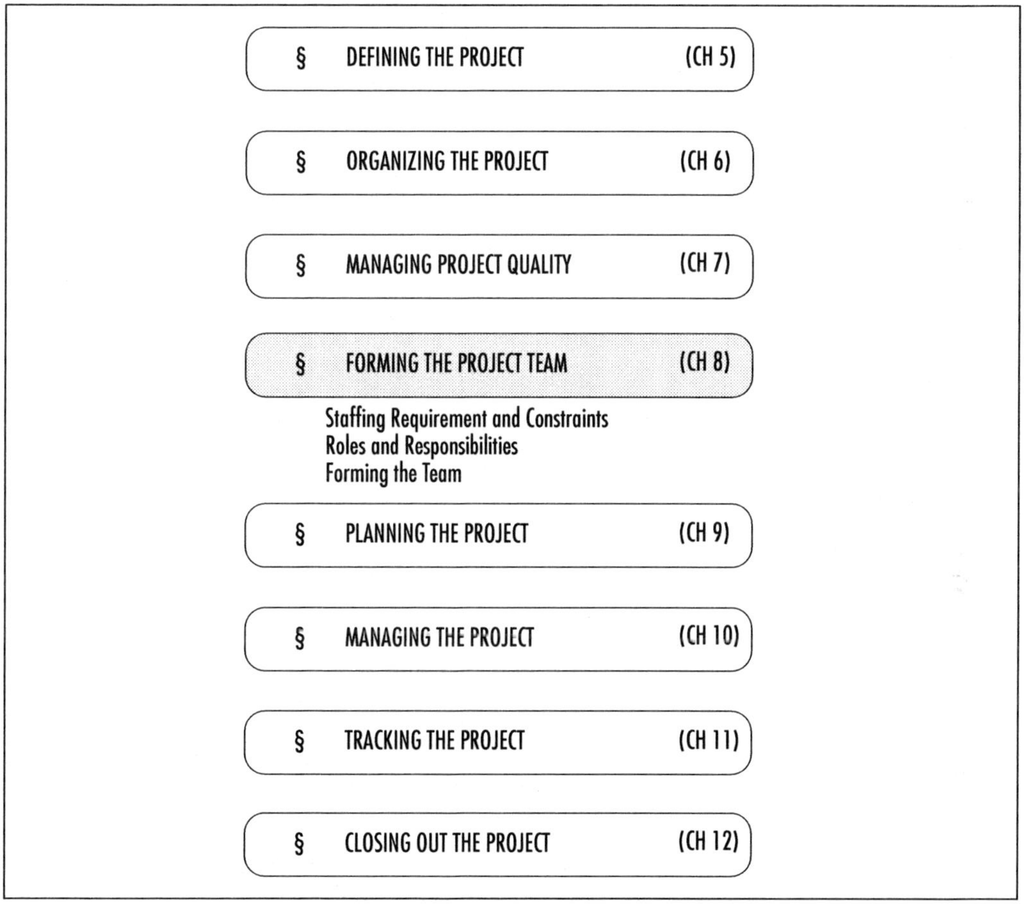

§	DEFINING THE PROJECT	(CH 5)
§	ORGANIZING THE PROJECT	(CH 6)
§	MANAGING PROJECT QUALITY	(CH 7)
§	FORMING THE PROJECT TEAM	(CH 8)

Staffing Requirement and Constraints
Roles and Responsibilities
Forming the Team

§	PLANNING THE PROJECT	(CH 9)
§	MANAGING THE PROJECT	(CH 10)
§	TRACKING THE PROJECT	(CH 11)
§	CLOSING OUT THE PROJECT	(CH 12)

Identifying Project Team Requirements

Let's start with the big picture. Your project team will be comprised of subject matter experts—people who can help define and deliver project results. These folks may be from your IT department or they may be from many different departments in the company. Your project team may rely on a mix of internal staff and external contractors. It may be comprised of people locally or globally. The first step is to define the kinds of people (skills, not personalities) you need, not the *specific* people you need. In some companies, an initial project team works on defining these requirements and then members of the project team are added or removed as needed.

You can begin by looking at the overall environment and looking specifically at these elements:

- **Organizational** Which departments, divisions, or sections of the company should be represented on the project team? Is there a budget issue (hiring freeze, cutbacks, etc.) that could impact your project? What about unions or collective bargaining issues that will impact team membership (or the project itself)?

- **Technical** What are the different technical specialties that should be represented on the project team? Are there different types of technologies (engineering approaches, software languages, equipment) that should be represented or that will have to be coordinated?

- **Logistical** Where are project team members located? Are they local, remote, overseas? How will you coordinate their activities? Much of this should have already been defined in IT project team processes in Chapter 6.

- **Interpersonal** What types of formal and informal relationships exist among team members (or potential team members)? Are there known relationships you can leverage or known issues you can avoid?

- **Political** What alliances exist among various stakeholders and how will these influence your project (for better or for worse)? Are there any people on the IT project team with political clout or any members on the team that seem to be out of favor politically? How will this affect your IT project?

In addition to these environmental issues, there are additional things to think about when you build your IT project team. Some of these elements may not be relevant to every IT project, but going through these elements helps you make sure you're building the most optimal project team you can within the organizational constraints. We all have experienced teams that had certain members because of politics or because of the company's organizational structure. While having these kinds of people on your IT project team is not optimal, these team members can be managed if you know what's what.

You may want to develop an organizational chart showing the relationships of potential or desirable team members so you can visualize the lay of the land. You may prefer a simple matrix or grid to depict team members and responsibilities or you may opt for the simple team roster. The key is to capture this list of current and/or future IT project team members and have an understanding of the five elements described above.

Roles and Responsibilities

Once you've looked at the five environmental elements, you should then begin to identify roles and responsibilities. Again, this can (and should) be done without a specific individual in mind and it's often better if you start out that way. The tendency for most people is to identify people rather than roles, responsibilities, and competencies. When you identify people, you may develop preconceived notions about roles and responsibilities based upon that specific person. Ideally, you want to identify roles, responsibilities, and competencies needed for the project then find people to fill those roles. You can then add roles, responsibilities, and competencies to your team list (org chart, matrix, or team roster). We'll look at this in a bit more detail in just a bit.

Competencies

Your IT project will undoubtedly require specific competencies throughout the lifecycle of the project. These may change from one phase to another (and probably will). Defining the required competencies and mapping them to roles and responsibilities can help you identify the specific people you'll need to make your project successful. If you define a software engineer role whose job it is to define end user requirements, you'll need to identify the specific competencies for that role such as the ability to interact effectively with end users, the ability to translate functional requirements into technical requirements, or the ability to negotiate with end users to help develop requirements that are feasible and useful.

Another type of competency to keep in mind are the workstyles we discussed earlier in the book. If you have a team full of *analyst* types, you won't have a balanced team. This can lead to blind spots (everyone thinking in the same way) and can actually make it harder to manage the team. Whenever possible, try to create a balanced team by including people who represent the four different workstyles we discussed (see Chapter 4). By having each workstyle represented, you'll gain access to different viewpoints and different approaches to the project. This can help add to the quality of your final project and even make managing the team a bit easier. You'll be able to utilize the unique skills and talents that members bring to the team. For instance, the *analyst* types can help define many of the details while others who may be more interactive can help craft and manage the project communications, or work with users.

Staff Availability

Now that you've identified your dream team, you have to find out if they're available for your IT project. In smaller companies, it's easy to determine if people are available or to shift things around so they will be available. In larger companies, it often is a matter of competing for team members with other projects and other priorities. It also means negotiating and working within a political framework to get the IT project team members needed. If you need assistance, your project sponsor can often help out by exerting his or her influence within the organization to help you get needed staff resources. If you cannot acquire the talent and expertise needed to successfully execute your project plan, your project is in serious jeopardy. This creates a significant risk to the project (we'll discuss project risk in more depth later in the book) and you should not proceed until you've addressed this problem in a satisfactory manner.

Identifying Project Interfaces

Project interfaces describe all the ways your project team interacts with others. You should think about how your IT project team members will need to interact with others in the organization throughout the project lifecycle. This will help you identify contacts, liaisons, resources, and allies within the organization that will interact with your project and project team. If you thoroughly identified stakeholders earlier, you have a jumpstart on this process, though not all project interfaces are stakeholders per se. For instance, you may need someone in the Payroll department to create a project code and to work with team members to properly code timesheets or other payroll information to be submitted. That person is not a stakeholder in the IT project, but is clearly someone with whom the project team members will interface. There may be other more significant interfaces you identify at this point or they could all have been identified during your stakeholder identification process.

You may already have an established project team for your IT project and if so, that's fine. You don't need to reinvent the wheel, but do take a moment to review the items just listed and compare them to your current project team to make sure all your bases are covered. As you know, once you've identified many of your IT project elements once, you can reuse and repurpose much of that work over and over again to save yourself time and effort. Just don't fall into complacency. Check your work against your formal process as you go to make sure you don't accidentally miss something that might be new or unique to this IT project.

Identifying Staffing Requirements and Constraints

We briefly discussed roles and responsibilities in an earlier section, but that was a more generic list of desired or needed roles and responsibilities based on project requirements. Now you need to identify specific *people* to fill those roles and take on those responsibilities. This often requires a bit of negotiation and salesmanship to get the right people on board with the project. Selling the project doesn't mean saying things that are false or misleading. Just the opposite. You should be able to present the project in a positive, enthusiastic manner and be prepared to describe the benefits to any team members that you need on the project. We all know that some team members don't really have a choice as to whether to participate in the project or not, but others do have options and if you need their time, talent, or cooperation (or you need their manager to release them to your project), you need to clearly make the case for what's in it for them. People don't care as much about how you'll benefit from their participation (well, everyone likes an ego boost now and then) as much as they want to know what's in it for them. If you can't clearly state that, you may have a hard time convincing them to participate. Forcing someone to work on a project they don't want to work on always yields sub-optimal results because you'll be dragging them along with the project rather than having them help lead the way.

Remember to look at staffing requirements in terms of internal and external: Internal/external to your IT group, to your division, to your location, or to your company. You may need consultants, vendor experts, industry experts, legal or financial experts, or experts on governmental regulations to assist in your project. Make sure you've looked thoroughly at your project requirements and defined the roles and responsibilities that will address all those requirements. Then look for the right people to fill those roles.

Constraints for staffing come in many forms, as most of you already know. Sometimes the ideal candidate is not available for another three months and the project has to get underway next month. Sometimes the ideal candidate simply does not exist. Sometimes you have two or three people who, together, have all the right skills and talents you need, but you can't grab all three for the project. Sometimes you can't seem to successfully navigate the political waters to acquire the talent you need. The list goes on and on in terms of staffing constraints.

Begin by identifying any known constraints, such as the need for a particular skill or talent at a particular point in the project (remember, the project team may shift over the lifecycle of the project as you move from one phase to the next). Keep in mind that since you have not yet broken down your project into the work units (we'll do that in Chapter 9), you may not have a complete list of required skills at this point. You may need to add or subtract resources once you've completed your Work Breakdown Structure (see Chapter 9).

Next, determine if the skills and talents you've identified for your project exist within your team, division, or company. If not, you're going to have to go outside the company for that skill. If the talent is internal, are they available for the project and can you get them assigned to your project? If the talent is external, was this figured into the project cost estimate and can you locate and afford to hire that talent? If your project depends on a rare talent that only four people in the world have, you not only will have more trouble locating, acquiring, and affording that talent, but you also have identified another very serious project risk (again, we'll tackle project risk later on).

Be sure to review your requirements, especially legal, financial, and governmental to make sure you have the expertise on your IT project team to address these requirements. You may need to bring in your corporate attorney or accountant or you may need to hire an industry or governmental expert to ensure you meet these types of requirements. You may need to put some of your team through training to address the need for specific expertise and we'll talk more about training in just a bit.

If your IT project is being conducted in an environment where labor unions are present, you may also have to contend with union requirements or regulations as a staffing constraint. For instance, if your IT project is developing a new program to run a particular manufacturing machine and you'll need to get the machinists to test the program for you, you may have to work with union leadership to get this done in a manner that complies with union rules and meets your IT project's needs.

Defining Roles and Responsibilities

Once you've identified the people with various skills and talents you need represented on the IT project team and you've worked to acquire those folks for your project, you need to organize them. By defining clear roles and responsibilities, you will create a framework within which team members can work. Most people like to have clear roles, responsibilities, and boundaries so they know what they should (and should not) do, what is and is not acceptable, and how to interact with others on the team. Clearly defined roles and responsibilities are absolutely essential for project success. You may have created some of the needed framework when you defined project processes; there may be additional information needed to help team members work in the most productive manner possible.

Rather than working with people's organizational titles, you may choose to define roles and responsibilities within the team structure. This can help create a sense of being part of a team and can help reduce problems based on organizational rank or title. For instance, if you have three people on the team that will all fill the same role (software engineer, for instance), call them "software engineer" for the project even if each of them has a different official title within the organization. As with the project itself, it may be helpful to define what is and is not included in each role. Setting role boundaries will help avoid overlap, conflict, and confusion later.

Once you've defined roles, you also need to define each role's responsibilities. Sometimes it's helpful to work on this with the team, other times a group discussion may simply lead to conflicts and arguments. Depending on the nature of your team, you'll have to decide the best course of action. If you define roles and responsibilities for the team, you will need to run this by team members for two reasons. The first reason is that you may have inadvertently overlooked important information for roles and responsibilities. The second is that by asking the team for input (and then using it), you'll help build the team's ownership in the project. If you simply define roles and responsibilities and hand them out, the team will have a much lower stake than if they can provide input and ideas. Usually this process also yield more clarity because team members can ask questions and clarify any gray areas.

Defining responsibilities typically includes defining deliverables or what each team member will be responsible for accomplishing. Again, the more clarity you start with, the better the result. Working with each member of the team to establish clear, well-defined responsibilities also helps ask and answer questions about conflicting roles, responsibilities, and deliverables. Avoid overlapping responsibilities and work with the team to clarify any issues before getting started on the project work itself. These responsibilities and deliverables also become part of the performance review proccess at project closeout (see Chapter 12 for details).

Another area to look at is required competencies. We discussed identifying required competencies at the higher project level, but once you've begun looking at specific people, you need to check your competencies requirements to make sure that you're getting the people with the skills you need.

Enterprise 128 ...

Hot Projects and Hot Shots

Putting together a project team can sometimes be a very easy, pleasurable task—especially when the project has high visibility or involves working with cutting-edge technology. On the other hand, there are more utilitarian projects that people will go to great lengths to avoid. These projects often need the same skills, talents, and enthusiasm, but putting together a project team for a mundane IT project can be a challenge. Here's your mission: don't go for the low hanging fruit. You may be tempted to grab just about any warm body you can for these lower priority, lower visibility projects, but that may put your project at risk. Taking whoever's available is the path of least resistance and yields the results with the least luster. Some IT project managers don't want to expend the energy required to sell a less exciting project to their talented IT staff (or to others outside the immediate environment), but that's a mistake. Ideally, you should try to ensure that assignments to exciting, highly visible projects are based, at least to some degree, on past participation on the mundane projects. By establishing a link between participation in mundane and exciting projects, you can help ensure you get a good, talented, enthusiastic mix on all your IT projects—even your brightest stars should spend time working on less exciting projects. Of course, things in the real world aren't always ideal, but you have to start someplace.

Acquiring Needed Staff

After you've defined required skills and competencies and identified roles and responsibilities, you have to go about pulling the team together before the project starts. If your project team comes from within your IT team, then you really don't have much to think about here. On the other hand, if you're pulling in resources from other departments, divisions, or companies (vendors, consultants, contractors), you have to give a lot of thought to how you pull it all together. First and foremost, make contact with the person's direct supervisor or manager and gain agreement about the person's participation in the project. Sometimes a person may agree to participate, but his or her manager has other plans such as other, higher priority assignments or issues with the person's work that you're not aware of. Start by contacting the person's manager for an official OK.

If your project requires the use of outside expertise, you need to include a staffing expense in your project budget. If you did not include this type of expense in your project estimate, make sure you add it now. You may also need to compare actual labor rates to the ones you used for estimating to make sure they're accurate. If necessary, discuss any changes or issues with the project sponsor.

Next, you need to think about some of the immediate next steps for your team. Here are a few additional considerations:

- Where will the team work? Will people have to travel to a central location for meetings or meet via phone or videoconference?

- What is the procedure to formally pull someone onto the project? Which managers need to be notified? How and when should they be notified? Are there political issues involved?

- What is the cost of each team member for the project and how will this be accounted for? In some cases, you may only need to track hours against the project. In other cases you may need to track specific payroll costs and will have to work with Human Resources, Payroll, or Accounting to manage this.

- When will the team be formally tasked with the project work and when is each team member available? Sometimes changing availability can impact the start or progress of a project to a significant degree.

- If external people are required, you'll need to identify how those people are acquired. Will you go through a staffing agency? Will you hire them on full-time? How long will you need to find and hire the specific skills and talents your project will require? Working with an experienced recruiter can help you answer many of these questions if you're not experienced in this regard.

- What will you do if the project start date slips? Which resources will be at risk? Which resources will be lost? What alternatives can you come up with to manage this scenario?

One thing to keep in mind with your project team: sometimes you are assigned people you'd rather not have on the team due to a variety of issues. For instance, some departments may toss one of their worst performers your way just to get him or her out of the way. They might give you their most contentious, least-knowledge-able person or they might give you the person just about to be fired. If you find yourself in a situation where you've been assigned someone who will be a serious liability to the project (or even just a non-contributor), you should sit down with your project sponsor and have an honest discussion. Don't let deadweight land on your project team without pushing back. In the end, you may not have any choice but to accept this team member, but hopefully your project sponsor will be savvy enough to understand the risks a non-performer brings to the project. You'll need to be tactful but honest with your project sponsor and most important, go prepared with the name of the person or people you *do* want. Successful projects depend upon a good project team and as the IT project manager, you should do your best to make sure you don't get stuck with any duds.

Cheat Sheet...

Good Technical Recruiters... Worth Their Weight in Gold

Whether you're trying to find permanent IT staff or temporary technical people for an IT project, you might consider establishing a relationship with an experienced technical recruiting firm. Even if your job is not to directly find or hire people (that may be solely within the Human Resources department), it won't hurt for you to establish a relationship with a good technical recruiting firm or technical recruiter. "A good recruiter has lots of contacts and resources and is a great source when looking for part-time, temporary or temporary-to-permanent IT staff," explains Chris Landi, President of TekWork.com, a technical recruiting company. "Rather than spending your time and money trying to advertise a position in the "right" places, one call to a good recruiter can get it all done for you, often with better results." Once you establish a working relationship with a good recruiter, your job of locating and retaining the right talent for your IT department or for your IT project will be much easier. If your firm has an internal technical recruiter, you should certainly start there, but having an established contact or two outside your own firm can help fill the gaps.

Forming the Team

You've now laid the groundwork for forming your IT team and should be ready to go. Once you've identified the IT team members, you're ready to officially form your team. As we discussed earlier, you'll need to organize your team. Some of this organization was discussed in Chapter 6 when we discussed how to organize your project. However, we'll briefly review some of those elements and add a bit more detail here. Remember, too, that once you've identified your work breakdown, your team requirements may change.

Team Roster

Creating a team roster may seem like a no-brainer, but you'd be surprised how many times it's overlooked. Create a team roster listing all the relevant information about each team members and distribute it to your team. You may want to list this on a team intranet site or simply distribute it as a text document via e-mail. Whatever you do, make sure you create a roster and distribute it to facilitate team communication. You can download a team roster template to give you a head start.

Training

Once you've formed the project team, you may find there is specific training needed in order for the project to proceed. A good example of this is if you're putting together a hardware and software package for point of sales systems and the system must track sales tax. The sales tax calculation will depend on local, state, and federal tax rules and one or more member of your team may need to be trained in how this works so that your systems will be fully compliant. Gather input from the team as well to make sure you don't overlook important training before the project gets underway. Make sure this training has been reflected in your project budget estimate and include the specific line item costs when you prepare your final project budget, which we'll discuss later in this book. If you're not sure if your team will require training (or how much training), build in contingency funds for training. If the training is triggered by using less experienced team members, you may also use this cost as leverage to get more experienced people on your team. Sometimes the time and cost of training is worth the investment (versus putting more experienced people on the team), sometimes it's not. This might be a point of discussion with the project sponsor, if in doubt.

Processes and Procedures

You should already have defined processes and procedures for your project, including how the team will interact, how often it will meet, what types of status and data reporting is needed, and how performance will be tracked and assessed. These should be discussed with the team and any modifications to procedures should be discussed and finalized. You want to have a fairly stable set of processes and procedures going into your project so you're not changing the rules in the middle of the project. Ensure that all team members understand the processes, and how their performance will be evaluated. When applicable, provide written documentation for reference.

Compliance

You should make sure that everyone is clear about legal, financial, or regulatory compliance issues. Since the team will soon begin working independently, it's critical that they understand these issues at the outset. It wouldn't help the project or the team to find out later that something was out of compliance. In some cases it results in rework, which adds time and cost to the project and can also reduce quality. In other cases, it could result in serious legal or financial repercussions. Preventing these kinds of lapses is important. Educate the team on these issues prior to starting project work to help everyone stay on track.

Team Meeting (Kick-Off Meeting)

Last, but not least, you should hold a project team meeting for the sole purpose of getting everyone together and on board with the project. Some IT project managers see this as an opportunity to get down to business, but if you can afford the time, you should really allow the first meeting to be more of a meet-and-greet. You should use the first team meeting to introduce everyone on the team (if they are not already acquainted) and give everyone a chance to talk a bit about his or her background and participation on this project. You should also discuss basic team information such as the team roster (how/when you'll distribute it), any team resources such as an intranet site that will be utilized for communication and where team members can find project information moving forward. During the kick-off meeting, you should review the project plan and objectives. Encourage team members to ask questions and also encourage them to read the initial project plan (the plan thus far) and come prepared with questions to a follow up meeting (or submit questions/comments via e-mail). It's important to begin creating a sense of ownership for the project plan as well as to begin to gather team input so the project plan can be as solid as possible before proceeding. Remember, should someone identify a major problem, don't get an attitude. This is the point in your project planning that you *want* to find problems (if they exist). Encourage and reward that type of input from your new team to create an environment that fosters input, honesty, and good information.

After you've done the "housekeeping" tasks, make sure you allow time for team members to get to know one another. If it's going to be a long project, you may want to schedule subsequent team building activities to get the team working together as a cohesive unit. If doing team-building sounds like sissy work, think again. Many large companies spend millions of dollars each year trying to figure out how to create more productive work teams. Productive teams are worth a small investment and if you're really not comfortable with this, contact a local consultant who specialized in team building and creating highly effective teams. One or two sessions with a team-building consultant can help your team change from a group of highly skilled individuals to a highly functional team—and you might actually enjoy yourself along the way. If you equate team building with a mushy group hug, think again. There are many fascinating and interesting team building sessions that help people learn about themselves and build a cohesive team.

The IT Factor...

Building Team Success

If *team building* sounds a bit too touchy-feely for you, you aren't up to speed on what team building can do for you. To build a sense of commitment to the success of the project, you must build a sense of commitment to the team. Since you, as the IT project manager, typically lack formal organizational authority, you need people on your team to be committed to the project's success. Gaining their commitment can come in part from getting people on the team to connect with one another. People are much less likely to drop the ball or point the finger when they've established a connection with other team members. "Getting people to work well together is more than just getting them in the same room," explains VirtualTeam Senior Consultant Lorraine Gutsche. "You need to create a shared sense of purpose and you need create an environment that encourages people to connect and contribute to the project. Without a strong sense of team commitment, your team members will continue to act as independent contributors. Independent work may be fine, but their efforts will yield less than optimal project results. You want optimal project results and a whole that is greater than the sum of its parts."

For more information on how to form and manage a highly functional team, refer to the end of Chapter 4 and review the section entitled "Managing High Performance Teams."

Team Technology

If you're using technology to enhance or foster team communication, make sure all team members have access to those resources and know how to use them. Just because someone is technically savvy in one area does not necessarily mean he or she is savvy in other areas. Don't assume team members know how to use technical resources unless it's very clear they do (e-mail, telephone, etc.). If you're using instant messaging, an intranet site, a collaboration software tool, or any other technology team members may not know how to use effectively, make sure you provide training. Most technical people don't like to admit there's something they don't know (or can't figure out), so don't ask for a show of hands to tell you who does and does not know how to use a particular tool. Instead, assume no one knows and provide training for everyone or check in with team members individually.

Managing Performance

After you've formed your team, you'll need to begin managing their project-related performance. You should have some of the processes and procedures already defined, but it's likely you'll need to work with your team to clarify or tune up some of these processes and procedures. Studies repeatedly show that people who are involved with setting their own performance standards are more likely to meet those performance standards—and that doesn't mean setting the bar so low as to be useless. Performance metrics have to be reasonable and achievable, but if members of the team can participate in setting those levels (even if that means giving feedback and modifying preset standards), they're more likely to work hard to achieve them.

You may need to work with team members' direct supervisor, managers, or HR staff to develop acceptable performance measurements that can be used both within the project team and by the person's manager as part of an overall performance evaluation process. In some companies, the PM performs an evaluation as part of the project closeout activities (see Chapter 12).

Finally, you need to think about what you'll do if people fail to perform to standards. There are many reasons for this type of failure—from not understanding roles and responsibilities to lack of ability to perform required tasks to political maneuvering and laziness. Your job as IT project manager is to shepherd this project along toward successful completion and along the way, you may have to deal with poor performance. These methods should be well defined in advance so you can simply implement your performance management processes and procedures, if needed. It will save you time and lots of aggravation.

Remember that there are essentially two causes of poor performance—the lack of ability and the lack of desire. Your job should be to try to determine where the problem lies. If it's lack of ability, the person may require training or may have to be replaced with someone more capable. If it's lack of desire, you have an entirely different problem on your hands. You can try to get the person to come around, you can talk with the person's manager, or you may have to replace that person as well. Your options as an IT project manager are a bit more limited than if you had formal organizational authority over team members, but the basics remain the same.

Recognition and Rewards

Finding appropriate ways to give recognition and rewards for team members is an important part of forming and managing high performance teams (for a review of managing high performance teams, re-read the end of Chapter 4.) As the leader of the team, an important part of your role is to keep everyone on the team moving forward toward a common goal and that means providing genuine recognition and rewards for project work. Perhaps you've experienced recognition and rewards that are not genuine—for instance when everyone gets the same recognition or reward regardless of contribution. These insincere attempts at recognition and reward usually backfire because the worst performers get recognition they don't deserve and the best performers are lumped in with the worst performers. If you want to find ways to demotivate people, that's your best bet. There are times when rewarding the whole team for a team effort is appropriate, but it should not be the only type of recognition and reward team members receive. However, if you want to motivate the team toward higher achievement, recognition and rewards must match the actual contribution in order to be perceived as genuine.

Recognition can come in many different forms and taking a look at how your company operates and its political environment can give you great ideas for how to provide meaningful recognition. In some companies, sending a global e-mail or memo to the person's manager touting someone's great project performance might be just the way to give them appropriate recognition. In other companies, the best way might be to provide a certificate of achievement; in other companies, it might be a pizza party held in their honor. Whatever you do, make it meaningful to the recipient.

As for rewards, these too come in all shapes and sizes from silly rewards to a free pair of movie tickets to a local theater or a gift certificate to a local restaurant. Some rewards are not monetary—such as when someone does a great job and earns a spot on a special project team or is assigned a coveted project task. Again, the rewards should match the contribution and they should be awarded in a fair and consistent manager to avoid demotivating your best performers.

Cheat Sheet...

Low-Budget Rewards and Recognition

These days, everyone's budget is strained, so you might have to be creative in devising fun and meaningful recognition and rewards for your team. If you have a creative bone in your body, you should be able to come up with something. If you don't, call upon one of your creative friends or coworkers for ideas. You can find plenty of ideas on the Web as well, but here are a few to get you started.

1. Create a Wall of Fame and post a picture of the star performer with a brief description of why the recognition is being given and how it impacted the team or project.

2. Hand out small, inexpensive tokens as kudos during team meetings. You could use different colored marbles for different types of tasks or small toy cars or just about anything that would make recognition fun and tangible.

3. Hand out points or tokens for various levels of achievement or contribution and allow team members to cash in those points for small prizes at the end of the project. Points might be good for a gift certificate to an online store or movie tickets or a miniature golf outing—whatever you think team members would enjoy that won't break the bank.

4. Create an award or trophy (the crazier the better) that travels to various team members' desks each week or month based on peer-reviewed performance ratings. Toilet plungers (unused) and bowling pins are two ever-popular trophies.

These are just a few ideas to get you started. Remember, there's no rule against having lots of fun while you're working hard. Recognition tops the list of things that cause people to feel satisfied with their jobs, so finding ways to give genuine recognition for a job well done is an important part of managing a successful project.

At the conclusion of this process, you should have your team members identified and acquired and you should have (or be planning) your first team meeting. Figure 8.2 shows the document that should be developed at the end of this process, the team roster.

Figure 8.2 Team Roster

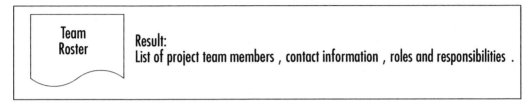

Summary

At this point in your project planning, you'll need to form (or have formed) your project team. You've clearly identified the project and its major deliverables so now you need the project team to begin contributing their ideas and expertise so the project gets off on the right foot. In Chapter 4 you learned about managing an IT project team and there's a lot of detail in that chapter that you might want to review. In this chapter, we discussed how to actually form the team.

You need to begin by defining your team requirements so you can be sure to include the right people with the right expertise at the right time in the right way. This is often best done without identifying specific people so you make sure you cover your project requirements before you get into specifics of people and personalities. Once you've identified these requirements, you can begin looking at specific people and identifying who you need and what constraints might have to be considered.

Clearly defined roles and responsibilities are absolutely critical to project success because they help everyone know exactly what they should be doing. Sometimes it's helpful to define roles using the "is/is not" structure we discussed earlier in the book. Well-defined roles and responsibilities also help you hold team members individually accountable for results. Clear performance guidelines improve project sucsess and help make the performance evaluation process fair and consistent.

Sometimes it can be a challenge to actually get the needed staff assigned to your project. With some high profile, exciting, cutting-edge projects, it's relatively easy to get top-notch talent to volunteer or be assigned to the project. In other cases, it's more difficult. If at all possible, link participation in mundane projects to participation in the high profile projects to ensure that even the most boring, routine projects get their share of talented staff. Avoid accepting known troublemakers on the team by having an honest discussion with the project sponsor. A successful project starts with a strong project team and allowing a known disruptive influence on the team without at least pushing back will put your project at risk.

Once you've formed the team, you need to do a little work turning it from a group of individuals to a highly functional team. There are numerous ways to do this (review Chapter 4) and with a little creativity and effort, you can find ways to forge a team identity that will help propel the project toward success.

Solutions Fast Track

Identifying Project Team Requirements

☑ Factors to consider when forming your project team include: organizational, technical, logistical, interpersonal, and political.

☑ Defining needed roles and responsibilities before identifying people to fill those roles will help you create an optimal team.

☑ Identifying needed competencies will help you select the people best suited to the project. It also helps you identify skill gaps you may need to look outside your firm to fill.

☑ Identifying constraints to staff availability is important so you can work with these constraints in your project scheduling (discussed later in this book). You may find you have to hire external staff to work around any significant availability issues.

☑ Identifying how your project team will interface with other parts of the organization may be required, depending on the nature of the project.

Identifying Staffing Requirements and Constraints

☑ Once you've identified high-level roles and responsibilities, you can begin looking for the appropriate people to fill these roles.

☑ Once you've identified specific people for various roles, you'll need to use whatever power and authority you have to get those people assigned to your project team.

☑ Sometimes the most desirable or needed team members are unavailable either temporarily or permanently. You'll have to look for these constraints and find ways to deal with them—either through modifying your project schedule or through hiring external staff to fill in gaps.

☑ Constraints can also be limitations on internal skills and talents that must be addressed through additional training or through additional hiring (temp, contractor, permanent, etc.).

Defining Roles and Responsibilities

☑ Once you've formed your project team, you need to assign each team member a specific role and set of responsibilities.

☑ Clearly defined roles and responsibilities help avoid finger pointing, turf wars, and other nonproductive human behavior.

☑ Responsibilities should be clearly delineated. Have team members work as a team to carve out appropriate roles and responsibilities so they begin to take ownership of the project.

Acquiring Needed Staff

☑ You'll need to work with selected team member's managers (if you're not their direct supervisor) to make sure they are released for project work when needed.

☑ Identify any procedural issues for pulling people onto your project team and work to get those in place prior to kicking off your first team meeting.

☑ Identify the cost of your team from a payroll standpoint. In some companies, you'll need to include labor hours or the fully burdened cost of each person per hour (the cost of salary plus benefits plus payroll taxes, etc.).

☑ If you'll be bringing in outside staff, you'll need to work with any external scheduling/availability issues and you'll need to add the cost of these folks to your project costs (we'll discuss developing your project budget later in the book).

Forming the Team

☑ Once you have identified and acquired your team, you should create and distribute a team roster. It helps foster team communication now and in the future.

☑ Identify any need for team training, whether formal or informal. Make sure the team has all the skills it needs, individually and collectively, to successfully complete this project.

☑ Hold a team (kick-off) meeting to introduce team members and to help everyone begin to form a sense of belonging to a team.

☑ If your team will be using non-standard technology, make sure everyone is trained and has equal access to these technologies. While it might be acceptable to assume everyone can use e-mail (though you should make sure that's the case), you shouldn't assume everyone understands how to use instant messaging, intranet sites, or collaboration tools. Provide training and documentation whenever possible to ensure everyone can use team project technology equally.

☑ You'll need to manage team performance, so make sure you have processes and procedures in place to monitor, measure, and evaluate individual and team project performance. Make sure you have identified how you'll handle poor performance before the project gets fully underway.

☑ Create genuine methods of recognition and rewards that will reward good (or great) performance. Look for opportunities to instill a bit of fun or humor into the process.

Frequently Asked Questions

The following Frequently Asked Questions, answered by the author of this book, are designed to both measure your understanding of the concepts presented in this chapter and to assist you with real-life implementation of these concepts. To have your questions about this chapter answered by the author, browse to **www.syngress.com/solutions** and click on the **"Ask the Author"** form.

Q: This is a book on IT project management, but you've spent two chapters talking about teams. Why?

A: Projects don't fail, people do. As an IT project manager, if you can't success-fully manage your project team, your project is in serious danger. Sometimes you get lucky and the project sort of runs itself, but the odds of that are worse than winning the lottery. We've dedicated two chapters on managing your project team—one from a more theoretical standpoint (Chapter 4) and one from a more practical standpoint (this chapter) in order to give you the tools you need to successfully manage your IT project team. Managing people is usually more complicated than managing technology and many IT project managers excel at the latter and fail at the former. Improving and honing people-management skills is part of improving as an IT project manager and will certainly be needed if you plan on moving up the corporate ladder in your career.

Q: I don't usually get to choose who's on my IT project team and who's not. How can I deal with a preassigned team more successfully?

A: Start by going through the steps listed in this chapter, including identifying roles, responsibilities, and competencies needed to successfully complete the project. Then try to map these requirements to your assigned team members. If there are any significant gaps, bring this to the attention of your project sponsor. If your project sponsor is truly interested in a successful project, he or she will help you fill those gaps either by assigning additional people, allowing you to hire temporary outside contractors, or by providing training to assigned team members. If you can't do any of that, make sure that the skill or competency gaps are noted as project risks (we'll discuss identifying and managing project risks later in the book) so at least no one can turn around later and say they were unaware of these shortfalls.

Q: Creating roles and responsibilities sounds like a lot of bureaucratic nonsense. Can we just get the team going?

A: It would be nice if we all could just intuitively know what to do and could instinctively get along with others, but unfortunately it rarely works that way. Creating clearly defined boundaries helps everyone. It actually reduces team stress when people know exactly what is expected (and not expected) of them. While it may take some extra planning effort on your part, it really will generate positive results once the project is underway. It doesn't have to be a long, drawn-out process by any means. See if you can reuse definitions from other (successful) projects. And, if it really works your last good nerve to create this from scratch, find someone on your team that has those strong analyzer qualities and ask them to create the initial roles and responsibilities document. Then, all you have to do is edit it.

Q: I'm not very comfortable giving public recognition or rewards to my team. Any suggestions?

A: A lot of people are uncomfortable in those situations, so you're not alone. However, managing a team involves a certain amount of public speaking. While you can talk to team members individually and in private to let them know how well they're doing, it usually has more impact to give them that recognition in a team, department, or division meeting. So if you're uncomfortable doing that, try writing down what you would say then practicing it in front of a mirror or with someone you trust to be kind and to help coach you (dogs can be a good stand-in because they rarely laugh out loud at you). Focusing on the specific behavior will also help because then you're not saying, "Hey, that Raina, isn't' she great?" Instead, you can focus on the actual behavior such as, "Raina wrote such clean code that she was able to meet Requirements 1, 2, *and* 3 with just 150 lines of code. Great job, Raina, thanks!" The more specific you are and the more focused on the task, behavior and benefit you are, the more comfortable you'll probably be handing out compliments. And get used to it—the more you hand out genuine compliments, the happier your team will be.

Chapter 9

Planning IT Projects

Solutions in this chapter:

- **Creating a Work Breakdown Structure**
- **Creating a Network Diagram**
- **Creating the Project Schedule**
- **Creating the Project Budget**
- **Identifying Project Risks**
- **Planning Project Communications**
- **Finalizing the Project Plan**

☑ **Summary**

☑ **Solutions Fast Track**

☑ **Frequently Asked Questions**

Introduction

Up to this point, we've done a lot of work to define the project clearly. If you've done all of this work diligently, your project is now resting on a very solid foundation. If you've skipped any steps, take time to go back and go through them to ensure your project doesn't have any gaping holes before we get into the detailed project planning in this chapter.

The only way your project can complete successfully is if it starts off successfully. In this chapter, you'll learn how to break the project down into manageable components so that you can not only plan the work, but you can develop a more realistic schedule and budget. By breaking the project down into its components, you can also verify your project scope and take this opportunity to make sure you don't have any missing elements.

As you develop these more detailed plans, you may come across new project risks that you were not previously aware of. As with other steps, some of these risks may be so significant that your project sponsor chooses to hold or terminate the project. More often though, the risks you identify give you the opportunity to figure out what you and the team can do to avoid these risks or what you'll do if these risks occur.

Many IT project teams come in with average to failing scores when it comes to project communication, so we'll end this chapter with a review of the communication plans you should have in place and how you should be progressing on those. This will help ensure you communicate appropriately (effectively and timely) with the necessary people to help make your project not only be successful, but to help it be *perceived* as successful as well.

As in other chapters, we will start with an overview of the IT project management process to keep track of where we are, as shown in Figure 9.1. Notice this is the final step before actually initiating the project, so you want to ensure you've got everything set before you pull the trigger.

Figure 9.1 IT Project Management Process Overview

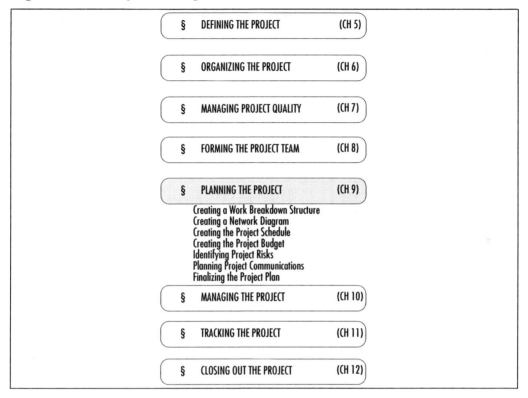

In this chapter, we'll introduce many new concepts and related terminology, so let's define some of the language we'll be using.

- **Completion Criteria** The standards or measurements used to define when a task (work package) is successfully completed.

- **Critical Path** The longest, least flexible path through the project. Any delay to tasks on the critical path put the entire project at risk of delay.

- **Critical Path Method (CPM)** A network technique using one time estimate for the calculation of the duration of the critical path.

- **Earned Value** The value of work completed based on the budget for that work. EV = % Complete * Budget At Completion (BAC).

- **Earned Value Management (EVM)** Integrates scope, schedule, and cost to give an objective, scalable, point-in-time assessment of the progress of the project. It calculates performance against plan and can be used to evaluate the project and identify serious problems earlier than other methods might.

- **Entry/Exit Criteria** The standards or measurements used to set the conditions or circumstances required to enter into or exit from a particular milestone or work phase.

- **Mitigation Strategy** A plan devised to avoid or reduce identified risks to the project.

- **Network Diagram** A graphical representation of the workflow of the project along with dependencies and constraints.

- **Program Evaluation and Review Technique (PERT)** A network technique using three time estimates for the calculation of the duration of the project. Each task has three duration estimates: best (B), worst (W), and most likely (ML). These estimates are used to determine the expected time using the formula: Expected Duration = (B + (4 * ML) + W)/6.

- **Percent Complete** An estimate of the amount of work completed compared to the total amount of work required.

- **Precedence Diagramming Method (PDM)** A method of creating a network diagram (mapping project work tasks) to indicate dependencies, constraints, and sequencing. Some variation of PDM is used in most project management software programs.

- **Slack** (also called **Float**) The amount of time an activity can be delayed without delaying the rest of the project.

- **Task** The term *task* and *work package* are used interchangeably. A task is defined as the smallest, most manageable discrete unit of work. Some organizations define tasks as units of the work package.

- **Triggers** The specific set of circumstances that must occur for you to put your alternative plans into action as part of your project risk mitigation strategy.

- **Work Breakdown Structure (WBS)** The hierarchical breakdown of the work in a project that starts with the highest-level deliverables and breaks them down into small, manageable work components (*tasks* or *work packages*).

- **Work Package** The smallest, most manageable, discrete unit of work within the WBS.

Enterprise 128 ...

Things are More Likely to go Wrong...

Here's another project management saying: "Things are more likely to accidentally go wrong than to accidentally go right." It's like a perfect golf shot or a perfect hit in baseball—it seems we can hit a horrible shot over and over exactly the same way, but when we hit that one absolutely perfect shot, we can't seem to repeat it (unless, of course, we're in the ranks of Tiger Woods, Annika Sorenstam, Derek Jeter, or A-Rod). Strange, but true. In IT project management, things *will* go wrong, that's a fact. The more time you spend in the planning stage (to a point), the more likely you are to see some of the bumps along the road and avoid them. You won't be able to avoid every single problem, but this phase—the planning phase—is often skipped or abbreviated and that means lackluster results for some projects and abject failure for others. This is time well spent and it doesn't have to take an inordinate amount of time. In fact, the amount of time you spend in the planning stage *should* be appropriate to the complexity, scope, and importance of the project. That said, don't short-change this step. It will improve your results substantially.

Now that we've defined a few terms, let's turn to the process we'll discuss in this chapter. You can see in Figure 9.2 the inputs, actions, and outputs from this step in the IT project planning process. We'll discuss each of these briefly here and then delve into more detail in the remainder of the chapter.

Figure 9.2 Inputs, Actions, and Outputs for Project Planning Step

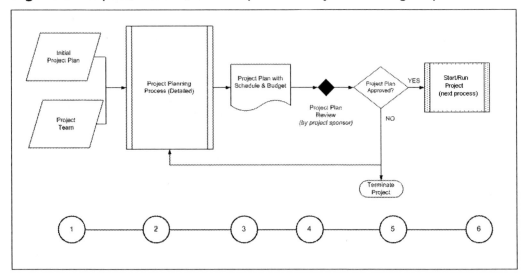

1. **INPUT** The inputs to this step in the IT project management process are twofold. First, the initial project plan must be used in order to ensure that the planning steps you take meet the project requirements including scope, time, cost, quality, and functional and technical requirements. The other input is your project team, meaning that at this point you should have identified and created your project team. While members of the project team may change over the course of the project, your initial team should be ready to go to help you with the planning stage of this IT project.

2. **ACTION** The action is to perform the IT project planning processes discussed in this chapter. These actions will help you create a detailed project plan from which you can develop a much more realistic and manageable schedule and from which you can develop your project's final target budget.

3. **OUTPUT** The output of this step is an updated and detailed project plan that includes your initial target schedule and budget. In some cases, the schedule and budget resulting from this process will be your final targets. In other cases, further refinement may be needed.

4. **CHECKPOINT** The detailed project plan, schedule, and budget should be reviewed with the project sponsor at this point to make sure you and the project sponsor are in agreement. Any areas of confusion, disagreement, or contention should be resolved before moving forward. If there are any known problems in the project plan at this point, they will only be magnified in the future, so they should be satisfactorily resolved now. If any modifications are made, the project plan should be reviewed briefly to ensure other elements aren't impacted by the change.

5. **DECISION POINT** If the project plan is approved, you'll be ready to actually launch the project itself. If the project plan is not approved, you may need to make revisions to the plan or be prepared to terminate the project (or perhaps place it on hold).

6. **NEXT STEP** If you have an approved detailed project plan, schedule, and budget, you're ready to begin project work. Once project work begins, your job is to manage the project and keep in on track and we'll discuss those tasks in Chapter 10.

Creating the Work Breakdown Structure

If you recall from your earlier work, you developed three to five high-level objectives or deliverables for the project. You also defined functional and technical specifications. If you didn't create specifications that were defined, discrete, and measurable, you need to do so before you head into this detailed planning work. If you have a well-defined project, creating the Work Breakdown Structure will create a much clearer and more detailed picture of the project. If you haven't created defined, discrete and measurable requirements for your project, your WBS will wander and you'll most likely experience scope creep right out of the gate.

Quality and WBS

One key point to remember as you begin creating your WBS is that you should refer to your project scope and your project quality plan. The scope of the project will ultimately be defined by the WBS, so keeping scope in mind as you create your WBS will help keep you and the team focused. Also, keep in mind your quality plan and quality metrics. These can be used in two ways. First, you may want (or need) to define additional tasks related to quality planning, quality control, or quality assurance. Second, you can define entry/exit criteria and/or completion criteria (both explained in a moment) for tasks based on quality standards or metrics. Quality is built into a project from the ground up and as you develop your WBS, you should keep your quality goals in the forefront of your mind. By keeping an eye on quality during this planning phase, you will continue to build quality into the project rather than have to come back and try to add it later.

Breaking Down Your Project

If you have very clearly defined project parameters, creating your WBS will not only be easier, but the end result will be a breakdown of work that maps to your project's requirements and outcomes. Let's start by using a generic example to explain how we're going to break the project down into its components. To use a very tangible example, if you were going to build a house, your three to five objectives might be:

1. House plan
2. Foundation
3. Framing
4. Exterior
5. Interior

You know that each of these high-level objectives or deliverables has a set of activities that must be completed in order to deliver that element. For example, the foundation deliverable might include surveying and marking the property to determine the correct position/location for the foundation. The foundation area must be excavated and forms to mold the concrete must be built before the concrete is poured. These are discrete elements of work (tasks or work packages) to be performed in order to deliver the foundation part of this plan.

The same holds true in IT project planning. Each of your major deliverables has work associated with it that results in the successful delivery of that element. Breaking the major deliverables down into their component tasks or work packages is called creating the Work Breakdown Structure. The process of breaking the major deliverables into smaller units is formally called decomposing the WBS, but we'll keep it simple.

The IT Factor...

Your WBS "Inventory"

"Many people underestimate the benefits, not to mention the challenges, of developing a good work breakdown structure. A good WBS provides the critical link between defining a project and achieving project goals. A WBS is not complete until work packages have been identified for all the tasks in the WBS. It's the work packages that translate projects into reality," explains Ralph Spitzen, Director of the Metals Industry Practice and The Center for Learning & Professional Excellence at TDCI Inc., an Ohio-based consulting firm. "Most projects within a given organization will have similar life cycles and thus similar requirements for work packages in each phase. Building an inventory of reusable WBS's is an important part of every IT project manager's toolkit."

Major Deliverables to Major Tasks

The first step in developing your WBS is to take each of your major deliverables and break them down into the major segments of work required to complete this deliverable. Using the house-building example, it means breaking down the foundation deliverable as we did a moment ago. Clearly, there are numerous steps that go into each of those major tasks, but for now we simply want to identify the major tasks. In some larger or more complex projects, you may choose to divide up the major deliverables and assign them to subject matter experts so they can develop the major tasks. As the IT project manager, you job is not to do all the project work or to know everything about everything. Your job is to make sure the project gets completed successfully, and that typically means finding the right people to do the various jobs. This can also save time by having people work simultaneously (rather than a big group exercise). Another potential bonus to getting your subject matter experts to work on this task is that they may use prior expertise to streamline the project tasks or they may uncover a problem no one knew about.

IT Factor ...

Organizing Your WBS

When developing your WBS, don't be concerned with the order in which tasks are listed at the outset. Make sure all tasks (work packages) are listed before you worry about the order, which will be developed later. If you start worrying about the order in which the tasks should be listed, you're likely to forget one or more important tasks. Most people think in a rather linear manner, so the task lists often come out in some sort of initial order and that's fine. Just don't spend time rearranging the list because sequencing comes later. Many IT project managers find it helpful to use a numbering system for tasks so that as they do move around later, it remains clear which tasks are part of a work package, master task or summary task. The most commonly used numbering system is as follows:

1. Major task 1
    1.1.   Sub-task 1
    1.2.   Sub-task 2
    1.3.   Sub-task 3
        1.3.1. Sub-sub-task 1
        1.3.2. Sub-sub-task 2
2. Major task 2
    2.1.   Sub-task 1
    2.2.   Sub-task 2
3. Major task 3
    3.1.   Sub-task 1
    3.2.   Sub-task 2
    3.3.   Sub-task 3

This type of number system helps because each major task is identified and all of the related sub-tasks are then numbered to keep track of their association with each other and with their major task. When the tasks are later rearranged to create the most optimal sequence and later, the schedule, it won't matter what order the tasks are in because your numbering system will help you immediately recognize their relationships. While you don't have to use this type of numbering system, it's one of the easiest to use to keep track of multiple layers

Continued

of tasks, which most IT project have. When you later assign tasks to owners, you can assign by number and you can have task owners for major tasks and all sub-tasks or you can assign individual owners to sub-tasks, whichever best suits your project's and team's needs.

Major Tasks to Tasks

There's a project management tool called the *8/80 rule*, which states that it usually is best to define tasks that take a minimum of 8 hours and a maximum of 80 hours. If you identify tasks that take 2 or 4 hours, you're headed toward a scheduling night-mare by creating unnecessary headaches for yourself. If you identify tasks that take less than 8 hours, you probably can (and should) roll them up into a slightly larger task that will take 8 or more hours. On the other side, you should avoid identifying any task (work package) that takes more than 80 hours. It's better to break those work packages down into smaller increments of work so they can be more effec-tively managed and tracked. So, the general rule of 8/80 applies here.

Taking your major tasks, have the team break them down into tasks that fall between 8 and 80 hours in duration. There may be additional, smaller tasks that must be accomplished, but for scheduling purposes, you should stick to the 8/80 rule. Let's look at an example. We'll use the house-building example again. If the house painter needs to paint the exterior, that might be a three-day job, so it would be listed as a task in the *Exterior* section of the project. That painter might break that task down into smaller tasks to help him or her complete the job. The painter might make a list that includes: prep all exterior trim, prime all exterior trim, paint all exte-rior trim, apply second coat to all exterior trim. Some of those tasks might take less than 4 hours and they don't have to be added to the project schedule. Paint exterior trim is the task on the schedule and the subtasks we just identified make up the task "Paint exterior trim." The task owner (we'll discuss task owners in a moment) will often break a task down into its components in order to complete the task, and that's a good thing. Trying to schedule all those subtasks would be akin to micromanaging the project and you'll create headaches for yourself and everyone else if you try to schedule and manage all those small subtasks.

Once you have delineated all your tasks, you should make a first pass at setting the duration for the task. Remember, duration and effort are not the same thing. A task might only take eight hours to complete, but you're allowing a duration of three days to allow the person to complete the task. If you can enter these durations for tasks now, do so. If you don't have enough data to determine duration for certain tasks, get the task owners busy (more on task owners in a moment) estimating the duration. You'll need duration for all tasks before you can determine your final pro-ject schedule.

As we mentioned earlier, you should not worry about the order or sequence of tasks at this point. Though there may be a certain amount of linear thinking that causes you to think of tasks in a particular sequence, you should not spend time now trying to place tasks in sequence as much as you should ensure that all the required work for the project is listed. We'll look at how to sequence tasks in just a bit, so for this exercise, just make sure all the work is listed and that they are somewhere between 8 and 80 hours in duration.

Cheat Sheet...

Defining Tasks Using Verbs and Nouns

The 8/80 rule helps you create tasks that are manageable and that's clearly your number one goal as IT PM. Another tip for managing your project is to have your team define your tasks using a noun/verb format. If someone is assigned the task of *"Cabling,"* he or she may have no idea what that means. If he or she is assigned a task that says "Install CAT5 cable", he or she now has a much better idea of the nature of the task. It will help everyone and it's easy to have your team write up tasks in this format from the start. A project's success is created one task at a time, so make sure each task is clear and concise.

Scope Check

Once you have created your WBS, you and the project team should step back and look at your project's requirements including scope, time, cost, quality, and functional and technical requirements. Check to make sure the work defined by the WBS actually matches the work outlined by the project requirements. Often in IT projects, this is where the first disconnect happens. Any gap between the project's requirements and the WBS is a problem. On one hand, you may find that the WBS defines more work than is in the requirements. This is a classic example of one type of scope creep. Somehow, in defining the deliverables in terms of actual work packages, the scope of the project expanded. Sometimes this happens because you can't always know the extent of work needed until you create the WBS. However, if this happens, you have to carefully look at the project and determine if the original requirements were insufficient and the tasks in the WBS should be included in the requirements or if the WBS should be scaled back to better meet the project requirements. There is no right answer here because the ultimate test of the project is whether it meets user/customer requirements. It's possible that by defining your WBS, you identified elements of the user requirements that were not actually specified but are needed. An example of this might be something like the program contains all the user's requirements but you forgot about the user interface that would allow the user to use these features (unlikely, but just one example).

The bottom line here is that this is an excellent opportunity to ensure your project requirements and project work are aligned and that they haven't started to spread around the middle. Keep your project lean and mean and take steps here to address any disconnects, gaps, or creep.

Remember, too, that your WBS essentially defines your scope. As you recall, scope is defined as the total amount of work in the project needed to meet the requirements. So, your project requirements should match your WBS, and your WBS should include only the work needed to meet project requirements and not a speck more. If they're not aligned at this point, you're going to be way off track at the other end of the project.

Task Owners

After the major deliverables have been broken down into the component tasks, each task should be assigned an owner. The rule of thumb is: *one owner per task or work package*. That doesn't mean that a team or group won't work on that task, but that one person is held responsible for that task. A task owner, by definition, is the person responsible for the successful completion of the task. That does not mean that the task owner must perform the work in the task. It means that the owner is responsible for making sure the task is completed according to task specifications (scope, time, cost, and quality for the task). The task details determine how the task will be completed and the owner is often the best person to determine those details. The owner may delegate the development of task details to others, but ultimately it is the task owner who should be held accountable for delivering these task details and later, delivering the task successfully.

How do you assign owners? There are several criteria you might use in assigning owners and ideally, your IT project team members will select tasks to take on based on their own areas of expertise and interest. If you have to assign owners, you should look for one or more of these criteria:

- **Expertise** Look for a subject matter expert who understands the components of the task. Those closest to the job often understand best what needs to be done. If you can get a subject matter expert (often called an SME) to own the task, its more likely the task will be well defined and well managed.

- **Experience** If you don't have a subject matter expert to take on the task, the next criterion might be experience in related areas. If you assign tasks to experienced team members, they can either figure out the required information or they know who they have to go to in order to get that data.

- **Existing Technical or Team Lead** This person may already have the formal authority on part of the project team and may be helpful in both defining tasks and determining to whom tasks should be delegated.

If you don't have a project team member with the expertise or experience to own the tasks, you have a problem. Remember, someone might be a peripheral part of the project team because he or she only works on one area of the project. How you define "project team" may flex and bend over the life of the project, so don't forget about people who might only participate in certain phases or steps of the project. If you need additional expertise, work with your project sponsor to identify resource needs to make sure you get the expertise you need. Lack of required expertise on a technical project can tank that project quickly. Having subject matter experts assist in developing task details (even if they don't later own them) might be your best bet in highly technical projects.

Cheat Sheet...

Task Ownership

The rule in project management is that a task should have one and only one owner. A task with more than one owner is less likely to be completed on time, on budget, and with the required quality. A task with no owners simply won't get done. More than one person can work on a task, but only one person should be assigned as the owner. If the task gets in trouble, you don't need a lot of finger pointing and "he-said, she-said." You need the task to be completed according to the specifications, period. One task, one owner.

Completion Criteria

Ideally, the task owner should create the completion criteria. *Completion criteria* are the standards or measurements used to determine that a task or job was completed according to specifications. These specifications include scope, time, cost, quality, and perhaps functional and technical requirements. Sometimes the completion criteria may be developed by a group or team or by the entire IT project team. You'll have to use your best judgment for which way to go, but often the task owner can create the completion criteria quickly and efficiently. The quality metrics you developed in Chapter 7 should be included in the completion criteria because it is through completion criteria that quality is managed (quality control) during the work phase of the task.

Let's go back to our painting analogy. The house painter knows how to do the job quickly and correctly (scope, time, cost, and quality) or you wouldn't be using this house painter. The painter is the best one to come up with the completion criteria for "Paint all exterior trim." He or she can make a quick checklist that can be used by anyone else to determine, beyond a shadow of a doubt, whether or not the job is completed within the scope, time, cost, and quality parameters. The completion criteria should be crystal clear: the job either *was* or *was not* completed successfully. This is important because you don't want a lot of discussion and debate on whether or not a task was successfully completed. If the completion criteria leave room for doubt, they need to be revised. The house painter knows that if the wood isn't prepped, the paint won't adhere, so properly prepping all wood surfaces to be painted might be part of the completion criteria for the task. It's possible that even more detail is required to specify exactly how the wood should be prepped. Does it include filling in gaps and nail holes? Does it include sanding the surfaces? Does it include wiping or washing down surfaces?

As you can see, the degree of detail depends on several factors.

1. Who is performing the work? If someone more experienced is performing the work, the completion criteria typically do not need to be as detailed. An experienced network administrator will know to take certain steps that might have to be spelled out to a less experienced net admin.

2. How complex is the task? The more complex a task is, the more detailed the completion criteria should be. Leave no room for doubt.

3. How critical is the task to project completion? Sometimes a task or deliverable is very critical to the project and therefore has little room for error. In these cases, more detailed completion criteria may be appropriate.

Let's not confuse the complexity or level of detail with the quality of the completion criteria. Just because you might opt for shorter, more concise completion criteria, it doesn't mean you're sacrificing quality. The needed level of quality should be delivered no matter what. You and your team will need to verify that the completion criteria for tasks drive that level of quality. The complexity of the task and the expertise of the person working on the task will typically determine how detailed the completion criteria need to be, but they should be as detailed as needed to ensure quality. As the IT project manager, you will ultimately be held accountable for project deliverables, so be sure you agree with task completion criteria. As the liaison between the stakeholders and the project team, you may also have a better perspective as to stakeholder and project sponsor expectations and needs. Your job is to ensure these needs are reflected in the task completion criteria.

Completion criteria drive quality. In the chapter on quality, we discussed the sources of quality in a project and we mentioned completion criteria. Completion criteria are the best tool to manage quality on a task-by-task basis. That's why they're so important to define well and to use as the measurement for whether or not a task is complete. The time your team spends in developing clear, thorough completion criteria for each task is time very well spent.

Entry/Exit Criteria

Entry and exit criteria are used to define the entry into and exit from particular project milestones. When developing your WBS, you may want to define entry and exit criteria. These are different from completion criteria in that you are not defining successful task completion, but rather successful phase or step completion. For instance, suppose your project is to develop a new program. You should wait to complete your requirements development before you have programmers begin writing code. Therefore, the entry criteria for the code development phase of the project could be the completed, accepted requirements list (note that the completed, accepted requirements list can also be the exit criteria for the requirements development phase). Entry and exit criteria are typically used to define entry and exit into and out of phases or steps of the project, but some companies choose to create these for all major deliverables, all major phases, or even all major work packages. Your decision should be based on the complexity of the project and the way your company operates.

Project Management Software

You'll notice that this is the first time we introduce project management software. Why? Because having project management software doesn't mean you can manage a project anymore than having Microsoft Excel makes you an accountant. Project management software is simply a tool that can make it easier to manage the project. Notice we didn't say define or plan the project but manage the project. Once the project gets underway, you have to track a lot of moving parts and that's where having a software program can really help; that's why this is the first time we've referred to a software program. For smaller projects, you may be able to track the project in Microsoft Excel, Microsoft Outlook (with calendar and tasks), or on paper (gasp). For anything with a lot of moving parts, a project management software program is almost mandatory. Large projects managed in Excel or on paper end up taking a disproportionate amount of time to track and manage and the cost of a PM software package quickly becomes justified. There are numerous online programs you can rent (ASP model) as well as numerous software packages you can purchase and install—either as desktop installations or enterprise-wide installations. A discussion of those software tools is outside the scope of this book, but a bit of research on your part will yield a vast array of choices. Talk to peers in your company or industry to find out what tool(s) they recommend since every software program comes with its own set of challenges. For instance, Microsoft Project has a lot of basic capabilities that help manage the project schedule but it is somewhat lacking in reporting flexibility and capabilities. (Microsoft Project 2003 addresses some of these issues; older versions can be a challenge.) Each tool has its limitations so you really just need to figure out which limitations are easiest for you to work with.

Once you create your WBS, you may choose to enter your tasks into the software program. Some people like to define their tasks and put them in sequence before entering them into the software program. Regardless of when you enter your task data, make sure you don't confuse the software tool process for the project management process. The software tool won't necessarily help you with your IT PM processes, it will simply track what you enter. The most helpful part of any project management software program is the ability to manage a changing schedule and to identify risks to the project via the critical path. We'll discuss critical path more in just a moment. The outcome of this step should be a WBS with task owners and completion criteria. The document is listed in Figure 9.3 and this should be added to your project plan for sponsor approval. The entire plan will be presented for project sponsor approval prior to starting project work, and we'll discuss this at the end of this chapter.

Figure 9.3 Work Breakdown Structure, Task Owners, and Completion Criteria

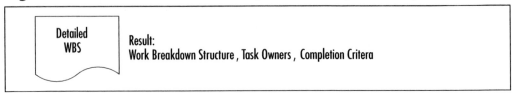

Task Details

The WBS and the tasks that are developed should contain enough detail that the project is very well defined at this point. While you have not yet developed the schedule or the budget, the work to be accomplished during the project (scope and requirements) should be evident in the breakdown of project work. The tasks should contain needed detail, and the following list contains some of the elements you may want to include in your task detail. Depending on the nature and type of project you're working on, some of these details may not be helpful, but this will give you a starting point for developing a template of your own for required task detail. You can also download the task detail template from the Syngress website.

Task details help define the task, the quality expected, and other details including:

- Task name (noun/verb format)
- Task number (if used)
- Task owner (one person)
- Task contributors (one or more people who may work on task)
- Task detail (longer description of task)
- Completion criteria
- Entry/exit criteria (if any)
- Quality metrics
- Requirements or specifications
- Required resources
- Task deadline (if any)
- Estimated start date
- Duration (length of time allotted for completion of task)
- Effort (amount of actual work time needed for completion)

- Estimated end date (based on duration)

- Cost (historical or calculated)

- Dependencies

- Constraints

- Related milestones or events (if any external events are tied to this task)

- Approval/signature needed (if any approvals are needed, these should be noted)

- Risks to task (if known)

- Triggers for implementing risk management plans (contingency plans)

- Amount of reserve needed (to be listed separately and not added to duration)

- Lessons learned (to be completed at task completion)

You can see from this list of task details that there's a lot of information to be developed, which is why it's best to have the task owner develop (or delegate the development of) these details. Remember, a task owner doesn't necessarily complete the work; he or she is responsible for ensuring the task is completed successfully according to specifications. If you're not sure the task owner will deliver, you've got to make some decisions about how to handle the situation because the success of the project is built upon the successful completion of tasks.

Functional and Technical Requirements

We discussed developing functional and technical requirements earlier in the book, but this is a good time to review those requirements. You may need to modify functional or technical requirements based on the development of your WBS. For instance, if your WBS defines a scope that is larger than your requirements, you've got scope creep starting. You should go back and modify your WBS so that the tasks only describe the total amount of work needed to meet requirements (scope, time, cost, quality, and functional and technical requirements). On the other hand, if your WBS doesn't fully address your functional or technical requirements, you have a disconnect and you'll need to modify your WBS to address all the requirements. This is where you have a great opportunity to check, double-check, and triple-check your project's scope and make absolutely sure it meets the functional and technical requirements. This is a stress point for projects and is a common point at which problems begin to develop. The problem is that when issues develop at this point, they often fly under the radar until they show up with a vengeance somewhere down the line. Identifying and correcting disconnects here is vital to project success.

Every IT project will have different functional and technical requirements, so there is no "one size fits all" in this case. However, functional and technical specifications do have common elements and if you'd like a framework against which to review your project's functional and technical specifications, you can download the requirements templates from the Syngress website.

Cheat Sheet...

Selecting Project Management Software Tools

Each project management software tool has its own "personality." The key to selecting the right program for you, your team, and your company is to look at the features and limitations of each and try to choose one that is the best fit. For instance, who will be entering and updating task information? One person or the whole team? Do you need a single desktop program or a shared, networked program? Do you need to facilitate collaboration or do you simply need to track task progress? Take a few minutes to create your own requirements document for your project management software solution and select one that will fill the bill.

Creating A Network Diagram

A network diagram is a tool that helps you and the IT project team graphically represent the nature of the relationships and dependencies of the project's tasks. Clearly, you can't create the network diagram until you've identified all the project work packages. You can't begin to create a realistic schedule until you know about all the work that must be done, but just having your WBS doesn't give you the whole picture. Once the work has been clearly identified, you can work as a team to figure out the logical sequencing of activities. The logical sequencing forms the foundation of the project schedule. We know, for example, that the house painter can't paint the trim until the walls have been put up and the walls can't be erected until the foundation has been poured and set. These are examples of *constraints* or *dependencies*.

Cheat Sheet...

Network Diagramming Methods

There are several different ways you can create your network diagram. We won't cover them in detail, but if you're interested, you can do some independent research to learn more about methods that interest you.

- **Arrow Diagramming Method (ADM)** Uses nodes to represent events and arrows to represent activity duration.

- **Precedence Diagramming Method (PDM)** Uses nodes to represent activity duration and connectors to show precedence and dependencies (this is a commonly used method).

- **Program Evaluation and Review Techniques (PERT)** Uses weighted average for duration to calculate project completion time/date. Average includes optimistic duration, most-likely duration, and pessimistic duration estimates.

- **Critical Path Method (CPM)** Uses sequential network logic with a single estimated duration for each task (rather than weighted averages). This is a method and should not be confused with the *critical path* itself.

- **Graphical Evaluation and Review Technique (GERT)** Uses probability sequencing and duration estimates. GERT is an advanced method of creating a network diagram.

Sequencing is a function of logical, desirable, and feasible timing for all project tasks. For instance, some sequence of activities might be logical but not desirable. Other sequencing may appear to be desirable, but it's just not feasible. The first step in creating a detailed project schedule is creating the sequencing for tasks and this is best done through a network diagram. There is no requirement that you create a network diagram; there are other ways you may have used in the past to create the optimal sequence for your project tasks, but a network diagram is a commonly used tool. There are four common methods of creating a network diagram, but we're going to focus on the most commonly used (and easiest to use) method: *Precedence Diagramming Method (PDM)*. Many project management software programs, including Microsoft Project, use some sort of PDM (various hybrids exist). You can create your network diagram by entering your tasks, sequences, dependencies, and constraints into your PM software tool and allow the program to create the network diagram for you, or you can create the diagram by hand. One popular method is to write the tasks on sticky notes and physically create your network diagram by placing the sticky notes on a white board and drawing lines for dependencies. This way, it's easy for everyone to see and visualize and it's easy to move things around. While it might sound a bit archaic, it's a very effective and efficient method for working with your team on task sequencing. We've thrown around three terms: sequence, constraints, and dependencies. Let's discuss them with regard to your WBS and your project schedule.

Sequence The sequence in which tasks should be started, worked on, or completed is your starting point. Most of the tasks in the project have some sort of logical sequence and that might be your best starting point. Once you've put tasks in their logical sequence, you have to begin thinking about other elements that will affect the sequence. Once tasks are in logical order, have the team look at the sequence and see if anything jumps out at them. For instance, someone might note that Task 4 logically follows Task 2, but it would be more desirable if it followed Task 5 instead. Someone might identify a logical sequence that is simply not feasible. Yes, it would be great if we could do Task 11 and 14 at the same time, but they require the same resource, so it's just not feasible.

Constraints Once you and your team have identified the most logical, desirable, feasible sequence, you have to begin looking at any constraints in place. You should refer back to your project document where you may have identified some project constraints early on. For instance, now that you're getting closer to knowing when the project will start and how long it will take, there may be constraints such as availability of key resources or outside vendors that will impact your schedule. One of the most common constraints is that a required resource is not available when needed or that two or more tasks require the same resource at the same time.

Dependencies Dependencies between tasks often mean that one task cannot start until another is complete. Using our home-building analogy, you can't put the walls up until the foundation is set. That's a finish–to–start dependency because Task A (foundation) must be finished before Task B (walls) can start. There are other types of dependencies, but this is the most common one and the default type of dependency used in most project management software programs. The four dependencies are depicted in Table 9.1 below.

Table 9.1 Task Dependencies

Dependency Type	Graphical Representation	Description
Finish-to-Start *Most common type of dependency*	Task 1 → Task 2	One task cannot start until a preceding task finishes. The walls of a house (Task 2) cannot be built until the foundation is poured and set (Task 1).
Finish-to-Finish	Task 1 / Task 2	Ideally, the two tasks finish at the same or nearly same time. For instance, if you're installing network cabling in a new location, the technician putting the wall plate on in each office (where the computer cable will connect in the wall to the network cable) can't complete the task until the network cable is pulled to that location. Ideally, as the cable is being pulled, the technician begins putting on wall plates so that when the cable-pulling is complete, so too is the face plate installation. In many cases, improperly terminated cables can result in network problems, so you'd want the pulling of the cables and the installation of the connecting wall plates to finish at about the same time.

Continued

Table 9.1 continued Task Dependencies

Dependency Type	Graphical Representation	Description
Start-to-start		When Task 1 must start before Task 2, but both can happen at the same time. This type of dependency is often used to indicate tasks that can occur in tandem once Task 1 begins. An example of this type of dependency is that ghosting drives and new desktop installation can run in tandem as long as the first drive is ghosted before the first desktop is installed. Once Task 1 (ghosting drives) begins, Task 2 (installing new desktop computers) can begin as well.
Start-to-finish		The start-to-finish *Rarely used* dependency is rarely used and it is somewhat unusual to find this type of dependency outside the construction or manufacturing arenas. In this type of dependency, Task 1 must start so that Task 2 can finish.

The IT Factor...

Network Diagramming Guidelines

There are a number of guidelines that you should keep in mind as you create your network diagram. These guidelines are designed to help you prevent overlooking key elements such as critical dependencies.

1. Use milestones to create a high-level diagram if you're not sure where to start.
2. Make sure all of the tasks are included in the diagram.
3. Make sure the relationship between a task and its dependencies is correct.
4. Make sure that all tasks that can be done simultaneously are shown in the diagram as such.
5. Look for hidden dependencies including entry and exit criteria and operational boundaries. Use subject matter experts to assist in this to ensure you're not overlooking critical data.

Milestones

If you're not sure where to start in creating your network diagram, begin with milestones. When do certain phases have to begin or end? If you know where your milestones are, you can then begin to put your tasks in the right order to meet these milestones. Two things to note: don't diagram the relationship between a task and a summary task (a summary task is comprised of all related sub-tasks) and don't diagram the relationship between summary tasks and milestones. Summary tasks are not actually tasks themselves, but a roll-up (summary) of groups of linked tasks. Link to the specific task that forms the dependency or to the milestone at the end of the group of tasks instead.

Creating the Diagram

Let's look at a portion of a network diagram, shown in Figure 9.4, created in Microsoft Project. Notice that you can't develop server specs until you've developed hardware specs (this may not be true in all projects, but it is true for this project).

The software specs in this case are dependent upon the hardware specs. The ordering of the enterprise application depends on the completion of the software specs (a finish-to-start dependency). Notice that once the hardware specs are completed, two paths are created. The top path that begins with "Develop software specs" is not on the critical path (in Microsoft Project's network diagram, all tasks on the critical path are shown in red, though you can't see red in this black and white diagram). The path that begins with "Develop server specs" is the critical path and is shown in red in the software program. A delay to any task on the first path will not necessarily delay the project (though it could) but a delay on the second path will delay the entire project.

Figure 9.4 Network Diagram

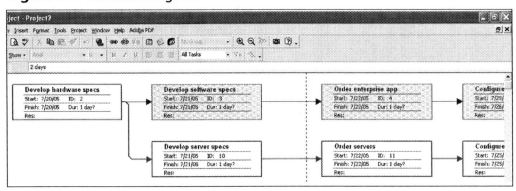

Your network diagram may be more bunched up or more spread out, depending on how many tasks of the project can run simultaneously. Look for places in the project where you can run tasks in parallel to decrease the overall length of the project where possible. Since the project management software programs are rather linear in nature, it often causes people to look at things in a very linear manner. This sometimes causes people to overlook the fact that many tasks can be started at just about any time in the project or that they have a lot of flexibility as to when particular tasks start or must finish. Keep this in mind as you sequence your tasks.

Critical Path

We've defined the *critical path* as the longest, least flexible path through the project. This does not mean the path containing the most "critical" tasks (however you define "critical") in the project but those that, if delayed, put your project schedule at risk. Remember when we defined our flexibility matrix? That comes into play here because if schedule is your least flexible element, you may have to come up with alternatives, such as hiring additional help, to meet your schedule. If your critical path puts your schedule at risk and your schedule is the least flexible element, you'll have to figure out ways to deal with this. On the other hand, if schedule is most flexible and budget is least flexible, you may need to re-arrange your schedule in a way that reduces expenses such as allowing more time for the completion of tasks so you don't incur overtime.

Having your network diagram available (either in the software program or on a white board) can help you identify problems in your sequence and high-level schedule. It can be an excellent way to visualize the project and determine the way to sequence tasks to meet project parameters. You don't have to have PM software to create your network diagram and to determine your critical path. Figure 9.5 shows a network diagram using a block diagram style. In this case, it's likely that Task 6 has an external constraint of some type that prevents it from starting any sooner than it does, though its start time is not dependent upon the other tasks in the project. In this case, both the second (Tasks 2,5,7) and third (Tasks 6, 8) paths through the project appear to be the critical path. However, by definition, the longest, least flexible path is the critical path, which in this case is comprised of Tasks 1, 2, 5, and 7. If Task 6 is delayed, it might also delay the project, and at that point the critical path might shift from Task 1-2-5-7 to Task 1-6-8. The point to remember is that your critical path may change through the life of the project if tasks are delayed to the point where they will push your entire project schedule out. Identifying these possible problem areas is much easier with a network diagram than if you were simply looking at all these tasks in a list of start and finish dates.

Figure 9.5 Block Diagram of Network

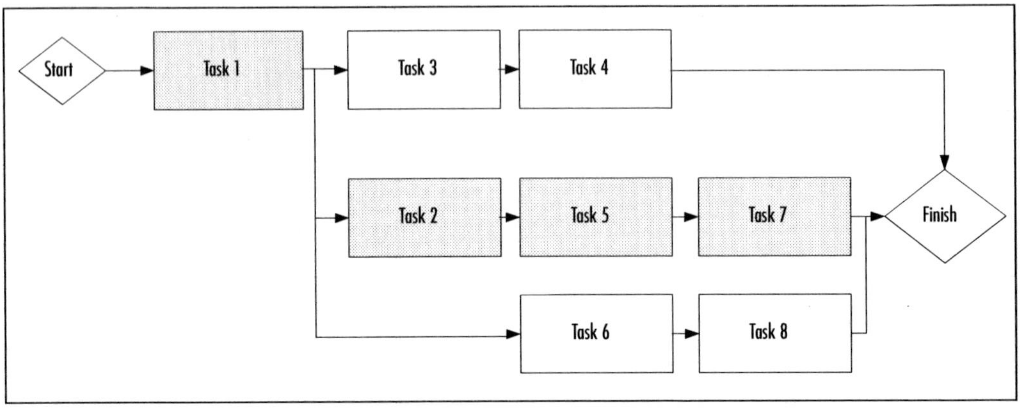

Slack and Float

You may have heard the term *slack* or *float* associated with project tasks or schedules. They are used interchangeably and refer to the amount of time an activity can be delayed without delaying the rest of the project. To use the information from Figure 9.4, we know that "Develop software specs" is not on the critical path. Still, if that activity is delayed long enough, the other tasks on that path will be delayed and they could eventually (if delayed long enough) end up on the critical path. Clearly, if any task in the project is delayed long enough, it could put the project at risk (if not, you might ask if the task should be done at all). Here's another example: suppose users need to be trained on the new features of an enterprise application that is going to be upgraded. Users are already familiar with the product and simply need a short four-hour training session to get them up to speed on new features. This training, hypothetically, could occur any time before the actual product rollout and not delay the completion of the project. Certainly, there are some optimal timeframes for training in this case, but the training can be said to have a certain amount of float or slack. For instance, it might be scheduled for one month prior to application rollout, but it might have two weeks of float meaning that it could be pushed out two weeks and still not delay the project. That gives you a bit of flexibility in case the training is delayed or in case the trainer is out sick for a week. Identifying slack in your tasks is an important part of scheduling because it will let you know where you have tasks that can be moved to accommodate problems that might pop up in scheduling. It also lets you know where you might have resources available to apply to problem areas if the going gets tough. Some people indicate slack on the task in their diagrams (if you use PM software, you can enter slack or float and it will be shown in the network diagram) so they can visually see where they have a bit of leeway.

Remember, tasks on the critical path almost always have zero float, which is how they end up on the critical path in the first place. If a task has no float, it is "least flexible" and cannot budge. Tasks with float are typically not on the critical path because the reason that they can be moved around a bit to accommodate other changes.

Applying Your Knowledge

Identify the slack or float that exists for tasks in your project. This will help you make decisions more easily when something changes (and it will). Understanding which tasks have float and which ones don't will help you make better decisions about how to allocate resources and will make your scheduling more efficient. Since the critical path may shift if too many tasks have zero float, make sure you know which tasks can shift around and which ones absolutely cannot.

Once you've identified duration and float (or slack, whichever term you prefer), you can add that data to your network diagram, as shown in Figure 9.6. Once you've added that data, you can easily calculate your critical path by adding up the longest, least flexible path. Using Figure 9.6, you can see that Tasks 1, 3, and 4 add up to 7 days' duration and have 6 total days of float. The second path, which includes Tasks 1, 2, 5, and 7, has a total duration of 11 days and 0 days of float. The third path, Tasks 1, 6, and 8 have a total duration of 5 days and 7 days of float. Clearly, then, the critical path is the second path. When you have these types of duration and float estimates, you can more easily visualize your critical path. Once you know which tasks are on the critical path, you can take steps to ensure that these tasks remain on schedule.

Figure 9.6 Network Diagram with Duration and Float

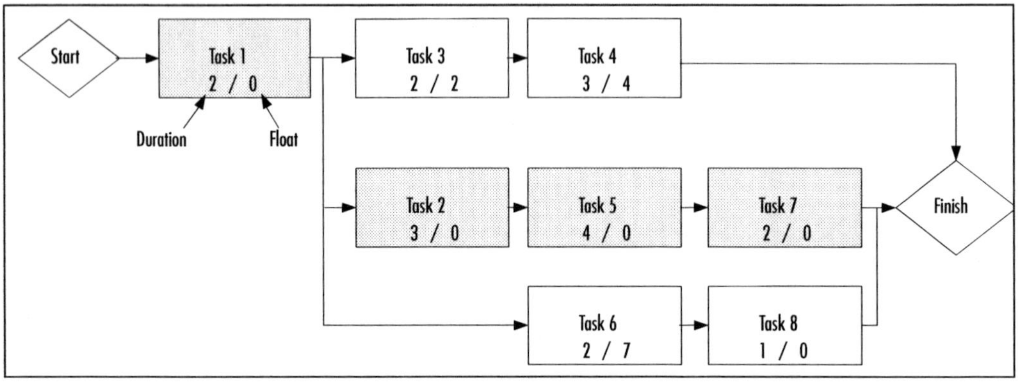

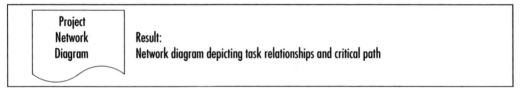

The result of this part of your planning should be your project's network diagram, which should be added to your project plan for final project sponsor approval. This document can be created by hand, in a program such as Proquis allClear, Microsoft Visio, or Microsoft Excel, or in a project management software program. It is represented by the document icon shown in Figure 9.7.

Figure 9.7 Network Diagram for Project Plan

Project
Network
Diagram

Result:
Network diagram depicting task relationships and critical path

Creating the Project Schedule

You've created a list of all project work (the WBS), estimated the duration of each task, and put them in the sequence that makes the most sense at this point. The question is, how long will these tasks actually take? The *sequence* of tasks may be dependent upon resource availability, but the *schedule* is definitely dependent upon resource availability. Some of that is related to the estimated duration of a task. If Resource A is needed for Tasks 1, 2, 5, and 6 (see Figure 9.5), you have a problem since Task 5 and Task 6 are currently sequenced to run in parallel. These are the types of conflicts that should come to light during the sequencing and/or scheduling phase. Since Task 5 is on the critical path, it means you'll need to find another resource to complete Task 6 if you don't want to put the project at risk. If some of the tasks have enough float, this may resolve the conflict, which is why creating a more detailed network diagram (see Figure 9.6) can reveal those elements as well.

You should document any assumptions you're making about your schedule so that you can be very clear about what is and is not going to happen. It might be acceptable to assume that a promised resource will be available when you need it, but if it might put your project at risk, you should list it as an assumption. We'll discuss risk later in this chapter, but for now, list any assumptions you're making about the schedule so that they are explicitly stated. If those assumptions are incorrect, your project team, subject matter experts, or the project sponsor can clearly see those assumptions and challenge or correct them.

Once you've sequenced your tasks, you can enter them into your project management software program so you can begin to develop your schedule (if you aren't using PM software, you can enter your tasks in Excel or in a table in Word, on a white board, or on a piece of paper). A sample project schedule is shown in Figure 9.8 and shows a Gantt chart, which is a graphical depiction of the schedule. The summary tasks are indicated by the long black bars that run from the start to finish of a group of sub-tasks, in this case in rows 1 and 9. These are the "roll up" of the tasks beneath them and are not in themselves distinct tasks.

Figure 9.8 Sample Microsoft Project Schedule

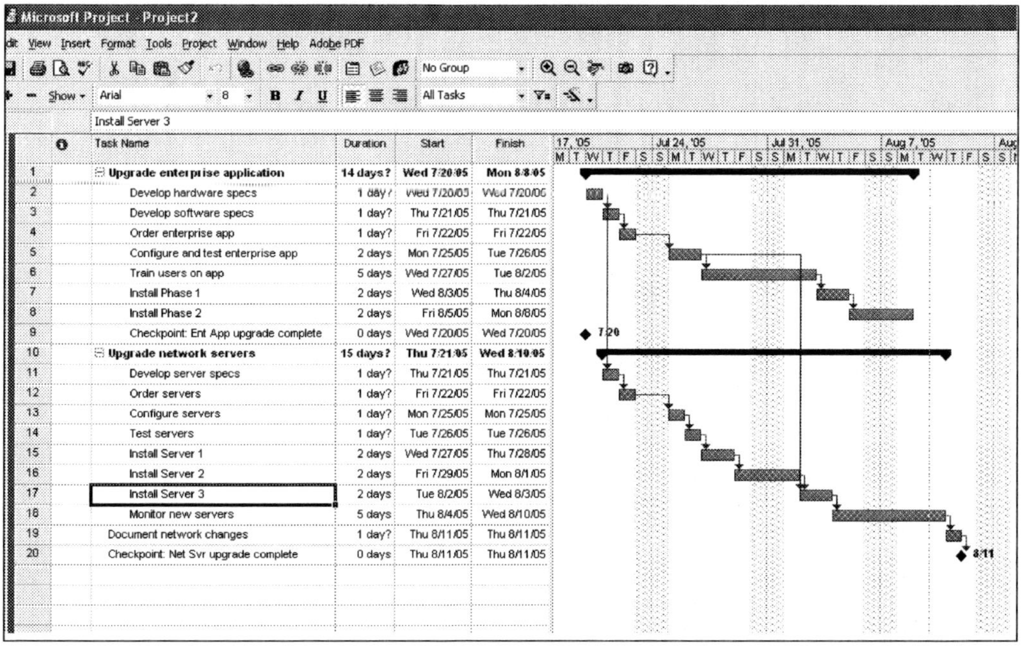

In creating your project schedule, there are several areas that might trip you up. We've listed a few common things to watch out for so your schedule has a good chance for success right off the bat.

1. Present timeline information in a format that matches the audience needs (executives need high-level milestones, while project participants need detailed schedules, etc.).

2. Identify areas of potential organizational conflict including vacations, holidays, company events, or other large project dates.

3. Identify areas of resource scheduling conflicts and resource competition (coordinate with other project managers, functional managers, vendors, etc.).

4. Provide supporting detail when necessary (risk assessment and contingencies for the schedule, resource requirements, timing or estimates, alternative schedules).

Skills and Scheduling

Placing tasks in their most logical and optimal sequence is the first step in creating your IT project schedule. The second step is to identify the resources needed for each of these defined tasks (or work packages). You have already identified needed resources and skills for the project, but now is the time you have to match those skills and resources (people and equipment) to specific tasks that are scheduled at defined times. There are a lot of moving parts at this point, so start by matching skills and resources to tasks. After you've created your optimal pairings, you can then go back through and look at areas where resources may be double-booked, have conflicting schedule requirements, or have no resources assigned. Remember, the first step is to create the most optimal schedule and then modify it to match reality. If you start with reality first, you will almost certainly miss opportunities for optimal scheduling.

Enterprise 128 ...

Start, Stop and Duration

Every task must have a start and stop date in order to have a duration. One inexperienced project manager wanted to create tasks that only had stop dates because he said he didn't care how long it took someone to get it done, as long as it was completed by a certain date. The problem was that he was managing the high-level tasks and was not looking at the lower-level tasks of the WBS. If all you care about are completion dates and someone else is actually managing the lower-level details, you may want to use milestones for those completion dates and roll up those lower-level tasks into a master project plan. One way or another, all tasks have to have a *start* and *stop* date in order for work to be completed on time. Milestones can be used to indicate required completion dates, but a project with nothing but milestones is a summary, not a project plan.

Schedules: Padding Versus Reserves

When it comes to building a project schedule (the same holds true for project budgets, which we'll discuss later in this chapter), many IT project managers are tempted to add in a bit of "fudge factor" to give them some wiggle room when things start to get off track. Many projects' schedules *do* start shifting to the right (later in time) once things get underway. However, that's no reason to pad your estimates. Let's look at the difference between padding and reserves.

Padding

Padding is the practice of taking an estimate and adding some number (usually dollars, hours, or percentages) to the estimate to give you some wiggle room. If you think a task will take 16 hours, you might record it as 24 hours to give yourself some cushion. There are two problems with doing that. First, you lose sight of how long you *really* think the task will take. Later, when you go back to review performance against plan, you really don't know what you're comparing. You'll know you're comparing actual against some number you made up, but what number and based on what? The second problem is that it becomes a bit of a problem having padded estimates all the way down the line. If David pads his time (or cost) estimates by 10% and Louisa pads her time estimate by 8% and Amadou pads his time estimate by 12%, you can see that your project schedule begins stretching out into eternity.

The danger? Your project sponsor might balk and consider canceling the project if you can't get it done any sooner than projected and you have no idea how long these folks *really* think things will take.

Another danger of padding is that in some instances, it becomes unethical or perhaps illegal. Though these are only time (or cost) *estimates*, they may become part of a contract, Statement of Work, Project Charter, or other legal document in which case there may be legal or ethical issues to consider.

Reserves

A better way to handle the uncertainty of time or cost in an IT project is to use a concept called a *reserve*. Rather than padding each task's time or cost estimate, you create a reserve amount (of time or money) for each major task. For instance, using our network upgrade project example, you might calculate 10% of your total server budget and add that to your server budget as a reserve. Then, if you need to upgrade a disk drive or add memory to one or more servers (or if prices increase by the time you purchase them), you're covered. You did not hide your estimated cost by randomly adding some amount to it. Instead, you listed your estimated amount and added to that a discrete, clearly defined reserve amount. You can do this with time as well. If your very best estimate is that it will take three days to set up and test each server, you have a nine day task (three servers, unless you create a separate task for each server setup). You might add one day to that task as a reserve amount. However, you don't change the task duration or time estimate, you add one day to your scheduled reserve. The reserve is an amount (percentage or actual number) that is placed into your schedule or budget to allow for time or cost overruns.

Reserve is then totaled up for each major task or objective and added to the schedule or budget. If a task ends up taking more time than scheduled, you deduct the overage from your reserve. If a task takes less time than scheduled, you can add the amount of unused time to the reserve. In fact, a reserve acts a lot like a savings account and should be used as such. Table 9.2 shows an example of schedule reserve for a hypothetical house-building project. Let's look at a few of the items in this table. The site location has a 15% reserve because it might take longer to get a site survey than you expect due to heavy market demand. Pouring the foundation has a 25% reserve because market demand for new housing is so high that concrete is in short supply. Framing has a low reserve because the framing takes only a few days and there are plenty of carpenters in your area. The exterior finishing has a 15% reserve because weather may delay some of the exterior tasks. Interior tasks will not be delayed by weather, so the reserve is 5%. Though landscaping may also be delayed by weather, it is a short job and has far more flexibility, so it's given a low reserve. Your total reserve, then, is calculated to be 24.25 days, which averages out to 11% of your total schedule (you may want to use a weighted average or the mean rather than a simple average). Thus, your optimistic schedule indicates that everything happens as you plan. The pessimistic schedule indicates you'll use every one of your reserve days. The "most likely" schedule is in between. There may be standards or industry practices in your particular field that are used for reserves and if that's the case, you can take some of the guesswork out of your project schedule. If you've done similar projects in the past (or even similar sub-sections or project phases) in the past, you can reuse those estimates. Make sure you look at project results versus schedules if you're using historical data so you can see what another IT PM thought would happen versus what actually happened. This will give you a good view into potential problems and may allow you to avoid some of those problems right from the start.

Table 9.2 Schedule Reserve Example

Task	Duration	Reserve %	Reserve Days
Site Location	90	15 %	13.5
Foundation	30	25 %	7.5
Framing	12	5 %	0.6
Roof	5	10 %	0.5
Exterior Finish	8	15 %	1.2
Interior Finish	16	5 %	0.8
Landscaping	3	5 %	0.15
Total	**164**	**11 % (average)**	**24.25**
Optimistic schedule	164		
Pessimistic schedule	188	(optimistic + 100% reserve)	
Most likely schedule	176	(optimistic + 50% reserve)	

You may need to educate your project sponsor about this concept and about how reserves work. It's important that the project sponsor support your efforts to run a "clean" project and that you be held accountable for the total schedule and total budget (including reserves) rather than individual task time or cost estimates. If your project sponsor is reluctant to do that, have him or her read this section of the chapter.

APPLYING YOUR KNOWLEDGE

Some IT project managers are hesitant to use the reserve method because they're afraid someone from management will knock their reserve amounts down and push them into shorter schedules and tighter budgets. Let's face it: whether you use a reserve amount or padded estimates, you're going to be pushed to do the project faster and with less money. The key is how you record and utilize the reserves. If you create discrete time and cost reserves, you can utilize the "savings account" notion and track your variance closely. This gives you cleaner data about your project and helps you hone your estimating skills. When you go back and compare plan to actual, you'll be comparing your (or someone's) best estimate with actual. You can use this data to troubleshoot your estimates so your estimates will be more accurate in the future. If you find the variance was an anomaly, you can make a note of it and move on. Padding obscures results, creating reserves clarifies them. To become better at your job, use reserves and avoid padding. This means you'll need to educate your team and get them to give you real estimates as well. Though this might require a bit of education, assurance, and commitment on your part, once the team understands how reserves work, they'll come around.

The deliverable for this planning task is a "final" schedule. The word "final" is relative here because one of the major responsibilities of an IT project manager is to manage the inevitable changes to the schedule that will occur. However, you have to draw a line in the sand and start somewhere and this schedule, once approved, will become the baseline against which you measure variance and progress. Figure 9.9 shows the deliverable as a schedule to be included in your project plan for final project sponsor approval, which we'll discuss at the end of this chapter.

Figure 9.9 Project Schedule with Reserves

Project Schedule

Result:
Baseline project schedule with reserves

Creating the Project Budget

With your WBS in hand, you can also develop a fairly detailed budget. The ideal situation is that the task owner will develop the task cost. For instance, a painter knows how long it will take to paint a room and he or she is also probably the best person to tell you how many gallons of paint it will take. The painter might also be well acquainted with the cost of paint and can give you a cost estimate that is fairly accurate.

There are some instances when someone in Finance or Accounting develops your project budget based on the data given. In those cases, you might be working with purchasers to purchase IT equipment or others outside your immediate IT project team. Some companies have Finance create the budget based on past experience and with limited input from the IT department. Clearly, there are pros and cons to each of these methods.

Also keep in mind there may be hidden expenses such as indirect costs or overhead that will be added to your project costs. Work with your Accounting department to determine what these additional costs might be and how you should account for them in your project budget.

It's a good idea to document assumptions you're making about costs for your project. If you assume that particular resources will be available or that a particular price range will be available for large purchases, you should note those assumptions. When the project sponsor reviews your budget, he or she can review the assumptions and clarify or challenge any assumptions that might be incorrect or unacceptable.

Ideally, you will create your own IT project budget based on the WBS. Once you have a list of all tasks to be completed, you can calculate the cost of each task. Some IT projects have to track time against the project as a fixed unit cost. For instance, software engineers may be billed to the project at one fixed rate and IT technicians at a different fixed rate. Other IT projects require specific cost data to be collected such as the wages and benefits cost of each individual software engineer as well as that of all other individuals working on the project. This is a much more detailed approach but yields a truer cost picture. In cases where the project is being billed or charged against some set resource (client, grant, investor funding, etc.), tracking costs with this level of precision may be very important. In other cases, labor is not even tracked as a cost because the company assumes it is paying wages and benefits as part of its overhead costs. So, in some projects, the only things that would count as costs are things that must be purchased such as servers, network cabling, test equipment, etc.

To create your IT project budget:

1. Create cost estimates for each work package (task) either by using calculations, historical data, or subject matter experts.

2. Roll up the cost of all tasks for the project. At the major task, deliverable, or phase point, add appropriate reserves.

3. Compare your calculated project budget with the project budget assigned or approved by the project sponsor.

4. Reconcile any budget differences through either increasing the budget or reducing the scope, increasing the time, or reducing the quality of the project (remember the four elements: scope = time x cost x quality? If the budget changes, something else also has to change).

To create your budget, go through each task in your WBS and add the cost of that task to your tally. Best practices suggest that you create a subtotal for each major deliverable and create a reserve amount at that level. For instance, you might decide that there's a low chance for budget overruns during the network design phase, so you give it a 5% reserve. However, you decide there's a high chance for budget overruns in the server testing phase (the phase where you purchase and test your servers), so you add a 20% reserve for that phase. During the installation phase, you are fairly confident that your costs are well known and you're comfortable with an additional 10% reserve for additional cabling or replacement parts. In your testing and monitoring phase, you may believe there is a low chance for budget overruns and you assign a 5% reserve to that phase. Thus, none of your estimates are padded and you've intelligently managed potential overruns by reviewing the likelihood of occurrence during each phase of the project. This is a cleaner, more effective way to manage your budget and it keeps everything aboveboard.

By going through your tasks and identifying budget items, you'll probably come up with a budget that is fairly accurate. However, sometimes in creating the tasks, task owners have omitted critical data such as the need for equipment or supplies. The reserve amount may account for that; you can also use the IT project budget checklist from the Syngress website to give you a running start.

Estimating Cash Flow

You may be asked to provide an estimate of cash flow during the project. Some companies require the IT project manager to provide this, others don't. Regardless, it's good to get in the habit of looking at cash flow since you may someday be called upon to develop a cash flow estimate. Companies often need this with large expenditures because they need to budget accordingly. If your project is short or fairly low-cost, this may not be needed. Figure 9.10 shows a sample cash flow diagram.

Figure 9.10 IT Project Cash Flow Example

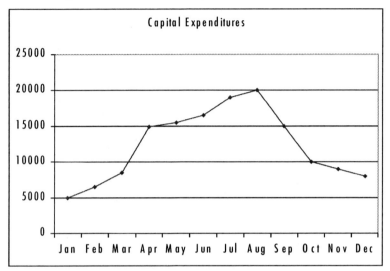

Implementing Cost Control

The degree to which you attempt to control costs is directly related to your flexibility matrix. Even if cost is the most flexible, you will still try to control your costs, but cost may increase to accommodate your least flexible parameters. For instance, if your schedule is least flexible then you may have to add people to critical tasks to stay on schedule. You may have budgeted for this because you were aware of the potential for this problem (we'll discuss risk management later), but this is one place where your costs can slip. If cost is more flexible than schedule, your reserves should reflect this (more reserve in cost than schedule) and you should make conscious, deliberate decisions to use your reserve to keep your schedule on track (rather than getting wrapped around the axle because your cost reserves are being used up).

That said, you'll need to work to contain and control your costs and that should start with a cost baseline. This is the total project cost broken down by phases, major deliverables, or tasks (as appropriate) with your clearly marked reserve amount or percentage. Next you should develop (if you haven't already) change control processes. Changes in the scope or nature of the project is the number one place costs creep (or stumble) into a project, so managing change is critical to managing costs.

As with scope management, you should have a clear process for managing changes to costs. A cost change control procedure need not be complicated or detailed, but it should require someone to note the original (baseline) cost, the new estimated cost, the reason for the change, and the people impacted by the change (if any). It should also have clear parameters for when a cost increase must be approved and by whom (cost reductions are both rare and welcomed, and they rarely need approval).

You can use the following list to help control your costs:

1. Control causes of change to ensure change is needed.

2. Control and document changes to cost baseline as they occur.

3. Control changes to the project and note their impact on project cost.

4. Monitor costs regularly and understand the impact of cost variances to the project.

5. Record cost changes in a timely manner to keep project cost data current.

6. Prevent unauthorized changes to the project or project cost baseline.

7. Communicate cost changes to appropriate stakeholders and get approval when needed.

The project budget should be developed and submitted for approval by the project sponsor along with the rest of the project plan. The budget is typically delineated in a spreadsheet and any notes or comments related to the budget can be included in the spreadsheet or as an additional document. It is typically a separate document (depicted in Figure 9.11) that is included with the project plan.

APPLYING YOUR KNOWLEDGE

Remember, your project has four elements: scope, time, cost, and quality. Previously, we discussed understanding the relative flexibility of each of these elements so you could better manage your project. If budget is your least flexible element, you should implement very clear, concise cost control processes in your project. You don't want team members approving budget expenditures without your knowledge unless those expenditures are within certain parameters. Creating clear guidelines for team members about budgetary items will help reduce your stress and will help keep team members inside acceptable parameters. If budget is your least flexible item, make sure your project sponsor is aware that other things may shift such as schedule, scope, or quality.

Figure 9.11 Project Budget with Reserves

Identifying Project Risks

By now it should be clear to you that there are many different kinds of project risks. The question is, which ones should you deal with? If you spent all your time addressing every possible project risk, you'd either end up in planning gridlock getting nothing done or you'd decide to scrap the project because you can't address all the risks. The key to risk management is to identify the risks that are *both* likely to occur and harmful if they do occur. Some project risks are highly likely to occur, but not particularly harmful, and you would deal with them as you would any minor inconvenience. Other project risks are not particularly likely to occur, but would be harmful if they did occur. This might include a natural disaster that destroyed the office building or destroyed the project work already accomplished. Most project risks fall someplace in between these two types of risks.

There are essentially three steps in IT project risk management: risk identification, risk quantification, and risk mitigation. Let's take a closer look at these three elements.

Identify IT Project Risks

The first step in planning for and managing project risk is to identify all known project risks. This is a good opportunity to get the IT project team together (make sure you have some *analyzer* types included, as they are often particularly good at this type of exercise) to identify risks. The first step is to determine what could go wrong with the project. Here's a list of potential problems to get you started, but you should certainly add to this list to address your project's particular risks.

- **External risks** War, civil unrest/disruption, economic fluctuations, political unrest/change, natural disasters, etc.

- **Organizational risks** Corporate cash flow issues, business disruption (strike, natural disaster, etc.), union contract status/negotiation, union contract terms, corporate shakeup, executive turnover.

- **Project risks** Resource conflict, budget constraints, vendor/supplier issues, technology changes, skill sets (training), shifting priorities, project sponsor change, risk to any task on the critical path, etc..

Remember that your IT project's risks come in many different forms—from external to internal. Make sure you scan the horizon for all potential risks that may impact your project. If you have people on your team who always see the dark side of things, this is their time to shine. Utilize that skill to root out potential problems. Don't let the meeting spiral down into endless negativity, though. Manage the team so that the outcome of this exercise is clear—a list of all potential project risks, not a doomsday report.

The IT Factor...

360 View of Risks

Project risks come in all shapes and sizes. It's important that you take a full view of project risks so you don't inadvertently miss any risks that have a high likelihood of occurrence and a high project impact. One method is to look at each task in your WBS and evaluate it for risk. While this might seem like a large task, you could ask task owners to identify risks to their tasks. These risks can then be compiled (there will likely be some overlap) to create your project risk list. There are types of project risks that are sometimes overlooked. The need for team training, the need to hire outside contractors, and the need for resources that are not available when needed are all risks to the project that might be overlooked or downplayed. We tend to look for (or recognize) the big risks and sometimes miss the smaller, but equally critical project risks.

Quantify IT Project Risk

Once you've identified your project's risks, you'll need to quantify and qualify them. Different companies have different ways of approaching this exercise, so if your company has a specific method for assessing risk, feel free to use that for your project. Otherwise, you should sort your list twice. First, you should go through your list of risks and sort them from most likely to occur to least likely to occur. If you want, you can use a numbering system and give the smallest numbers to the risks least likely to occur. Use a numbering system such as 5 = highest likelihood and 1 = lowest likelihood (or 50 through 1 if you want to use a somewhat "weighted" scale).

If you sort that list in descending order, you should end up with the risks with the highest likelihood of occurrence at the top of your list. Next, go through your sorted list a second time. This time, rank the risk in terms of the impact to the project should that risk occur. Again, use larger numbers for those with the highest impact and use the same numbering system as you did for your likelihood rating (5 = highest impact, 1 = lowest impact for example). Now, tally up the totals for each risk. Your resulting list should have the risks with both the highest likelihood of occurrence and the highest impact to the project listed at the top.

The next question that naturally arises is how many risks should you plan for? Clearly, you can't (and shouldn't) plan for every single risk. How far down you plan is a matter of your project's precision. If you recall from our discussion earlier in the book, precision is how much planning and detail are required for any given step in a project. If your least flexible element of the project is project scope, you should look at your project risks with that in mind and deal with all risks that put your project's scope at risk. You may also look at your sorted list and see a natural dividing point. For instance, you might find that your sorted list has 10 project risks with a combined score of 25 or higher because the next risk on the list has a combined score of 12. That gap clearly denotes a change in the nature of the identified risks and might be a natural stopping point in terms of planning (we'll discuss planning for project risks in just a moment).

Finally, make sure you look at your project's critical path tasks and critical path schedule and compare them with the project's identified risks. Make sure that you've accounted for risks to the critical path and that those critical path risks are on your list of risks to plan for. It's likely they're accounted for because their impact to the project, should they occur, is the highest. If these risks have a low likelihood of occurrence, you can still choose to plan for them since they could put your project schedule at risk. This is where using a little human intelligence can come in quite handy. After you have your double-sorted, prioritized list, look through it and decide what you will and won't plan for. You should plan for risk to whatever degree is appropriate for your project. If you look at NASA's Space Shuttle missions, where human life is at risk, the risk management process is clearly more rigorous (as it should be) than it would be for a server network upgrade. Don't get paralyzed at this point trying to identify and plan for every possible risk, but do use your best judgment to determine how far down your risk list you should plan.

Mitigate IT Project Risk

Once you've made a determination as to which risks you're going to plan for, spend time with the project team identifying your mitigation strategies. *Mitigation strategies* are alternate plans or strategies you devise to minimize or avoid (mitigate) the defined risks. Essentially, you are answering three key questions: "What can I change in the project to reduce or avoid this risk?" "What will I do if this risk occurs?" and "How will I know if this risk occurs?"

Alternate Plans

Ideally, the best risk mitigation strategy is to avoid the risk altogether. In some cases, simply identifying a risk provides you (and your team) with alternative ideas about how to approach a particular task. If you can change a task to avoid a risk altogether, you're far better off. Since it's not always possible to avoid risks, your next course of action will be to make alternate plans in case that risk occurs. For each selected risk, you should identify what you'll do if that risk occurs. For instance, suppose the project you're working on relies upon a particular technology that is in a state of change. There is a risk that the technology you've selected will be the technology that falls out of favor (perhaps the change is occurring during your definition or planning phase) and you'll need to re-tool to use another, competing technology. That's a serious project risk that has both a high likelihood of occurrence and a high impact to the project. It almost certainly impacts your critical path. So, what should you do? In some cases, you may choose to delay the project just a bit until it becomes clear which technology path you should take. In other cases, it might mean developing two paths, using both technologies, until it becomes clear which direction to head. If you can select the "right" technology by doing further research, you're that much better off. If you can't, you will have to plan for the best and worst case scenarios.

Creating alternate plans may yield some fascinating new alternatives that end up becoming so desirable that you modify the project plan to utilize these new alternatives or you develop ideas for another related project. The exercise of developing alternatives helps you understand and manage project risk and sometimes leads you down new paths to better alternatives for this project or other projects. Let's look at an example.

Risk Avoidance (or Countermeasure)

Let's say your project is to upgrade the network infrastructure including upgrading a customer relationship management (CRM) application that will use a three-tiered database model. One of the risks you've identified is that a legacy application not slated for upgrade has to tie into this new application and it lacks the proper interface to do so. Clearly, this problem has a high likelihood of occurrence and a high impact to the project. It is likely the interface task is on the critical path as well.

What alternative plans can you and your team devise to address this? There are many possibilities, though only a few may end up being feasible, logical, desirable, or affordable (four elements discussed in Chapter 2). For instance, you may choose to upgrade the legacy application prior to moving forward on this project; you may choose to write a custom interface to link the legacy and the new applications as part of this project; you may choose to purchase a third-party interface; you may choose to outsource the development of a custom interface; you may choose to incorporate the functionality of the legacy application into this project (which requires going back and revising your entire project plan including creating a new problem and mission statement, and revising functional and technical specifications, scope definition, Work Breakdown Structures, etc.). As you can see, there are a range of choices (you'll probably be able to think of several other viable alternatives on your own) and there is no one clear direction to go unless you go back to your project definition and look at the problem the project is trying to solve. At that point, the best alternative may become clear. In any case, you must choose your best option and plan accordingly.

Risk Mitigation (or Reduction)

Let's look at another scenario. Suppose there are three high-profile projects being planned that all have roughly the same start date. All three projects at one point or another require the skills of four software developers. You are the IT project manager for one of these three projects and though you have some great political pull in your organization, you realize there's a high likelihood that these four developers will be busy when your project needs them. You've talked with the other IT project managers about the timing of their projects and when they'll need these developers, but you also know that timing on projects shifts around a lot. Without the efforts of these four developers, your project is at risk. With a high likelihood of occurrence and a high impact to the project, this risk must be planned for. Though you may have some strategies in mind to avoid the risk altogether, you also know there's a chance these developers could be available (of course, we're assuming for this example you don't have a Project or Program Management Office overseeing the allocation of all project resources). One of your risk mitigation strategies might be to identify external contractors with the requisite skills to perform this work should your internal developers be unavailable when needed. You may also determine that the work the four developers must do can actually be done in parallel with other work and you may be able to modify your task sequence (and therefore schedule) if these developers are busy when you originally needed them. You might also decide to use outside contractors for this key work regardless because you can't risk not having these developers available. All of these may be viable alternatives, depending on your project's mission and deliverables. All of these potential solutions reduce your risk as it pertains to the four developers. Some of them reduce your risk to zero (by deciding to use contractors regardless of internal staff availability), but increase your costs.

Keep in mind that some of these strategies introduce new risks, so you have to watch for secondary risks. For instance, if you choose to use outside contractors, what happens if those contractors simply decide they don't want to work on your project because they got a better offer or better project from someone else? What happens if those contractors fail to deliver as promised? What happens if those contractors don't have the skills you thought they had? There are a number of new risks you've introduced. Again, many of these can also be mitigated—using contractors with whom you have worked in the past, contractors who come highly recommended by peers or associates, etc. Still, there are new risks and when you come up with any alternative plans, you must also assess those risks and address them to the degree possible.

While it might seem that you could identify risks and alternatives and the risks of those alternatives and so on for eternity, you really just need to be aware of the fact that new plans create new risks and you should evaluate the pros and cons before you head off in a new direction. Using the developer example, you might decide that you will line up four external contractors, and you'll actually have one of the contractors start some of the work and you will use the internal developers as they become available while the external contractor continues uninterrupted. Whatever arrangement you choose, make sure you've looked at the new risks you're introducing and try to find a balance between the known risk (your four developers may be busy) and your new unknown risks (the reliability of untested external contractors).

Triggers

Once you decide which project risks you're going to address and what you'll do to address those risks (either by avoiding them or by minimizing their impact), you then have to identify triggers. *Triggers* are the specific sets of circumstances that must occur for you to put your alternative plans into action. Using the example of the four needed software developers who may be busy when you need them, you'll need to identify when you will implement "Plan B." For the sake of argument, let's say you chose to identify two external contractors you could use if your internal developers were busy. You realize it will increase your costs, but you also know that you'll have these two contractors' full time and attention so you may get more productivity from these two than you might otherwise get from two equivalent internal developers (who may be constantly interrupted with questions, pulled into meetings, etc). You're only going to use these two external contractors if the internal developers are busy because your project sponsor does not want to pay for external services if at all possible. When do you decide it's time to use those contractors? Obviously you don't wait until the day the task is scheduled to start to find out those needed resources are busy. At what point will you decide to use those contractors? Under what circumstances?

The trigger point for using your contractors may be the projected availability of the four internal developers one month prior to the beginning of the work package to which they are assigned. It might also mean that two months before that work is to begin you work with a technical recruiting firm to locate the developers you need or that you contact contractors you've worked with in the past and get a verbal commitment from them. Whatever arrangement you make, you must decide on the timing of the trigger and what will happen when that trigger occurs. That way, when it becomes clear that three of the four developers will not be available when your project needs them, you have a calm, clear plan for moving forward. Add trigger points as milestones to your project schedule.

Applying Your Knowledge

Triggers should be clear, unambiguous statements that either yield a "Go" or "No Go" decision. You and your team members should be absolutely clear when a trigger point has been reached and what the next steps should be. This helps reduce the number of times you'll be "running around with your hair on fire" trying to figure out what to do when problems strike.

Risk Mitigation Plan

Your risk mitigation plan should be a list of tasks that are at risk, the level of risk, the alternate plan, and the trigger point. You may choose to add a few elements such as who makes the decision to use the alternate plan (the task owner, the project team, the project manager), who needs to approve the alternative plan (if it involves an expenditure, does the project sponsor have to sign off?), what the cost of the alternative is, etc. You can use a format similar to the one shown in Table 9.3 or you can use whatever format suits you as long as it contains these critical elements. Be sure to have clear alternatives and triggers so you can easily implement "Plan B" if the risk occurs and make sure you add in the cost of the alternatives to your budget as an additional reserve amount that is clearly delineated. These details should be captured in a document (depicted in Figure 9.12) and included in the project plan.

Table 9.3 Risk Mitigation Plan Elements Example

Risk	Level	Alternative	Trigger
Four developers unavailable during Phase II of project development.	95	Contact recruiter to secure two developers with defined skill set.	45 days before start of Phase II, currently slated for February 12, 2006.
Deployment team may be unable to deploy application using current technology.	85	Purchase interface upgrade from XYZ Company.	Evaluate deployment technology interface at the completion of Phase I, currently slated for October 1, 2005. If needed, purchase upgrade by November 1, 2005.
Customer training requires new scripting for Web-based training.	40	Contract Web development company to develop new scripting.	Determine need for scripting at the conclusion of Phase II, currently slated to end on March 20, 2006.

Figure 9.12 Project Risk Mitigation Plan

Planning Project Communications

If you've gone this far into your project planning and haven't communicated with anyone outside the IT project team yet, you've created a huge information void within your organization. If your definition and planning phases only take a few days or a week, you may not need to communicate before this point. Most IT projects take a bit more planning and if weeks have gone by without a peep from IT about the project, people start making assumptions—mostly negative ("They don't know what they're doing", "This project will never get off the ground"). Even if rumors don't start flying, you've missed a good opportunity to keep people focused on and excited about the project. Remember, a large portion of project success is defined by the *perception* of success by the people involved. Perception is greatly influenced by communication, so learn to communicate more frequently even if you don't know all the details.

One of the most common reasons given for failing to communicate is that there were just too many unknowns. Most people don't like saying "I don't know" and techies may be some of the most reluctant. The objection is, "If I don't know what's going on yet, what should I communicate?" It's not as difficult as many people make it and there are plenty of ways of saying "I don't know" that don't sound quite so clueless. A simple e-mail letting people know you're in the planning stages of the project and that you expect to have more detailed announcements in the coming weeks might be sufficient. For instance, you could say, "We are in the planning stages of Project XYZ. We expect to have a detailed plan available for review by our executive team by next Friday. In the meantime, you may be hearing from some of our IT project team members as they gather additional data to nail down the details of this project. Thanks for your cooperation and we'll keep you posted as things move forward." What have you really said? Basically that you don't know enough to tell anybody anything but you will by next Friday. That's a long way around "I don't know," but it provides project visibility and lets people know you *are* moving forward.

There's a saying in project management that "no news is no news" (as opposed to the saying "no news is good news"). No news means you have no information and when you're working on a project that's in the planning stages, it also means your project visibility slowly (or sometimes quickly) fades into the background. This might mean you have difficulty securing promised resources because managers forgot about your project. It might mean that the expenditures are going to be delayed because Purchasing forgot to take the necessary steps to procure needed resources. There are many more reasons to keep your project visible, so communicate regularly during the definition and planning stages because project work is not yet visible to the rest of the organization.

APPLYING YOUR KNOWLEDGE

Remember, every IT project involves people, technology, and business. Communicating effectively impacts all three, but it impacts people the most. People plan and implement projects, people get project work done, people determine the success of the project. Communicate well and your project will be more successful.

Project Communications Moving Forward

From this point forward, you should have your communication plans in place for your various stakeholders and you should begin implementing those plans. From the planning phase through project completion, you should communicate regularly (at appropriate intervals for each audience) with your stakeholders. This is one area that many IT project managers fail in and it's a huge opportunity to influence the perception of the project. With a bit of planning and practice, you can improve your project communication skills and the payoff is almost always far greater than the investment.

Your communications plans and activities should include the following audiences:

- IT project sponsor
- IT project team
- IT project stakeholders
- Company
- Executives

Communication Checkpoints

There are various checkpoints you may want to use for your project communications. Sometimes project phases are good checkpoints, other times you might want to use project milestones. Whatever checkpoints you use, make sure you identify them and use them. Some IT project managers create communication sub-plans so they can roll their communication planning into their project plan. That's a great practice but it's not always required. If you have someone on your IT project team who is a good communicator, you may delegate project communications planning and implementation to this team member. Together decide on your communication checkpoints and have a team member own that schedule. That means updating the schedule as the project schedule changes and communicating some of those changes to project stakeholders as well. If you feel like you're over-communicating, that's probably good since most IT project managers under-communicate outside of their immediate IT environment. An e-mail everyday is probably overkill but an e-mail every week or two may be quite appropriate. Table 9.4 outlines one method of managing communications; you may choose to use other methods suitable to your project and organization. As with any task, if the task doesn't have an owner, it probably won't get done, so make sure you ask for a volunteer or assign these tasks to someone on the IT project team and ensure that person takes ownership of these crucial tasks.

Table 9.4 Communication Plan Overview

Target Audience	Frequency	Method	Owner
Project team	Daily	E-mail updates	Project team, as needed
Project sponsor	Weekly	E-mail updates (submit progress report as part of project processes)	Project manager
Unit Directors	Bi-weekly overview, monthly detail	Bi-weekly overview via email, monthly presentation at Director's meeting.	Project Manager
Project Deployment Team	Monthly overview until 60 days from project completion, then weekly	E-mail updates, then weekly meetings.	Project Communication Lead (person from IT project team to fill this role)
Project Operational Transfer Team	Monthly overview until project completion then weekly until transfer complete (est. 90 days)	E-mail updates, then weekly meetings.	Project Communication Lead
Project Users, Customers, Stakeholders, or Company-wide	Every two months until project completion	Update in company newsletter, targeted e-mail to user groups.	Project Communication Lead

Cheat Sheet...

IT Project Communications 101

Still feeling a bit squeamish about project communications? One way of countering this is to utilize internal communication resources. "Companies often have a person or department that can assist with project communications," explains Lisa Mainz, Operations Manager for ShopNatural.com. "Look around to see who's putting together the corporate newsletter or who sends out corporate updates and press releases. Someone in that department may be willing and able to help you with project communications, especially a junior staffer who's anxious to learn and grow on the job. Utilizing existing corporate resources will reduce your workload and might improve your project's reputation in the process."

Remember, there are different work styles and there really *are* people who enjoy and are good at communicating. Find them, utilize them, and learn from them. Learning to communicate more effectively might not be on the top of your "To Do" list, but it is well worth the investment.

The deliverable from this part of your planning process is a more detailed communications plan that includes communication milestones or checkpoints. Making sure that communications are planned into the project helps you and the project team communicate effectively and regularly with less effort. This document, depicted in Figure 9.13, should be included in the project plan submitted to your project sponsor for final approval.

Figure 9.13 Project Communication Plan with Checkpoints

Project Communication Plan	Result: Detailed project communication plan with milestones or checkpoints

Finalizing the Project Plan

The time has come to finalize the project plan so work can begin. Though you've put a lot of work into your project up to this point, the actual tasks of the project have yet to begin. This is your last checkpoint before work on the project commences, so this is the point at which you finalize your project plan and take it to your project sponsor for approval. If you've been bringing recommended elements to your project sponsor along the way, your final project plan should be approved with few, if any, changes. Keep in mind, though, that things change constantly. It's possible that since your planning began, your company has a new strategic mission, a new customer, a new priority, and a new problem, and your IT project's priority fell from 2 to 200. It happens and there's not much you can do about it. Your project sponsor may be pleased with the plan but not ready to begin project work for a variety of reasons.

Your project sponsor may also want minor or major changes made to the project plan. If that's the case, you need to go back through the necessary steps to make the required changes. Remember, your job as IT project manager is to ensure the successful completion of the project. If you believe your project sponsor is requesting (or demanding) changes that put the project at risk, you need to say so. Sometimes the project sponsor may think his or her idea is marvelous when in reality, it would tank the project. While you need to be diplomatic in your delivery, it is very important that you voice these concerns now, before the project work is officially underway. If your project sponsor insists on changes you think create serious risks to the project, do the same type of risk assessment we discussed earlier in this chapter. Assess the likelihood and impact of the risk, develop alternatives (including the costs to the budget and schedule) and present this to your sponsor so he or she can make an informed decision about the requested changes. Don't just blindly agree to changes—push back if you think you should. You were selected to be the IT project manager because someone (usually the project sponsor) thought you were the right person for the job—and that includes using your skills, knowledge, and expertise to push back against ideas or changes that put your project at risk. Of course, some project sponsors just don't want to hear it, so push back to the degree necessary, but also know when to back down. You should note exceptions, risks, and other concerns about proposed changes then do your best to make them happen if that's the final decision.

If you refer back to Figure 9.2 at the opening of this chapter, you'll notice in Step 5 that there is the option to terminate the project. While it might seem like a big waste of time or a huge disappointment to cancel the project at this point, the upside is that you will have spared your company the time, cost, and sometimes embarrassment of embarking on a plan that shouldn't have gone forward for any one of a number of reasons. You might also be freed up to work on an even better project, especially if your planning efforts are recognized and appreciated. Though it may not be likely the project will be cancelled at this point, you just never know and if you're mentally prepared for that possibility, you'll handle it like a champ if it does occur.

You should also take a moment to go back through your project plan and make sure everything is set. Sometimes data is missing or some portion of the plan needs to be revised or reviewed prior to finalizing. This is also a good time to get your team together to finalize the project plan and to update or revise project procedures. Many of the procedures you defined at the outset may still be perfectly fine for the project, but you may have identified needs for changes to procedures or additional project processes needed to bring this project to a successful conclusion. Review processes and procedures in light of all the project detail you now have and make any needed adjustments before finalizing the plan and proceeding.

Once you've completed your review, the project plan should go to the project sponsor for approval. If modifications are necessary, make those changes and resubmit your plan with changes. In a perfect world, the approved plan is the final project plan where no further modifications are made except to the schedule once work is underway and perhaps to the budget. The project problem, mission, and solution statements should be set. The project's functional and technical requirements should be clearly spelled out and set. The project's quality plan, communication plan, and operational transfer plan (if applicable) should be set. The risks should be identified, alternatives should be created, and trigger points should be set. The project schedule and budget should be set as baselines so variances from these plans can be measured and managed. You should be ready to get started on your project's tasks. The final result, then, is an approved project plan, depicted in Figure 9.14. We use the word "final" rather loosely—on one hand, you must set a baseline; on the other hand, many elements will change. So, we'll assume the "final" project plan is what is used to set the baseline and we'll agree that changes of one kind or another will more than likely occur.

Figure 9.14 Final, Approved Project Plan

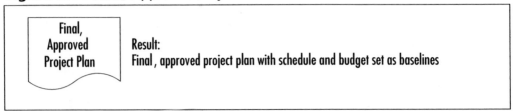

Final,
Approved
Project Plan

Result:
Final, approved project plan with schedule and budget set as baselines

Applying Your Knowledge

By finalizing your project plan and "etching it in stone," you provide you and your IT team with a great learning tool. All the work you've done up to this point is a compilation of your collective expertise, skills, talent, and knowledge. Clearly, the project plan is a living, breathing document—but keeping an unchanged copy of the "final, approved project plan" as your project baseline can help you later when you're looking at final project results. We'll discuss project wrap-up later in this book, but for now, keep in mind that a final copy of this document should be saved for later review. Once you finalize the project, you can compare plan to actual and update your data so you know what worked and what didn't work. The process of comparing plan to actual will help you improve your project management skills exponentially.

Summary

The project plan is your roadmap to success and in this chapter we stepped through creating the needed details that will help guide your project once work begins. The Work Breakdown Structure is one of the most key elements of any project plan because it delineates, in a very detailed manner, the work that must be done to accomplish the project's objectives. Some might argue that if you were only going to implement one project management process it would be the creation of the WBS and task details. The WBS defines the scope of the project. If work is not in the WBS, it's not in the project. The various task details including task owner, entry/exit criteria, and completion criteria round out the WBS and give you and your project team a very clear picture of the work to be accomplished. Remember that quality is managed, in part, through completion criteria (which may include quality metrics), so keep your quality plan front and center as you create your WBS.

The network diagram is a great way to help your project take shape and form. By using a network diagram, you can begin to chart out your critical path and identify potential scheduling problems. Most project management software programs will generate a network diagram automatically once you've entered your tasks based on your WBS. The network diagram is a useful way of sequencing your tasks as a precursor to creating your project schedule. Create your project schedule from your ideal or best-case sequence, not the other way around. Using both duration and float, you can create a more detailed network diagram that helps you see where you have opportunities to modify your sequence (or later, your schedule) to manage constraints.

The schedule must take into account resource conflicts and constraints at several levels, which is where having a project management software program can be quite helpful. You and the IT project team will have to evaluate these various constraints and make choices about how to sequence and schedule project tasks to meet the project's objectives, including deadlines and timelines. We introduced the concept of reserves, which are added at top-level phases or tasks, not to each individual task. It is important for a variety of reasons to add reserves rather than padding estimates, whether they are time or cost estimates. The most important reason is so you and your team have an accurate estimate, not a wild estimate based on everyone's individual padding methods.

The project budget is developed based on the cost of each task, which can be generated based on historical results or on calculations. Again, we used the concept of reserves to provide flexibility in the budget while maintaining clarity about costs. A cash flow projection is often needed (or required) and can help you and your company manage large project expenditures. Cost control measures should be put in place for a project of any size, but more attention should be given to this process if the project is long, complex, expensive, or if cost is the least flexible element of your project.

Identifying and managing project risks is an important undertaking and one that is often skipped in IT project management. Risks to the project as a whole or elements of the project (scope, time, cost, or quality) should be identified. These risks should be sorted according to two criteria: likelihood of occurrence and impact to the project. Using a weighted rating system may be helpful if there are numerous risks to be evaluated. The risks with both the highest likelihood of occurrence and the highest impact to the project should be evaluated. It's a bit of a judgment call as to where to draw the line, but that's where you, your IT project team, and your subject matter experts come in. Once the list of risks is defined, you and the team should identify alternatives. Alternatives provide you a means to either avoid the risk altogether or minimize it to an acceptable level. Sometimes alternatives that are identified in this step are great ideas that improve the overall project. Once risks and alternatives (also called mitigation strategies or contingency plans) are developed, you should identify triggers that allow you and your team to know, in no uncertain terms, when a risk has occurred and what steps should be taken. As the IT project manager, you can then respond to these "emergencies" with preconceived plans.

Also as part of your project planning, you should add detail to your communications plans. You should have developed communications plans as part of your project processes and procedures, but now that you have added project detail, you can modify your plan as needed. Ensuring that project information is communicated regularly and to the right people in the right way will help avoid rumors that tend to crop up with no real information is available.

The final project plan should be a comprehensive plan that includes all the work and detail we've discussed up to this point in the book. You should review project elements in light of the project detail created as a result of this planning phase. Check that the requirements match the scope and the WBS. Check that your processes and procedures are still adequate for the project. The finalized plan should be brought to the project sponsor for final approval prior to initiating project work. The project sponsor may want to make changes at this point, but if you've regularly brought portions of the project plan to the sponsor for review, discussion, and approval, there should be few, if any, changes at this point. Keep in mind that one possible outcome of this step is to have the project delayed, put on hold, or cancelled altogether. While disappointing, this does happen and it's better to have the project cancelled before project work commences than afterward. Finally, keeping a final copy of the project plan saved in a secure location can be helpful for later review. This establishes your baseline for the entire project and can be used to compare plan to actual. The "active" final project plan should be a living, breathing document that is updated as approved changes occur.

Solutions Fast Track

Creating a Work Breakdown Structure

☑ The Work Breakdown Structure is created using the project's major deliverables or objectives.

☑ Project quality must be built into the project and you can implement quality control through the WBS.

☑ Duration is the amount of time you'll allow for a task, while effort is the amount of actual work or time the task will take.

☑ Project tasks should follow the 8/80 rule. Any task or work package that is less than 8 hours in duration should be rolled up into a higher level task that will be more than 8 hours in duration. Any task or work package that is longer than 80 hours should be broken down into smaller, more manageable tasks.

☑ The tasks defined in the WBS define the total work of the project; therefore, the WBS defines the project scope. This is an opportunity to compare your WBS to your project scope statement(s) to ensure they are describing the same work.

☑ Completion criteria describe what a completed task looks like or is comprised of. This is one way quality is managed in a project.

☑ Entry/exit criteria can be used to define when tasks or phases can begin and end. This is another quality control method.

☑ Tasks should be placed in optimal sequence at this point. Resource constraints and other limitations should not be introduced at this time.

☑ Numbering tasks using a numbered outline format (1, 1.1, 1.2, 1.2.1, etc.) can be helpful in tracking tasks.

☑ Review functional and technical requirements to make sure they are addressed by your WBS.

Creating a Network Diagram

☑ The network diagram is a visual depiction of the sequenced tasks in the project.

☑ Duration is the amount of time the task is allotted for completion. Float is the amount of flexibility in the timeframe for completion of the task. These can be used together to help sequence and schedule tasks.

☑ The network diagram will help you see the project's critical path. Identifying tasks on the critical path will help you make better decisions about various project constraints.

Creating the Project Schedule

☑ The project schedule is developed only after you've created an optimal sequence.

☑ The project schedule takes into account resource conflict, limitations, and constraints.

☑ Project management software is very helpful in creating and managing the project schedule.

☑ Schedule based on task duration, not effort.

☑ Identify needed resources for each task, then resolve sequence/schedule conflicts based on resources constraints.

☑ The reserve is like a savings account. If a task takes longer than planned, the extra time is subtracted from the reserve. If a task takes less time than planned, the amount of unused time is added to the reserve.

☑ Add reserve amounts to high-level tasks, not to each individual task. The reserve amount (days or percentages) should be clearly spelled out, not embedded in other time estimates.

Creating the Project Budget

☑ The project budget is developed by adding the cost of each task. The cost of each task can be developed using historical data or through calculation.

☑ A cash flow estimate helps show when large project expenditures will be needed so you, the team, and the company can plan accordingly.

☑ Cost control measures are important in any project to prevent costs from spiraling out of control. The larger, more complex, or more expensive a project is, the more important these controls become.

☑ If cost is your least flexible project parameter, cost controls should be very detailed to afford you the ability to closely manage project costs.

☑ Reserves for the budget are developed just as they are for time reserves in the schedule. Additional amounts (dollar amounts or percentages) can be added to high-level tasks. The reserve amounts should always be clearly spelled out, not embedded in other costs.

Identifying Project Risks

☑ Every project has risks unique to that project. Spend time as a team to identify these risks. Pay particular attention to risks that affect tasks on the critical path.

☑ Risks should be sorted based on both the likelihood of occurrence and the impact to the project.

☑ Decide as a team how far down your risk list you should plan.

☑ For each risk chosen, investigate ways to reduce or avoid the risk by changing the project plan or the risk element. Typically, the best option is to try to avoid the risk in the first place. The second best option is to have a contingency plan ready to go should the risk occur.

☑ For each risk, develop an alternate plan that you will implement if the risk occurs.

☑ For each alternate plan, develop a trigger so you will know exactly when the risk has occurred and exactly how (and when) you'll put your alternate plan into action.

☑ Review each alternative plan for potential new risks and plan accordingly.

Planning Project Communications

☑ IT project communications are vital to the perceived and actual success of the project.

☑ Ensure that you and your team have a solid communications plan and make adjustments as necessary based on the detailed project planning you've done.

☑ If you and your team are not good at communicating, look for resources within your company that can assist you.

☑ Communicate regularly about the project, even if you don't have definitive information.

☑ Communicate with the appropriate frequency and method for the audience.

☑ Assign an owner to communication tasks so you can be sure they get done.

Finalizing the Project Plan

☑ The final project plan contains all the elements we've discussed to this point in the book.

☑ The final project plan should be brought to the project sponsor for approval.

☑ If the project sponsor requests or requires significant change, discuss this in depth to ensure the sponsor understands the implications of change at this point.

☑ Sometimes projects reach this stage and are delayed, put on indefinite hold, or cancelled altogether. While this is disappointing, it is better to cancel a project in the planning stage than in the work stage.

☑ Keep a separate copy of the final project plan for your archives. You can use it later to compare plan to actual results. This will help you improve your IT project management skills.

☑ An archived copy of the final project plan may be useful for later use. Reusing project processes, procedures, or part of the Work Breakdown Structure can help you avoid "reinventing" the wheel.

Frequently Asked Questions

The following Frequently Asked Questions, answered by the author of this book, are designed to both measure your understanding of the concepts presented in this chapter and to assist you with real-life implementation of these concepts. To have your questions about this chapter answered by the author, browse to **www.syngress.com/solutions** and click on the **"Ask the Author"** form.

Q: The information described in this chapter—in this entire book so far—is very enlightening, but I know I'm never going to be able to implement this level of planning in our organization. Should I just toss this book out?

A: First, no, don't toss the book out—there's a lot more good information to come. Second, you don't have to implement all of these processes at once. Granted, that would be ideal—to start a fresh project and build it from the ground up using these IT project management processes. But that's just not how the real world works. Most people approach change one small chunk at a time. If you have ever tried to make any kind of change in your life, you know that if you try to tackle too big a change, you'll simply revert to your old ways. Instead of giving up, finish reading through this book, then go back and find the one process or procedure you think will have the greatest impact on your project's success. Choose that one process or procedure and use it for a while. Then, just begin to work your way through all these processes until, slowly but surely, you have a full-blown IT project management process implemented. If you can't implement all of these steps at once, don't worry about it. Anything new that you do implement will help improve project results. For instance, in the past, you probably created a detailed list of work to be done (your version of a WBS). So, this time, have task owners create completion criteria so everyone will know when a task is successfully completed. That's a fairly easy change to make and what you'll probably discover is that your team latches on to these things because completion criteria (for example) make team members' jobs easier. Any time something makes life easier, we tend to use it. So, look for processes you can add that will make your IT project team's job easier and you will probably find very little resistance. Finally, keep the word *kaizen* in mind—it means small, incremental, continuous improvement. That's what this is all about.

Q: I've never used a network diagram before, but it looks interesting. How can I create one if I don't have a project management software program?

A: One method taught by a prestigious project management program suggests using sticky notes (often referred to by the trade name "Post-Its"). If each task is written on a note and the duration and float are added, you can create a network diagram on any surface to which sticky notes will stick. Some people prefer index cards. A whiteboard can be helpful, but remember that you probably don't want to erase and re-draw over and over as you move things around, so the white board can be useful either as a surface for the sticky notes or as a place to record your final version of the network diagram before transferring it to paper or electronic format. A whiteboard (or blank wall) can be very helpful in looking at the network diagram as a whole. Some people who are visually-oriented may spot problems with the diagram immediately. Others may find the sequencing tasks easier if they are more tangible (using paper rather than the computer). There are plenty of ways to create the sequence (and thus, the schedule) without using project management software; get creative. You will find, however, that once you have your sequence and schedule that you may want to find a PM software tool to manage the schedule unless you have a fairly small project.

Q: I've used Microsoft Project in the past but with mixed results. Any suggestions?

A: Yes, two comments. First, having Microsoft Project doesn't make you a good project manager any more than having Adobe Photoshop makes you a graphic artist. Project and Photoshop are tools to help those who already have some level of expertise. So, your experience with Microsoft Project may be the result of not having the project management skills needed to effectively use the tool. Second, Microsoft Project is one of many different project management tools available. Each tool has some wonderful, unique features and some inherent limitations. You may need to look around at your choices to determine which tool is most appropriate for your project, your team, and your budget. You can install enterprise or desktop applications or you can use Web-based applications, all depending on your needs. Now that you've learned more about IT project management, you may want to go back and give Microsoft Project another try (it sounds as though you already own it so you might as well try using it again). You might be surprised by how differently you approach the tool now that you have new skills under your belt.

Q: Our company's Finance department creates our project budgets for us, so I'm not inclined to want to create a budget or a cash flow projection. Is there any reason I should?

A: If you're comfortable with the way in which your IT project budgets are created and that works for you, feel free to leave well enough alone. On the other hand, if you ever go to work for another company, having experience creating and managing IT project budgets might be helpful or required. It's up to you whether or not you want to take on creating your budget, but you might want to get your feet wet so you gain experience in this area. If you're held accountable for a budget you don't create, that can cause some strange problems, so that's another reason you might want to get involved.

Q: It seems you could plan for risks of risks of risks. What's a reasonable point at which to draw the line?

A: You're right that you could probably spend the rest of your life trying to plan for and avoid risk, but you'd never get anything done. It would be like saying, "There are risks involved with travel"—that statement is true, but some travel is more dangerous than others. Flying in a poorly maintained single engine aircraft is far riskier than flying on a commercial airliner. Riding a motorcycle without a helmet at top speeds in traffic is riskier than driving in a mid-sized sedan. Everything we do has risk, the question is how much risk are you willing to accept? Companies typically have different "risk personalities", meaning that some companies are willing to accept more risk than others. The same holds true with IT project managers. Some IT PMs love the adrenaline rush of running around trying to solve some big problem; others avoid those kinds of situations. So, there is no single, right answer, but you should look at your own tolerance for risk (as well as your company's) and plan accordingly. Avoid analysis paralysis and do draw the line on risk planning at a reasonable point. If you feel that you're beginning to spin your wheels, find someone on your project team (or in close proximity) that has some of that *doer* personality. He or she will help you cut to the chase and get moving.

Q: I usually work with the same project sponsor and she never wants to review any part of the project plan until I submit the final project plan for approval. However, she always wants major changes at that point. How can I manage this?

A: That is a tough situation because you seem to lose on both ends. One suggestion is that you might bring less detail to your project sponsor more frequently. It's possible you are providing so much detail each time that she doesn't have time to review it, so she's created a process to limit the amount of detail she has to manage. The higher up one is in an organization, the more this is likely to be true. Rather than assume your project sponsor doesn't want information before the final project plan, try providing far less detail. Think of providing sound bites for your project sponsor throughout the defining, organizing, and planning phases. That way, you can keep her up to date without inundating her with details. Many successful IT project managers find a balance between getting things done and working on detail work (the *doer* versus the *analyzer*) and you may need to modify your communication style a bit to work more effectively with your project sponsor. In addition, you may want to take a look at past projects and see if there is a pattern to the types of changes required by your project sponsor. Does she always want a change in scope, time, cost, or quality? What are the reasons for past changes? It's possible that she consistently wants projects that have tighter timeframes or higher quality. If you can see where the disconnect is by looking at past projects, you may be able to come in more closely aligned on this and future projects. Finally, if you use the methods discussed in this book, it's possible that your project sponsor will not have as many changes. For instance, it will be very quick and easy to get her to sign off on the project problem statement. Once you agree to the problem, you can agree to the mission. Once you agree on the mission, you can agree on the selected solution, and so forth. These small checkpoints throughout the project planning process are designed to gain agreement and maintain alignment so changes don't come at the end of the planning phase.

Chapter 10

Managing
IT Projects

Solutions in this chapter:

- Initiating Project Work
- Monitoring Project Progress
- Managing Project Change
- Managing Project Risk
- Managing the Project Team

☑ Summary

☑ Solutions Fast Track

☑ Frequently Asked Questions

Introduction

If you've followed all the steps leading up to this chapter, congratulations! Your IT project should be sitting on very solid ground. Your planning activities will help everyone stay focused during the project work phase and will help make sure the scope, time, cost, and quality requirements are met. In this chapter, we're going to discuss strategies for managing your IT project. We'll talk about getting the project started and how to monitor and control project progress. We will cover more detailed, technical tracking techniques separately in Chapter 11 along with common project problems and solutions. Where appropriate, we'll mention some of the detailed tracking techniques in this chapter and refer you to Chapter 11 for more detail.

Managing your IT project is much easier when you have a clear vision of the project, developed from your efforts at defining, organizing, and planning your project. In this chapter, we'll look at how to supervise the project elements, including monitoring project progress, managing change and risk, and managing your project team.

As with previous chapters, we'll begin by taking a look at where we are in the process, shown in Figure 10.1. It is clear that up until now, no actual project *work* has been done (yes, planning *is* work, but not the actual work of the project). Though there are a lot of planning activities, they all contribute to your ability to manage your project during this implementation and work phase. As your project moves forward, you'll begin to recognize and reap the rewards of your planning efforts.

Figure 10.1 IT Project Management Process Overview

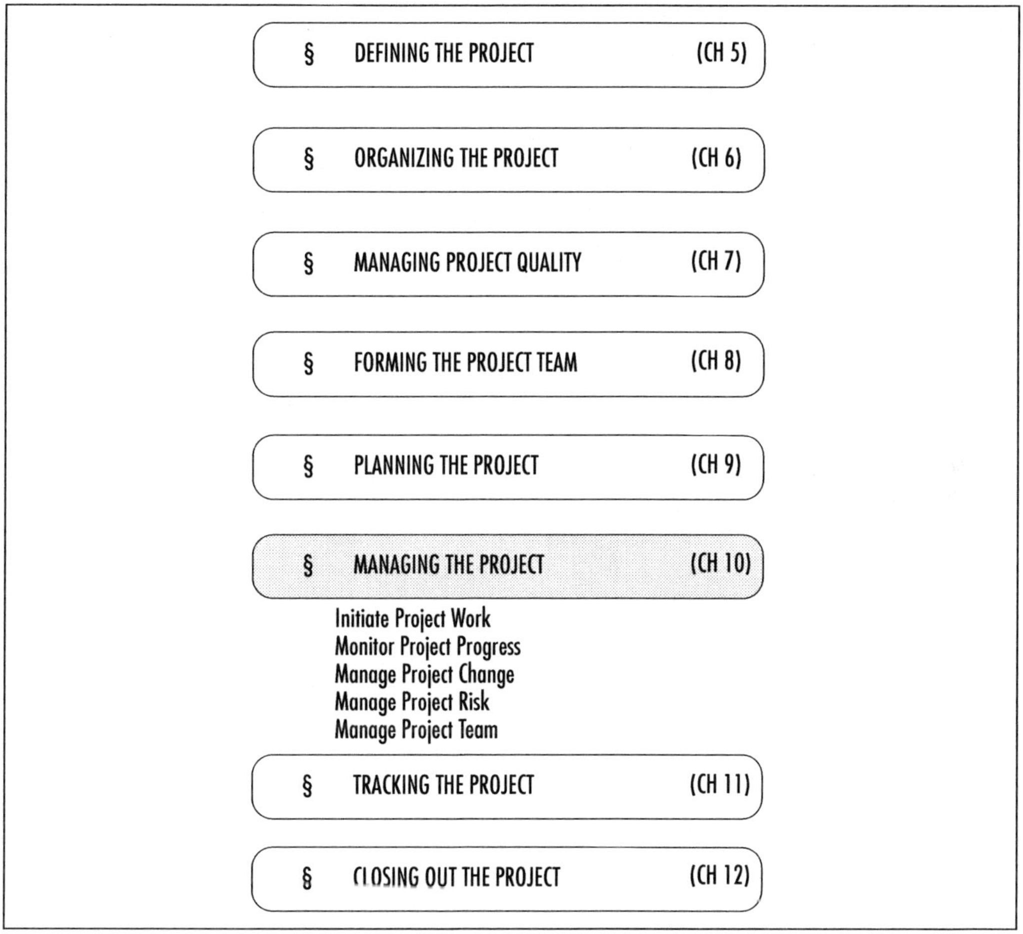

```
┌────────────────────────────────────────────────────────────┐
│                                                            │
│   ╭──────────────────────────────────────────────────╮     │
│   │  §     DEFINING THE PROJECT              (CH 5)   │     │
│   ╰──────────────────────────────────────────────────╯     │
│                                                            │
│   ╭──────────────────────────────────────────────────╮     │
│   │  §     ORGANIZING THE PROJECT            (CH 6)   │     │
│   ╰──────────────────────────────────────────────────╯     │
│                                                            │
│   ╭──────────────────────────────────────────────────╮     │
│   │  §     MANAGING PROJECT QUALITY          (CH 7)   │     │
│   ╰──────────────────────────────────────────────────╯     │
│                                                            │
│   ╭──────────────────────────────────────────────────╮     │
│   │  §     FORMING THE PROJECT TEAM          (CH 8)   │     │
│   ╰──────────────────────────────────────────────────╯     │
│                                                            │
│   ╭──────────────────────────────────────────────────╮     │
│   │  §     PLANNING THE PROJECT              (CH 9)   │     │
│   ╰──────────────────────────────────────────────────╯     │
│                                                            │
│   ╭──────────────────────────────────────────────────╮     │
│   │  §     MANAGING THE PROJECT             (CH 10)   │     │
│   ╰──────────────────────────────────────────────────╯     │
│            Initiate Project Work                           │
│            Monitor Project Progress                        │
│            Manage Project Change                           │
│            Manage Project Risk                             │
│            Manage Project Team                             │
│   ╭──────────────────────────────────────────────────╮     │
│   │  §     TRACKING THE PROJECT             (CH 11)   │     │
│   ╰──────────────────────────────────────────────────╯     │
│                                                            │
│   ╭──────────────────────────────────────────────────╮     │
│   │  §     CLOSING OUT THE PROJECT          (CH 12)   │     │
│   ╰──────────────────────────────────────────────────╯     │
│                                                            │
└────────────────────────────────────────────────────────────┘
```

We've already defined most of the project management terminology that we'll be using, but a few new terms will be introduced in this chapter including:

- **Baseline** The starting point or basis against which progress or change is measured.

- **Deliverable** A measurable, verifiable work product, result, or capability.

- **Project phase** A phase is generally characterized by the delivery and approval of one or more project deliverables.

- **Variance** The amount or percentage a result differs from the plan or baseline.

The input to this stage of the project is your final, approved project plan and the outcome of this stage is the completed project. The actions within this stage are shown in Figure 10.2.

Figure 10.2 Inputs, Actions, and Outputs for Project Management Step

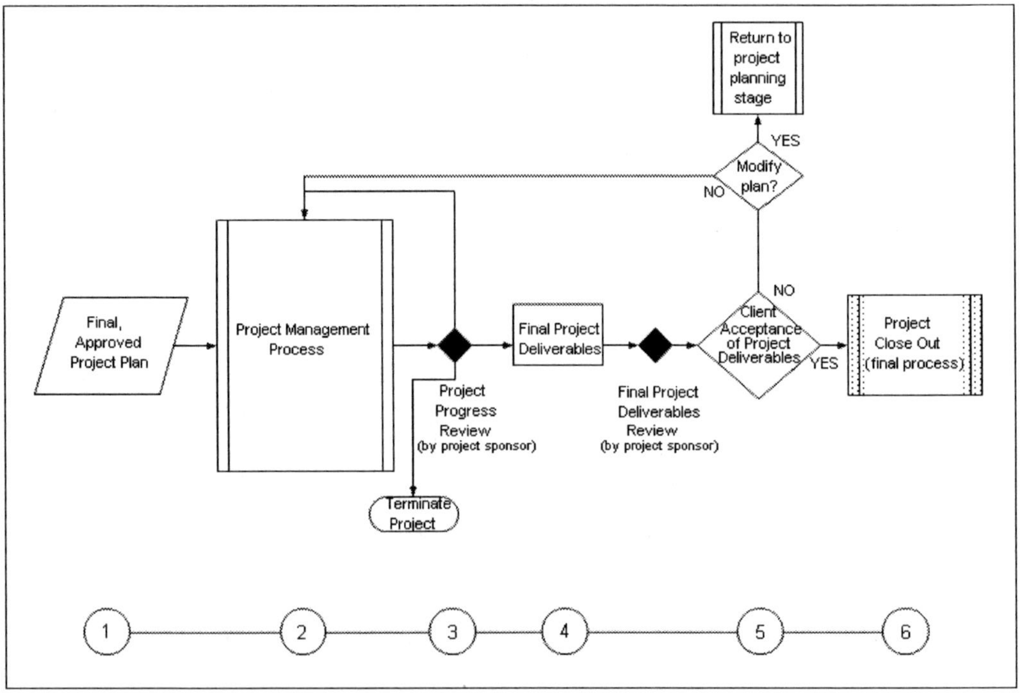

1. **INPUT** The input to this step in the IT project management process is your final, approved project plan. This plan should include, at minimum, the problem, mission, solution, scope, functional and technical requirements, schedule, budget, Work Breakdown Structure, task details, project processes, and procedures. Sub-plans such as training, communications, testing, and operational transfer plans should also be included as needed. This is the plan from which you'll create your baseline and against which you'll measure progress.

2. **ACTION** The process of actually managing the project work-in-progress is the phase we'll be discussing in detail in this chapter. It is during this phase that the plans are used so that work progresses according to plan. During this phase you must also work to ensure that your scope does not expand (scope creep), a common problem in this phase. Changes that occur to schedule, budget, or scope must be managed so final deliverables meet

scope, time, cost, and quality metrics as well as functional and technical requirements. Technical project tracking processes are discussed in detail in Chapter 11.

3.   **CHECKPOINT** The first checkpoint is the project progress review by the project sponsor. This review will happen multiple times during this phase and each review should result in the project sponsor approving results of the work in progress, requiring changes to the project (which flows back into the project management process and/or may require changes in the project plan), or a decision to terminate the project. Terminating the project at this point would be a very serious decision, but there are times that projects are cancelled at this stage. Cancellation at this point might be due to changes in the company, the market, or the product, or due to dissatisfaction with project results to date (above budget, behind schedule, under quality, below scope). In some projects, these checkpoints might also be used with clients or users to ensure the project is progressing as expected. You can modify this process to include client or user approval, if needed.

4.   **OUTPUT** Assuming the project progresses as planned and the project sponsor approves project progress, the output is the final project deliverables. These may be delivered in stages or phases or they may be delivered all at once, depending on your IT project.

5.   **DECISION POINT** Once the project's final deliverables are complete, the project work is complete. The project's deliverables should be brought to the client/user for approval if this is part of your project plan (some projects will not have a discrete user acceptance process). If the client approves the deliverables, this is typically the point at which client billing for final project deliverables occurs and operational transfer plans are put into effect. If the deliverables are not accepted at this point, you will most likely have to go back to your project plan to determine where you went wrong and make modifications. You'll most likely need to go through the planning and managing steps again for at least part of your project. If you have worked with your clients/users as suggested throughout this book, there is a much higher chance the client will accept deliverables without problems. If the client does not accept deliverables, it should raise a flag in your organization and within your team because it indicates there was a communication problem at some point in the project planning stages. You should look closely as where and why the disconnect occurred. This is a serious problem that should be analyzed fully.

6. **NEXT STEP** If the client accepts project deliverables, your next step is
   to close out the project. Closing out the project is discussed in Chapter 12.

The project management or implementation phase of our process includes reviewing the plan, starting project work, and managing, monitoring, and measuring project work, as shown in Figure 10.3. If any work varies from the plan, corrective action must be taken and work (new work due to correction or repair of earlier work) must be undertaken. The final project work includes delivering the project results to the end user or customer for approval and acceptance. Once project deliverables are accepted, responsibility is typically transferred to the user/customer or to another group responsible for installation or deployment, beta testing, or operations. Periodic reporting occurs during the Work, Monitor, and Correct steps shown in Figure 10.3, but final reporting is also required. Reporting includes status and progress reports from your team to you as well as progress reports from you to your project sponsor, user/client representative(s), executive team, and/or company. The diagram shown in Figure 10.3 can represent the entire implementation (work) cycle of a project or the implementation of one phase of a project. These steps are iterative and continue until all project work is completed, approved, and accepted. We'll discuss these elements in this chapter.

Figure 10.3 Implementation phase overview

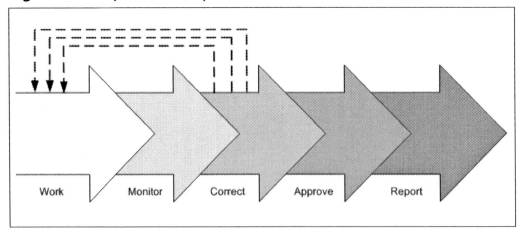

Initiating Project Work

Your project plan has been approved, your project team is in place and you've gotten the official "ok" to proceed. Getting project work going and monitoring its progress is your next step. The purpose of all the planning you've done is to be able to control your project once work gets underway. *Control* is the process of comparing where you are to where you were supposed to be so you can make corrections as you go. It's like driving a car. If you're in control of the car (driver), you use the accelerator, brake pedal, and steering wheel to make small corrections as you go so that you stay in your lane heading in the direction you decided to go. You speed up, slow down, or stop as needed to stay in the flow of traffic, to avoid hazards, and to arrive safely at your destination. You may occasionally alter your original course because of road construction or a major delay en route. Maintaining control of your project is a similar process that will require you to speed up, slow down, swerve or stop from time to time in order to drive your project to successful completion.

Start of Work Announcement

Though you may have already held a project kick-off meeting to get your project team together and aligned, you should hold a meeting to mark the start of project work with your team. You should review project processes and procedures, clarify next steps, and review first deliverables and milestones with the team. In addition, you should send out an announcement to your company or department that project work has commenced. This is a key communication that helps everyone know you are moving out of the planning stage and into the work stage (which counteracts those who complain that "all we ever do is plan, we never get anything done") and also lets people know that the resources they committed to this project will now be called upon. If your project relies on outside resources including equipment, vendors, or contractors, be sure to let them know the project has commenced. In some cases, you'll need to re-verify time estimates, bids, quotes, or lead times to ensure the numbers you're working with are still accurate.

This is a good time for team members to verify their own next steps and to ensure the resources they need for their first tasks are lined up and ready to go. Remind team members of when first status reports are due, review procedures for change and issue management, and ensure everyone knows how to update the status of their tasks (both schedule and budget) based on the project management system you're using (Microsoft Project, a Web-based PM tool, tasks in Microsoft Outlook, e-mail, etc.).

Implementation of Project Plan

The project should get off to a smooth start if your project plan is sound. Work should commence on initial tasks as scheduled. Your job as IT project manager, at this point, is to monitor and manage all the moving parts. You should check on project progress regularly. Your status reporting intervals should be frequent enough that big problems won't sneak up on you, but not so frequent as to drive your team crazy. You may need to adjust your status reporting interval once project work is underway to accommodate the actual needs of the team and the project. All work should proceed according to the project plan and it's important to make sure this happens right from the beginning. Starting out on the right foot helps the team learn and apply the project procedures and helps you verify that everyone is using those procedures. If you or your project team develops bad habits at the outset, your project is at greater risk.

APPLYING YOUR KNOWLEDGE

Remember that project success is defined as much by the perception of those involved in the project as it is by the deliverables. Take this opportunity to promote your project as you begin work. For instance, you might send an e-mail blast to the company or set up a presentation for the executive team. Let everyone know how well the planning stage went, how the plans will set the project up for success, and when you'll have updates for them. Setting the stage for project success starts early and now's a great time to initiate your communication plan as well.

Monitoring Project Progress

There are numerous ways you can monitor project progress. There are also some more technical methods for tracking project status. In this chapter, we'll stick to the less technical methods and if you're interested in more rigorous tracking methods, you'll find them (along with common project problems and solutions) in Chapter 11.

As you monitor your project, you have to ask four essential questions:

1. What is the actual status of the project work?
2. What is the difference (or variance) between plan and actual, and what caused it?

3. What should be done to keep the project on track?

4. What have we learned that we can use moving forward?

In this section, we'll first talk about how to gather project status data. Then we'll talk about variance to the project. Finally in this section, we'll discuss the steps you can take to deal with the variance.

Cheat Sheet...

Gathering Lessons Learned

Ideally, you should have a section in your task data called "Lessons Learned" so that lessons learned can be captured by task owners (or those working on tasks) as work progresses. Capturing these lessons in the task is ideal because that information can be captured immediately while memories are fresh. Those thoughts and ideas tend to fade over time the further we get from the task that sparked the learning or insight. Capturing lessons learned for the project can be a simple matter of having task owners or team members collect lessons learned for completed tasks on a periodic basis and reporting them or capturing them in a central document. Recording this data in real time, or at least while project work is in progress, helps you and the team learn quickly. A lesson learned in one area might save time or money on an upcoming task in another area. Sharing this information during team meetings can be a great way to learn as a group and make subsequent tasks or projects more successful. These lessons learned should also be captured at the project close-out, which we'll discuss in Chapter 12. Don't wait until your project is complete to gather this data, however, because your current project work may well benefit from someone else's lesson learned.

Reporting Project Progress

Reporting project status is one of the processes you should have delineated back when you were defining project processes. Status can be communicated in a variety of ways. In the next section, we'll discuss exactly how to measure progress, but for now, let's focus on the methods of communicating progress.

Team Meetings

One of the processes we discussed earlier in the book was gathering project status updates from the team. One method that most IT project managers use is the project team meeting. Team meetings not only help people stay focused on the project, they help build that sense of teamwork that can be crucial to project success. Well-run team meetings also give people the opportunity to stay up to date on the overall project progress and gather information that may be helpful in accomplishing their work. Sharing best practices or lessons learned benefits the whole team and can help others avoid similar problems. In addition, team meetings are a good place to discuss project status because changes to one task or work package can impact many other tasks down the line. Having everyone in the same room (or tied in by video or phone) to discuss status and changes can help resolve issues before they get out of hand. Team meetings are also where problems should be raised, discussed, and resolved. Having this regular forum for project work helps prevent side conversations and agreements from occurring. It's not uncommon to have one or more members of the team approached by a member of the user community to request a "small change" to the project. These are very dangerous to a project plan and should be avoided. By holding regular team meetings and encouraging team members to discuss these kinds of requests and issues, you can keep everything aboveboard, manage these requests through your standard project processes and hopefully avoid (or manage) scope creep.

Status and Progress Reports

You may ask for status or progress reports during team meetings or you may want those sent to you via e-mail prior to the meeting. Whatever method you've developed for gathering project status and progress, make sure you use it consistently. One common occurrence is that project status reports are consistently required at the outset of the project, but as time wears on, everyone gradually gets a bit lax in their reporting and before you know it, you have no current project data. Current data is the only way you can control the progress of the project, so it's the key to project success at this point.

The best way for people to report on status and progress is to record their activities in real time. Studies consistently show that the longer the interval from work to recording, the more inaccurate the recording is. Encourage team members (task owners as well as those doing task work) to record their work as they're doing it. Their data will be much more accurate and it will give you a better view into the status of the project. If people wait until the end of a work week to record details about their project work, there is a very strong likelihood that the data will be skewed one way or another. If you've ever waited a month to fill out an expense report from a trip you took, you know how difficult it can be to re-create the data. You have to go back through your e-mail, calendar and receipt files. It takes very little time to record activities in real time and it provides the most meaningful data. Encourage team members to be truthful in their reporting as well. The tendency is to minimize problems so we don't have to deal with them, but eventually the problem flares up and it's far more difficult to deal with it once it doubles or triples in size. Consistently look for bad news—the good news will jump out at you with little effort. That doesn't mean taking a pessimistic attitude toward the project; it means that if you don't look for the bad news, you might not see it until it's too late. If you and your team have a good attitude toward bad news, you might devote a portion of your team meetings to "the bad news you'd rather not tell us" where each team member is asked to divulge something about their section of the project they might not otherwise share.

Cheat Sheet...

Microsoft Outlook Journal

One useful tool that is available to many people is Microsoft Outlook Journal. The journal function allows you to create a new journal entry and record the task name, task type, start time, duration, and notes. If someone creates a new journal entry at the start of a task and starts the timer, the timers will continue to record work time until the timer is paused or the journal entry is saved and closed. Those journal entries can be e-mailed to the IT project manager or simply used as a way to capture work data for later compilation into a progress report. It's a great way to record work effort in real time with very little effort.

Issues Logs

Part of reporting status and progress is creating and managing an issues log. There are many different approaches to issues logs, but they essentially all have the same function—to track problems that arise. Each issue should have a brief name and description, a category (the part of the project in which the problem was found), an owner (who will take action to resolve the issue), an origination date (when it's entered in the issues log), a recommendation date (the date a recommendation is due), a resolution date (the date resolution is due), and a completion or close-out date (when the issue was considered resolved). If it's helpful, you can create an issue numbering system so issues can be grouped or referred to by number since unique issue names may become cumbersome. Remember, too, that there may be some issues that require no action. These should be noted and closed as *resolved* with comments as to why no action was recommended or taken. While this might seem obvious, it's easy to get in the mind set that each issue requires some change. Though that's often the case, the option of doing nothing should be considered. Some issues actually do resolve themselves. Some people find it helpful to use a spreadsheet to track issues. Some companies have specific software designed for issue tracking (in software development, there are usually issues logs *and* bug or defect logs). Whatever system you implement, make sure it's easy for team members to add issues (if you want them updating the log) and make sure it's easy to find, sort, and analyze issues as well as to quickly and easily determine the status of issues (open, closed, pending, at risk, critical, etc.).

Bugs or software defects can be considered issues, but more often they are tracked separately in a bug tracking system. An issue might be that the code specified for Part 4 doesn't interface with one of the legacy systems. A bug might be that the code written for Part 4 doesn't work as specified. Essentially, an issue in software development is typically related to functional or technical specifications whereas a bug is a problem with code written to a specification. Bugs or defects should be tracked in a similar manner as issues, but they generally go through a different resolution cycle. Bugs or defects typically are sent back through the work cycle for repair either during current work or as a separate work cycle. You can download a bug tracking template if you don't already have one.

There are three common problems with issues logs worth discussing: *no owners of issues, no follow up*, and *lengthy or repeated issues discussions*. Let's look at of these problems briefly.

No Owners of Issues

Just as a task without an owner will not get done, an issue without an owner will not be resolved. Issues should be assigned owners so that they can be researched and resolved. As the IT project manager, you are the default owner of all tasks. It's safe to assume you don't want to do all the project work single-handedly, so check to make sure all tasks have appropriate owners. The owner should be responsible for researching the issue and making recommendations for solutions. Depending on the type of issue, the owner may recommend the solution or bring the problem to the team for discussion. Once recommendations are made, the owner (or team) should make a decision on a course of action and implement that action.

No Follow-Up

If no one is checking the issues log on a regular basis (that's typically the job of the IT project manager), then it's likely people will stop updating the issues log. Worse, they may stop taking action on issues and that puts your project at risk. Part of each team meeting should be a review of the open issues and updates relevant to the issues log. Don't spend a lot of time on this. A quick update should suffice such as, "Hey, Phoebe, what's the status of Issue 123? Do you think you'll have a resolution by Thursday?" Make sure you touch upon each open issue so that owners are held accountable for closing issues in a timely and reasonable manner. Otherwise, as your attention to the issues log wanes so too will theirs.

Lengthy or Repeated Issues Discussions

We all know how painfully boring it can be to sit through a lengthy discussion that does not involve us. It's why some people start ducking out of meetings or not showing up in the first place. If an issue requires lengthy discussion by the entire team, it should be on the agenda as a separate agenda item whenever possible. If an issue prompts discussion, it might be worthwhile to discuss it as a team, but if the issue does not impact a majority of the team, don't make everyone sit through an irrelevant discussion. Table it and have the interested parties discuss it outside of the regular meeting time.

Going through the issues log should not be a long, arduous, and painful process, though in some companies that's exactly what it is. Make sure the issues log is used as a tool and that you use it as intended. If your issues log is long (in some large projects, the issues log can become very lengthy), you may have a separate issues log meeting. In some cases, you may break it down further and have issues log meetings for subsets of the project team to avoid discussing endless detail on a topic a majority of the team does not need to know or hear.

Also, avoid rehashing the same issues over and over. Determine a course of action, request updates, and move on. If an issue keeps coming back up, it's important that you, as the IT project manager, take a look at this and figure out why you keep discussing it over and over. This problem often occurs if notes are not kept that capture the discussion and decision points. It's important that you develop a course of action and resolution for issues because rehashing those issues repeatedly is a waste of time and will de-motivate the team quickly (not to mention the risk it injects into the project).

Managing Escalations

Sometimes problems occur in projects that require the assistance, input, or decision of someone higher in the organization. Your escalation procedures should be well established before work commences so that task owners and team members know how and when to escalate issues. Your issues log is certainly the starting place for raising, tracking, and managing issues, but sometimes these issues require additional input for resolution. Make sure the criteria and process for escalating issues is clear to all team members. On one hand, you don't want to "cry wolf" and escalate every little issue you and the team run into. On the other hand, executives hate surprises so it's important to understand how, when, and why you should escalate issues. This is one part project management, one part change management, and one part risk management. Issues that are difficult or impossible to resolve that impact the project's overall scope, critical path, or functional deliverables should certainly rank high on your list of potential escalation candidates. The criteria you and the IT project team establish should have been reviewed and cleared with the project sponsor so you know exactly which issues should be brought to a higher level in the organization.

Using team meetings, status and progress reports, and issues logs, you have three fundamental tools at your disposal to know what is going on in your project. You're probably familiar with the data processing saying "Garbage in, garbage out." Your project data is only as good as the data people put into it. Current, accurate data will help you recognize problems quickly and take appropriate corrective action. You can download an issues log template from the Syngress website if you don't already have a format you prefer.

Risks and Contingency Plans

We'll discuss managing risks and contingency plans in more detail later in this chapter, but during the course of your project work, you should keep your risk management plan handy and make sure you're aware of your risks and trigger points. Ideally, you should have placed milestones in your project plan to remind you of potential or upcoming risks and trigger points. For example, if you know that only Joaquin can write a particular section of code, you should have a checkpoint prior to that work package to check that Joaquin is available for this task at the scheduled time. It wouldn't be helpful to find out the day before work on that task is to begin that Joaquin just took off for a month in Mali. Make sure you review your risk management plan and keep an eye on your trigger points. Build them into your schedule if you haven't already so that risks and associated triggers are kept in the forefront.

Remember, too, that implementing "Plan B" is a change to your project and must be addressed through your change management procedures. During the risk management planning phase, you should have identified the major areas that might be impacted by your "Plan B," but once work commences, the picture may change. Make sure you look ahead and think about how potential contingency plans might impact the project at this point and going forward. While you won't have time (nor would it be advisable) to plan this way for every single risk, you usually get a sense for which risks are most likely to occur and which require additional thought.

Determining Project Progress

To manage your project, you must know where you wanted to be (that's defined in your project plan) and where you are (current project status). The current project status is something that people sometimes think means progress against budget (if *cost* is the least flexible element) or progress against schedule (if *time* is the least flexible element). However, if you measure a project's progress against just one parameter, you have a very lopsided picture of the project. Let's look at an example.

Suppose Patty was assigned a task to write a particular section of code for a new application. The schedule estimates that it's 10,000 lines of code and that it should take her fourteen work days to accomplish this. For the sake of this example, let's assume Patty makes $25/hour. At the halfway mark, on day seven, Patty has 7,000 lines of code complete. What is the status of the task and how does that impact the project? You could say that since she's seven days into the task that she must be 50% complete (schedule). However, she has 7,000 lines of code written, you could also say that she is 70% complete (lines of code or deliverable).

What if we also included the fact that Patty has spent 84 hours on the task because she worked 12-hour days instead of 8-hour days (7 days x 12 hrs. = 84 hrs., 14 day x 8 hrs. = 112 hrs.)? You might say, well, she's expended 75% of the hours needed, so she must be 75% complete. You might also say that if she's 75% complete at the half way point that she must be ahead of schedule. Which, among all these statements, is actually correct?

Let's look at the cost factor. The total cost of this task was estimated to be the cost of Patty's wages—$25/hr x 112 hours or $2,800. Patty has completed seven days of work, but she incurred overtime on all seven days. The current tab is (($25 x 8) x 7) + (($37.50 x 4) x 7) or $2450. That's about 87.5% of the total budgeted cost. If she is on salary, the cost of an 8-hour day and a 12-hour day would be the same and she'd have expended 50% of the task budget (remember, we're talking about *cost* here, not effort). Clear as mud, isn't it?

Let's recap: Patty is 50% complete, 70% complete, 75% complete or 87.5% complete, right? Patty is on time, ahead of schedule, or behind schedule. That's not very helpful, is it? What if we also said that Patty ran into a huge problem and that although 7,000 lines of code are finished, she now estimates that it will take 25,000 lines of code to complete this task? Suppose working all that overtime to get this task completed caused Patty to make several key errors in the code and the remaining work might take twice as long? Suppose Patty is a genius (which we all suspected anyway) and she actually found a better way to write the code and it's complete at 7,000 lines of code? What is the status of the task now?

As you can see, there are a number of variables to consider. There are always these kinds of variables and it's impossible to know absolutely everything. Some task progress will be much more tangible and easy to assess. In other tasks, like Patty's, tracking progress can be a bit more elusive. You can see by this example that by tracking more than just one element (more than just *time* or just *cost*), you can at least get a much better idea of the actual progress. Getting Patty's perspective on her progress and remaining work can be very helpful and can be an important part of understanding progress, especially in knowledge work.

Project Progress and Knowledge Work

Knowledge work (the work done in many IT projects) is quite different from other kinds of work. In fact, work in knowledge areas (such as programming) does not progress along a linear path. Its path looks more like the trajectory shown in Figure 10.4. Thus, progress may appear to be slow or lagging in the early stages of work and the work gets completed quickly at the end. Knowledge work often follows the 80/20 rule—80 % of the work is accomplished during the last 20%of the project. Stated in reverse, it typically takes 80% of the task time to accomplish the first 20% of the work. This is partially attributable to the learning curve associated with most knowledge work.

Figure 10.4 Progress Curve for Knowledge-Based Tasks or Work

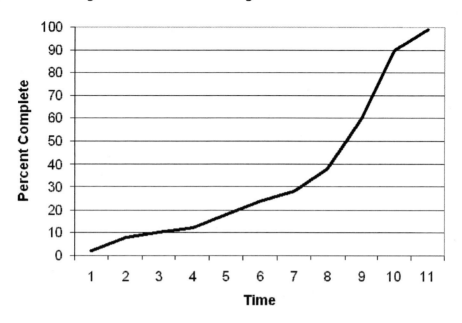

As you can see, there can be a lot of difficulty determining project status for just this one task. The challenge, of course, is to figure out how to accurately determine the task and project status in a relatively fast and simple manner. If you don't take scope, time, cost, and quality into account, you won't have a clear picture at all, so let's look at some methods you can use to account for these different measurements.

There are several methods used to track project progress that give a clearer view of things. We're going to discuss the basic ways to do so and we'll discuss some of the more advanced methods including *Earned Value Analysis*, *Cost Performance*, and *Schedule Performance* (among others) in Chapter 11. The methods in this chapter (Chapter 10) are suitable for many IT projects, but some projects (or some companies) require the more rigorous tracking methods discussed in the next chapter.

Percent Complete

Percent complete is probably the easiest method for assessing project progress and it's one many people use. If you're going to use percent complete, you should track both percent of *budget* expended and percent of *schedule* expended. When possible, it is ideal to also track percent complete of the deliverable work itself, though this is not always feasible. If you track against both cost *and* time, you will instantly have a better picture of what's going on than if you just tracked cost *or* time. Since percent complete is often a judgment call, it's not always an accurate measure, but it's often the best (or only) measure we have.

If we use our earlier example of Patty's code development task, we can say that she is 70% complete because she has 7,000 of 10,000 lines of code complete (*deliverable*). We can also say that she is 75% complete because she has expended 75% of the hours (*effort*) allotted for this task. Since she's completed 70% of the code and expended 75% of the time, we might actually conclude that she's running a bit behind because we would expect to see 75% of the work completed once 75% of the effort had been expended. Are we in trouble on this task? It's difficult to know since Patty might have figured out a way to do this task with 7,500 lines of code, she might run into a problem that causes her to be delayed in completing the final lines of code, or she might have to spend significantly more hours to complete the code (according to scope and requirements) on time. We also know that for knowledge work, it can take longer to complete the early stages of the task so Patty might make up the time on the back end and come in ahead of schedule. Again, Patty's the subject matter expert in this case, so her perspective about the task's progress should also be taken into account.

In this case, *effort* and *duration* are quite relevant, so we might choose to focus on Patty's hours compared to duration. For instance, she has expended 75% of the estimated hours (*effort*) in 50% of the duration (*schedule*), so we might conclude she is ahead of schedule. If she had expended only 25% of the hours at the 50% mark in duration, we could reasonably conclude Patty was behind schedule.

Remember that the original time and cost estimates were developed based on subject matter experts' opinions (possibly Patty's own estimates for this task) or on historical data. However, they were still *estimates*. So, the estimate of what it would take to complete the task is really an educated guess and the estimate of where the task or project is now is also a bit of an educated guess. You could spend hours and hours of time trying to nail this down more exactly, but in many cases these educated guesses are as good as it gets (well, from a cost/benefit perspective, they are as good as it gets). So, percent complete isn't perfect, but it does give you some idea of what's going on, especially if you use percent complete for schedule *and* budget and include percent complete of deliverables when possible.

> ## Cheat Sheet...
>
> ### Where Are We?
>
> As your project data is updated and you begin to gather information, make sure you actually look at it and analyze it. If you have someone on the team that is an *analyzer* type, this might be a good task to delegate, especially if data analysis is not your strong suit. The key is to look at the data with an impartial eye. Sometimes it's a matter of "the glass is half empty" versus "the glass is half full," but many times you can learn important information about your project status by taking some time to analyze the data. Using the example of Patty's code writing, should we be concerned that she's expended 75% of the allotted time and delivered only 70% of the code? Past experience will probably give you the answer, but this is something worth noting. The fact that she's at the 7-day mark (50% of allotted duration) is an important additional element, isn't it? Looking at the data in terms of actual versus schedule for time, cost, and deliverables is crucial. As you can see from this example, looking at only one metric will give you a very skewed view of your project.

Variance

Measuring variance is another commonly used method to measure project (or task) progress. Variance is typically represented as a percentage over or under plan. By definition, *variance* is the amount a result differs from the plan or baseline expressed as a positive or negative number (or percentage). A positive variance means the *actual* is better than the *plan*; a negative variance means the *actual* is worse than the *plan*. Variance can be an extension of the percent complete method because variance can use actual numbers or percentage of completion for measurement. First, let's recap the data for this task, shown in Table 10.1.

Table 10.1 Recap of Sample Task Data

Plan	Actual
Duration: 14 days	Current duration: 7 days (50% mark)
Planned effort: 112 hours	Current hours: 84 (vs. 56 expected)
Planned cost: $2800	Current cost: $1400 (vs. $1400 expected)
Planned work: 10,000 lines of code	Current work: 7,000 lines of code (versus 5,000 expected)

For instance, we could say that Patty has expended 84 hours at the halfway mark, so she is 28 hours over the effort estimate, a -28 hour variance (*plan minus actual* or 56—84). We could also use percentages and say that she has expended 75% of the hours at the 50% mark and therefore has a -25% variance (50% - 75%) on estimated hours. Without knowing how much work she's accomplished, though, her actual hours don't tell us the whole story.

Some IT project managers like to manage using variance because they can focus on the things with the greatest variance. One method is to calculate variance and assign a risk category to that variance. Any task falling into a medium to high risk variance category gets extra attention. An example of this type of categorization is shown in Table 10.2. You can modify this to suit your needs, but the point is that anything with a large or significant variance from plan should be investigated immediately—that includes things that are reported as significantly *under* budget or *under* schedule. For example, tasks that have a variance of 51% or more may require work on the task or project to halt until the problem(s) can be resolved. Anything that has a significant variance should be investigated because it can mean only one of two things: your estimate was wrong or your task/project is at serious risk. If you're have a large variance *under* estimates you shouldn't assume things are going extraordinarily well (though you should be open to that possibility). Rather, you should wonder if the scope or quality is being met, if someone skipped a step or forgot a key work package component, or if someone is simply fudging the numbers to make themselves look better (yes, unfortunately, that does happen). Of course, you need to also be open to the possibility that someone was innovative, creative, or flat-out brilliant and came up with a better solution that took less than half the estimated time. It can happen, but remember, things are more likely to accidentally go wrong than to accidentally go right, so keep a healthy dose of skepticism handy when reviewing variances.

Table 10.2 Sample Variance and Risk Categorization

Variance	Category	Action
Under 51% or more	Red Alert	Investigate/ Halt Work
Under 26% - 50%	Red—High Risk	Investigate Immediately
Under 11% - 25%	Yellow—Medium Risk	Continue/ Analyze
Under 0—10%	Green—Low Risk	Continue/ Monitor
Over 0—10%	Green—Low Risk	Continue/ Monitor
Over 11% - 25%	Yellow—Medium Risk	Continue/ Analyze
Over 26% - 50%	Red—High Risk	Investigate Immediately
Over 51% or more	Red Alert	Investigate/ Halt Work

Let's return to our example of Patty the code writer. Let's recap the stats on this task and look at the variance at the same time, as shown in Table 10.3. The various data described earlier is summarized in the table. By noting the scheduled or planned versus the actual and noting the variance, you get a better picture of what's actually going on in this task. As you can see, the *Expected* column is the calculation of where we should be at this point. Part of the task detail might be a progress checkpoint at the halfway mark, other times this data will be developed on the fly. You might choose to create these kinds of checkpoints (milestones) for all tasks on the critical path so that you can analyze these tasks more thoroughly.

Table 10.3 Task Stats

Item	Total Scheduled	Expected	Actual	Difference	Variance	Status
Duration (days)	14	7	7	0	(None)	Green
Effort (hours)	112	56	84	28	- 50 %	Red
Deliverable (code)	10,000 lines	5,000 lines	7,000 lines	+ 2,000	+ 40%	Red
Cost (dollars)	$2,800	$1,400	$1,400	0	(None)	Green

You might look at this and ask why effort and deliverable are at red status when the deliverable appears to be *ahead* of schedule. The key is that according to the framework laid out in Table 10.2, anything that is out of variance by 26% or more should be looked into. In this case, there's a simple explanation—Patty is getting ready to go on a four-week vacation to the Mediterranean and wanted to complete her task early in case there were any issues with her code. She's been working overtime (she's salaried, so there's no additional incremental cost) to complete her work early. That may be the only explanation needed. Let's look at another scenario. Suppose Patty completed those 7,000 lines of code in just four days, but she's been stuck on the 7,001th line of code for three days. She's expended 75% of the allotted time to accomplish about 70% of the work, so that would normally look like things were moving along. In truth, she's come to a dead halt. Will your variance report tell you that? Not in this case, but since you're looking into these large variances, this information should come to light. By noting the variance and investigating it, you can find out whether Patty is truly ahead of schedule or whether this variance might be an indicator that something is going wrong. Patty's input on task progress would indicate whether she is at a dead halt or whether work is progressing as expected.

What about scope and quality? Are those in or out of variance? Scope and quality are both defined within the task. The total amount of work to be accomplished for Patty's task should be clearly delineated in a requirements document and again in the task detail. Although we've talked about an estimated 10,000 lines of code, the scope and quality information will define what that code should do (one could write 10,000 lines of code that do nothing or do the wrong thing). The entry/exit criteria or completion criteria should be clearly delineated, as should the quality metrics. Although it is possible that Patty's code is poor quality or does not address the scope, you have to assume that because Patty was given the task that she is capable of understanding and delivering on the requirements. As the IT project manager, you can't micromanage every project task so you have to trust others to get their work done according to specifications.

That said, there *should* be built-in checks and balances and in an IT project, this often is accomplished using entry/exit criteria, completion criteria, quality metrics, and through testing tasks or phases. The task owner (whether that's Patty or the Director of Software Engineering who assigned Patty to the task) is responsible for performing to specifications and your job is to ensure each task is making required progress. The point is that you usually cannot clearly quantify scope or quality as easily as time or cost in terms of how much variance there may be from plan until a task is complete. For instance, if Patty's code turns out to be 9,945 lines of code but does not address one required feature, the scope has been reduced. Could you have known the scope was being reduced when the task was, say, 75% complete? Maybe, but not as easily as you could determine that the task was on schedule or on budget. The same goes for quality. There's often no reasonable way you can know if Patty's work meets or exceeds quality standards until it's tested, which is generally a separate task or phase. Thus, it will be difficult to know if there is significant variance in Patty's work in terms of scope or quality until it's completed. Most IT projects have built in ways to determine if there are variances to scope or quality once a task is complete, but generally do not try to track that during task work itself. In some cases, you may be able to track variance to scope or quality within the confines of the task. If it's possible and useful, you certainly can do so, but don't expend too many cycles on this. Instead, make sure you have good quality control processes to ensure that scope and quality are met before a task is marked complete and make sure the right people are assigned to the right tasks.

One final note about task progress: There are certainly unknown elements that could derail this task's progress. Patty could get sick or win the lottery and not come back to work. Patty could run into problems with the last segment of code and not be able to complete it on time or she may have to expend twice the number of hours to get it completed on time. There are a lot of variables with some types of tasks and you can't account for all of them. However, your risk planning should have addressed the known risks, especially if Patty is the only person who can write that particular code (resource risk), and if that task is on the critical path (schedule and project risk).

Applying Your Knowledge

Some projects require very rigorous tracking and we'll discuss some of those methods in Chapter 11. However, for many IT projects, simply tracking time, cost, *and* deliverables is a big improvement over current methods. Task owners are responsible for tracking and reporting this data. The person(s) performing the work must track their progress and report it accurately to the task owner (if the task owner and person doing task work are not the same person). It doesn't have to be complex to be useful and in many projects, *anything* is an improvement.

Managing Variance

When you discover a variance in your project (plan versus actual), there are really only four possible courses of action. You can choose to ignore the variance if it's minor or a one-time issue. You can take action to address the issue, or you can modify the project plan to accommodate the issue. Finally, you can choose to cancel the project in response to unacceptable levels of variance. Since so much of managing your project *is* managing variance, we're going to discuss this in more detail in the upcoming section titled "Managing Project Change."

Managing Related Plans

Whether your training, communication, quality testing, or operational transfer plans are internal or external to your project plan (tasks within your project or checkpoints that refer to external plans), you need to keep track of the timelines and deliverables related to these plans. Two common complaints about IT projects is the lack of communication and the lack of attention paid to training plans. Both of these are easily addressed through your project plan, which we discussed earlier in the book. During the implementation/management phase of the project work, it's important for the IT project manager to monitor the coordination of these plans. You can improve both the perception and the reality of project success by communicating effectively at appropriate intervals. You can also help by making sure that changes in this project are mapped with these related (or external) plans so that changes in one will be appropriately reflected in the other. Timing is everything and that's certainly true with these types of related plans, so make sure that you (or someone on your team) is managing or watching over the interaction between your IT project plan and these related plans. It's often helpful to delegate this to someone on your team and it can be set up as a recurring task within the project plan to ensure these plans remain visible. Also be sure to address the impact of changes in your project plan on these external plans. You should be aware of what the impact will be on the external plans if several key project tasks are delayed and be sure to coordinate with these external plans so things don't get out of sync.

The IT Factor ...

Timing is Everything

When managing your IT project, it's important to keep an eye on these external (or related) plans such as training, communications, testing, operational transfer, etc.. Since the timing of these is related to project progress, those responsible for related plans rely upon accurate and timely information about the status of the IT project. "The timing of the training is particularly difficult because if it comes too early, participants forget what they learned. If it comes too late, participants may be expected to use new features or products they're not trained on, resulting in frustration and low morale. It may be a difficult balance to achieve," explains Kim Nagle, Learning & Development Manager at Canyon Ranch. "Many users have different training needs and often have diverse schedules that must be accommodated. A one-size-fits-all approach to training is usually not effective and by working with your company's training or HR department, you can develop training plans and schedules that meet the needs of the IT project and the users. While it may be tricky to coordinate everything, the effort pays off in increased user satisfaction, higher productivity and a more positive perception of the IT project."

Managing Project Change

Managing change is one of the major jobs for the IT PM and IT team during the work phase of the project. When change occurs, the first step is to look for the root cause of that change. Is it the project definition? The plan? The WBS? External factors? If you don't look for the root cause of the change, you will miss opportunities to improve your project management skills. Change means that something is not going according to the plan, but we all know that plans are rarely perfect. Assessing what is causing the change will help you not only address this issue, but may also help you foresee additional issues that might stem from the same root cause. During the course of the project, the scope, schedule, budget, quality, or requirements can change. The impact these changes have on other tasks and on the project as a whole can range from negligible to extensive. "Manage change or it will manage you" is very true in project management. In this section, we'll look at these and discuss how to deal with change so it doesn't derail your project.

Change Due to Variance

Earlier, we said that if there was any variance, we needed to look at the cause of the variance and then decide what to do. We really have four primary choices in terms of dealing with variance and they are:

- **Ignore the variance** You can choose to ignore the variance, and in some cases this is the best option. When would you choose to ignore the variance? If a task is not on the critical path, minor variances to its schedule may not be all that important to the outcome of the project. If a task's variance on cost is easily explained and you have the reserves to handle it, you may choose to do nothing. Minor price variations of supplies are an expected source of variance and can usually be ignored. Let's be optimistic for a moment. Perhaps something comes in ahead of schedule or costs less than anticipated; you might choose to ignore the variance, though you might want to investigate so you can learn how to repeat that kind of success. Don't be fooled, however. When a task comes in far ahead of schedule or far under the estimated cost, it could be a sign of trouble, as mentioned earlier.

- **Take appropriate action to address the source or effect of the variance** Most of the time when you identify schedule or cost variance, you'll need to take steps to address the variance. These steps could include shuffling resources around, modifying the project schedule, reducing project scope, cutting costs on another task, etc.. The appropriate action should be evaluated in terms of any additional risk it may bring to the project and what impact it will have on other tasks and the project as a whole.

- **Revise the plan to reflect the variation** Sometimes the variation is such that it requires a revision to the project plan. An example of that might be that a component you were going to use in the project suddenly jumps in price by 500% due to a manufacturing plant going off-line (due to strike, natural disaster, etc.). You may need to go back and revise the plan to deal with this variance in cost. You might choose to select a different component or build the component in-house. These all require changes to the project plan and each change should be carefully thought out before being implemented because changes to the project plan (at this point) come with greater risk. There's a saying that "Problems are often born of solutions"—sometimes we fix one thing and break four others. This is especially true in software development, but holds true in all types of IT projects.

- **Cancel the project** One of the options that people hate to consider at this point is canceling the project. However, sometimes it's better to cut your losses and move on. If a variation to the project schedule will delay the project to the point that it's no longer useful, it should be cancelled. An example of this might be a project to develop an interim software solution until the network servers are all upgraded. Once the upgrade is complete, the interim solution will be scrapped and a permanent solution will be installed. If the network upgrade is supposed to take 24 months and the interim solution is delayed and isn't going to be available until month 18, it might not be worth finishing the project. Another example is when a project gets in trouble financially due to cost overruns that make it impossible or inadvisable to complete the project. While sound planning can help you avoid some of these scenarios, it can't prevent them completely and sometimes the most prudent course of action is to cancel the project.

Now, let's turn our attention to areas that might have variance, why they might have variance and what you can do to manage variance to get your project back on track.

Changes to Schedule

Managing change to the project as a whole is part of change management and it should follow your established guidelines for change management developed in your definition and organization stages. By monitoring the project schedule, reviewing performance and status reports, and managing change requests, the IT project manager can control the project schedule to the greatest extent possible. However, the project schedule is one of the parameters that almost always shift as work progresses. The question is, how do you manage these changes without going crazy or putting your project at risk?

The schedule is the number one thing that tends to change in the implementation phase of the project because we can't know with absolute certainty how long tasks will actually take. Ideally, using subject matter experts and historical data, your estimates are very close to actual. Still, there are unexpected things that always pop up that make changes to the schedule almost a foregone conclusion. Resources become unavailable even if they were previously assigned to the project, resources get overbooked, people leave the company, delays in preceding tasks require resources to be shuffled around—the list is almost endless.

Managing schedule changes means staying on top of current task progress and looking ahead a step or two in the project to make sure resources are lined up. Your risk management planning should have addressed the major risks to your schedule and that planning should have looked closely at all risks to the tasks on the critical path. You should have a "Plan B" identified for tasks on the critical path and you should understand the impact of delays or changes to the schedule of these tasks. If change is required, assess the impact on other tasks and to the critical path before implementing schedule changes. Sometimes a solution creates more problems than it solves, so don't jump too quickly. Look first for optimal solutions and then look at the reality of your situation. By looking first for the "best case scenario" you might spot an opportunity or two that you would otherwise have missed. Granted, some schedule changes are simply pushed on you—a task is delayed and it's not clear it will be late until the very last minute. These types of changes are difficult to manage but you should strive to *respond* rather than *react*. Responding is a rational action based on new information; reaction is typically an irrational or poorly planned action based on new information. Your first step, after assessing the situation, is to see if there are tasks that can be rearranged in order to accommodate the schedule changes. Sometimes these exist and the schedule can easily be modified without changing the project parameters (scope, time, cost, quality).

There are two commonly used methods you can use to get your schedule back on track if things really take a turn for the worse: crashing and fast tracking. *Crashing* occurs when you add more resources to the project to ensure it completes on time. Clearly this has an impact on your budget because additional resources cost additional money. Hopefully your reserve amounts will cover all or most of this additional cost should crashing become necessary. The danger of crashing is that adding more bodies does not always translate into more work being completed. A good analogy is that a race horse doesn't go any faster with two jockeys than it does with one (and in some cases, it goes slower). In software development, there is a point at which more bodies will mean less work accomplished, so caution should be used when deciding to crash a project schedule. Make sure that more bodies really *will* help. An example of when this might work well is when you have to install 50 servers in five locations. In that case, more bodies may well get the job done faster.

Fast tracking occurs when tasks that normally would be done sequentially are done in parallel (at the same time). This allows tasks to be done either at the same time or with some overlap. An example of fast tracking might be that servers will be installed as soon as they pass final QA testing rather than once all the servers for a particular location are ready to go. The danger to fast tracking is that you risk rushing things and this increases risk, especially to quality. Rework is often the result.

Applying Your Knowledge

You would typically crash or fast track your schedule if schedule (time) was your least flexible project parameter. There are risks with both methods and neither assures you that your project will still complete on time. If schedule is not your least flexible project parameter, you may do well to simply push your completion date out rather than incur the risks these two methods bring to a project.

Changes to Budget

The budget is managed first by creating realistic estimates for the cost of the project (not necessarily the estimates your boss wants to hear). Once the initial budget and reserve amount are decided upon, a baseline should be established. Monitoring the cost of each task and the total, cumulative cost of the project regularly is the key to keeping project costs under control. You can use percent complete, variance, or some of the techniques we'll discuss in Chapter 11 to analyze where you are with your project budget. If the project budget starts getting off track, you'll need to start rearranging things to stay on track. Remember, though, that you should keep your flexibility grid in mind as you decide what to do. If budget is your *least* flexible item, you may have to push your schedule out so you incur fewer costs in a given period of time or so you incur fewer costs overall. You may also have to go back to the planning stage to determine how you can accomplish the remaining work for less. Budget issues stem from four types of problems: flawed estimates, accounting anomalies, permanent variances, and minor variances.

Flawed estimates require a new estimate to be created. This is known in the formal project management world as generating a new Estimate to Complete (ETC) because you know that the original estimate was simply wrong. This new estimate should specify the additional amount needed to complete the project as well as the actual cost to date. If known, it may be helpful to note why the estimate was flawed as well as any lessons learned so you and the team can avoid these errors in the future.

Anomalies are like hiccoughs—they come out of nowhere, they take you by surprise, and there's not much you can do about it. These types of situations are one-time events that significantly impact your budget, so you *will* have to account for them after the fact, though you can't plan for them before they occur. Your reserve amount might cover the cost of an anomaly, but you might choose to make this a discrete line item so your reserve amount can be used for the normal budget variances that will occur. Here's an example of one such scenario. You've ordered fifty new servers and as they arrive (five at a time) your team begins to unpack, configure, test, and install them. It's not until you have 35 servers installed that they start failing and you discover there was a manufacturing problem and *all* the servers are all defective. The vendor is willing to replace them immediately, but you've already spent a large portion of your budget (and schedule) unpacking, configuring, testing, and installing *these* servers. In order to complete the project on time, you contract with an external IT company to come in and assist with these tasks on the replacement servers. This unplanned event blows your budget out of the water. It's not an estimating error but an anomaly that is unlikely to occur again in the future (if it does, fire that vendor). All you can do is deal with the anomaly. These types of variances can be small or large, and what differentiates anomalies from other types of variances is whether they could not have been reasonably foreseen and are not likely to occur again. Large anomalies can cause projects to be cancelled at this stage, but small anomalies can usually be incorporated into the project.

Permanent variances are variances that are expected to be typical for the remainder of the project. An example of a permanent variance is that the materials you needed have gone up in price by 20% but that price increase is locked in for another 12 months, so while you are protected against any further increases the remainder of your project will show a -20% variance (remember, a negative variance means your *plan* is better than your *actual*) on this line item. Another example of a permanent variance is if the people assigned to the task are not as skilled or competent as expected. They make take more time to complete tasks (more paid hours), you may have to provide additional training, or you may have to bring in outside contractors to assist. This causes permanent variances moving forward unless other actions can be taken. Permanent variances may or may not be addressed by the reserve amount. In some cases, the permanent variance should be added to the cost of the project and the reserve left intact to account for other minor variances that may occur. How it is handled is a matter for you, your project sponsor, and your Accounting department to decide upon.

Minor variances also occur in projects, which is why you created a reserve amount in your budget for each phase of the project (or each major deliverable). These are to be expected and you may choose to set a threshold for "minor" so that you and the team are clear what minor means in terms of a budget variance. Certainly you don't want to get pulled from a meeting if the cost of a task will exceed budget by 5%. By the same token, 5% variances can add up quickly. Define acceptable variances and closely monitor your reserves.

Cheat Sheet...

Bring in the Reserves

Remember when you created your schedule and budget based on your WBS and your best estimates for time and cost? You created reserves for each based on a number of factors. When evaluating change to the project, make sure you remember your reserve amounts. Most minor variances can be dealt with from the reserves. Major or unanticipated variances often have to be handled differently. Typically these major variances must be added to the overall project schedule and/or budget rather than being handled through reserves. This will help you keep the project on course by leaving you with reserves to provide flexibility to address the day-to-day variances that occur. You may have to "spend" your entire reserve amount if the variance is huge, but that means that every other task (both time and cost) will have to hit dead on for the project to complete as expected. The odds of that are about the same as winning the state lottery, so be wary of using up your reserves for large, unexpected variances (your project sponsor may require you use your reserves respond to a large variance, but that won't change the fact that minor variances will still occur).

Changes to Scope

Changes to scope can be *managed* or *unmanaged*. Unmanaged changes to scope are often referred to as scope creep. *Scope creep* occurs when the amount of work expands after the project plan has been agreed upon and approved. One of the ways this occurs is through team members interacting with users or stakeholders and informally agreeing to changes outside of project meetings. Another way this occurs is when executives or your project sponsor insert work into the project after the plan is set. Your first line of defense is to make it clear to your team that the only changes to the work of the project that are made are those discussed and agreed upon in project team meetings. Your scope of work is modified when a proposed change is approved and incorporated into the project plan. For instance, if you have a permanent budget variance, you (you, the team, project sponsor, stakeholders) may decide to reduce the scope of the project so that the final budget is closer to the planned budget. This would indicate that budget is least flexible and scope is somewhat (or most) flexible. Another time you may choose to reduce scope to meet schedule requirements or hard deadlines. You may choose to increase the scope in order to accommodate market or user changes or to incorporate a leading edge technology that just became available. However, increasing scope also means something else has to change. Remember the relationship between scope, time, cost, and quality. When your scope increases, you'll have to increase your schedule, increase your budget, or reduce your quality to accommodate this change. In some cases, you may be able to add scope without impacting schedule or budget, but those instances are few and far between.

Requested changes almost always impact scope in one way or another, so the logical starting point is your Work Breakdown Structure. Remember that your scope is essentially defined by the tasks in the WBS, so managing your scope means managing the tasks of the project. Change might be in the amount of work requested, changes to the attributes of the deliverables, or changes to the methods used to create the deliverables. Each of these changes should be evaluated to determine the change to the WBS so that you will know where tasks need to be added, removed, or modified to accommodate the change. Then you should evaluate whether the requested change is logical, desirable, feasible, and affordable. You also need to understand how this increased scope will impact the remainder of your project, especially as it relates to schedule, budget, resource allocation, and tasks on your critical path. Once you understand the nature and impact of the requested change, you can make a determination as to whether or not (or how) to implement the change.

Reviewing status and progress reports can also lead to change requests. It's possible that as work progresses, it becomes clear that the project will not be able to deliver on one or more objectives as it currently stands. This might become clear through reporting and analysis of progress reports. It's also possible that through progress reporting you discover the project is on better footing that you planned and you *can* accommodate that last-minute, "must have" feature that users have been clamoring for.

Cheat Sheet...

Scope Creep 101

One of the most common problems that happens in projects is scope creep. Scope creep is sneaky and it often happens when you least suspect. When managing a project, it's important to continually keep an eye on scope. Every time you consider making a change, you should ask what effect the change will have on scope. There are a lot of changes that can happen in a project that have a relatively low impact, but changes that impact your scope ripple through your project and become magnified. To avoid the ripple effect of scope creep, make sure you continually ask if changes will impact scope and then decide whether that's acceptable or not. Be sure to understand how and where that ripple effect will occur.

Managing Change Requests

Change requests typically involve changes to scope, but they can conceivably involve changes to schedule, budget, or quality. Changes to functional or technical requirements usually fall in the category of scope change. Change can come from verbal or written requests, from inside or outside the organization, or from legal or regulatory requirements. Regardless of the nature of the change request, one of the most important tasks of an IT project manager during this phase is to manage change requests. If your team is constantly shooting at a moving target, it's unlikely the goals of the project will be met. Change control is the way you prevent the moving target syndrome. Though we discussed change management earlier in the book, it's worth repeating at this juncture.

First, your change management process should be clear about how change can be requested, how change is evaluated, and how change is made to the project. Most change requests fall into one of four categories: errors or omissions, risk response, value-added, or external events.

Errors and omissions are perhaps the most common source of change requests in a project. Through the project management process, you've attempted to reduce or eliminate the need for rework due to errors or omissions, but they sometimes still occur. The error or omission might be due to a forgotten or overlooked task in the WBS (one that should be in the WBS and is not), an overlooked or forgotten feature of the project deliverables (functional specification error), or an error in the technical specifications discovered during the work phase. Changes that address gaps or shortfalls in the project must be assessed based on their impact to project scope, schedule, budget, quality, requirements, and risks.

Change also occurs when you have to respond to project risk (*risk response*), whether planned or unplanned. If you have to implement "Plan B" for a particular work package or project phase, that forces change on the project. Having to develop "Plan C" on the fly due to unforeseen circumstances also forces change on the project. The degree to which change occurs as a result of implementing contingency plans should be part of the risk management and assessment phase. If it wasn't assessed at that time, make sure you and the team take a look at the impact of Plan B to your project's scope, schedule, budget, requirements, and quality before implementing it. Even if you assessed your risks associated with Plan B, it's always a good idea to re-evaluate them based on the current project status and data since many things change between *planned* and *actual* as work progresses.

Value-added change requests are just that—they are changes that will add value to the project such as a change that will reduce the overall cost of the project or a change that will shorten the project schedule by two weeks or a change that will add functionality, usability, or other desirable features to the project. Value-added change is typically a positive thing, but it should be scrutinized just as any other change should be.

External events can drive change requests as well. If you're developing a software product that deals with finance, you may have to change your specifications in response to changing local, state, or federal laws. These are external events that should have been assessed during the risk assessment phase ("What external factors might impact your project?"), but these kinds of changes cannot always be known in advance.

Requesting change to the project should be a formal process. You can download a change request template from the Syngress website if you don't already have a solid change request process in place. The elements of a change control system include:

- Document requested change and reason for request.

- Evaluate impact of requested change on scope, schedule, budget, requirements, quality, and WBS.

- Determine whether or not to implement change.

- Determine approval levels needed (if any).

- Determine if any special communication is needed with respect to the requested/approved change.

- Integrate the change into the project plan.

- Update any related external plans impacted by the change (training, operational transfer, etc.).

- Document lessons learned, if applicable.

Taking Corrective Action

Any corrective action you take is, by definition, a change to the project. It's important to understand this so you don't inadvertently introduce new problems into the project. If you recall from our discussion about quality in Chapter 7, change becomes riskier and more expensive the further out in time you go (that is, the further into the project work you get). Each change carries its own unique set of risks and it's your job as IT project manager to weigh the risks and the benefits of the change. Once you've evaluated the reward relationship, you can make an informed decision as to the proper course of action. Some changes may be mandated (by the project sponsor, stakeholders, or legal requirements) and you have only two choices: make the required change or terminate the project. In some cases, you may choose to terminate the project because to incorporate the required change would cause the project to fail. In other cases, you have to determine the impact of the required change and modify your project plan (including scope, schedule, budget, requirements, quality metrics, WBS, and task details) to reflect that change. Corrective action could (and often does) introduce new problems, so don't take corrective action without fully assessing the impact on the project.

The IT Factor...

Responding to Change

When the folks at NASA and the Jet Propulsion Laboratory were preparing the Mars mission, they had a hard deadline because there were only certain times the rocket could be launched when the planets were properly aligned for the mission. During the course of the project, the team creating the landing system discovered they'd underestimated the actual weight of the Mars vehicle (designed by a different team) and had to go back to the drawing board to redesign a landing system that could accommodate the weight of the vehicles. They didn't have a choice about making this change nor did they have a choice about the

Continued

schedule. In their case, the schedule was the least flexible item, and quality was a close second because it wouldn't do to meet the deadline and have the Mars vehicle crash and burn as it landed on the surface of Mars. Their team raced against the clock to get the project completed. Another team responsible for the software systems had the launch and landing software tested and ready to go, but were unable to complete the surface navigation software in time. However, they knew that they had a small window of opportunity to complete this task without putting the mission at risk because the navigation software had two flexible features the rest of the mission did not: it was not required to be completed at launch (no *finish-to-start* dependency with launch) and it could be modified on the fly by beaming the new software code up to the vehicles once they were en route to Mars or even on the surface of Mars.

This is a great example of how projects progress. Errors, omissions, and changes will occur, even when it *is* rocket science. The key is how well you assess your options and how innovative you can be in responding to change.

Managing Project Risk

Once you have a risk management process in place, you need to actively monitor the project for those risks. However, the risks you identified and planned for are not the only risks your project will encounter. We discussed the risk and cost of changes in later stages of the project plan and even if those risks and contingency plans were assessed and "planned" for, they may still have secondary effects you were not aware of. This cycle of project risk is shown in Figure 10.5. You can see that even if the risk is identified and "Plan B" is implemented, you may still be creating secondary risks. Sometimes those risks are minor, sometimes they're major but you've accounted for them, and sometimes they're major and completely unexpected.

Figure 10.5 Project Risk Cycle

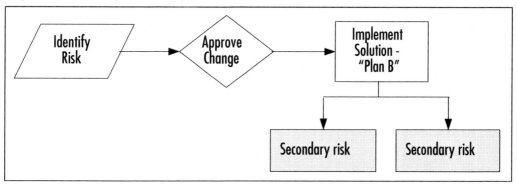

Risk monitoring and control occur in this phase of the project lifecycle. The methods of managing risk include:

- Having and using a risk management plan

- Communicating project risks

- Actively monitoring for new risks

- Assessing impact of scope change

As you move from one phase to the next or one set of deliverables to another, you should review your risk management plan and be aware of the risks your team identified. If a risk was anticipated, it should not come as a surprise simply because you (or your team) forgot to review your risk management plan. It's sometimes helpful to add milestones to your project schedule either to indicate places where risk has been identified, trigger points for identified risks, or simply as a reminder to review your risk management plan periodically. You should also periodically discuss and review project risk in your project team meetings, especially risks to your critical path tasks. This discussion can include risks that are pending, coming up, or just discovered. It can also be used to discuss the potential secondary risks discovered as a result of one or more changes to the project. Another risk management tool is the Earned Value Analysis, which we discuss at length in Chapter 11. This can help assess project progress and identify overall project risk. One final tool for managing project risk is the monitoring or measuring of performance against specification. If the project team does not have the skills and talents necessary to accomplish the project work, your project is at risk. This may not have been an identified risk during your project risk evaluation process, so it might crop up only as work gets underway.

What can you do to manage risk? We've previously discussed developing contingency plans for project risks that have the highest likelihood of occurring and the highest impact to the project. We can manage risk through:

- **Workarounds** Workarounds are ad hoc responses to risks that were not planned. Workarounds should be assessed to determine whether secondary risks exist and if those risks are acceptable.

- **Corrective actions** Corrective actions are actions you take to keep your project on track. Often corrective actions are minor tweaks you make as part of your day-to-day IT project management. Any type of corrective action typically carries secondary risk, which should be identified and assessed.

- **Change requests** Changes to the project work or project plan due to risk should be brought through the standard change management process. These changes should be reflected in the project plan and accounted for in the scope, schedule, budget, requirements, or quality metrics of the plan.

- **Risk response plans/updates** As identified risks occur and contingency plans are implemented, these changes should be documented and reflected in the updated project plan. Sometimes during the course of project work, the risks or risk priorities shift. If this occurs, the risk management plan should also be updated to reflect new risks or new priorities for those risks.

Remember, when assessing changes and risks, it's important to keep your critical path tasks in mind. Risks and changes to tasks on the critical path require careful review of potential ramifications. Risks and changes to tasks that are not on the critical path also require careful assessment, but by definition, changes to these tasks will be less dramatic, at least to the project schedule, than tasks on the critical path. Finally, keep in mind that changes to tasks can place them on the critical path, so evaluate change before implementing them to keep your project on an even keel.

Managing the Project Team

We've discussed how to manage and motivate a project team at length earlier in this book, so we're not going to repeat that material here. If you are new to IT project management or new to management in general, you may not feel comfortable managing a group of people over whom you have no direct authority. If that's the case, you should review earlier material on managing highly effective teams and you should seek the advice and guidance from a more experienced project manager. That said, we will discuss some of the common problems project managers run into in managing the team and we'll give you a few pointers to use to help overcome those problems.

Effective IT Project Management

If you don't like working with people, you're probably always going to have mixed emotions about project management. Projects don't just happen, people make them happen and the project manager's job is to ensure that those people have the time, skills, tools, and motivation needed to get the project tasks done. The job of an IT project manager is one part manager, one part communicator, one part negotiator, and one part cheerleader. To manage the project successfully, you'll need to manage people successfully. Some IT PMs just naturally work well with people, others struggle a bit. We're not going to give you a short course on management here, but we can give you a few tips to make your job as IT PM just a bit easier. Keep these principles in mind as you work with your team.

- **Share information** Information is power, so share information with your team. You will empower them to do their jobs and you will develop a two-way trust that can help when the going gets rough. If you can't share certain confidential information, tell them that rather than side-step the issue. Otherwise, share as much information as is reasonable and prudent. Hoarding information will eventually hogtie the project.

- **Find ways to motivate** It's often argued that you can't really motivate anyone, they have to motivate themselves. That said, there are things you can do that will inspire others to do a good job for your project. Find ways to let people on the team know that their contribution is meaningful and appreciated. Let them know you understand their situation (if they're working overtime to get the job done, etc.). Thank people for small and large contributions to the project. Find ways to align project work with people's work personalities (see earlier chapters in this book for more detail).

- **Remove obstacles** One of the ways a manager can inspire commitment and hard work is to be committed to removing as many obstacles as possible for the project team. If team members are having difficulty gaining access to a room needed to set up a lab, take that task on yourself. Make it happen and let the team continue to work on their project tasks. If you see your job as IT PM as the person responsible for removing the roadblocks to success, you'll do your project and your team a great service. Don't take on everyone's battles—certainly team members will have to deal with their own issues, but do work to remove obstacles that impact your project when appropriate.

- **Don't take it personally** Whether someone does a good or bad job, whether they're early, on time, or late, don't take it personally. Most of the time, work performance issues are unrelated to the IT project manager (and unrelated to the project itself sometimes). As a manager, you have to develop a bit thicker skin. Continue to focus on the outcome. Continually ask yourself, "What outcome do I want and will this action help me get the outcome?" If the answer is no, stop. If the answer is yes, continue. Focusing on behavior, results, and outcomes—not personalities—will help you manage the project and your team.

- **Foster cooperation, not competition** We live in a competitive world and many companies encourage competition—either implicitly or explicitly. On a project team, however, competition is usually a negative force causing people to withhold information, hoard resources, and generally work as individuals rather than as a team. You pull together a project team because you need the project work to be greater than the sum of its parts. If that wasn't the case, you wouldn't need a team at all and you could simply hire contractors to do work and be done with it. Most projects require problem solving, innovation, and other skills that are greatly enhanced by team membership. Look for ways to encourage team members to cooperate and only reward cooperative (not competitive) behavior. Some competition may be fine if done in the spirit of making the project better, but don't let it rule the team.

- **Foster exceptional project work performance** In order for individuals on the project team to do a good job, they must have five things:

  - A clear understanding of the purpose, goals and objectives for the task (or project).

  - A plan for how to achieve the goals and objectives.

  - The skills, resources, and time to do the job.

  - Feedback on performance.

  - A clear understanding of his or her authority to make decisions and take corrective action to deal with variances to the plan.

The last bullet point is particularly important because team members must be empowered, to some degree, to make decisions in order to complete tasks successfully. Have you ever called an 800 number about a problem with a credit card statement and gotten that person that says, "You are correct. This charge posted twice. However, I am not able to fix the problem." It drives most of us nuts because we're required to jump through three more hoops to get the problem resolved simply because the person to whom we first spoke did not have the authority to resolve the problem. This will drive your team members nuts as well when they face problems they know how to resolve but lack the authority to do so. A person without information cannot take responsibility. A person cannot take responsibility without authority. When someone is responsible for a deliverable but is not given the authority to get the job done, they will typically either seize authority or fail. Neither is an ideal outcome.

The IT Factor...

Power On The Front Lines

Most people these days are familiar with Federal Express. Years ago, they became innovators in their field for a number of reasons, but one of the reasons that still stands out is that the people who answered their phones were actually empowered to fix problems. This was quite different from the way others companies ran at that time. The typical response was, "I'll have to talk to my supervisor," or "Call back tomorrow," or "There's nothing I can do about that." At FedEx, people who answered the phones were given a defined amount of authority. They could credit you for a package that arrived late. They could send a courier out for a missed or late pick up. They could actually DO something about many of the problems they fielded. This not only improved morale, but it helped build the reputation for quality that FedEx came to be associated with. Customers and employees alike were more satisfied and it's a fair bet to say that costs went down because fewer people had to call in multiple times, so fewer operators were needed. Delegate responsibility *and* a defined amount of authority to get the work done. If you hand out responsibility without authority, it will backfire and reappear as morale, productivity, or quality problems. Besides, if you can't trust your team with both responsibility *and* authority, you have a bigger problem to address.

Dealing with Project Team Issues

As an IT project manager, you'll have to manage the performance of team members even when you lack the formal authority to do so. Review Chapter 4 for more in-depth information on this topic. In this section, we're going to focus specifically on issues that may crop up during the work phase of the project. As with other topics, the list is not intended to be exhaustive, but to cover some of the most common issues that arise. If you run into issues you don't know how to handle, beeline it to your HR department or your manager for some impartial advice or coaching. Whatever you do, don't let project or team issues simply slide. They tend to only get bigger and more complicated with each passing day.

Deliverables

If project team members fail to meet deadlines for deliverables, the project schedule will begin to slip. How much it slips obviously depends on how much each task slips and whether or not it's on the critical path. Failure to meet deliverable deadlines can indicate that team members:

- Have too much work to do

- Have run into a problem completing the work

- Lack the skills required to complete the work

- Lack the motivation to complete the work

Many experienced managers know that most performance issues typically boil down to two root problems: competence and attitude. If someone is *incapable* of completing the work, your job as IT project manager is to either reassign that task to someone who is qualified or provide the training, tools, or resources needed for the current person to complete that work. If someone is *unwilling* to complete the work, you have to either talk with that person to change his or her attitude or remove him or her from the team.

As the IT project manager, you may be hesitant to take action related to performance, especially if you lack formal organizational authority. However, performance problems by team members put your project at risk, so it is incumbent upon you to deal with these issues clearly, directly, and immediately. Some problems do just go away, but performance problems are usually not among them. If you're not comfortable discussing these problems with a team member, go to your Human Resources manager (or equivalent) and ask for advice and language to use in dealing with these issues. Having the right language to use to address the issue in an appropriate manner can be the biggest challenge and a good HR person can help you out.

As mentioned earlier in the book, your project processes should include a performance evaluation process (typically performed at project close out and discussed in Chapter 12). Managing performance, like managing your project, is a daily task not just something you do when closing out the project.

The IT Factor...

Human Resources Are Part of Your Team

New managers of any kind (including IT project managers) tend to feel like they should have all the answers. In truth, no one has all the answers. A great way to learn how to become a better manager is to talk about your challenges with your manager or with someone in Human Resources. "There's usually someone in the HR department who can coach you on how to deal with a variety of problems that come with managing people," explains David Getman, Human Resources Director for Canyon Ranch. "HR staff help managers by providing an impartial view of the situation, by discussing the problem and potential solutions, by helping the manager understand the organizational or legal implications (if any), or by coaching the manager on how to handle a situation. Often simply providing some suggested language to use is a tremendous help. HR can be a very valuable part of your team and it's a resource many people forget when they're busy managing their project."

Quality

If team members are completing tasks below the required level of quality (performance to specifications), your project is in serious risk. You can refer back to Chapter 7 for a thorough discussion of quality, but in this section we'll discuss how team members may contribute to quality problems and what you can do to address these issues. Quality problems can be performance issues, but they can also point to process or specification issues. Your first task, then, is to determine the root cause of the quality problem. Quality problems tend to fall into one of three categories in IT project work: performance-based, process-based, or specification-based.

Performance

Performance issues can be the cause of poor quality work from team members. In some cases, the person doing the work lacks the skill or ability to do the task, in which case you have to reassign that task or provide training, coaching, or guidance. In other cases, quality issues may stem from a lack of understanding about requirements or a lack of attention to requirements. In either case, your job as IT PM is to review the requirements for the task(s) and ensure the team member has the capability and resources to complete or rework the task so it meets quality standards.

Process

Process issues can also create quality problems if the defined process or procedure is incorrect. Some procedures may be developed at the outset of the project and may require refinement or modification during the course of the project. Other procedures may not be obviously incorrect but yield sub-optimal quality results. If you're confident the team member has the skills and capabilities to accomplish the task and understands the specifications, you may want to check the process they're using to determine if this is the root cause. The team member may be performing work in the wrong order, may be receiving work in the wrong order, or may be following incorrect procedures. For instance, if a procedure was written up for installing a disk drive in a server and it stated that the drive should be installed with power on, this may be incorrect and yield a high number of initial drive failures. The team member may faithfully follow procedure but that is what leads to the quality issue.

Specifications

Many IT projects have specifications, both functional and technical, developed at the front end of the project during a feasibility study or during the definition stage. Sometimes the specifications end up being slightly off or flat out wrong. Sometimes specifications change after the project is defined, sometimes an error is made in writing the specification, and other times the specifications are correct but impossible to meet. Quality issues that stem from problems in the specifications are the most serious because they typically mean that one or more parts of the project plan will have to be revised and this almost always impacts scope, schedule, and budget (we know it will impact quality because that's what prompted the action in the first place).

Communication

Teams often experience communication problems at one point or another. We all know people who are excellent communicators and others who have difficulty stringing together a coherent sentence. Good communications are crucial for a successful project as you and the team try to manage many moving parts. If the team is having difficulty communicating, look for root causes. One of the important elements we discussed at length in Chapter 4 was differences in styles. People with different work styles communicate very differently and this can lead to frustration and miscommunication. Someone from Marketing might naturally talk more and speak in "big picture" terms while someone from Engineering is busy worrying about exactly what the Marketing person means because it's not quantifiable or because it seems vague. These kinds of style differences can be managed, but it takes a good team leader to recognize these problems and address them. Often the best course of action in these situations is to use active listening skills, paraphrasing speaker's messages and acting almost as a translator so your team can find that middle ground. Also keep in mind if you're communicating across electronic links (phone, video conferencing) and across time zones and cultures that extra attention must be given to team communications.

Dealing with Project Team Meeting Issues

Having an agenda can help keep the meeting on track, but someone (that is, you, the IT project manager) has to manage the meeting. In some companies, the task of moderating or facilitating the meeting rotates so that each team member has a turn at running the team meeting. In other cases, if you have someone on the team who's good at facilitating meetings, you may ask him or her to be the team meeting moderator on a permanent (for the project) basis. A well-run meeting can help avoid many of the problems we'll discuss next so it's worthwhile to learn to run an effective meeting or to find someone who is good at it. Your HR department may offer classes, tips, or coaching on running effective meetings and it's a great skill to have.

Even if you're great at running meetings, some problems will probably crop up. While there's no standard set of problems, here are a few you might encounter and what they might indicate.

- **Team members miss project team meetings**

  Problem: People miss scheduled meetings either because something unexpected came up or because they are purposely avoiding the meeting. In the latter case, they may be skipping the meetings because they feel the meetings are not productive or because they are scheduled at a time that is difficult to break away.

  Solution: Make sure your project team meetings are short and to the point. Make sure you have an agenda going in and that you stick to the agenda. Team members can socialize before or after meetings, but don't let the meeting itself turn into a schmooze-fest. Make sure meetings start and end on time and accomplish their objectives. Talk with missing team members one-on-one to determine the reason for the team member's absence.

- **Team members arrive late or are ill-prepared for team meetings**

  Problem: Team members may arrive late or be ill-prepared because they occasionally run late or because they are not placing a priority on these meetings. They may simply have too much work to do to arrive on time or to be prepared, but these should raise warning flags for you. If they have so much work they cannot arrive on time and prepared, they may not be giving their attention to your IT project (assuming they have multiple priorities and projects, which most people do).

Solution: Again, if the meetings are well-run, people are less likely to arrive late or ill-prepared. If the meeting starts on time and covers the agenda items, people are more likely to attend and be prepared because they know they will be called upon to discuss their data. Many project teams produce a status report based on the outcomes of the previous meeting, which helps keep everyone on the same page. If a team member is ill-prepared, talk with him or her one-on-one to determine if there is a misunderstanding about what is expected for team meetings. If they have too much work on their plates, you need to work with them to find a solution that will allow them and your project to be successful.

■ **Team members bicker during team meetings**

Problem: Team members seem to disagree on everything during team meetings. They cannot come to consensus and some seem to play devil's advocate just for fun.

Solution: This problem can occur when team members represent different corporate interests such as Marketing and Engineering. If the root cause appears to be a difference of perspective, you might assign the opposite point of view to the team members and ask them to argue "the other guy's" case. This often helps people see things from the other's point of view and helps bridge gaps. You might also schedule an additional meeting to hammer out these differences so things can move forward. Make sure you stick to the meeting agenda and request (require) that team members discuss things in a positive framework.

■ **Team members do not participate in team meetings**

Problem: Team members come to meetings but do not participate or participate minimally. When called upon they reply with "I don't know" or "I'm not sure" or "I have no opinion." This is sometimes caused by people feeling the meeting is a waste of their time or that the meeting is a hostile environment in which to interact. Other times it is caused by people feeling nervous talking in front of a group or they may simply be shy and not assert themselves in the conversation.

Solution: Make sure the meeting is effective and also make sure you foster a positive communication style. Ask people to focus on behaviors and tasks, not personalities. If a team member is simply not comfortable talking in the group, draw him or her into the discussion at points where their expertise would be useful. Make sure to call upon team maters who are not voluntarily talking. Ask open-ended questions that require a longer response than "I don't know" to get all team members participating.

■ **Team members interrupt, talk too long, meander**

Problem: Team members interupt each other or don't stay on topic. Interrupting others can be a sign of poor manners, excitement, or lack of awareness. Regardless of the root cause, you should encourage team members to be respectful of others and that means allowing others to finish their thoughts or statements. On the flip side, there seem to be people who seem to be unaware that they talk non-stop. These folks can go on and on and say little, if anything, of importance. Oddly, the best way to manage these people is to interrupt because otherwise they will dominate a conversation, often without even meaning to do so. However, the person to interrupt should be the moderator or team meeting leader.

Solution: One of the jobs of the moderator is to make sure the meeting stays on track so the moderator can and should politely interrupt people who go on and on. If everyone understands the role of the moderator, they are less likely to take offense if they are interrupted. Finally, you can hold "stand up meetings" where there are no chairs in the room. This can facilitate focused communication and information sharing and provide a needed change of position for people who sit all day long.

Applying Your Knowledge

Create an atmosphere that is positive and conducive to teamwork. That means not allowing team members to be rude or disrespectful of others' opinions. It also means drawing out the quieter, less talkative members of the team. If someone complains, ask him or her to phrase it in terms of a problem/solution so that they have to provide a recommendation for change. This causes people to take responsibility for their communications and helps build a more productive team atmosphere. If someone does not participate, specifically call upon them and ask an easy, safe, open-ended question. If someone tends to dominate the conversation, politely interrupt them and call on others. Don't let poor team communications hold your project captive.

How to Deal with Interpersonal Issues

Entire books have been written on this topic, so we can only point you in the right direction here. As stated earlier, your HR department can be a great resource for guiding you through the process of dealing with a wide range of personnel type issues. Of course, don't go marching into HR thinking you can dump your problems on their doorstep—not so. They're there to guide and coach you, not to do your job for you. When dealing with team issues, you should start at the top and work your way down. What that means is that you should not get involved with or be concerned about interpersonal issues that do not impact your project's goals, objectives, and deliverables. The most advisable course of action with interpersonal issues is for you to take each party aside individually and discuss the problem candidly. Find out what that person is willing to do differently to improve the situation. Do this with each person involved. Then, set a meeting with all parties to discuss the problem and the agreements you've forged. By discussing the issues individually, you give each person the opportunity to safely vent their frustrations without adding fuel to the fire. By gathering everyone together after that, you bring people back together to re-create their relationships based on their agreements. If this all sounds a bit too touchy-feely for you, remember that if your team doesn't work well together, your project may fall apart. If you're not comfortable doing these things, get some assistance from your HR department. Whatever you do, don't ignore these kinds of issues because they will eventually affect everyone on the team, not just the offending parties.

If a person refuses to acknowledge his or her part in the problem or if they're unwilling to change, you might consider removing them from the project team because interpersonal issues can pull a team apart quickly. Of course, that's in the ideal world—in the real world you may not have the authority to remove someone from the project. However, if the problem puts the project in jeopardy, you should have a serious discussion with your project sponsor and encourage him or her to allow you to replace one or more people on the team. If the project is worth doing, it's not worth putting in jeopardy because of one or two unruly or incorrigible people.

Finishing Project Work

The exit point from the project implementation or work phase is the project close-out. We'll discuss closing out the project in Chapter 12. The deliverable from this stage is the entire set of project deliverables as well as an up-to-date project plan showing the baseline and actual-to-date information. The deliverables and project plan are depicted in Figure 10.6 and are the output or result of this phase of the project. There may be additional data that you add, revise, or update during the close-out phase and we'll discuss that in Chapter 12. Before we head into Chapter 12, we'll discuss some of the more technical project tracking methods in Chapter 11 as well as common project problems and how to address them.

Figure 10.6 Deliverables from this Phase

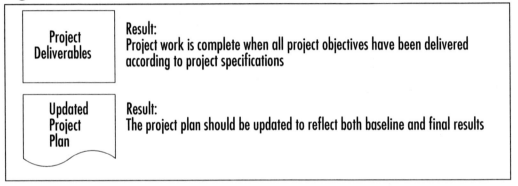

Summary

After you've defined, organized, and planned your project, you're ready to begin project work. The process of implementing your project involves starting work, monitoring progress, managing variance, and reporting status. These are iterative processes that continue until all project work is complete. For the most part, these activities are described in your project processes and procedures at the outset of project planning.

Project status can be monitored through the use of team meetings, status reports, and issues logs. Throughout this process you should capture lessons learned so you and the team can learn in real time. When problems do arise, they can be handled through standard project processes including team meetings, status reports, issues logs, bug tracking and escalations. Progress can be stated as percent complete, but it's important to use the percent complete of tasks, time, and cost in order to get a balanced view of progress.

Variances to the plan will occur as things move and shift. Managing these changes is one of the jobs of the IT project manager. Variances can be measured by percent complete versus expected at any given point in the task. At the halfway point in any task, the time and cost should be roughly 50% of total. Significant variances (over and under) should be investigated thoroughly.

When change occurs in a project, you have four possible responses: do nothing, repair the problem, revise the plan, or terminate the project. If change occurs to your schedule, you can choose to crash or fast track your schedule. Both techniques deal with schedule problems, but both introduce their own unique set of risks to the project. Each method should be evaluated prior to implementing. Changes to budgets also can occur and there are four sources of budget changes: flawed estimates, anomalies, permanent variance, and minor variance. Each has a different impact on your project and some may end up causing the project to be terminated. The reserve created for schedule or budget can be used for minor variances, but larger variances may have to be treated as more separate, discrete elements depending on their size and impact to the project.

Change to the scope is the most dangerous because it often creeps in unnoticed (hence the term *scope creep*). Managing the scope is another important job of the IT PM. Scope is defined through the Work Breakdown Structure and the task details, so keeping an eye on changes in this area will help avoid scope creep. Define and enforce change control procedures so that work is not added to your project without the team knowing and accepting these changes. Remember that increases in scope almost always result in a change to the schedule, budget, or quality.

Change requests are prompted from four primary sources of change: errors/omissions, risk response (implementing your "Plan B"), value-added, or external events. All change is a risk to your project, so it's important to evaluate the impact of change on project parameters (scope, time, cost, quality) as well as the impact on the functional and technical requirements.

During your planning phase, you should have worked with the project team to identify and plan for risks (based on likelihood of occurrence and impact on the project). During the work phase, you may run into those risks or other unexpected risks. When these problems occur, you have four possible responses: workaround, corrective action, change request, or risk response. Since each of these involves some change to the project, each should be evaluated before being implemented to avoid introducing secondary risks and new problems.

Managing the project team can be a challenge for first-time IT project managers and for those who would rather talk to computers than to human beings. Honing your people management skills will help you become a better IT project manager. Keep your manager, project sponsor, or HR department in mind when looking for assistance in dealing with team personnel issues. The success of the project is dependent upon the skills, talents, and motivation of the IT project team. If performance or quality issues exist, look for the root cause. Determine if the person has the skills, time, and resources to properly do the job. If the problem is one of attitude or motivation, you face a different challenge, but you must deal with the issue if you want your project to succeed. Keys to managing your team well are to delegate, share information, and provide the authority commensurate with the responsibility so team members can effectively do what's asked of them. Deal with team communication, performance, or interpersonal issues quickly because they will only flare up later and put your project at risk.

When you and the team have completed all project work, you're ready to announce project completion, deliver it to your user/customer and begin the project close-out phase. We'll discuss project close-out in Chapter 12 after discussing a few more technical ways to measure project progress and ways to troubleshoot common project problems in Chapter 11.

Solutions Fast Track

Initiating Project Work

- ☑ Initiate project work with an announcement that project work is underway.
- ☑ Hold a team meeting to ensure team members understand project processes, procedures, and next steps.

☑ Regularly monitor project status and progress through team meetings, status reports, and bug tracking and issue logs.

☑ Capture and share lessons learned as you go along to help avoid common errors or pitfalls along the way.

Monitoring Project Progress

☑ Status reports and team meetings give you a good view into the project progress.

☑ The issues log should be used to manage issues that arise. Assign every issue a priority, an owner, and due date so issues actually do get resolved.

☑ Progress can be recorded as percent complete, but percent complete for progress, time, and cost should be measured to give a more balanced view.

☑ Variance can be measured as the difference between what was planned and actual results. Large positive or negative variances should be flags that you investigate.

☑ Large variances can cause a project to be cancelled.

Managing Project Change

☑ Variance is a change to the project and should be managed as such.

☑ You have four possible responses to variance: do nothing, repair the problem, change the project plan, or terminate the project.

☑ Changes to the schedule can often be accommodated via the schedule reserve. Larger changes may require you to crash the schedule or fast track the schedule.

☑ Crashing and fast tracking both come with inherent risks that should be understood and evaluated prior to implementing either of these methods.

☑ Changes to budgets stem from four primary causes: flawed estimates, anomalies, permanent variance, and minor variance.

☑ Changes to budgets can sometimes be accounted for via the budget reserve. Other times the change must be listed as a separate line item and dealt with separately.

☑ Drastic changes to schedules or budgets can cause the project to be terminated if the changes cannot be accommodated or if those changes make the project undesirable.

☑ Changes to scope often sneak in and cause scope creep. Using standard project procedures including change management procedures, you can manage scope during project work.

☑ Your change management procedures should allow you the ability to deal with changes that stem from the four primary sources: errors/omissions, risk response (implementing "Plan B"), value-added, and external events.

Managing Project Risk

☑ Review your project's risk management plan at the outset of project work. It might have to be revised as project work progresses due to new or changing risks.

☑ Include milestones in your project plan for places where you want to review your risk plan or places where risk might occur.

☑ Evaluate "Plan B" before implementing it. Look for secondary risks the contingency plan might inject into your project.

☑ All change carries risk and all risk mitigation techniques carry the possibility of secondary risk. You cannot plan for all risk, but looking for risks will help you avoid many of the obvious ones.

☑ As project work progresses, risks can change and shift. Keep an eye out for new risks resulting from other changes in the project and update your risk management plan as needed.

Managing the Project Team

☑ Successfully managing people is key to managing an IT project. Hone your people management skills for greater project success.

☑ In order for team members to accomplish their work, they must understand what is required, have the time, tools, and talent to accomplish the work, and must be motivated to do the work.

☑ Team members must be given the information, responsibility, and authority to complete their work.

☑ Deal with team performance, quality, or attitude problems quickly and effectively. These kinds of problems rarely go away on their own and they typically just get bigger and more complicated over time.

☑ Use your manger, project sponsor, and Human Resources department as resources to assist you in managing your team.

☑ Managing a team over whom you have little direct or organization authority can be challenging, but by focusing on creating a positive, productive environment, your team and your project will fare better.

Frequently Asked Questions

The following Frequently Asked Questions, answered by the author of this book, are designed to both measure your understanding of the concepts presented in this chapter and to assist you with real-life implementation of these concepts. To have your questions about this chapter answered by the author, browse to **www.syngress.com/solutions** and click on the **"Ask the Author"** form.

Q: In our company, our issues log discussions run on and on and I just want to run from the room. Any suggestions on how to deal with this?

A: Issues log management can be tricky because you're dealing with issues that have come up that are unexpected. If they were expected, they would have been planned into the project (assuming you planned your project). This often makes people nervous because sometimes the issues log is viewed as a scorecard as to how many issues cropped up in one area or another. When people get nervous or defensive, long discussions can ensue as people try to cover tracks or explain away problems. The best defense in this case is a good offense. The key is to focus on the outcomes. Issues log discussions often devolve into theoretical discussions or discussions of issues tangential to the core problem. Keep focused on the issue and the outcome. Don't allow discussion to get off course. If an issue cannot be quickly resolved (you could set a 5 minute timer, if needed), table it and move on. Tabled issues might require additional, separate meetings for review and resolution so that the issues log review doesn't become a painful and unproductive experience. If you're not in charge of the meeting, you might gently suggest this method to the meeting leader as a way to perhaps make more productive use of people's time.

Q: It seems that even though we plan for various risks, they always seem to sneak up on us anyway. What can we do to avoid this?

A: It's hard to keep your eye on so many moving parts, so it's understandable that some things might be overlooked. However, project management is a process that is intended to reduce errors and omissions, and you can create better project management practices to help avoid this problem. In your case, you've done a great job identifying project risks, but then no one manages the risk plan. Two possible solutions come immediately to mind (if you think of others after reading this, that's fine too). The first is that you can delegate the task of watching the risk management plan to someone on your IT project team who would do a good job at that task. Sometimes just delegating some of these tasks is all that it takes to keep better control of your project since there is only so much you, as the IT project manager, can do. Second is to add milestones to your project at the point where you've identified triggers. If one of your project risks is that a vendor might ship parts late, you should add a milestone (check-point) for the point at which you need to check vendor lead time, another milestone for the point at which you need to order from the vendor, another milestone at the point the vendor should ship, and another milestone at the point where you would implement your contingency plan. While that may seem like a lot of milestones to add for one risk, it will help you easily manage your project's risks as you manage your overall plan.

Q: You didn't discuss Earned Value Analysis and it's my opinion that percent complete or variance are relatively useless measurements. Any comment?

A: Yes, we'll discuss EVA in Chapter 11 for those that require a more technical analysis of project progress. While percent complete and variance can be somewhat subjective, they are useful tools in many projects that do not require more rigorous methods of evaluating project progress.

Q: It seems that in every IT project, our scope gets out of hand before we know what hit us. Typically, we get requests from all sides—users, managers, the project sponsor, even executives—and we really don't have a choice to say "no." What can we do to better manage this?

A: Sounds like you have a bad case of scope creep. Fortunately, there is a cure, though in your case it might be a slow process. The key is to educate everyone about the impact of scope creep. You might start by reviewing past projects. Compare actual results to planned results and calculate how much extra time and money these projects cost. If possible, compare the desired (defined, planned) quality to the actual quality. Somewhere in those historical results is the answer you're looking for. You will likely find that the cost always goes through the roof or your team never meets deadlines or your project results are viewed as having poor quality. Since you now understand the relationship between scope, time, cost, and quality, you'll need to educate your executives and managers about this and work with them to understand and utilize your change management process. It also seems there may be challenges to your project definition early on. If your projects are not addressing user/customer, business, and executive needs, they will be pushed around. If they were well-defined and your company simply deals with frequent change, you should become a bit more forceful (if possible) in implementing and managing your change control process. Educate everyone about how, when, and why change will be considered, evaluated, and implemented. Help them understand what change does to the project and help determine appropriate priorities. It's possible that your firm is comfortable with a project being over budget, delivered late, or having less-than-desired quality, but once you explain how you can do a better job for less money and in less time, you might catch a few people's attention.

Q: I am really not comfortable dealing with people. I thought being an IT project manager would let me manage *projects*.

A: I'm assuming the question in there is that you're not sure what to do now that you've discovered that managing IT projects is really more about managing people than managing technology. For you, the excitement and satisfaction may come from the definition of the project including the functional and technical specifications, perhaps creating the WBS and the tasks. In that case, you might be better off working on the team as a subject matter expert than as the IT PM. If you're interested in improving your people skills, a project can be a great way to do that. Sit down and talk with someone who's known to be a solid project manager and talk with him or her about techniques you can use to manage your team. Managing people is a skill you can learn, especially if you continually focus on the desired outcome, but if you really don't like working with people, you're always going to find being an IT project manager a bit of an uncomfortable challenge.

Chapter 11

Tracking IT Projects

Solutions in this chapter:

- **Technical Tracking Tools**

- **Testing Project Deliverables**

- **Preparing for Implementation, Deployment, and Operational Transfer**

- **Resolving Common Project Problems**

☑ **Summary**

☑ **Solutions Fast Track**

☑ **Frequently Asked Questions**

Introduction

In Chapter 10, we discussed how to manage your project once work gets underway. Monitoring and measuring project performance can be a challenge, especially if you use *percent complete* or other less technical measurements. We've all been involved in at least one project where everything seemed to be rolling along in the "green" zone and a week or two before project completion, all hell broke loose and the project suddenly was in the "red" zone. How do these things happen? Depending on whether you're in an optimistic or pessimistic mood, your assessment of the percent complete can change in part because percent complete is a judgement call. In this chapter, we're going to review a few more technical approaches to measuring project progress. Even if you don't plan on using them, you might find it useful to read through the material. You might be surprised to find that these are measurements you understand and could easily implement. If you choose not to read through the more technical measurements, skip to the middle of the chapter and pick up reading where we discuss common project problems and their solutions. Understanding and resolving project problems is part of keeping your project on track so you'll find helpful information in this section. It's not meant to be the definitive list of potential project problems—every project is unique (by its very definition) and every project will encounter different problems. However, there are commonly occurring themes and these tend to crop up frequently. Being prepared for the common problems can be seen as part of your risk management strategy. Plan for the common problems and respond to the uncommon problems. You'll sleep better at night having some of these strategies in your back pocket.

As in previous chapters, let's look at where we are in our IT project management process. Figure 11.1 shows tracking as the last step before project close-out, discussed in Chapter 12.

Figure 11.1 IT Project Management Process Overview

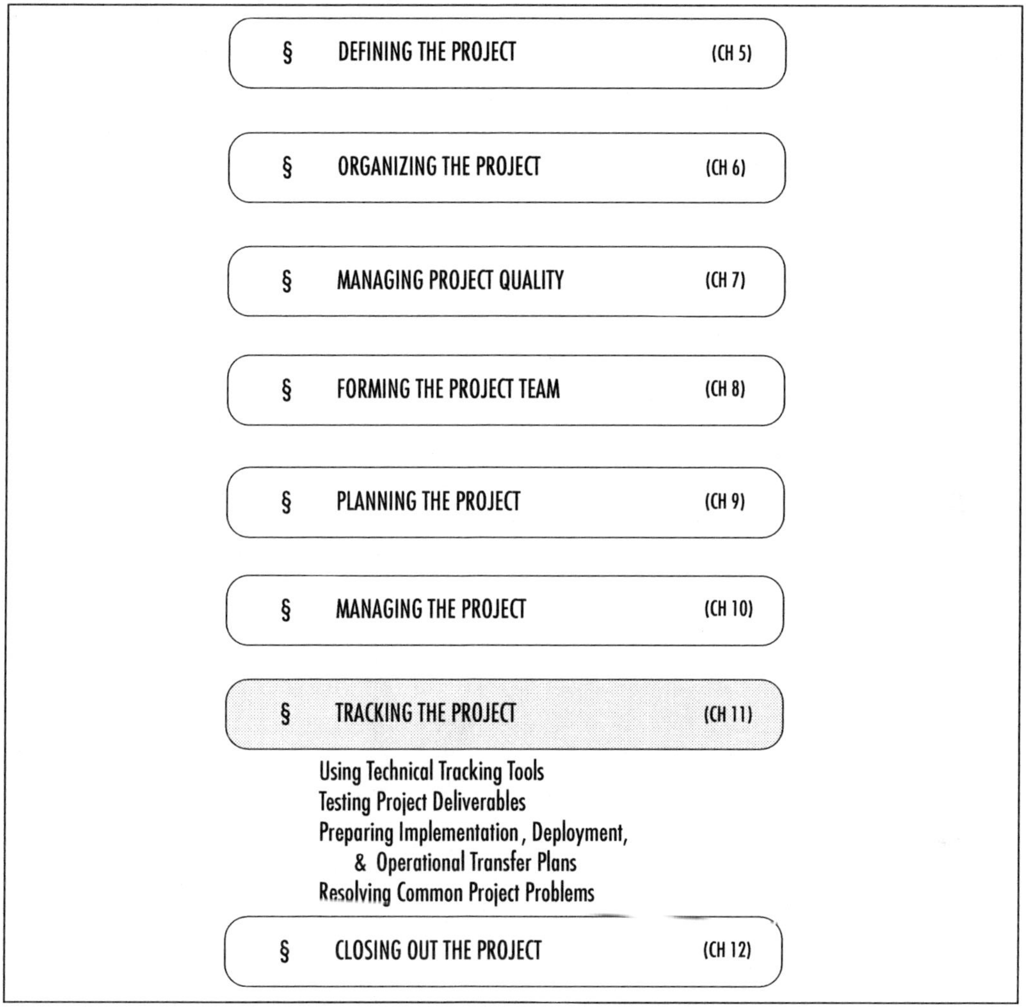

Before we head into the chapter material, let's define new terms you'll encounter in this chapter.

- **Actual Cost** The actual cost of all the work you completed.

- **Cost Performance Index (CPI)** The ratio of the cost of work accomplished compared to the cost of work planned. A positive value indicates the project is under budget, a zero value indicates the project is on budget, a negative value indicates the project is over budget.

- **Critical Ratio** The critical ratio (CR) is found by multiplying the schedule performance index (SPI) by the cost performance index (CPI). If the project is proceeding according to plan, the CR should be at or near 1. Any number above 1 indicates the project is making better than planned progress. Any number below one indicates the project is falling behind.

- **Earned Value** The planned cost of all work you have completed.

- **Earned Value Analysis** The analysis of the earned value of a project to indicate current project status and to forecast future project status.

- **Planned Value** The planned cost of all work you expected to complete.

- **Schedule Performance Index (SPI)** The ratio of work accomplished compared to the work planned. A positive value indicates the project is ahead of schedule, a zero value indicates the project is on schedule, a negative value indicates the project is behind schedule.

Tracking the project to maintain control, taking corrective action based on tracking data, and resolving common project problems are all part of managing the IT project, but are discussed separately in this chapter in order to clearly focus on these aspects of IT project management. For some IT projects, using a simple percent complete or variance reporting will be sufficient; for other IT projects, more detailed tracking and analysis is required and we'll cover these techniques in this chapter.

Figure 11.2 shows the inputs, actions, checkpoints, and outputs from this stage of the project lifecycle. It is the same diagram used in Chapter 10 since the tracking and control steps occur during the management phase of the project.

Figure 11.2 Inputs, Actions, and Outputs for Project Management Step

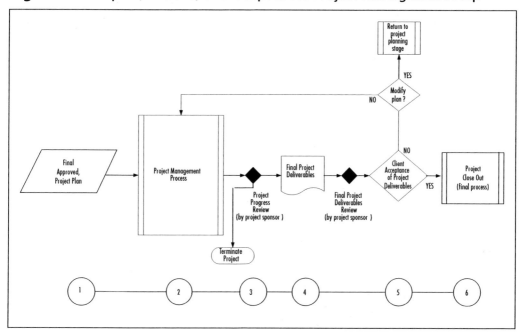

The discrete steps are delineated in Chapter 10, but it is important to note the project management process includes implementing the project, monitoring and tracking the results, and taking appropriate corrective action in an iterative manner until all project work has been successfully completed. In this chapter, we'll look at steps involved in tracking and controlling the project as well as the steps for preparing for final project deliverables and close-out.

Technical Tracking Tools

Percent complete and variance reporting may be all you need to track and manage your project. In some cases, though, you may want or need more detailed views of project progress. There are numerous metrics you can utilize for measuring project progress including earned value analysis, schedule performance, schedule performance index, cost performance, cost performance index, estimate at completion, and critical ratio. All of these metrics measure planned outcomes to actual outcomes at specific points in time to reveal data about progress as well as to help you forecast project results based on current trends. These metrics can be intimidating, even to experienced project managers, but in truth, they are simple mathematical calculations. The challenge with these metrics is often in collecting the data rather than in crunching the numbers. Many project management information systems, such as Microsoft Project, will calculate some of these numbers for you. Of course, you have to enter the correct data and keep it up to date as the project progresses in order to get any meaningful data about performance.

IT projects fall into two basic categories, roughly grouped as physical- or knowledge-based. Physical projects are those that involve running cables, upgrading servers, installing applications, etc. Knowledge projects are those that involve working on a more intangible level with information and knowledge, such as creating a new process or a new application. Clearly, physical projects have knowledge components and knowledge projects may have physical components. The key is that it is usually easier to track physical projects than knowledge projects. If the project is to upgrade 15 servers or transition the company from traditional phones to voice over IP (VoIP) phones, there are many physical elements that can be easily tracked. Tracking these physical elements usually gives you a fairly clear view of how the project is going. If the project is less tangible - for example, developing a new software application—it can be hard to know in advance how many lines of code it's going to take or how long it will take to complete each phase. You may be able to break a knowledge project down into manageable stages so that each segment of completed code can be measured, but it's usually a less exact science than managing a physical project.

Does that mean you should not attempt to track the progress of a knowledge-based project? No. It means that it is a more inexact science and you'll need to rely upon your team's collective knowledge and expertise to have a feel for how things are *really* going. If you recall from Chapter 10, knowledge work typically follows a curve that might lead you to believe things are falling behind early in the project when, in fact, they are right on target. Keeping an eye on both the actual project work and the technical metrics we'll discuss in this section can help you fine-tune project work to ensure it completes on time, on budget, and with the required functionality and features.

Earned Value Analysis

Some people hear the term Earned Value Analysis, or EVA, and run screaming from the room. Many experienced project managers still avoid using EVA because they never learned it, never understood how it could benefit them, or never got a chance to try it out. Whatever the case, take a few minutes to read through this material—especially if you have avoided EVA with every ounce of your being. You may be surprised to find it less daunting and more useful than you thought.

Earned Value Analysis is a method of assessing project progress. The Project Management Body of Knowledge (PMBOK) defines earned value as the value of the work that has been completed based on the budget for that work. Therefore, an EVA would be an analysis of the work that's been completed compared to the budget for that work. EVA also includes another important element, one we discussed in some detail in Chapter 10—*scope*. By integrating scope along with time and cost, you gain a more objective, scalable point-in-time assessment of project progress. EVA is not only useful in assessing the current state of the project, but for forecasting the likely state of the project as you move out in time. Think of it like this: if you start out on a 3,000 mile road trip and you've decided to navigate solely by compass, a variation of 5 or 10 miles away from your primary direction may not mean much on day one or day two, but by the end of your trip, you're going to be so far off course that it will take a monumental effort to correct it. EVA is like your project compass in helping you to determine how far off course your project at completion may be based on how far off course it is at the moment. To state that more positively, it can show you how close you'll come to your targets based on where you are today.

Components of EVA

Earned Value Analysis asks three critical questions to assess project progress:

1. How much work did you plan on completing? (Planned Value)

2. How much work did you actually complete? (Earned Value)

3. How much did it cost to complete that work? (Actual Cost)

Planned Value (PV) is budgeted cost of work you expected to start and finish at a particular point in time. It is the cumulative cost of all planned work to a particular point in time in your project. Earned Value (EV) on the other hand, it the sum of all budgeted costs for tasks completed at this point in time. Actual Cost (AC) is the actual cost of all completed work at this point in time.

Enterprise 128 ...

Alphabet Soup

One of the reasons people shy away from EVA is that it uses a lot of letters in formulas and the letters don't really help you remember what's what. If you're going to use EVA, make sure you understand the difference between PV, EV, and AC. If you don't understand them and use them correctly, your data will be way off and you'll be reporting incorrect information. At that point, you're better off reverting to percent complete. EVA is used for a particular point in time, so all the metrics you use have the same time span: start to the selected point in time.

- Planned Value is the planned cost of all work you expected to complete.
- Earned Value is the planned cost of all work you did complete.
- Actual Cost is the actual cost of all the work you did complete.

Keep these straight and your EVA will be right on target.

Applying Earned Value Analysis

Let's walk through an example so you can see how EVA can help you assess the project. Let's assume you're working on a small eight-week project that is estimated to cost $80,000. Let's keep this simple and say that you have eight tasks, each scheduled to be one week long and costing $10,000. At the midway point of the project, you want to assess where you are. You know that you are at the midpoint of the project, so if everything is on track, you would expect to see that you have 50% of the work completed and 50% of the costs incurred. Three of eight examples are present in this example.

To calculate the Planned Value, you have to add up the planned cost of all work you expected to complete to date. Figure 11.3 shows the formula for calculating PV. Using the formula, we can see that PV = 50% x $80,000. In our scenario, the PV is $40,000. You can only calculate the cost of the work you planned on accomplishing by the particular point in time (ours is the 50% point) if you know the planned cost of each task or work package (which you should have in your budget).

Figure 11.3 Calculating Planned Value

$$PV = Planned\ \%\ Complete \times Total\ Project\ Budget$$

To calculate the Earned Value, you have to add up the value of all planned work that has actually been accomplished at this point in time. The EV formula is shown in Figure 11.4. Don't confuse EV with *actual cost*. EV is the planned cost for all work completed at this point in time. Our actual work complete is 37.5% (three of eight equal tasks completed, for this simplified example). So, our formula is EV = 37.5% x $80,000. The EV of this project at this point in time is $30,000. Notice that if you just added up those three completed tasks' costs, the result is the same as when we use the EV formula. This should help you grok the formula a bit better.

Figure 11.4 Calculating Earned Value

$$EV = Actual\ \%\ Complete \times Total\ Project\ Budget$$

Next, we need the Actual Cost. Let's say that the actual cost for these three tasks comes to $38,000. OK, we now have our three metrics, it's time to put them to use. First, we can calculate the cost variance for the project. Figure 11.5 shows the formula for determining the cost variance. We can now calculate that our cost variance is CV = $30,000 - $38,000 or CV = $8,000. This indicates that we are $8,000 over budget at this point in time.

Figure 11.5 Calculating Cost Variance

$$Cost\ Variance = Earned\ Value - Actual\ Cost$$
$$CV = EV - AC$$

Next, we need to calculate the schedule variance to determine how we're tracking with our schedule. This formula is shown in Figure 11.6. Using the formula SV = EV—PV, we can calculate that SV = $30,000 - $40,000 or SV = -$10,000. You might ask how -$10,000 indicates a schedule variance and that's a good question. Using EVA, you look at your schedule in terms of the planned or actual cost of work. So, in this scenario, we have a $8,000 cost variance and a -$10,000 schedule variance. That means that your project is both over budget and behind schedule. In a relative sense, you are more behind schedule that you are over budget because your schedule variance is larger (even though negative) than your cost variance.

Figure 11.6 Calculating Schedule Variance

> Schedule Variance = Earned Value - Planned Value
> SV = EV - PV

Your goal is to have a zero or positive variance for both cost and schedule. Any negative number indicates a problem. Of course, the larger the negative number, the bigger the problem and the more attention you'll need to give to figuring out what's going wrong.

The IT Factor...

EVA the PMBOK Way

The Project Management Institute, a non-profit organization dedicated to advancing methods of project management, publishes the Project Management Body of Knowledge, referred to as the PMBOK (sometimes pronounced *pim-bok*). In the PMBOK method, the calculations are the same, they just use more letters. Our system uses the old PMBOK lettering system, but does exactly the same calculations. For the record, the current PMBOK uses:

- BCWS—Budgeted Cost of Work Scheduled (equates to our PV).
- BCWP—Budgeted Cost of Work Performed (equates to our EV).
- ACWP—Actual Cost of Work Performed (equates to our AC).

Studies have repeatedly shown that people can remember up to three things at a time, which is why we stuck to the two-letter acronyms rather than using the PMI's four-letter acronyms. If you're studying for your PMP or CAPM certification, be sure to review the PMBOK for the latest changes and terminology. The intent of this chapter is not to help you pass a certification exam, but to understand and apply the concepts presented.

Schedule Performance Index

We all know that IT projects rarely just hum along smoothly. There are always bumps in the road and understanding how you're performing against schedule is one of the things an IT PM needs to know. A recent survey of CIOs indicated that only about 10% of important IT initiatives came in both on time and on budget. Of those initiatives, about 50% were able to deliver on schedule or budget, but not both. The success rates we discussed at the beginning of this book clearly hold true and it seems as if project success is still an elusive goal. As you know, the longer a project runs, the less likely it is to be successful, especially as needed resources are siphoned off to be used elsewhere. The schedule performance index is a good tool to use to help you see your schedule trend as positive, negative, or neutral. The formula for calculating SPI is shown in Figure 11.7. In our example, SPI = $30,000 (EV) / $40,000 (PV) or SPI = 0.75.

Because the SPI (and later, the CPI) are ratios, the perfect point to be at is 1. SPI will equal 1 when the earned value and planned value are the same ($40,000 divided by $40,000 is 1 and that would indicate the project is right on schedule). Any number greater than 1 indicates the project is ahead of schedule. Any number less than 1 indicates the project is behind schedule. Of course, the further the SPI is from 1 on the down side, the bigger the problem you have. Remember, though, sometimes a large positive variance (an SPI of 1.9 or 2.5 for instance) could indicate problems as well, so keep an eye on all large variances on either side of 1.

Based on our calculation, how far off schedule are we? Well, we're about 25% behind schedule based on an SPI of .75. Is this good or bad? Well, it depends on whether your schedule is your least flexible project parameter and whether you can pull in extra resources to get the work done on time or perhaps there's simply a learning curve in the first half of the project and you're confident you can make up that time simply because you're at the top of the learning curve (meaning the team or people performing the work have learned just about as much as can or should be learned at this point, and will make fast progress from here on out).

Figure 11.7 Calculating Schedule Performance Index

Schedule Performance Index = Earned Value / Planned Value
SPI = EV/ PV

Using Schedule Reserves

If you are behind schedule, you can choose to use some of your schedule reserve. Using schedule reserve can be done in a number of ways, but often it means that you make a "withdrawal" from your reserve and update your project plan. For instance, if you determine that your project is about three days behind schedule, you can reduce your schedule reserve by three days and update your project plan to indicate it is now "on schedule." If you look at your schedule performance in another month and everything is perfectly on time, your schedule indicators will reflect the project as being on time rather than still three days behind because you used some of your project reserve to address this one-time event.

The use of schedule reserve in this manner prevents you from "dragging along" a slip in the schedule throughout the remainder of the project. At project close out, you can compare actual to planned and include use of your reserves in your analysis.

Cost Performance Index

The cost performance index is the same type of ratio as SPI, only it tracks your progress against budget. The formula is similar to SPI and is shown in Figure 11.8. To calculate our CPI for this sample project, we insert the relevant values so that our CPI = EV/AC or $30,000 / $38,000 or CPI = 0.789. As with our SPI, a value of 1 means we're spot on, a value greater than one indicates we're below budget (doing better than budget), and a value less than one indicates we're above budget (doing worse than budget). In this case, we're under 1, which means we're over budget. Also similar to SPI, the relative size of the number should be considered when evaluating the CPI. If we were at 0.38, we'd be performing far worse against budget than if we were at 0.789. Of course, to have a CPI of 1.14 would be wonderful, but a CPI of 4.2 should set off a few alarm bells.

Figure 11.8 Calculating Cost Performance Index

> Cost Performance Index = Earned Value / Actual Cost
> CPI = EV/ AC

Using Budget Reserves

Just as with schedule, you can choose to use budget reserves to adjust your project's budget. If you are $8,000 over budget, you can "withdraw" or deduct $8,000 from your project's reserve amount and apply it to your budget. Now when you calculate performance against budget, you'll be calculating it against the budget plus the additional reserve amount. Essentially, adding your reserve amount at this point brings you back to a CPI of 1. Doing this allows you to accurately see the progress of future project work without constantly having to reference the deficit created to this point in time. So, if you are at the halfway point in your project and you're behind budget (or schedule), you can use reserve amounts to get you back to even. Then, if you calculate your progress at the 75% mark, you can tell how the work between the 50% and the 75% mark is progressing. If you don't use reserve amounts and you're gaining or losing ground, it might be difficult to determine how this segment of work is going versus earlier segments of work. You can certainly calculate all these figures for various points in time—you could choose to calculate the values for just the work from 50% to 75% and do the same calculation. It's mostly a matter of preference as to how you approach these calculations. As long as you understand that you "drag along" past deficits (or gains) into your current point in time, you can manage these numbers in whatever way makes the most sense to you.

Estimate At Completion

Now that we've calculated our schedule and cost performance, it would probably be helpful to understand our trends. If things continue as they are, how far behind schedule will we be? How much over budget will we be? To determine that, we need to calculate estimate at completion, or EAC. The EAC is a pretty simple calculation that is shown in Figure 11.9. The EAC is determined by taking the total planned project budget (BAC) and dividing it by the cost performance index. In the example we've been using, EAC = $80,000 / 0.789 or EAC = $101,394. This means that the project will come in about $21,000 over budget if the trend remains the same. This calculation should be done prior to adjusting values using reserves so you can identify potential trends.

Figure 11.9 Calculating Estimate At Completion

Estimated At Completion = Project Budget / Cost Performance Index
EAC   = BAC/ CPI
* BAC = budget at completion or total planned project budget

APPLYING YOUR KNOWLEDGE

As you can see, these calculations are a bit more precise than percent complete or even variance. They can be used to give you a very clear picture of what's going on in your project. We can manage what we can see, so having this type of visibility into project performance can be incredibly helpful.

One of the most valuable aspects of these numbers is understanding, relative to perfect performance, how your project is performing against time and cost. The EAC is a great tool for understanding how much your budget variance will impact your final cost. Often when a project starts running over budget, a manager or executive will demand, "How much will this cost when it's all said and done?" Using these values, you can project a final cost based on the trend and make an informed decision about moving forward on the project (or not). One potential pitfall to watch for is that EAC will project your problems into the future because it will use the current trend to forecast the future. If you have a one-time event that impacts your budget, pull from your reserve amount, recalculate then calculate your EAC to get a more realistic view of the likely cost at completion. If you don't make this adjustment, the EAC calculation will assume your current run rate will continue into the future and that may not always be accurate.

Critical Ratio

Now that you've calculated all kinds of numbers to help you track your IT project's progress, you can calculate one final ratio that gives you an overall view of the project. You might choose to calculate this number on a periodic basis and chart it to give senior management a single point of reference for project progress. The *critical ratio* (CR) is derived by multiplying the cost performance index (CPI) by the schedule performance index (SPI), as shown in Figure 11.10. This ratio shows the overall progress of the project taking both cost and schedule into account. A ratio of 1 indicates the project is right on target; a ratio of greater than 1 indicates the project is doing better than plan; a ratio of less than 1 indicates the project is falling behind plan.

Keep in mind that it is possible to have your CPI less than one and your SPI greater than 1, which could mathematically cause your CR to be equal to 1. If you think about the implications of such a scenario, you realize that if your project is over budget but ahead of schedule, your project progress is probably acceptable because more than likely, the budget overruns are accounted for in the additional effort expended to bring the project in ahead of schedule. The reverse is also true. If your project is behind schedule but under budget, you might also have a CR of 1. In this case, the budget hasn't been expended because the work has not been done. This scenario, however, could raise a flag if you have a hard deadline or external constraint.

Figure 11.10 Critical Ratio

Critical Ratio = Schedule Performance Index x Cost Performance Index
CR = SPI x CPI

APPLYING YOUR KNOWLEDGE

As an IT project manager, your job is to guide the project toward success. While you're mired in the details of the project, you still need to communicate project progress to your project sponsor and sometimes to corporate executives as well. To avoid sharing too much detailed information or sharing information that is not helpful to decision makers, use EVA, SPI, CPI, and CR to indicate project progress. By boiling the project down to a few meaningful metrics, you'll assure executives that the project is on target (or provide them with remediation plans if it is falling behind) without inundating them with project details. Providing too much detail almost always invites micromanagement and to avoid that, provide these high-level but accurate metrics.

Testing Project Deliverables

Without testing project deliverables, it would be impossible to know if your project was on track or not. If the results of project work are not regularly reviewed and tested, where appropriate, you may end up at the completion of your project with deliverables that do not address the required project scope or fail to deliver required functionality (quality or performance). Therefore, part of tracking project progress is testing results of project work.

In some projects such as software development, testing may be a discrete function outside the project plan. For instance, at each delivery point, the project may have a milestone indicating a deliverable is sent to testing. The project may also have a second milestone indicating when results from testing will be reviewed so that action can be taken. The action is usually binary—either proceed or revise. If revision is required, the project's scope and specifications (functional and technical requirements) should be reviewed to determine why there is a difference between what was specified and what came through testing.

In some projects, the testing component is included in the project plan. This is common in more physical-based projects such as upgrading infrastructure or replacing servers, applications, or network components. In these cases, testing may occur in a lab environment to ensure the required configuration meets the project's specifications and works as intended. Once tested and approved in the lab environment, the solution may be implemented in the live setting and additional tests may be conducted to ensure everything is still working as expected. In these cases, testing tasks are built into the project plan and are conducted as project tasks.

Whether testing is part of the project plan or is part of an external project plan, testing is critical to managing and controlling IT project progress. Thought it's done from time to time, it would be pretty risky to put everything together and implement the solution without testing results at periodic intervals during project work. Often, pressure to get a product to market or into the hands of users forces IT project managers to compress testing, which is unfortunate. Sound testing is part of quality control. Remember from our earlier discussion on quality, the cost to fix a problem once the project's deliverables are in the users/customers hands is 100 times the cost of fixing that problem in the design phase. If a problem is found in the unit testing phase, the cost is only 10 times the cost of finding it in the design phase. If the problem is found in the integration testing phase, the cost is 30 times the cost of finding it in the design phase. As you can see, 10x or 30x is still far less expensive than 100x. If you are the IT project manager and you're being pushed to shorten or even skip the testing phases of your project, you may want to pull out Chapter 7 and explain to your project sponsor or corporate executives the costs (both direct and indirect) of doing so. You might not win the battle, but you might find a solution that addresses both the management team's and your concerns. At the very least, your executive team and project sponsor can make an informed decision about testing once you've laid out the costs and risks for them.

You and your IT project team should have developed a testing plan either as part of your project processes in the organization or planning phases of your project, so we won't repeat that information here. There are numerous types of test plans and testing that can occur in an IT project. In this section, we'll look at the various types of tests and discuss how the results impact this phase of the project lifecycle.

The result of any kind of testing should be a clear understanding of how well your project's deliverables are performing against requirements. Your test and quality plans should clearly define the next steps for various types of results. For instance, results that vary from specifications just a bit may be sent back through the project work cycle to be fixed, or they may be deferred (as may be the case in software development projects). Results that vary significantly from specifications may be considered "show stoppers" and may cause project work to halt until the cause for the variance is determined and corrected. Understanding the results of testing and having plans for understanding and managing the results will help keep your project on track. If you are unable to assess the results of your various testing plans as it pertains to overall project progress, your project is at risk. In that case, you should step back and reassess your testing plans and assess what each test is designed to show and what the results will tell you about the project.

Unit Testing

Unit testing is done throughout the project work phase. Testing can be done on hardware, software, processes, and procedures throughout the project work cycle Results of unit testing are your first indication of project progress. If deliverables at this point fail unit testing, this should raise a flag for you. If unit testing progresses smoothly, your project deliverables are off to a good start. A unit test is a good way to test a small portion of the deliverable early in the process. It is typically performed by the person doing the work. If a technician is supposed to configure 18 new servers, he or she should test each server to ensure the configuration is correct and works as expected. The work should not be considered complete until a unit test has been performed. Unit testing can be specifically added to entry/exit criteria or completion criteria. It is reasonable to expect the unit testing has been completed before the task owner designates the work as complete.

For example, suppose that you are having a house built and at the moment the plumber is installing the water lines. You would have (and should have) a real expectation that the plumber will have tested his work to make sure that there are no leaks before saying the job (task) is complete. The same attitude belongs in your IT project.

Integration Testing

Integration testing is the next logical step after unit testing. Integration takes your unit deliverables and begins putting them together and testing how well these components interact. It could be a situation where you have tested several disk drives and are now testing them in a RAID system or as a cluster. It could be where you take several segments of code related to the user interface and test them together to see how they work. These tests are usually referred to as *functional* or *black box* tests, meaning that the tester is not going through component by component or line by line looking at the internal functionality, but is looking at inputs and outputs only. In a hardware project (or physical project), the integration testing may overlap with implementation and deployment phases.

Usability Testing

Usability testing is done in a controlled environment to ensure that the project results can be used in the real world. These tests may involve bringing select users into a lab or test environment to use the project's results in order to see how the user will interact with the product. The results of this type of testing can help an IT project team refine the project's deliverables and can also be used as input to performance test plans. Usability testing is important to ensure the product is usable, but it should not be utilized in lieu of sound functional and technical specifications. Fixing usability issues once project work is underway is 10 to 30 times more expensive than creating excellent specifications early in the project cycle. That said, if there was an error or omission made in the project definition phase, it is easier to fix it after reviewing usability test results than once the product is in the user's hands.

Acceptance Testing

Acceptance testing is usually the final phase of most quality assurance processes. Acceptance testing may be performed in-house by testers or project team members to verify that the required features and functionality work as specified. In other cases, acceptance testing is done by a group of users to verify that the features and functionality work as they expect it to. Acceptance testing should be well defined going into the project because users have a habit of forgetting what they specified at some point in the past. IT projects can run from several weeks to several years and users may forget, change their minds, or leave altogether. Therefore, it is critical that acceptance procedures be clearly delineated and agreed to by the user/customer before the project commences. In some cases, you will need to modify the project acceptance testing plan or criteria (based on required changes to the project over time). In all cases, though, the acceptance criteria and test plans should be clearly delineated and agreed to by the user/customer to avoid end-of-project disagreements about what is and is not acceptable.

The result of this type of testing is the assurance (either by internal staff or by external customers) that the project results are suitable for use in the real world and that it performs as expected. Sometimes acceptance testing is combined with beta testing. Acceptance testing is often tied to payment when the project is for a client.

Beta Testing

Beta testing is a limited release of the project's deliverables to a selected group of users. Often the beta test group includes knowledgeable or expert testers who will use the project's product as users would. In the case of hardware projects, beta testing may come after a limited rollout of the project's results before implementing across the enterprise. The results of beta testing may result in project rework, but it may also result in notes for future releases. Most beta testing plans provide some definition or description of different levels of problems or bugs found during the beta testing process, as described earlier. Bugs or defects classified as show stoppers can impact your final delivery date and should be investigated thoroughly. Those bugs or defects classified with lower priorities will generally be put back in the work pipeline for repair during the normal project cycle. Some bugs or defects may be deferred to later project phases or later releases.

Regression Testing

Once errors and defects are found, rework should address the problems. At this point, the revised project work is again tested to ensure that the changes made to fix the defect did not introduce new problems. If you recall from our discussion of project risk, making a change to the project in order to address a risk often introduces secondary risk. The same is true in the project work itself. Any revision to address a problem or defect has the possibility of introducing new problems or defects into the project. Regression testing is used to verify that the identified problems have been fixed and that no new problems have been introduced.

Performance Testing

Performance testing can take many different forms. For instance, you can perform stress or load testing to see how a component performs in actual use. This is often done on hardware components to ensure that a disk drive or server can handle the load that will be placed on it once in production. This can also be performed on software components such as stress or load testing a database application to ensure that it will perform fast enough when 100 users are requesting data from the database. The four main types of performance tests are stress, load, stability, and reliability.

Stress and Load Testing

Stress testing attempts to replicate the stress placed on the system (hardware or software) once it's in a production environment. Load testing is a form of stress testing that places various loads on the system (read requests on the disk drive, login requests on the server, calculation requests on an application, for instance) to ensure that it can perform under pressure. Many systems look great on paper and look fine in development, but come to a screeching halt when placed under a realistic load. If a database application takes 10 minutes to return a simple query, users are not going to be happy and stress and load testing can begin to help you identify problems before you put the project's deliverables in the hands of users.

Stress and load testing can sometimes be accomplished as unit tests during the work phase of the project. Other times, stress and load tests require a more integrated approach and are performed as project work nears completion.

Stability and Reliability Testing

Stability and reliability tests are generally run on fully integrated systems to ensure that they don't crash or halt intermittently over time. These types of tests are stress and load tests performed over a longer period of time, typically days or weeks, and sometimes months. For instance, problems with database applications may only show up after a period of time. Memory leaks in an application or problems with particular locations in physical memory may only show up after an extended period of time. Problems with heat can impact hardware components over a period of time and those problems might not show up if a stress or load test is run for just a few hours. This type of testing can also include a "test to fail" process where the system is intentionally placed under load until it fails to determine the actual stress or load limits. It also helps to determine how to recover from the damage caused when the failure occurs and steps that can be taken to make the crash a bit more graceful.

Stability and reliability testing are sometimes performed in parallel or in conjunction with beta testing. These types of tests are performed on the integrated results of the project and are therefore performed during the latter stages of the project work cycle.

Benchmark Testing

Benchmark testing, or *benchmarking*, is the process of testing hardware or software against specific performance standards. This testing can be performed during unit and integration testing. If you are installing new network cable, you might unit test the cable to ensure it can carry the volume of traffic its specification indicate (to verify the specification and the cable are correct) and you might also test it in the test or production environment to again verify it is performing according to specifications. In the realm of software development, you might unit test to make sure that a procedure call actually works as specified and you might again test in an integrated test environment to ensure the application runs quickly and delivers the results as expected. A benchmark can be used to define the minimum standard of performance and can be included in entry/exit criteria, completion criteria, and quality metrics.

Security Testing

In today's environment, security testing should be part of just about every IT project. Security testing should cover two key areas: that the project deliverables meet security requirements and that if attacked, the system(s) can handle it gracefully. If a security problem does crop up, you want your hardware and software to deal with it intelligently. For instance, some database errors can give hackers additional information needed to continue penetrating the system. By forcing errors, hackers learn more about the design of the database and learn better how to infiltrate the system. These are the kinds of problems that can be discovered through security testing so that if a hacker does force an error, the error does not provide additional information for hackers. That's an example of a system handling an attack gracefully rather than laying out the welcome mat for intruders.

Many third-party companies specialize in testing security for companies and this might be something worth considering, especially if security is paramount to your particular IT project. Often internal "group think" sets in, which means everyone approaches the project from the same perspective. When this happens, it can be difficult (or impossible) to identify potential security problems. Sourcing this to an external firm can help overcome a sometimes myopic approach to security testing.

> ## Cheat Sheet...
>
> ### Security versus Usability
>
> Being impervious to attacks can sometimes be impossible and there is a balance between security and usability that must be achieved. The most secure network (or application) is one that is not connected to the Internet and does not allow user access. Not a very useful network, but very secure. Your IT project may need to take security elements into account, and if so, be sure to keep usability in mind. If you require 28-letter complex passwords, users will simply write them down, defeating the purpose of strong passwords. If you lock a system down so it is user-unfriendly, users will either try to circumvent the system, stop using it, or become very frustrated. None of those scenarios is an indicator of project success.

Preparing for Implementation, Deployment, and Operational Transfer

Your project is coming down the home stretch. Deliverables are coming out on schedule, results are being tested and verified and everything looks good. A few pieces of rework here and there, a couple of tweaks to the schedule and you can see the home stretch in front of you. Now what?

One of the areas that some IT project managers overlook at this point are the connections to external plans such as implementation, deployment, or operational transfer. Depending on the nature of your project, you will have to contend with one or more of these types of plans. As with testing, these plans are sometimes discrete phases of your IT project plan and other times they are external plans tied to your IT project. If they're internal, you're far more likely to manage them in terms of updating the schedule and communicating key data such as delays, changes, or requirements. When they're external, these same elements can cause major issues. It's important that throughout your project you place milestones to remind you and the project team to update or communicate information regarding these additional plans.

Implementation

In some IT projects, implementation is a phase of the IT project that describes how the project's deliverables will be implemented (this is sometimes the same as a deployment plan, depending on the IT project). This might describe a phased approach or an "all or nothing" approach. The implementation plan may be discrete tasks within the project plan that follow testing tasks. If a separate implementation plan exists, you should have milestones within your IT project plan indicating points at which you need to communicate about the implementation or points at which you need input from the implementation team. Many IT project managers are good about keeping an eye on implementation because that's essentially where project success is defined. However, it's easy to let critical information or important changes slip through the communication cracks when it comes to implementation. A flawless implementation can greatly increase the *perception* of project success, so it's important that your management activities during this phase address implementation. In some cases, management or oversight of the implementation phase can be delegated to a team member. Make sure your implementation plan includes plans for a rollback in case things go wrong. A clear roadmap for rolling back the implementation will help keep people cool, calm, and collected if the going gets rough during implementation.

Cheat Sheet...

Delegating Project Management Tasks

During the work phase of the project, you're mostly likely going to have your hands full just keeping track of the issues and changes in the project and managing the critical path tasks. Rather than taking on the world, you can delegate portions of the management task to others. If you recall from our discussion earlier in the book on managing high performance teams, many people on a team find satisfaction in gaining new experiences or skills, while others enjoy additional responsibility and authority. Delegating management of these end phases such as implementation, deployment, or operational transfer, whether they're part of your formal IT project plan or part of external plans, can be just the opportunity junior team members are looking for. Finding members of your project team that would enjoy the tasks associated with managing these sub-plans can provide a coveted opportunity for a team member while at the same time offloading some of your management tasks. It's a win-win situation that can help build project management skills in your IT department. Word to the wise—delegating means handing over responsibility and authority, but it doesn't mean handing it off and never thinking about it again. Allow others to do the job while you check on progress occasionally and provide support and assistance as needed.

Deployment

A deployment plan describes how the hardware or software will be installed, tested, and turned over. This may be the same as an implementation plan in some projects. In other projects, a deployment team is responsible for product deployment, whether internally or externally. As with an implementation plan, the deployment plan should be kept up to date with the IT project plan so that changes are reflected in these plans. It's not uncommon for a change to be made (especially during the testing phase) that requires a change or update to the deployment plan. If this is not properly communicated, the deployment team will be unable to start or complete the deployment in a timely and satisfactory manner. As with your implementation plan, your deployment plan should include a discussion of potential risk as well as related contingency plans. A rollback plan should be included in case deployment goes terribly wrong. In that case, the deployment team should have a clear cut plan for rolling back to the last known good state.

Enterprise 128 ...

Don't Just Lob It Over the Fence

Sometimes an IT project team can be so exhilarated to complete a project and so exhausted by the process that they almost lob it over the fence to the deployment team, which can cause all kinds of problems. A software development company (whose name is not used to protect both the guilty and the innocent) was working on a major product release. When the code was complete and sent for integration and regression testing to the test engineers, all the developers rejoiced and decided it was a great time to take a break from all their hard work. Friday noon rolled around and most of the senior developers packed up in a few vehicles and took off for parts unknown for a no-e-mail, no-cell phone camping trip....The only problem was that critical changes required for this customer installation were not included in the final released code. That meant the deployment team would be unable to install the released code on the customer's machines. The deployment team discovered this as they began to create their installation disks for the customer, around 1:00 P.M. that Friday. With most of the developers gone, the deployment team had to scramble. They pulled together a few of the software engineers who'd not gone camping along with one of the senior testers. They cobbled together an installation CD that would work so the deployment team could jump on an airplane Sunday afternoon. It took all Friday

Continued

night, all Saturday and part of Sunday morning to fix the problems, but the deployment team's dedication to making this beta deployment a success made all the difference. Ultimately, the deployment team had to perform some tricky on-site changes and install an overlay to the code to get everything set for the customer.

Lesson Learned: Don't assume because tasks or code is complete that everything is just fine. Make sure that your implementation or deployment teams have what they need to get the job done. After all, the project isn't complete until the user has signed off on it and implementation or deployment is that critical link between code complete and a satisfied user.

Operational Transfer

Operational transfer is the process of handing off the project's deliverables to the user on a permanent basis (sometimes referred to as *project cut over)*. It assumes that the implementation or deployment has been successful and that you and the IT project team are ready to pass ongoing management of the project's deliverables to another team or to the user/customer.

The operational transfer plan is a document that describes how the deliverables of the project will be integrated and managed. The goal is to have a smooth, seamless transfer of the project's deliverable to the permanent team that has responsibility for this on an ongoing basis. It is used to help define the people and processes needed in the functional arena to ensure success. Remember that how well the project is handed off is a large part of user and stakeholder perception about the success of the project, so mistakes here will impact the perception of success even if the project meets or exceeds all other expectations.

An operational transfer plan should include:

- Tasks to hand off the project's deliverables

- The strategy to be used during handoff

- The key resources needed

- Task owners

- Timing of transfer tasks

- Cost of transfer tasks

- Schedule for transfer

- Risks and contingency plans for risk

- Formal acceptance of handoff by customer/client/user

If this list looks familiar, that's good. It is a scaled down version of a project plan. In fact, you could use the entire IT project management methodology described in this book to create an optimized operational transfer plan. Though many organizations do not do so, there are clear benefits to stepping back and starting at the beginning. What is the problem to be solved? What is the mission or objective? What are the potential solutions? What are the criteria for selecting the best solution? If you step through the IT project methodology we've discussed, you'll find that you have a clear, concise, and easy-to-manage operational transfer plan. Many IT project managers avoid going through the same IT project management process described in this book for any number of reasons. However, doing so will yield far better results for your IT project and for the users/customers to whom control is ultimately transferred.

In order to develop an effective operational transfer plan (which often can be done in parallel with later stage project work tasks), you should follow several key steps, listed here.

1. Identify and involve key functional and process owners to help define the plan.

2. Perform a needs analysis to determine the needs for both an operational plan and long-term, ongoing operation of project deliverables.

3. Define requirements for final operational test and for trigger points for transfer.

4. Prepare for transfer of all relevant IT project assets. This might include source code, installers, system configuration, and documentation. Ensure all relevant documentation is accurate and current.

5. Where intellectual property is concerned, ensure that ownership of property rights is clearly determined and agreed to. For example, does the copyright transfer to the owner or remain with your company?

6. Determine support that will be required after transfer. Clearly list responsibilities for ongoing support—who is responsible for the activities and costs of on-going support?

7. Determine the logistics of the actual operational transfer.

8. Determine changes to user/stakeholder processes and procedures created by this operational transfer and modify processes/procedures as needed.

9. Understand risks to operational transfer and develop contingency plans.

10. Tie your operational transfer plans to training plans, support documentation, release notes, and Service Level Agreements (SLAs) where appropriate.

11. Create a handoff checklist with roles and responsibilities clearly delineated to avoid gaps.

12. Keep your operational transfer plan updated and include milestones that tie into the IT project plan so both plans are kept up to date and in sync.

Operational transfer is an area where many IT projects fall on their faces, which is unfortunate because it's a huge opportunity for success. A smooth transition can improve your project success rate tremendously, so make sure your IT project plan includes an operational transfer component. You may choose to create a separate operational transfer plan and tie it to your IT project. The time and effort you spend creating this transfer plan will help in terms of fewer customer complaints, higher user satisfaction, and a higher overall perception of the project's deliverables.

Resolving Common Project Problems

In this section of the chapter, we're going to discuss common project problems and provide ideas for addressing these problems. Obviously, we can't cover every possible scenario, but we will cover some of the common problems. By recognizing common problems, you may be able to head them off at the pass. As you continue to hone your IT project management skills, you will probably intuitively avoid these more common mistakes. As part of your lessons learned activities in your IT project, you may want to add to this list and keep it handy as you manage future IT projects. We can't always avoid mistakes, but at least we can avoid making the same mistakes over and over again.

Problems with Scope

As you know, scope is the total amount of work to be accomplished on the project, so defining scope is fundamental to the project work and to the project's success. Problems with scope come in two primary flavors: problems with scope definition and problems with scope management.

Vague Scope Definition

At the outset of a project, during the definition stage, it's possible that not enough detail is yet known to clearly define the scope of the project. During the definition stage, you should strive to create as much detail about scope as possible. The scope document or definition should clearly describe the circumference of the circle of project work, while not necessarily providing great detail. It should answer the question, "How will we know when we've finished our work?" or to use the travel analogy, "How will we know when we get there?"

Possible Solutions: Add or develop specific, measurable criteria to the scope document if it is vague. Many organizations call these SMART goals - *specific, measurable, attainable, realistic,* and *time-based* (some people use *tangible* as the last element). Instead of "Improve system uptime" as a scope statement, quantify that by putting some numbers in to it. "System uptime will be 99.95% overall uptime with no more than 30 minutes per week for unscheduled downtime." Even if you later discover the goal is not possible, you have drawn a line in the sand and everyone knows what the project is all about. This detail allows you to push back on any proposed changes that might increase scope. If you have a sound change management process defined (and in place) for your project, you can better manage proposed changes to the project that will implement scope.

Scope Not Feasible

Sometimes despite our best efforts, we discover, as we're midway through the project, that the scope is just not feasible. Often projects start out sounding great, but once we get into the functional or technical requirements phase, things start looking bleak. Projects that include "discovery" work are most susceptible to this problem, though all projects by their very nature are vulnerable to this risk.

Possible Solutions: Be sure to clearly define project specifications and proposed approach. At the moment the project's scope (deliverables) are deemed not feasible, you should notify your project sponsor. If there is a business need driving this project, you may need to go back to the drawing board. If not, you may want to recommend this project be cancelled. There is no sense in chasing after a result that is not possible or feasible. If you recall from earlier discussions, part of your evaluation of the project at each step should be to ask whether the project (or any element) is *logical, feasible, desirable,* and *affordable.* If you've been asking this all along, you're less likely to wind up in this situation. However, if you cancel a project that is no longer feasible, you can at least be viewed as part of the solution instead of being viewed as the part of the problem.

Errors in Approach

Sometimes despite our best project planning, we select the wrong approach. The scope may be well defined, but how we choose to deliver on that scope may be wrong. Often the wrong approach is embedded in the technical specifications, derived from the functional specifications. If you define a specific set of functionality and then choose the wrong method of providing that functionality, your project can get off track quickly. If your technical specifications assumed or specified a

Windows-based solution but other components only work on a UNIX platform, you have an error in the approach.

Possible solutions: To the degree possible, look at functional and technical requirements closely to ensure you don't have a disconnect. If an error in the approach is discovered after project work commences, you have two choices. One is to stop project work and go back through your planning stages. This can be time-consuming and politically perilous, but can ultimately yield a more satisfactory result. A second option is to sit down and figure out how to address the problem at this juncture through change control methods. Ideally, your schedule and budget reserves should help cover the additional time or money required, but that may leave the rest of your project work exposed to time and cost risks. Whatever you do, sit down with your project sponsor immediately to address this issue before it gets out of hand, becomes a political minefield, or blows up in your (or the project sponsor's) face. Getting out in front of this kind of issue is the best approach because regardless of how painful it is now, it will only hurt worse as time goes on.

Scope Creep

We've discussed the dangers of scope creep repeatedly throughout this book. When an IT project scope keeps expanding, it makes it virtually impossible to meet any measure of success. That said, don't be afraid of change. Sometimes changes are innovative and ultimately reduce the time or cost of a project or increase the quality or perception of the project. Large changes are those that are most dangerous and should be brought through your formal change management process.

Possible solutions: First, educate everyone involved with the project about the dangers of scope creep. Gain agreement from the IT project team to use the change management process to manage scope changes. Avoid making changes to scope without fully analyzing the change and assessing it in terms of its impact on the project as well as on the time, cost, and quality of the project. Push back on your project sponsor if he or she insists on changes to scope once project work has begun. If change is required, be sure to let everyone (including executives and the project sponsor) know how the change impacts the project.

Problems with Quality

Any problem with quality can be called a bug or defect. The term *bug* is used more often in software projects and when a machine running questionable code acts strange, it's often said to be "acting buggy." We'll use the terms bug, error, or defect interchangeably in this section. For more on software bug tracking and management techniques, you can download the bug tracking template from the Syngress website.

In some projects, quality metrics are very clear-cut. In other projects, quality tends to be more subjective and your role is to be the arbitrator or final authority on all issues related to the project. This means making decisions in a timely fashion, having clear policies, and sticking to them. There are several common problems you may run into regarding project quality that we'll discuss in this section along with possible solutions.

Initial Results Do Not Meet Quality Standards

If the first project deliverables (or early versions of them) do not meet quality standards, you have a problem. Quality defects at this point are signs of bigger problems. The good news is that problems you discover at this point are easier and less expensive to fix now than later.

Possible solutions: Regardless of the direction you take, you must address the quality issue immediately. In some cases that might mean halting project work until the source of the problem can be discovered and remedied. The logical starting point for your inquiry should be at the task—did the person performing the work understand what needed to be done and did he or she have the skills, tools, and resources to accomplish that work? Was unit testing performed and were the results acceptable? If a team member is submitting sub-standard work, look more closely at that person. Task owners (and those doing the work) are responsible for submitting work that meets scope and quality standards. Unit testing should find errors or problems early. If unit testing is flawed or not occurring, this must to be remedied immediately. If several team members are submitting sub-standard work, the problem is more likely in the project plan itself. If you suspect a problem in the plan, begin by reviewing the tasks that came in under standards to see what (if any) quality standards, entry/exit criteria, or completion criteria were defined. In some cases, the answer is staring you in the face—no quality metrics or criteria associated with tasks means the work of defining the WBS was not fully completed. Go back and fill in all necessary details before proceeding. If your examination of the tasks doesn't reveal any problems, the problem is most likely in the functional or technical specifications. Review these specs in light of the task problems discovered and modify plans as needed.

Work Delivered Outside of Scope

Sometimes work that is delivered is outside the scope of work. To those performing the work, it may be considered an enhancement. To those testing the work, it might be considered a bug. Which is it and what do you do about it?

Possible solutions: First, check your scope statement and your project definition. Look at functional and technical specs related to this issue. First determine whether this issue is a bug or an enhancement. If it is a bug, it should be noted in the bug tracking system and fixed. If it is outside the scope but not a bug, you have to decide if you want it to remain there or not. Some "enhancements" may seem trivial at the time, but as you get deeper into the project, they end up having a long reach and impacting many other parts of the code. This type of scope creep may appear to be innocent at first, but you should carefully consider whether or not to let it stand. Even a seemingly innocuous enhancement can end up causing bug-like behavior when it interacts with other parts of the project. If you are unable to clearly understand the implications on the project, you should probably treat it as a bug and have it fixed to avoid later problems. In some cases, it really is an enhancement and may increase the final quality of the project. Analyze then select a course of action and stick to it. Vacillating on important decisions will eventually reduce your effectiveness as an IT project manager.

Fixing The Wrong Problem

When reporting any type of error or defect, it's important that the source problem be identified, reported, and resolved. If it's not, a lot of time and effort can be expended running after the wrong problem. Here's an example. You're staying in a hotel and you notice water on the floor in the bathroom. You report "water on floor in bathroom." The hotel manager sends someone up with a mop and bucket and mops up the water. However, the water soon returns. The manager sends someone back up with a mop, and so it continues. The real issue is not water on the floor, but a leak that is causing water to be on the floor. If you had reported "a leak that leaves water on the floor" the manager could have sent a plumber instead of a janitor. The same is true with quality problems in your project. Always look for the root cause and address it.

Possible solutions: The symptom is likely to be one person saying they fixed a problem (developer, tech) and another person (tester) saying the problem still exists. This can lead to bad working relationships on both sides and this type of back and forth should be quickly managed. The tester is looking at the product from the user point of view, while the developer or tech is looking at it from the project point of view. When these situations occur, you may be able to locate the underlying problem easily. If not, get several developers/techs and testers in a room to brainstorm about what could be the underlying cause. By getting the team to work together on this issue, you are subtly acknowledging the issue is bigger than any one person. This helps people "save face," an important element in effective team work. If the developer/tech feels he or she is being insulted or that their work is being questioned, he or she may become defensive and not fully participate. Make it clear that the work is fine but that there is an underlying problem that has to be discovered. Using their expertise, you can find that problem and fix it.

Problems Reappear

This issue is almost exclusively found in the software arena where a tester reports a bug, it gets fixed and later, the problem reappears. This is a likely sign that source control procedures are not being followed. Developers do most of their work with a local copy of the code running on their machine. This code may contain one program or hundreds, depending what is being developed. If one developer (George) fixes a piece of defective code, while another developer (Lorraine) has a copy of the bad code running on her machine then this can happen. George finds and fixes the bug and checks the code back in to the system library. Now Lorraine, who was working on another issue, checks her code back in. If the source library protocols are not followed correctly, Lorraine's code will overwrite George's fix and will reintroduce the bug back into the code.

Possible solutions: If you find this happening, meet with the developers (or development manager) and ask them to identify how this happened and what changes they will make to their source control procedures to avoid this issue in the future. Don't assume this is a one-time event. If one problem reappears, it may have been a one-time problem, but investigate it thoroughly. Process and procedure problems may initially appear as a single problem, but they will grow over time and you'll find that you have multiple problems reappearing. By the time this happens, you've got considerable confusion and frustration with the developers and a real risk to your code. This is a very serious problem that can create major havoc with the project. It can also create real morale problems when issues keep cropping back up. The good news is that most software projects have source control tools available and when used in a disciplined manner, they can help you avoid these kinds of issues.

Problems Cannot Be Resolved

Sometimes problems that crop up cannot be quickly or easily resolved. They may appear first as quality issues, but upon further investigation, they reveal deeper design problems. These instances may be rare, but when they occur, an IT project manager may spend several sleepless nights worrying about what to do.

Possible solutions: First, gather the team and discuss the issue. In this type of scenario, the more people looking at the problem, the better. Begin with an organized search for the problem by looking at the scope statement, the functional and technical specifications, the technology, and the chosen approach to the project. If the problem cannot be found, begin brainstorming about possible sources of the problem. Encourage the team to be really creative at this juncture to make sure that they cover every possible angle. If you encourage this type of investigation, it's likely the problem will be found. You may need to halt project work while this problem is being investigated to prevent the problem from rippling through the project. Be sure to gain project sponsor approval for delaying or halting the project and adjust your schedule accordingly. Once the solution is found, assess its impact on your schedule, budget, critical path, scope, and project requirements. Determine if the solution is feasible within the constraints of the project. This may require you and the team to go back and modify the project plan or simply modify some of the tasks, processes, or procedures within the project. If the problem cannot be resolved, the project should be tabled until resolution is found or terminated. Continuing on while your project is hobbled by an unsolvable problem of any size significantly reduces your chance of success. Some problems allow us to keep working while we find the solution; other problems are best solved when everyone stops work in other areas and focuses on addressing this one issue.

A final word on this scenario. It's wise to always try to separate out "discovery" work from "production" work—meaning you should not try to invent a new technology and put that new technology to work in the same project. A discovery project is far more uncertain and will have many more stops and starts than a production project. Don't start the production project until discovery is almost complete. This will help avoid unsolvable problems in some instances.

Problems with Schedule

Problems with the project schedule are often the most challenging because you're dealing with tasks both on and off the critical path. Changes to the project schedule can put the project at risk due to a variety of issues. Let's look at common schedule problems and possible solutions you can use to address them.

Late Start

Sometimes you can start project work already behind schedule due to earlier changes or delays or due to shifting requirements. Normally, you start the project schedule clock ticking once work gets underway, but if you have external milestones or deadlines to meet, it may not matter when your schedule "officially" begins. Late starts can start you off on the wrong foot, so try to avoid starting your project behind schedule.

Possible solutions: In some cases, you may be able to adjust your schedule to reflect the changes or delays that cause the schedule problem. Be sure to document the causes of the delay, especially if they were out of your control or outside your realm of authority or influence. Talk with your project sponsor to get approval for modifying the schedule to adjust for the unavoidable delay. If possible, you may find ways to shorten your project schedule. Sometimes analysis reveals opportunities to do tasks in parallel that were missed earlier. Sometimes you may choose to crash or fast track your schedule (discussed in Chapter 10), but these are serious actions that come with a certain degree of risk. Whatever you do, don't promise to make up lost time if you're not 100% certain you can do so. The rule of thumb is "under promise, over deliver." If you make a promise you can't keep, your credibility and political capital will fall. If you make a promise and deliver it with time to spare, you'll look like a hero. One word of caution about that: don't under promise to the point where your project sponsor thinks you're incompetent. If something should take a week and you promise it in three weeks and deliver it in two days, you will gain a reputation as either a terrible estimator or someone obsessed with covering your rear end. Neither view is flattering, so lean toward the pessimistic view of reality when coming up with new schedule commitments.

Floating Start Date

This problem can be similar to a late start, but it's a bit trickier to address sometimes. The start date is set then moves then gets set then moves again. A floating start date is dangerous because resources committed to your project can become unavailable if your start date keeps floating around.

Possible solutions: First, check that the project is aligned with corporate needs. If it's somewhere out in left field, you'll have trouble getting necessary commitments for the project to move forward. Along those lines, also check on the project's priority. It may be aligned with corporate goals, but it may have slipped down in priority due to other changes in the corporate business environment. Sometimes the start date floats because the planning stage drags on and on. In this case, set a hard deadline for completing planning so the start date can be set. Don't spend time creating detailed plans for work that is 6 or 12 months out. Create high-level plans for later phases, but don't spin your wheels creating detailed plans for distant dates in the future. Things will likely change by then and you probably don't have enough information to create a detailed plan. This sometimes leads to planning paralysis, so make a commitment to complete planning, don't shoot for detail on distance phases, and draw a line in the sand and get going. If you're wishy-washy on setting and sticking to your start date, you're going to have trouble throughout your project with deadlines and deliverables so learn to make and keep commitments. If your start date does float or change, you'll have to double check that needed resources are still available. Finally, if you can't pin down a start date, you might consider canceling the project.

Floating Completion Date

Some projects get off to a great start but seem unable to complete. These projects just seem to go on and on with no end in sight. A floating completion date means you've got one or more problems in your project that you should address immediately.

Possible solutions: First, look at tasks on your critical path. Which ones have slipped and why? Next, determine what is currently causing the float. When you can't pin down a completion date, it means that there is uncertainty, especially regarding tasks on the critical path. Next, check your scope statement and requirements. Double check that scope hasn't expanded while you weren't looking. Scope creep is the most common reason for a floating completion date, so be sure to check that. Review your WBS. Does your WBS define all the work that has to be done? If not, additional work may be going on that is needed, but not actually defined or scheduled. Another problem with the WBS is that tasks lack adequate detail and work packages or assignments become vague. Tasks should have plenty of detail in them, including entry/exit criteria or completion criteria. A task without these criteria could simply go on forever. Define what a completed task looks like so it can be completed. Also, double check that all tasks have owners. Some tasks may not have owners through oversight or through miscommunication and those tasks will not get done. These may be the tasks that keep floating around your project schedule and never get started because no one is taking responsibility for them. Floating completion date can also occur when you have a project that combines discovery and production. Separate the discovery portion of the project from the production portion and only begin (or continue) production work once the discovery portion is completed.

Missed Deadline or Deliverable

Missed deadlines or deliverables happen to everyone once in a while. The key is how and how well you handle these inevitable problems.

Possible solutions: It should not come as a surprise to you, your project team, or your project sponsor that a deadline or deliverable will be missed. That would be the equivalent of driving 80 mph right up to the edge of a cliff before applying the brakes—not a wise choice and almost always ineffective. Make sure you encourage (require) your team to keep you apprised of potential problems. If you recall from Chapter 10, encouraging your team to bring you the bad news will help you manage the project more effectively. Once you're aware of problems that cannot be corrected in a timely manner (that is, those that will cause you to miss a deadline or deliverable), work with your team to develop contingency plans, alternatives, or solutions to the problem. Determine what caused you to miss the deadline, what impact it has on the project, and what you can do to recover. Once that information is prepared, talk with your project sponsor. Over time, IT project managers that deal with problems in a responsible and proactive manner are given more responsibility and respect. Letting problems creep up on you and your project sponsor will not only put the project at risk, it could very well put your career at risk as well. It's often not whether problems occur, but how well you deal with them that will determine your success—both in your project and in your career.

Everything on the Critical Path

One common statement is "all tasks in the project are critical, so they're all on the critical path." While it is true that all tasks in the project are important (or they should not be in the project plan), it is not true that all tasks are on the critical path. By definition, the tasks on the critical path are those tasks that, if delayed, would delay the entire project. Conversely, these same tasks, if completed ahead of schedule, would cause the project to finish early. Let's look at an analogy. If you were driving from San Diego, California to Richmond, Virginia, there would be tasks that would be more important than others. For instance, getting gas would be on the critical path because if you delayed getting gas, you'd run out of gas someplace and you'd be delayed getting to Richmond. On the other hand, you may have a task defined as "clean bugs off windshield." This task will be done intermittently throughout your project, but delaying cleaning bugs off the windshield will not delay the project until the windshield becomes so filled with bugs you cannot see and have to slow down to drive. This task, then, can be done just about anytime within reason. If, however, it is delayed beyond a reasonable point, it can land on the critical path. Understanding the nature of critical path tasks helps you properly define them.

Possible solutions: If you believe all tasks are on the critical path, you have made an error in the defining your task dependencies, durations, and/or float. In almost every project, there are tasks that are not on the critical path that can be done just about any time. If you're installing a new server, you need the power to be in place before you can fire it up, but you don't need the nameplate that attaches to the server cover telling you the server's name. If all tasks in your project are on the critical path, review your task dependencies. If a task is not really dependent upon previous task(s), remove the dependency. If a task is not going to take as long as the duration in the plan indicates, adjust it to reflect reality. If tasks have no float defined, they may end up on the critical path. Add appropriate slack or float to reflect the reality of the situation. It's not uncommon that things shift after the initial project plan is created and updating dependencies, duration, and float to reflect reality will help you see your *real* critical path.

Nothing on the Critical Path

In some cases, you might think that there are no real dependencies. Using the server example, you might think "We can get that power installed anytime before next month" or "We can borrow backup tapes until ours come in." While these statements are true, they are misleading. Every project has tasks on the critical path.

Possible solutions: If you have a project plan showing no critical path tasks, something is wrong. Start by looking at dependencies. Ask what would happen if a task was delayed for a week, month, or longer. Once you understand the impact of the delay, you can determine whether a task is on the critical path or not. Also check duration and float. If you were loosy-goosy with duration and float estimates, it may appear that everything can move around to accommodate change. Review your duration and float estimates, especially for tasks you've determined would be a problem if they were delayed too long. This will help you begin to identify tasks that truly belong on the critical path. The overriding question is, "Will this delay the entire project if delayed?" If yes, it's on the critical path. The secondary question is, "Which tasks is this dependent upon and which tasks depend on this?" Once you've accurately identified dependencies, you'll begin to see your critical path emerge.

Problems with Budget

Some companies pay little attention to a project budget, while others review it with a fine-toothed comb. Regardless of how your company deals with IT project budgets, your job as IT project manager is to manage the funds allotted to you for the project. When a project ends up sideways due to its funding, the chances for project success are reduced significantly. Keep in mind that if cost is your least flexible project parameter, you should carefully and frequently review project costs to avoid these common problems. And, if you discover a problem with the budget, let your project sponsor know immediately. It's better to bring this problem to your sponsor than to have your sponsor bring it to you. Let's look at problems common to budget management and possible solutions you can use.

Funds Expended Up Front

An unfortunate but common scenario is you're halfway into the project and 3/4 of your funds are spent. This is an indication of one of two problems. Either there was a significant variation or you're not doing a great job managing your budget. Remember, though, that scope, schedule, budget, and quality are all interrelated. If you increase scope or quality or reduce schedule, your budget may burst at the seams. That might be perfectly acceptable to all parties involved—the key is to gain explicit approval for such variances *before* they occur. If budget is the least flexible project parameter, you will have to explain why you have this type of variance. There may be a good reason such as purchasing equipment needed for a later phase of work at year-end for accounting purposes or to take advantage of a special pricing deal. These will net out at the end of the project but should be carefully reviewed.

Possible solutions: The first step is to look at what caused (is causing) the additional burden on your budget. In Chapter 10, we discussed sources for budget variance and what you can do to adjust for them. Some budget variances may simply be incorporated into the project (after analysis and agreement). Other budget problems will cause the project to be selected for special review (not a good thing). If your project risks cancellation because of these budget variances, you will have to do your best to make the business case for why the project should continue (if, in fact, it should). Sometimes the budget variance is a logical consequence of earlier, agreed-upon actions. Sometimes the budget variance is due to some value-added activity that will pay off at project completion. Other times, there may be no reasonable explanation for the variance and the decision to move forward or cancel may rest solely with the project sponsor or the Finance department. If the problem is because you've done a poor job managing the budget, you should review your cost control procedures and make adjustments to ensure you have tighter control of your budget moving forward. If your reserve amount can handle the variance, you may be able to salvage the project if your adherence to budget moving forward is greatly improved. Hold weekly budget review meetings and insist on giving your personal approval for all expenditures over a certain (low) amount to help you get your budget back on track.

Assets Moved Off Project

Sometimes you'll purchase assets of the project that will sit idle for some period of time due to changes in the project schedule or other unanticipated changes. Occasionally, those assets will be appropriated by some other department or team and suddenly your new servers or new routers or new whatever are in someone else's domain or department. Sometimes someone sees hardware sitting around unused and sees it as a bone yard for scavenging parts.

Possible solutions: The key is to determine why the assets were taken, who took them, and why. This is not an exercise in finger-pointing, but a fact-finding mission. If the assets were taken for a higher priority project, that's fine. If they were used for spare parts, that's also ok. The key is to understand how and why they were taken so you can build the business case for getting them back. Talk with your project sponsor about the situation to determine the best course of action. Sometimes the best resolution is to take a hit to your budget and go purchase new equipment. This would be done with your project sponsor's explicit approval. If possible (depending on your corporate culture and accounting system), you may be able to assign the cost of those appropriated assets to that other division or department so your budget won't take a hit. If you have to use your reserve amounts to deal with this type of situation, document exactly what happened so there is not any question about the loss of corporate assets. If the servers are now in another location or were used for spare parts, make a note of that. You don't need corporate controllers coming back to you asking if you took three or four servers home with you.

Too Many Approvals To Spend Your Budget

Part of defining your project is to agree with your project sponsor as to what, where, how, and when you can spend your IT project budget. However, some companies have so many approval layers and so much red tape that it becomes a project in itself just to get approval to spend IT project funds. In these cases, delays in funding approval can throw the schedule off, causing a ripple effect throughout the project.

Possible solutions: If it's taking too long to get approval, consider asking your project sponsor for a monthly allocation that you can spend. Make sure it's not a "use it or lose it" allocation so that it can pile up for a month or two or three for large, upcoming expenditures. If that's not feasible, consider asking your project sponsor for a "fast track" funding option so that you can get project expenditures approved in a more timely manner. A third possible solution is to ask for an increase in the amount you are authorized to spend, at least for the duration of the project. It might be that in normal circumstances, you'd need approval for each expenditure over $500, but for the duration of the project, your limit is increased to $1000 or $1500. If none of these options is acceptable to your project sponsor, you should try to document the business case for modifying the spending limits or approval process. There is a cost to schedule delays—both tangible and intangible—and a polite reminder of these consequences for your project sponsor might prompt the change you need.

Shrinkage

Experienced IT project managers are familiar with shrinkage. It often stems from a memo from the CEO that begins "Due to changes in the marketplace, we're cutting all project budgets by 15% effective immediately…." Ouch. All that diligent project planning seems to fly right out the window. Since you're aware that there is a relationship between scope, time, cost, and quality, you immediately know that if your budget is reduced by 15% you will need to reduce scope or quality or increase time to adjust for the budget change. The question is, what do you do next? No matter what course of action you take, whining about the cutback is not likely to change the outcome and it's a sign of poor leadership. Look for ways to meet the new requirement and position yourself as part of the solution, not part of the problem. You may not be happy about the requirement to cut your budget, but you have to deal with it as the IT project manager.

Possible solutions: First, review your flexibility grid. If budget is your least flexible (and it was just reduced by 15%), you know that something else must be most flexible. Begin by looking at that parameter to determine what you can adjust. For example, if cost is least flexible but schedule is most flexible, you may find that by stretching out your schedule, you can reduce the cost of the project. If not, you have to move up your flexibility grid to your next most flexible parameter. Once you've determined your approach to cutting your project budget by 15%, you need to assess the risks associated with making the proposed changes. Ideally, you and the team will devise two or three possible solutions and prioritize them (remember, canceling the project may be one of them). Once you and the IT project team have developed your recommendations, you should meet with your project sponsor to discuss proposed solutions.

Problems with Staff

At several points throughout this book, we've discussed working with your IT project team from recognizing and managing differences in work styles and cultures to providing the necessary ingredients to create a highly effective team. Despite your best efforts, teams sometimes run into problems. If you find yourself with a problem related to your project team, you might find solutions in this section. If not, be sure to turn to your manager, another experienced IT project manager, or your friendly HR department for advice on resolving personnel issues.

Matrix Organization (Who's Staff Is This Anyway?)

One of the most common team-related problems you may run into is conflict over who belongs to whom. When someone is pulled from a department to work on a project team, to whom do they report? Who holds them accountable? What are their priorities? These kinds of unresolved problems cause stress for the person caught in the middle and reduce productivity and the quality of their work.

Possible solutions: Discuss the project with the functional or departmental managers who will be lending staff to your project. Explain to them the project's objectives, what you'll need the selected person to do, and what your timeframe is. Come to mutually acceptable agreements about how you'll handle conflicting priorities before they crop up then rely on your agreed-upon procedures when these issues arise. Anticipating and planning for these kinds of problems goes a long way toward avoiding them. If they can't be resolved in this manner, sit down and have an honest, open discussion with the manager explaining what is happening and how it impacts the project. Rather than expecting the other person to give in to your demands, come prepared with several possible solutions along with your recommendations. This will help resolve sometimes sticky issues by showing you're willing to work through problems, arrive at the table with potential solutions, and give a little.

Whiners

A whiner isn't someone who brings up the negative or downside of a situation. It's someone who does that and never looks for the solution. They can be irritating at best and few, if any, people want to work with people like this.

Possible solutions: If you have a whiner on your team, you need to assess whether they're adding enough value to the team to justify keeping them on board. Whiners can de-energize entire teams and take the energy, excitement, and enthusiasm for a project and deflate it quickly. If you can't or don't want to remove the team member, you'll need to manage this behavior. First, require that your team make meaningful statements about the problem that are specific, measurable (if possible), and realistic. For instance, saying "The code from Section Seven is garbage" is not meaningful by any measure. A statement such as, "There are fourteen critical errors in the code from Section Seven," is far more useful. Next, require that every time a problem is mentioned, a solution must also be offered. It doesn't matter much if the solution is feasible or desirable as long as problem is offered with a suggested solution (or two). This will prevent problems from just being lobbed out for the team to deal with. Instead, some thought will have to accompany problem statements. Who knows, you might also find a great solution along the way by requiring the naysayer to consider possible solutions. Make this a rule for everyone, not just your whiners. Meaningful problem statements paired with possible solutions will change this dynamic quickly.

Big Biters

People who take on too much can cause major or minor problems for projects because they typically lack self-awareness as to how much they should commit to, based on their time and skills. If you don't manage these folks, they can tank your project by signing on for more than they can handle then failing to deliver (scope, time, cost, or quality) on those deliverables. Self-confidence and enthusiasm are wonderful traits in measured doses.

Possible solutions: Encourage "big biters" to take on small segments of work until you verify whether or not this person has the time and skills to deliver. In some circles it's referred to as "trust and verify," meaning that you place a small amount of trust in the person and verify whether that trust was justified or not. If it was, you can place additional trust and verify that level and so forth. By carefully managing the big biter, you can help them grow in awareness of what they can and cannot do while keeping your project safe from the "over promise, under deliver" syndrome many big biters bring with them.

Belt and Suspenders

We all know someone like this—almost completely risk-averse. Their avoidance of risk could come from prior bad experience in which they got burned or it could simply be their personality or work style. The *analyst* types we discussed in Chapter 4 can sometimes really have problems with change and risk. If you have these types of people on your team and your project requires some level of risk, you're going to engage in a tug-of-war with them throughout the project process.

Possible solutions: If you are working on a risky project, these risk-averse people are not good fits for your team. If you cannot replace them with team members more comfortable with risk, try to find parts of the project that will utilize their skills and talents. Since these kinds of people can be very good at spotting problems (they look for risk so they can avoid it), you can engage them fully in your risk assessment and management tasks as well as some of your detail work such as creating the WBS and task details, helping manage the costs and schedule of the project, and other less risky tasks. By assigning more mundane roles to these folks, you utilize their innate talents while offloading some of the routine project management tasks to someone else, freeing you up to work on tasks that may require more of your bandwidth. Don't let their fear of risk or failure rub off on the team, though. Keep the project moving forward, and if you find they are causing delays due to risk aversion or through planning beyond a reasonable point (analysis paralysis), take action to move them off the task or out of the way to keep forward momentum.

Personal Conflict

As we discussed in Chapter 4, your role as IT project manager includes creating a positive work environment for your team. This is especially true when dealing with people of different ages, backgrounds, cultures, and languages. Your HR department is probably your best resource for advice on handling sensitive issues, but we'll discuss some possible solutions here as well.

Possible solutions: First, you should have a zero tolerance policy for rude, intimidating, belittling, or disrespectful behavior. Some behaviors can lead to a hostile work environment and may lead to legal issues down the road. If you're unsure or if you're concerned, consult with your HR department immediately. Do not discount or trivialize these issues because they not only cause immediate problems, but they can have serious long-term consequences as well. That said, you may encounter conflicts between team members that are impacting the team but are not serious enough to bring to your HR department. To resolve interpersonal conflict you can:

- Talk privately to each individual involved in the problem. Listen to each individual's perspective. Conclude the conversation by asking them what they would change about the situation and what they would be willing to change. This sets the stage for a negotiated settlement and helps them understand they will likely have to give something to resolve the situation.

- Once you have each person's perspective along with their lists of what they would like to see changed and what they'd be willing to change, put together a recommended solution (or two or three, if possible). Gather everyone in the room and discuss solutions based on the information they gave you.

- Once a resolution has been forged, enforce it.

- If anyone reneges on the agreement, address it with them immediately.

- Remove people from the project who are unable or unwilling to resolve personal conflict through negotiation and mediation. They'll steal project time and energy and wear everyone out in the process.

Problems with Project Sponsor

Taking time to develop a strong, open, and honest relationship with your IT project sponsor can pay off handsomely down the line—when things go right, you'll get appropriate credit and rewards, and when things go wrong, you'll get appropriate political cover and support. Keep it real with your project sponsor and always be the one to bring the bad news to the sponsor. If your project sponsor hears bad news from another source before you report it, your credibility begins to erode. Most people hate being ambushed by bad news, so make sure you stay on top of things and communicate with your project sponsor in a proactive and timely manner. That said, there are problems that can crop up with your project sponsor, including the ones listed here.

Project Report Grows Lengthy

Sometimes a project report ends up getting longer and longer until it begins to rival *War and Peace*. This is not productive for you as the IT project manager and it's probably not helpful for your project sponsor either.

Possible solutions: What to include in the status report should be determined at the start of the project, but it is often not well defined or not known in advance. Try including just four basic elements when reporting project status:

- What has been accomplished since the last report

- What is planned to happen during the upcoming period until the next report

- What items have missed the schedule or are over budget and what their status is in a summary format

- What items are of concern that have to be addressed

The goal is to provide a one- or two-page summary of the project status and make sure any items that are a risk to the project are seen by management so they can be acted on as early as possible. If you provide too much detail, you also risk having the project sponsor (or other executives) begin to micromanage your project for you.

Meetings Become Rehash of Prior Decisions

Sometimes meetings with project sponsors become reviews of decisions previously made. Constantly reviewing previous decisions makes it difficult to get any forward momentum going and it puts your project at risk because, conceivably, every decision made could be reversed.

Possible solutions: If you and your project sponsor keep rehashing the same decisions, it could be a sign that the sponsor is nervous about the project. If that's the case, ask yourself:

- Are your project status reports accurate?

- If you were in your project sponsor's shoes, would you be nervous?

- Are you making decisions above your level of authority?

- Have you taken risks that have not panned out?

- Has your project sponsor been hit by any surprises or unexpected bad news regarding the project?

If your project sponsor feels he or she is not getting straight answers or the level of detail needed to accurately assess the project's health, he or she might begin to go back over old decisions with you. Go over your concerns with the project sponsor, give specific examples of the problem and really listen to the feedback you get from your project sponsor. If your project sponsor is a real hands-on type of person and can't seem to let go of these decisions, you may need to create a more detailed process for signing off on decisions so they do not have to be revisited. For instance, you may need to keep detailed notes about how, why, and when the decision was reached, what the environment was, and what factors went into the decision. Then, if the sponsor wants to revisit a decision, you may be able to discuss the document you have and ask what has changed to cause you to revisit the issue.

Can't Arrange Meetings with Sponsor

Project sponsors are often busy people like the rest of us. If you are unable to schedule time with your project sponsor to discuss project progress, one of three things is likely wrong. It's possible the project has slipped in priority and you don't know about it. It's possible the project sponsor's priorities have changed even if the organization's haven't. It's also possible that the project sponsor is just too busy and meetings with you fall off their "to do" list.

Possible solutions: If possible, first determine if the organization's priorities have shifted away from your project. If it seems that's the likely cause of the problem, insist on a meeting and let the sponsor know that you realize priorities may have shifted. If the sponsor wants to avoid this session because he or she doesn't want to deal with the negative impact, your mentioning this might pave the way to an honest and useful discussion. If the project sponsor's priorities have shifted and you've been able to discern that, it might be time for a different project sponsor. In that case, you should identify your desired or optimal replacement sponsor and define your rationale for such a request. Then, contact your project sponsor and let him or her know that you believe the project might do well to transition to another person due to this sponsor's workload, commitments, new direction, etc. Be very careful not to make this about the project sponsor failing as a sponsor, but about the changes that have occurred within the project sponsor's work or environment that make changing sponsors a logical action. Finally, if your project sponsor just claims to be too busy, be ready to be incredibly flexible to get some face time with the project sponsor. Come in early, stay late, offer to go get sandwiches for an in-house meeting, arrange a video call or cell phone call while you (or the project sponsor) is traveling, talk on Saturday morning at a local coffee shop. Do whatever it takes to get face-to-face with your project sponsor on a fairly regular basis. Be creative and offer solutions such as offloading non-critical tasks (signing project time cards, for example) to someone else with proper authority or look to bring on a project co-sponsor to take up some of the work. Whatever you do, do *not* assume that just because you can't get a meeting that the project sponsor is just fine with what's going on. Remember the old project management saying, "No news is simply no news."

Project Sponsor Pressure

The project sponsor is under pressure regarding the project just as the IT project manager is. The key difference is that the project sponsor will pass that pressure on to you and sometimes you feel as though you may buckle under the pressure. Here are some simple solutions that can help you deal with that type of project pressure.

Possible solutions: First, be prepared. Make sure your project data is up to date, that your team provides you updates that are accurate and timely, and that you, in turn, provide accurate, timely, and meaningful data to your project sponsor. If your project sponsor is up to speed on the progress of the project and understands the risks, challenges, positive, and negative events, he or she will be able to properly explain (and in some cases, defend) project results to corporate management or executives. A good offense is the best defense, so make sure you're on top of your project's status. If your project sponsor has signed off on the major components of the project as you've gone along (as suggested throughout this book), you should have an easier time dealing with some pressure because you can take these decisions points back to your sponsor to spark his or her memory. If you're getting pressure to complete the project sooner, for instance, you can discuss scope and schedule with your project sponsor and come to agreement as to how to proceed or how to fend off further schedule pressure. If you've developed a good relationship with your project sponsor, you can have an honest, open discussion about what the drivers are and together develop a plan to address these added pressures.

Cheat Sheet...

Being On Top of Your Game

A project manager has lots of pressure and your sponsor will certainly provide a share of it. You can control this pressure by being organized and having an iron-clad reporting system. "On my projects, I produce a weekly status report on Fridays. I stay as late as possible to get it done on Friday, but if it is not done, I finish it on the weekend," explains Nels Hoenig, Quality Assurance Project Leader for TDCI, Inc. "My publish date is Monday at 9:00 A.M. This hard date keeps me focused. It also means my sponsor knows she can count on being prepared for her staff meeting at 10:00A.M. I hold my team responsible for having their reports to me by end of the day on Thursday and I am very strict about this. Since I'm not pestering them 25 times a week on status questions, they deliver their status updates on time and we all can spend the rest of our time on the items that are critical or that can become critical if not resolved. This also gives me Friday to chase down and solve any issues that need to be addressed prior to finalizing my report."

Nels also produces a monthly project report that provides a high-level view of the project. It includes information on budget and schedule including plan versus actual. He also includes good and bad news about the project so that everyone remains up to date and helps ensure that everyone hears the same message.

Problems with Project Vendors

We haven't focused on managing vendors, since vendors take so many different forms. However, vendors should be treated as part of the project team from the beginning so they are included in key project communications including timelines and deadlines. Written contracts should be used to clarify costs, timelines, and deliverables. Someone on the project team can be assigned as the vendor liaison (or several team members, depending on the number of vendors) to oversee the vendor relationship. Most vendors want to do a good job and will work cooperatively with you to define portions of the project they'll be working on and to help develop specifications for work. Be sure to develop *acceptance criteria* that will indicate to the vendor when *you* will sign off on or accept *their* deliverables. Define early delivery bonuses and late delivery penalties. And remember to get a vendor point of contact and all contact information including name, address, phone, cell, e-mail, etc. so you know who to contact for routine or emergency communications. It's helpful to spell out in detail which process will be used to resolve disagreements to be sure that everyone is on the same page (and to avoid surprises). Contracts written by attorneys as well as standard (boilerplate) contracts often contain these details, but it's a good idea to make sure they're included in your contracts. Despite your earnest efforts, you may still run into vendor problems. Here are a few common problems and potential solutions.

Vendor Does Not Deliver As Promised

The biggest problem facing an IT project with regard to vendors is when a vendor does not deliver as promised. Whether it's needed test equipment, software code, or new servers for the upgrade, vendor delays can put your project behind schedule quickly. If the product or service the vendor is providing is critical to the project (tasks that depend on these are on the critical path), you should have identified them as risks and developed contingency plans for these scenarios. Any external event (including vendor deliverables) over which you have little (or no) control presents a project risk and you should include these in your risk management plans.

Possible solutions: The first step is to find out why the vendor did not deliver as promised. Is the issue quality, quantity, or delivery altogether? If the vendor shipped defective parts, it's the same problem as not shipping at all. Your contract should specify your remedy should you have problems with the deliverable including reordering on an expedited track. If the vendor is unable or unwilling to deliver the items, you will have to locate an alternate vendor and expedite the order if possible. Don't wait until the shipment is delayed two weeks to check on it. Check on deliverables before they are due so you know if there is a snag in the process. If there is to be a delay, see if you can schedule other work around the delay so you don't end up pushing your entire schedule out. If the vendor short-shipped items, you may be able to begin work in a staggered manner instead of waiting for all parts to be present. In some IT projects, this presents problems and introduces unacceptable risk. In other IT projects, a staggered start on this part of the project work is acceptable and causes only a few rescheduling events.

Obviously, if you have continued problems with the vendor—not only in terms of deliverables, but in terms of their attitude toward addressing problems—find another vendor. Projects can be delayed or can fail altogether because a vendor was unwilling to address issues or unable to deliver as promised. Don't get into the mindset that this was a one-time event. If a problem occurs and the vendor handles it promptly and appropriately, you can chalk it up to "mistakes sometimes happen." If mistakes happen frequently or the vendor is slow to resolve issues (or completely unwilling), find a new vendor because things will rarely get better.

Product or Service Does Not Meet Specifications

When a vendor's product or service doesn't meet project specifications, there are several potential problems that could be the root cause. Before blasting your vendor, be sure to look at your own project plan first to determine what your specifications actually are. You may find the vendor met your specifications, but you (and the project team) were mistaken about the specs. This can happen when specifications change or when a subject matter expert (including someone from the vendor company) recommends a different or better way to approach a specification.

Possible solutions: First check that the vendor's deliverable really doest not meet specifications. It's embarrassing to blast a vendor only to find out later you were wrong. Once you're sure the vendor's product is out of spec, talk with the person on your IT project team that worked with that vendor. Review the vendor paperwork. What you want to find out is if you properly communicated the specifications to the vendor in the first place. If you told the vendor there was a 5/8" clearance and it's really on 3/8", the problem is on your end and you'll need to work with the vendor to find an appropriate solution. Once you've determined that your specs are correct and that the vendor was given the correct specs, you obviously need to contact the vendor. Ask them to review their specs and processes to determine what went wrong and what they can do to remedy the problem. Be clear about timelines, deadlines, and costs when talking with them so they know exactly what they'll need to do to resolve the issue. If the issue requires research on their part, get them to commit to a follow up meeting or phone call on a specific day and time. This will put clear boundaries on their research and resolution period and will not push your schedule into an interminable "float". Also, by telling them what the problem is and asking them for the resolution, you put the onus on them to resolve an issue they created. In some cases, they may come back with a better resolution than you would have requested. If you find the vendor is unwilling to admit to their error, review the specifications and contract with them. This helps you be sure the problem is on their end and essentially pushes them into accepting responsibility. If they still will not resolve the issue, you may have to escalate it to your project sponsor or even to legal counsel for resolution, if appropriate. If they are not cooperative, you will have to continue to push for resolution with them and simultaneously identify a new vendor to fill in. As soon as possible, sever the relationship with the non-responsive vendor. Put them on your "do not use" list for future projects. Mistakes are one thing, refusing to take responsibility for errors is another matter altogether. The first can be fixed, the second is an attitude or company culture problem that goes to the core and will rarely, if ever, change.

Vendor Does Not Communicate

Communicating effectively with vendors is a key part of effective vendor management. If you have a vendor with whom communications are difficult or impossible, this should raise a red flag for you because it means if you run into a problem down the line, you'll have a very difficult time chasing down someone to respond to your issues.

Possible solutions: Make sure you have the correct vendor contact and current contact information. Insist on a personal e-mail address (as opposed to "customer service," "marketing," "sales," or "info") and a cell phone number. If you are unable to reach your contact, call the main vendor phone number and ask for that person's supervisor. If unavailable, ask for the next person up the line until you get a human being on the phone who can respond to your concerns. Be politely persistent. If the vendor contact says he or she will return your call at 10:00 A.M., get on the phone at 10:05 A.M. and call them. If they do not answer, leave a message and state another time you can be reached or provide an e-mail address. Don't let communications slide, insist on timely responses, and escalate issues in a timely manner. Sometimes your contact may have left the company or gone on vacation without your knowledge, so leaving repeated e-mails or voice mails will not resolve the issue. Therefore, if you don't get a response in a reasonable timeframe, start working you way up the ladder. It might make your vendor contact angry, but your job is to get your project completed on time. Be polite but persistent. If the error is yours or you jumped the gun in escalating, apologize and move on. One incident like that, though, is often enough to spur your contact to respond in a more timely manner in the future.

The IT Factor...

From the Vendor's Perspective

"Most vendors want your business and they strive to create a mutually beneficial relationship," explains Sonal Rana, Systems Analyst with an international consulting firm. "When problems crop up, it's often a case of miscommunication rather than ill-intent. Stepping back from the situation and approaching it from another angle can help you resolve the matter. Start with the mindset that everyone has good intentions and something went wrong along the way. If you start off blaming and accusing, you're not likely to get an honest answer or a positive result. When dealing with companies from other countries or cultures,

Continued

keep in mind that words and phrases may not have exactly the same meaning or intent. Cross-cultural communications can be complicated, so check for understanding by having the vendor explain to you, in their words, what they believe is expected of them. This can help you avoid simple miscommunications that end up delaying an entire project."

Problems with Customers/Users/Stakeholders

Problems with customers, end users, or stakeholders (whatever the case in your IT project) come in several different forms. In some cases, the user (we'll use "user" here for all those terms) isn't clear what the project deliverables are supposed to be and is therefore displeased with the results. In other cases, user requirements have changed and the deliverables don't meet user needs. In still other cases, the user gets stubborn about some elements of the project.

Users Are Not Pleased with Project Results

At some point during the project work and reporting, it becomes clear that the user is displeased with the project. This is a difficult situation that can cause problems both in terms of real and perceived success of the project.

Possible solutions: It is during the definition of project scope and functional requirements that the project begins to meet user needs. Users (or a select subset of users) should be involved with defining these specifications from the start. Two things should happen at that point: the user is clear about what is and is not included in the project and the IT project team is clear about what the user needs and wants. Having a formal approval process for functional requirements that the user signs off on is very helpful in preventing the users from changing their view of the requirements of the project once work is underway. It can also be helpful to review this document with users periodically throughout the project lifecycle to ensure that user requirements are the same.

User Requirements Have Changed, Project Doesn't Meet Needs

Sometimes major unanticipated changes happen in the user world that might require you to go back and redefine functional requirements. What was acceptable two or three months ago is now only part of the picture. This type of change is a major event in your IT project. Let's look at how you can handle this.

Possible solutions: If major change occurs in the course of the project, you can use the approved functional requirements document as your starting point for discussion rather than reinventing the wheel. First determine what has changed in the user environment and map it to deliverables in your functional specifications. Next, figure out what has to change to accommodate user needs. Assemble the project team and step back through the relevant definition and planning steps, including defining the new functional and technical specifications, as well as defining new scope, time, schedule, and quality parameters. Look at the risk to work completed to determine how these changes will impact work already completed—will you have to redo work or can you implement change moving forward? Finally, put all this together in a report or analysis and discuss the results with your project sponsor. Delivering a project that no longer meets users needs is a useless and wasteful exercise, but you must assess how much of the change (if any) you can accommodate. Remember, there may be times when canceling the project is your best bet. Other times, you may need to drastically revamp (that is, start from scratch) your IT project plan. The better job you do on the front end defining requirements and getting user buy-in, the less likely this scenario is to occur. That said, the unexpected can happen in the user's world just as it can in your world and by devising thoughtful responses and solutions, you'll be seen as a problem solver and team player.

User is Picking and Choosing Among Deliverables

This problem is most common when the user is an external client who is being billed for services. Sometimes during the definition or delivery phase of the project, the user starts nitpicking project details. In some cases, they might agree to large expenditures and then nickel-and-dime you to death on small details. It can happen at the outset of a project, sometime during project work, or when work is being delivered.

Possible solutions: Help the user understand the end-to-end benefits of the project proposal or project plan. Define the functional specifications based both on user need and project need and educate the user about project needs. A good example is if the user agrees to buy an expensive new tape backup unit but doesn't want to buy new tapes so they insist you spec out a tape drive than can use their current tapes. Your job will be to educate the user and this often means making the business case for your decisions. If the tape backup drive you recommend is more reliable, handles more data, is faster or more secure, make sure you educate the user about this, especially if you believe they're starting to nickel-and-dime the project. The cost of new tape might be the real issue for the user/client, so try to figure out what the real objection is to your plan is and address that. If the user is reluctant to pay for new tapes, do the math for them. Figure out the cost of a new set of tapes and compare that to potential backup issues (slow backup due to rewrites, bad backups due to tape errors) as well as the cost of a total system outage because of worn out, unreliable tapes.

Enterprise 128 ...

Penny Wise, Pound Foolish

Sometimes users demand the very best from an IT project. They're happy to spend thousands (or tens of thousands) of dollars on the latest hardware and software. They want top-of-the-line everything and are willing to pay you over-time to get everything ordered, tested, and installed in record time. During the project definition phase, however, they become reluctant to spend an additional $100 or $500 on some critical part of the solution. "What some clients fail to realize is that it's usually a case of pay a little now or pay much more later," explains Chris Compton, President of TCR Solutions, an IT service firm. "When we recommend the customer purchase a $500 UPS system to avoid problems with power outages that occur every year in the summer as part of an upgrade pro-ject, they sometimes balk. Later if the system goes down, it often costs 10 or 20 times the cost of the UPS when you add up the replacement cost of hardware, the cost of our time to replace and reinstall everything, and the lost productivity," says Compton. "We've begun developing business case scenarios for our clients to help them understand the cost of prevention vs. the cost of recovery. In every case, prevention has a much higher ROI (return on investment). We've begun to build this into our IT project proposal phase to help clients make better long-term decisions."

    <u>Lesson Learned:</u> When your users, customers, or clients balk at taking the right steps to ensure project completion or success, make sure you step back and help them see the bigger picture. Like life insurance, you don't buy it because you want to use it; you buy it because you hope you never have to use it. If your cus-tomers want to play the odds, make sure you've made the business case and then documented the decisions thoroughly to prevent these short-sighted decisions from coming back to bite you and your IT project team.

The Impossible Project

Sometimes users, stakeholders, project sponsors, and others insist on what essentially can be called an "impossible" project. They want you to accomplish too much work in too little time with too few resources. This is a disaster waiting to happen and you don't need to be the poor sucker who walks into that one. First, you should learn to recognize "impossible" projects early on so you can try to avoid becoming involved with them. They are:

- Projects that combine discovery with production
- Projects that are poorly defined or planned and lack adequate detail
- Projects whose plans have been modified by management (shorter schedule, lower budget, higher quality, and/or increased scope)
- Projects with wrong or inadequate staffing
- Projects that keep slipping the start date
- Projects that are underway but show no sign of progress
- Projects that "depend on you to save them"
- Projects that appear to have political problems
- Projects that have no meaningful organizational support

One common problem is that a confident or experienced IT project manager may think, "I can fix this," especially if you have a knack for fixing problems in projects. However, to step into a troubled project is really a huge career risk for several reasons. You could be being set up to fail, either intentionally or not. You could be saddled with a terrible project that will prevent you from working on a project that could be successful and add value to the company and to your career. You could become so mired in this troubled project that you get pigeon-holed and moved off into some obscure career corner of your company.

Possible solutions: Though it may sound deceptively simple, the best solution is to avoid these projects whenever possible. Keep your ego in check and don't rush in to save the day. Instead, look for opportunities to apply your skills and expertise to a new project so you can build it properly from the ground up. If you do get saddled with one of these impossible projects, follow these guidelines to help maintain your sanity and your sterling reputation:

- Don't overcommit. Promise less than you think you can deliver across the board. Unfortunately, even these scaled-down commitments may end up being ambitious.

- Don't commit to any project parameters until you're confident they're correct. That includes scope, time, cost, and quality, as well as functional and technical requirements.

- Present your worst-case, most pessimistic scenarios and estimates. Normally this is not a wise course of action because you want to be viewed as an IT PM who can come up with accurate estimates. However, when dealing with an impossible project, your worst-case scenario is most likely correct or not close to bad enough. Don't compound the issues in this project by taking a more moderate view of things.

- Identify where this project fits into corporate goals and priorities. If it's not a high enough priority or if it's not aligned to corporate goals, try to persuade the powers that be to cancel the project or redesign it.

- Find ways to get others to have a vested interest in the outcome. There is power in numbers and if you can get enough influential people to have a vested interest in the project results, you might then find enough organizational clout to actually get the project moving in the right direction. If you're the only one with "skin in the game" you're in a very risky position and it will be your career, and yours alone, that tanks if things go bad.

Summary

In this chapter, we looked at additional tools for tracking and managing your IT project. The more technical metrics that can be used, such as Earned Value Analysis, are often avoided by even experienced project managers. Sometimes its because the process of gather the numbers for analysis is too cumbersome, but often times it's because in the heat of managing the project, these tools are forgotten. Using EVA and the related metrics including SPI, CPI, and CR can help you communicate project health to your sponsor or to your executive team. It helps you avoid discussing details at great length and gives you a quick birds' eye view of the project. Like any numbers or metrics, the data can be manipulated or used in unintended ways, but when used appropriately, they can help you better manage your project and forecast future results more accurately.

Testing is another part of tracking and controlling your project. Testing occurs at various stages of project work and there are many different kinds of testing used in IT projects, depending on the nature of the project itself. A solid testing plan can help find problems earlier in the work cycle and problems are less difficult and less expensive to fix earlier in the project than when they're found at the end of project work or when found by the user.

IT projects typically have external plans that have to sync up to them including implementation or deployment plans, support plans, or operational transfer plans. If these tasks are not part of your formal IT project, it's important to keep the people involved with these external plans up to date regarding your project's progress. Changes in your project's deliverables, scope or schedule can greatly impact these related plans. Developing a communication channel with these external projects can help make sure everyone is on the same page and that all expectations regarding deliverables and timelines are clear and unambiguous.

A detailed and well executed handoff plan help promote a positive perception of the project. It sends the signal that you managed the project well throughout the lifecycle. The user will judge the success of the project in large part through the handoff experience, so it's important to do this well.

There are all kinds of problems that can occur in managing your IT project, many of which can be prevented or minimized simply by using the project management methods we've discussed throughout this book. Problems will still crop up, even in the best planned projects, so we discussed the kinds of problems and possible solutions to a whole host of problems. By understanding what kinds of problems can crop up, you may be able to avoid some of these problems. If not, you can refer to this section to get ideas for resolving problems that sneak up on you and threaten your project's success.

The formulas used in this chapter are repeated here for easy reference:

Planned Value (PV) = Planned % Complete x Total Project Budget

Earned Value (EV) = Actual % Complete x Total Project Budget

Cost Variance (CV) = Earned Value (EV)—Actual Cost (AC)

Schedule Variance (SV) = Earned Value (EV)—Planned Value (PV)

Cost Performance Index (CPI) = Earned Value (EV) / Actual Cost (AC)

Schedule Performance Index (SPI) = Earned Value (EV) / Planned Value (PV)

Estimate At Completion (EAC) = Project Budget (total project budget) / Cost Performance Index (CPI)

Critical Ratio (CR) = Schedule Performance Index (SPI) x Cost Performance Index (CPI)

Solutions Fast Track

Technical Tracking Tools

- ☑ Earned value analysis (EVA) is a method of assessing project progress using calculations involving planned and actual work progress metrics.

- ☑ Planned Value (PV) is defined as the planned percent complete times the total project budget.

- ☑ Earned Value (EV) is defined as the actual percent complete times the total project budget.

- ☑ The Cost Variance (CV) is defined as the earned value minus the actual cost.

- ☑ The Schedule Variance (SV) is defined as the earned value minus the planned value.

- ☑ The Schedule Performance Index (SPI) is calculated by dividing earned value by planned value (PV).

- ☑ The Cost Performance Index (CPI) is calculated by dividing the earned value by the actual cost.

- ☑ The Estimate At Completion (EAC) is determined by dividing the total project budget by the cost performance index.

☑ The Critical Ratio (CR) is calculated by multiplying the SPI by the CPI.

☑ An SPI value of greater than 1 indicates your project is ahead of schedule. A value of less than of 1 indicates your project is behind schedule.

☑ If your schedule gets off track, you may choose to carry the deficit (or surplus) forward or use your schedule reserve.

☑ A CPI value of greater than 1 indicates your project is under budget. A value of less than of 1 indicates your project is over budget.

☑ If your cost gets off track, you may choose to carry the deficit (or surplus) forward or use your budget reserve.

☑ Estimate At Completion uses the cost performance index and the total project budget to determine a new estimate for the real cost of the project at completion.

☑ EAC can be used to determine whether or what a project should (or can) go forward. A project estimated to be too far over budget at completion may be cancelled.

☑ The Critical Ratio can be used to gain an overall understanding of project progress and can be used to effectively communicate progress with upper management.

Testing Project Deliverables

☑ Unit testing is often performed on project deliverables as soon as they are ready. Integration testing tests the performance of multiple project deliverables to determine how (and if) they work together in an integrated fashion.

☑ The person performing the work should perform some type of unit testing as part of the task to ensure the scope and quality requirements are met.

☑ Usability testing is typically performed in a controlled environment to ensure the project results are usable from a customer/user perspective.

☑ Acceptance testing is used to determine whether or not the user will accept project deliverables. The functional specifications are typically tested in acceptance testing.

☑ Beta testing occurs when the product is in the final stages and is close to release. Beta testing can turn up major (show stopper) and minor (revision) errors and defects.

☑ Beta testing may include some form of user testing in their environment to test functionality.

☑ Regression testing is performed after errors and defects have been identified and reworked. Regression testing is done to ensure that no new errors or defects have been created as a result of addressing earlier errors.

☑ Performance testing can include stress, load, reliability, and stability testing to ensure the project's deliverables can work in real-world conditions.

☑ Benchmark testing tests hardware and software against defined standards.

☑ Security testing ensures the project's deliverables meet security requirements. One element of security testing is to make sure that if attacked, the project's deliverables respond appropriately to avoid providing additional information to intruders.

☑ Security testing is often outsourced to get a fresh set of expert eyes looking for security weaknesses.

Preparing for Implementation, Deployment and Operational Transfer

☑ An implementation plan describes steps to be taken to install or implement the project's deliverables.

☑ A deployment plan describes steps to be taken to deploy the solution across the enterprise.

☑ In some cases, the implementation and deployment plans are one and the same.

☑ Both implementation and deployment plans should include rollback plans in case things go wrong. The original state should be defined so rollback can occur.

☑ Operational transfer is the process of permanently handing off operations of the project's deliverables.

☑ A well written operational transfer plan will follow the same steps as an IT project plan to avoid errors and omissions.

☑ Training, support documents, users guides, release notes, and Service Level Agreements should all be defined within the operational transfer plan.

Resolving Common Project Problems

☑ Problems with scope include vague scope, scope not feasible, errors in approach, and scope creep.

☑ Problems with quality include initial results failing to meet quality standards, work delivered outside the scope of the project, fixing the wrong problems, problems that reappear, and problems that cannot be resolved.

☑ Problems with schedule include late start, missed deadline or deliverable, everything on the critical path, and nothing on the critical path.

☑ Problems with budget include funds expended up front, assets moved off project, too many approval points, and shrinkage.

☑ Problems with staff include confusion over who's in charge of project staff, whiners, big biters, belt and suspenders, and interpersonal conflict.

☑ Problems with the project sponsor include lengthy reporting requirements, rehashing previous decisions, inability to schedule project review meetings, and pressure to complete the project faster, for less money or with more scope.

☑ Problems with vendors include late delivery, unacceptable quality, and poor communications.

☑ Problems with customers/users/stakeholders include users not being pleased with project results, changing user requirements, picking and choosing among deliverables, and setting impossible demands.

Frequently Asked Questions

The following Frequently Asked Questions, answered by the author of this book, are designed to both measure your understanding of the concepts presented in this chapter and to assist you with real-life implementation of these concepts. To have your questions about this chapter answered by the author, browse to **www.syngress.com/solutions** and click on the **"Ask the Author"** form.

Q: Why don't you use the PMBOK acronyms for EVA and other technical analysis?

A: The material we presented adheres to PMI standards and material presented in the PMBOK with one notable exception—the letters we use to indicate the various measurements. In our opinion, it's easier to remember what two letters stand for and the point of the material was to make it highly useable for you. If you're concerned with passing a formal certification exam, you should adhere to the PMBOK standards. If your concern is simply your ability to use these metrics, stick to the two-letter system so you'll be more likely to remember (and therefore, use) these metrics.

Q: If my project is under budget but behind schedule, my project could still be in trouble. Using the metrics provided in this chapter, I could come up with a ratio of close to 1 that would indicate my project was just fine. Any comment?

A: It's true that when using ratios, you're dividing one number by another and in some cases, their equal and opposite deviations from 1 can offset each other. In the case you describe, you stated that your project was under budget (ratio > 1) and your schedule was behind (ratio < 1). While these might offset, you know going into this analysis that you are under budget and behind schedule. That information alone helps you better manage your project. These numbers can't manage your project for you nor can they think for you (though we all sometimes wish they could), but they can help guide you toward understanding where your project risks are, what your overall project health is, and help you focus in on the problem areas. Using your scenario, you can look at your budget variance and assume it is because you are behind schedule. However, you may be behind schedule because of a problem making approved budget expenditures. If you can't spend your budget, you can't do your work and you can fall behind schedule. Understanding where you are helps you understand what to do to fix problems that arise and these metrics are just one of many tools you can use to manage your IT project.

Q: It never fails that our development and testing teams do a great job but completely disregard our deployment team's deadlines and deliverables. This leaves the deployment team swinging in the wind and having to deal with angry or frustrated users. Any suggestions?

A: This is a serious problem that requires resolution because over time, your company will lose credibility with users. There are a few different ways you can address this, depending on the people involved, the customers, the project, and the corporate culture in which you're working. One way to work on this is to get engineers and testers in front of users or customers. Engineers and testing engineers can become a bit isolated from the real world application and getting them out of their offices and onto a user site and be a real eye opener. Another possible solution is to bring this to your project sponsor for escalation. Remember that your testers' goals are to find issues early in the cycle and send them back for repair before the project is released to the user. Code (or other work) with lots of problems is not the fault of the tester, though the tester sometimes gets blamed for delayed or missed project deadlines. Meeting deadlines for deliverables is everyone's responsibility and the team must work together to make sure all phases run smoothly. The developer and testing teams need to be held accountable not only for deadlines and deliverables on their own work, but for working cooperatively as part of a larger team to help the company succeed. Every time your deployment team has to backpedal with the customer, your entire company suffers. While it may sound a bit dramatic, everyone's jobs depend upon satisfied customers so the developers and testers are putting everyone's jobs at risk by ignoring deployment deadlines. On the flip side of that coin, the deployment team needs to communicate effectively with the developers and test engineers. That means listening to what *is* and *is not* possible, working together to create realistic schedules and negotiating to find mutually satisfactory and realistic goals.

Q: We work with external vendors on a lot of our IT projects. Most of them don't use formal project management. Do you have any suggestions for how to get them on board with our IT PM process?

A: That's a great question. Your vendors do not need to use project management methods in order for you to work successfully with them. However, once they begin to see the power of IT PM in the way you handle your projects, they may start showing interest in your processes and procedures. Until that happens, you can clearly set up processes and procedures for working with your vendors. Those procedures may include contractual (legal) elements, but at minimum, you should specify the vendor contact, vendor deliverables, vendor schedule, vendor cost, and vendor quality metrics (scope, time, cost, quality). This will help keep communications with your vendors clear, concise, and focused. It should ultimately help them do their job better because they won't have to second guess what you want or spend an inordinate amount of time trying to figure out how to meet your needs. A good vendor relationship is a two-way street, so you may need to adjust a few of your project's processes to accommodate a vendor's needs, if appropriate. Over time, the vendor will likely see the benefits of your IT PM process and may even inquire as to what system or methodology you use. Sharing your process will help your vendor do a better job and create a positive win-win relationship.

Q: My project sponsor almost always pushes me to deliver faster, better, cheaper. Despite my repeated discussions with my sponsor, this never seems to change. Can you provide any advice to help me out?

A: Some project sponsors seem to think that if they don't put the constant squeeze on you that you won't turn in your best work. If that's the nature of this problem, you may want to have a candid conversation with your sponsor and let him or her know that you are constantly working as hard as you can and that pushing you harder only adds stress. The project sponsor may be unaware that his or her actions are perceived as pushing (they might think they're encouraging or coaching) and they may change their approach. If the project sponsor is pushing because they really do need the project faster, better, or cheaper, you may want to ask the sponsor what changed since the original project definition (which they signed off on). This may cause them to realize that the project is on target and they're just getting jumpy. You may want to communicate more proactively with your sponsor if this is the case, because he or she may not feel they're getting enough current information so they push you. Sometimes a pushy project sponsor makes us retreat because we don't want to deal with the constant push and that can result in less frequent or less meaningful project communication. This leads the sponsor to get even jumpier and pushier and the cycle escalates. Don't allow the sponsor to bully you into creating a project plan that is better, faster, cheaper, and unrealistic. If you commit to a plan, make sure you're fairly confident you can deliver. If forced to commit to the better, faster, cheaper plan, make sure you document your concerns and reservations. Document what you believe the risks to the project are in this approach. Finally, if you continually have a problem with the sponsor pushing for better, faster, cheaper on every project you do, even after he or she has signed off on the project plan, learn to ignore those pushes and continue project work at the agreed upon pace…either that or find a new project sponsor who better understands the role of project sponsor.

Chapter 12

Closing Out
IT Projects

Solutions in this chapter:

- Closing Out Project Activities

- Preparing Final Documentation

- Final Project Sign-Off

- Review Lessons Learned

- Administrative Closure

- Final Team Meeting

☑ Summary

☑ Solutions Fast Track

☑ Frequently Asked Questions

Introduction

Before you pop the champagne cork and begin your celebration dance, you have a few more details to attend to. In this chapter, we'll look at project close-out activities. While you might think these are "throw away" activities that are optional, they're really not. Through properly closing out the project, you ensure users are satisfied and that the deployment, maintenance, and support activities are set up or in place. You also complete project documentation including updating final stats, and calculating total schedule, effort (hours expended), cost, and other project metrics. You wind down project activities and announce closure. Finally, you provide feedback to your team and an opportunity to wind down the team on a positive note.

While you might be exhausted by this time in your project, reserve just a bit more energy for properly closing out the project. Two things about project closure are absolutely true. It's a thousand times easier to do it now than in a month when your boss hounds you incessantly for the data *and* you can get your project team to help you close up shop so you can all go celebrate together.

As with previous chapters, let's look at the IT project management process overview and where we currently stand. This is shown in Figure 12.1 and indicates we're in the last phase of the project management process. This is important to keep in mind because close out *is* part of the IT PM process, not an annoying add-on.

Figure 12.1 IT Project Management Process Overview

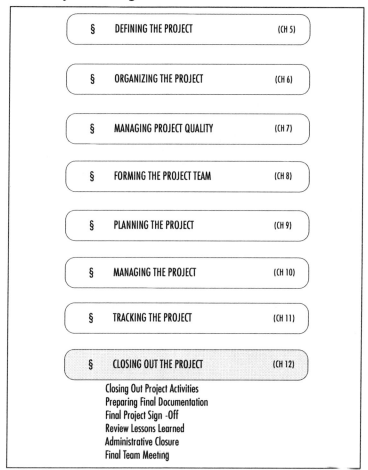

Since we won't be introducing any new terms in this chapter, let's look at the inputs, actions, and outputs from this final phase of IT project management, shown in Figure 12.2.

Figure 12.2 Inputs, Actions, and Outputs for Project Close-Out Step

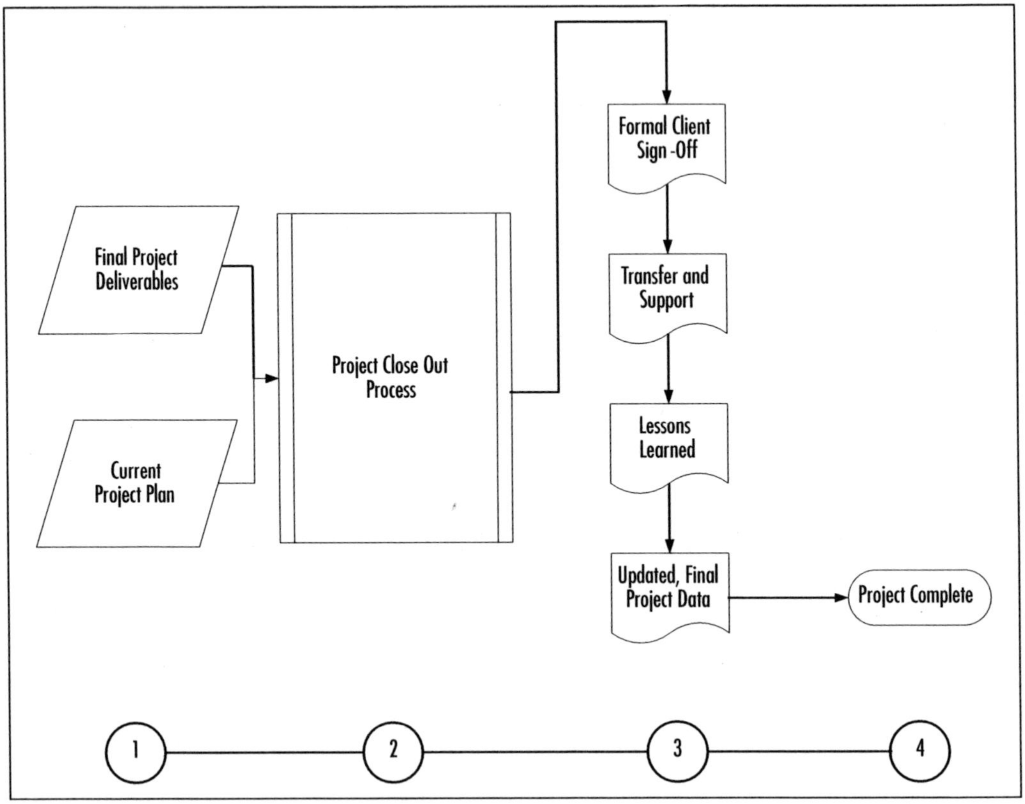

1. **INPUT** The inputs to this phase are the final project deliverables and the most current project plan. The project deliverables must be deemed fit to deliver to the user/client/customer, so they are necessary inputs to the close-out stage, though there are additional activities we'll undertake in this phase related to project deliverables. The project plan should be a living, breathing document and it should be kept relatively up to date throughout the project work cycle. The current project data is an input and during this phase, we'll finalize that data.

2. **ACTION** The actions in this close-out phase are related to updating project data and documentation, making sure that deliverables are formally accepted and that the ongoing operations or support processes are in place. Lessons learned are captured and reviewed before performing final team activities.

3. **OUTPUTS** The outputs from this cycle are the various documents needed to update and close out the project including lessons learned, client acceptance documents, updated project data, and updated project documentation, among others.

4. **PROJECT TERMINATION** This marks the formal completion and end of your IT project.

Closing Out Project Activities

There are a number of project activities that require finalization or close-out once project work is completed. These include closing out the project issues log, addressing lingering change requests or work orders, and dealing with bug reports.

Issues Log

Despite your best efforts, it's likely there will be issues on your issues log that are pending or still open. The first question you should ask is: Is the project really complete? In some cases, an issue left open means that one or more deliverables might be incomplete or not up to quality standards. However, in most cases, leftover issues (whether pending or open) can indicate issues that were indirectly related to the tasks such as an ongoing issue with a tracking system or with a vendor. These issues may not ultimately impact the scope, time, cost, or quality of the project, but at the time they were raised, someone believed the issue was important enough to track it.

Hold a final issues log review meeting and look through all issues that are either pending or open (that is, all issues not closed). As a team, decide what to do with each issue. Some issues simply may not have been updated, while other issues may have resolved themselves. Other issues may require follow up and some issues may simply be irrelevant at this point. Don't just assume that the items on the issues list are irrelevant because you've determined the project is complete. Go through each line item and make a definitive decision about the issue. If it is no longer relevant, close it as unresolved with brief comments to note that no action was taken but that you are closing the issue. Your issues log should end up with no open issues at the end of this session. Any issues that the team feels should remain open should be transferred to some other tracking system so the issues log can be finalized and documented. The reason for this is simple—no one, including you, is likely to look at the issues log for a project that is complete. Rather than losing important issues that may still need to be addressed (a vendor issue, a corporate accounting issue, etcetera), transfer it to a more appropriate venue for resolution now that the project is winding down.

Change Requests/ Work Orders

It would be odd to find open change requests or work orders when your project work is complete, but it does happen. Review any open change requests or work orders to determine if your project work truly is complete or not. As with the issues log, review all open orders and determine why they're open. Some may be open only because the documentation hasn't caught up yet and the issue is resolved. Others may cause you to look more closely at project deliverables to make sure everything is in order. As with the issues log, don't just leave these items hanging. Close them with a notation as to why they were not addressed in the project. In some cases, these items may cause charge backs to the project (the client reducing the fee they'll pay you because some portion of work was not included in the final deliverable).

Bug Reports

Bug reports are like the issues log with one major exception. The development team may choose to defer fixing some bugs to later versions or releases. Therefore, it is critical that all open or pending bugs be updated (where applicable) and transferred to the bug tracking system for safekeeping. When the next round of development fires up, these bugs should be readily available so the functional and technical specifications can be written to address the most urgent (or desirable) bug fixes.

Preparing Final Documentation

At the end of each project, there are numerous project documents that should be prepared including a finalized project plan, variance reports, support or training documents, and more. Here's a list of some of the types of documentation you may need to prepare:

- Project reports and documentation
- Project closure report
- System and configuration documentation
- Program code
- Instruction manuals
- Training manuals
- User documentation

- Test criteria and results

- Regulatory information (test and results documents proving conformity to legal specifications, etc.)

- Acceptance or product certification

This list is not exhaustive but should clue you in to the types of documentation you should prepare as you close out your report. As we've discussed previously, it's always easier to document these things as quickly as possible so you don't have to expend tremendous effort later trying to remember project detail and fill in the gaps. In some cases, there may be legal requirements for the timing of these documents, so keep those in mind as you move forward.

In addition, there are probably different formats you'll need to use to distribute these documents. Here's a starter list to get you thinking about the possibilities:

- Printed hard copy

- Soft copy (network location with link, e-mail attachment)

- DVD or CD

- PowerPoint or multimedia presentations

- Online documentation (Adobe's PDF is a popular format for this) for downloading, viewing, and printing

- Help files and FAQs (within the product or online)

- FTP sites (for downloads)

- Video, audio, Web conferencing

- Intranets and extranets

Take a look at your communication plan and determine who needs which documents and what type of project close-out communication is appropriate for the various stakeholders. You might need to create a formal report for your project sponsor or develop a presentation for corporate executives. Think about all the people you need to communicate with and which method of communication will be most convenient for them. Remember that project success is determined, in part, by the perception of success so use this communication opportunity to create a positive impression of your project outcomes.

Technical Documentation

For IT projects, system and configuration documentation is critical. The internal deployment/support team or an external vendor (to whom operations are transferred) will need this information. To develop appropriate documentation, first determine who the intended audience is for each type of documentation. Look at the user environment to determine the best format and method of distribution. If in doubt, ask. For instance, it wouldn't make sense for you to create Help files and FAQ on a website if none of the users have Internet access. Assign owners for these tasks (if this falls within your project area) and make sure these documents are generated. If preparation of these documents is outside your area, be sure to keep your IT project team in the loop so they can provide information to the folks preparing the documentation. There are three primary types of IT projects and each has slightly different documentation needs: software development, desktop applications, and network infrastructure.

Software Development Projects

The program code itself must be thoroughly documented along with the versions of any plug-ins or external applications used. The configuration of the operating system the code has been tested on and the version and configuration information about any other software used in the development, testing, or support of the product should be documented. Relevant backup and recovery procedures should also be documented where needed. If bug fixes were included, the bug numbers and descriptions should be listed. If any temporary workarounds were included, those should also be documented along with notes about how to unwind those changes.

Desktop Applications

Documentation about the applications licensing, versions, configurations, and images (disk images, often referred to as *ghost images*), as well as configuration and images of the operating system should be prepared. If any workarounds are required, these should be noted along with how to back out of the workarounds once a fix is installed.

Network Infrastructure

Documentation should include version and configuration information for all relevant network infrastructure components such as network servers, application servers, Web servers, print servers, routers, gateways, firewalls, proxy servers, wireless access points, etc. Include any unique information regarding these components such as order of start up or shut down or special steps needed to properly install, configure, troubleshoot, or maintain this equipment. Backup and recovery procedures should also be well documented (and tested). Record currently installed firmware versions and workarounds, if used. Where applicable, also provide diagrams and/or updated blueprints showing network configuration such as subnets, cabling, router configuration, etc.

Final, Updated Project Plan

The project plan that you've used throughout this project to help you stay on course should be fairly up to date with the latest versions of schedule, budget, variances, issues logs, and whatever else you included in your project plan. Take time to gather the final data for the project and update the project plan one last time. This will enable you to finalize numbers in terms of plan versus actual. This data will be needed both for the project closure report (see next section) and for your communications with your project sponsor, stakeholders, or corporate executives. Have the team look at the project schedule and budget reserves to determine how close (or far) your estimates were from actual. This is a great opportunity to improve your estimating skills through examining planned estimates versus actual, looking at how you calculated reserves, understanding how reserves were used, and learning what you can do better next time.

Project Closure Report

You should prepare a project closure report. This report should be distributed to the project sponsor, appropriate stakeholders, and key corporate executives (if appropriate). This report should adhere to the following guidelines:

1. Include a brief statement of project background and objectives.
2. List members of the project team and contributors including name, department, title, project role, and next project assignment (where applicable).
3. State reason for project closure (completion, postponement, cancellation).
4. List planned and actual project deliverables. Discuss the gaps, if any.
5. List planned and actual project schedule. Briefly discuss changes that impacted final delivery date.
6. List planned and actual project budget. Briefly discuss any variances.
7. Identify project ROI (return on investment), if possible.
8. List any outstanding risks as well as related contingency plans, if applicable.

9. Include a summary of lessons learned (discussed later in this chapter).

10. Discuss methods or processes developed during the project that could (should) be reused and why.

11. Discuss external (organizational, departmental, procedural) limitations or problems that impacted the project and provide suggestions for improvement.

12. Identify ongoing support or maintenance needs, plans for or status of operational transfer.

13. If needed, identify next steps. This might include moving onto the next phase of a multi-phased project, filing required legal documentation (copyrights, patents, conformance to regulatory requirements, etc.), or moving any open tasks to a post-deployment plan.

14. Obtain formal project closure approval from the project sponsor.

A project closure report is a summary of the entire project at a high level. Avoid delving into detail in this report. The updated *project plan* should include all the project detail and this data should not be simply copied and pasted into the project closure report. Think of this report as a summary that you could look back over in a few years. It will tell you all the salient information about the project without delving into detail that in two or three years will be completely irrelevant to you.

One important note here—if a project is cancelled, it's especially important to formalize the close-out so that you and all those involved are aware the project was cancelled and not just forgotten. Projects are cancelled for many reasons, some of which we've discussed throughout this book. If your project is cancelled, go through the project closure report process to document the project and to obtain formal approval to cancel the project. This avoids the type of miscommunication where perhaps you thought you were told to cancel the project but were, in fact, told to put it on hold temporarily. It also should capture the reason for canceling the project and on whose authority. If someone comes back to second-guess this decision, it should be well documented and defensible.

Final Project Sign-Off

Before you get too antsy to move on, remember that you need to obtain final project sign-off and transfer any operational, support, or training issues to the responsible parties. Let's look at these briefly.

Formal Project Sign-Off

Formal sign-off is truly the end of the project. In a sense, the work's not done 'til the project sponsor says so. Typically, you should present the project sponsor with your project closure report, an updated copy of the project plan (if appropriate or required), and obtain formal agreement the project is complete.

What if the project sponsor does not agree with you that the project is complete? There are several steps you can take to address this scenario.

1. Accept project with variance noted.

2. Accept project with compensation to user/customer/sponsor for omissions or variances.

3. Continue project work until variances are addressed.

Clearly you want to avoid any of these scenarios because it means that somewhere along the line, something was misunderstood or miscommunicated. If you discovered open change requests or work orders (discussed earlier), you may have realized too late that there were portions of the deliverables missing. This means there is a gap in your project management process that you should find and repair. However, it doesn't have to mean the end of the world either. Work with your project sponsor (who is sometimes an external customer paying for the project) to define acceptable next steps, generate a plan for accomplishing those next steps, and move along. It might be a bit deflating to think you're finished only to have another "to do" list, but it happens. When you move into a brand new house, you often go through and find things that need to be finished. This is often called a *punch list*, not because it makes you want to punch the wall (though it might), but because each item is "punched" as it is completed. The same may be required in some IT projects though the goal is to have a clean finish with no additional "to do" items. If you discover additional items, it's very important to figure out where you went wrong, not to blame the guilty parties, but to discover how you can fix your process to prevent this type of error in the future.

Operational Transfer

The process of transferring responsibility to another party for project deliverables should be well planned. This improves the perception of quality of your project and helps make everyone's life easier. Think about the last time you bought a new car. If the dealer just pulled the new car out of the lot (dust, window smudges, windows stickers, and all) and tossed you the car keys, you probably would have wondered about the car, the dealer, and the quality. On the other hand, most dealers make a big deal out of delivering the car. It's washed, polished, the windows are clean, the tires inflated, the tank is full, and they sit you down and explain every last detail of how the car works (most of which you promptly forget because you really can't wait to get behind the wheel). This whole experience can add to or detract from your car buying experience just as the project handoff can. Remember, throughout this book we've discussed best practices to give you the knowledge to deliver the best IT project you can. It's not always this tidy in the real world, but it's what you should aim for.

In Chapter 11, we discussed preparing for operational transfer as part of your managing, tracking, and completing project work. Earlier in this chapter, we discussed some of the documentation you might need for a smooth transfer. Now, let's look at some of the steps you can take to successfully hand off the project. Some of these steps should have been completed during project work. This list is a checklist you can use to be sure you have all your bases covered:

- Begin with a final operational test to make sure everything actually is complete and in working order.

- Identify your contact point for operational transfer so you can coordinate the transfer of information and processes.

- Develop warranty information (express, implied) and how warranty issues will be handled.

- Develop documentation detailing ownership of copyrights or other intellectual property. You may need your corporate attorney to draw up these documents on behalf of your company.

- Contact the Training department to determine training needs. This might include train-the-trainer sessions, support documentation, or other assistance in defining and developing training materials.

- Clearly document who is responsible for operations, support, fixes, warranty issues, etc. Using the *is/is not* framework we used to define scope earlier in the book can be helpful to avoid making incorrect assumptions about roles and responsibilities.

- Formally transfer code, configuration, and other relevant documentation to your contact.

- Set a transfer date and develop specific transfer procedures with your contact, if needed.

- Communicate the transfer date to all relevant parties including project sponsor, stakeholders, and the project team.

- Perform any other activities that may have been contractually listed as handoff items (usually this is with external, paying customers).

- Manage user/customer/client perception. The perception of success has been built throughout your project, so be sure to end on a high note. Make the handoff a more visible affair by having a walkthrough, a demonstration, or a ribbon cutting ceremony. Making the handoff a more formal, visible affair helps build a positive perception of the project and the competence of your project team. If possible and appropriate, think of an innovative, interesting way to formalize the handoff so your user/customer/client remembers it in a positive light.

Cheat Sheet...

Project Audit

Whether or not your company requires a project audit, it's a good habit to get into following the completion of a project. An audit is an examination of the project's goals, achievements, deliverables, and metrics. It examines compliance with scope, time, cost, and quality requirements. It measures variance from functional and technical specifications. It documents final variance in terms of schedule, cost, and scope. It's a good habit to get into, but it should not turn into a major flog-fest. Problems will always crop up in a project, which is why every project has a project manager. Your job is to do your best to guide the project to successful completion through often treacherous terrain. Taking the opportunity to audit your project will build strong IT PM muscles. No pain, no gain.

Dispose of Project Assets

During the course of your project, you may have acquired various tangible assets. That might include chairs, tables, desks, computers, lab or test equipment, temporary office space, etc. At this point, you should determine the status of all project assets and the appropriate disposition of those assets. Here's a partial list to get you started:

- Pack up and vacate temporary office space.

- Pack up and vacate temporary conference rooms.

- Pack up and vacate labs or other temporary project space.

- Clean up after yourselves in all of the temporary locations you occupied (no sense in ruining your reputation at this late date).

- Properly dispose of unneeded project documentation through shredding or other appropriate disposal mechanisms (if documents are part of legal or regulatory requirements, file and store them appropriately).

- Dispose of (transfer, sell, reassign) hard assets including servers, desktops, laptops, cell phones, PDAs, test equipment, or any other equipment acquired specifically for the project.

Review Lessons Learned

We've emphasized lessons learned throughout the project lifecycle because capturing what you've learned as you go is the most efficient and effective method by far. The lessons learned meeting should be somewhat informal and should not devolve into a project audit. Have everyone gather their lessons learned (if you have not been gathering these in a centralized location periodically throughout the project) and have everyone prepare a brief presentation (5 minutes) to discuss the most important or useful lesson learned, the craziest lesson learned, etc. Compile and discuss the lessons learned, including what worked and what didn't work, which might include:

- Project definition process

- Project organizing process

- Project planning process

- Project execution

- Project scope, schedule, budget, and quality

- Project communications

- Project controls

- Project documentation

- Project tools or technology

- Project office, location, amenities, etc.

Do not allow the session to spiral down into a blame session. Share what worked and what didn't work. Focus on the behaviors, processes, outcome, and problems, not specific people or personalities. Take this to the next level and get the team to discuss how these lessons learned can be incorporated in the future. It's not enough to simply list what you've "learned"—the real learning comes from understanding how that information can be applied in the future. When well managed, this session can be interesting, enlightening, and extremely useful. Once you've talked through your lessons learned, capture the final data and include it in a document to be included in the final project plan. This will help IT teams on future projects and will provide practical historical data for planning, estimating and managing future projects.

The IT Factor...

How Organizations Learn

If you've ever worked in an organization that learns from its mistakes and gets better at what it does, you know what an energizing work environment that can be. "Companies that value organizational learning not only tend to become more successful over time, they attract and retain talented individuals," explains Dr. Gary J. Frost, Vice Chancellor at National University. "Organizational learning takes many forms but the common element is the desire to learn in order to generate optimal results. For employees, it can create a positive and motivating atmosphere in which to work. For organizations, it can create a more competitive position in the marketplace by continually improving products, services and processes."

Administrative Closure

Administrative closure is catchy term used for *doing the paperwork*. We all know that most projects are not considered complete until several reams of paper have been printed, forms have been filled out in triplicate, and fourteen file boxes have been filled with documents we'll never look at again. OK, that's the downside view. The upside is that there *are* important documents that are actually *useful* that should be completed during project close-out. We'll look at the common categories, but your organization will no doubt have additional or different requirements for paperwork. Create a list of required paperwork as you begin your close-out process (you can define it in your processes and procedures during your project organization phase if you're really on top of things). Past projects may give you some insight into what to use, but remember that past projects may not have used a solid project management methodology and might be incomplete from your new IT project management perspective. If you've been keeping your project data up to date, you shouldn't have much difficulty completing the administrative closure activities. Any shared team project data on network servers, drives, or intranet locations should be removed, archived, or deleted, as appropriate. Don't leave a physical or electronic mess behind.

Security

Make sure you address all security issues. The rule of thumb in any kind of security is *grant enough to get the job done* (and not a speck more). In the case of your project, additional permissions may have been granted and wherever possible, those special permissions should be revoked at project closure. If your team was granted special building or network access, that access should be revoked (unless it's still needed and appropriate). If your team was granted special access passes, passwords, or access to sensitive or confidential data, need for this access should be reviewed and, where appropriate, revoked. As you know, most network break-ins or compromise of confidential data happens from the inside of companies, so be sure to restore appropriate security permissions to project team members to avoid creating security gaps.

Paperwork

The kinds of paperwork you should complete at this point will vary from company to company and from IT project to IT project. To get you started, here is a general list of paperwork you may want to complete as you close out your project:

- Gather, organize, and file (or archive soft copies) of all project status reports sent to you by your team.

- Gather, organize, and file (or archive) of all project progress reports sent to your project sponsor.

- Finalize and file (or archive) the final, updated project report.

- Complete performance reviews (discussed in the next section) and distribute to appropriate personnel (team member's managers, HR department, etc).

- Complete and submit final project time cards or time tracking information.

- Ensure all billing for the project is complete including receipt and payment of vendor invoices and receipt of payment for project invoices (when an external customer is being billed, for instance).

- Close out project contracts with vendors and suppliers.

- Complete paperwork for the transfer or disposition of project hard assets such as test equipment or other physical resources.

- Assist in any post-project audits (financial, legal, process, regulatory, investor, etc).

Proper Disposition of Paperwork

File final copies of project plans and related paperwork. Think twice before shredding documents. If you're confident they are no longer needed, will not be needed in the event of a lawsuit or other legal action, and if they're sensitive or confidential in nature, they're good candidates for shredding. Consult with your firm's legal counsel before shredding documents if you're not sure. Shredding documents to cover your tracks is often illegal and almost certainly unwise. A great question to ask yourself is: would you do this if you knew you would get caught? If the answer is no, you probably shouldn't do it. That includes entering false or misleading data in reports, changing data after the fact, and shredding certain documents (by the way, if your company is involved in any kind of lawsuit, talk to your attorney before shredding any documents, even if they're completely unrelated to the lawsuit. Shredding can give the appearance of impropriety even where none exists).

In many cases, shredding unneeded documents is just fine and preferable to them simply being thrown into the trash. For all documents that will be preserved, use your company's document management system for storing and archiving documents. If none exists, you can store your files in hard or soft copy, but be sure they are well marked. Include the project name, project manager, project sponsor, client (if any), dates of the project, brief description of the project, and brief description of the stored documents. Whatever you do, make sure you file final copies of documents (mark them as such) so no one is wondering exactly which version is stored. Pick a system and stick with it or work with the appropriate people at your company to develop a system for company-wide use.

Regulatory Issues

During the definition of project specifications, you may have identified legal or regulatory requirements associated with your project. If so, you will probably also have to fill out paperwork to satisfy these legal or regulatory requirements. For example, if your project deliverables include shipping technology overseas, you may need to fill out export paperwork or certifications regarding the equipment and the legal export of certain technologies. If your project is subject to legal or regulatory requirements, you should already be aware of them. Some requirements stipulate project specifications or deliverables. Other requirements may simply be end-of-project reporting requirements. If you're not completely certain, talk with your project sponsor, legal, or financial advisor about potential requirements. If in doubt, ask. Failing to conform to requirements can cause massive legal and financial problems down the line.

Personnel Performance Reviews

Not all IT project managers will be required by their organizations to provide performance reviews for team members, so this may or may not be part of your project close-out activities. However, everyone needs feedback about the work they've done and as the IT project manager, you're in the best position to provide that feedback from a project perspective. During the organization phase of the project, you defined various processes and procedures for the team to use. During the planning stage, you defined the work to be accomplished, the timelines, budgets, deliverables, and quality required. You have all the elements, then, for providing performance feedback. You may choose to formalize team performance requirements, especially if you will be required to conduct a formal performance review at the conclusion of your project. Check with your HR department regarding an appropriate format and for guidelines on conducting the session if you've never conducted a performance review before. There are organizational and legal guidelines that should be followed.

Performance Review Elements

What elements should you include in the performance evaluation? Again, it depends on how your company runs, and if there is a defined process, you should consider using that. If none exists or you want to create one specific to IT projects, here are some general guidelines:

1. Team member name, title, role on team, or reason for being selected for the project.
2. Date team member started on project.
3. Date team member finished on project (or left project).
4. Primary project role.
5. List of responsibilities for project work including deliverables, timelines, costs, and quality.
6. Performance of responsibilities.
7. Performance related to teamwork including:

- Attendance and timeliness at team meetings
- Participation in team meetings
- Collaboration and cooperation with team members
- Assistance provided to team members
- Effectiveness of interpersonal communications

8. Performance related to paperwork and reporting including:

- Completeness and timeliness of status reports
- Timeliness of time cards or project time reporting
- Completeness and timeliness of updating project task status

9. Participation in any special activities including:

- Managing the issues log
- Managing the change request log/process
- Managing the bug reporting and tracking process
- Managing the communication plan and project communications
- Maintaining the project plan and schedule changes
- Managing vendors

10. List of new skills gained during project.

11. Discussion of overall strengths and contribution to project.

12. Discussion of specific weaknesses, impact to project, and recommendations for improvement.

13. Summary of overall performance.

14. Performance grade (if used) such as: Exceeded expectations, Met Expectations, Below Expectations.

15. Project manager and team members' signatures and date.

Performance reviews or evaluations should be a positive experience for both parties. The team member should come away from the session having a better understanding of his or her strengths and weaknesses. They should feel good about their contribution to the team and have clear ideas about how to improve performance in the future.

The IT Factor...

One For All

One company has as part of its performance evaluation criteria the requirement that a person excel in his or her job *and* assist others in excelling in theirs. This dual requirement ensures that teamwork is as valued and rewarded as individual performance. A strong team is comprised of strong individuals and individuals should be strengthened by team membership. All for one and one for all.

Delivering Performance Reviews: Below Expectations

Certainly, not all team members will exceed expectations and you'll need to be prepared to deliver more difficult news to underperformers. One thing that is absolutely key to a successful performance evaluation, even if the performance was sub-standard, is that the information in the review should *never* be a surprise. Performance should be measured, evaluated, and managed throughout the project cycle. At the first sign of trouble, take steps to manage performance (just as you do with your project). For instance, let's say that Alex is a smart, talented, nice guy who thinks that team meetings are a waste of time. As a result, he skips the second team meeting. Don't wait until Alex skips the third and fourth and fifth team meetings to address this. Team meetings should be productive events (so make sure they are) and Alex's absence makes it difficult for the team to form a bond as a team, communicate to everyone on the team at the same time in the same manner, assign duties based on team availability, and update team members regarding concerns, issues, or potential problems. That's not fair to the rest of the team and allowing this behavior to continue will demoralize the others ("Alex gets to skip, why should I have to attend?"). Don't use the performance review session as the place to *address* this issue. Talk with Alex, explain that team meetings are not optional and that should he have to miss a meeting for a legitimate business need, he should let you know in advance. This nips the behavior in the bud and lets Alex know that the team is expected to work as a team and participate as defined in the guidelines for team membership. If Alex's behavior continues to be a problem, you should continue to address it. That may include removing Alex from the team if the behavior continues. At performance review time, you will be able to then recap the issues rather than address them for the first time.

Delivering Performance Reviews

During the performance review session, focus on behaviors, work habits, and deliverables. In Alex's case, you might say, "Your attendance at team meetings was spotty, you missed 8 team meetings in a six month period. We discussed the importance of attending and participating in team meetings several times. The below average rating in this area reflects this issue." That's clear, unemotional, and states the facts and the behaviors. Choose language that is not accusing but that clearly states the facts. Don't try to sugarcoat them or minimize them. If you've addressed Alex's behavior in the past, these statements will not come as a surprise. If you hold Alex accountable for being a responsible team member, he may perform better in the future and become a star player. If you don't hold him accountable, his bad behavior will continue.

Keep this in mind as well: Everyone needs to retain their dignity. Unless someone has willfully been causing problems (in which case you may have removed them from the team), most people are trying to do the best they can. Factors such as problems outside of work, health issues, conflicting job expectations or requirements, and more can cause work performance to slip. Provide everyone the ability to retain their dignity even if you are giving them a "below expectations" review. With practice, you'll become more comfortable and competent delivering all kinds of performance reviews, but if you're new to this, talk with your HR folks for guidance on how to deliver this type of review. They can give you tips, help you avoid common pitfalls, and perhaps most important, provide appropriate language to use during the review.

APPLYING YOUR KNOWLEDGE

The performance evaluation process can be a bit scary for first-time managers or for people who are more often on the receiving end of reviews. The cardinal rule of any performance evaluation process is that results should never be a surprise to the person being reviewed. Just as you don't wait to the end of the project to determine if your schedule, budget, and deliverables are on track, you shouldn't wait until the performance evaluation session to track performance. By defining, monitoring, and managing performance throughout the project lifecycle (sound familiar?), you'll generate better project results, foster team commitment and high performance, *and* be respected as the team leader.

Even if your company does not require a formal performance review, you may choose to sit down with each team member and provide formal or informal feedback. Everyone likes to hear how well they did and many people are open to constructive feedback so they can grow and learn. Use this opportunity to finish out your IT project leadership duties on a strong, positive note.

Final Team Meeting

The final team meeting should not be one where you discuss the IT project details. You should have already covered those issues during meetings to close out the issues log or update/create project documentation. The final team meeting should be used to help everyone recognize the contribution they made to the team, the project, and the company. It should be a fun, relaxing time and should be scheduled at a time all team members can attend. Figure 12.3 shows the flow chart for this process. A detailed discussion of the flow chart elements follows.

Figure 12.3 Final Team Meeting Process

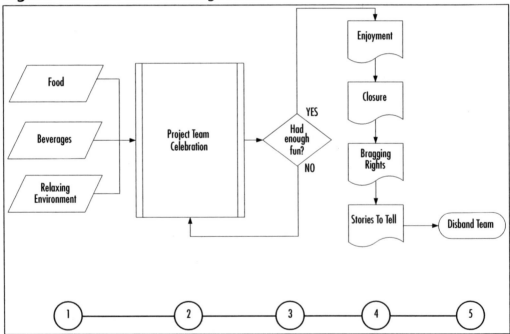

1. **INPUT** The inputs for this final phase of the project are food, beverages, and a relaxing environment. Gather the team for the final team meeting in a location that provides the opportunity to relax, unwind, and talk.

2. **ACTION** The processes involved in this step are described in the section that follows.

3. **CHECKPOINT** The checkpoint is used to determine whether everyone on the team has had enough fun. If not, activities return to the project team celebration and continue in an iterative manner until all celebration is complete. When celebration meets completion criteria, the process results in the following outputs.

4. **OUTPUTS** The outputs from this final step in the IT project management process are: enjoyment, closure, bragging rights, and great stories to tell. Ensuring these outputs meet quality and quantity standards for your team will bring the project to a successful end.

5. **NEXT STEPS** The final step in this process is to thank everyone for their diligent efforts and disband the team.

While done in jest, the steps listed above are actually recommended steps to take with your team. You've worked hard, you've overcome obstacles individually and as a team, and you should celebrate your successes. A good leader understands the value of recognizing individual and group efforts even when things don't turn out perfectly. Focus on the positive during this final meeting. Some IT project managers like to hand out certificates of recognition, awards for outstanding service, or monetary rewards. If you're not good at party planning, find someone on your team who is (or get advice from your HR team) and plan a memorable, enjoyable event. Here's a quick checklist to help you celebrate in style (for all types of budgets):

■ Go out to lunch as a group (everyone chips in to pay the bill) or have a potluck.

■ Ask everyone on the team to come to the meeting (lunch, dinner, donuts, whatever) with a success story, silly story, or "believe it or not" story from the project.

■ As the IT project manager, prepare a short positive story about every team member to highlight their work, their personality, or the wins (or losses) they had during the project.

■ Hand out t-shirts, mugs, toys, prizes, certificates, and awards. If your budget can accommodate it (the real reason you try to manage your budget in IT PM), provide higher-end gifts such as customized jackets, embroidered polo shirts, sports bags, hats, or cash bonuses.

- Arrange for a team outing like going to the movies or bowling as a group. Make sure all team members will be able to participate in the selected event.

- Snap a group photo, (edit in anyone not present for the photo) and distribute a team photo to everyone on the team. Hang a copy in your office or in an appropriate location in the building.

- Create a mock newspaper or magazine cover with your team's "headlines" on it and distribute to the team. Hang a copy in your office or in an appropriate location in the building.

- Get creative, get silly, have fun, recognize and reward your team's efforts.

Once you've held your final team celebration, you're ready to disband the team and send them on to their next assignment.

As the IT project manager, you've had to work hard from start to finish to steer this project toward successful conclusion. At times it may have seemed like no one appreciated your hard work or your role in the success. At other times, it may have seemed like you were the whipping boy or girl since you seemed to take the heat no matter what. That's life as an IT project manager. You've got to love the challenge of organizing and managing all the moving parts. You've got to enjoy (and be good at) communicating with all kinds of people to find solutions to problems, middle ground in standoffs, and resolution in heated arguments. A great IT PM is a strong leader, negotiator, manager, counselor, accountant, scheduler, mediator, and communicator. If you bring those skills to the table and apply the techniques and processes we've discussed throughout this book, you'll be headed for success in the wild, wooly world of IT project management. With that, we'll close out *this* project and wish you all the success you can handle.

APPLYING YOUR KNOWLEDGE

"Leadership is not about the leader; it is about how the leader builds the confidence of everyone else. Leaders deliver confidence by espousing high standards in their messages, exemplifying these standards of conduct they model, and establishing formal mechanisms to provide a structure for acting on those standards." -Rosabeth Moss Kanter, Professor of Business Administration, Harvard Business School
    Adapted from Confidence: How Winning Streaks and Losing Streaks Begin and End, by Rosabeth Moss Kanter. Copyright 2004 by Rosabeth Moss Kanter.

Summary

In this final stage of IT project management, the project work is complete and project activities wind down. Rather than letting them simply fade away, it's better to formally close the project out. This will vary from company to company (or IT project to IT project) and, in some cases, may be dictated by legal or regulatory requirements.

The first steps in closing out the project are to make sure all project work is complete and that any and all open issues are resolved. The issues log, for example, should be examined and all issues should be given a final disposition so nothing is left hanging. The same holds true for other logs or tracking devices such as change requests or bug tracking.

The final project documentation is important and should be completed in a timely manner. It might be needed or useful for historical purposes. Many IT project managers go back and review past projects when developing new project plans so they can use procedures, processes and lessons learned. The documentation might also be needed for the operational transfer phase or it might be needed for auditing purposes. Completing it in a timely manner will make the job much easier rather than having to re-create data and remember facts and figures long after the project is closed.

The project should also be formally signed off by appropriate parties. This ensures that everyone is on the same page with regard to project completion, project deliverables, and next steps. During this phase of work, you might also be preparing, reviewing, or revising the operational transfer plans so that ongoing support for the project's deliverables can be transferred seamlessly.

Hold a lessons learned meeting to gather the lessons learned captured throughout the project lifecycle. This is an opportunity for the team to share what they've learned and to understand how this new knowledge might be applied. A good lessons learned meeting is not an hour of finger-pointing, but instead an opportunity to learn as a group and grow in your ability to plan and manage IT projects.

Every company requires a certain amount of paperwork and this should be completed during the project close-out phase. This might include final project time cards, performance reviews, final billing, paperwork to transfer project assets to another department or division, or filing legal or regulatory paperwork. Also revoke any unnecessary security permissions or access to maintain tight network and building security. You should conduct project performance reviews with individual team members and use the opportunity to discuss the contributions and strengths the person brought to the team. You can also use the opportunity to identify learning opportunities so the team member can grow professionally.

Finally, you should hold your last team meeting. Depending on your company policies and your budget, you can have an on-site or off-site meeting; you can arrange a special event; you can provide awards, plaques, certificates, bonuses, or gifts to show appreciation for the team's efforts. This is a time to celebrate the project's successes and to send the team off to their next assignments.

Solutions Fast Track

Closing Out Project Activities

- ☑ Issues logs may still have open issues. Review issues to determine whether further project work is required. The issues in the log should each be addressed and specifically resolved or closed as unresolved.

- ☑ Review any open or pending change requests or work orders. This might indicate you still have project work to complete. Otherwise, close, cancel, or transfer all open requests or orders, as appropriate. Unfinished work orders may cause project charge backs or contractual issues.

- ☑ Bug reports should be updated to indicate which bugs were included in the release and which are still open or pending. This data should be formally transferred to a centralized system (if not already there) to be used for future revisions or releases.

Preparing Final Project Documentation

- ☑ Technical documentation should be completed. This will vary widely depending on your IT project. It may include system or configuration information, source code, versions of third-party software used, serial numbers, or specifications for equipment.

- ☑ The project plan should be updated to reflect final data. Gather all relevant data so you can analyze plan versus actual results.

- ☑ Prepare a project closure report, which recaps and summarizes the project and its results. This report is typically provided to the project sponsor, corporate executives, and in some cases, the user/customer/client (when appropriate).

Final Project Sign-Off

☑ Projects should be formally signed off as complete by the project sponsor or user/client/customer (as appropriate).

☑ The project may be signed off in one of four states: accepted, accept project with variance noted, accept project with compensation to user/customer/sponsor for omissions or variances, or continue project work until variances are addressed.

☑ Operational transfer generally occurs after final project sign-off. In some cases, it may begin before or long after formal sign-off.

☑ Operational transfer should specify a number of details including contacts for transfer, roles, responsibilities, warranties, ownership of intellectual property, support agreements, and more.

☑ The point of transfer is an excellent opportunity to present your project's deliverables in a positive light to the user/client/customer. Use the transfer event to increase the positive perception of the project.

Reviewing Lessons Learned

☑ A project audit might be conducted to analyze project results. An audit should not be conducted at the same time as a lessons learned meeting.

☑ Lessons learned should be gathered throughout the project lifecycle. If they're captured just at the end, many important lessons learned will probably be forgotten or overlooked.

☑ Your lessons learned meeting should not spiral down into blame and accusations. Keep it positive and focus on what was learned and how that information can be used in the future.

☑ Capturing, analyzing, and incorporating lessons learned is one important way organizations become "learning organizations" and improve their products, services, and processes over time.

Administrative Closure

☑ Any special permissions granted to the members of the project team, such as special building or network access, special passwords, or access to confidential files should be revoked (as appropriate) as part of the administrative closure.

☑ Paperwork may include gathering and filing project status or progress reports, closing out vendor and supplier contracts, finishing up billing paperwork, or completing paperwork for post-project audits.

☑ Regulatory requirements should have been identified during the project definition and organization phase. However, if you're not sure if there are legal or regulatory issues with your project, contact your project sponsor or legal or financial advisor.

☑ Failing to comply with legal or regulatory requirements (including reporting requirements) can cause huge legal and financial problems down the road. If you're unsure, ask.

☑ Performance reviews should include elements related to individual and team participation during the project.

☑ If you're unsure of how to conduct a performance evaluation, work with your project sponsor or HR department. There are legal and professional guidelines to which your reviews should conform.

☑ A strong IT project manager uses the performance evaluation process to help team members grow through recognizing strengths and providing coaching to improve weaknesses.

Final Team Meeting

☑ Create a relaxed, enjoyable atmosphere to celebrate success.

☑ Depending on your corporate guidelines and budget, provide awards, certificates, gifts, or bonuses.

☑ Send your team off feeling good about the project's successes.

Frequently Asked Questions

The following Frequently Asked Questions, answered by the author of this book, are designed to both measure your understanding of the concepts presented in this chapter and to assist you with real-life implementation of these concepts. To have your questions about this chapter answered by the author, browse to **www.syngress.com/solutions** and click on the **"Ask the Author"** form.

Q: Once our projects are complete, people run as fast as they can for the nearest exits. Any suggestions for how to get people to assist with project close-out activities?

A: Yes, there are several ways you can accomplish this. First, you can define close-out activities during your project definition phase so that it is clear to everyone that these activities are *part* of the IT project. Also, you can add close-out tasks to your project plan, assign owners, and create entry/exit or completion criteria for these tasks. Adding milestones for the completion of these tasks will also give visibility to the importance of close-out tasks. You can add elements to performance requirements so team members clearly understand their roles and responsibilities during project close-out. Finally, you can use good old peer pressure, friendly cajoling, and the reminder that "the party doesn't start until the paperwork's done."

Q: We don't have any formal system for managing project documentation once projects are complete. Do you have any suggestions?

A: That's an excellent question. Many companies lack formal document management systems, so IT project managers are unsure of how to store or archive this data. Begin by asking what format and location will be most useful to your company based on how people work. For instance, if most people don't use computers, network storage of files might not be useful. If most people have computers, would an intranet site, network storage location, or good old CDs be your best bet? If you decide to store the documents electronically, pay attention to the file format. Ironically, documents written thousands of years ago can still be read, but files written 10 years ago sometimes cannot. Choose a fairly universal file and storage format if you store documents electronically. Including keywords or other metadata will make the documents that much more searchable. To create a storage system, define the steps, formats, procedures, and technical specifications for the system and document them so you (and others) will use them consistently.

Q: Our Training department always seems to expect us to develop training materials for them. What suggestions do you have for how we might better address this issue during project close-out?

A: If training is a function external to your project, you should have a point of contact within the Training department with whom you coordinate the development of training materials. Using your IT project management skills, you (or a member of your team) and the training contact can develop a training project sub-plan (or external plan). Defining roles and responsibilities, listing tasks, and assigning owners can be a great way to help develop the needed plan and identify who needs to do what. Most likely, someone from the Training department will need to sit down with someone from the project team in order to transfer the required knowledge from which training materials will be developed. Be willing and able to assist as far as possible to make the task of developing training materials easier. In some cases, it might be helpful and desirable to have one of the trainers participate as a tester. This not only helps the trainer become familiar with the product, but it helps testing by bringing in the user perspective. Plus, the trainer participating in testing gives you another tester (usually from someone else's budget). Remember, the Training department has many other obligations and deliverables and they've had to wait for your project to complete before developing materials. That might put them in a time crunch, especially if your project did not complete on schedule. Work cooperatively with Training and remember that the better the training, the better your project will be received and perceived. Using the framework of IT PM, you should be able to set clear, firm boundaries that will help the training folks understand and own their deliverables more appropriately in the future.

Q: I dread giving performance reviews. I don't do it very often and I never know what to say, especially when someone's performance was less than stellar. Do I *have* to do this as part of IT PM?

A: You may not *have* to give performance reviews but you really *should* make yourself do it. As you continue up the career ladder, it will be a regular part of your job so you might as well learn how to do a performance review now. If you're really uncomfortable with the whole thing, write up the review as you would if you were going to just e-mail it to your boss or HR for review. Be honest but polite about the person's performance. Focus on behaviors and outcomes, not people or personalities. Next, contact HR and ask if someone would help you prepare for the review. Bring the paperwork and discuss your views of the person's performance. Then, have the HR rep role-play with you. You might feel silly doing it, but you will absolutely feel more confident afterward. The HR person can play devil's advocate, can respond to your constructive criticism in "negative" ways, and coach you on how to handle various reactions. Once you've done this a few times, you'll feel more confident about delivering reviews that help people grow professionally.

Q: My friends and colleagues would not describe me as a gregarious, outgoing person. I'm not really comfortable with this whole team meeting party concept. I'm more of a *"Thank you!" on a Post-It ™ note* kind of guy. Any suggestions?

A: No one ever died of embarrassment, so take a risk, loosen up, and have some fun. If you *really* think heading up a fun event would totally be outside your comfort zone, gather your most outgoing, fun-loving IT project team members for a little planning session and assign the role of "master of ceremonies" to the guy or gal who will do the best job ensuring everyone has a good time. That way, you can fade in to the background if you need to, but you'll still provide your team with a memorable close-out event.

Index

Numerals

8/80 rule, 345–346

A

AC (actual cost), 463
Acceptance criteria, 246, 258, 295
Acceptance testing, 474–475
Achievement, 116–117
Acronyms, 466, 517
Actions, project. *see* Project steps
Actual cost (AC), 463
ACWP (Actual Cost of Work Performed), 466
Adjustment of management, 133–134
ADM (arrow diagramming method), 355
Administrative closure
  paperwork, 536–537
  personnel performance reviews, 538–542, 550–551
  regulatory issues, 537–538
  security, 536
Advancement, 120
Advantage, competitive, 2, 36
Agendas for meetings, 136
Air conditioning, 113
Aligning IT with corporate strategies
  competitive advantage, 36–40
  description, 34–35
  execution and efficiency, 37
  innovation, 38–40
  leveraging technology, 37–38
  strategy *versus* tactical concerns, 35–36
Alliances, building, 99
Analysis
  SWOT (strengths, weaknesses, opportunities, and threats), 46–47
  trends, 47–49
Analyst work style, 125, 131–132, 277, 419
Announcement of start, 407
Approval of proposals, 197–200
Approval procedures, 268–269
Approvers, 224
Arrow diagramming method (ADM), 355
Assessing progress, 415–416
Assets

disposal of, 533–534
  exchanging, 88–89
Assigning people, 116–117
Assumptions, 213
Attitude, negative, 158–159
Attractive people, 78
Availability of staff, 314
Awareness training, cross-culture, 138

B

Bad news, communicating, 89
Barter, influencing by, 81–82
Baseline, 286, 403
BCWP (Budgeted Cost of Work Performed), 466
BCWS (Budgeted Cost of Work Scheduled), 466
Behavior, 114
Benchmark testing, 286, 477
Beta testing, 475
Boomer Generation, 145–146
BPI. *see* Business process improvement (BPI)
Budgeted Cost of Work Performed (BCWP), 466
Budgeted Cost of Work Scheduled (BCWS), 466
Budgets
  changes, 428–430
  creating, 371–372
  estimating cash flow, 372–373
  implementing cost control, 373–374
  reserves, 469
  see also Problems with budgets
Bug reports, 526
Building alliances, 99
Business case, 94
Business process improvement (BPI)
  Capability Maturity Model (CMM), 3
  description, 2
  International Standards Organization (ISO), 5
  Project Management Institute (PMI), 2–3
  Six Sigma system, 4–5, 27
Business requirements, 239
Business strategies. *see* Strategies, business

C

T

Syngress: *The Definition of a Serious Security Library*

Syn·gress (sin–gres): *noun, sing.* Freedom from risk or danger; safety. See *security.*

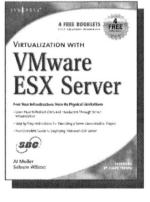

SYNGRESS®